WITHDRAWN
UTSA Libraries

Types of Rural Economy

BY THE SAME AUTHOR

★

La riziculture dans le delta du Tonkin
1935

Misère ou prospérité paysanne?
1936

Le problème agricole française
N.E.L., 1946

Les leçons de l'agriculture américaine
Flammarion, 1949

Voyages en France d'un agronome
Génin, 1951 et 1956
(prix Olivier de Serres)

Révolution dans les campagnes chinoises
Le Seuil, 1957

TYPES OF RURAL ECONOMY

Studies in World Agriculture

by

RENÉ DUMONT

*Professeur à l'Institut National Agronomique
et à l'Institut d'Etudes politiques*

METHUEN AND CO. LTD
11 New Fetter Lane
London EC4

Économie Agricole dans le Monde *was first published in Paris in 1954, by Librairie Dalloz. The present translation is by Douglas Magnin, Head of the Geography Department, Erith Grammar School*

First English language edition published in 1957
Reprinted twice
Reprinted 1970
1.4

SBN 416 58490 X

First published as a University Paperback 1970
1.1
SBN 416 18280 1

This title is available both as a paperback and as a hardboard edition. The paperback edition is sold subject to the condition that it shall not, by way of trade or otherwise, be lent, re-sold, hired out, or otherwise circulated without the publisher's prior consent in any form of binding or cover other than that in which it is published and without a similar condition including this condition being imposed on the subsequent purchaser.

*Distributed in the U.S.A.
by Barnes & Noble Inc.*

Preface

This book is the work of an agronomist who has indulged his interest in economic problems in moments of leisure from his professional work, but too late in life to have acquired a really profound knowledge of them. Our starting-point was in 1934 when, speaking from the tribune of the Senate, President Caillaux declared that the efforts of agricultural technologists had had the nefarious result of 'surfeiting the market'. When, in the following year, in October 1935, the Laval decrees did away with the *Offices agricoles* in the departments, which had pursued the cause of progress too efficiently, our interest became fully aroused.

If these assertions were true, then surely it was also necessary to abolish agricultural teaching, and every agronomist with the welfare of his country at heart should have looked for another career. Moreover, we had ourselves witnessed the famine in Northern Annam in the autumn of 1931 and seen the unsold consignments of rice piling up on the wharves at Saigon while the authorities refused to succour the famished, thus sowing the seeds of the recent conflict. As early as February 1934 we were unable to pass without comment a proposal put forward by the Association of Wheat Producers in France, which suggested that the 'surplus' rice in Cochin-China should be bought up, like Brazilian coffee, and dropped into the sea. This noble grain, all too scarce in the bowl of the Tonkinese peasant, hindered the marketing of coarse grains at a 'fair' price when it was poured into our pig troughs and fed to our calves and our poultry. Only wheat, the vine, and sugar-beet, which were all being over-produced, were well protected, and this served to aggravate the lack of balance in French agricultural production. Confronted with such a situation, the agricultural specialist unwilling to give up his work was forced to seek other solutions.

In this book we have made a rapid perusal of a few of the types of agricultural practice to be found in various parts of the world. The examples studied are an arbitrary selection, as we have dealt with those regions which we have actually visited.[1] We have never been able to understand a system of agriculture without seeing it for ourselves, and

[1] Except the U.S.A. and France which are the subjects of our two most recent works.

this first-hand experience is no doubt the main justification for our presumption. In this century of air travel, however, rapid journeys often prevent the absorption of an adequate fund of knowledge and may well lead to the formulation of arbitrary, and sometimes perhaps inaccurate, generalizations.[1]

After indicating the natural, economic, and human conditions of a regional complex, we shall describe a few of its villages and discuss a few ideas in an attempt to evaluate the possibilities of the agricultural system and to determine the best ways of ensuring a progressive type of development. Our aim is not to delve deeply into the varied problems which will present themselves but to provide a fairly broad but admittedly rather fleeting view of them for farmers, for experts in agricultural and economic subjects, for students of agronomy, rural economics and geography, and also for the intelligent man preoccupied —as he should be—with the future of mankind; and the reader, whoever he may be, may sometimes find the focus of the picture a little unusual.

As we have been unable to avoid countless sins of omission and have intentionally avoided some matters of great importance, we do not presume to offer this work as a comprehensive treatise. Towards the end of our career, having filled in some of these important gaps (U.S.S.R., South America) and accumulated fresh material and pondered upon it, we shall try in another work of synthesis to remedy some of the deficiencies of this first essay. This book is, in effect, a preliminary exercise and we hope that constructive criticisms will be freely offered, for they will help in the preparation of the final work.[2]

[1] 'It is dangerous to write about a country when one has only seen it in passing during the course of one or two field trips', writes a German colleague. But how else can one even attempt a work of synthesis?

[2] Each chapter has been revised in the light of criticisms by several acknowledged experts on the region concerned and the whole book has been thoroughly scanned by Denis Bergmann. We extend our thanks to all those who have given us so much help, and apologize for being unable to mention them all.

Contents

PREFACE   *page* vii

I   ESSENTIAL CRITERIA AND AGRICULTURAL POLICIES   1

    1. Agriculture defined as man's transformation of the rural environment. 2. Intensification and mechanization, climate and soil. 3. The agricultural undertaking and the human factor. 4. Types of farming: productivity. 5. The search for improvement. 6. Hunger, rising population, soil destruction, and neo-Malthusian economics. 7. Remedial measures can be effective.

II   THE EQUATORIAL RAIN FOREST IN THE NORTH OF THE BELGIAN CONGO   18

    1. Favourable climate, poor unstable soils, low level of cultural development. 2. The collecting economy, plantations and forest fallow of the Mayumba Massif. 3. Human effort and malnutrition; the vicious circle resulting from an inefficient use of land. 4. The failure of continuous cultivation and the improved Bantu system. 5. Directed peasant farming—spread of the savanna checked. 6. Better use of the forests—plantations and permanent rice-fields. 7. Intensification, mechanization, and industrialization.

III   THE TROPICAL SAVANNA OF AFRICA FROM CHAD TO THE RIVER CASAMANCE   61

    1. Drier climate, occasionally more fertile soils, the trading system. 2. A cereal-growing village near the River Shari and its concentric rings of cultivation. 3. Growing use of animals; local handicrafts. 4. The impoverishment of soil by badly administered cotton schemes. 5. The beginnings of intensification and poverty in the North Cameroons. 6. Difficulties of continuous cropping in the Sudan and the need to overcome them. 7. Improved rice-fields from the Niger to the Logone. 8. The Office du Niger—irrigated rice—a directed economy. 9. Priority for irrigated cotton on the Egyptian model in the Kouroumari region. 10. Soil exhaustion due to ground-nut cultivation in Senegal. 11. The difficulties of mechanization and the possibilities of mixed farming.

IV   THE OVERPOPULATED COASTAL PLAINS OF MONSOON ASIA IN NORTHERN VIETNAM   125

    1. Chinese and Indian civilizations: fertilized and irrigated rice-fields in continuous cultivation. 2. The concentration of property: excessive rents, usury. 3. A 'one-buffalo' farm in the

upper Delta. 4. A 'half-ox' farm of the lower Delta: indigent farmers and their poverty-stricken labourers. 5. Priority for intensification: water, fertilizers, type of farming. 6. Industrialization, emigration, and birth control. 7. Progress in China more rapid than in India.

V SHEEP AND CEREALS, TREES AND WATER IN NORTH AFRICA   164

1. Mediterranean aridity and the dangers of erosion. 2. Nomadic and sedentary peoples, colonization, demography. 3. The shepherd of the high Algerian plains and the fight against hunger. 4. Concentric belts of cultivation in the Tunisian Sahel at M'saken, near Susa. 5. Arboriculture, overpopulation, and emigration in Kabylia in Algeria. 6. The traditional type of cereal cultivation in Chaouia in Morocco. 7. Mechanization and the Paysanat (S.M.P.). 8. Irrigation and its difficulties; the latifundia. 9. A settler combines stock rearing and cereal cultivation in the upper Cheliff. 10. Mechanization, intensification, and industrialization in underdeveloped countries.

VI ARID PLATEAUX AND *HUERTAS* IN SPAIN   209

1. Unfavourable environment, slow development. 2. *Secano* or dry cultivation in the Saragossa Steppe. 3. Difficulties implicit in the intensification of *secano* cultivation. 4. Microfundia and latifundia; agrarian reform. 5. Colonization: the new village of Ontinar del Salz. 6. Congestion and falling productivity in the Murcian *huerta*. 7. The Guadalquivir; the future of southern Spain. 8. Intensification and decongestion in the rural areas.

VII OVERPOPULATION AND UNEMPLOYMENT IN THE ITALIAN COUNTRYSIDE   229

1. Too many people living on too few resources. 2. Mandatory labour laws and high rents on a *cascina* in Lombardy. 3. Poverty in spite of high yields on the drained lands of Ferrara. 4. A well-to-do owner-farmer and a poor *métayer* in Tuscany. 5. The *métayage* system in danger in the Valle di Chiana. 6. The latifundia of the Maremma and agrarian reforms. 7. The inadequacy of these reforms; solutions outside the sphere of agriculture.

VIII PASTORALISM DOMINANT IN THE VAL D'ANNIVIERS IN THE SWISS ALPS   264

1. Age-old meadows occupying the best land. 2. The byre-barn on the irrigated meadows. 3. Two types of land use in retreat—arable land and *pacages*. 4. Encroachment of the alpine pastures on the *mayens*; cheese the main product. 5. The vines of the Rhône Valley provide the ready money. 6. An agricultural economy in recession. 7. Extension of pastures and intensification

CONTENTS

on the meadows. 8. The size of farms and industrialization in the high valleys.

IX THE STUBAITAL IN THE TYROLEAN ALPS. CULTIVATION MODERNIZED   310

1. Milk, butter, and flour the basis of life. 2. The richest sector—the sunny side of the main valley. 3. The wet meadows of the valley bottom. Haymaking by hand. 4. The retreat of arable land and cereals on the *Schadenseite*. 5. The retreat of cereals and arable even more marked in the higher valleys. 6. The alp and *mayen* combined—individual herding, butter-production. 7 Outdated practices and intensification in highland and lowland zones.

X BAVARIAN AGRICULTURE—INTENSIVE AND MECHANIZED, BUT FARM UNITS TOO SMALL   339

1. Old and new methods east of Munich. 2. Heavily manured grassland in the zone at the foot of the Alps. 3. The Hallertau—distinguished by its hop-gardens. 4. The difficulties of farming on the Danubian marshlands. 5. Colonization and the uncertain future of the uneconomically small Bavarian farms.

XI THE BELGIAN FARM—WELL KEPT BUT UNDERSIZED   360

1. Bouvignies on the loess of Hainaut, and the part-time farmer. 2. Flanders south of Ghent; tiny holdings and 'satellite farms'. 3. Intensive farming at Brecht on the heaths of the Campine.

XII THE RECOVERY OF ENGLISH AGRICULTURE; RAPID MECHANIZATION   376

1. From the disappearance of the peasantry to the 'stick and dog' farming of the present century. 2. Arable cultivation, grass leys and milk bring renewed prosperity to two villages in south Shropshire. 3. The 'urbanization' of the English countryside. 4. New House Farm and the marginal areas. 5. From the smallholding to the large arable farm. 6. The Boyne Estate and Burwarton Castle. 7. A brave and difficult adventure.

XIII INTENSIFICATION IN THE LOW COUNTRIES: ITS POSSIBILITIES AND LIMITATIONS   406

1. Overpopulation and the conquest of the land; education and capital. 2. The specialized grass-milk farms of North Holland. 3. The triumph of selective breeding in Friesland. 4. A State farm on the North-east Polder. 5. The conquest of the eastern heathlands and the rural exodus. 6. Horticulture—market near the point of saturation. 7. Lessons to be learnt from the Netherlands; technique and equipment, austerity and independence.

TYPES OF RURAL ECONOMY

XIV AGRARIAN REFORM IN EAST GERMANY 437
   1. The breaking up of the large estates. 2. A new peasant in Saxony-Anhalt, delivery norms and the plan of production. 3. A machine hiring station (M.A.S.) in Brandenburg and its differential tariffs. 4. A State farm in Saxony and agricultural research. 5. The old-established peasants of Saxony-Anhalt. 6. Towards collectivization.

XV HUNGARY—AGRICULTURE IN A PEOPLE'S DEMOCRACY 465
   1. Rural overpopulation in an environment of unevenly distributed resources. 2. Mezokovesd, a poor 'agricultural town'. 3. Gollo, a rich village in Transdanubia. 4. The shanty-town of the new settlers at Eloszallas. 5. The isolated *tanyas* of Kecskemet, the Bugac *puszta* and the 'Bulgarian' gardens. 6. The early days of the producers' co-operatives—recent developments.

XVI FROM THE SLOVAK PEASANT TO THE CZECH CO-OPERATIVE AND THE SOVIET *KOLKHOZ* 492
   1. The Slovak farm, still too small and overcrowded. 2. A townsman-wine-grower. 3. Colonization and the uphill movement of vineyards in Moravia. 4. The four types of producers' co-operatives. 5. Machinery stations and State farms. 6. Collective farms south of Moscow and a Ukrainian *sovkhoz*.

CONCLUSION: MALTHUSIAN ECONOMICS RESPONSIBLE FOR THE WORLD'S HUNGER 516
   1. Small farms and collectives—the archers *versus* the tanks. 2. Priority for 'real' and not simply 'economic' food requirements. 3. Symptoms of European and French decadence; the revival of Malthusianism. 4. Food-production lagging behind population increases. 5. The fight against hunger, the categorical imperative of modern times.

INDEX 539

I

Essential Criteria and Agricultural Policies

1. Agriculture Defined as Man's Transformation of the Rural Environment

1. The principal aim of agriculture may be defined as follows: to supply mankind with food and with those raw materials which are of animal or vegetable origin.[1] Evidently some of these requirements can be provided in other ways and the earliest mode of subsistence was simply by gathering the products of untended nature. Today, fishing is still an invaluable resource, and together with hunting it still forms the mainstay of certain primitive economies. As late as 1936 there was an old peasant woman at Murols in the Auvergne, who gathered wild hazelnuts from the hedgerows, shelled them on the hearth and, after two months of spare-time work, produced three or four litres of 'wild' oil. Her only concession to progress was the use of an old mechanical press. There are few of us who have never gathered wild berries, picked dandelions from the meadows in the spring or mushrooms from the woods in the autumn. We have often, without realizing it—like Monsieur Jourdain—imitated the example of the old peasant woman.

The difference between mere collecting and agriculture is that the latter endeavours to modify the natural environment so as to secure the most favourable possible conditions for various useful species of plants and animals whose utility is further enhanced by a conscious process of selection. Agriculture tempers the extremes of the climate; with irrigation the farmer fights aridity; he houses his animals and protects his market gardens with frames and glass against wind and cold. Above all, agriculture modifies the soil. Unlike climate, this should not be regarded as part of the natural endowment of a region,[2]

---

[1] See *Bulletin de la Société française d'Economie Rurale* (December 1949) for a more detailed definition.

[2] In this work, however, we have conformed with the usual practice of regarding soil as part of the physical environment.

the only exception being the case of certain virgin soils which have retained their original vegetation of grass or forest and which have provided the basis for pedological classification. Our own soils are highly artificial. In many cases they have been worked with plough and harrow for thousands of years, corrected for deficiencies and enriched with manure and every kind of fertilizer, natural and artificial.

Agricultural science is the practical farmer's consultant. Its domain is the whole range of organic life utilized by man. It raises the productivity of useful species by methods of selection which were once empirical but now rely increasingly on the science of genetics. It transforms the living conditions and, more particularly, the feeding of animals. Thus the stage of development of any rural economy can be estimated by noting the degree to which the natural environment has been changed and the techniques employed to this end.

In a region developed on an extensive basis, the original features are only slightly modified and are still very apparent. In the case of a pastoral economy, where the grazing animal forages—and concentrates—the natural produce of the grassland, there is no modification whatsoever and there is very little even in the permanent grasslands of Western Europe, to which the term 'natural' is often applied with good cause; indeed, as is still all too often the case in Normandy,[1] rational methods of management, with fertilizing and other forms of improvement, are on the whole unfortunately absent. So long as the soil is not actually worked, permanent grassland remains, in effect, natural grassland; in the strict sense of the term therefore it is not a form of agriculture, the symbols of which are the plough and 'ager', the ploughed field.

2. Intensification and Mechanization. Climate and Soil

2. We must now examine the distinctions which are usually made between the two main methods of raising the level of agricultural productivity. Intensification aims primarily at high yields even if they are costly in terms of labour and the maintenance of soil capital (by means of improved seeds, fertilizers, etc., whereby biological processes are modified). This is the method which must be urgently applied in overpopulated areas where the overriding consideration is that the productivity of the scarce factor—that is, of the land—should be increased. The soil is cultivated repeatedly and with such minute attention that the commonest implements are often the rake and the spade; the land

[1] In Norway 'cultivated', i.e. fertilized, grasslands are classified separately.

is heavily manured and the water resources are carefully husbanded. The net result is a greatly modified landscape, and a good example of an intensive system of this type, with high yields per unit of area, is found in a typical market garden, where the climate is completely artificial and the soil is transformed by massive additions of fertilizing substances. The same practices, though to a lesser degree, can be recognized in the Spanish *huertas*; here, however, the climate is extremely favourable.

At the other end of the scale, mechanization aims at cutting down labour and increasing its productivity. In every type of operation, cultivating and harvesting included, human energy is replaced as far as possible by the work of animals and the power of machines. The hand tool is replaced by the motorized implement. The combine-harvester does all the work which previously was performed by scythe and sickle, flail and winnowing basket. It is in sparsely populated regions such as the 'new countries' that this type of mechanization is most needed, for, contrary to the general situation elsewhere, these are sometimes afflicted by a dearth of men on the land, and the special attribute of the machine is that it increases the farm-worker's daily output.

3. Although mechanization and intensification have so far been discussed separately, they are not mutually exclusive. In fact, they often occur in combination. For instance, if a tractor is used to increase the number of times a field is cultivated when only a short season is available for such operations, its use will result in higher crop yields, and it can therefore be regarded as an agent of agricultural intensification. Conversely, scientific fertilizing not only raises the productivity of the land, but also ensures a higher output per unit of labour employed. At opposite ends of the scale the 'intensive mechanization' of the English lowland contrasts with the 'extensive mechanization', with fewer machines to the square mile, of the much less densely populated West of the United States.

In analysing the features of a particular kind of agricultural economy, we shall first make a rapid examination of the relevant features of its so-called 'natural' environment. First and foremost, the climatic conditions will be described, for these are not susceptible to modification by man, except at great cost.

Although there can be no question that soils in their virgin state are a product of the action of climate on the rocks at or near the surface, it has been established that when dealing with cultivated soils, account must be taken of the changes brought about by generations of farmers whose work of fertilizing, liming, and water-control has culminated in an overall improvement of the edaphic conditions which some economists often regard as a form of capital. Admittedly, some farming systems have merely exploited the soil and brought about a deterioration of their most valuable resource. Unfortunately, such practices are as common among the 'primitive' Africans as they are among 'civilized' Algerian settlers and North American farmers. Facts such as these pose the problem of soil conservation which is a question of paramount importance for the future of mankind, for soil erosion is the swift result of overpopulation, unenlightened farming practices, and the dangerous over-liberal doctrine of production at the lowest cost. In this matter, a *laissez-faire* policy can no longer be tolerated.

3. The Agricultural Undertaking and the Human Factor

4. Whether it be farm, estate or collective, it is the individual undertaking which, by its work on the land—present and past—turns the forces of nature to advantage. For the most part, however, agriculture is still the domain of the family enterprise and is therefore carried on by a great multitude of highly dispersed units of production, some of them quite small and many of them very small indeed. The provision of machinery is thus inherently more difficult and costly than in manufacturing industry, where the trend is for ever-increasing concentration, while the discontinuous use of farm equipment heightens the contrast still further.

In some advanced types of economy, both capitalist and collectivist, the scale of agricultural enterprise is being increased, though more rapidly in some areas than in others. This is a significant trend; it is generally accompanied by the introduction of an appreciable volume of machinery and agriculture is therefore brought into line, in certain important respects, with manufacturing industry. In dealing with a particular type of farming, we shall therefore give some indication of the average size of the undertakings concerned. For instance, in the capitalist world, the family enterprise is the rule, and it gives ample proof of vitality when there is no shortage of space or of capital, as in the United States.

The farm unit operates in the context of a legal system which regulates the appropriation and disposal of the various factors of production, including the land. It also determines the farmer's relationship with the moneylender, banker, or financier and, if he does not own the land himself, with his landlord. The law may either help or hinder the modernization and equipping of the countryside, but is notoriously slow in adjusting itself to technical developments and is, in consequence, rarely of much assistance. We shall indicate in outline some of the legal conditions which favour progressive farming.

Each individual farm is conditioned by its economic and social setting. Fertilizers, tractors, and machines are the products of highly organized industries characterized by the efficient use of man-power and mass production methods, and commanding all the resources of modern technology. Apart from the natural environment of a region, therefore, its degree of industrialization stands out as the most important criterion in any evaluation of its agricultural future. Quite apart from the fact that it manufactures equipment for sale to the farmer, industry breaks down the barriers of self-sufficiency and precipitates the transition to a commercial economy by creating in its labour force a market for farm produce which, saving periods of depression, is well endowed with purchasing power.

Having already amassed a great fund of capital, an industrial region can the more easily continue to accrue its wealth. Moreover, increments generally accumulate more quickly in manufacturing industry and commerce than in agriculture, where the returns march in slow rhythm with the seasons. Thus, whereas the methods of former times demanded hard manual work most of all, today the farmer needs the modern tools of his craft, but almost inevitably lacks the means to buy them, and this is the most formidable obstacle which bars the way to rapid progress. The land is rarely short of hands, but very often it has neither capital nor machines.

5. The density of population is another important element in our analysis. When the density is high, the law of diminishing returns hinders the necessary intensification of production unless better techniques are constantly evolved and applied, but this is rarely the case in underdeveloped countries where research and education are both limited in their scope. In areas such as Spain and the Far East, where industrialization is still in a very early stage, there is the problem of finding useful outlets for the superabundant labour of the countryside where low productivity is all too often the rule.

Where the density of population is very low, the problem of rapid development is one of finding enormous quantities of equipment as quickly as possible. But this is not always practicable, and there is always the risk that the materials will be misapplied or used inefficiently, as may so easily happen, for example, in the administration of transport services.

A large part is also played by the educational system, and in this connexion standards of professional training are of particular significance, for successful intensive agriculture demands a very high level of competence. Whereas a large undertaking needs to fill only a small number of key posts, the proportion of highly qualified men needs to be very much greater when every farmer is the manager of his own small family enterprise.

When all these factors have been considered in turn, a clear picture will emerge of the conditions under which the farmer has to operate, and at this juncture it will be appropriate to study the broad features of his techniques of production; in a general survey such as this we cannot concern ourselves with the minutiae of his methods. We shall, however, attempt to classify various systems according to their degree of intensiveness, with particular emphasis on permanent improvements, such as schemes of drainage or irrigation, on the frequency of soil working, and above all on methods of fertilization.

In some cases, no attempt whatsoever is made to fertilize the soil, and instances of this neglect are to be found in many primitive societies and even sometimes in those generally considered to be 'civilized', although here this adjective hardly seems appropriate. The next stage is when fertilization is practised sporadically; its value is hardly understood, and it exists mainly as a convenient method of waste disposal. In the final stage, soil enrichment, in one form or another, is practised consciously and for its own sake. So long as transport remains difficult and expensive, however, only the ground in the immediate vicinity of the home is affected. The first kind of fertilizer to be used is generally the residue of ashes from the hearth, and only later is the value of night soil, animal droppings, and plant remains, which are all available on the farm itself, fully appreciated. The most advanced stage of all is reached when fertilizers are brought in from outside the farm especially, when, like chemical fertilizers, they are the product of a factory process.

The degree of mechanization in an economy is indicated by the relative proportion of work done by hand, by animals, and by machines, respectively. A small proportion of manual labour obviously points to an advanced stage of development. In a primitive system, man is the beast of burden, but later he becomes a director of operations, driving the tractor which pulls or drives the machinery; furthermore, the efficiency of the latter in the performance of its highly specialized functions is constantly being improved. At the same time the need for equipment increases and fresh improvements are continually added to the work of the past.

4. Types of Farming: Productivity

6. The more he improves the physical environment, the greater is man's freedom in choosing the plants he wishes to cultivate. Having increased the volume and reliability of crop yields, he can also afford to add to his list of domestic animals. Thus, technically, he may select the precise combination he wishes to pursue[1] from a very large number of possible enterprises. In other words, he chooses a 'type' of agriculture or animal husbandry,[2] and the description of these types, together with the varying rates at which they have been developed, is an integral part of the study of the different forms of rural economy with which they are associated.

In subsistence farming, where nothing is brought in from outside, there is generally an even greater variety of produce than in the primitive type of economy, where a wide range of necessities is supplied by collecting rather than by agriculture. Similarly, subsistence farming is more varied than modern commercial agriculture, which has grown up thanks to improvements in communications and methods of distribution—although the efficiency of the latter is more open to doubt. Commercial agriculture is free to specialize in one or several of the products best suited to the overall conditions.

Once certain crops have been selected, they will often be cultivated on the same land year after year, and the form of the rotation will be designed to make tillage and fertilizing as convenient and economical as possible. The sequence sugar-beet, wheat, and barley, for instance, represented the basic rotation practised in Northern France during the latter part of the nineteenth and the early part of the twentieth centuries. Land utilization, on the other hand, is the proportion of a given area devoted to each crop: 25 acres of sugar-beet, 25 of wheat, and 25 of barley in 1953-4, for example.

Type of farming, crop rotation system, and land utilization are the appropriate criteria for the classification of modern rural economies. When properly balanced, they facilitate soil conservation and avoid extremes of seasonal labour demands. At one time, however, the same land was not cropped continuously, and even today in some backward areas periods of cultivation are separated by long intervals of fallow.

---

[1] But he is increasingly forced to produce at the lowest possible costs by economic factors.

[2] Bergmann defines them in terms of: type of product (crop and animal) and factors of production employed (land, labour, capital).

Thus cultivation may be either continuous or intermittent, and the former is characteristic of all the more advanced kinds of farming, except in semi-arid regions.

7. In Africa and Asia especially the rearing of animals is still carried on by nomadic herdsmen who practise no form of agriculture whatsoever. They rely solely on the unimproved pastures and undertake seasonal migrations in areas where the climatic régime restricts plant growth at certain times of the year. Such an economy becomes more intensive as its interest in crop production increases; its animals then provide power for tilling the land and manure for fertilizing it.

Such a system is more productive and certain commodities plentiful at one time of the year can be stored for use when needed; hay, for example, bundles of leafy twigs and various other items culled from forest, steppe, scrub, or low-lying marshland. Next, certain fields may be set aside for cattle and converted into permanent grassland. This, however, may be a retrograde step for it is often associated with a fall in productivity.

The introduction of rotation grasses, roots, kale, and other fodder crops, however, always represents a very real advance, although even here, as in the case of direct food production, the intensiveness of the system will depend on how much the land is cultivated and fertilized. Later, the fodder crops may be supplemented by the purchase of feeding-stuffs—mostly industrial by-products and often rich in proteins—like cattle-cake, bran, and offal. Finally comes the use of various substances, such as mineral salts and vitamins, advocated by modern science. Once this stage is reached, selective breeding can safely begin for, although pedigree animals are more delicate, the farmer is now in a position to give them the care and attention they need. It was during the eighteenth century that these techniques of selective breeding and large-scale fodder-crop cultivation began to be applied, first in England and later in the rest of Western Europe.[1]

Except in its very highly specialized forms—like pig-rearing and poultry-keeping, which rely almost wholly on purchases of feeding-stuffs—animal husbandry is generally an integral part of the modern type of farming system. The size of the animal population will, of course, determine the volume of fodder crops to be grown and the size of reserves needed to tide over the season of restricted plant growth. Apart from the Equatorial zone, a modern system of intensive farming should provide for a high density of animals in order to satisfy the growing demand for meat and milk derivatives from the more advanced

---

[1] Cf. *La Géographie de l'élevage*, by Paul Veyret (Paris, 1951).

and highly industrialized countries. The extent to which an agricultural system meets this need will enable us to evaluate its stage of development. On a number of occasions we have already pronounced most unfavourably on the position in regions which do not conform in this respect (density of cattle too low in the Paris Basin, for example).

8. The various ways in which different types of farming are carried on and the proportion in which the various factors of production are employed result in different levels of productivity. The effectiveness of a given type cannot be measured exactly, but estimates can be made in terms of yield per unit area or of yield per working day (productivity of labour). The number of working days required to produce a certain quantity of a specified crop can be used as a basis of comparison between the various kinds of rural economy, and the most representative unit is the hundredweight of grain.[1] But only large differences between the indices thus obtained are of any significance.

In a modern economy, agriculture can feed a large number of people while employing a relatively small labour force,[2] but although this feature is characteristic of the advanced countries the reverse is true of primitive economies. Except in countries like England which import large quantities of food, the efficiency of a nation's farming bears an inverse relationship to the proportion of the working population employed on the land. This, however, is only true if the soil is not being exploited wastefully. A further characteristic of modern farming, and of specialized farming in particular, is that the greater part of the produce is marketed. In a primitive economy, on the other hand, almost everything is consumed by the producer himself.

5. The Search for Improvement

9. The agricultural scientist is not content merely to describe the general principles of an agricultural system. The identification and description of the various types are his starting-point, for he is constantly seeking to raise current levels of productivity by increasing the resources available and improving the manner of their employment. The facts must be thoroughly known and understood before the question of improvement can be considered, and it was the disregard of

[1] This is not to imply, as some have suggested without proof, that technical progress is limited to this type of product.

[2] Food products make up about four-fifths of the world's agricultural output, by value. But industrial raw materials, and, foremost among them, textiles, must also be taken into account if a true picture of overall agricultural productivity is to emerge.

this basic precept which cost the first European agronomists their repeated setbacks in the unfamiliar environment of the tropics.[1]

Accurate information about the environmental conditions and historical antecedents of an agricultural system must be supplemented by an appraisal of the human and material resources available, and by an examination of actual and potential markets. Only then can the agricultural scientist begin the task of synthesis—the most difficult of all his tasks—which alone will enable him to formulate proposals for improving the existing state of affairs.

The various types of agriculture and animal husbandry have emerged after long processes of trial and error and under conditions which made the direct satisfaction of domestic needs a far more compelling necessity than it is today. They are now feeling the effects of the revolution in transport, but in very varying degrees, and in the light of these changes it will be interesting to consider what systems are really appropriate to the various regions studied. This is not always an easy task, for numerous factors are involved and the situation is sometimes in a state of rapid change. In this work, therefore, a dynamic approach has been attempted whenever possible. Physical factors such as climate and soil—rapid erosion and intensive fertilization excepted—change but slowly. Human and economic conditions, on the other hand, are subject to rapid fluctuations.

It follows that readjustments to changing circumstances must be made much more promptly in the future than they were during the slow-moving centuries of the past. Among the various trends of recent years, some, like the cultivation of steep slopes, are positively dangerous and threaten to destroy the soil itself. Others, like allowing land to revert to grass, especially where such factors as low rainfall or permeable soils are present, are retrogressive and lead to a decline in productivity. Current trends, therefore, are not always correctly orientated, but fortunately we shall find many areas where real progress is being made.

The present generation of agricultural scientists is faced with a new and urgent task—namely, the problem of the rational utilization of the soil. The study of this problem, sometimes known as 'geonomy', is receiving considerable attention in the English-speaking countries, in

---

[1] The first recommendations which wree made to improve riziculture in Indochina were based on our knowledge of wheat cultivation in the temperate zone. We have therefore studied the traditional methods (see our *La culture du riz dans le delta du Tonkin*) before reaching any conclusions as to their merits or demerits.

the U.S.S.R., and in Czechoslovakia and other people's democracies, but in France research has hardly yet begun.

10. After careful consideration of all the evidence, it may in some instances appear that the only course is to abandon certain areas now cultivated, a course which may sometimes involve the migration of people to other areas. Obviously, such a step could be justified only in terms of the advantages that would accrue to the people directly concerned. Geonomic studies will have their greatest value, however, and will be most strongly encouraged when they form the basis of a centralized and compulsorily enforced plan, for thus their recommendations can be put into effect without delay. But they are still worthwhile if individuals are merely advised of their conclusions and retain their freedom of action. A compromise solution is to offer subsidies to those who conform with farming principles declared to be in the national interest. This is the policy favoured in the Soil Conservation Programme of the United States.

The problem of deciding how best to utilize the soil in a particular area is fraught with difficulties, and the reader is advised to examine critically the particular solutions suggested in the following chapters. The rate at which development should proceed, whether intensification or mechanization be the point at issue, is an even more delicate problem. Only those who have specialized for many years in the study of a micro-region can possibly commit themselves with any degree of certainty in this matter, but all the same it offers a fruitful field for research. For our part, we shall confine our attention to general principles, emphasizing only the major steps which must be taken to utilize resources more efficiently and marshal fresh instruments of production. It is fairly easy, as we have seen, to recommend in a general way whether priority should be given to mechanization or to higher yields per acre, but detailed proposals are a far more difficult matter.

Every country needs in fact to increase both its yields per acre and the efficiency of its agricultural labour, for the one affects the overall volume of production, while the other, considered in conjunction with prevailing price levels, determines the standard of living of the rural population (subsidies apart). Pausing here and there to consider briefly how various social, economic, and legal systems could facilitate development, we shall try to show in what general direction progress might be sought. Finally, apart from the size of farm units and the degree of industrialization, we shall also be concerned with the availability of assured markets for agricultural produce.

6. Hunger, Rising Population, Soil Destruction, and Neo-Malthusian Economics

11. 'To produce as much as possible with the minimum of effort is the acme of economic behaviour', wrote the physiocrat Quesnay, and whatever the economic structure, any worthwhile scheme of development must work towards this goal. Naturally, many farmers are still haunted by the memory of economic depressions, especially of the crisis period, 1929-36. Since the beginning of 1951, however, the policy of economic Malthusianism,[1] which creates scarcity to force up agricultural prices, has again begun to find favour in certain official quarters in France. It is no longer proposed, as in 1932-4, simply to destroy wealth. Now the policy is to stifle production, more or less surreptitiously, by such devices as reducing purchases of fertilizers and equipment. This unfortunate trend is reflected in the substantial yearly increase in the acreage of rough pasture at the expense of arable land, which is jeopardizing the French economy today.

We can understand some of the motives of the small minority of farmers' leaders who ally themselves dispassionately with these policies, although they do so by preaching them to the peasant rather than by setting the example themselves. Their attitude is one of protest against industrial Malthusianism, of reaction against the notorious producers' ring. Industrialists, being neither so numerous nor dispersed as farmers, can restrict output without recourse to legislation and can hold the consumer—including the farmer—to ransom at will. By opposing such practices, the farmers' organizations would win the approval of the community at large and link their own interests with those of the country as a whole. In the highest quarters, however, one discerns a growing *rapprochement* between industry and agriculture. One may well ask whether its sole purpose is to promote the public good and achieve that rational and continuous development in the whole field of national production which is the only real criterion of a country's wealth.

The farmer obviously has the right to refrain from producing so much as to bring about his own financial ruin. On the other hand, a limited fall in prices can be partially offset by increasing production and lowering the cost per unit of output. Indeed, the only way to satisfy the consumer and avert loss to the producer, whose profits are

[1] 'Malthusianism' is a term frequently used by French economists to describe actions which have the effect of reducing output or even of preventing its increase.

directly related to prices, is to improve the techniques of production. Government interference should be inspired by the desire to raise productivity by a better use of natural and human resources. Instead of bolstering up the inefficient producer, efforts should be made, as in England, to help the progressive farmer by subsidizing his attempts at modernization. Above all, the distribution of a country's purchasing power must be regulated to ensure that all production destined for home consumption finds a market. This precludes a *laissez-faire* policy; but many farmers who demand security of price still insist on calling themselves 'liberals'.

12. The neo-Malthusians would deprive mankind of one of its fundamental sources of pride and self-respect—namely, the satisfaction of working to increase the wealth of the community. The farmer and the agricultural scientist are particularly concerned, and, but for such motives, this book might never have been written. The world urgently needs to increase its agricultural output, and the task is made more difficult by the rapidity with which it must be accomplished. There are three main facts which, while they confirm the imperative need for greater production, demonstrate the shortcomings of a neo-Malthusian policy. The first of these is the prevalence of malnutrition in many parts of the world. Since the Hot Springs Conference, when national governments were declared responsible for ensuring that certain minimum standards of nutrition were everywhere maintained, studies by the Food and Agriculture Organization have revealed that nearly two-thirds of the world's population is actually short of food. The stark hunger of millions of children in Asia, Africa, Central and South America, and southern Europe (Spain, Yugoslavia, southern Italy, Rumania, Greece, and Albania) is a horrifying theme—which even the cinema has generally avoided.[1] But when great decisions are being taken it is a fact to be remembered.

Hunger is a rare phenomenon in countries like France which, by reason of better farming practices or lower population densities, are relatively prosperous. But even here one may find qualitative deficiencies in the diet among large sections of the community, especially among the lower-paid workers in industry and, paradoxically enough, among agricultural labourers. The position is worse in the environs of towns, in western France, and in the uplands. Deficiencies of protective foods (animal proteins, vitamins, calcium, phosphorus, and other mineral

---

[1] See Josué de Castro's excellent *Géopolitique de la faim* (Editions ouvrières, 1952). However, we hesitate to accept the author's contention that lack of proteins and fertility are cause and effect.

salts) have frequently come under the notice of dietetic surveys, and we shall refer to some of these in due course. The worst affected are the poorer classes, but such deficiencies can also be observed in other sections of the community, for ignorance also plays its part.

Even if France selfishly refused to envisage schemes of mutual aid with other countries and tried to isolate her economy, she would soon find that self-sufficiency was impracticable and that a rapid expansion of agricultural production was one of the essential factors in settling her balance of payments. This, of course, is on the assumption that she wishes to retain her national sovereignty, her economic, and thus also her political, independence. Contrary to general opinion, if the purchasing power of the country as a whole became really adequate, the market for food would reveal itself to be comparatively elastic. It takes seven to eight vegetable calories to produce an animal calorie. Thus, replacing a proportion of the bread and potatoes in the diet with meat and cheese would multiply, in the same proportion, the number of original vegetable calories consumed.[1]

13. The second vital consideration is the annual rate of growth of the world's population—2·5 per 1,000 at the end of the seventeenth century, 10 per 1,000 today.[2] In some European countries, in the U.S.S.R. since 1932, in North America and in Australia agricultural production has more than kept pace with population growth and nutritional standards have risen fairly rapidly. The problem of underdeveloped countries, however, is still acute, especially where they are overpopulated. Their position has been aggravated by the part they have played in exporting foodstuffs to more prosperous regions, and many of those which are already liable to famine are seeing their situation worsening as population continues to increase much more rapidly than food production. The plight of the Indian Union, where, according to certain British economists, the supply of food per head has decreased by nearly a third during the last century, is no less than tragic.

The third, and by no means the least, cause for alarm is the rapid destruction of soil, which has affected a considerable proportion of the world's agricultural land and which has resulted from the use of techniques inappropriate to the environment. There have been heavy losses of fertility, while erosion by wind and water, lateritization, and even leaching and podsolization, have all played their part. North America, which of all countries in the Temperate Zone has witnessed soil erosion on the largest scale, has also contributed the first detailed studies of the

[1] On this point see our *Le problème agricole français* (N.E.L., 1942).
[2] Marcel Reinhard, *Histoire de la population mondiale de 1700 à 1948* (Paris, 1949).

problem and of possible remedies. Soil erosion has not yet sealed the fate of the world; there are remedies. The danger, however, is underlined by the enormous resources and the heavy expenditure needed to repair the damage in severely affected countries, which are often poor and in no position to finance the necessary projects themselves. For greater effect, the traditional techniques of conservation, like terracing and contour farming, should be supplemented by the application of soil correctives, such as lime and organic matter.

If the nations of the world should ever really want to help each other, here is a sphere where the possibilities of international cooperation might be first exploited: in the fight against famine for the present, and in conserving the soil resources of the world so as to save future generations from the threat of want. Effective action, carried out on a scale commensurate with the magnitude of the danger, would cost a little less than the world is now spending on armaments. Having little propaganda value, the dangers of soil erosion are sometimes completely ignored, as in Spain and Brazil, while elsewhere the resources deployed are insufficient for the task, as in North Africa. The Soil Conservation Programme of the United States and the Stalin Plan for the Transformation of Nature of the U.S.S.R. are the most considerable projects yet undertaken, but even these do not seem bold enough to ward off the danger.

7. Remedial Measures can be Effective

14. The world is at a turning-point in its history, and while there are some who regard the future with foreboding, others look forward with confidence. Both views are probably too extreme. The pessimists of the American school are right in pointing to the tragic side of the situation, which reveals itself as soon as one tries to imagine the world 100 years hence, if trends in food production, soil erosion, and population growth continue as they are today. Added to this is the exhaustion of reserves of essential soil minerals, accelerated by wasteful methods of sewerage and refuse-disposal in our vast urban agglomerations, where little thought is spared for the problem of restoring all this food-derived material to the land. Unaided by the destructive force of war, these factors could bring the world to the threshold of a terrible famine.

The optimists of the Soviet and Catholic schools have equally good grounds for refusing to countenance the possibility of man's annihilation. They stake their belief in the tremendous potentialities of concerted action by the agricultural sciences. These would have a much better chance of success if they could operate in an economic structure able to deal with the rapid increases in production, and the Age of Abundance which would follow.

The chronic fear of a limited and easily glutted market would have to be removed. *Laissez-faire*, or even reliance on the ludicrously inadequate efforts being made today, is bound to vindicate the pessimistic view. Failing international action to protect the tropical and subtropical regions of Africa and South America, where the world's largest remaining reserves of undeveloped land are situated, the final disastrous chapter in the history of soil erosion will undoubtedly be written. This book, however, is intended to be a warning call, not a cry of despair.

The optimists go too far when they condemn the idea of birth control. They simply reveal their inability to appreciate the difficulties of raising production in countries like India and other parts of monsoon Asia which are both overpopulated and underdeveloped. Unless international aid—approximately on the scale of the world's armaments expenditure in 1954—is forthcoming, at least a generation must pass before enough local capital to initiate all the urgently needed schemes of improvement can be accumulated. In the meantime the production curve would never be rising steeply enough in relation to the rate of population increase to ensure a rapid rise in general standards of nutrition. Finally, we prefer the idea of human happiness to that of mere numbers. We shall refrain from commenting on the ethics of those who, while opposing birth control, advocate various forms of economic Malthusianism, ranging from the destruction of wealth to the restriction or even the stagnation of production.[1]

15. We prefer the optimistic view, provided that the size and difficulty of the task are not underestimated, especially in the early stages. We are hopeful enough to believe that if enough encouragement is given to research and to all kinds of investment, a rapid increase in food production will follow. Fortified in this faith—it is difficult to prove—we consider that a thorough analysis of the difficulties involved will be an important contribution to the overall objective. Our belief is not a certainty, and its realization will depend on the efficient use of every resource. The *laissez-faire* policy of a liberal economy aims merely at minimizing the cost of current production, and thus disqualifies itself from the rôle of mobilizing every available means in the fight against hunger—a task which appears profitable only when viewed from a

[1] See our '*Diverses formes du malthusianisme agricole*' in the *Revue Internationale* (June 1946); and also '*Quatre âges de l'Agriculture*' in *Cahiers des Ingénieurs Agronomes* (June 1951), and our reply in *Petit Cahiers* (November 1951).

REMEDIAL MEASURES CAN BE EFFECTIVE

national or world standpoint. Those who object to central direction on the Soviet model would be well advised to settle their differences and give their urgent attention to setting up forms of economic organization which will work efficiently.

It is not an easy matter. Demographic and social considerations force the pace, but the agricultural scientist advises extreme prudence. Tropical farming techniques which can be applied without the risk of soil impoverishment have not yet been perfected. It is high time that the enormous damage inflicted by the robber economy of the first settlers was repaired, and that the generations of the future should cease to be sacrificed on the altar of present-day convenience or self-indulgence.

We have now reviewed the main aspects of our study and the essential considerations which will receive attention during our analysis of several different kinds of rural economy. Inter-tropical Africa—a highly important nerve centre in the future development of the world—will be our starting-point.

II

The Equatorial Rain Forest in the North of the Belgian Congo[1]

1. Favourable Climate, Poor, Unstable Soils, Low Level of Cultural Development

16. The luxuriant vegetation of the dense or so-called 'rain' forest (not 'virgin' forest, for it nearly always comprises secondary growth which has often re-established itself after a period of cultivation) has for many years led to the belief that equatorial conditions are ideally suited to the growth of all plants, and consequently to agriculture. The area with which we shall be concerned in this chapter stretches on either side of the Equator but extends a little further into the Northern Hemisphere than the Southern. It is a very humid region, generally with more than 60 in. of rain, and includes the central part of the continent and a sector of the Atlantic seaboard. Further east, in the same latitude, the climate becomes much drier.

Even in a region with rain throughout the year—in the vicinity of Stanleyville, for example—a decrease in the winter rainfall soon checks the growth of vegetation; inadequacy of rainfall rapidly becomes a limiting factor. In the south of French Equatorial Africa (A.E.F.), between Brazzaville and Dolisie in the Middle Congo, on the margins of the drier region of Gabon, neither of the two rainy seasons, here distinctly marked, provides the optimum amount of rainfall for many crops; not even for the ground-nut, which is hardly an exacting crop.

Here the fully developed equatorial forest has already given way to its degraded form, the savanna grassland, with only a scatter of trees. The true equatorial region, however, whether it has one or two rainy

[1] Field studies in December 1949 and January 1950 at the request of the Compagnie française pour le développement des textiles. On the basis of what had actually been achieved in the Belgian Congo we examined the possibilities of extending the cotton acreage in French Equatorial Africa and the North Cameroons.

18

seasons, is characterized by its fairly abundant and generally reliable rainfall. Not until the tropical zone is reached does one find a really distinct and prolonged dry season. In the centre—that is, in the Congo proper—the two rainy seasons, spring and autumn, are distinguished from the two so-called dry seasons only by an even greater degree of humidity.

This climate, with its continuous heat and very small variations of temperature, undoubtedly favours a great profusion of plant growth. On the other hand, when soil is no longer protected by a continuous forest cover from rain-wash and solar photo-oxidation, its rapid destruction is assured by factors inherent in the climate. The dense rain forest which flourishes in such a climate is found in the centre of the Congo region, but at its margins, on every side, the forest is threatened by the advance of the savanna, which is favoured by the activities of man.

17. In Central Africa the soils are largely derived from the rocks of the Archaean and Palaeozoic basement and from the soft Lubilash sandstones,[1] or, in the centre of the Congo Basin, from old alluvial deposits. The great majority of them are more highly acid and much poorer in essential plant foods than the soils of temperate regions. It is a mistake to assume a high degree of agricultural potential on the evidence of vigorous forest growth. The low humus content and the absence of a good absorbing medium, due to the type of clay (kaolinized and greatly inferior to the montmorillonites of temperate latitudes), result in the rapid eluviation of essential soil substances.

Although the soils are stable so long as they support a vegetation cover, as soon as the forest is cleared the organic matter is broken down too quickly to permit a great deal of humification. As the climate allows bacterial processes to continue without interruption, nitrogen losses are extremely heavy. The soluble minerals also disappear very rapidly, while hydraulic erosion (the carrying away of soil particles by run-off) is facilitated. The latter assumes dangerous proportions even on gentle slopes with a gradient of more than 1/125. On the other hand, soils developed on newer sediments, along watercourses and bordering the coast, and those derived from recent volcanic rocks, are more fertile and call for the earliest possible development.

The climatic conditions themselves are ideal for plantations of cacao,

---

[1] 'The enormous extent of these sandstones of continental origin are the curse of the tropical regions. The sandy soils which develop on them have little value.' P. Gourou in *Les Pays Tropicaux*, 1948. Is not this work unnecessarily pessimistic on occasions?

oil-palm (*Elaeis guineensis*), rubber, and cinchona; all these are adapted to strongly acid soils and are more or less confined to the equatorial zone. Coffee, bananas, and manioc are also typical, but they are found in tropical regions as well. It is, however, difficult to find extensive areas anywhere in Africa where the soil is rich enough for the establishment of large modern plantations and where high yields would conceivably offset the heavy initial costs. The Compagnie générale des oléagineux tropicaux, a partly public, partly private corporation formed in France in 1947,[1] is having difficulty in finding a site for its projected oil-palm plantation.

On the whole, this natural environment is distinctly less favourable to plant growth than the equatorial zone of the Far East, which enjoys a better climate and a higher proportion of very fertile soils derived from recent volcanic rocks. It is therefore not surprising to find that European plantations concerned with the crops already referred to began in South-East Asia, especially in Indonesia, several decades before they were initiated in Africa.

18. Another factor is the difficulty of communication in so vast a continent, which has helped to delay both the discovery of the interior, incomplete even at the end of the last century, and subsequently its political conquest by European powers. The first phase was one of exploitation pure and simple, and even now, apart from the extreme north and south, the rational development of the continent as a whole has scarcely begun. In the equatorial zone, the native people found on our first arrival were of Bantu stock. They are more advanced than the Pygmies, but their organization of production is still primitive: division of labour is almost non-existent; only the blacksmith and the potter have fairly specialized functions.

There is hardly any tradition of spinning and weaving, and there is little in the way of local handicrafts. Until the arrival of Europeans, clothing was of the most primitive kind. Its more recent general use, associated with the import of cotton goods, is highly prejudicial to health, as the sun's rays, which promote the assimilation of calcium, are thereby intercepted. In the small, primitive, self-sufficient communities of the region, where each group provides for itself alone, commercial activities were restricted to an absolute minimum until recent times. The well-known 'mute trade' with the Pygmies, which consisted of the exchange of meat for the products of cultivation (grains, roots) or of local handicrafts (spear-heads, pottery), was always on a limited scale. As their external trade was very small, these communities were

[1] This company will be mentioned again at the end of Chapter III.

unable to engage in either saving or investment. In the villages, at least four adults out of every five are still engaged in farming or collecting activities.

The land is still under collective ownership and generally belongs to the 'tribe', which in this sense includes the living and the dead. Through the jurisdiction of 'land chiefs', the tribe apportions the land among the heads of families.[1] Consequently, the cultivator's right to the use of land is precarious and, indeed, it disappears as soon as he abandons his plot to the spontaneous growth of vegetation. Originally, the land chief decided which areas were to be cultivated, and for how long. This communal tradition prevented practices destructive of soil fertility and maintained a primitive régime of soil conservation—this without selling anything outside and without any sure guarantee against famine.

Work on the land is still generally a matter for the patriarchal family, often enlarged, especially when its head can afford a large number of wives. His wealth thus grows as a result of the work of women and children, and, were it not that consumer goods are nearly always preferred, this would permit a start to be made in the accumulation of capital. In addition to the field belonging to the head of the family, where everyone must work, the youths and women tend their small individual plots, the produce of which belongs entirely to them. This enables them to vary their diet or to treat themselves to small luxuries or even to save up for their dowries. Finally, when there is a lot of urgent work on hand (clearing, hoeing, weeding), additional help is obtained from 'age brotherhoods', gangs of young people working to the rhythm of music and receiving food and drink for their labours, who are in actual fact exploited. We are dealing here with a communal and highly organized system of agriculture; we shall see that it is fairly well adapted to the natural conditions.

19. Education as we know it in Europe is not at all widespread, especially in the villages. The decline of tribal institutions is sometimes accompanied, before the introduction of modern teaching, by the complete disappearance of initiation, a very practical form of instruction and of great value in tribal life; the plants indicative of the degree of soil fertility are no longer so well known to the younger generation as to their elders. In the French colonies (now Union Française) education has been greatly handicapped by the decision—a throwback to

---

[1] This is merely a schematic outline, which is also valid for the tropical zone, but the local variations are much more complex than this description suggests. For further details see *Paysans d'Afrique Occidentale*, by Henri Labouret (1941).

the old 'colonialism'—that teaching should be conducted only in French, which is, after all, a foreign language to the African.

The use of native languages, which are often very diverse, is certainly fraught with difficulties. A solution might well be found if the system used in the Belgian Congo were widely adopted. The idea is to group those languages with a common basis over large areas into simple, precise 'languages of communication' which could be enriched gradually so as to adapt them to modern conditions. Belgian Congo officials have to learn three of these languages, and they can therefore dispense with the interpreter, that fearful barrier between the French administrator and the native people, depriving them as he does of all direct, human contacts. It is true that the interpreter often serves his own interests, but he can frequently make mistakes in all good faith when it is not merely a question of translation, but of communication between two entirely different mentalities. In the Belgian Congo, with its ingenious language system, the average Bantu cultivator already appears to be making more rapid progress than in the French colonies, but a knowledge of French will still be an asset to those who need to learn modern techniques. The Belgian idea seems preferable even to the 'basic French' which is now being tried.

The intellectual calibre of the native peoples has long been assessed in the context of our own racial prejudices. These are more virulent in South Africa and the United States and, while they enjoy less popularity in France, they are prevalent among the European settler communities. An old missionary in the Belgian Congo once exclaimed, 'After forty years in Africa, how sad to conclude that the black man has no soul!'[1] Already in the sixth century, at a time when woman was considered an inferior being, there were men in holy orders asking whether she had a soul; and even now our dominant religion does not admit the equality of the sexes (priesthood, etc.). Be that as it may, we ourselves have found in the Southern States of the U.S.A. a situation typical of societies with an oppressed minority; for we have met coloured university teachers of great technical ability with higher moral principles than the whites.

In the settler communities there are scores of sayings which impute all the notorious 'native' shortcomings to all the indigenous peoples, with hardly any distinctions, from the Mediterranean to the Equator

---

[1] An ageing bishop is said to have declared: 'When I die I shall ask God to open up the skull of a Negro and show me what there is inside.' It is true that only a small minority of missionaries feel like this, but we gained the impression that such men were less of a rarity in the Belgian Congo than elsewhere.

or from Senegal to Tonkin: they are dishonest, untruthful, lazy. . . . As for thieving and lying, the police evidence is biased, and they should be viewed against the background of mean living conditions; and it is as well to remember that the incidence of petty crime has yet to be compared with its prevalence in other societies. With regard to laziness, the frequently permanent conditions of undernourishment and the unremittingly serious incidence of endemic disease are a sufficient explanation.[1] Malaria and dysentery make exertion almost insufferably difficult. In spite of this, the African, and more frequently still the Asian peasant, can sometimes find considerable reserves of energy. But if great efforts are demanded of him, and he is not provided with an adequate diet and the necessary minimum of sanitary amenities, his mortality rate becomes alarmingly high, as, for instance, during heavy portage work, or when the Congo-Ocean railway was built—'Every sleeper cost a corpse', wrote Albert Londres.

Another obstacle to progress is the increasing lack of understanding shown by Europeans who, sometimes with the best intentions and with completely unselfish motives, want to impose their own conceptions of happiness. They would appreciate the true value of the native ideals if they scrutinized them more carefully and understood them more thoroughly. For instance, there existed, especially in music and sculpture, a unique indigenous art form which has, indeed, contributed to our own within the last fifty years. But now it is already declining, for we have tried to make its exponents conform with our own preconceived notions. The Belgian official forces the master potter, heir to centuries of tradition, to plant a row of coffee trees.

Finally, measures of racial segregation are too widely applied. An incident which occurred at the hotel near Aketi Station, a railhead on the Itirumbi, a Congo tributary in the north of the Belgian Congo, will serve to illustrate the point. Agbessi Banga,[2] my chauffeur and friend, was standing in front of the hotel, for I had not dared to invite him to our table, and I brought him a glass of mineral water. The hotel manager angrily pounced on me, declaring that such conduct was forbidden by the laws of the Congo. 'This is not a French colony!' he cried, in exasperation.

A fundamental feature of the human background in the region under consideration is the low density of population, which often falls to from five to ten per square mile; this could even, in the last resort, vindicate

---

[1] P. Gourou, *Les Pays Tropicaux*, Chapter II; de Castro, *Géopolitique de la faim*.

[2] He was from Dahomey and well-educated, speaking English as well as he spoke French. He looked after his car with the tenderness of a mother.

the moderate levels of production. But there are large areas east of the Congo in Ruanda-Urundi (Belgian since 1919), as in southern Nigeria and the Lower Congo, where densities reach 250 and even 1,000 per square mile. As the agricultural system is not adapted to these high densities, they pose a number of extremely difficult problems.

Now that the environmental conditions have been briefly described, let us turn to the question of native agriculture and to the possibilities of its future development.

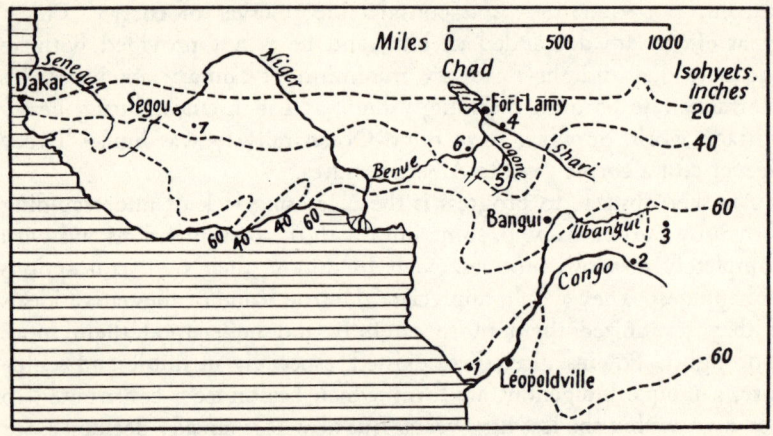

FIG. 1. Sketch map to show villages studied in French Equatorial and French West Africa and the Belgian Congo.

1, Pene Niolo; 2, Yangambi and the Turumbu; 3, Bambesa and the Baboua; 4, Morio near Bouso; 5, Bebedjia; 6, Be near Garoua; 7, M'Pesoba.

2. The Collecting Economy, Plantations, and Forest Fallow of the Mayumba Massif

20. From the lower Congo River port of Boma, former capital of an independent Congo, the road and the small railway run due north as far as Tshela, an administrative centre quite near the borders of A.E.F. and Cabinda, a Portuguese enclave. Ten miles S.S.W. from here is the village of Pene Niolo,[1] situated in the Mayumba Hills, which hardly deserve to be called 'mountains' in spite of their comparative ruggedness. Pene Niolo comprises two separate hamlets, each sited on a hilltop, with not a single isolated building. The more important of

[1] Fig. 1 gives a general idea of the location of the various villages studied in Chapters II and III.

the two was built five years ago, when the older site was abandoned because the soil of the land around it had become completely impoverished. In this area, however, the scope for such movements is strictly limited by the pressure of population on the land. The village has 300 inhabitants who eke out a living from some 800 acres. The density, therefore, is about 250 per square mile, thus exceeding the regional average, which is itself exceptionally high for the Congo.

The seventy-five families with their 157 children under sixteen[1] give some idea of the high rate of population increase. They occupy fifty-four huts, strung along each side of a track. These are rectangular in shape, for the conical type is only found outside the forest zone. The huts are rebuilt about every ten years. Wooden stakes are used for the walls and maranta leaves for the roof and, on average, about one month of work per year is needed for repairs and rebuilding. Only the village chief has a hut with walls of wooden boards, but the school hut and the chapel are rather more elaborate.

One has to stoop to enter one of these huts (Fig. 2), and just inside there is a hollow in the ground for the fire. Above this a few maize cobs, protected from insects by the smoke, hang from the roof. Beyond are a low bed and a heap of roots. Coming from the Sudan one is struck by the absence of large stocks of food, for the 'reserves' are either still in the ground or not yet picked from the tree. Food is therefore available at all times, and there is no periodically recurring season of short rations. The bedroom, surrounded by a partition and projecting into the living-space, contains two beds and a handsome coffin which serves as a clothes' chest while awaiting its final destination. There are two wood piles near the door of this room, while a third, the largest, is opposite the porch roof at the back of the hut. Of the two narrow passages on either side of the sleeping quarters one is used as a storeroom and the other as a shelter for poultry. Behind the hut is the inevitable latrine, decreed by law, but not always used.

Some huts are reserved for men; others for women, girls, and young children; and, finally, some are set apart for boys, who are divided into age groups and brought up separately from the time they are seven or eight years old. The diagram shows a small hut for four boys.

We noticed a blind old man, who, obviously sensing the presence of a European, was lamenting the fact that no one had come to weed his field as local custom demands. It was explained to us by M. Halut that

[1] These figures are approximate. There is no registration of births, and the children—and likewise their parents—do not generally know their own ages. The measurement of time is still rather a vague notion.

the old man was a kind of outcast who, as a youth, had refused to help the old people and was now paying for his sins. Among these comparatively prosperous tribes of the Mayumba, the sense of unity had remained strong.[1] In other regions the outcast often finds employment in one of the towns, sets himself up as a craftsman or trader or seeks work in one of the many nearby European plantations. We have often been guilty of disrupting the traditional framework of tribal custom without setting up anything in its place.

21. The first source of food is from a belt of bananas and plantains, the fruits of which are eaten raw and cooked respectively. The trees stretch along the slopes on either side of and below the village (Fig. 3). In virtue of their situation, they receive some of the cinders from the hearth, a certain amount of domestic refuse and night soil, and even the waste water from the huts. Thus they benefit—not altogether fortuitously—from a form of fertilization, but their yields remain low because they are left to grow too old and are seldom transplanted. Growing next to them are pineapples and a few fruit trees (orange, native pear, or kola); oil-palms are generally found with these, and there may be a few coconut palms. Growing wild in the space between this 'orchard' and the village there may be other useful plants: a few gourds and shrubs of capsicum; very often a variety of *Lycopersicum*, which is

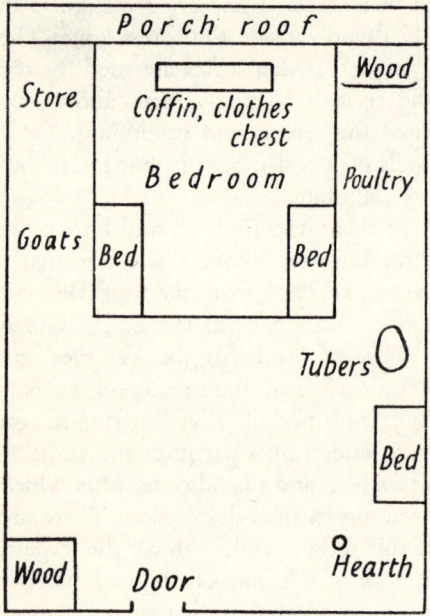

FIG. 2. Diagram of a hut (11 ft. 6 in. × 18 ft.) at Pene Niolo, in the Mayumba, Belgian Congo.

[1] According to Portères, in French West Africa the fields of those who were mobilized in the First War were cared for by their neighbours, but this did not happen during the War of 1939-45.

similar to the tomato, but hardy enough to stand the steamy heat without being affected by mildew (Fig. 4).

This is not really cultivation in a European sense, for it consists merely of tending plants which have grown spontaneously from seed. On the other hand, this garden belt is somewhat reminiscent of the ring of gardens, hemp-fields, and orchards which from time immemorial has been a feature of the typical village in the open-field areas of northern Europe. We were shown the village's first real garden, started in autumn, 1949. It is in the form of a square, enclosed by a fence of horizontal bamboos, sown with maize, ground-nuts, and 'tomatoes', and fertilized with fowl and goat droppings. The contrast with Asia is remarkable. Asked whether they make use of night soil, the villagers vigorously protested that they did not eat the products of their own dung!

Apart from goats and poultry there are a few sheep with hairy coats, and these, together with pigs, are the characteristic domestic animals of equatorial regions. About ten years ago various small breeds of cattle were introduced by the missions. Some of them have been loaned to villagers and the calves are equally divided between the two parties. As in Guinea and Casamance, these animals are of the Dahomey and N'dama breeds and are resistant to sleeping sickness. Elsewhere, the Somba or so-called 'lagoon' breed is more important. Cattle are thus penetrating into the equatorial zone—the only region, apart from desert and tundra, from which they were still traditionally absent.[1]

The density of animals is very low—lower than in any other agricultural system. The main sources of animal proteins are: game, obtained only by organizing veritable hunting expeditions into the jungle, and much more difficult to come by, therefore, than in the savanna; salt-water fish in coastal districts, either dried, smoked, or salted—but it is much less important than in South-East Asia;[2] and, finally, fresh-water fish.

The Belgian Administration is now making great efforts to introduce pisciculture in small lakes and ponds (bran and other by-products of milling are sometimes used as feed), and is concentrating on the *Tilapia*

[1] Rather belatedly, stock-rearing is now making progress in French Equatorial Africa, notably in the savanna country of the Lower Congo in the Dolisie and Loudima districts and on the Bateke plateaux north of Brazzaville.

[2] In March 1953 two trawlers were bringing their catch each week to Boma and Matadi, and the fish was being sent as far as Leopoldville. A salting and drying factory was under construction at Matadi.

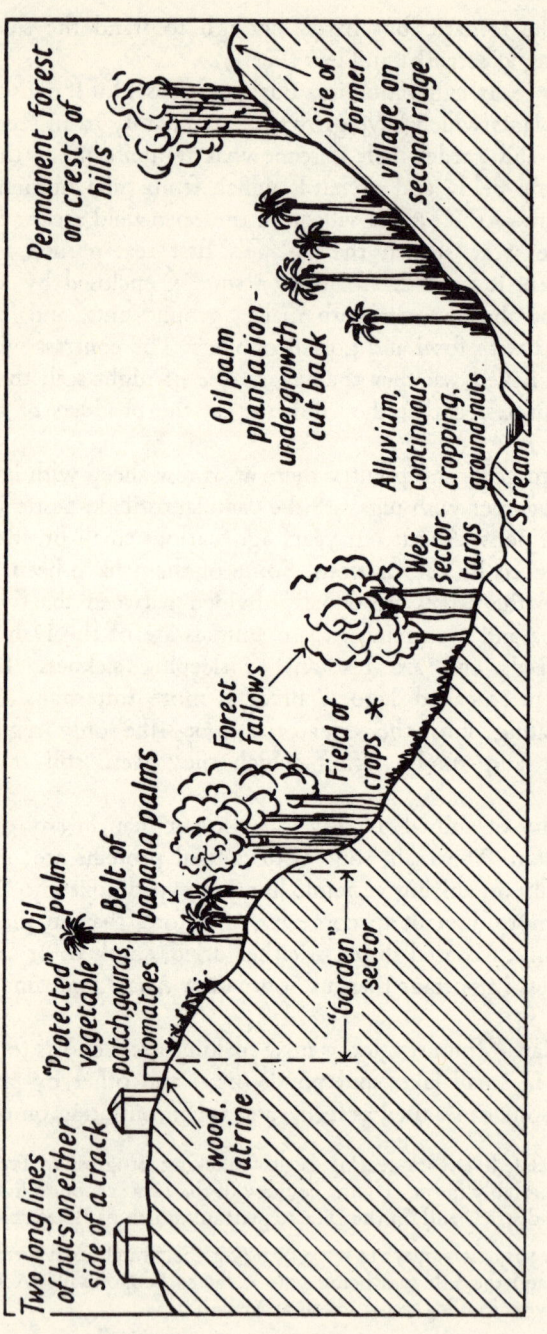

FIG. 3. Diagrammatic cross section of Pene Niolo and its vicinity.

macrochir, a native variety of flat fish.[1] In order to overcome the shortage of animal proteins, which is a matter of crucial importance for the future of these peoples, reliance is being placed on increasing the supply of fish rather than the number of domestic animals. Even though cattle are more numerous than in many other parts of the equatorial zone, where they are often practically unknown, stock rearing is still of only very minor importance.[2] Plants, whether cultivated or not, are the essential basis of the food supply.

22. Leaving the crest of the hill, one may follow the steep, slippery footpaths, their clayey surfaces puddled by the rain, down through the fetid heat to the 'voluntary' plantation of oil palms which is maintained nowadays simply by cutting back the undergrowth. In the early days of plantations the ground used to be completely cleared, but this laborious method was abandoned when its evil consequence became apparent, for the bare soil rapidly deteriorated. Later, the soil was protected with leguminous cover crops which were frequently cut, and thus they provided green manure as well. Nowadays the wild vegetation which protects the sloping ground is merely cut back sufficiently to accommodate the growth of the palms.

A collective palm plantation covers some 42 acres of ground on the far side of the next ridge. This is a 'compulsory' plantation, imposed on the village by the Administration, which supplies first year plants. These are set in rows 30 ft. apart in one direction, 18 ft. in the other, under the direction of native foremen who indicate where the holes are to be dug. At first $1\frac{1}{4}$ acres of compulsory plantation were assigned to each H.A.V. (*homme adulte valide*), but the control of so many small units became impracticable, and each village is simply given a block acreage. The villagers share the crop amongst themselves with no apparent difficulty, but the elders no doubt make quite sure of their part first.

In addition to these plantations, oil-palms are scattered throughout the territory of the village. They are given a certain amount of attention and are spared when the forest is being cleared, although the Baboua do not take even this precaution. Collecting bunches of palm fruits is

[1] These feed on plankton. Other types of fish, feeding on plant foods, are also used. The Belgians have established fishermen's schools near the large lakes of the middle Congo.

[2] 600,000 cattle, 1,500,000 sheep and goats and 200,000 pigs are the official figures for the 590,000,000 acres of the Belgian Congo; even so, the majority of these animals are in the drier east, outside the forest zone.

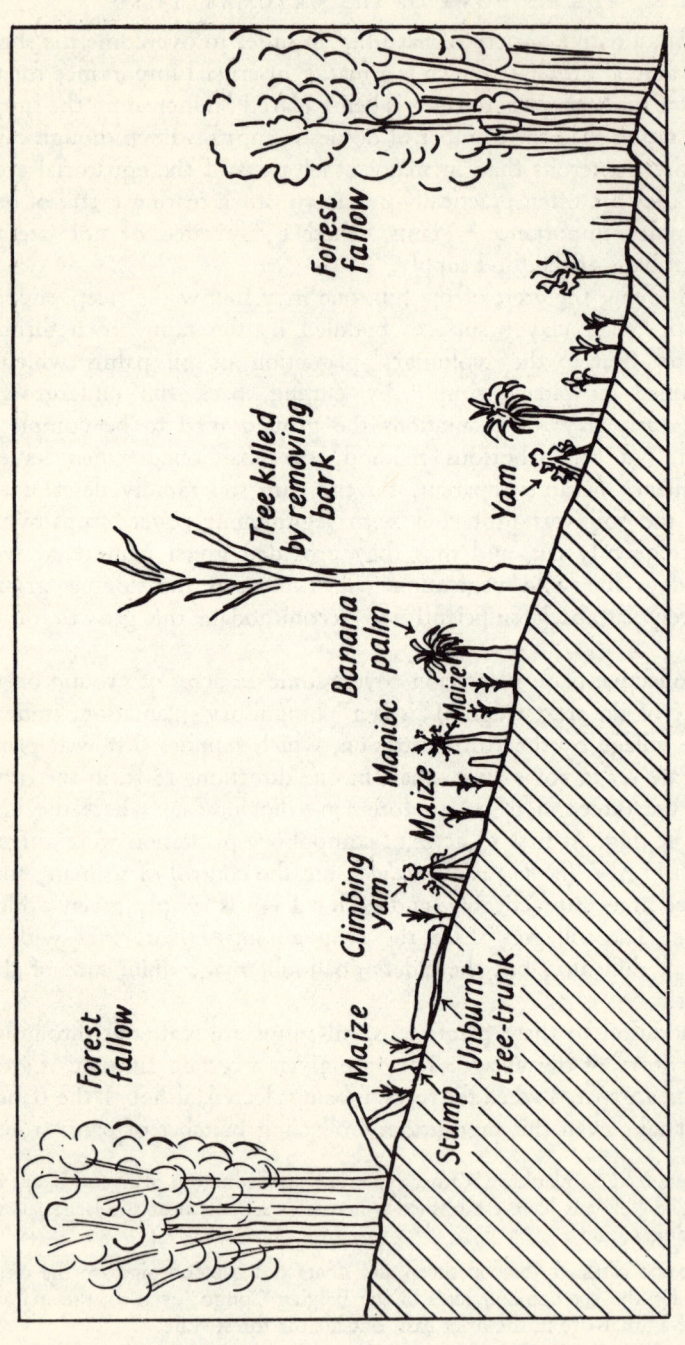

FIG. 4. Diagram of a 'field' at Pene Niolo, littered with stumps and tree trunks and a few dead trees; seeds are sown in planting holes.

THE ECONOMY OF THE MAYUMBA MASSIF

the main work performed by the men.[1] If they worked full time, they could each gather fruit at the rate of well over ½ ton a month during the eight months when the tree is in full bearing and perhaps at half this rate during the other four months—a total of 6 tons a year. In actual fact, however, they average only about 3 tons. The fruit is collected in lorries by a nearby oil mill.[2] It also possesses its own plantations of carefully selected palms which are set out along the contour levels to minimize erosion. This type of alignment has not yet been applied to the compulsory native plantation.

During the autumn of 1949, three tons of fruit was fetching 1,350 Congo francs, or about £10.[3] On the experimental station near Gimbi, casual labour was paid 4 Congo francs a day, plus rations worth about 33·50 a week. Some of the latter were resold to save up for a wife—or to buy beer. The sale of beer, which is a product of European industry, and consequently very dear, is favoured by the prohibition on native brewing which, unbelievably hypocritical as it may sound, is forbidden on moral grounds.[4] In the eastern part of the Congo, alcoholic drink is usually made from bananas, but here the fermented sap of the palm is used to make palm wine. As the liquid already begins to ferment in the bowl set to collect it, the impetuous drinker is not always in a fit state to climb down the tree; he may fall and hurt himself—sometimes fatally.

The poll tax was 144 Congo francs, but only 40 for fathers of four children.[5] Monsieur Halut, the young Belgian agronomist from Boma who acted as our guide, pointed out the serious consequences of this reduction. It had no doubt already stimulated the birth-rate, and yet the population is even now overtaxing the resources of the land under the present system of cultivation. Measures appropriate to areas of sparse

---

[1] This is not the only product of collecting. The secondary forest and the remnants of the original forest cover, but more particularly the former, supply not only game and fish, but building materials, bark and fibres, and even vegetables (shoots and leaves of various kinds) and tubers (wild yams), some of which are poisonous.

[2] At the beginning the factory scales were always 'light'.

[3] In March 1953 the price per pound rose from 0·20 to 0·35 Congo francs, and there was a bonus of 0·02 francs for good-quality fruit.

[4] The sale of imported liquor more than doubled between 1946 and 1952 in French West Africa. Is this one of the benefits of 'civilization'?

[5] 'In Senegal taxes and interest on loans of seed account for a tenth of the family income', according to Portères.

population are not necessarily applicable elsewhere.[1] The existence of four sewing machines in the village indicated a certain standard of living, but the people were greatly troubled because they had not been able to graduate to the second rung in the ladder of prosperity, the symbol of which is that almost magical machine, the bicycle. Now, however (1953), its use is becoming fairly general, so M. Halut informs us.

23. The cultivated areas are scattered throughout the district, except on the hilltops, where remnants of the virgin forest are left untouched as a precaution against erosion. Clearing is effected during the dry season, which lasts from June to September. First the smaller trees are cut about 3 ft. from the ground as the small axe or machete which is used could not cope with the thicker part of the trunk. The large trees —there are very few of them left here—are killed simply by removing their bark. The drying wood is burnt in October, shortly before the rains, and burning is sometimes repeated twelve months later. Although the twigs and small branches catch fire and burn, the ground remains littered with stumps and tree trunks. To a European it looks more like a scene of battle than a cultivated field (Fig. 4). The work of clearing is shared between the sexes: the men fell the trees and hack the trunks into shorter lengths with their axes; the women cut the branches, heap them up, and set fire to them. But all the subsequent work of cultivation is done exclusively by the women.

No digging is needed, for the soil has been enriched with ashes and aerated and loosened by roots during its period of forest cover. Here and there, in holes dug with a hoe about 4 ft. apart, maize,[2] manioc cuttings and pieces of yam are planted side by side. The yams are generally set where a stump or a dead tree offers some support for the twining stems. Banana cuttings may be planted either at this stage or a few months later, but in any case during the rains.

There are sometimes two crops of maize, the first being harvested in January or February, three to four months after sowing. Taros (*Colocasia*), which are grown in the wet bottom lands, and yams are lifted after eight months, at the beginning of the dry season in June. According to the very precise official figures, some 27 sq. yds. per family are devoted to taros. The field then gradually returns to its former wild condition, but during the period between about fifteen months and

---

[1] Since the beginning of 1952 family allowances have been granted to workers at the rate of half a food ration for a wife and a quarter for a child. The weekly ration is fixed at 43 Congo francs in the Mayumba region.

[2] This cereal is characteristic of the forest zone, but as yet its cultivation has not become general. It reached the central Congo from Egypt.

TOIL AND WANT—RESULTS OF AN INEFFICIENT SYSTEM

three years after the first planting, the women continue to collect bananas and manioc roots as they need them. The manioc is second only to the oil palm as a source of income for the natives, as the village has to send a regular supply to the prison at Tshela.

3. Human Effort and Malnutrition. The Vicious Circle resulting from an Inefficient Use of Land

24. With the help of small hoes with heart-shaped blades and short handles, the villagers cultivate a clearing for about eight months. This period is followed by approximately two years of collecting. During this time the maniocs and banana palms provide a gratuitous return, but they are not tended in any way and the undergrowth begins to reach considerable proportions. This secondary growth may be left for anything between five and twelve years before it is cleared again, but the principles followed by the old land chiefs are not applied as scrupulously as in former times. Apart from 110 acres of clearings which are either cultivated or reverting to forest but still productive, the village lands comprise 50 acres of oil-palm plantations, between 60 and 75 acres of hill-top forest, and 30 acres occupied by the two groups of village buildings and their immediate surroundings. In the absence of a detailed survey, these are only approximate figures.

A good 50 acres are probably cleared each year. Since 1917, the administration has, in theory, worked on the basis of at least $\frac{3}{8}$ acres of beans, $\frac{1}{4}$ of manioc and the same of bananas, per H.A.V.[1] The area thus defined represents sixty days' work, and may sometimes add up to $1\frac{1}{4}$ acres in all. Although the men are legally responsible for attaining these figures and run the risk of prison in cases of default, all the cultivation is done by the women. They sometimes find it difficult to cope with the task, but their more regular work seems to give them a better physique than the men. In practice, every family looks after nearly $1\frac{1}{4}$ acres of oil-palm, merely keeping the undergrowth in check, and collects bananas from another $\frac{1}{4}$ acre. About 200 sq. yds. of the latter are taken up by some thirty plantains, while 117 banana palms account for the rest. In addition, cultivated land and recently cleared areas where manioc can still be collected each cover about $\frac{3}{4}$ acre.

The details of land utilization are even more complex than this account suggests. Each family cultivates its own tiny plot in the horticultural belt near the village where, on average, each has 9 sq. yds. of sugar cane, $3\frac{1}{2}$ of pimento and 14 of pineapples. Providing food for

[1] Decree on crops grown compulsorily for educational reasons.

the family is the primary and was until recently the only purpose of this 'garden' cultivation, and this explains the variety of produce. Even so, production falls far short of requirements, for, apart from all its cloth, the main items which the village has to buy are fish and rice. The first of these emphasizes the absence of livestock in the economy, while the second is of great significance and will be discussed in a later section.

25. The other main features of this Bantu system are as follows:

The lack of fertilization, apart from the horticultural belt which is not an important feature of this district.

The system of temporary cultivation. The eight months of cultivation are sometimes repeated for two or three years in a row, but sooner or later each area reverts to a collecting economy for two years. This in turn is followed by five to twelve years of forest fallow. Until 1914 there was an analogous system in the forest clearings of the Ardennes, where two years under cereals and another two under rough pasture were followed by a twenty-year period of brushwood and coppice. The trees help to restore fertility by bringing eluviated material back to the surface and protecting the soil from deterioration by exposure to the sun and from erosion.

Complete dependence on manual labour and on the work of women in particular. Conditions today are still unfavourable to stock-rearing, while stumps and fallen trees would make ploughing well-nigh impossible. Digging a few holes in the ground is in fact the only preparation for sowing and planting. The soil is never tilled, and the lack of power limits the area which can be cropped to $3\frac{3}{4}$ acres per family at the very most (including the area from which produce is merely collected).

The interplanting of crops, which ensures an adequate and continuous cover of vegetation for the soil. At first most of the ground is occupied by the quicker-growing crops, and the hoeing received by these also benefits the crops with a longer cycle which need to be protected from the competition of weeds in the early stages. When interplanting is practised to the extent found here, it becomes impossible to practise rotations as we know them.

The fact that collecting is more important than cultivation. Palm fruits and many other items of food, building materials and various raw materials are collected from the forest. A 'semi-collecting' economy is practised in the palm plantations and the old clearings with their bananas and manioc.

TOIL AND WANT—RESULTS OF AN INEFFICIENT SYSTEM

The negligible role of livestock in the economy and the absence of fodder and industrial crops.[1]

This is a balanced system, and if the periods of forest fallow were long enough the fertility of the soil could be maintained. Overpopulation prevents this from being the case. The available evidence suggests that fallow periods should last at least twelve years, and there is every indication that yields are already falling where the intervals between cultivation are too short. This applies especially to areas near territorial boundaries, where the villages on either side try to affirm their rights by frequent use of the land.

There are two important exceptions to the sequence of cultivation, collecting, and forest fallow. Plantations of oil-palms and other tree crops allow the land to be used continuously and without ill effect so long as the soil remains covered and protected from erosion. These plantations constitute an artificial forest comparable in many ways with the rain forest itself. Secondly, on sandy alluvial deposits, which are found mainly in areas of braided streams, ground-nuts can be grown year after year without recourse to forest fallows. A two-year rotation of ground-nuts and maize is possible where there are more fertile loams.

26. Although fairly well balanced, the system is not very productive. Apart from palm oil, a few tons of manioc are the only surplus, and the purchase of food from other areas is absolutely necessary. The serious food shortages common in the northern part of the tropical zone are absent here, thanks partly to the maize crop, which helps to tide over periods of scarcity. Nevertheless, food is often in short supply and is invariably deficient in quality. The lack of calcium and of animal and even vegetable proteins is particularly marked. A rough estimate of the daily ration of an adult male illustrates the preponderance of starch and carbohydrates in the diet: bananas (over 2 lb.), manioc (over 1 lb.); very much smaller quantities of beans and ground nuts ($4\frac{1}{2}$ oz. together), and of maize and palm oil ($1\frac{3}{4}$ oz. each). The almost complete absence of meat and cereals is especially noteworthy, but the proportion of fats is adequate. As far as we could judge, however, the figure

[1] Although the cultivation of fodder crops is almost entirely absent in the inter-tropical regions, thirty miles east of Tshela each native family grows about $\frac{1}{4}$ acre of *Urena lobata* on the newly-cleared—and consequently the richest—land. On the other side of the frontier in French Equatorial Africa, an organization known as Sofico and financed by the Corporation française de jute is undertaking a scheme for the large-scale cultivation of Urena by Europeans in the savanna country of the Niara valley in the Middle Congo near Dolisie. The conditions are thus different from those east of Tshela, and probably rather less favourable.

of $1\frac{3}{4}$ oz. for oil seems to have been considerably surpassed at Pene Niolo.

The quality of the food is thus particularly deficient, and it cannot provide enough energy for the cultivation of an adequate area. This creates a vicious circle which will be broken only when human energy can be supplemented by the power of animals or machines, but, as we shall see, this involves all manner of practical difficulties. The whole economy is very delicately poised. As at Taza in Morocco (where the tragic year 1923 is remembered as 'the year of the road'), a severe food shortage followed the construction of a road, which employed all the men of the village at the very season when they should have been clearing the forest.

The primary objective of the system is to produce food. Here, however, as in the eastern part of the Congo, the high population density has resulted in the curtailment of forest fallows and the process of soil deterioration seems already to have begun.[1] The situation is thus far from satisfactory. The palm plantations have increased the efficiency of labour in the production of an export crop and their product is ousting 'wild' oil from the market. In the next stage modernization must reach the land devoted to food crops and increase yields without endangering the soil. An attempt to do this is being made at the headquarters of the National Institute for Agricultural Research in the Belgian Congo (I.N.E.A.C.) at Yangambi. To reach Yangambi, which is in the central part of the Congo basin, we went by car via Boma to Matadi. From there a plane brought us across the forests, where the sky is nearly always overcast, to Leopoldville and then to Stanleyville. We finally reached the research station after another car journey which took us downstream along the right bank of the Congo. We had travelled from latitude 5° S. to about 1° N.

4. The Failure of Continuous Cultivation and the Improved Bantu System[2]

27. One can easily imagine the horror of the first Belgian agricultural scientists, fresh from the rich open fields of Hainaut or the intensively cultivated sandy soils of Flanders, when they first beheld the native

[1] This is particularly true of the environs of the larger villages, the growth of which is encouraged in the cause of administrative convenience; it is true also of areas which border important routeways and which can therefore produce export crops more economically.

[2] Studied under the able guidance of MM. Muller and Henry.

fields strewn with debris and the enormous areas left under forest. On the first experimental plots at Yangambi, the forest was cut down, burnt and uprooted. The soil was ploughed deep (as in Hesbaye) and, as a precaution, sown with *Pueraria, Calopogonium*, and other leguminous crops which had proved their worth in plantations. These were used as green manure and various grasses (*Pennisetum purpureum*) were sometimes sown as well. The land was ploughed a second time and then cultivated on a two-year rotation. As the region has rain throughout the year, with only a slight abatement from December to April, it was possible to introduce four breaks into this rotation. A crop of upland rice was followed by two of manioc and one of ground-nuts. This was followed by a leguminous cover crop. In this manner it was hoped to begin continuous cultivation on the pattern of temperate agriculture. The ant-hills, which occupied about a third of the area, were not cultivated. The soil was exposed to the harmful effects of chemical photo-oxidation for more than half the time—for thirteen months out of twenty-four to be exact. Deep ploughing, expensive as it was, impaired the soil structure. The absence of a vegetation cover for so much of the period increased the amount of percolation, and the removal of plant foods from the topsoil was thus accelerated. The cover crops themselves did not have any apparent effect in improving the soil and their woody stems decomposed too slowly. Bacterial activity was hindered by excessive insolation and was unable to keep up an adequate supply of humus.

The yield of every crop fell rapidly. The ears of rice did not swell. The 150 acres on which the experiment had been conducted had to be abandoned after a few years. Too far from the edge of the forest to be reseeded quickly and with the micro-climate of its soil reduced almost to aridity, the area was still only thinly wooded ten years later. The Belgians frankly recognized their mistakes. Their notions of farming in temperate regions were obviously out of place in the Congo. In 1940 they decided to start again, but this time they took the Bantu system[1] as their only sure starting-point and tried to improve it.

To study these improvements, we shall examine what was done in the area of the Turumbu tribe, who live on the right bank of the Congo where the system of land use is similar to that at Pene Niolo. The forest clearings produce upland rice, manioc and bananas, and there is the same sequence of two years' cultivation followed by a

[1] 'Which no scientifically proven method is as yet capable of replacing', according to J. Henry in *Les bases théoriques des essais de paysanat indigène au Congo belge*.

period of semi-collecting from clearings rapidly reverting to forest.

28. First of all the system of clearing was reorganized, and a planned economy or *paysanat dirigé* was imposed on the district. The natives were directed to clear parallel bands each 110 yds. in width and orientated from east to west (Fig. 5). In this manner an adequate acreage of cleared land is obtained, while the narrowness of the bands ensures the rapid regeneration of the forest once the land is abandoned. The forest fallow is thus retained in the absence of a better solution. A fresh belt of ground is brought under cultivation each year, but is separated from the last by a stretch of forest of the same width—110 yds. Over a nine-year period, every 'even' belt is cleared in turn and then the 'odd' numbers follow in sequence, starting with the line of forest which separated the first two clearings.

Let us take an example to see how the system works. The undergrowth is cut in November and December 1953 (six days' work per acre). The large trees are then felled and not merely stripped of their bark (fourteen days). After the branches have been piled up (sixteen days), burning takes place in January and February. There are three burnings in all, and each time the debris is collected together and heaped up again (eight and four days). Clearing alone thus accounts for some forty-eight man-days of work per acre.

In March 1954 planting holes are dug about 18 in. apart. A variety of maize which ripens in four months is sown in clumps and, in theory, the crop is weeded in May. The cobs are subsequently carried to the village, which is often over half a mile away, in head-loads of 90 lb. to 100 lb. Here they are tied in pairs and hung to dry on a line stretched between two stakes. Between twenty-eight and thirty-two days of work bring a return of some 8 cwt. of grain per acre.

Upland rice,[1] which needs more moisture than maize, is sown in July and August about the time of the heavy rains. It is planted in small holes 8 in. apart and the soil is disturbed as little as possible. It is sometimes interplanted with maize and invariably with one-year-old banana shoots, which are set about 4 yds. apart. These in their turn are intercalated with manioc cuttings in September. In December the rice is cut and tied into small sheaves which are dried by placing them against a support of horizontal stakes, and then threshed with sticks. About as much work is needed as in the cultivation of maize and an acre produces 8-10 cwt. of paddy which gives 5-6 cwt. of rice with a high proportion

[1] The ground is not levelled, and the crop depends entirely on rainfall, as opposed to the Asian type of riziculture in flooded fields which have to be levelled and embanked (Chapter IV).

of broken grain after it has been husked with a mortar and pestle.

The bananas will begin to bear fruit in April 1955, and the manioc will be ready about a month later. These two will continue to bear fairly heavily for about a year and give between 3 and 4 tons—half fruit and half roots—to the acre. They are the staple items in the native diet.[1] As we have already seen, a second cereal has been added to the traditional rotation. The most important innovation, however, is that in April 1956 the ground will be thoroughly hoed and weeded in preparation for the sowing of maize and ground-nuts in May. These will be ready for harvesting in August.

After another hoeing, this will be followed by another crop of ground-nuts,[2] sown in September-October and ready by the following January-February. In the meantime, Abroma, a tree yielding fibre from its bark, will be sown in October to assist in the recolonization of the area by spontaneous vegetation. This secondary forest will be cut in April and again in December 1957, and will then be left until the autumn of 1971 before being cleared again. Clearing will thus take place at eighteen-year intervals, and fourteen years of forest fallow are interposed between periods of cultivation. The task of clearing a second time will be much easier, for the forest will be less tall and will consist mainly of umbrella trees. The work of cutting and piling up the branches preparatory to burning will take about half the time, or about twenty-four man-days per acre.

29. Good progress has been made already, and the prodigious task of clearing the forest is now rewarded by a span of four years of cultivation. Satisfactory plants for the commercial production of fibre, however, have not yet been found. Abroma, which has been tried as an experiment, is a stinging plant and gives a fibre of mediocre quality. Moreover, it is estimated that 520 man-days per acre are needed for the complete cycle,[3] and this still seems excessive. A monogamous family can only cope with half its allotment of $1\frac{1}{4}$ acres, which would take 650 days of really hard work. Partly because of the climate, a typical family with three or four children, some of whom are working part-time, finds this programme of work much too onerous, and it is never

---

[1] Together with a little more grain than at Pene Niolo.

[2] At the time of our visit this idea had not yet been translated into fact, as the Turumbu, being very fond of the nuts—and not having any—had eaten the quota which they had received for seed.

[3] Manioc demands the most work, not because it is difficult to grow, but because of the time taken in carrying it in bowls, peeling, steeping, and drying; in other words because of the post-cultivation operations.

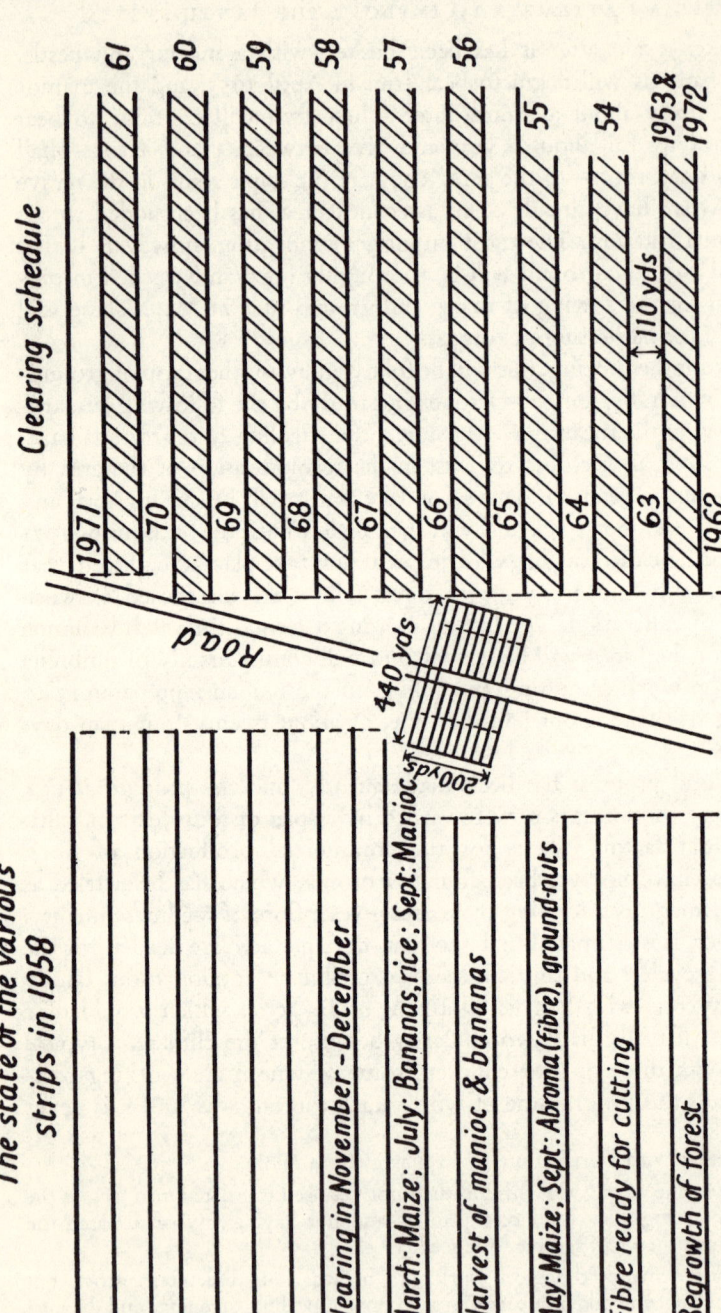

Fig. 5. The Turumbu Paysanat, showing the layout of the village of Yalibwa. The date for clearing each strip is shown on the right. 18 families live in the hamlet, 9 on either side of the road and each has a section of a strip to clear, the size depending on its 'labour force'.

fulfilled in practice. When we visited the area in January 1950, strenuous but unavailing efforts had been made to keep up with the clearing schedule—efforts, incidentally, which belied the Negro's unjust reputation for laziness.

As a result of all this work, the Turumbu have no time to spare for hunting, their nets stay at home, and game has become a luxury, so rarely does it appear on the table. Pig-rearing, introduced in an attempt to ensure a regular supply of meat, was not a success. The supervised economy is not innocent of waste. After oil has been extracted from the pericarp of the palm fruit, the oil-rich kernel is often thrown away or used as fuel. Again, the siting of the first few villages along the roads made them a rather striking feature in the landscape, but the people themselves would often have preferred an entirely different arrangement. In particular, the distance from the well is often so great as to make the carrying of water, which is a matter of great importance in all these primitive societies, quite unnecessarily laborious.[1]

These apt criticisms were first made by Professor Baptist of the Université agronomique at Ghent, but they do not detract from the great achievements of the scientists at Yangambi. They have fearlessly attacked the most difficult of all the problems with which science is faced at the present day, and their experiments could hardly have been expected to meet with unqualified success all along the line. They themselves do not consider the present situation to be satisfactory, but their efforts to determine the best times of sowing and the best cropspacings have increased the yields to such an extent that the food supply, although expensive in labour, is more than enough for the sparse population of the region. They are now turning their attention to the selection of improved strains, which the Turumbu are required to propagate.

Under present conditions, with its distance from the coast and even in some places from the river, this area is well outside the range of economic transport costs for the import of chemical fertilizers. The thirty-five miles of lorry transport from Yalibutu to the river port account for 25 per cent. of the value of the rice exports; a quarter of the money paid to the producer goes in paying for the first stage of the journey! It would be ridiculous to advocate the purchase of fertilizers to a man who cannot afford a pair of shoes and who consoles himself for the lack of a bicycle by painting one on the door of his hut. In a region far removed from distribution centres and major lines of communication, where commercial agriculture is frustrated by heavy freight

[1] This matter was remedied in 1952 by the sinking of wells.

charges, the import costs are also very high, for they are regulated by the same inadequate modes of transport.

30. Most of the Belgian agronomists accept these arguments. In the present circumstances they are justified in doing so, but it would be a great mistake to leave things as they are. Fertilizers were one of the decisive factors in the success of the T.V.A. In the Congo the opportunity for an economic use of fertilizers could be created fairly quickly by prospecting for local deposits of phosphates, developing hydroelectric power for the manufacture of nitrates, and organizing an efficient transport system which would ensure, among other things, better prices for the producer. The way in which the British have encouraged the use of granulated superphosphates in Nigeria is relevant in this connexion. The more easily accessible areas near the rivers could be the first to change to a really intensive form of agriculture.

The enormous amount of work which the improved Bantu system entails naturally leads one to think in terms of mechanization. First, bulldozers would be needed. They would have to be fairly powerful to be of any use in clearing the forest, but light enough to avoid damaging the soil structure by excessive ramming. Unfortunately, these two important requirements are mutually contradictory. Complete clearing of the forest, including the removal of stumps and the levelling of ant-hills, would be so costly that it would certainly not be possible ever to repeat it again. The forest fallow would have to be replaced by some form of grass fallow; in other words, the rain forest would have to give place to savanna. As the ground is more productive after a period under forest, cattle would have to be introduced to make the soil both fertile and productive, even though it remained under grass. In this manner some respite might be gained from the tyrannical cycle of cultivation and forest fallows. It would be worth a try.

It might be possible to alternate grass fallow with a rest period devoted to the growing of valuable timber—shinglewood, for example. Even the umbrella tree is excellent for pulping purposes and could be utilized if transport facilities were available. These and many other ways must be tested by experiment, for none of them can offer the prospect of quick and sure success. Indeed, the improvements already effected in the Bantu economy are designed merely to tide over, without detriment to the soil, the transition period which must precede the establishment of a system of intensive and continuous cultivation.

This process of development will have a better chance of success if the recent alluvial soils of the flood plain and of the many islands are given over to food production. Here, a 'mixed-farming' system with livestock and grass fallows would have a better chance of showing satisfactory yields, and the riverside location, especially when the bulky nature of the commodities concerned is taken into account, would greatly reduce costs of transport. On the other hand, the commercial plantations, where clearing the forest is an initial and non-recurring task and whose products (cacao, coffee, rubber, palm-oil) are valuable in relation to their bulk, could be established on the plateaux of the interior.

In 1952 it became apparent that because of transport difficulties the cultivation of food crops for sale was not a very profitable business[1] (annual income of 3,000 Congo francs for the most efficient producers, according to J. Henry). Thus nearly a third of an acre of coffee shrubs per cultivator was henceforth incorporated in the scheme. The shrubs were planted in the mixed sandy and clay lands of the plateau, and to assist in the management of the crop they were grouped in a few large blocks. In 1953 the planting of some 2,500 acres of oil-palm began somewhat nearer the river. Even more significant from the point of view of future trends was the fact that a grass sward (*Cynodon dactylon*, *Digitaria*, *Brachiaria*) had been established and that it was already supporting a number of beef cattle, which, it was hoped, would eventually be used as draught animals.[2] The system was beginning to bear some resemblance to the intensive farming of Western Europe.

The horticultural belt has not been forgotten. A number of different kinds of fruit trees have been planted, including citrus trees, native pears, rambutans, and avocado pears, the fruit of which has a high fat content. Suitable rotations are being worked out for different kinds of soil; for instance, on low-lying sandy soils maize, ground-nuts, and manioc are grown in preference to bananas and rice.

Before taking our argument any further, we shall give an account of the cotton research station to the north-east of Yangambi at Bambesa, which is in latitude 4° N. and near the limit of the rain forest.

5. Directed Peasant Farming—Spread of the Savanna Checked

31. Even without the heavy financial burden of supporting a European administration, modern equipment could never be bought out of the proceeds of cultivating food crops alone. Thus, the possibilities of cash-crop cultivation may be profitably examined as long as the

[1] The 1952 report shows increased purchases of bicycles and sewing machines, which, at the time of our visit, were very much fewer than in the cotton areas.

[2] Ten light carts were introduced in 1953.

primary objective, that of suppressing hunger, is not forgotten. Cotton does not succeed in the centre of the basin, but it can be grown near the margins of the forest north of about 2-3° N., where the dry season is sufficiently marked to permit ripening. During the period 1922-3 cultivation was started in the Bambesa region by Cotonco, a large commercial undertaking closely associated with the Société générale de Belgique, which obtained a monopoly[1] of cotton-ginning throughout a large region in the northern Congo. Capitalist enterprise in the development of this area contrasts with the State planning of the Yangambi scheme.

The forest was already in retreat, for the native Baboua avoided the strenuous work of clearing as much as possible. They cropped the same land over and over again, and the results were soil exhaustion and a very rapid fall in yields. Afterwards the secondary forest growth re-established itself very slowly and the process was further hindered by the length of the dry season, which here lasts more than four months. There was therefore some extension of the grass savanna, which was ravaged by fire at the end of every dry season, at the expense of the forest. As the area of cultivated land was limited, however, the damage did not affect a large area.

The introduction of cotton gave a fresh and dangerous impetus to this trend. To make sure of a large crop, the agents of Cotonco, who had wide powers in these matters, caused large new areas to be cleared for the cultivation of cotton. In the absence of local surveys, however, there was no proper basis for control and the new crop spread all too fast. The result was the creation of arid micro-climates inimical to spontaneous reafforestation. On the other hand, cotton represented a new source of wealth. The tax levied on the crop—in reality a tax on the producer—provided the funds for the construction of a road network, and thus delivered the native from the tyranny of portages which had previously taken such a heavy toll.[2]

[1] Is this why the directors are so much in favour of free enterprise?
[2] The European coffee-planters of Uele export their produce along a route paid for entirely by native cotton-growers. So as to improve the road before a visit from a Minister, the natives were mobilized for a fortnight just at a time when their attention was urgently needed on the land. Sowing was delayed, and yields probably suffered a drop of about 20 per cent., or nearly 1 cwt. per acre. It would be much easier to mechanize road-making and maintenance than the work on the land, but the burden still lay heavily on the shoulders of the natives. Mechanization should be a priority task in the Belgian Congo, as in the rest of inter-tropical Africa, but it would cost the Government twice as much as it has to spend on roads at present. It would be interesting to know how much

DIRECTED PEASANT FARMING AT BAMBESA

Agricultural scientists began—and with good cause—to accuse the system of promoting the rapid deterioration of the soil. The yield of crops grown after savanna fallow often fell to only 60 per cent. of those obtained on land cleared of forest. The Administration and the company in question soon saw the need for action, and the outcome was the planning of the Baboua economy or *paysanat*. M. Lecomte, the manager of the Bambesa station, who, with his colleagues, greatly assisted us in our work, declared that even the education of the native cultivator and the raising of crop yields were subsidiary to the all-important task of saving the soil.

32. A thorough survey of relief, drainage, soils, and vegetation is carried out on the basis of field traverses 1,100 yds. apart in one direction and 2,200 in the other. The territory of each 'clan'[1] is then defined, and for this purpose fishing preserves are the most useful criterion, for where land is fairly plentiful these are delimited more precisely than the territorial rights to cultivation. The identity of each tribe or clan is confirmed by genealogical and ethnographic investigation, and on all this evidence each is allotted a precisely delimited area of land. Then for the first time each family is given hereditary title to the use of a certain tract of land, which generally covers 25 acres. Twenty-two of these will be involved in the system of land rotation.

At Yangambi the strips of land were distributed among the Turumbu in accordance with local customs. Each family was allotted a portion of the strip proportional to the labour force at its disposal. Every time another belt of land was cleared, the proportions were liable to vary according to changes in family circumstances. Those who were so minded were also free to undertake the cultivation of land in excess of their normal entitlement. Here, however, the aim was to encourage the idea of the 'small family holding', considered to be the fundamental basis of all society. A form of European land tenure which has yet to prove itself adaptable to modern techniques has thus been imported

---

this 'economy' was really costing in terms of production from the land, where it sometimes has disastrous consequences. Even though the position has improved, M. Houssiaux of the Cotonco organization tells us that many a chief has acquired a fine house by mobilizing the men liable to *corvée* in his clan—at a probable cost of 500 tons of cotton each time. The peasant who actually owes his chief thirty days of labour a year often furnishes rather more. J. Henry also criticizes 'the frequency of useless *corvées*'.

[1] The men of a clan have to take a wife from outside it. The clan consists of the descendants of a common ancestor: thus the Baboua are 'the people of Boua'. For further details, see *Le paysanat Turumbu*, by J. Valleys.

into a continent with completely different social traditions.[1] Among many of the white people in colonial territories the universal supremacy of European ideas is an unquestioned fact.

Sixteen thousand small farms were established at the beginning of 1953. There are parallel tracks 2,200 yds. apart, and where the land is suitable the space between each pair is divided into rectangular holdings each 1,100 yds. in length and with 110 yds. of frontage.

In practice, no attempt is made to utilize steep-sided valleys, marshy bottom lands, or areas of infertile soils. The exact proportion of poorer land which has to be used depends on the population density, which varies from thirty to sixty-five per square mile. Reckoned on a basis of four persons per family and holdings of 25 acres, 22 of which are cultivated, the theoretical upper limit of density is 100 to the square mile. In practice this means that in areas with thirty persons per square mile the poorest two-thirds of the area can be ignored, but where the density rises to sixty-five, even land of mediocre quality has to be cultivated.

33. The rigid pattern of rectangular fields makes it impossible to allow for irregularities of terrain, and simple soil conservation techniques like contour ploughing and avoidance of steep slopes cannot be put into effect. The dispersed pattern of settlement results in many families living at some distance from springs, and they are obliged to use wells, which are less convenient for some purposes (e.g. washing). Around each dwelling, and separated from the road by a hedge, is a small 'home' field, which occupies all the frontage of the holding and stretches back for about 65 yds. Part of it is kept clear as a drying space, while the rest comprises a kitchen garden, with taros and tomatoes, a cluster of oil-palms, and an orchard of mangoes, pineapples, papayas, and bananas. It is a small family replica of the village horticultural belt found elsewhere. The space allotted for the garden is not always used as it should be, however, and it often remains completely uncleared. The huts themselves are not always spaced at regular intervals and sometimes stand in groups of half a dozen or more, forming small hamlets. For many years to come the people will have to continue bringing in the harvest along the narrow tracks by carrying it on their

[1] J. Henry makes the following apt comments: 'The philosophical concepts of the colonizer must not determine local solutions. . . . Far from acting as a stimulus, the immediate introduction of private property in a native community would be an obstacle to progress in agriculture. . . . It would be accompanied by usury and debt, and would lead the peasant into a condition of slavery. . . . The traditional system is a better guarantee of security for the worker on the land than private ownership can ever be.'

heads. The *paysanat* is therefore torn between the need to keep each hut as close as possible to its fields and the desire to encourage community life by grouping native dwellings together. Here, again, will the traditional hierarchy of tribal life, which also exploits the native to some extent, have to be demolished completely before new loyalties can replace it?

On its allotted space each family is free to build its own house. This first hut is always rectangular in plan and comprises the hearth and the kitchen. Inside, one may see a bunch of palm fruits, from which the oil will shortly be extracted, and next to them a basket which men carry by passing the straps over their shoulders, whereas the women support them on the forehead. There is also a mortar in *Chlorophora* wood and a pestle. The latter is found everywhere in Africa and has many uses—crushing plantains, husking rice, grinding manioc and maize into meal, and separating the oily pulp from the kernels of the palm fruits after they have been boiled. A smaller pestle is used for vegetables, and maize and manioc are sometimes ground on a flat stone with a large egg-shaped pebble about 8 in. long. A hunting net hangs down from the wall,[1] and bags of ground-nuts are laid above the hearth on the criss-crossing laths of the ceiling. On the floor are baskets full of cotton lint from the last harvest. Some families do not bother to collect the whole crop if they get enough money from the first picking.

The hut is not really a 'home', because the Baboua live out of doors as much as possible and only use their huts for sleeping at night and sheltering from the rain by day. The beds have palliasses made from banana leaves, and sometimes have mosquito nets, cotton sheets, and even blankets. The latter are almost unheard of in the villages of French Equatorial Africa.

Commercial agriculture is helping to raise the standard of living. The women, who formerly went quite naked, can now buy themselves loincloths, but much heavier losses of body salt result from the increased perspiration. Apart from the sewing machine, the most treasured possession is the bicycle. There are several of these in the village, and although in some countries like the U.S.A. they would be a sign of poverty, here they are an indication of wealth. They are valued as toys and as vehicles for taking goods to market. Great efforts have been made to increase the number of buying centres, but in some

---

[1] The richer families had saucepans, cups, scissors, plates; a blacksmith even owned a spade. There are many signs of a higher living standard than among the Turumbu, who have remained concerned only with food crops.

cases distances of up to six and seven miles will still have to be covered. This is a serious matter when one considers that an average family, with $2\frac{1}{2}$ acres under cotton, will have up to 16 cwt. to carry in 55-lb. loads, and that this may represent a journey of nearly 400 miles. Other valued possessions are the piano-accordion and the gramophone, for the Baboua are a musical people, and there are as yet no radio facilities. The shot-gun is an even greater luxury.

Nowadays, alcohol is made from plaintains soaked in water or from maize, and no longer from oil-palms, which are still common enough in the forest, although many have been destroyed in the course of clearing operations. The average family income did not appear to reach the official estimate of 2,500 Congo francs announced in 1950.[1]

34. Whereas a bachelor has to grow $\frac{3}{4}$ acre of cotton each year, the typical family has to clear a rectangle 55 yds. deep along the whole of its frontage of 110 yds. The following year they tackle the next rectangle, thus creating in two years their section of the 110-yd.-wide cleared belt of land. During the third and fourth years, a similar area, separated from the first square by 110 yds. of forest, is cleared in the same way. Thus, the last of the 'odd' bands of the 'property' (inalienable, for land rights can only be inherited) is cleared in the tenth year, and after this the work is resumed from the first stretch of forest, which was left nearest the hut. The system is thus similar to that of the Turumbu (Fig. 6).

The result of the rigid geometrical pattern is that poorer land cannot be avoided, and another disadvantage is that when the first half-band of 55 yds. has been cleared, it does not leave much light, for the crops which are then immediately sown. Furthermore, although in theory the corridors of land should each be cleared simultaneously, in actual fact they often remain punctuated by sections of uncleared forest, for some families work more slowly than others. In some cases, there are complaints from larger or more energetic families that their allocation of land is much too small. It is difficult at this stage to say definitely which is the better of the two systems, the Yangambi or the Bambesa. The best course is to allow both to develop along their own lines and to encourage the adoption elsewhere of methods proved successful in these pioneer schemes. The principles underlying the Yangambi system, however, do seem to provide for greater flexibility and to be more easily adaptable to native traditions.

The forest is cut down between October and December, and there follows an initial year of 'voluntary' cultivation. The colonist is advised

[1] It exceeded that of the Turumbu.

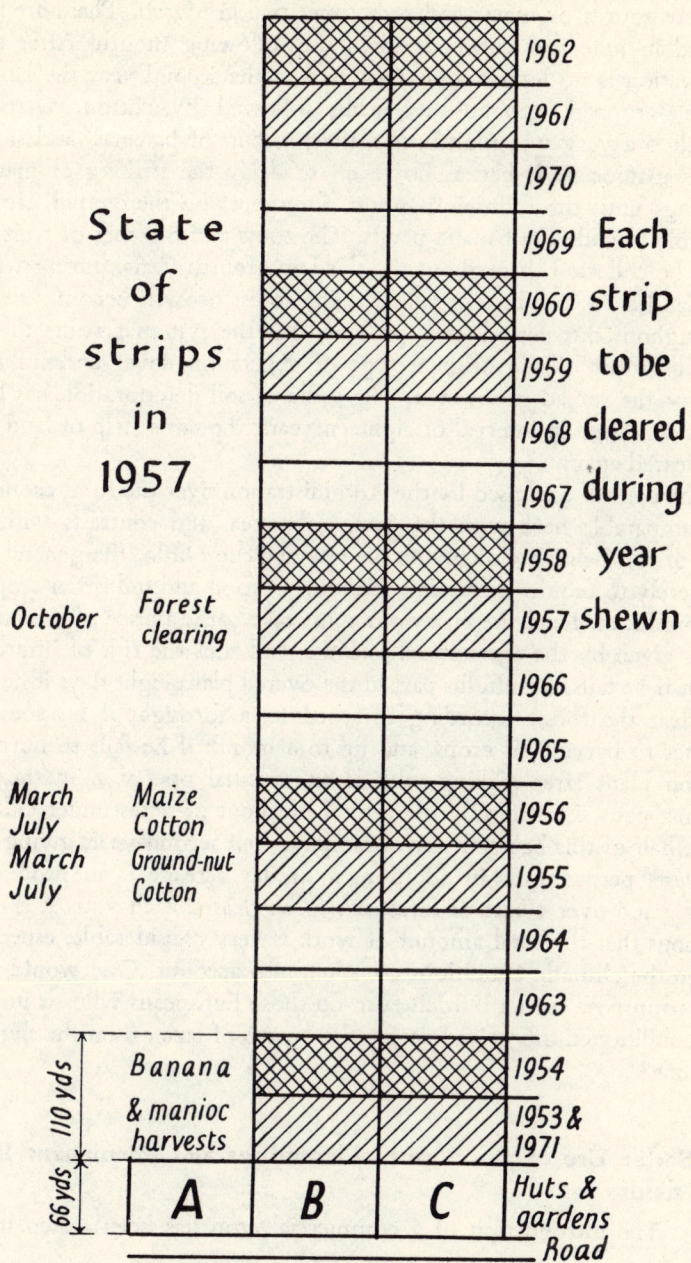

FIG. 6. The Baboua Paysanat.

to sow gourds or maize and sometimes rice in March. These are harvested in June and cotton is sown the following month. After this, cultivation is no longer voluntary, and in the second year the land is double-cropped, ground-nuts being followed by cotton. October, which is a very wet month, sees the planting of bananas, and sometimes manioc. It is better, however, to delay the striking of manioc cuttings until the following spring, for otherwise their rapid growth is liable to stifle the banana plants. The roots and bunches of fruit can then be collected throughout the third and fourth years, during which the land is in 'productive fallow'. The forest growth becomes denser throughout this period, thus proving that the system favours the reestablishment of the original type of vegetation cover and militates against the spread of savanna. The cycle of soil deterioration has been stopped. After an interval of eighteen years, the same strip of land will be cleared again.

The control exercised by the Administration over the rural economy is comparable here with the Yangambi area, and contrasts with the rest of the Belgian Congo. As we saw at Pene Niolo, the general rule is merely to require a certain minimum of food and industrial crops to be produced. Here the cultivator must take some notice of the advice he is given by the agricultural scientist, and runs the risk of imprisonment if he fails to fulfil his part in the overall plan: eight days if he fails to clear the forest according to schedule, a fortnight if he does not bother to harvest his crops, and up to a month if he fails to burn the cotton plant after picking—this is an essential operation in the war against pests. Each family has a total of about $2\frac{1}{2}$ acres under cultivation, half of this being first-year land and half second-year, giving two harvests per annum. In addition, a similar acreage is in productive fallow and over 1 acre of forest has to be cleared each year. It is quite obvious that the total amount of work is very considerable, especially when the climatic conditions are taken into account. One would hesitate to impose such a burden even on those Europeans who sit in their air-conditioned offices and accuse the Negro of laziness on the slightest pretext.[1]

6. Better Use of the Forest—Plantations and Permanent Ricefields

35. The introduction of a commercial crop has been a step in the

[1] M. Lecomte informs us that the $1\frac{1}{4}$ acres of compulsory cotton are often exceeded—without any coercion whatsoever.

right direction. The choice of cotton reflects the desire of the colonial power to make certain of its sources of raw material rather than the wish to provide for the basic needs of the native population. The Belgians, in their search for greater economic independence, are naturally anxious to control the supply of raw material for their textile industry, and in order to achieve this they are encouraging the cultivation of cotton in the only intertropical colonies they possess. In the case of a planned world economy, the cultivation of cotton would no doubt be concentrated in tropical and warm temperate countries, where the factors of production do not have to be diverted to maintain an expensive system of forest fallow—always providing that synthetic fibres did not quickly replace cotton altogether.

In a world where the demand for cellulose is constantly increasing, and where the supplies available from the temperate forests are becoming inadequate, it seems regrettable that every acre of burnt-over land in the equatorial region involves the waste of enormous quantities of humus, of 600-900 lb. of nitrogen and of 120-400 tons of wood, not to mention the forty-eight days of human labour spent in felling and stacking. Finally, it takes another 50 days' work to produce 1·2 cwt. of a fibre[1] which consists essentially of cellulose. The fibre thus obtained is admittedly superior to anything which can at present be made from wood, but the situation is bound to change as new processes are evolved. It is easier, however, to point to the anomaly of the situation than to suggest practical remedies. The establishment of timber mills would necessitate an enormous capital outlay, but the present lack of means for keeping up a constant flow of raw material would often make such ventures uneconomic. The all-important requirement is cheap transport from forest to factory, and floating the timber downstream is the only way in which this could be achieved at present.

There is, moreover, no immediate intention of exploiting the forests near the rivers, either for saw-mill timber or for power-generation. Even the ashes are not fully put to use. Much of their value as fertilizers is lost because they are not spread evenly over the ground, and this may lead to toxic effects in areas of excess. As for timber, only the valuable hardwood trees are exploited to any extent, and then only when they occur near the coast, for they have to be singled out laboriously from mixed stands. With modern machinery, however, practically any

---

[1] The average for French Equatorial Africa is well below 1 cwt. of fibre per acre, and only the Indian Union has lower yields. The yield of raw cotton, with the seed, is about three times as much as for fibre alone. Arizona has an average of $5\frac{1}{4}$ cwt. of fibre per acre, with maxima of up to 15 cwt.!

kind of wood can be pulped nowadays, and this suggests a possible use for the secondary forest, where the bulk of the trees are of umbrella type. In this way the forested areas near the rivers could be made productive and the waste of land and effort now implicit in the forest fallow system could be greatly reduced. This would only be a temporary solution, but it could be applied while the best way of establishing a productive grass fallow—or even a system of annual rotations not harmful to the soil—was still being worked out.

36. The attempt to find systems of continuous intensive cultivation appropriate to equatorial regions will involve a protracted period of trial and error. Fortunately, there are already two ways in which continuous production from a given area can be achieved without endangering the fertility of the soil. The first method is the growing of tree crops under a plantation system which aims at the creation of an artificial and commercially productive forest. If due care is given to such points as shade, contour planting, and adequate cover of ground vegetation, the fertility of the land can be maintained. Furthermore, the products of these plantations are specific to the equatorial zone and their development in areas outside this zone is out of the question. The ideal conditions for cotton, however, as we have seen, are found in higher latitudes. Finally, the work of making these plantations is far less arduous than that of periodic clearing and cultivation for annual crops, while the returns are very much higher.

The first modern plantations of *Hevea* and oil-palm were made in the Far East, particularly in Indonesia and Malaya, at about the turn of the century. Significant developments in the Belgian Congo did not occur until the 1920s, while French Equatorial Africa still lags far behind. From the very first, high yields have been the main objective of the intensive methods employed by the large commercial companies which have undertaken this type of enterprise. Capital and equipment have been poured into each small selected region on a very large scale, and the Far East has remained, in virtue of its generous endowment of rich soils, the most favourable region for this type of exploitation. By comparison with the primitive system of collecting wild products from the forest still practised at Pene Niolo, this type of economy at its best results in a ten- or even a twelve-fold increase in the productivity of native labour.

One must go to French West Africa to find people who still advocate the primitive type of system. They cannot see that the fate of wild rubber production in the face of competition from plantations of budgrafted *Hevea* has any relevance to the production of palm-oil. 'The collecting of wild rubber, which was resumed during the war, emptied the villages of French West Africa, and in 1944 3,500 tons were produced, whereas the output of the Firestone plantation in Liberia was 25,000 tons' (J. Dresch, 'West African Problems', *Boletim cultural da Guine Portuguesa*, January 1950). In Oubangui, the production of wild rubber is on the same insignificant scale. As students at the *Institut d'Agronomie coloniale* from 1927-8, we were exhorted to study various latex-secreting lianas which had even then been commercially obsolete for twenty years.

The effect of the plantation system is to make the native an employee, and from a social point of view the wisdom of this transformation is debatable. Then, again, there are few areas in equatorial Africa where the soils are good enough to encourage the plantation type of economy. Business interests are only attracted by land which will give good returns for the money required to develop it. The agricultural scientist, on the other hand, is concerned primarily with the needs of the native peoples, and consequently with the conservation, and the development to appropriate levels of intensiveness of the great mass of average quality land, which will inevitably account for the bulk of production in the future.

Large-scale undertakings begin by removing the whole of the natural vegetation cover and exceptionally favourable conditions are needed to attract them. But the semi-modern type of plantation has much more modest requirements. Small pockets of land can be cleared by the natives and the undergrowth periodically slashed with much less trouble, and this seems the logical line of development in most of equatorial Africa, where the soils are so often rather less than fertile. The oil-palm would be particularly well suited to this kind of system, for it gives phenomenally high yields, which are unsurpassed by any other crop. During the course of certain experiments in Malaya over 2·4 tons of oil per acre were recorded, and although yields such as this can only be obtained under the best conditions, there is no reason why native African production should not achieve something like 4-8 cwt. per acre, which still makes this an interesting proposition. In the British and Belgian colonies at least, the need to stimulate native production of this kind has been recognized.

There is no reason why our supply of valuable commodities from equatorial regions should not continue to expand, so long as certain precepts are observed: the social consequences of an increased emphasis on commercial crops must be studied; sites must be chosen with care and priority given to the richest areas available; trees must be planted immediately after clearing, without the interpolation of field crops. Cacao is another crop with distinct possibilities. A larger demand may well result from a general rise in living standards, for North America, with less than one-fifteenth of the world's population, consumes one-third of the total crop. An advantage of the cacao plantation is that the plant itself needs to grow in the shade of larger trees, and the soil is the more easily maintained in consequence of the double protection it enjoys.

The future of natural rubber is much less certain, threatened as it is by the synthetic rubber industry, which is constantly cutting its costs and improving the quality of its products. Rubber can also be obtained from various plants of the temperate regions, such as *kok-sagyz*, which is cultivated in the U.S.S.R. as an insurance against the cessation of imported supplies, but the yield from such sources is very low indeed, and the *Hevea brasiliensis* would rapidly establish a monopoly in the free rubber market. Unlike palm-oil, cacao, and rubber, the production of coffee is not virtually confined to equatorial regions. Indeed, the finest *arabica* type can be grown successfully only in tropical areas and at a considerable height above sea-level. The crop has no harmful effect on the soil, but poor methods of cultivation have resulted in serious damage to millions of acres in South America, and even in Africa similar effects have already been observed.

37. Even if a certain amount of capital could be accumulated out of local resources along these lines, equally if not more important is the need to improve the general standard of nutrition. The grave shortcomings of the unbalanced diet, with its excess of carbohydrates and deficiency in animal proteins, have already been noted. The latter could be alleviated by pisciculture, sea- and fresh-water fishing, by distributing more guns as an encouragement to hunting, and by introducing animal husbandry. The food from manioc and bananas should be supplemented by growing various protein-rich leguminous crops like ground-nuts and soya beans which are now in great demand. Sugar cane cultivation could also be extended, although, as we shall see, the need for this is even more urgent in the Far East.

The principal cereal of the temperate lands is wheat, whereas in intertropical regions rice plays the dominant role. But the cultivation of upland rice is a powerful factor in soil erosion, and this is, unfortunately, extremely apparent in French West Africa. Wet rice of the Asiatic type must therefore be developed wherever valley bottoms and other reasonably flat areas can be levelled without too much effort, and irrigated or drained as the circumstances demand. The effect of the water is to protect the soil, and large fluctuations in yield are thus avoided. As it will take some time to instil Asiatic habits of systematic fertilizing, the most suitable areas at first will be the low-lying flood-plains which are enriched with silt from the swollen rivers of the rainy season. Allowing fallows to revert to bush, and later on the use of green manures, will be sufficient to maintain soil fertility in higher flood-free areas which prove rich enough to warrant development. Fertilizing will be absolutely necessary, however, wherever the rainfall régime, supplemented by small irrigation projects, is such as to permit double-cropping. Unfortunately, the introduction of wet paddy is likely to be delayed, owing to the cost of such projects and the lack of credit facilities.

This point will be examined in more detail in connexion with tropical regions where the same kind of problem arises. Soil fertility,[1] likely cost of development, and proximity to areas of comparatively dense population are the chief factors which must influence decisions on the relative priority accorded to different regions. The question of existing population densities is relevant, because rice cultivation along the lines suggested is the means whereby the pressure of population could be relieved, and the transfer of people to the new areas would be facilitated if the distances involved were kept to a minimum. The relief of congestion in areas where the soils are now severely taxed would in itself constitute a measure of land conservation, while the rice consumed in the new areas and the smaller dependence on maize and bananas would represent a welcome advance in dietetic standards. The adoption of continuous cultivation from the start would go hand in hand with the complete abolition of forest fallow and clearing and would permit much higher population densities than can safely be supported at present. Finally, mechanization could eventually be grafted on to this type of system with comparatively little difficulty.

It is certainly likely to succeed in low-lying regions, such as river flood plains, and this consideration leads us on to assert that it is towards these more promising regions that movements of population should be encouraged. Until now such migrations have occurred only in the interests of European-owned plantations and mines, and they have often taken place under appalling conditions, especially in areas like the Lower Ivory Coast, where the neglect of medical facilities and native dietary habits has had tragic consequences. Curiously enough, any scheme which is strictly in the interests of the native population is sure to find all kinds

[1] Thus the Ivory Coast should have priority over Mauretania and the Niger. In France, on the contrary, the time has come for efforts to be concentrated in the underdeveloped regions.

of high-principled arguments levelled against it by the very people who have benefited from the mobility of native labour in the past.

7. Intensification, Mechanization, and Industrialization

38. Here, then, are the two agricultural systems which must now be exploited to the full and which can give the breathing space required to perfect techniques of much wider application. These will enable the land to be cropped year after year without inundation. It now remains for us to consider how quickly these processes of mechanization and intensification should take place.

The overpopulated parts of the equatorial zone will be considered first, because, although they are comparatively restricted in extent, the problems here are most acute. The urgent necessity for increasing crop yields has already been stressed, and a partial but immediate solution is the better use of natural fertilizers, such as wood ashes, plant refuse, and, to a lesser extent, animal and human waste products; always providing that such measures, by increasing the demands on labour and local transport facilities, would not entail a worsening of the situation. In any densely populated areas like Kivu, where soil erosion has already begun, the only possible remedy is the use of chemical fertilizers, the purchase of which will have to be subsidized by governments.

Elsewhere, where the cost of fertilizers is now considered to be prohibitive, the time will come when the status of the soil can no longer be restored economically under forest fallows. These become ineffective when overshortened, but sufficient time can be allowed for the natural process of soil regeneration only in areas of very sparse population. Even so, the system is tolerated only because of the poor living standards and the low productivity of labour. When the standards of living begin to rise, forty-eight days spent in clearing and burning 1 acre of forest will no longer seem worthwhile. At the same time, local manufacture will greatly reduce the cost of chemical fertilizers, although their general introduction here appears to be rather less urgent than in tropical Africa and monsoon Asia.

A similar argument can be applied to mechanization. The importance of this question is enhanced by the severe limitations on the use of animals and by the inadequacy of human labour alone in coping with the task of raising production. At the moment, tractors and other modern equipment have to be imported at great expense, and the same applies to fuel oils while, paradoxically enough, large sections of the forest are continually being burnt to waste[1] and hydro-electric power possibilities remain untapped. The first phase of capitalism and the attendant rise in living standards will naturally conduce to a situation where skilled labour becomes increasingly available and all kinds of operations, such as mechanical maintenance work, can be carried out with local resources. Most important of all, a higher price will have to be paid for labour.

Enormous quantities of equipment are needed, but their availability from European countries is now greatly restricted by the burden of defence programmes. Consequently, a careful scheme of priorities must be devised to ensure that the slender resources are applied where the greatest benefits, in terms of higher production, are likely to accrue. The recourse to imports of material is handicapped by the lack of funds in the territories themselves, and while complete self-sufficiency is neither advisable nor practicable the only solution is for materials to be manufactured, as far as the economics of the situation will allow, where they are needed—that is, in the colonies themselves. Whatever the circumstances, the modernization of agriculture cannot be effected nearly so rapidly unless a general policy of industrialization is pursued simultaneously. Any country whose economy is based exclusively on produce from the land balanced by imports of manufactured articles must pay the price of low standards of living,[2] agricultural stagnation, and possibly even of political tutelage.

Manufacturing industry, merely by employing labour, can obviously help to relieve the pressure on the land in areas of high population density, and it thereby becomes an instrument of soil conservation. So far this consideration does not appear to have been borne in mind when areas have been selected for development. The equatorial zone has no immediate prospect of reducing its essential dependence on the produce of the land. It therefore seems logical to ask that at first industrialization should aim not so much at making profits as at bringing much-needed benefits to the land and its workers. This does not imply that the laws of economics should be disregarded. On the contrary, industrial production must be carefully attuned to its market, but the situation will involve a series of most delicate adjustments. The policy of industrialization must be designed in such a way as to bring the greatest possible benefits to the territories concerned, and the problem of its implementation

[1] Which could be used to actuate stationary gas-operated motors—a more sensible method than using petrol or oil in the equatorial regions. In the increasing use of these latter one detects an element of Malthusianism, a desire to limit their availability on the market. Cf. P. H. Mensier's article in *Oléagineux* (January-February 1952).

[2] E.g. the Balkans until 1945.

39. Native and European have a common interest in the industrial development of the equatorial region. In the early days when the *Pacte colonial* was still in force, the building of factories was prohibited in order to promote the flow of raw materials to the colonial power and to preserve the colonial market for manufactured goods. On the other hand, Belgian private interests have shown more enterprise than the French in equipping what is after all their only colony. Facing the scattered and village-like settlement of Brazzaville across Stanley Pool, Leopoldville has the aspect of a modern capital city.

In the Belgian Congo, the spinning and weaving industry absorbs an appreciable proportion of the cotton crop, but in French Equatorial Africa, as late as 1949, sanction was refused for an interesting scheme which envisaged the establishment of local cotton manufactures. Industrialization of the Congo makes it necessary to increase the available supply of power, and though poor in coal the area has great possibilities for the utilization of hydro-electric power. Unfortunately, however, the available sites are expensive to develop and distribution over a region as sparsely populated as this is also bound to be costly. From the agricultural point of view, electricity means synthetic nitrates, which could put an end to forest fallow once and for all.

One of the engineers employed by Cotonco had evolved a small scheme for a portion of the River Uele upstream of Bambili. The falls here would produce about 500 h.p., which could be used—

- to supply electricity to the cotton-ginning machines and to the nearby native villages;
- to recharge the accumulators of electric-motor-driven lorries at night, thus finding a use for current at a time when it is often wasted, and also making imports of fuel oil, which are so expensive here in the interior, unnecessary;
- to start off small local industries making furniture, bicycles, kitchen utensils and similar items which would supply the needs of the native people.

It is most important that small schemes like this, requiring only a modest allocation of equipment, should not be overlooked when plans are drawn up on a much wider regional basis. Collectively, they are capable of effecting, at a low initial cost, a substantial rise in levels of productivity (e.g. by improving hand tools) and standards of living.

INTENSIFICATION AND INDUSTRIALIZATION

That industrialization is the necessary starting-point for agricultural improvement is a theme which will recur again and again in this book. Unfortunately, however, many of those who flock to the towns seek in vain for employment and only too often the Negro peasant becomes an out-of-work idler or, in other circumstances, the parasitic dependent of a successful parent. Once the food supply is assured, the surplus rural population should be able to find industrial work of higher productivity in the towns, but the 'Negro villages' of Brazzaville and Bangui, the 'Bidonvilles' of Casablanca and Djibuti, and the 'work camps' of Matunga near Bombay evoke a picture of poverty and squalor. These examples only emphasize the crying need for an abundant supply of the basic necessities of life.

40. If progress in cultivation is difficult to promote, it is very much easier to improve the methods used in the preparation and processing of various products, even when they are destined for home consumption. The small Japanese type of rice-thresher,[1] a hand-operated maize-stripper, a foot pestle on the Asian model instead of the present hand implement, hoe blades with sockets for fixing the handles, the sickle in place of the knife which cuts one ear of rice at a time—the adoption of all these improvements would represent a great advance. Transport also could be made much easier by the use of a light type of rickshaw with tyres; this would be preferable either to the cart, which would be too heavy, or to the wheelbarrow, which would be equally tiring. The rickshaw would enable a man to pull about 2 cwt. of cotton at a time along the paths, which would require a little more attention than at present. This, however, would not offset the advantage over the present method of carrying 50-lb. or 60-lb. loads on the head. This is traditionally performed by women, but men would not be debarred from pulling a load, for this is considered more dignified.[2]

Small-scale improvements such as these, inspired mainly through studying the much more ingenious methods of the Asian peasant, would have a marked overall effect on the productivity of agricultural labour. Certainly, to begin with, money could be spent more profitably in promoting such minor changes of method than in equipping the large plantations with machinery. This is not to argue against large-scale mechanization, but as it cannot in the course of a few years be applied to the whole of African agriculture, it is as well to remember

---

[1] For this machine and various other tools which might be introduced into Africa, see *La culture du riz dans le delta du Tonkin* (Paris, 1935).

[2] But in French West Africa human traction is prohibited; yet one would have thought it represented an advance on portage.

that the less spectacular kinds of reform are equally worthy of attention, and that they are often likely to give better results. They can be quickly developed, however, only in the context of a directed economy, but it is worth emphasizing that any restrictions can be justified only if they lead to rapid progress. Some of those which are imposed today would be difficult to justify on any grounds.

J. Henry has shown that at Turumbu, only 27 per cent. of the work was formerly spent on actual cultivation, 4 per cent. was spent on clearing forest, 13 per cent. on transport, and over half, 56 per cent., on the preparation of produce (drying, soaking, threshing, husking, grinding). Now maize-strippers, ground-nut-decorticators, and a rice mill have been introduced. The task of spreading improvements of this kind and of training the Negro in sound agricultural techniques still offers tremendous scope for action. The real revolution in equatorial agriculture will come later, and will involve the adoption of systems of continuous cropping which do not endanger the soil. Then, and only then, will this region be able to contribute substantially to the world food supply, perhaps not so much as South America, but certainly more than it does today. It will then be in a position to act as a reception area for some of the excess population of Asia, particularly for Indians, many of whom have already emigrated to South and East Africa. It will undoubtedly be a long time before these plans are eventually fulfilled, but a greater effort is capable of accelerating the process to an appreciable degree.

In conclusion, one cannot but endorse the opinion of H. Green, the Rothamsted expert on tropical soils: 'An appreciable output of exportable commodities, a general and progressive improvement in soil fertility, and a continuous rise in the standards of living are objectives which must be successfully pursued at one and the same time . . . while not forgetting to encourage any social reforms which are really desirable and resisting those that are not . . . and failure anywhere along the line may lead to disaster.'[1]

[1] *African Soils*, Vol. I, p. 12. The non-specialist is referred to Gourou's *Les Pays Tropicaux* for Chapters II and IV, and to our *'La mise en valeur agricole de l'Afrique tropicale'* (*Economie contemporaine*, January-February 1951) for Chapters II and III. The agricultural scientist is referred to *Comptes rendus de la Semaine Agricole de Yangambi*, published by the Institut National pour l'Etude Agronomique du Congo belge (Brussels, 1947), and 'Comptes rendus de la Conférence Africaine de Goma' (1948), published in the *Bulletin Agricole du Congo belge* during the course of 1949. Consult also the laboratory of tropical agronomy (Professor Portères) at the Muséum d'histoire naturelle, Paris, the Bureau interafricain des sols (Dr Guilloteau), and the journal of the latter, *African Soils*, printed in French and English. For social and cultural problems see *Présence Africaine*, the journal of the Institut français d'Afrique noire de Dakar.

III

The Tropical Savanna of Africa from Chad to the River Casamance[1]

1. Drier Climate, Occasionally More Fertile Soils, the Trading System

41. North of the equatorial zone of Africa, the wet season becomes shorter and the rainfall diminishes and becomes less and less reliable. Beyond Lake Chad and the Niger bend, complete aridity prevails. There are two clearly marked seasons, and only one crop per year can be obtained where the rains last less than six months. When they last less than four months and the total is under 30 in., failure to sow both commercial and subsistence crops at the beginning of the rains is to court disaster. There is thus a most pronounced peak demand for labour at this season.

The rest of the year is completely rainless,[2] and the length of this dry season increases to the north—from four months at Bangui to nearly eight at Fort Lamy. Temperature variations also become significant. In the Chad region, variations of over 60° F. commonly occur during the course of a single month, and at sunrise in January the temperature is often down to 48° F. and none too pleasant for people not accustomed to cold and who are at best only scantily clothed. The

---

[1] It should be noted that this area includes the greater part of West Africa, except for the coastal region between Gabon and Guinea, which is part of the forest zone; also the northern half of the area misnamed 'French Equatorial Africa', that is the Chad and most of Oubangui-Chari except for a narrow band in the extreme south. We visited the area twice in 1950: January-February in French Equatorial Africa and North Cameroons; October-November in Senegal, Casamance, and Sudan.

[2] One can sleep in the open without discomfort—provided one has a mosquito net.

humidity[1] is much too low for the establishment of high-yielding tree plantations, and as for wild tree products, they are confined to various oils which can be collected from drought-resisting species like the shea and certain rues. Desiccating winds like the *harmattan*, their force no longer broken by the forest, blow across the thinly covered soils with disastrous effect and encourage the extension of desert conditions towards the south. The climate, however, favours the rearing of animals, cattle in the south and zebu cattle in the drier north. Enormous areas which are otherwise too arid for cultivation without irrigation are given over to grazing on a very extensive scale, for no other form of land utilization is possible.

42. Whereas the climate becomes increasingly difficult away from the forest and towards the desert, the soils, on the contrary, tend to become richer. Wherever this grassland region receives less than about twenty inches of rain, the soils, according to the pedologist Georges Aubert, are characterized by a high proportion of humus. They are subjected to very little leaching, and the processes destructive of organic material are slowed down or halted during the dry season. They are richer in soluble minerals, contain more bases—like calcium, which promotes crumb structure—and are less acid than equatorial soils.[2] As in the Southern Ukraine, the arid climate is the only curb on agriculture. In the tree savanna further south only the upper layers of soil contain a little organic material. Leaching becomes more marked towards the Equator, and the hydroxides of iron are precipitated below the surface, but so long as the illuviated zone remains below the ground and the surface is protected by vegetation, the soil remains fairly productive.

The grass savannas, however, are ravaged every year by fires.[3] They may be lit for various reasons—to assist hunting, to facilitate travel, to kill parasites, or sometimes just for sport, as Agbessi, our driver, did one day. But they do tremendous damage, for only a few trees survive, and at the beginning of the rains the soil is so devoid of protection against erosion that even quite gentle slopes are subject to dissection.

[1] One day at Fort Lamy we left a strip of stamps on a table and were unable to find them a few minutes later. We eventually discovered that the drying gum had made it curl into a long, thin cylinder which, at first, we had failed to recognize.

[2] On the whole, the soils are intermediate between those of the equatorial and temperate zones (M. Ferrand).

[3] By lighting them earlier, an attempt is being made to reduce the damage done by fires. The vegetation, still humid, then burns less fiercely.

When the surface soil has been removed, the iron-rich horizon which is thereby exposed becomes indurated and forms a hard crust known in Guinea as *boval*, which we have found as far as the area east of the Ubangi. As in these circumstances, repeated cultivation favours soil erosion, many villages are encircled by an absolutely sterile 'iron halo'. The true laterites of the forest zone, consisting mainly of aluminium hydroxide, are comparable in many respects and are the result of similar circumstances. The formation of this hard pan, together with the soil erosion which gives rise to it, is the most potent cause of soil deterioration in the region.

In former times, the region was covered with a type of forest, remnants of which are still found near Boali, north-west of Bangui. It was adapted to the drier conditions, but the upper branches of the trees formed a continuous crown of foliage. Since this type of vegetation has given way to tree savanna the soils have become poorer, and the acidic nature of the underlying rocks, which are mostly granites, gneisses, sandstones, and quartzites, has not helped to check the process. Near the margins of the rain forest, the savanna grasses like elephant grass (*Pennisetum purpureum*) grow to considerable heights, but much smaller species replace them towards the north. All these grasses, with their shallow roots, are very much less effective than the forest in minimizing the leaching action of percolating water. Moreover, the greater part of the ashes left after savanna fires is dispersed by the wind and thereby lost to the soil. The richest areas are still those with 'alluvial and colluvial soils in river valleys and at the base of the slopes' (Aubert), where excessive humidity, however, sometimes hinders their development.

The people themselves are taller than the inhabitants of the forest, and many tribes are noted for their fine physique. This is no doubt due, in part at least, to hunting and stock-rearing, which provide both meat and, even more important, milk in the native diet. The Saras of Rei-Buba in the Northern Cameroons are often over 6 ft. 6 in. in height. Furthermore, much more advanced peoples than are ever found in the forest zone have built up empires of considerable importance. Tropical Africa has witnessed the flowering of more than one civilization; indeed, they have been many and varied as the studies by Théodore Monod at the Institut français d'Afrique noir at Dakar have demonstrated convincingly. This, incidentally, is a work which has been written in a spirit of humane understanding which could well serve as a model for others.

Various arts and handicrafts flourish. In particular, spinning and weaving are much more highly developed than in equatorial Africa.

There is obviously a correlation with the length of the period of agricultural inactivity which lasts almost as long as the dry season. Mohammedanism, spreading out from the desert margins, is gaining more and more at the expense of primitive animism. Society is more highly stratified, polygamy is often traditional, and money-lending, with its attendant evils, is firmly established, particularly in the coastal zone, which is comparatively open to commercial contacts.

The individual works for himself. He tills his own field rather than sharing in the cultivation of a holding run on patriarchal lines. The young man earns his future wife's dowry himself by working in the fields. He chooses her himself, and is not necessarily obliged to obtain her father's consent. The French, believing theirs to be the 'most advanced' legal system, tried to encourage the private ownership of land in Senegal, but were not successful outside the urban centres. In his thesis on the ground-nut,[1] Fouquet has shown that in 1928 little more than seventeen acres of land, consisting of forty-five separate holdings, came under private ownership, and for rural areas this was a record year.

The impact of European influence on the native economy is much more important and dates from an earlier period than in the heart of the continent. One may well ask whether it has always been beneficial. In his *West African Problems*, J. Dresch shows that the 'trading economy' which reserved the local market for manufactures to the industries of the colonial power and prevented the territories themselves from exporting anything but raw materials, remained operative right up till the last war. West Africa began by supplying slaves for shipment to America—the so-called 'ebony trade'; later there came various wild products, like gum arabic, ivory, rubber, oils (shea and palm), wax, honey, and valuable woods. The supply of each of these commodities became exhausted in turn, sometimes quite rapidly, and there followed the export of cultivated products: coffee, cacao, and bananas from the forest margins, sisal, cotton, and, most important of all, ground-nuts from the savanna.

In return, the companies who buy these commodities furnish cotton goods, hardware, soap, perfume—and alcoholic liquors, which are more concentrated and harmful than the native brews. These companies have a virtual monopoly and are mostly very large concerns, like C.F.A.O. and S.C.O.A. in the French colonies and Unilever, the world-wide vegetable oils combine, and its subsidiaries, in the British. In good

[1] *Oléagineux* (January-February 1952), an analysis of Fouquet's thesis by Stéphane Guyot.

years profits are sometimes comparable with the nominal capital, and, as Dresch has emphasized, 'they are distributed as dividends to shareholders and are hardly ever invested in Africa'. The very large profits from trading discourage the sinking of capital into productive enterprises, and before the war private commercial investments exceeded the sum total of money invested in plantations, mines, and manufacturing industry.

We shall now examine in more detail a few selected localities in this enormous area.

2. A Cereal-growing Village near the River Shari and Its Concentric Rings of Cultivation

43. Travelling north-west from Bambesa via Bangassu in Oubangui, one enters the Chad Territory and reaches the River Shari a little upstream of Fort Archambault. Further downstream is Bouso, a local administrative centre, and striking north-west from the right bank of the river here one crosses savanna country to reach the village of Morio. This is situated in a region which receives all of its 28 in. of rain between mid-May and the end of September. The village comprises a fairly scattered collection of huts and gardens surrounded by enclosures. Abdulai Kader, with his wife,[1] cultivated a series of holdings at varying distances from the village.

The home field near the hut comprises a little over $\frac{1}{4}$ acre, and is bounded by a fence of matted wild grass. It is heavily fertilized with animal manure, but the cinders from the hearth are thrown away, as their value is not appreciated. The land is sown with maize during the rainy season, year after year. So long as it is not too ripe, it is eaten straight away, but the ripe grain is ground into flour. Various 'industrial' crops are grown along the fences and the walls of the huts. String and fishing nets are made from ambaria hemp (*Hibiscus cannabinus*). The hard shell of certain Cucurbitacea is soaked and then dried to make the calabash which in Central Africa is the universal substitute for the basin and the bucket which are found in the French Sudan, where cultivation is on a bigger scale. The earthenware jar, more fragile than the calabash, nevertheless competes with it to some extent.

Locally grown indigo is used to dye the narrow lengths of cloth (2-8 in. wide) known as *gabacs*, which are woven by the men from locally grown cotton. Kader buys these at the market and his wife

[1] His sister-in-law lives with them since her recent divorce, but, in accordance with local custom, she will remain a full year without working.

makes his clothes from them. Only towards the Cameroons, nearer the Islamic influences, does one find the broader strips of cloth, sometimes over 2 ft. wide, which are there woven by the women. The Egyptian thorn is employed in tanning leather, castor oil for preparing hides, and there are several other plants with similar uses. The gardens also provide vegetable products, such as *gumbo* and various medicines. Near the hut, the villagers take their siesta under a roof supported on wooden poles upon which ground-nuts are spread to dry. These supply the householders with about 5 pints of oil a month, and there is generally a small surplus for sale. Five pints have in any case to be provided each year for the Administration, which buys at 23 francs C.F.A. per pint[1]—a price very advantageous to itself.

A short distance away is the hut belonging to Kader's sister-in-law, which is partly surrounded by a roofless enclosure for the ass and its foal. Eight goats and two kids are housed in a covered shed near the hut belonging to the head of the family and his wife; the huts here are circular with a conical roof. On either side are five or six granaries, made of matted stalks of grasses which, at the end of January, contained about 2 tons of sorghum and spiked millet. Such large reserves were entirely absent in the forest zone. Kader is a large producer, and has no children. He therefore sells as much of his grain as he can before the harvest, when food is short and prices are high. Further west, near the River Logone, the granaries of the Banana tribe have walls made of unbaked clay mixed with straw and dung and supported on stones to keep out white ants.

Behind the garden with its varied produce, but still quite near the hut, is an open field belonging to what we have called the first concentric ring of cultivation. In its first year it was sown with maize, but since then it has given successive crops of early red sorghum, or 'children's millet'. This is sown at the end of May, and a very careful watch is kept on the crop, for it is harvested in August, which is a critical time of year from the point of view of food supply. The field is rarely manured, and bears an unbroken succession of crops. Sorghum, however, is a less exhausting crop than maize. The continuous and occasionally intensive cultivation of the home field under a rotation different from that of more outlying areas thus figures more prominently than in the forest zone.

A second ring of crop land extends some 300 yds. beyond the first, and here the rotation comprises two years of mixed cultivation, with

[1] The franc of the Colonie françaises d'Afrique (C.F.A.) has been worth double the French franc since 1943.

lines of red sorghum 3 or 4 yds. apart, interspersed with ground-nuts[1] at 16 × 28 in. intervals. This is followed by two or three years of fallow. Considering the complete absence of manuring, the rest period seems rather short, and the miserable weeds of the fallow fields lend support to this view. The scant growth of vegetation on the fallow simplifies the work, for sorghum is first sown broadcast (like the wheat in Kabylia), and only then is the ground hoed. The soil is thus broken up, the weeds are removed, and the seeds are covered over, all in the one operation.

44. Since 1944 manioc has appeared in the area. Though formerly confined to more humid climates, it has steadily spread from the equatorial region into higher latitudes and now at Kano in Northern Nigeria its northern limit reaches right into a wheat-growing area. Wheat has spread from the semi-arid margins of the Sahara and is carefully tended and irrigated from the sub-surface flow of rivers whose beds are quite dry in the winter. Manioc, on the other hand, although a native of the wet forests, is planted on unirrigated slopes, for the cuttings are struck at the height of the rains, with the result that its roots have a good chance of quick growth and penetrate deep into the ground. Wheat, which would be attacked by rust during the rains, is not sown until the dry season is well under way, and irrigation is then obviously indispensable.

Manioc has certain advantages. It is a hardy crop less liable to damage from locusts and, planted during the rains, it forms a valuable addition to the food supply. It benefits the poorer people especially, for it is available in winter and spring and during the period of food shortage before the cereal harvest. But although capable of growing on impoverished soils, it can lead to their complete exhaustion, and from this point of view its cultivation is a hazardous investment. There are as yet undeveloped possibilities in the use of its leaves which are rich in protein. In the meantime they are often greatly relished by the goats which are normally short of grazing during the dry season. Fencing is therefore essential if reasonable crops are to be obtained. In spite of its possibilities, however, manioc still enters hardly at all into the diet of the region. The diet still has an almost exclusively

[1] Sometimes replaced by the stone ground-nut (*Voandzeia*), a kind of leguminous food crop; by various types of gourd, etc. Like millet, the ground-nut prefers sandy soils, whereas sorghum is better adapted to heavier soils. Further east one also finds the following biennial rotation in this 'ring': red sorghum—ground-nut. Here the fields are left level, but where the soil is thin it is banked into ridges 30 in. wide; further east these are sometimes replaced by conical mounds 6 ft. wide at the base. The pattern is everywhere more complex than our description suggests.

cereal basis, and it depends on one main harvest and the keeping of large reserves.

The rapid impoverishment of the surrounding land which is brought on by over-frequent cultivation was formerly counteracted by moving the whole village to a fresh area as soon as serious soil deterioration set in. Here, on the east side of the Shari, there is no lack of land. The density of population is only about three or four per square mile and is so low as to have prevented the introduction of cotton, for the collection of small quantities of fibre from many scattered centres of production would have been uneconomic. But when the Service Géographique has determined the position of a village on a map, the Administration does not take kindly to the idea of subsequent changes of location. The official pressure which is exerted to avert such changes is thus an important factor in the impoverishment of land, and until a scientifically devised system of perennial cropping can be introduced, permanent forms of rural settlement should be strongly discouraged. With its distance from the coast and from possible sources of equipment, the region will probably have to wait a long time before the intensive methods presupposed by permanent occupation of land can be applied.

45. The 'bush fields' are the last, but by no means the least important area of cultivation. The fields of the whole village are grouped together in order to facilitate the watch against birds, which is kept from high observation posts. This arrangement also promotes a certain rivalry between the different families. The fields lie at some distance from the village, generally at between one and three miles, but never more than five. The villagers, whose community spirit is apparent in the exploitation of this outer zone, clear large sections of the savanna, and the first crop to be sown on the rich virgin land—as everywhere from the Oubangui to the Chad—is sesamum, the traditional source of oil for domestic purposes. Ground-nut oil is tending to replace it, however, and where this is the case the first crop is spiked millet, or *dokhone*, as it is known here. The latter, which was introduced long ago, has certain advantages over sorghum or great millet, which is the only truly native cereal, for its grain is more highly esteemed and its ears are less subject to damage by birds. It is either grown for two or three years in succession, or, more frequently, alternated with sorghum. After this the land remains fallow for three to five years, which is barely long enough, especially as there are tracts of virtually empty land a little further to the east.

The few trees of the savanna are cut down in the cool season and burnt about mid-March. This requires only six days of work per acre —one-eighth of the labour needed in the Congo forest to perform the same task. When the first rains begin in June, the men merely scrape out planting holes about 1 in. deep and 1 yd. apart in the light earth. The women then sow about a dozen seeds in each hole and pull the earth over them with their heels. This year the Kader family sowed 10 acres in this manner, and it took them only four days. They worked without eating from first light until six in the evening and had their only meal, mainly boiled millet, when the day's work was finished. Soon after the crop begins to sprout, the thicker clumps are thinned and the sparser ones are made good with the thinnings. It takes five or six days to do this for 10 acres.

The bane of tropical agriculture is weeding. Here it is done by earthing up the individual clumps. This requires about thirty days of hard work and is repeated again if the weeds are really bad. Throughout the region stretching from Senegal to the Chad, it is at this stage that much land under sorghum or millet, or even under ground-nuts or cotton, is abandoned. It is not an arduous task to sow 2 or 4 lb. of grain to the acre, but keeping the field reasonably clear of weeds later on is an entirely different matter.

Millet is harvested in two operations. The man walks through the field breaking the stalks near the ground with his foot (four days), and his wife follows him, cutting the ears (six days). A stack is made in the corner of the field with help from other families; with three helpers —that is, five workers in all—this takes two days. Threshing is done with sticks whenever the grain is needed, and again there is mutual help: about fifteen men can thresh 1 ton of grain, the yield of about 6 or 7 acres of land, in a day.

3. Growing Use of Animals. Local Handicrafts

46. Until now we have only seen human labour employed in the cause of agricultural production, but here we find animals being put to use. The technique of their employment, however, has not progressed very far as yet, and for the most part they serve as beasts of burden. On the day appointed for the transport of grain to the village, about ten donkeys, each carrying 130 lb.,[1] are lent by neighbours, and three men drive them to and fro between field and village. The harvest from 10 acres of land can be dealt with in this way during the course

[1] As compared with 350 lb. for the *salmée* or traditional ass's load in the French Midi, where the animals are larger and better fed.

of a day. Although the village of Morio owns its beasts of burden, however, the people of neighbouring villages, a little to the east, do not. They rely on the nomadic herdsmen, who come south during the dry season and hire their zebu cattle, which carry loads of 220 lb. at a time. For transporting the grain a few miles from the field to the granary, these nomads often earn 10 and even 15 per cent. of the total harvest, and their reward for a few days' work is greater than the cultivator's return on a whole season of labour. The nomad still despises the villager and continues to exploit him, and even in Sardinia and Provence we find a similar clash of interests between herdsman and farmer. The stubble, dry leaves, and the weeds which have sprouted up again are grazed by the zebu cattle and they manure the fields to some small extent, but the value of controlled grazing and systematic manuring does not seem to be appreciated.

In the western part of the Chad, near the narrow northern strip of the Cameroons, the agriculturalists, who here sometimes have nomadic forebears, are constantly buying cattle and increasing their herds with the money they earn from cotton. Goats, however, are the main form of livestock, and they exist in far greater numbers than in the forest zone. Taken in conjunction with the plentiful game of the almost empty area[1] to the east, the milk obtained from these goats helps to explain the much better health of these people as compared with the forest-dwellers. Goat meat is eaten only on ceremonial occasions; an example is the goat sacrifice made to the 'spirit of millet' before the new grain is eaten, in order to expiate the act of 'killing' the grain.[2] The sale of kids helps to find the money to buy a wife, and the herd is regarded as a reserve upon which to draw for the purchase of any major item, such as a shirt or a pair of trousers.

After a fermentation process similar to that used for making beer, a special kind of sorghum furnishes a slightly alcoholic (4 to 6 per cent.) but fairly nutritive (yeast, vitamins, etc.) beverage known as *dolo*. The average daily consumption of a man in good health is probably a little over 2 lb. of sorghum and nearly 2 pints of *dolo*, which represents about 10 oz. of grain. It may occasionally be true that drinking accounts for more grain than eating, but Europeans are quick to castigate the

[1] In the course of a journey across this region, the only hunter we had in our party could have shot several hundred wild fowl and dozens of antelopes every day, but he killed no more than the party needed for food. Our native escort, which was made up entirely of men from the forests, consumed on occasions 9-11 lb. of meat per head in a day.

[2] If he did not take this precaution, the peasant would have a poor harvest the following year! Normally only old or injured animals are eaten.

native for such habits, and it adds piquancy to the situation when their remarks are made, glass of whisky in hand.

47. With his enclosed garden, his ground in each of the two rings of cultivation and his share of bush fields, Kader and his wife hoe-cultivate a total of 14 acres, which is much higher than the average. This calls for about sixteen days of work per acre, reckoned on the basis of two days for a third of the task of clearing, six for two lots of weeding, and eight for jobs like sowing, thinning, the harvest, transport, threshing, and scaring away the birds. The resulting yield is about 4 cwt. of sorghum or 2½ cwt. of spiked millet per acre.[1] Taking everything into consideration, something like five days of work—it may vary between about four and seven—are needed to produce 1 cwt. of grain.

This is a better figure than the average. In the Ivory Coast, on the edge of the forests, the savanna has a greater density of trees than at Morio, the grasses have long rhizomes which must be hoed out laboriously before sowing, and head portage is the only means of transporting the crops. Clearing takes longer, the weeds are more troublesome, transport over the long distances often involved is much less efficient, yields are only about 4-5 cwt. per acre and, on average, ten days are needed to produce 1 cwt. of grain.[2] This figure, though one of the lowest we have ever personally observed, is still much higher than for even the most productive of the various economies which rely on collecting grain from wild grasses. Until the beginning of the century, lyme grass was still collected by men on camels in the Mongolian steppes, but a man would have barely 175 lb. of grain after a month at work.

More time has to be spent on weeding than in the forest zone, but much less on clearing, transport, and food-preparation, and although the harvest is much less bulky it is of considerably higher value. Peak periods in the demand for labour, such as sowing, harvesting, and most of all weeding, are much more clearly marked. Even if Kader and his wife, who each spend perhaps 110 or 120 days in the fields, have little to do during the winter, they find it very difficult to keep up with the work in the summer.

Further to the east, local handicrafts, by providing an occupation

[1] The maize on the 'home' field gives him over 3¼ cwt. from little over ¼ acre, or 12 cwt. per acre, which demonstrates the great possibilities of intensive cultivation.

[2] The general average would be between twenty-four and thirty-two days per acre, and about seven days per hundredweight.

which can be carried on in the winter, help to even out the seasonal demand for work. A *gabac* of cotton, measuring 22 yds. by 4½ in., and weighing nearly 1¾ lb., can be exchanged for a weaned kid or sold for 250 francs C.F.A. It takes nearly 9 lb. of raw cotton to make, and the fibre is separated with a cylindrical rod which is worked over a slightly hollowed wooden log. This process takes about five days, on the basis of five or six hours' work a day, spinning occupies twice this time, and weaving the material on a primitive loom can be completed in the course of a single day.

From a strictly economic point of view, the weaving process is the only one which can claim to be in any degree productive. The provision of a little co-operatively owned equipment would be a start in raising the level of productivity. A few spindles and saw gins, even though they would necessitate carding to restore the alignment of the fibres and even if they were obsolete European equipment, would soon make an appreciable difference. But all those concerned with the cotton trade, even the peripatetic Hausa merchants whose services sometimes double the price, are unanimously opposed to such ideas. At the time of our visit, the local material, which is very strong and heavy, could still be sold at only four-fifths of the price of imported cloth—in spite of the primitive and inefficient manner of its production. The economic advantages of the modern factory are here outweighed by transport costs, but even more by the costs of distribution via a succession of middlemen.

Although of much less significance than in the forest, collecting still furnishes certain roots and is important as a means of obtaining oil, particularly from the fruit of the *Balanites egyptiaca*, or *ijelij*, which is a native of this part of the savanna. A little further south, at Bebedjia, as we shall see, a similar role is played by the shea tree (*Butyrospermum parkii*).

Kader and his wife have a certain amount of initiative, and sell their grain—at the 'black market' price of ten francs C.F.A. a pound in the winter of 1949-50—to Fort Lamy. Their ass and the nearby river combine in solving the transport problem most satisfactorily. Kader allowed us to inspect his hut, and we found a leather suitcase, two locally-made strips of cotton, a piece of imported cloth for his wife, and a sum of 3,020 francs C.F.A.[1]—and this was at the season when he had only

---

[1] A horse, which was customarily bartered for a native boat, was worth 15,000 francs C.F.A.; a wife was worth 'about' 8,000 francs C.F.A. Further east, where the use of money was less prevalent, the latter cost about a cow (3,500 francs), plus 1,500 francs C.F.A.

GROWING USE OF ANIMALS. LOCAL HANDICRAFTS

just begun to sell his produce. On the other hand, there was not a single sewing machine[1] in the village, and there were some who had never even heard of a bicycle. The general standard of living is thus vastly different from that in the cotton areas of the Belgian Congo.

48. In some of the neighbouring villages, the area under cultivation was definitely smaller than at Morio, though still comparing favourably with the average for the tropical zone as a whole. The animists appeared to be more energetic and often accounted for over 5 acres per man in addition to some 2 or 3 acres per woman or youth. The Mohammedans seemed phlegmatic by comparison, and in some cases a family would cultivate no more than 5 acres in all, while a rather indolent bachelor might content himself with $1\frac{1}{2}$ acres. It is apparent that the harvest is barely sufficient to keep the people in food and drink, and there is little or no sale of produce. The average family is hardly aware of the meaning of commercial exchange.

As the climate offers no hindrance to stock-rearing, one may envisage the use of animals for draught purposes, and certain parts of the Sudan have already given a lead in this matter, as we shall see. With draught animals at its disposal, the region could expand its production of cereals fairly quickly. This would do away with the food-shortages in the towns, which were still apparent at the time of our visit. There are still large tracts of cultivable land awaiting development, and it would not be difficult to increase the agricultural area without incurring the risk of soil erosion; but this depends on the village-dweller no longer remaining in permanent occupation of particular localities and reverting to his former habit of migrating to fresh land about every ten years. This would permit longer fallows to alternate with periods of cultivation. The latter could then, for example, follow a scheme of two three-year rotations separated by a two- or three-year fallow interval. The nearness of the river is a good argument for extending the acreage under cereals, as it provides an ideal method of transporting bulky commodities for sale in the towns or among the nomads further north.

East of the Shari, in the area delimited by Melfi, Aboudeya, and Am-Timan, there is plenty of good land with adequate rainfall, but the population density is only 3·5 per square mile, and only 1 per cent. of the surface is cultivated. The truly 'equatorial' portion of French Equatorial Africa should one day be able to obtain all its meat cheaply from here. The nomadic grazing, which is after all the primitive stage in an evolution towards ranching on the American model, could be greatly developed, especially by making use of the swampy regions

[1] They were still only found in the larger settlements.

which provide fodder at the only difficult time of the year—namely, at the end of the dry season. Later on the system could be developed a little further; the harnessing of animals and the proper use of their manure would make it possible to start cultivating a few crops. The third stage would be to substitute forage crops for natural pasture, but considerable time must elapse before this becomes possible. For the present it is best to concentrate on introducing the improved and higher-yielding strains of millet and sorghum which are now being evolved.

Further to the north and north-east, rainfall decreases and becomes very much less reliable. Here are the zones of endemic famine, and from Mongo and beyond, the 'food is scarce after a dry summer', and by the following spring the people are in no condition to work hard in the fields. In spite of this, the density of population is about eight per square mile. Anomalies such as this are by no means unusual. Farther west, for example, on either side of the frontier of the Cameroons, there are several overpopulated areas, and the juxtaposition of these with comparatively empty lands naturally leads one to think in terms of population transfers. Morio itself has already received so many 'Sara' immigrants from the 'Mesopotamia' between the rivers Logone and Shari to the south-west that they now make up 28 per cent. of its population.

4. The Impoverishment of Soil by Badly Administered Cotton Schemes

49. An economy which is essentially subsistence in nature, like the one we have just described, cannot possibly supply the wherewithal for equipping a country. Cotton cultivation began about 1922 on the banks of the Uele in the Belgian Congo, and as a result of official pressure it reached the Ubangi in 1924 and the Chad area in 1929. The early years of the cotton crop are painful memories in the minds of the older folk. The schemes were administered on a collective basis, and payment for the crop produced by a village was made to the chief, who sometimes condescended to pass on a few trifling sums. Moreover, villagers could think themselves lucky if the scales were true. Another criticism was the fact that collecting centres were so few and far between. Baskets of cotton, each containing about 50 lb. and carried on the head, often had to be taken distances up to twenty or thirty miles, and in some cases even up to sixty miles.

These abuses have now been stopped, and the money is paid direct to the producer, except in the case of the chiefs, who, as their fields

THE EFFECTS OF BADLY ADMINISTERED COTTON SCHEMES

are cultivated under a kind of feudal system, receive payment without doing any of the work. Nowadays, the weighing machines are reliable, the administration of payments is closely controlled, and the distance to the collecting centre rarely exceeds ten miles; unquestionably there has been some progress. The effect of cotton in generalizing the use of money was the subject of comment by the administrator at Lere, who pointed out that a greater degree of social distinction had resulted, and also an increase in polygamy. For instance, the drunken Azina, self-styled 'King of the Banana Tribe', who rules a canton east of Kelo, can afford to buy European liquor thanks to the levy he collects on cotton grown in his district and to the crop cultivated by his thirty wives; their royal title does not save them from labour in the fields. The chief of the canton of Lere has 230 wives; only thirty of them have any marital status, and he has five children!

An example of how the compulsory growing of cotton sometimes works out in practice can be given from the village where the cotton research station (I.R.C.T.) is situated, 160 miles south of Bouso. This is the settlement of Bebedjia, sited on the East Logone-West Logone interfluve between Doba and Moundou. One of the village elders, a man of the 'Sara' race, who is chief of one of the sections, rejoices in the possession of two wives. One is the mother of five children and is therefore exempt from the 'cotton imposition', but the other, with two children only, and three of the children themselves are liable for compulsory cultivation. The family allocation is five 'cords' of cotton.

Every adult and adolescent is obliged to undertake the cultivation of a square of cotton $\frac{9}{10}$ acre in size, and the term 'cord', which originates in the method of marking out this area with a 66-yd. length of cord, is now also applied to the square itself. At Bebedjia, the 'cotton-boy' charged with the task of measuring out the required areas was so animated with zeal—it would have been interesting to discover its cause—that he doubled the statutory square and allocated each person a rectangle measuring 66 yds. by 132. These irksome 'double cords', which are not unusual in the Pala region, are counted in the returns as squares of the prescribed dimensions, and the actual yields of cotton must therefore be considerably lower than the official statistics suggest.

From its nine acres of compulsory cultivation the chief's family harvested about $\frac{1}{2}$ ton of raw cotton during the season of 1949-50. Sold at 5·50 francs C.F.A. per lb., it enabled the chief to buy a pair of trousers and a loincloth for each of his wives—and to pay his taxes. He was wealthier than average for the region, for the better harvests of previous years had provided blankets, a mosquito net, a quantity of cloth and a horse. But his yield of 120 lb. of cotton to the acre was barely half the average in the Chad region and only a quarter of that obtained in the forest zone of the Belgian Congo.

The cycle of cultivation consists in turn of clearing, digging the land with a hoe, sowing, replacing the seeds which fail to sprout, three further diggings, and earthing up the plants. Picking, at the rate of 33 lb. per picker per day, is very slow. There follows the endless process of sorting the cotton seed by seed into two grades according to quality. Then it has to be carried to the village and from there to the market—in this case, near at hand—where it will be sold after hours of waiting in long queues. At the end of the whole laborious process, some 56 days of work, each of six or seven hours, have been expended on each acre of land. It is a sad reflection that the result of all this effort is a mere 120 lb. of raw cotton. With a good harvest, conscientious picking, and the market nine miles away, the total number of work days in some instances may rise to over 200.

50. Here, then, a man's gross salary in 1950 was equivalent to 12 francs C.F.A. (24 French francs) a day, whereas the regional average was between 15 and 20 francs C.F.A. Moreover, Arab merchants were offering loincloths measuring 1 yd. by 6, at 1,500 francs C.F.A.,[1] the price of 275 lb. of raw cotton. In the Belgian Congo the same length of material was sold for the equivalent of only 60 lb. of the raw fibre, but it cost the average cultivator between seventy-five and a hundred days of work to produce this amount. In spite of the higher price he received and the better system of marketing, he still earned only $2\frac{1}{2}$ in. of cloth in a day of six or seven hours spent toiling under the tropical sun. At Bebedjia, in similar terms a day's work is worth less than 2 in. of cloth. When equated in this way, the abysmally low level of agricultural productivity becomes clearly apparent especially when compared with European standards.

At Morio, it took Kader forty days of work to produce 700 lb. of millet, which sold at the same price as raw cotton. In other words, the return on his labour was eight times higher than at Bebedjia. Near Yagoua in the Northern Cameroons there is a man who has 95 sq. yds. of ground, and from this in the dry season he produces 600 balls of tobacco of the *Nicotiana rustica* variety, which sell at 5 francs apiece.

[1] In the shop at Bebedjia we even noticed a 3-yd. length (the form in which it is most commonly bought) priced at 2,200 francs C.F.A. This length is regarded as the 'poor person's loincloth'; 3,000 francs for the whole length was the lowest price observed in the Chad that winter. In 1951-2 cotton was paid 11 francs C.F.A. a pound, and the price of the loincloth had fallen considerably. The result was an appreciable improvement in real earnings.

Careful irrigation, fertilizing, and transplanting permit him to obtain three crops a year, and the financial return from this tiny holding is equivalent to that from $2\frac{1}{2}$ acres of average cotton land in the Chad region, which would yield about 550 lb.

The advantages of modernization by the introduction of an export crop are thus debatable. In the winter of 1949-50, 1 lb. of raw cotton sold for 5·50 francs C.F.A., and brought the Government 5 francs C.F.A. in the form of export tax and other levies. At the same time the current price in French West Africa was 11 francs C.F.A., and the export tax almost negligible. In spite of this, hardly any of the crop entered into overseas trade, because the political climate no longer permitted the imposition of compulsory schemes of cultivation.

It is not difficult to imagine the European farmer's reaction if he had to sell his wheat for little over half its value. In this part of Africa the low price of cotton acted as a brake on production. Schemes of agricultural improvement were held back, and part of their value was wasted. The native cultivator would produce even less, the deficit varying from place to place according to the character of the tribe, if the pressure of official compulsion was slackened. This occurred in 1946, and production fell by 50 per cent. One official we met did not attempt to conceal his adherence to the old school of thought—he still jails the whole family if a native fails to weed his crop thoroughly. Although compulsion also exists in the Belgian Congo, there is far more in the way of technical assistance.

51. The situation is aggravated at Bebedjia by the low yields. Women were digging the land with a mere stump of a hoe. Originally 6 in. across, the blades had been worn to a width of little over 1 in., so that the effectiveness of the implement was reduced by about two-thirds. More than four and a half years after the war, the basic tool of hand-cultivation had not yet been supplied in sufficient quantities. We earnestly hope that the effort to rearm is in no way related to this deficiency. As for the cotton plants, expert opinion suggests that a density of five per square yard would give the best results. The practice here is to plant only two, and the exposed soil is subject to an accelerated rate of deterioration. Furthermore, sowing was not completed until 1 August, which was much too late to ensure a good crop.

Cotton is resown after only two years of fallow, and is followed by sorghum in the second year, millet in the third, and even after this a second crop of sorghum is sometimes taken in the fourth year. Whereas the rich soil of freshly cleared land was once invariably devoted to food crops, such as sesamum, beans, ground-nuts, or cereals, it is now compulsorily sown to cotton destined for export to Europe. In some years this has led to veritable famine conditions. In the Lere district in 1950, cash-crop cultivation resulted in a scarcity of grain, and the purchase of sorghum to remedy this deficiency accounted for more than a third of the earnings from the sale of cotton. Another causative factor in this particular situation was the cumulative impoverishment of the soil. Too much cultivation of the same land in a village where 1,000 acres of the best soils have been taken over by the experimental station has resulted in dangerously short periods of fallow. The cycle of soil deterioration has begun, and this is partly responsible for the low yields. M. Grondard, the director of the forest service, has asserted that 625,000 acres of tree savanna are cleared each year to make room for cotton, and that the inadequate time allowed for soil recuperation between periods of cultivation bodes ill for the future. On rich land, at least seven years of rest should be allowed after three of cropping, and in poorer areas, especially if the grass is fired each year and the vegetation cover therefore remains too sparse to promote the restoration of fertility, periods of up to fifteen years may be necessary.

Cotton should not be imposed on the kind of land which is farmed at Bebedjia. The official argument is that if an exception were made it would be resented by neighbouring villages, and they would be unwilling to grow any more cotton themselves. This is an admission that the cotton acreage is maintained entirely by compulsion. In this region, the prescribed cotton acreage has been doubled arbitrarily, although, as we have seen, this is by no means unusual. The very fact that the acreage of cotton imposed is based on the number of workers on the land, men and women included, means that the area devoted to commercial agriculture is largest where the fertility and the food production potential of the soil are already strained to their utmost. Pending the introduction of a balanced system of continuous cultivation in this part of the savanna zone, never more than one-fifth of the area should be cropped at one time.

Unfortunately, we were to find areas in an even sorrier plight than Bebedjia. Near the Logone, to the east of Kelo, the village of Leo-M'boro produced a mere 53 lb. of raw cotton to the acre in 1948-9. Most of the fields belonging to the village are situated in a poorly drained depression which is quite unsuitable for cotton especially in wet years. But it has to be grown. In 1950 the people had not had enough time to tend their own crops. The harvest suffered and, being unable to buy any grain, they had to go hungry. The empirical rules

THE EFFECTS OF BADLY ADMINISTERED COTTON SCHEMES

of the old land chiefs were vastly superior to a system which, when food is short in the towns, diverts to other uses land which should be producing cereals. If, in the cause of justice, all must share the burden of compulsion, the crop selected should be suited to the environment. Near Lere, on either side of the road to Pala, we observed yet another disastrous example of short-sighted management. The representative of the cotton interests had insisted on the rows of plants being earthed up even when they followed straight down the steepest slopes, on gradients of one in five and one in four. The resulting erosion has laid bare the underlying rocks, and the yields of cotton have fallen practically to nil.

52. The exercise of authority is substituted for the provision of technical aid, and we have seen a few of the results of this policy. Perhaps the worst predicament of all is that of certain villages in Oubangui which have had to conform to the general rule in French Equatorial Africa of siting themselves in close proximity to the roads. Lacking funds for the purchase of a little cement, and therefore unable to build their roads along the valleys where small bridges would have been needed to cross the streams, they have built their routes along the interfluves. The villages have therefore had to be moved to hilltop sites, where they border the roads at intervals of a mile or so, and the rich land previously cultivated at lower levels is no longer accessible. The density of population is only five per square mile, but the cultivated land is now on slopes so steep as to make soil erosion inevitable.

Near Bozoum-Bocaranga there is now a triangular pattern of three roads, each forty miles long, with villages spaced along them. What consternation there would be if the farmers of an English county were told that they must confine their operations to the land bordering a few main roads! Even so, with their modern means of transport, they would not be handicapped as severely as the African.

The only people satisfied with things as they are are the administrators of the old school, who will not tolerate the technical expert unless he is relegated to subordinate status. The situation suits their purposes admirably: labour gangs for road maintenance can be recruited so conveniently; they can be inspected without even having to leave the official car; alternatively, a 50-yd. walk at most brings one into the refreshing shade.

Another kind of situation is coming to a head in the area of the Fianga lakes, near the Cameroons frontier, where there are nearly 250 people to the square mile. Among the Tabouris of Dablaka on the edge of Lake Tikem the practice of continuous cropping, which elsewhere is confined to the vicinity of the huts, has now been extended to the whole of the cultivated area. This has been done without recourse to fertilizing, which is the indispensable adjunct to such a system. As the compulsory acreage under cotton has increased in proportion with the growth of population, the tribe has been forced to grow two crops a year on the same land—white sorghum followed by cotton. Originally the land was rich. Notwithstanding its fertility, the Tabouris used to move on after fifteen or twenty years of cultivation had taken their toll. Today such movements are very severely curtailed by the scarcity of land.

Sorghum is sown year after year on the wetter land nearer the lake. The strip of land adjoining the lake is flooded in the late summer, and bears an abundant growth of bent grass which represents a valuable reserve of grazing towards the end of the dry season. It enables cattle to survive from March, by which time other sources of food have been exhausted, until the June rains. During the rains, cattle can graze the scrub or sometimes they are taken further north. At the beginning of the dry season they feed on the stubble.[1]

53. From French Equatorial Africa, France obtains well over a tenth of her supply of cotton, but the methods of cultivation employed are often in process of destroying the soil. France's desire to reduce dependence on the U.S.A., for whom the export of cotton is an effective tool of economic pressure, is a powerful stimulus to the full development of the resources she controls. But the effort made so far has aimed solely at serving the interests of the colonial power, and the welfare of the colonial territories themselves has been completely ignored. The cotton-grower who supplies the factories of Roubaix or of the Vosges stands to gain less than the primitive weaver of the area east of the Shari. The productive effort of the native peoples should at least have been rewarded with effective measures of soil conservation and the establishment of local industries catering for local needs.

In 1948, when the monopolies of the ginning companies were being renewed, one powerful group requested permission to establish an integrated plant for spinning, weaving, dyeing, and cotton-seed oil production instead of retaining their ginning rights in the best area.

[1] On the credit side of this 'cotton policy' is its continuity. Near the boundary between Oubangui and the Cameroons the natives began to wish they could return to the German administration of former years, in spite of its authoritarian rule and inflexible policies; they tired quickly of the whims of various French officials, one of whom wanted to increase coffee production, another the acreage under bananas, while yet another favoured rice cultivation . . . and now all efforts are being concentrated on cotton. An enormous amount of effort has been wasted through the lack of consistent policies.

They could have sold their wares most profitably at the buying centres where the natives bring their raw cotton, for distribution costs would have been negligible.[1] Commercial interests, however, were powerful enough to engineer the rejection of this commendable scheme. It should be remembered that the women of the Banana tribe, who actually grow the cotton, do not use any kind of cloth material. Many of them wonder what possible use can be found for the white cotton bolls. In the equatorial zone clothing may have harmful physical effects, but here it becomes a real necessity. On a cold January morning, when the temperature may fall to less than 45° F., the children and the old people shiver with cold as they come out of their huts and crowd round the miserable fire. Blankets imported from Europe, and likewise mosquito nets, which could play an important part in the campaign against malaria, remain luxuries which only the wealthy can afford. Fires are often lit underneath the beds during the cool season, but this practice is extremely injurious to health, especially in view of the lack of ventilation in the huts.

The poorest grade cotton, which nobody even bothers to pick, together with the tangled fibres discarded by the ginning machines and the lint which still adheres to the seed when the fibre has been removed, could provide all the raw material likely to be needed for blankets of local manufacture similar to those made at Leopoldville by the Belgians. The pressed cotton seeds furnish a good-quality oil for culinary purposes. The residue or cake has a high protein content and, after certain precautions have been taken, could be fed to cattle. In Texas it is even used as a chocolate ingredient.

Whereas oil and cake mills are rapidly appearing in the Belgian Congo, in French Equatorial Africa some of the cotton seed is burnt as fuel for the engines driving the gins. This is a shocking waste, but most of the seed is burnt in heaps outside the factories when it could be used to make food for cattle or even fertilizer for the land. Not even the ashes are taken back to the fields. It is hardly surprising that this form of robber economy is resulting in severe damage to the soil.

54. The cotton-ginning companies, though they hold monopolies which guarantee profits far more effectively than peasant wages, have not devoted any of their resources to the equipping of the country. Admittedly, this would involve a financial risk, but surely the ability

---

[1] The poorer peasants, who only buy in very small quantities, pay costs of distribution at a disproportionate rate. Sugar, for instance, is sold by the lump at 1 franc C.F.A. each; similarly the Andalusian agricultural worker's children buy their sweets singly.

to do this is the main justification of the capitalist system in its expansionist phase. Sample checks are made to find out which varieties of seed give the best yields and the longest staples. The companies are supposed to be guided by these tests when laying seed in store for the next season's crop, but they often fail to take even this elementary precaution.

Apart from the essential technical improvements which have been indicated,[1] changes are needed in the distribution of both population and crops. A serious study of the suitability of certain areas for different crops could not hope to solve the complex problems of adaptation all at once, but at least some of the more glaring anomalies of the present situation would soon be put right. The wetter areas could thus be given over to food production and people attracted from the congested districts towards those which are still awaiting development. Among the latter are the area east of the Shari, where cotton and millet could be grown without endangering the soil, and the Chad 'Mesopotamia', where rice, already cultivated near Laï, could be introduced.

The extra rice would help to feed the higher areas now overpopulated, which, provided they were paid a proper price for their cotton, could then abandon some of their food-producing acreage. In the U.S.A. cereals fetch about a third of the price of raw cotton. It has been proposed that large quantities of rice could be sent to the coast from the Logone for export, but the land distance involved obviously makes this quite impracticable. Cotton fibre, which is ten times more valuable than rice, and possibly ground-nut oil, are the only export commodities which could stand the cost of transport.

Compulsion in the Belgian Congo goes hand in hand with a degree of material assistance which has assured the Negro peasant who is willing to make the necessary effort of an adequate supply of food and a number of amenities which he could not previously afford. Cotton has improved the lot of the natives in the best parts of Oubangui and the Chad Territory, but even these areas have often paid the price of soil impoverishment, and the standard of living is still lower than in the Belgian Congo. Bicycles, gramophones, and sewing machines are still practically unknown. As yet the few agricultural scientists of French Equatorial Africa have not been granted the status they deserve and not enough weight is given to their opinions. It is impossible to justify an authoritarian rule which leads to the ruination of the soil.

[1] These are studied in more detail in our report to the Compagnie française pour le développement des textiles, submitted in 1950, but not published.

5. The Beginnings of Intensification and Poverty in the North Cameroons

55. The nucleated village of Be (Fig. 7) is situated between Garoua and Rei-Buba[1] on the banks of the Mayo-Kebi, an affluent of the Benue. The latter is in process of capturing the Logone, to the detriment of the Chad region. The *saré*[2] field, fertilized with cattle dung (but still not with ashes), produces alternate crops of sorghum and ground-nuts, the latter being in part destined for export. The ground-nut is cultivated also where the soil is sandy. Next to the hut itself is a patch of manioc, protected from the depredations of goats by a strong fence. An area sited about 50 yds. from the hut is manured only occasionally. It is thrown up into ridges and supports a more complicated rotation. Sweet potatoes[3] are grown for two or three years in succession during the rains, and are followed by sorghum and then by two or three crops of ground-nuts sometimes mixed with beans or, on very poor sandy soils, with stone ground-nuts.

Away from the village, near the foot of the hills, the higher land always carries sorghum and rice is grown in the depressions. The village is inhabited by people of the Foulbes tribe, who were once nomads, later came under the influence of Mohammedanism, and are now sedentary. Nowhere in its territory is there any fallow land. As there is plenty of good land, the people can clear whatever areas they choose without restriction. Red millet is sown on the light land sloping towards the river; below it a stretch of sandy loams at the limit of the floods is used for rice,[4] and still nearer the river a clayey hollow is double-cropped each year: a quick-growing variety of maize, sown in late May, is harvested when the floods reach this level in August, and a 'late flood' sorghum of the *muscuari* type, sown in September in a nursery bed on higher land, is transplanted here in early October

---

[1] On seeing the Sultan of Rei-Buba's retinue, with its mail-clad horsemen and its foot soldiers armed with bows and leather shields, one is agreeably reminded of the Middle Ages—until one remembers the burden of taxes borne by the peasant; even the interpreter, in the presence of his master, has to prostrate himself, his face in the dust.

[2] Local term for 'hut'.

[3] At Ouro Taro, six miles to the east, sesamum is the first-year crop.

[4] Sown in planting holes in June, a score of seeds per hole and the latter 16-24 in. apart. It would be better to shorten these intervals and sow fewer seeds in each hole. The field is weeded three times and in October the crop is harvested with sickles—in the early morning, so as to reduce shedding.

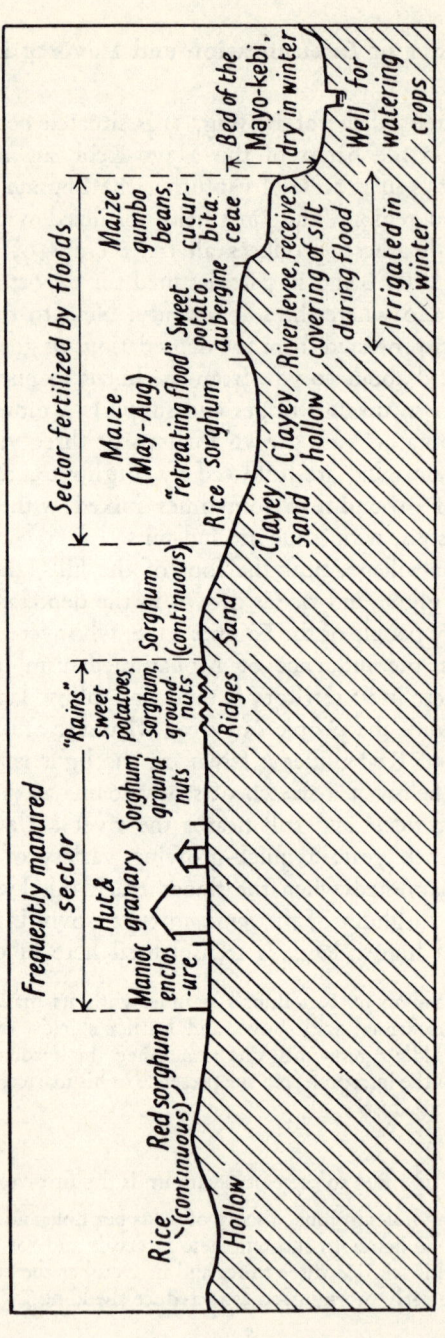

FIG. 7. Diagrammatic cross section of Be, North Cameroons.

when the flood water subsides. It is harvested in the middle of the dry season in late February-March without having needed any weeding whatsoever.

On the banks of the river itself, alluvium, which is enriched every year by further deposition, is used for intensive market gardening. Flooded in the summer, this strip of land is irrigated in the winter by drawing water with calabashes from below the dried-up bed of the stream. The higher part, where the castor-oil plant is subspontaneous, is set with cuttings of sweet potato in November. These are taken from plants in the *saré* field and are ready by the end of February or March. Next to them, round aubergines are cultivated on a large scale for sale in Garoua. The distance they travel to market does not compare, however, with the onions grown at Binder in the Chad, which are taken to Bangui and even as far as Duala in the Cameroons. On the lower ground, dry-season maize is inter-tilled with a great variety of fruits and vegetables, such as gumbo, various Cucurbitacea (marrows, pumpkins, calabashes), and beans.

56. The following list indicates what an average cultivator, without giving overmuch attention to garden crops, might expect to have for sale each year:

   300 lb. ground-nuts at 6·50 francs per lb. (1950 prices).
   550 lb. sweet potatoes at 120 francs per basket of 55 lb.
   440 lb. millet at 4·50 to 5·50 francs per lb.

This represents an income of well over 5,000 francs C.F.A. which is used to buy cotton, either locally grown or imported from the Chad, for spinning and weaving, and perhaps also a little rice (about 20 lb.) and some cloth. If he can save any money, he will probably use it to buy goats, forty of which are needed here to pay for a wife, and cattle. He will then indulge in what Veyret[1] has called 'sentimental' livestock rearing. His animals are a sign of wealth, and he would never resell them. The animals are kept so long before being slaughtered that this form of stock-rearing is quite irrational from an economic point of view.

Even the manure sometimes accumulates in great heaps. After explaining its possible uses to the chief of a neighbouring canton, we received the following reply: 'I am old and shall soon die. Then when passers-by see this great dunghill, they will think of me and will say to themselves, "He was a great chief, for he must have had a great herd of cattle to leave such a pile of manure." ' The possible use of this fertilizer as a commemorative edifice had heretofore not occurred to us.

[1] *Géographie de l'Elevage* (N.R.F., 1951).

If he is really rich, a man may buy a horse, which he will tend with great care, even fetching him fresh grass from the marshes during the dry season.

With its *saré* fields giving ground-nuts for export and its riverine lowland furnishing large quantities of vegetables, the system can best be described as dominantly horticultural. Although the only form of fertilization is that effected by the regular deposition of river silt over a restricted area, there are no apparent signs of the soil becoming impoverished. This is due to its preponderantly alluvial origin and to the slower rate of eluviation as compared with the much wetter equatorial region. In spite of the number of domestic animals, there is no systematic manuring of the land, and if this practice continues to be neglected sooner or later the village will undoubtedly be forced to move. The opening up of suitable markets would give a tremendous scope for the development of animal husbandry in association with the cultivation of crops. Finally, local handicrafts, such as pottery, weaving, and dyeing, have a relatively important place in the life of the village.

57. Returning northwards towards Guidder, one finds a much higher density of population, often reaching seventy-five per square mile, as compared with only two or three at Rei-Buba. Furthermore, the distribution is extremely uneven, and there are concentrations of 500 per square mile and more, both in the mountainous east and in parts of the region further west. The people are Kirdis, pagan tribesmen forced back into the hills by nomadic and Mohammedan invaders, and their dire shortage of land poses some difficult problems. By arranging large stones in rough alignment along the contours, they have built rough terraces on the steep hill slopes which they are forced to cultivate. The earth which does slip down is brought up again in baskets.

At Kola, between Mokolo and Mora, they grow white sorghum, sometimes in rotation with millet, without ever resting the land. In 1953, the whole area will be under white sorghum, and if there is a good harvest it will provide enough grain for two years. The 1954 crop of pearl millet, which fetches a better price, will then be sold, but large marketable surpluses are exceptional. The terraces receive the benefit of a certain amount of cattle dung, and some of the domestic refuse and ashes. Grass, branches in leaf, and other similar material are also used as fertilizers, a practice which could profitably be extended to the cultivation of green manures.

Unfortunately, owing to the lack of money, most of the cattle dung and goat droppings are burnt, while ashes are immersed in water, from which salt is then extracted by evaporation. The main product of this process is sodium carbonate, which, for domestic purposes, is a poor substitute for ordinary salt, which they are unable to buy. Rather less than half the families keep one or two 'hut' bullocks, which never leave their stalls and are sacrificed at the 'feasts of the ancestors'. As the whole village then slaughters its animals, much of the meat is wasted. Asses are used as pack-animals; there are more goats than sheep.

The population is increasing rapidly, owing mainly to the advent of modern medicine before the introduction of scientific agriculture, which in any case is slower in achieving tangible results. This sequence, unfortunately, is common to many of the world's underdeveloped countries, and it portends ill for the future. If they move to the plains, the Kirdis return to the yoke of their erstwhile Mohammedan rulers, the 'Lamido' chiefs, whose subjects are the herdsmen of this far-stretching grassland region. The Kirdis have a social organization which is both primitive and patriarchal, and, given the opportunity, the more powerful lowlands chiefs are quick to exploit them. This discourages them from moving to the much less crowded plains, where in other circumstances they would be able to live more prosperously. A more rational distribution of population must be encouraged by every possible means: by restricting the exercise of despotic powers by the lowland chiefs, by means of financial incentives, etc.[1]

The land which the Kirdis cultivate does, however, extend as far as the foot of the mountains, and here three-year fallows alternate with periods of six years under crops. Cotton makes its appearance, together with white millet and ground-nuts, and has spread rapidly since 1950,[2] thanks to an efficient system of collecting the crop. There are also rice-fields in the low-lying hollows. The poverty of resources obliges the Kirdis to eat even the bran of the millet, which the Foulbes discard. Meat is very seldom eaten, and fats are very scarce indeed. The great majority, who never have any surplus of cereals, earn money to pay their taxes and for the purchase of a few trifles by processing their produce to the greatest possible extent. They sell their cotton as strips of cloth (*gabacs*), their ambaria hemp as rope, and their tobacco in balls. Fine leatherwork is made from goat-skins at Maroua. Occasionally they can manage to spare 50 lb. or so of ground-nuts, or perhaps 20 lb. of millet for sale.

The significance of these small quantities is further emphasized by

[1] The financial outlay could soon be recouped by taxes on the larger yields.
[2] Until then the North Cameroons exported practically nothing apart from a few thousands of tons of ground-nuts.

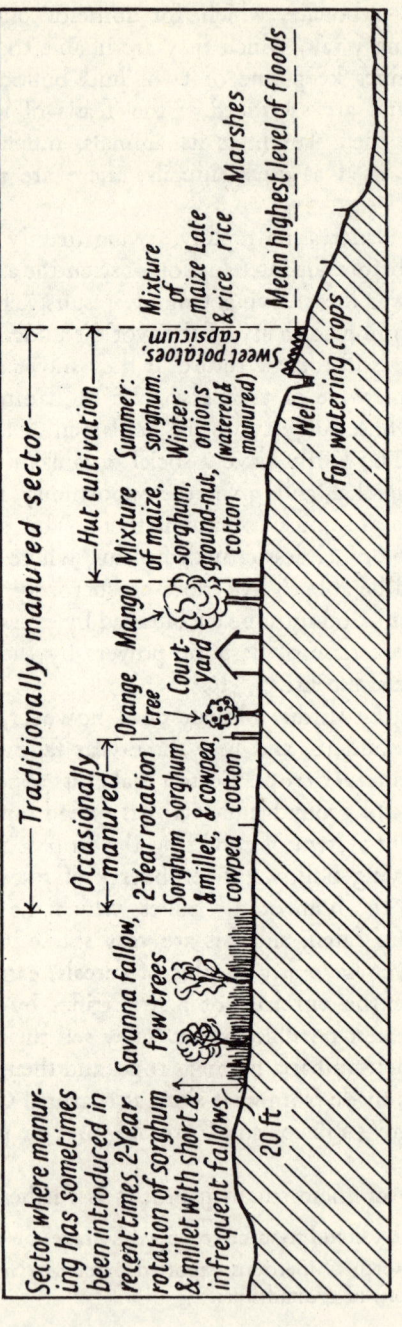

FIG. 8. Diagrammatic cross section of M'Pesoba, French Sudan.

the appearance of a typical Kirdi market. The economy is on the borderline of subsistence, and if the harvest falls very slightly short of expectations shortage is soon translated into famine and the payment of taxes becomes a terrible hardship. Here, then, is a case for urgent action. The first essential is the introduction of intensive cultivation with ox-drawn ploughs and the systematic spreading of manure. The latter would obviously be much easier in the plains, where cartage can be used, than on the hill terraces, where everything has to be carried. A start has already been made with some of the less primitive people and the results have been encouraging. A further step could be taken by erecting at Garoua slaughterhouses as modern as those of Fort Lamy. By creating an accessible market for meat, this would stimulate the transition from 'sentimental' animal keeping to commercial livestock rearing. The resulting premium on quality would lead to improved feeding and to the breeding of better animals. Indeed, the mixed farming system, which has so successfully maintained the soil fertility of temperate regions, could profitably be applied to practically the whole of the tropical zone.

6. Difficulties of Continuous Cropping in the Sudan and the Need to Overcome Them

58. A thousand miles to the west lies the town of Segou, situated on the Niger in latitude 13° N. From the road to Bobo Dioulasso a little to the south-west of Segou, on the far side of the Bani, a tributary of the Niger, one may see large fields of up to 7 acres devoted to the growing of calabash. The crop is sown at the end of the rains, and the ground is cultivated during the dry season to conserve the moisture in the soil, a practice reminiscent of the dry farming of North Africa. After soaking and subsequent drying, the hemispherical shells make useful receptacles. In the scattered villages in the north of the Niger they are still sold in exchange for their volume of sorghum, the size of the container being regarded as the criterion of its value.[1]

At M'Pesoba, fifty miles from Segou, the walled enclosures produce oranges, mangoes, and a few tomatoes. Livestock such as goats, sheep and poultry are comparatively plentiful. On the higher ground, the gardens often have a mixture of maize, quick-growing sorghum, ground-nuts, cotton, and gumbo (Fig. 8). Although harvested in this order from September till the end of December, they are all sown

---

[1] They were much sought after during the war owing to the shortage of enamel bowls, and at Bamako they fetched three times their volume of grain.

at the same time in mid-June, by which time there is always plenty of rain. In some cases ambaria hemp is grown instead of gumbo and ground-nuts.

Lower down, near the limit of the summer floods, sorghum occupies the ground from June until October, and then, after the soil has been dug to a depth of about 8 in., a kind of shallot is planted; for ten days the crop is left under a cover of stalks of great millet, and it benefits from a copious application of manure. During the dry season, the water table is 3 ft. or so below the surface, and the crop has to be watered with calabashes night and morning. On the lower slopes the land is ridged for sweet potatoes, while further up there are nurseries for capsicum. The double-cropping system of this market garden below the village is in the hands of specialists and is reminiscent of the *Ceinture dorée* of Brittany, but the total area is only about 6 or 7 acres.

The flood level varies unforeseeably from one summer to another, and along the zone which is inundated in some years but not in others maize seeds are sown in holes at intervals of 18 in. in rows 3 ft. apart during the very first rains in June. Ten days later rice is sown between the maize and covered with $\frac{1}{2}$ in. of moist earth. A normal flood which allows both crops to ripen satisfactorily arrives when the rice is already 2 ft. high and covers the field to a depth of 1 ft. or more for a period of twenty days. A higher flood level results in the loss of the maize crop, but greatly favours the rice, which is then harvested at the end of November. If the water does not rise as high as usual, there is a good crop of maize which is ready by September. Having to make the best of such variable conditions, the cultivator often has good grounds for craving the tax-collector's indulgence. Nearer the marshes, where the water often lies for two months, a crop of late rice can be grown, as it is adapted to the greater depth of flood water.

On the land which rises towards the plateau on the other side of M'Pesoba, the more accessible fields are manured, and the area so treated is rather larger than in the Chad. The use of ashes, night soil, and also of animal manure permits a system of continuous cultivation. Sorghum alternates with either cotton or millet and is always interspersed with cow-pea. A hundred yards or so further away, however, manuring becomes sporadic and the absence of fallow is reflected in yields, which, according to the older men of the village, are declining steadily. The appearance of striga, a parasite which is liable to attack indifferent crops of sorghum, confirms this view.

About 1925 a piece of land which lies further from the village was divided, at the instigation of the director of the experimental station, into privately owned holdings. A portion of it has remained in continuous cultivation since 1926, mostly with alternating crops of sorghum and millet, which are both sown mixed with beans. Another sector, exhausted after twenty years of cultivation, is being allowed to rest for six years and the grasses which sprout again after the fires of the dry season are grazed from December to May.

59. One villager, who cultivates on a large scale, has four men and seven women of his family to help him with his 50 acres.[1] In addition, four old women look after the spinning and weaving, and he hires two permanent helpers, who are paid 600 francs C.F.A. a month; food, living quarters, and clothing are also provided. At the busiest time of the year, when weeding is in progress, he recruits fifteen to twenty youths (an 'age brotherhood'), who are employed for five days and paid only in kind—that is, they receive fairly good meals, mainly millet with goat and dog meat, the latter being eaten here as in China; if the group is large enough, he may even slaughter an ox for them. As the people are Mohammedans, they drink no millet beer and there are two 'rest' days in the week.[2] On Fridays no work is permitted, except in the gardens; on Mondays only cotton and ground-nuts receive any attention, for, unlike sorghum, they are not traditional crops and the religious taboos do not apply to plants which have only recently been introduced.

This particular cultivator has two donkeys, which are used mainly for taking goods to market, and forty-seven head of cattle of all ages.[3] Of the latter, eight are draught animals which can be harnessed to the plough or to any of the four carts which he possesses, and this is the first case so far encountered of animals being used in this manner on a fairly large scale. It is obviously far superior to the use of pack animals as a means of transport. The carts are the indispensable adjunct to the plough, and their only purpose is to bring 40 or 50 tons of manure from the village every year. This is spread over the 6 acres of land devoted to the crop at the head of the rotation: a mixture of sorghum, maize, and cotton, grown for two years in succession and twice manured during this period. These are followed by cereals, which are sometimes mixed with beans. As the women would vehemently refuse

---

[1] About 32 acres of millet, $7\frac{1}{2}$ acres of sorghum and beans, 5 of cotton, $2\frac{1}{2}$ of ground-nuts and cotton, $2\frac{1}{2}$ of maize and cotton, $2\frac{1}{2}$ of rice.

[2] Most of the townsfolk are Mohammedans, but the Miniakas, who live in the villages, are still mostly fetishists.

[3] Plus a varying number—generally larger than the number of cattle—of sheep and goats.

to carry manure,[1] the role of the cart is absolutely essential in these operations. On the other hand, the suggestion that carts should be used to take grain to market—the nearest is over a mile away—is regarded as ridiculous; tradition demands that the women take it on their heads. Modern methods are readily applied to tasks connected with enterprises of recent origin, but where there is a customary precedent it is followed without question.

This villager, with his 50 acres of land, operates on the largest scale yet observed in our study, and his existence implies a certain degree of class distinction. Every year he sells about 2 tons of raw cotton at 9 francs C.F.A. a lb., and this is his largest single item of revenue. In addition, he can market some 770 yds. of woven cotton strip 6 in. wide at 18 francs C.F.A. a yard. He also earns 10,000 francs from ground-nuts, 6,000 francs from rice, a little from the sale of butter collected from shea trees, but he sells hardly any grain. In view of the unreliability of the climate, he prefers to keep his granaries well stocked. In comparison with the poverty observed in the North Cameroons uplands, here is wealth indeed.

This, however, is obviously not a representative case. The reasonably well-off peasant family with three men, two women, and three children cultivates about 10 acres: 7 of sorghum or millet, 2 of ground-nuts and a little cotton. They can sell about 1 ton of grain (7,500 francs), 4 cwt. of ground-nuts (2,000 francs), 3 of cotton (3,000 francs), and in addition about twenty chickens (2,000 francs). A flock of fifteen or so ewes and goats, with a ram and a he-goat, enables them to pay their taxes from the sale of five or six lambs or kids; the sale of each animal pays for one person's tax, which is here 320 francs per head. Probably another five kids could be marketed in an average year, thus adding some 1,500 francs to the family income. The women gather the wild fruit of the shea tree, and after their domestic requirements have been satisfied there is generally a surplus of butter, 200 lb. of which would fetch 3,150 francs. A little cotton yarn and a few woven strips would, at 1950 prices, have brought the family income up to 20,000 francs C.F.A. per annum.

The land chief who still exercises his functions in this region makes a levy of 33 lb. of millet per family, in default of which he curses the land. The witch-doctor earns a little more than this for frightening

[1] The manager of some mines in the southern part of the Belgian Congo put the manure from his pit ponies at the disposal of his workmen. The women thereupon protested to the local official at the idea of having to carry such an offensive substance. The contrast with Asia is striking.

away the devils. The blacksmith, according to the amount of work he does, may be paid anything from five to twenty sheaves of sorghum after the harvest. These services are an indication of a fairly advanced society. In addition, the family must find the money to buy blankets and suitable feast-day attire: trousers and flowing cotton gowns for the men, loin-cloths and smocks for the women, and sometimes even gold ornaments for those who can afford them. Everyday clothes are spun, woven, and sewn at home. All things considered, the standard of living is very much higher than in the Chad region.

60. M'Pesoba is known particularly for its four new settlements, established in connexion with a small experiment in rural planning. Thirty-two settlers, grouped into four hamlets[1] of equal size, have each been allotted a 30-acre holding, known as a 'quarter' of land. These holdings are arranged radially, with the hamlet in the centre, as in some of the co-operative villages in Palestine. Four fields of 5 acres each follow a compulsory rotation of manured cotton, manured sorghum, ground-nuts, and fallow, but in estimating the quantity of grain needed by the village no account was taken of the large amount of beer which is drunk here. Consequently, on the remaining 10 acres, where there are no restrictions, sorghum is grown without manuring year after year. This land has therefore been quickly exhausted, and the same process is now being repeated a little further afield.

Each 'farm' has from two to four oxen, which, when they are being used for ploughing, are kept in the yard. The manure is thrown into a pit and dries quickly in the sun, its value thereby being diminished. The settlers earn enough money to buy a fairly large number of animals, but although there are over twelve head of cattle per holding of 30 acres, this figure gives an entirely false impression. Like everywhere else in tropical Africa, the keeping of animals is not in the least integrated with agriculture. Whereas some fifty to sixty cattle return to the hamlet at night after being in the charge of a herdsman by day, the rest are grazed far away by Peuhl nomads,[2] and are hardly ever near the village. Thus only the night manure of a proportion of the animals is ever collected for use in the fields.

The fallow land is ploughed in September, and is thus left devoid of vegetation throughout the dry season. Excessive exposure to the sun

---

[1] A small chain is stretched across the entrance to each house near the ground; if the devil tries to come in he breaks his neck.

[2] 'Whose implement of cultivation is the box of matches' (to set fire to the scrub). Cf. the Corsican shepherds in *Revue du Ministère de l'Agriculture* (December 1952).

and deflation by the *harmattan* winds, which often blow at nearly forty miles an hour, play havoc with the soil. Similarly, the millet stalks are removed in March, which is too early, for the leaching action of percolating water is obviously greatly intensified on the arrival of the rains wherever the ground is unprotected. The prevalence of striga in the sorghum crops is an indication of soil exhaustion.

Machines for dehusking millet have been supplied, but the resulting flour is regarded as inferior to that produced by the traditional 'wet' process, which makes use of a mortar and pestle. Grain mills would be just as labour-saving and would also provide flour very similar to that of the traditional process.[1] At the hamlet of Boudy-Bougou, which, owing to its better soils and greater use of manure, is the showpiece of the scheme, the yield of raw cotton reaches 450 lb. per acre, in spite of extremely thin sowing. On the other hand, at Francis-Bougou, the yield of 175 lb. is indicative of the less favourable conditions, and several of the settlers have already left; manure is now hardly used at all, and on slightly sloping ground every storm opens up a few more gullies, which rapidly increase in size. But the white-haired official to whom we suggested a few well-known conservation measures, such as contour ridging, retorted: 'We had enough trouble teaching them what a straight line was, and now you want us to start all over again!' It is this same straight line, which some are pleased to regard as the symbol of European superiority, which has unleashed the destructive force of soil erosion.

In areas of sparse population, the system of allowing a proportion of land to lie fallow can still be resorted to, but, as A. Rénard has emphasized, this land is ravaged by bush fires which we have been unable to suppress; it is swept by strong winds and by the dust storms which herald the approach of the winter and leached by the downpours of the rainy season. It is, in short, no more likely than cultivated fallow to help very much in the maintenance of fertility. It is true, as Guillaume

[1] M. Ringelmann, who taught agricultural engineering at the Institut Agronomique, used to delight in telling us how he made a small machine for husking millet, about the turn of the century, at the request of the Bishop of Haute-Volta, who wished to see the day of rest properly observed. The machine, which worked on the same principle as a coffee-grinder, reduced the time taken to husk millet by four-fifths and several hundred models were made and distributed to the most deserving parishioners. Their husbands, before departing on long portages, allotted their faithful spouses the usual quantity of grain to be treated during their absence, thus assuring that they would be fully occupied in 'healthy' pursuits. They had failed, however, to allow for 'the increased productivity due to the introduction of modern equipment', and the women had plenty of time on their hands—which the devil exploited to lead them into temptation. 'And yet they were my very best parishioners,' sighed the Bishop.

has pointed out, that intensification is sometimes associated with a decline in the productivity of labour, owing to the extra work necessitated by fertilizing. In many areas, however, like the region of the Chad lakes, at the foot of the mountains in the Northern Cameroons, in the Sudan round Segou and Baroueli, and in the Bobo and the Mossi country, the density of population makes it inevitable that the proportion of cropped land should exceed the 20 per cent. of the total area which Viguier has defined as the 'condition of equilibrium'. A. Rénard asserts that, especially since the fall in grain prices of 1952-3, the peasant, with his increased liabilities, can no longer live on 3·75 acres of land, which is the present average per worker. The demographic situation makes the modernization of agriculture absolutely essential.

In virtue of the favourable conditions for animals and consequently of the availability of manure, it would appear that the transition to continuous cropping, which has been practised for the last twenty-seven years at the M'Pesoba Experimental Station, is easier here than in the equatorial region. The essential condition is that adequate steps should be taken to guard against soil erosion. The greatest difficulty is that the means of spreading technical knowledge quickly and of ensuring its application over large areas simply do not exist. While experiment is still proceeding, with the object of confirming the validity of certain techniques and improving the application of others, efforts should be made to expand the area under rice, for here the state of our knowledge is much more complete.

7. Improved Rice-fields from the Niger to the Logone

61. Returning to Segou and thence following first the Niger and then its distributary, the Diaka, downstream, one passes through Diafarabe and eventually reaches Penga. From the left bank of the Diaka one may then travel by canoe across the delta of the Niger, which in mid-November is still flooded. The rice-fields are all dug with a *daba*, which has a triangular head 8 in. broad, 10 in. long, and 2-4 in. thick. Its effect is to bury the weeds; this work, which is completed between the retreat of the waters in December and the arrival of the rains at the end of June, is performed at the rate of 1 acre per twelve nine-hour days. About the beginning of July, when the soil has been well moistened, the rice is sown broadcast at 50-5 lb. per acre. Sometimes the seeds are then covered with a sprinkling of soil by using the *daba* to break up clods of earth held over the ground.

The sowing often drags on too late into the season Rice will not survive unless it has already reached a good height before the flood arrives about mid-August, for it cannot withstand complete immersion for more than four or five days. Sown in good time, it will be 10-12 in. high when the floods begin, and its growth will then keep pace with the rise in the level of the water. From mid-September onwards, when the depth of water may vary between 30 and 60 in., the paddy field is weeded once, twice, or three times, and each occasion necessitates two or three days of work per acre. These operations are also sometimes undertaken rather late, for fear of uprooting the smaller shoots; sowing in rows would solve this particular problem. The grain is cut with sickles about 8 in. below the ear. The early rice is sometimes harvested from canoes and the sheaves, approximately 1 ft. in diameter, are brought in either by canoe or on rafts of plaited straw. The late varieties, which are cut after the flood has retreated, are often left to dry in stooks. The paddy is threshed with sticks. It is then boiled to loosen the grain and husked with a pestle.

The cultivated land is frequently in private ownership. The landowners are Peuhls, and they employ Rimaibe slaves who so far have failed to win their freedom. The clustered villages are built on small hillocks completely surrounded by water during the floods. One finds very little in the way of *serai* cultivation (gourds, gumbo, ambaria hemp), the reason being that so little of the lower land is free from flooding. The straw huts are usually hemispherical in shape, but sometimes there are flat roofs. All the villagers have both sheep and goats, which feed on wild rice in the summer (*Oryza barthii*). Sometimes they own cattle and more rarely horses, which feed on *bourgou*, another aquatic grass. Head-portage is now most exceptional, and the transport of rice from field to hut and from hut to market is by means of donkeys. A family with three men would cultivate nearly 40 acres of rice, which is three times as much land as in the unirrigated areas, and about a third of the crop would consist of an early variety. The surplus is sold by the *saval* or calabash, which holds 9 lb. of husked rice, at Tenenkou Market.

Ploughs are used extensively. There are 100 of them in the nearby holy city of Dia alone, which is an important centre for commerce and handicrafts.[1] Two men with two pairs of oxen, generally ill-trained, take about four days to plough an acre.[2] When, as generally happens

[1] The weaving of cotton and wool (beautiful embroidered blankets or *kasa*), the cloth being marketed locally; there are blacksmiths who make *dabas*, mats of various kinds, etc.

[2] The men and their team could be hired at 200 francs C.F.A. per day (in November 1950).

after four or five years at the most, a rice-field becomes choked with weeds, it is rested for three years.

62. The irregularity of the floods, which may rise or subside too early or too late and spoil the crop in either case, is the main cause of uncertainty, but a great advance was made when basin irrigation was introduced. This was facilitated by the presence of two dikes running at right angles to the Diaka opposite Dia and Tenenkou respectively, with a levee bordering a stretch of the river between them. The gaps in the latter were filled, and the fourth side of the rectangle completed at comparatively little cost. Sluices in the levees enable the fields to be lightly flooded earlier than would otherwise be possible. Alternatively, they may be used to hold back the early flood or later in the year to prevent the water from subsiding too soon.

The degree of irrigation control thus achieved has meant that bad harvests have been reduced from six to only two or three per decade. Furthermore, the fact that this area was already settled has enabled much of the heavy building expenditure incurred by the Office du Niger in colonizing new lands to be avoided. However, certain essential parts of the scheme have not yet been completed. The Dia canal outlet at the 'fishing suburb' of Dia-bozo, for instance, is still in need of a lock so as to enable the breach in the embankment to be closed without preventing the passage of native craft. By such means, the scheme could be made far more effective.

The Service de l'agriculture du Soudan, which has undertaken the project under the sure guidance of M. Viguier, and more recently of M. Rénard, is now planning to extend the irrigated area and to carry the campaign against weeds a stage further. Various species of wild rice are particularly troublesome, and it is hoped to tackle this problem by tractor-ploughing during the cool season. The lower probability of crop failure alone is unlikely to balance the heavy cost of dike construction, nor is the resulting grain surplus large enough to constitute an insurance against the uncertainties of unirrigated farming in the surrounding regions.

Only the cultivated land is privately owned, and the opening up of new areas with the help of tractors is therefore bringing more land under private control and is reinforcing the position of the ruling families. The feudal system appears to be particularly oppressive in this Islamized region, the more so as it is officially favoured. Even though the chief of the canton of Dia has not added to his own personal estate, his brother, it seems, was not forgotten, for he received large sums of money from other users of the land, as did the land chief. Thus may economic progress sometimes work to the detriment of social justice. Finally, the scheme provides for three mechanical rice-mills, which are now being installed. They will undoubtedly reduce the long task of the husking by hand and improve the quality by reducing the amount of spoilt grain.

The logical corollary to these developments is the introduction of improved varieties of plants. The floating rice used until now has been of a red-grained variety. The trade wants 'white rice',[1] but the agricultural expert insists that introduced varieties must be at least as good as those which are already being grown, especially in point of resistance to disease. In areas of slightly undulating relief or where other factors make water-control difficult, the young plants could advantageously be sown in nursery beds and subsequently transplanted. This would save work, because it would take less time than weeding, which would no longer be necessary. The seedlings could be transplanted whenever the water reached the required depth. The exact time would vary according to the height of each field and, however flood conditions might fluctuate from year to year, the existence of fields at different levels would almost certainly ensure that some portion of the area was flooded to a suitable depth when the rice was ready for transplanting. This method is traditionally used in the flood plain of the Niger itself downstream of the delta as far as the Nigerian frontier; it could profitably be extended to the region further upstream.

63. These schemes appear to be fulfilling their objectives admirably; they are encouraging a more fruitful use of the best soils, are not costly when balanced against the increased productivity, and are likely to prove an insurance against famine for the people of the region. And this is being achieved without any serious loss of soil fertility in the richer areas. It is also significant that these improvements are taking place in the *sahel* zone, where, owing to the low and uncertain rainfall, which is everywhere less than 20 in., unirrigated crops[2] are subject to frequent failures. This makes the full development of available resources all the more important. For the older inhabitants of Segou, the year 1914 evokes the memory of a terrible famine rather than that of the outbreak of a world war; 30,000 tons of paddy grown

---

[1] It sells better. Very white grain is obtained by removing the vitamin B_1-rich outer layer—to the detriment of health.

[2] Millet in sandy areas, sorghum if clay is present. Nine miles north of Sokolo in the village of Farabougou, which is in the northern part of the Office du Niger's projected Kouroumari sector, the food situation appears to be critical; and the number of cattle appears to have declined as a result of epizootic diseases.

on 75,000 acres of irrigated land could have made all the difference.

In spite of its better access to the coast than the Chad region, the delta of the middle Niger is not likely for many years to be able to export its rice, owing to its inferior quality, but the only serious criticism which can be levelled at the present scheme is its excessively slow rate of progress. There are many other spheres where prudence is still the best counsel, but here is a region whose development is being guided along lines which are thoroughly understood from both economic and technological points of view. There is a strong case, therefore, for prompt and urgent action. When the valleys can feed more people, the higher ground, with its more precarious balance of soil conditions, will be able to produce export crops, such as cotton and ground-nuts, with far less risk of impoverishment.

In the vicinity of Bongor in the Chad Territory, another system of rice cultivation has been practised on the flood plain of the Logone since 1926. The flood water generally reaches a depth of between 2 and 3 ft.,[1] and the ground is first prepared in March and April by uprooting the weeds, which are more troublesome here than in the middle Niger. They are heaped up into long lines, which are then covered with earth. The ridges are then burnt and the strips of ground about 5 ft. wide on either side of them are sown broadcast. Finally, earth and ashes are spread over the seeds to a depth of 4 or 5 in. to protect them from the birds. Along the line of the ridges themselves, where the soil is more generously enriched with ashes, two or three rows of rice are sown in clusters. The composite strips thus formed are about 4 yds. wide, and are separated from each other by untended and unfertilized ribbons of ground about 2 yds. wide where the weeds grow unchecked. The system, with its selective fertilizing, is reminiscent of traditional methods found in some of the poorer parts of Western Europe.[2]

Although rice cultivation began there a very long time ago, one does not find the same attention paid to fertilizing in the middle Niger delta. The explanation is probably that the soils are richer and the ruling classes are Peuhl and Moorish herdsmen who do not concern themselves overmuch with agriculture.

8. The Office du Niger—Irrigated Rice—a Directed Economy

64. The relative fertility of the grassland soils, which are prevented

[1] Millet of the ragi type was formerly cultivated in these flood-liable areas.

[2] E.g. in Morvan (*ouche*) and Brittany (*terre chaude*). The fodder, grazing, and stable litter furnished by the heaths enriched—either directly or indirectly—the fields near the farm.

only by lack of rainfall from becoming extremely productive, has already been emphasized. M. Bélime was the person who realized the irrigation possibilities offered by the distributary channels of the old delta downstream of Segou. He saw that a slight raising of the river level would be necessary, and his efforts eventuated in the construction of the Sansanding Barrage and the establishment of the Office du Niger. At first, the object was to grow rice and cotton, but the former was given priority as a result of the last war.

Agriculture has been modernized by irrigation under the aegis of a directed economy, and the Negro cultivator follows a set plan of work on the land entrusted to him. The first settlers arrived about 1936, and were 'volunteers' appointed by their village chiefs. They came from the region south of the Niger bend, many of them from the Mossi country. At first they came as if they had been condemned to penal servitude, but they accepted the new situation fairly quickly when they saw how much greater were the yields than those which they had been accustomed to expect from unirrigated land. Since then there have always been plenty of volunteers to take up the new land as it became available. But the rate of new investment is slowing down and the full possibilities of the scheme, with its barrage and two trunk canals, have not by any means been exploited to the full. A much larger area than the present 65,000 acres could be irrigated, and the economics of the scheme can be summed up by saying that its capital is beginning to depreciate without ever having been fully used.

The efficient use of labour has sometimes been handicapped by a density of population surplus to the requirements of irrigated agriculture. At the village of Siguinogué, in the Kokry sector, where rice is grown year after year, the official returns for 1950[1] show 605 Mossis dependent on 1,100 acres of paddy. There were even large families with little more than 1 acre of crop land per head. In cases like these it may be observed that a land/population ratio almost comparable with that in the Far East has been induced.

A definite class structure is emerging as a result of the employment of hired labourers—who carry nearly the whole burden of work—by the officially designated settlers. During 1950, there were about fifty hired

[1] The actual figures are generally 10-20 per cent. higher. Since our visit the population of the village has been reduced to 545 (in 1952), 131 of whom are workers; this for 1,345 acres, including new extensions. In the March-April 1950 issue of *Agronomie Tropicale* (p. 464), P. Viguier observes: 'The numbers involved in the first colonization did not allow a single course in the rotation to be set aside for fallow or even for a crop which would benefit the soil. This could lead to a dangerous situation. . . .'

men working in the rice-fields of Niémina. Half of them had been engaged for the whole year, and expected to earn their food and between 5,000 and 8,000 francs C.F.A. The remainder had been taken on mainly to assist with harvesting and threshing, and were due to leave again at the end of six months. The sixty-five settlers themselves hardly work at all, except at the busiest times of the year. Instead of investing their profits in the improvement of their land and the purchase of equipment, they have set themselves up as shopkeepers, selling, for instance, kola nuts to the workmen employed on canal construction and maintenance. The tragedy is that money—which is scarce in these poverty-stricken countries—is being invested in the comparatively lucrative business of distribution, or in moneylending. The latter, as we shall see, is even more flourishing in Asia. The disparity between the rich and poor, however, is not so marked as in the Gezirah region of the Sudan Republic.

65. According to Aubert, the effect of irrigation on the rich land of this region is to reduce the proportion of organic matter, which is rapidly consumed, and also of such bases as calcium and magnesium. The net result is that the soil structure begins to break down, and the working of the land consequently becomes more difficult. This tendency is, in fact, unavoidable, but it can be corrected by using lime and green manure. The division of the land into square $2\frac{1}{2}$-acre plots made things worse and eventually the fields had to be relevelled so as to make the embankments parallel to the contours. But many of the settlers, not bothering to keep the embankments in proper repair, simply made up for their loss of water by increasing the flow from the canals, in some cases to as much as 1·5 or 2 gallons per second per acre instead of the 0·8 gallons actually necessary. This wasteful habit reduces the size of the area which could be irrigated with the water available in the canals, and it also encourages the spread of diseases and of marsh plants and may even give rise to salt incrustations near the surface. The situation will be improved by the drainage works which are being undertaken.

More serious is the fact that little use is made of animal manure. The huge *zeriba*, or wall of dried earth, at San Koura, which encloses a yard for keeping the cattle at night, accumulates a layer of manure nearly 3 ft. thick over the course of about ten years. It is left exposed to the rain and the sun, except for the occasional load which is brought to the land adjoining the huts. Even in a 'new' region the lack of integration between animal husbandry and agriculture is hardly surprising when one recalls that in the older settled areas the 'home field' is the only parcel of land which the African traditionally manures. Settlers of the Miniankas tribe adapt themselves somewhat better to the techniques which are demanded by a system of continuous cultivation. The Office encourages the ploughing in of rice straw in the paddy fields, with the addition of nitrates, and the use of animal manure for vegetables or tobacco, where it pays better. A wise plan would be to encourage the system adopted by the Miniankas of Niémina, who ingeniously saved themselves the trouble of rebuilding their derelict *zeriba* by making use of thorn fences to enclose their cattle on the rice-fields from December to August. In this way the land is fertilized without any extra work. Even if the nitrogen is not wholly replaced, the process of soil impoverishment is at least very strongly checked, and at less cost than if chemical fertilizers were used. During the day, the cattle feed on straw left in the fields, and the curb on their movements cuts down the amount of damage their trampling does to irrigation and drainage works.

If the cattle were kept in enclosures near the village at night and moved periodically, a complete belt of gardens could be systematically fertilized. This is actually done by the Balantes of Casamance,[1] and the standards of a European-planned economy should certainly never fall below those of any native agricultural system. An adequate supply of fertilizers for the 'garden belt' would be assured even if full use were made of ashes and human waste products, but the latter are not used at all, being either dispersed haphazardly or buried in holes in the ground. The transport of this material to the arable land beyond the gardens would, of course, necessitate the use of many more carts and draught animals.

Other easily available ways of fertilizing the land are also ignored. Ashes have already been mentioned, and the same applies to other forms of domestic refuse. Part of the explanation for this is the unnecessarily long distance between the huts and the gardens. Even the weeds which grow on the retaining banks of the paddy fields are not turned into the ground, and the same excuse certainly cannot apply here. Indeed, the abandonment of unirrigated farming with its long fallows in favour of intensive irrigated agriculture represents an abrupt change from the traditional methods of Africa to those of monsoon Asia, and the process is not an easy one.

66. In 1945, as soon as the war was over, opinion everywhere favoured the mechanization of agriculture. In Africa the recognition of its possibilities was long overdue, and it came to be regarded as the panacea for all evils. The Office du Niger, in addition to its work in connexion

[1] See our *'Etude de quelques économies agraires au Sénégal et en Casamance'* in the May-June 1951 issue of *Agronomie Tropicale*.

with the recently settled villages, undertook the cultivation of rice at Molodo, north of the barrage, under a system of direct control and complete mechanization. The varieties of rice which were sown, however, although hardy and high-yielding, were better suited to hand-reaping than to the use of combine-harvesters, which can operate efficiently only if the whole crop is ready at the same time. Furthermore, the combine can only be used on really firm ground, so that the irrigation water has to be drained away earlier than usual, to the detriment of the size and sometimes of the quality of the crop. By the time it is harvested, the grain is therefore too dry and brittle, so that much of it is spoilt in threshing.

Owing to its distance from the coast, this area will only ever be able to export rice of high quality, and at any rate for the present mechanization appears virtually to preclude this very condition. It seems that in the poorer, non-industrialized regions, where capital and equipment are sorely needed, priority should be given to measures such as the introduction of mechanized ploughing and irrigation, which are destined to raise the volume of production, rather than to those which, like the use of combines, reduce the demand for labour. Sauvy has epitomized measures of the latter kind as *progrès récessif*. Nevertheless, in sparsely populated regions, the use of harvesting machinery can be recommended in so far as it reduces the peak demand for labour to manageable proportions.

But this is not quite the case here. Indeed, in January 1951 surplus labour from the Kokry rice sector finished the work of harvesting by hand at Molodo, where the combines had quickly been put out of action. The purchase of machinery does not appear to have been justified in terms of increased returns, and it would probably have been better to aim at the lower level of mechanization represented by binders, which are simpler, cheaper, and capable of working on softer ground than combines. Threshing machines, which are used to thresh the grain grown by the native settlers, have already been introduced.[1] Another application of machinery which would undoubtedly prove its value would be the use of tractors for ploughing cotton land and paddy fields. They could be employed to even better advantage if accompanied by improvements in land drainage, which would reduce fluctuations of crop yields.

---

[1] As the women were responsible for threshing, the men were opposed to this measure (which cost them a certain amount of money), until the women, completely overtaxed by the size of the harvest, which was larger than they had ever known in the days of dry crops, went on strike.

67. The village of Nara, with its population of 400, has a total of twenty-eight families. In all there are 140 children under fourteen. The people are Bambaras, and they cultivate some 740 acres of rice. There are nearly 500 cattle, a rather higher figure than the average, and a third of them are cows and heifers. For the whole of the Kokry Basin the proportion is only one in five, and in some villages, such as San Koura, only a tenth of the adult animals are cows. The preponderance of oxen is related to the need for draught animals, but with the increased use of tractors for ploughing—and a fair acreage of the paddy land is now tractor-ploughed—the pattern is changing. For the future, therefore, cattle-rearing must be promoted with the object of producing meat and milk, and for this purpose the herds must comprise a majority of cows. In addition to the cattle, there are about ten horses and donkeys, 100 goats and 2,000 or 3,000 head of poultry.

The family of Bandiene Tangara is a large one, and it farms its 70 acres better and lives better than the average. It has forty-four people altogether, twenty-seven of them adults, with thirteen men and fourteen women. The large gardens[1] here are manured, and grow maize, millet, ambaria hemp, and cotton in the rainy season and capsicum, calabashes, tomatoes, sweet potatoes, and various spices, all carefully watered, at the beginning of the dry season. They grow tobacco, garlic, and onions, which thrive under the perpetually moist soil conditions on the edges of stagnant pools. The whole system is thus reminiscent of the 'garden agriculture' of Binder in the Chad or of Be in the North Cameroons.

The prosperity of these settlers, as compared with the inhabitants of unirrigated areas, is apparent from the clothes they wear and from the presence of a few gold ornaments. The latter were even more numerous among the wives of workers at Kokry. As at Niémina, among the new class of employers, the consumption of millet beer, and even in some cases of wine, is on the increase. Furthermore, although the soil sometimes appears to be hardening and although wild rice is a troublesome weed, the yields are still good, but not so high as those of the first few years. The average of 14 cwt. per acre is three or four times as great as the yields of the traditional type of unirrigated cultivation, and the amount of work per acre is only very slightly larger.

Subtracting the 3 cwt. which are taken by the Office to defray general expenses and costs of irrigation, the settler is still left with a

[1] The gardens vary in size according to the place of origin of the people: quite nearby, at Lafiala, the Samogo cultivators tend their rice-fields more carefully, but gardens are entirely absent from the vicinity of the village.

far larger crop than he could ever have obtained in his native region. Before the tractor was brought in, when the peasant still relied on ox-drawn ploughs, hand weeding, and sickles for harvesting, twenty-four days of work per acre (mechanical threshing included) yielded 11 cwt. of grain. This corresponds to 2·2 days per cwt. and compares most favourably with the 4·5 days noted for the Turumbu, which was very much higher than the average for the equatorial region, and with the five days per hundredweight of millet, which is a less valuable grain, observed in a particularly favourable instance in the Chad. In Tonkin we shall see that more than eight days of work are sometimes needed to produce a hundredweight of grain.

68. The work of the Office du Niger is having good results, but there is still plenty of scope for improvement in the greater use of natural manures of local origin and in the more efficient control of water. The latter problem which is now being tackled involves improved methods of water distribution and better land drainage. Owing to the lack of some system of siphoning out the water from below the embankment near the Niger, the rice-fields on the lower ground often have too much water in the rainy season; the crop is thereby endangered and the yields are reduced. Such areas remain marshy even in the dry season, and their moist soils therefore encourage the spread of wild rice. In areas of comparatively low population density, good drainage would permit rice to be alternated with an unirrigated crop, and this would prove an economic method of checking the growth of weeds. Asiatic methods of uprooting each individual weed by hand cannot be adopted here, and such a plan would be in line with methods of rice cultivation in North America, where labour is at a premium. Then again, the Negro settler is still being subsidized, for his water tax does not cover the real cost of irrigation. As in North Africa, it is most difficult to defray the heavy expenditure of an irrigation scheme by growing nothing but food crops, especially as irrigation must always be supplemented by drainage works.

Although the quality of the rice, especially the Bentoubala variety, is undoubtedly superior to that of the naturally flooded areas, it is still not good enough to make its export from French Sudan worthwhile under normal conditions. The irrigation of certain sectors enables enough grain to be grown comparatively cheaply to satisfy the local demand and to reduce appreciably the intensiveness of cultivation in the unirrigated upland areas. But such schemes, designed solely for the cultivation of rice, appear like the use of combines to be fundamentally uneconomic. The actual return is less than proportional to the investment.

A better utilization of resources is certainly called for in the irrigated sector of Kokry, but it is too low-lying for successful cotton-growing. One solution might be to extend rice-growing to the portion of the Niono cotton area where the drainage problem is most acute. We have already expressed our misgivings,[1] however, regarding an extension of irrigated rice on to the even lower region to be served by the Macina Canal, which runs parallel to the Niger. Here wild rice would probably be more difficult to keep in check and heavy expenditure would be incurred by the necessity for building dikes.

9. Priority for Irrigated Cotton on the Egyptian model in the Kouroumari Region

69. Once a number of irrigated sectors of the Diaka type have been established and the food supply of French Sudan has been assured, the time will be ripe for the Office du Niger to give priority to cotton. The region could supply not only the local market, but French needs as well. France has far more right to expect a return from her investment here than in the Chad, where export crops are being won to the detriment of the soil and of the people themselves. The Sahel Canal, which runs northwards, carries water not only to the Molodo rice area, but also to the Niono cotton region. At Kokry, in theory at least, each head of a family was given $7\frac{1}{2}$ acres of paddy land, and we saw that because of the enormous size of these patriarchal families some very high population densities had resulted.

At Niono, on the other hand, every male worker is entitled to 15 acres: 5 of these are under cotton and $2\frac{1}{2}$ under rice. In theory the remainder consists of 5 acres under a leguminous crop for green manure, which alternates with cotton, and $2\frac{1}{2}$ acres where fallow and rice alternate. As only half the land is actually cultivated, one might expect a population density about half that of Kokry, but the official figures for 1950 showed an average of 1·2 workers and nearly five inhabitants per 15-acre holding, which represented a density of two-thirds of that of Kokry. The threat of overpopulation had already begun to appear, and the official figures understated the case.

The lack of preliminary research has led to the inclusion of land which, as at Riziam, is too light for cotton. Ground-nuts are now cultivated here, although the 22 in. of rainfall would be just sufficient to grow them without irrigation. South of Niono, two former settlements are now in ruins: the soil was too infertile and could not be relied

[1] In an unpublished report to the Office du Niger submitted at the end of our work there.

upon to produce even the crop dues for the Office. Here, the dues are fixed at 175 lb. of raw cotton per acre, rising to 250 lb. per acre if tractors are used for ploughing, 265 lb. if the fields are also ridged, and 280 lb. of chemical fertilizers are employed. Another settlement, the village of Kouia, inhabited by Miniankas, manages to survive mainly by concentrating on horticulture and selling its produce to the nearby 'urban' centre of Niono.

The well-to-do family of Yaya Dambélé comprises four men, two women, and five children. They cultivate three holdings, and thus have 15 acres under cotton[1] and 7½ under rice. Yaya has 2½ acres of garden, and although horticulture is not by any means found in every village, he asserts that his family would not otherwise be fully occupied. His garden produce often exceeds the 15-acre cotton crop in value. It can be heavily manured, thanks to the large herd of cattle, and rice is sown in the hollows during the rains; elsewhere the crop consists of a mixture of maize and sorghum and an assortment of tomatoes, capsicum, and gumbo. The more lucrative crops are taken in the dry season, and include tobacco, onions, and tomatoes. The number of animals is exceptionally large: twenty-three cattle, two asses, ten goats, and a horse. The last is the most highly prized. It is used only for riding and is a mark of social standing.

The drainage is obstructed by the physical build of the region, and it is this, more than any other factor, which has led to the abandonment of the land. Difficulties of drainage in a somewhat less serious form are unfortunately common to the whole of the Niono sector. About every five years (1939, 1945, 1950 . . .) more than half the crop is lost through excessive humidity,[2] while two other years out of five see the crop affected to a lesser extent and the harvest either slightly or appreciably reduced in size.

70. Rice is more tolerant of poor drainage than cotton, which is an exacting crop. Whenever one of the factors in intensive agriculture is deficient, the productivity of the others is adversely affected. The heavy expenditure on green manures and tractor ploughing was certainly not recouped in 1950, for instance. The rice-fields, on the other hand, are highly productive, and average about 16 cwt. of grain to the acre, but

---

[1] In fact, apart from the 'official' fields of the head of the family—taxes are paid only on these—the women and children have their own small 'illicit' fields.

[2] In 1950, some settlers—at Keleguemogo, for instance—resumed sowing three times altogether, weeded three times and tried to rid their land of excess water by every means in their power. Furthermore, in this case at least, the soil was fertile, but their valiant efforts were of no avail.

the crop is essentially for domestic consumption, and the family income is derived from the sale of cotton. A wise plan would be to concentrate on rice in those areas which are more difficult to level and drain satisfactorily while devoting to cotton the more easily exploited west bank of the Molodo Channel (a natural continuation of the Sahel Canal). The latter area, however, has been officially earmarked for rice cultivation, although no valid reason for this decision is apparent.

M. Zahan, an ethnographer whom the Office had the wisdom to employ for the study of human problems, accompanied us to the village of Tenkedogo, which is inhabited by Mossis. These people are still closely linked with the customs and traditions of their native villages, even to the extent of parting with considerable sums at the behest of their parents[1] and of their old district chiefs. The system of buying wives has died out, however, and has been replaced by one of 'exchange of daughters' between the various family groups. Families related either in this way or merely by 'jocular kinship' are committed to mutual economic assistance.

Girls born in the new irrigated lands and accustomed to the less arduous life, the better food, and the more abundant supply of cloth are no longer willing to return to their ancestral villages, even if they receive a direct order from the chief to do so. The presence of bicycles in all except three families indicates a much higher standard of living than among the growers of unirrigated cotton of the Oubangui and Chad,[2] who in 1949-50 received only half the price given for cotton here. Some of the cotton is ginned at home, in spite of the fact that the ginned fibre is obtainable at the works run by the Office: 'The women must be kept occupied,' assert the menfolk.

At the start of the scheme especially, those who were still in awe of the traditions sometimes found it very difficult to find a wife if they happened to encounter opposition from their former chiefs. They would have thought it degrading to marry a woman of the local Bambara tribe. More recently, however, social barriers of this kind have tended to disappear; young girls and even the married women will willingly follow a worker employed on one of the various schemes, so long as he is earning plenty of ready money.

71. The 'government' of the village, as in all Mossi communities, is

[1] At harvest-time, parents who have remained in their villages send several members of the family to the new areas. The latter return with many gifts, sometimes even with horses.
[2] The physical productivity of work seemed to be three or four times higher than in these areas, owing to the greater reliability of harvests which has accompanied the introduction of irrigation; with a better system of drainage, productivity could well become six times as high.

in the hands of a chief and four elders. They are the village's representatives in the Native Agricultural Association. In effect, this is a co-operative society acting under supervision, responsible for selling the produce of the locality and also for buying its miscellaneous requirements, such as implements and consumer goods. The idea of a co-operative system is unexceptionable, but certain influential persons connected with the Office appear to have assumed only too readily that the supervision, which is obviously necessary at first, should continue for a prolonged period instead of being brought to an end as quickly as possible.[1] There is thus a danger that the excellent idea behind the scheme will eventuate in something which is no more than a convenient administrative device instead of leading to the formation of a commercially educated *élite*.

There is scope for the improvement of the educational system by making the content of teaching less remote and more closely related to the direct interests of the younger generation. Emancipation of the Negro is being retarded by the insufficient number of rural schools and by the insistence on French as the medium of instruction. If progress is to be made, village organizations must be placed in the hands of a non-feudal rural *élite*, which only schooling and co-operation can ever hope to create. As far as vocational training is concerned, the present system will continue to be inadequate so long as there are chiefs of sectors lacking in agricultural training and unable to speak the native languages. Here, as in Morocco, where the Beni-Amir scheme is modelled on the Office du Niger, the chief is regarded merely as a kind of enforcement officer. Because a technical adviser has not been appointed, the workshops at Markala, where apprentices are trained, are not serving their purpose satisfactorily. The practical value of technical education and the essential part it must play if the full benefits of a modern irrigation scheme are to be reaped are points which have not always been fully appreciated by the Office. Nevertheless, even if more could have been achieved, given larger resources, the progress made is indisputable, especially when the enormous difficulties inherent in any scheme of colonization and irrigation are taken into account. In a letter, M. Coyaud describes the Negroes' joy when the water first arrives as being a pleasure to watch. Indeed, in its work of modernizing African agriculture on the basis of water control, the Office du Niger has undertaken a most interesting task.

[1] One often finds the same attitude, on the political plane, in Vietnam, as in North Africa and Sudan; Nigeria, which adjoins the latter, has already been granted a very considerable degree of autonomy by the British.

72. The moment has now arrived when, on the basis of past experience, irrigation can be rapidly extended to the Kouroumari zone, north of Niono. This would simply be making the most of facilities which already exist. The Sahel is dry enough to favour long-stapled Egyptian cottons, and it could thus become a key area from the point of view of the French economy. A more thorough preliminary survey than has hitherto been undertaken would ensure that soils too light or too compact for cotton were avoided. Indeed, a group of Russian refugee land surveyors who are at work in the area have already put forward a soil classification which utilizes native knowledge of the locality. It also adopts the vernacular terminology, which is often much more appropriate than the pedological terms in general use. The accumulated experience of traditional native agriculture, which is being lost elsewhere, has thus been preserved. But it is doubtful whether enough attention will be paid to the conclusions drawn because the desire to keep the administrative machinery as simple as possible favours the idea of a single farming system for the whole sector. The wisdom of such a course seems questionable in view of the variety of soil conditions; the 'danga wheat' soils, for instance, are ideal for cereal growing, but not suitable for cotton.

A large portion of the land useless for cultivating could be planted with trees to good advantage. The twofold objective would be first to provide a source of timber which could be exploited methodically by the settlers and, secondly, to reduce the danger of erosion by breaking the force of the wind. The settlers of some of the older and now overpopulated sectors are already beginning to be short of timber, and we saw instances of rice being husked dry because of the lack of wood to effect the usual preparatory boiling. As in Asia, rice straw would be used as fuel, much to the detriment of the soil, if appropriate measures had not been taken. Provided that no special drainage problems are likely to arise, a start should be made with the sector west of Kouroumari. Complete levelling and perfect drainage are essential, in spite of their cost. There is no other way of avoiding the stagnation of soil water, which affects the longer-stapled varieties of cotton so severely. These give a more valuable crop, but they are less resistant to diseases, such as black-arm, than the medium-stapled American types grown at Niono. The latter are quite suitable for local weavers.[1]

There have been suggestions that some of the surplus population of

[1] It is worth remembering the need here for local handicrafts which are capable of making much better use of the labour available during the season of unemployment on the land than is possible at present.

North Africa, from southern Morocco in particular, should be brought in in order to develop this new area. One hesitates, however, to endorse an idea which involves immigration on such a scale. How could people of Mediterranean origin ever stand up to the summers of this region, which not only combine great heat with high humidity, but also call for the hardest work of any season in the year? Leaving aside the question of possible racial frictions, it must be recognized that the first duty of the Office du Niger is to alleviate the pressure of population in the Mossi country. This it must do by recruiting settlers from that locality, where the soil is already suffering from the effects of shortened fallow periods. The fear is sometimes expressed that settlers will not volunteer from the Mossi region in sufficient numbers, but it should be remembered that the overcrowded 'new' areas themselves, where the rate of increase now attains 3 per cent. per year, ought to be regarded as an important source of recruitment for the future.

Until now new arrivals have always found their quarters ready built for them. When they arrive at the beginning of the winter, however, soon after the harvest period, it would be more sensible to let them build their own homes, especially as they are allowed to draw rations until they have taken their first crop. In this manner they could plan most of their buildings in accordance with their own individual tastes and tribal customs. In every single enterprise of rural colonization throughout the world, the cost of building homes appears to count for an unnecessarily large proportion of the available resources. Moreover, from the point of view of the development of the factors of production, which by their very nature are entitled to first consideration, this expenditure represents a total loss. The Office could limit itself to providing reception camps, public buildings (including schools, which one now seeks in vain), roads, bridges, wells, and water-holes for stock. Wherever water can be found fairly near the surface, the intention is now to build a larger number of smaller villages, so as to reduce the distance to the fields.

The story of unirrigated cotton in French West Africa is one of a long series of setbacks. The attempt to extend this type of cultivation is liable to accelerate the complete ruination of the plateau areas wherever a serious attempt is not made to increase the volume of food production from the low-lying valleys. It seems preferable to concentrate our scant resources on the irrigation of 125,000 acres in the Kouroumari region. If half this area were devoted to Egyptian cotton, some 8,000 tons of long-staple fibre, representing nearly a third of France's requirements, could be harvested each year. Further into the

Sahel zone towards Mema, the soils become richer in humus, while, owing to the lower rainfall, which also acts as a check on black-arm, leaching becomes still further reduced.

73. At the time of the Liberation, grandiose but ill-considered projects were put forward for the construction of barrages and other costly works in the 'Mesopotamia' of the Chad, along the low-lying valleys of the Logone and Shari. It would be better, however, first to complete the network of channels in the Niger scheme, where the constructional works are already in place, and thus to make better use of the resources which are being frittered away at the moment. The final stage of the scheme, which depends on agreement between the countries concerned, would be to build reservoirs on the upper Niger. These would not only provide electricity, but would also bring perennial irrigation and double-cropping to the region. An alternative to double-cropping would be the cultivation of crops, like sugar cane, which have a long growing season. The more liberal use of fertilizers, both organic and chemical, would be the essential condition of this type of farming, which would have to approximate to that of monsoon Asia in the intensiveness of its methods. This would be the only way of checking the deterioration of soil structure and offsetting the losses due to leaching.

Later on, the introduction of forage crops into the rotation would allow breeds of cattle with better meat- and milk-producing qualities to be reared. To do this, the problem of seasonal shortages of food would certainly have to be overcome and feed of high protein value, such as grain, fresh hay, silage, cotton-seed, and ground-nut cake, would have to be provided. Of much greater consequence, however, in view of the present state of animal husbandry, is the provision of a market for meat by the construction of modern slaughter-houses. This would bring the Peuhl herdsmen into the orbit of economic exchange, and would accelerate the changeover from 'sentimental' to commercial cattle-rearing. The emphasis would be on the production of prime beef, and the animals would be slaughtered as they attained their maximum value.

Already the liking for gold ornaments evinced by the Peuhl women is stimulating commercial exchange, and this is a factor of no small importance in the development of the great resources of the Sudan region. The disadvantage of the present system is not only that the older animals have lost much of their value as meat, but also that, by consumption of fodder, they prevent the rearing of young. Tropical Africa could produce all its own requirements of animal proteins if its cattle were put to better use, and the growing of fodder crops would allow twice as many animals to be supported. It must be remembered, however, that any developments such as these are bound to take time.

The prospect of progress in this field is very much more hopeful than in equatorial Africa, but so far only the European market has been envisaged as a suitable outlet, and this point of view seems to be ill-advised. The temperate countries are themselves much better suited to rearing, and their means for purchases from abroad are likely, if anything, to decrease. The Sudan, however, is very well placed for supplying the coast of French West Africa, as is the Chad for sending meat to Brazzaville, which it has already begun to do by air. Only a very small and preponderantly European proportion of the population is now actually supplied, but there is a vast potential market. The meat problem here can unquestionably be solved much more readily than in monsoon Asia.

Whatever advances there may be in this direction, there is no doubt that the Chad will one day become the scene of an irrigation project similar to that of the middle Niger. The ground must therefore be prepared well in advance, and the urgent need at the moment is for an experimental station, better equipped than the present one at Ba-Illi, which is on a very small scale, capable of determining the techniques, types of crops, and methods of fertilizing best adapted to the local conditions. Only thus can the checks to progress and lulls in development which the Office du Niger has experienced through lack of preliminary research possibly be avoided. The soils most likely to benefit from irrigation must be carefully examined, and on the basis of this evidence the most favourable sites for dams and, later, for barrages can be determined. The execution of such a scheme requires the formulation of a development plan which lays down the relative importance of expenditure under different headings, assesses the priority to be given to each part of the scheme, and estimates the crop increment which can reasonably be expected. The work of the Office du Niger has sometimes suffered from over-optimistic forecasts of production. In future, therefore, every effort must be made to increase the reliability of such estimates. It is clear that in the meantime, before any large-scale project can be launched, small and inexpensive improvements, like the building of embankments to retain the flood water for a longer period, could be effected; even these could have important results in improving the local food supply by greatly extending the rice area. In this matter of food supply there is absolutely no excuse for delay. The

Chad cotton-grower pays enough in taxes to deserve some improvement to his land in return.

10. Soil Exhaustion due to Ground-nut Cultivation in Senegal

74. The valley of the River Senegal could well have been given priority over the Niger in the matter of irrigation. The production of food—rice in particular—should be rapidly developed, as has already been done at Richard-Toll at the mouth of the river, in response to the growing demand from nearby towns, such as Dakar. The advanced stage of soil erosion which is already evident in the region also calls for similar action.

G. Aubert writes:[1] 'In the more northerly regions where leaching is reduced, the soils (ochre-coloured and *dior* soils) are endangered by another factor: wind erosion. The process of soil deterioration can thus be summarized as follows: under a vegetation cover of tree savanna, a certain degree of equilibrium is maintained between the formation and the wastage of humus. At the same time, the bases are eluviated only to a fairly small extent.

'When cultivated for the ground-nut, the soil remains bare for the whole of the dry season after the harvest. What is left of the plant is generally burned, and the loss of humus is therefore not compensated. The soil, now poor in humus, loses its cohesiveness; the wind, which is very strong in the dry season, can thus perform its work of erosion more easily and, as the finer material is deflated, the proportion of coarse sand in the soil rises. When, after a few years of cultivation, the land is left in fallow, the humus content increases again, but not to its original level. The spontaneous vegetation consequently does not flourish as well as before on this partially impoverished soil. And so on....

'This process has been accelerated in recent years by the continuing increase in the demand for ground-nuts for export, so that the Negro cultivator has been encouraged to reduce or even to abolish altogether the fallow periods during which the soil rests. The result has been that in some places north of Louga and in the vicinity of Sine the illuviated horizon, which was previously at some distance below the ground, has been exposed at the surface by wind erosion. Such soils should be taken out of cultivation and the regrowth of the natural vegetation should be deliberately encouraged or at least allowed to take place spontaneously. It must be admitted that this will be a very long process.'

[1] *Encyclopédie de l'Afrique Occidentale Française*, chapter entitled 'Sols'.

The oil-mill at Louga in Cayor was built in 1931, when the process of soil erosion here was already well advanced. This is yet another example of a free economy in which no thought was spared for the preservation of natural resources nor for the future of the people. In a study of several villages in central Senegal,[1] we have observed what appears to be the beginning of the same cycle of erosion already described, and it is significant that the port of Rufisque now hardly exports any ground-nuts, 85 per cent. of the Senegalese crop now being dispatched from Kaolack further south.

It would appear that a certain abandonment of cultivated land must accompany the introduction of intensive agriculture. The latter would be facilitated by prompt action in promoting an irrigation scheme in the Senegal Valley and by extending the cultivation of ground-nuts towards the south. This extension is actually taking place quite naturally, without the help of outside stimuli, but further expansion is limited by the Ferlo 'desert' in the east and by the frontier of British Gambia in the south. Beyond Gambia is Casamance, which has a fairly large population of rice-cultivating Diolas near the coast, but the density of population thins out rapidly towards the interior.

75. The Compagnie générale des Oléagineux tropicaux,[2] or C.G.O.T., formed to implement the objectives of the Commissariat au Plan in modernizing agriculture overseas, started operations at Sefa on the right bank of the Casamance slightly upstream of Sedhiou in the autumn of 1948. The idea was originally inspired by the Tanganyika Ground-nut Scheme, but fortunately a later start was made, while the financial resources were more limited and the plan less ambitious, so that valuable lessons were derived from the painful experiences of the British undertaking. During the summer of 1949, 3,300 acres of heavily wooded savanna country were cleared before any adequate soil survey had been made; consequently, certain areas had to be abandoned later on owing to the steepness of slopes or to the presence of laterite below the surface. Also, the work of clearing was carried on into the dry season, when the ground becomes very hard, and great inconvenience was caused through tree trunks breaking and stumps thus being left in the ground.

The complete mechanization of ground-nut cultivation was the object of the scheme. Even in the United States this has only been achieved

---

[1] *Agronomie tropicale* (May-June 1951).

[2] A part-public, part-private company; industrial interests provided a tenth of the initial capital, the State the remainder. All subsequent capital has been furnished by the latter, so that the influence of the oil companies is disproportionate to the amount of money that they actually provided.

very recently, for the ground-nut was long regarded as a poor man's crop. Moreover, circumstances are entirely different when the soils are extremely light and perennial cultivation is possible from the very first. In Casamance, with its rainfall of over 50 in. occurring during the five months of the wet season, the main erosion factor is surface run-off rather than wind. Contour ridging is essential in some areas where the gradient exceeds 1 in 125, and field boundaries, belts of woodland, and also some of the roads have had to be realigned at right angles to the slope.

Pennisetum subangustum, a weed which is capable of choking any field crop with its vigorous growth, is proving most difficult to control with mechanical methods alone. It will survive unless it is completely buried in the ground, and whereas the native accomplishes the task easily enough by hand, the operation is most difficult to perform mechanically. Owing to the climate, the right conditions for sowing are of short duration. This means that a tremendous amount of machinery which virtually lies idle for the rest of the year must be used to prepare the ground during the limited time available. Finally, the rainfall is rather high for the successful cultivation of ground-nuts.

More serious are the doubts which still exist regarding the possibility of continuous and wholly mechanized cultivation ever becoming a sound economic proposition. The cost of cultivation is greatly enhanced by the purchase of large quantities of mechanical equipment, the restriction of their use to a very limited area, and the employment of a large body of highly paid European experts. Furthermore, clearing is such a costly process that it makes mechanization incompatible with a system of periodic forest fallows.[1] On the other hand, the best way of using green manures is not at all certain, for when bacterial activity is severely reduced by intense insolation the problem is to know how the necessary humification can be induced. The presence of a navigable river may well facilitate the import of chemical fertilizers, which is hardly feasible in the interior of the continent, but it cannot be taken for granted that even these can solve the problem of maintaining soil fertility.

76. There had been no field experiments until 1948. There were still far too many unknown factors in both the agricultural and economic

[1] The C.G.O.T. has perfected a comparatively inexpensive method of clearing by employing a heavy chain drawn by two large tractors. But somehow the fallen tree trunks must then be removed, for no useful purpose has been found for them as yet. As the trees consist of species which have successfully resisted savanna fires, they are difficult to burn. Poisoning with arsenate of soda is to be tried.

spheres to justify the launching of such a costly undertaking on a large scale, and the decision of the directorate of the Plan to go ahead demonstrated a lack of prudence reminiscent of that shown during the early stages of the *paysannat* projects of Morocco, which will be described in a later chapter. The management of the scheme was not put into the hands of agricultural scientists, even though they were frequently consulted, and the original notion of passing straight to the mechanized cultivation of ground-nuts on a large scale without graduating through less ambitious stages proved unworkable. To make the best of an unhappy situation, the whole scheme had to be turned into a pilot project with the limited objective of pointing the way for future development in Casamance.

Twelve thousand five hundred acres were cleared in the summer of 1950, and in the autumn of the same year we were invited to study the whole affair. We recommended that a halt should be called on any further development, and this advice was eventually accepted a year later after further difficulties had been encountered during the summer of 1951. Neither the last weeding, performed in September, nor the actual harvesting have as yet been satisfactorily mechanized. Such problems could have been tackled on a much smaller budget by establishing, in the first instance, a well-equipped experimental station which could have devoted the first five years wholly to research. It could have been followed by cultivation on a semi-commercial basis on some 2,500 to 4,000 acres—or rather less than the acreage occupied by the Agricultural Services scheme north of Kaffrine in southern Senegal. What in fact happened was that between 1949 and 1951 the Government, having for several decades refused to help with research, suddenly made available a volume of capital which was altogether disproportionate to the task. It was like building a factory before the methods of manufacture had been fully worked out.

Professor Portères, after visiting the area in 1951, suggested with some diffidence the following rotation: green manure (spiked millet or wild *Pennisetum*), a cereal (maize or sorghum), ground-nuts, a fibre (ambaria hemp, urena, or sunn hemp). It is impossible to envisage the success of an exhausting rotation of this kind with three saleable crops unless the soil is already rich in humus and chemical fertilizers can be readily applied. The introduction of sisal would have the advantage of prolonging the employment of machinery well into the cool season.

Our imperative need for vegetable oil-seeds should have ensured that the techniques applied to their production were sound. The success of the oil-palm, introduced to Malaya and the East Indies in 1910 and to the Belgian Congo in 1925, has been amply demonstrated. M. Julia[1] has shown that plantations can be mechanized without encountering the difficulties that are involved in the case of the ground-nut. The advantages of collecting large bunches of fruit as compared with digging up small nuts from below the ground are obvious and have been proved conclusively by past experience.

The oil-palm, however, matures fairly slowly, and, ignoring the time taken in surveying and clearing new land, a plantation begins to yield heavily only after about ten years. Indeed, in view of the declining production of ground-nuts from Senegal and, more particularly, of the dangers of soil erosion, it is wiser to look elsewhere than to the tropics for future European supplies. Much can be done by intensifying French agriculture and developing the large-scale cultivation of autumn-sown rape, for which a temperate climate is ideal. In this manner, 5-6 cwt. of oil could be obtained per acre, compared with only about 1 cwt. of butter—more than 15 per cent. of it water—now produced from the pasture lands of Normandy; this is symptomatic of the backwardness of some aspects of French farming. In Senegal, by comparison, 1 acre of land under ground-nuts would yield about 2 or 3 cwt. of oil.

11. The Difficulties of Mechanization and the Possibilities of Mixed Farming

77. The above survey has once again emphasized the urgent need to develop modern irrigation schemes in the low-lying river valleys and coastal regions. In this manner the uplands would be relieved of much of their burden of food production and the beneficial practice of fallowing could be continued until reliable techniques of continuous cultivation had been evolved. Only these will ever allow large numbers of people to be supported or enough capital to hasten the equipping of the country to be accumulated.

The problems which need to be resolved before such plans can be translated into fact deserve immediate attention, for the intertropical regions of Africa and America, together with a small portion of central Asia, constitute the largest remaining reserve of new land in the world. In temperate latitudes, areas still available for cultivation occur only in North America and Siberia, and are much less extensive. In view of

---

[1] *Projet de création de plantations mécanisées de palmier à huile*, a paper which has been duplicated (December 1950) by the Institut de recherches sur les huiles de palmes et les oléagineux.

THE FUTURE—MECHANIZATION AND MIXED FARMING

possible future increases in the world's population, it is of the utmost importance that the resources of these regions should not be frittered away by hasty schemes of exploitation before appropriate methods of development have been determined. Inasmuch as the unsatisfied demand for their products is large—and the native peoples deserve first consideration here—these regions must nevertheless be opened up rapidly, and capital and skill must therefore be freely put at their disposal.

The question will then be whether to aim at a concentration of effort in certain areas on the model of the Office du Niger or C.G.O.T., or whether to spread resources more thinly over larger regions. The first need is obviously to ensure that the basic minimum of equipment is everywhere provided; it is lamentably true that some African peasants do not even now possess hoes worthy of the name. First carts, and then cultivators and horse-drawn hoes—which P. Viguier has indicated as being more urgently required than ploughs—could be manufactured by the local craftsmen of Senegal and Sudan. The transformation of the primitive 'flood' irrigation of the low-lying valleys and plains into basin irrigation could be effected during the cool season, but modern terracing equipment would speed up the work considerably.

78. On the higher ground, where fallows of tree savanna alternate with periods of cultivation, the advisability of using tractors is still debatable, for we would hesitate to endorse the practice adopted by the C.G.O.T. of removing the stumps completely. They can, however, be used with greater facility in the irrigation basins, which are, of course, devoid of trees. The introduction of modern methods of water control would greatly increase the benefit to be derived from their use.

Elsewhere, the need for tractors is conditioned by the proportion of forest vegetation or by the need, as in the ground-nut areas of Senegal, to use green manures as a measure of soil protection. In the latter case, their services are indispensable, but once the crop had been turned into the soil they could be transferred to other areas to perform the selfsame operation. The native could then be left to grow his crops, using improved traditional methods. The advantage of this system would be that it would avoid too rapid a social upheaval.

The complete mechanization of agriculture would initiate a series of drastic changes in the native social structure. It would, for example, lead to the establishment of workshops and a host of other innovations which are part and parcel of a large-scale agricultural enterprise. Until now the very small unit has been the rule in the indigenous agriculture of the intertropical regions, and only the capitalist enterprise has been characterized by a large scale of operation. It makes no difference whether the venture is backed by government or private interests; the native is always an employee. This is true of Sefa and Molodo, as it is of Malayan or Sumatran plantations. For the future, however, the native must be offered something better than subservience. Co-operatives must be established and rapidly allowed to become completely independent as a step towards bringing really large enterprises under native control. It is impossible to mechanize an individual holding, but co-operation would enable modern equipment to be used by the existing native communities. On this count alone, therefore, it would be unwise to precipitate the breaking up of tribal units.

As yet there are not even the beginnings of local industry, and complete mechanization is therefore bound to be very costly for a long time to come. We would prefer to see pilot schemes, such as Richard Toll in Senegal, the C.G.O.T. and the Office du Niger, making a thorough study (in collaboration with native communities) of the possibilities of partial mechanization as applied to native co-operatives instead of pursuing the objective of complete modernization. At Kaffrine, in the south of Senegal, this principle has actually been adopted, but a great blunder was made in turning over all the proceeds from the sale of produce to the religious chief of the Mouride community. The money is distributed according to his fancy, and his subjects, the Talibes, who are the real producers, never receive more than a fraction of their share. Technical improvements may thus bring in their train the increased exploitation of labour.

79. Local handicrafts are more in evidence in the Sudan than in Senegal, but on the whole they make a very small contribution to the economy during the season of agricultural unemployment. A greater variety of crops would help to lengthen the working season for both men and machinery, and the importance of sisal in this connexion is that its leaves have to be cut in the cool season, which makes it an ideal ancillary crop to the ground-nut. With regard to the latter, the problem of soil conservation would be easier if only the oil were exported. The residue,[1] which has a high protein content, could be used locally with

---

[1] The sale of these residues as cake to the European farmer has for many years contributed to the impoverishment of tropical soils to the advantage of the temperate regions, even though the latter are incomparably more secure from the dangers of soil destruction. It is time that these abuses ceased, and that we began to produce for ourselves animal feeding stuffs with a higher content of nitrogen.

THE FUTURE—MECHANIZATION AND MIXED FARMING

advantage as human food or, failing this, as animal fodder. This might well lead to a close association between cultivation and livestock-rearing, and to the establishment of a tropical variety of that mixed farming which is a feature of the advanced agricultural systems of Western Europe.

Meanwhile, experiments now in progress could be used to evaluate the relative advantages of mechanizing different operations, on grounds of increased volume of production, lower costs, or easier execution. Judging by the setbacks which have been experienced at both Sefa and Molodo, the operation least in need of complete mechanization is harvesting, for it needs the most expensive machinery, which is only employed for a very short time. This is especially true of regions like Casamance, the old delta of the middle Niger and the lower Senegal, which are destined to play the part of reception areas for the surplus population of adjacent regions. An overall redistribution of population designed to strike a better balance between local densities and natural resources would prove less costly than total mechanization.

All things considered, machinery is needed here more urgently than in the river deltas of Asia. In the latter, owing to the extremely high densities of population, the imperative need is for intensification and the replacement of human energy by mechanical power must be preceded, or at any rate accompanied by, a vast programme of rural decongestion by industrialization. More thought should therefore be given to the priority of different kinds of modernization. The peasant could work longer on the land if dikes and roads were constructed with modern equipment. Then again, the mechanization of post-harvest operations discussed in the previous chapter is a comparatively simple matter: for example, the lorry can easily be substituted for the ass, and the barge for the canoe. The employment of tractors in the characteristically small fields, dotted about with trees and bushes, will be far more problematic, and the difficulties will be further aggravated if no attempt is made to prepare the social structure to meet the changes which are bound to follow.

The encouragement of mixed farming and of the more general use of draught animals is another worthwhile task which is by no means easy to accomplish, except perhaps in west central Senegal. Here the Sereres practise a biennial rotation of millet and ground-nuts with no fallows, which appears to have no harmful effect on the soil, even where the population, reaching 125 and even 200 per square mile, is really excessive. The explanation lies in the fact that their animals are grazed in the cultivated fields, which are therefore well manured. The bare land is also protected between harvest-time and the next sowing by a leguminous tree (*Faidherbia albida*), which comes into leaf during the dry season, thus also providing valuable fodder. It loses its leaves in the wet season and does not therefore interfere with farming operations. The excessive density of population is the only reason for the poverty of the people in this region, which is one of comparatively large resources.

Poverty is an obstacle to the introduction of horse-drawn hoes and seed-drills which would do away with losses in production due to tardy sowing and ease the burden of work at the busiest time of the year. Four months of field cultivation is really too short a period for the soils of the region, and it is at this time that the horse-drawn hoe would render invaluable service. Such measures would enable the Senegalese to extend the area under food crops, such as millet, without the cultivation of ground-nuts, the basic commercial crop, being affected. Once adequate reserves had been built up, the early but poorer yielding types of grain which are now forced on the cultivator by the aggravation of food shortages towards the end of the growing season could be abandoned in favour of better varieties. Eventually the peasant will be able to face the busy time of the year without being weakened through want of food, which is certainly not the case at the present.

The modernization of agriculture in the tropics is making little progress, although the task appears to be easier than in the equatorial region. The Senegalese still use a type of hoe introduced over a century ago, which enables them to cultivate no more than about 4 acres per head. Ground-nut yields have not risen for the last fifty years, and in recent years only about 400,000 tons have been marketed as compared with 500,000 to 600,000 before the war. Furthermore, the economic balance of the country is being upset by the emigration towards the towns, which makes the future prospect of the rural districts bleaker than ever. In a world of rapid change the stagnation of agricultural activity which is a fundamental feature of tropical Africa must not on any account be tolerated.[1]

The long season of agricultural inactivity and the more enlightened character of the people inhabiting the region incline one to the opinion that industrialization could be implemented in the tropical much more easily than in the equatorial zone. Modern milling machinery is already in use, and the next step will undoubtedly be the establishment of textile factories supplied with local raw materials. Eventually, chemical

---

[1] Cf. *Aménagement de l'économie agricole et rurale au Sénégal*, by R. Portères, a report (duplicated, 1952) to the French West African Government.

and engineering works will be able to meet local demands for the fertilizers and machinery needed for the modernization of agriculture.

80. The continent of Europe, whose transient ascendancy in the industrial field has left a permanent legacy of overpopulation, has now lost its place as the world's political and economic centre of gravity. Remorse is useless, attempts to turn back the clock are doomed to failure, and the only realistic course is to adopt a policy of readjustment to the new situation. Because the volume of her manufactured exports has declined, Europe can no longer rely on importing from intertropical areas commodities such as cereals which she can just as easily produce herself. These areas have the advantage in the matter of sugar and oilseed production and more particularly where certain plants such as sugar-cane and oil-palm are concerned. But in Brie, winter rape gives more oil than do ground-nuts in Senegal. In the south of France, moreover, the latter have begun to be grown together with cotton, and in Hungary, as we shall see in a later chapter, the cultivation of cotton has been developed very rapidly during the last few years.

Towards the end of the last century it was sometimes thought that, taking its lead from England, Western Europe was destined to become the workshop of the world, and that in consequence she could afford to neglect her agriculture and rely on imports of food. The course of events has proved this argument to be utterly fallacious, and Europe now faces the prospect of rapidly intensifying her agriculture as the only alternative to economic disaster. She will be obliged more and more to limit her economic demands on intertropical countries to the supply of commodities botanically limited to their environment, such as stimulants and possibly natural rubber, certain fibres, and part of her requirements of vegetable oils and sugar. But even this will be possible only if Europe herself pays for at least a portion of these imports with agricultural products appropriate to her own climatic conditions. Foremost among these are milk derivatives, especially powder made from skim-milk. Indeed, the latter should be distributed by the authorities concerned to the children of intertropical regions, first priority being given to the sparsely populated areas.

Europe can find in Africa a field for action with more permanent results than in Asia, which is already virtually autonomous. The prime condition is that, while there is still time, the native, instead of being merely exploited, should be given the status of an equal partner. To promote further efforts on the part of the native, the old 'treaty economy' must be replaced by a policy of really rational development. There have already been signs of this transformation since the war, but the tempo is still far too slow. It is pointless to deny that an enormous programme of capital investment, non-profitable in the narrow view and comparable in scale with the current volume of defence expenditure, will be needed to carry out this policy. To provide for both—African developments and defence—would result in a lowering of the European standard of living, especially among the poorer classes, which no one has the right to demand. We would prefer to see the money which the two opposing camps are now spending on armaments used to aid the world's underdeveloped countries. Failing this, Europe's role in world affairs will shrink to something more in keeping with her place as the smallest of the five continents, a mere peninsula in the massive outline of Asia.

If the outside help essential to rapid progress in the tropics were used as an instrument of subjugation, it would fail utterly as a means of procuring economic advance, for the only sure starting-point is the willingness of the African people themselves to make a sustained effort. This they will not do until they are convinced that their own true interests are at stake.

IV

The Overpopulated Coastal Plains of Monsoon Asia in Northern Vietnam[1]

1. Chinese and Indian Civilizations: Fertilized and Irrigated Rice-fields in Continuous Cultivation

81. West of Phu-Ly in Tonkin (now known as Northern Vietnam) the delta of the Song-koi or Red River ends abruptly against an almost vertical limestone escarpment. The 'intermediate' region on the west, with barely five persons per square mile, finishes right on the edge of the delta with its stoneless silts tens of yards in thickness, and with a population density of between 1,300 and 2,600 per square mile. The average is actually about 1,200, but the figure rises in the south and west, and in a certain canton quoted by P. Gourou[2] actually reaches a rural density of 4,430 persons per square mile. The interior rather resembles Africa, with forests and large areas of savanna dominated by *Imperata cylindrica*, the relative abundance of these two elements in the landscape depending on the extent of clearing rather than on latitude. There is no equivalent to the Sahara, and the humid region extends much further north than in Africa. The dry season is always in winter, but at Hanoi in Northern Vietnam (latitude 21° N. as compared with

---

[1] From 1929 until 1932 we had the task of trying to improve rice cultivation in the deltas of Tonkin and Northern Annam. Our research reports were published in the *Bulletin Economique de l'Indochine* and, more fully, in *La culture du riz dans le delta du Tonkin* (Paris, 1935). We have also had the opportunity to study the following areas at first hand: Yunnan (Kunming region); the Canton region; central Annam, and, for a short time, Cochin-China and Cambodia; Ceylon; the southern part of the Deccan as far north as Madras. This chapter, however, is based mainly on our observations in the Tonkin Delta, where we worked for three years.

[2] *Les paysans du delta tonkinois* (E.F.E.O., 1936). A village in Haute-Marne (*Voyages en France d'un Agronome*, Chapter 12) which has a population of 100 and an area of 2,500 acres would have 17,300 inhabitants at this density per square mile.

12° N. for the Chad) there is no month with less than seven rainy days. The drought season is more marked, however, in Cambodia, the lower Mekong Valley, northern Annam, and in the north-west along the Chinese frontier. With these exceptions, the whole of Indochina has more than 60 in. of rain.

Here, then, regional differences appear to derive from the contrast between the lowlands and the interior, and are not associated with latitudinal position. In the littoral plains stretching from the Indian peninsula[1] and Indonesia to north-central China as far as the Hwai-ho a little to the north of the Yang-tse-kiang—that is, from the Equator to the warm temperate regions—one finds an extremely ancient agricultural civilization characterized first and foremost by a high density of population. Generally speaking, as rain occurs during a considerable proportion of the year there is a long growing season, and in some areas vegetative growth is continuous throughout the year. Only in the extreme north does the lowering of winter temperatures, which is quite discernible at Hanoi,[2] prevent double-cropping. Where conditions are favourable for irrigation, two crops can be obtained each year throughout the tropical region and even beyond.

The soils of the lowlands have their origin for the most part in the denudation of the hills and mountains of the interior. When first cultivated they are fairly rich, but their fertility is considerably lower in areas of long-established settlement, particularly as the land has sometimes been protected from flooding in order to grow two crops a year. Diking, mainly a question of raising the river levees, appears to have been practised before the eleventh century in the Red Delta and the fields have thus been protected from flooding in the summer, which is by far the wettest season. Under the French régime public works have completed the projects of the Emperor of Annam, but the result is that the river silts, instead of being spread over the low-lying areas fertilizing them and raising their level, are now washed straight into the sea almost in their entirety. If this did not happen, the surface of the Delta would be raised by 0·2 in. every year and a great deal of money could be saved in fertilizers.[3] Were it not for the dense population it would be possible to flood a whole series of basins, the surface of which

[1] In the rice areas—that is, in the eastern half of the country, on its western seaboard and in the irrigated lowlands of the Indus.

[2] Mean temperature of coolest month: Saigon, 79° F.; Hanoi, 63° F.

[3] The river is raising its bed between the dikes and the danger of flooding is increasing constantly. Experience in the Po Valley shows that in the long term view diking alone is impracticable.

would thereby be raised and fertilized, but such measures would reduce the cultivable area.

In the interior of Indochina the soils are often vastly superior to those of Africa. In parts of south Annam, Cambodia, and Cochin-China, the soils are developed on young basic volcanic rocks, such as basalt and dacite. On the whole, the climate also is more favourable for plant growth. The tribes of the interior, however, who are often racially distinct from the people of the plains, practise a type of shifting agriculture similar in certain respects—in the communal ownership of land, for instance—to the African systems. Modern plantations of rubber, tea, and coffee came earlier to this region than to Africa, but they are obviously of a kind. In this chapter, however, we shall dwell rather on those features which are characteristic of the Far East and more particularly on the agriculture of the low-lying plains. 'The foci of civilization in Asia are the vast "Mesopotamian" lowlands of alluvial origin'—thus does René Grousset begin his *Histoire de la Chine*.

82. Ever since the fourteenth century B.C., when Chinese civilization began to spread into lower latitudes from the Great Northern Plain, it appears to have been characterized by a system of settled agriculture which contrasts strongly with the shifting cultivation of Africa and the upland regions of tropical Asia. The early development of a continuous cropping system was made possible by the complete removal of the natural vegetation, including the uprooting of any stumps remaining in the ground, and by the improvement of yields achieved by the use of fertilizers. The cultivated area soon became concentrated in the lowlands because of the practice of clearing steep slopes, which meant that parts of the uplands became unfit for agriculture. About the beginning of the Christian era, this system, with its animal-drawn iron plough, penetrated into Northern Vietnam (Tonkin), no doubt replacing the Indonesian type of riziculture still found in Madagascar, which had previously been known in the Delta.

The latter already represented an advance on the hoe-cultivation of forest clearings and, although the ground was merely trodden by animals, the land was levelled to facilitate the retention of water. Indeed, water control is one of the most significant criteria in appraising the intensiveness of an agricultural system. As in Oceania, where primitive methods were used to irrigate the terraces on which taros[1] were grown, the practice in China is to bring water straight from the rivers. On the other hand, the Indian system, which is typical of drier lands, is to

[1] Edible tubers of the Colocasia genus.

build large storage reservoirs as a safeguard against shortage of water in the dry season. The dams need constant attention, and when in time of war labour cannot be spared for this purpose the reservoirs become breeding places for malaria, a factor which helps to explain the depopulation of certain areas; the former rice-fields of Angkor in Cambodia, for example, are today covered with forest.

Whereas in northern Vietnam animals are used exclusively for ploughing, they play a much more prominent part in the Indian system, as exemplified in Cambodia, where there is greater emphasis on rearing and shepherds tend their transhumant flocks in the uplands. In the lowlands there is much more evidence of the use of animal power for various purposes, including transport and the drawing of water. Associated with the larger number of animals is the fact that they are yoked in pairs, whereas in northern Vietnam they are generally used singly, a practice which appears to have originated with the Chinese. It was from the same people that Europe copied the horse collar, which is first recorded as having been used in the sixth century in the border region between Turkestan and China. The cart of northern Vietnam, especially in the form of the wheelbarrow with its load more or less balanced on a single solid wheel, has a similar origin.

The peoples who now inhabit Vietnam established their settlements at various altitudes where temperature conditions approximated to those of the areas from whence they came. Thus the Meos, who migrated from Szechwan, have sited their villages at higher altitudes than the Mans and higher still above the Thais, who came from the upper Yangtse and Canton regions respectively.[1] In India and Africa the dominant crop may be taro in one locality, millet in another, and this diversity is the natural result of regional variations of climate. In the lowlands of the Far East, however, the situation is quite different, for rice, which is of Indo-Burman origin, is grown everywhere almost to the exclusion of all other food crops.

2. The Concentration of Property: Excessive Rents, Usury

83. This ancient agricultural civilization, which, though more advanced than our own in the Middle Ages, remained static for centuries until the year 1911, is marked by a much greater degree of social stratification. The absence of an alphabet and its replacement by a complicated list of characters which takes several years to learn has meant that culture was the prerogative of a privileged wealthy class. On the whole

[1] Historical data supplied by A. G. Haudricourt.

PROPERTY, RENTS AND USURY

there was little distinction between the landowners, the mandarins, and the warlords.

Private ownership of land, which has existed for centuries in these lowlands, is an aspect of native intertropical agriculture which we have not so far encountered elsewhere. In Africa there are many tracts of land which cannot be developed for want of labour, but here the situation is reversed. The Chinese exercised their authority, however, to avoid the over-concentration of land into the hands of a few individuals, and ever since about 1000 B.C. in the days of the Chou Dynasty an Imperial decree has defined the permissible minimum of land to be held communally as follows: 'In order to prevent the exploitation of the poor by the rich, at least one-ninth of the area must be preserved as common land and shared equally by all those who contribute personal taxes to the State.'

In 1397 the Emperor of Annam[1] decreed that no one was allowed to own more than 10 *mâu* (1 *mâu* = 10 *sao* = a little under 1 acre), and that any land held in excess of this figure must be handed over to the State. Only the members of the royal family were exempt—and they profited handsomely. The law stipulated that any area left unfarmed automatically became public property. It would constitute a great step forward if this formula were applied in France today, for it would resolve the legal problem of how to bring her abandoned land back into production.[2] A law of the Leis provides for the punishment of those who open up new land on their own authority and an Act of 1808 'forbids officials and rich persons to profit from the poverty of the people or from people leaving their villages by usurping land or paddy fields by right of purchase....'

These wise laws were soon abrogated after the French conquest. According to Gourou, 'there is no doubt that ever since the beginning of the French régime the large estate has been making considerable progress ... restrictions have been removed and have sometimes been replaced by measures which favour its extension, such as the granting of concessions; all existing property has become inviolable.' We have described elsewhere[3] how, near the borders of the Delta, especially in the province of Bac Giang, vast concessions of land temporarily abandoned owing to civil disturbances were made to French and Annamite landowners at the turn of the century. Since 1900, therefore, peasants who once owned the land, returning to their former homes, have been

---

[1] Quoted by P. Gourou in *Les paysans du delta tonkinois* (p. 135).
[2] Europeans are the 'civilizers' of Asia—we were forgetting!
[3] *La culture du riz dans le delta du Tonkin.*

forced to pay high rents to the new landlords, who have provided nothing in return either in the way of equipment or land improvement. Asked about the reason for this, one of the beneficiaries, evidently surprised at such a question, replied, 'It would be too much trouble.'

The granting of these concessions was rightly regarded by the Annamites as an outrage, for it was contrary to an ordinance promulgated in 1824 by the Emperor Minh Mang, whose sense of justice and interest in the public good were exemplary. He decreed as follows: 'Land belonging to abandoned villages will become part of the territory of adjoining villages and will be cultivated by their inhabitants on condition that they pay the taxes. If the previous owners should return, they may resume ownership of all their land and rice-fields except any portions of them which were previously uncultivated and have been brought into production by the new occupants.'

84. Control of the mandarin by the people, which formerly restrained his exacting demands, disappeared with the establishment of French authority. When a mandarin had abused his powers, his house was burned to the ground; or else, on the day of his departure from the province, the people would come in silence and perfume the route he had to take with their excrement. This action alone was sufficient to incriminate him and, according to the law, it was then his responsibility to prove his innocence. But in 1930 we witnessed the case of the mandarin of the *huyen* of Vinh Bao, an area which specialized in the profitable business of growing tobacco, who arrived crippled with debts and was able, after a few months had elapsed, to buy a luxurious American car. The overall trend has been for the emergence of huge estates, especially in the crowded and poverty-stricken lower Delta (Thai Binh) at the expense of communal land,[1] and even more, of smaller private property. Once a man has begun to make money, he can, unless he has a prodigal son, rapidly amass a fortune.

The whole process is favoured by the high level of farm rents. The journalist Nyuyen van Vinh made a shrewd comment on the position when in 1931 he said: 'The landlord is king and the poor fight each other for the tenancy of his rice-fields.' The rent was often a fixed amount, and before the Civil War it generally represented the equivalent of about half the harvest, and this was paid for the land alone, buildings and equipment excluded! When the land was infertile it would be about a third of the harvest, but at the opposite extreme

---

[1] 'Thanks to a misapplication of the royal decree of 4 June 1923', observes Gourou; in Cochin-China the grants were not to interfere with the full utilization of the land, but this condition was ignored.

in productive areas, the figure would often reach 60 per cent., as in Japan. When a crop is completely spoilt by floods the landlord has no claim on the *métayer*, but under the tenant system the rent is still due. The tenant is then obliged to borrow, but the rate of interest is so high that he has little hope of ever being able to pay the money back.

Like the Italian *métayer*, who, however, has the advantage of not having to provide his farm buildings and all his equipment, the tenant is obliged to bring his landlord gifts of no mean value and furnish a certain amount of unpaid labour. Against this system, with its feudal exploitation of the under-privileged, must also be set the fact that the landowner, like his nineteenth-century counterpart in the Allier, according to E. Guillaumin, showed himself averse to all innovations, such as the introduction of fertilizers, feeling no doubt that any change in the established order was bound to threaten his own position. The attitude of the land-owning class was that the poverty of the *métayer* was axiomatic, part of the natural order of things, and that the social order was not, therefore, a subject where rational argument could be profitably applied.

The actual value of the land depended partly on the density of population, and very considerably on the fortunes of the village rather than on any question of fertility or transport facilities. Sometimes the land was almost priceless, especially if men who had made their money elsewhere returned to their native villages and bought land for the sake of social prestige. If, on the other hand, the countryside had been impoverished by a series of floods, the price would fall very low indeed. Gourou cites cases from Hung-Yen where, in 1931, property was being ceded to moneylenders in repayment of debts at between 10 and 20 per cent. of its mean value. The former owner, who stayed on to farm the land, would then have to pay a yearly rent of 10 piastres (100 francs at the time) per *mâu*, which was the price he had received for the sale of the same land.

85. In this crowded plain, constantly under the threat of flood-burst or drought, the supply of essential foods was often severely endangered. The custom of borrowing was therefore much more widespread than in Africa. The indigent peasant had frequent recourse to the moneylender, in spite of the exorbitant rates of interest, for this was often his only alternative to abandoning the land altogether or even to starvation. Indeed, the acceleration of social development in certain directions has resulted in the increased exploitation of the poor. A tenant[1]

---

[1] According to Gourou, half the revenues of large landowners in Cochin-China came from rents and half from usury. The thrifty tenant who did not ask for loans was expelled because he was a poor investment.

or an employee who needs a small sum to pay for seed, to help with the taxes, or to tide over an illness, and who borrows it from his landlord, is overwhelmed with gratitude if he is not charged more than 3-4 per cent. interest per month. Even when property is offered as security, the moneylender generally charges between 6 per cent. and 10 per cent. per month. Every part of a month counts as a whole, so that a loan for two months and twenty days, from 20 February until 10 May, would count as four months. Moreover, if money is urgently needed just for a few days, the interest is sometimes 3-5 per cent. per day.[1]

From India to China these high interest rates have put a brake on all development, for industrial profits simply cannot compete. Similarly, they have prevented all manner of land improvement, such as irrigation, drainage, clearing, and levelling, and even the purchase of chemical fertilizers. Advance in agriculture has also been handicapped by the virtual absence of a rural middle class and by the traditional contempt for the man who works with his hands. The upper class did not often condescend to show any interest in such 'menial tasks'.

The agricultural credit schemes inaugurated by the French administration charged 1 per cent. per month on loans. They were undoubtedly of great service to the rural community, but the title deeds which were required as security were often already in the hands of a moneylender, who held them as a guarantee against the debts owing to him. He would sometimes take the deeds to the bank himself, thus obtaining money more cheaply than he ever could from one of the big Chinese credit firms,[2] and enabling him to lower his own interest rates. The situation in southern China was entirely similar, and the prevalence of such extortionate practices was brought to light by Mao Tse-tung's first wartime measures, which were designed to soften the blow of reform as much as possible for the mass of the people. By giving effect to the Chiang Kai-chek penal code of 1930, which until then had remained a dead letter, they brought rents down to 37·5 per cent. of the harvest.

---

[1] While we were away for a fortnight, our boy pawned a perfume-brazier and loaned the money thus obtained, at 5 per cent. a day, to vegetable-hawkers (these women carry their trays, weighing 44 lb., on their shoulders).

[2] In his *L'utilisation du sol de l'Indochine française* (Paris, 1940), Gourou describes a comparable situation in Cochin-China where the S.I.C.A.M. (similar to the credit scheme mentioned above) loaned money mainly to speculating moneylenders and big dealers in land. It thus facilitated the concentration of property, which was the very tendency it was set up to combat.

PROPERTY, RENTS AND USURY

For the peasant class as a whole, the situation was further worsened by the oligarchic organization of the virtually autonomous Annamite Commune. This was a little republic in itself, solely responsible for both land and capitation taxes, greatly to the benefit of the rich, who always had a powerful voice in the village councils. The schedule of duties payable on imported goods was such that French manufacturers could sell their goods here very profitably: in some cases at twice the price they would fetch on the Chinese market which was open to international competition. Just before the war, the piastre was tied to the French franc in a way which meant that Indochinese grains could find a market only in France. Furthermore, the high cost of transport and the profits made by middle-men brought the price paid to the producer down to a very low level—down to 5 francs a hundredweight about 1934. The poor *nha-que*[1] was the unfortunate victim of all too many factors which diminished the rewards of his labour.

Owing to its rising population, the Tonkin Delta ceased to export rice in 1932, but maize exports continued until 1940. Moreover, if one is to judge from the minimum reasonable requirements of the inhabitants, none of this grain should ever have left the country. Indeed, the Tonkinese were persuaded to go short of rice themselves so that they might have the currency to buy abroad; the volume of such purchases remained, however, very small. It is true that a stage of social development had been reached which was well in advance of that of tribal Africa, but although the artisan and commercial classes were both very much larger, the craftsmen were still sorely in need of equipment, while the merchants were far more numerous than the services they rendered to the community appeared to justify. A large proportion of the region's business interests, the wholesale trade especially, was controlled by Chinese merchants, who often combined trading with moneylending.

---

[1] I.e. 'peasant'. Y. Coyaud, the author of that remarkable work *Le riz*, informs us that these low prices, which had fallen by four-fifths, made the payment of taxes, which fell by only a tenth, a terrible hardship. In order to pay them, the peasant was forced to sell a considerable part of his harvest, and even his draught animals. The market value of the latter fell in consequence, and a buffalo would fetch as little as 50 francs (16s. 6d. in 1934). During the food shortages of 1943-4, a bowl of rice, which was almost priceless, was sufficient to pay the greatly increased taxes which were then current. The Annamite administration of former times was not so large as it later became under the French, and taxes were paid mainly in rice; these two factors respectively lightened the burden of taxation and made for less variation from year to year in the charge on the peasant.

3. A 'One-buffalo' Farm in the Upper Delta: Low Productivity

86. On the left bank of the Red River and of the Canal of the Rapids, the upper Delta includes several stretches of higher land which rely on the rains of the summer for their water supply. In the winter water is raised from the river by manual labour, which effectively limits the irrigable area to the lowest portions of the region. Nevertheless, some land-hungry peasants are willing to go to enormous trouble to irrigate their fields and Coyaud actually cites the case of land at Hadong, near Hanoi, being irrigated by means of eleven relays of men who carried up the water in scoops from one level to the next. It took twenty man-days to bring up the water for 1 acre of land. It is only in this lower-level zone that the double-cropping of rice can be practised, and even here it would be impossible but for the use of nursery sowing and subsequent transplanting.

Whereas the clayey parts of the higher land, which are too hard to work when dry, are left fallow in the winter, the remainder is under 'dry' cultivation, which relies solely on the rainfall. Thus, whereas in France, Brittany and Flanders apart, double cropping is the exception, and 8 per cent. of the area is still in fallow, in Asia it has been practised for at least 2,000 years. Sometimes even a third crop is obtained by taking a catch-crop of 'three-moon' rice between the two main harvests.

Thus in the summer, around each village with its spiky wall of bamboo hedges, one finds a great open field devoted solely to rice, but in the winter some land is devoted to other crops. According to Coyaud[1] about a fifth of the area is then under dry cultivation, as opposed to four-fifths under 'fifth-month' rice, so called because of the month— May or June—in which it is harvested. The fields, which may vary in extent from 350 sq. yds. to $\frac{1}{2}$ acre, have all been exactly levelled so that the depth of water is the same everywhere. They are bordered by banks of earth 6-10 in. high which may be as narrow as 8 in. in the overcrowded lower Delta; here they are sometimes more than 20 in. wide, and the paths between the various villages are sometimes no wider. On market days the uninterrupted lines of peasants who throng them give an impression of swarming, ant-like humanity.

Outside the villages, the open countryside stretches away in a featureless plain devoid of landmarks except for one or two isolated trees or an occasional temple. A few ponds often surround the village and, apart from clay for building purposes, they provide fish and aquatic plants, which are eaten by both men and animals. Behind them, a

[1] *Le riz* (Saigon, 1950), archives of the Office indochine du riz.

LOW PRODUCTIVITY IN THE UPPER DELTA

prickly bamboo rampart, its two or three entrances carefully closed each night, completely surrounds the village. The houses, together with their barns and courtyards, are set amid a lush tangle of fruit trees, ornamental shrubs, and tiny gardens. Only a small part of the ground occupied by the settlement is devoted to vegetable-growing, but although the villages themselves are extremely compact they actually cover one-twelfth of the total area of the Delta. The average commune is very small, with a little over 500 acres of land and barely 1,000 inhabitants, although some of them are much larger than these figures suggest. Quang Phuong Ha (in Nam-Dinh province), for instance, had an exclusively rural population of 18,500 in 1930. Such 'rural townships' are not a unique phenomenon, and we shall find them again in Hungary, Tunisia, and elsewhere.[1]

87. Yves Henry[2] describes a holding of 3·2 acres at Nam-Xuong, in Bac-Giang province (Fig. 9). This is rather larger than the majority of farms in Tonkin, which vary in size from $1\frac{1}{4}$ to $2\frac{1}{2}$ acres and average a little over 2 acres, as compared with $8\frac{1}{2}$ for Cochin-China. This particular holding has a further advantage which puts it well above the average, for the farmer has the sole possession of a buffalo, an animal better suited to the lowlands, which is used for draught purposes. It is used with a harness which puts the weight on the animal's withers, unlike the much less efficient type of yoke still used in France, which, putting the strain on the head and neck, involves the cervical vertebrae and makes the work very much harder. The work on the land has been carried on with the help of animals, used singly, for nearly 2,000 years; they draw the plough, which looks rather like the tine of a modern cultivator, and they harrow, but they are never used for anything else.

Man is still the principal beast of burden in the Delta. He completes the preparation of the land by digging or hoeing the corners of the field and by breaking the clods of earth with a wooden mallet. He raises irrigation water in the dry season with scoops, with buckets on ropes, and with the foot-operated chain pump. Everything that has to be carried, whether it be manure for the fields, grain for storage in the barn, or produce for market, is taken in a pair of baskets which are attached to a piece of wood carried across the shoulder (fruitless attempts were made to introduce the Dutch or Norman *juk*, which distributes the weight more evenly over the whole shoulder). Rice is cut with a

---

[1] See Gourou for an excellent and comprehensive description of the Tonkin village, its houses, its surroundings, its life, etc.

[2] *Economie Agricole de l'Indochine* (Hanoi, 1932).

hook or a sickle, and is often threshed merely by beating the small sheaves against a stone. One has to visit the southern part of Vietnam to see animals commonly used for transport purposes where water communications are lacking, and in Cambodia, for instance, the human porter is replaced by pack animals and carts.

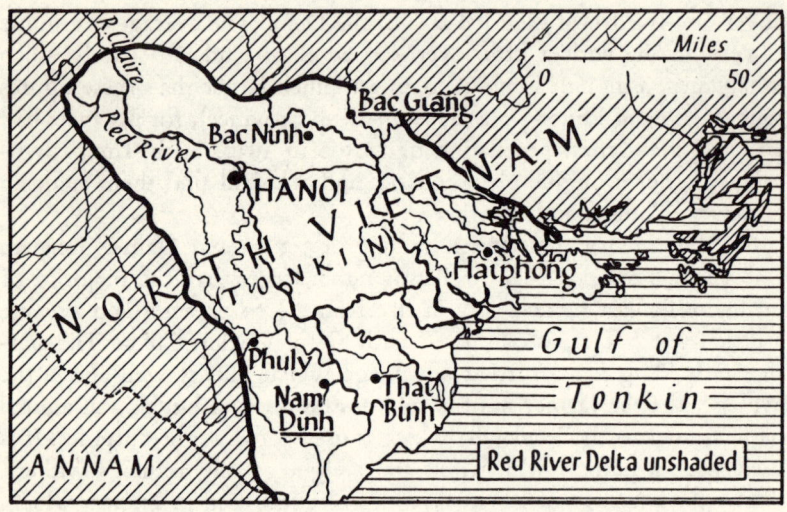

FIG. 9. North Vietnam (Tonkin).

According to the size of the farm, the animal is worked several hours a day for forty to seventy days a year. During the rest of the time it is turned out during the day to graze the field embankments, the borders of the paths, the sides of the larger dams, the cemeteries, and any other available waste ground. When it is needed for work, however, a certain amount of fodder is provided, but unfortunately the rice straw, which is the basis of the feed, is also needed as fuel for cooking purposes. The children are therefore given sickles and sent out to collect blades of grass, some of them hardly 1 in. long, wherever they can find them; it takes many hours of this work to provide the animal with a single meal. Taking its lower nutritive value into account, grass is often sold on the markets at a higher price than rice bran during the ploughing season. The situation can be summed up by saying that animal power is not employed more freely because of its cost in terms of human effort. Not least is the time taken in minding the animals, a task generally given to the children, but this custom is disappearing as a result of the spread of education. Alternatives will have to be found, and one recalls the effects of compulsory education in the southern French Alps, where the flocks—now unfortunately greatly reduced in size—had traditionally been cared for by young shepherds.

Before the war, the Tonkin Delta had about 500,000 oxen and buffaloes on its 3,000,000 acres of cultivated land. Of the latter, well over half was double cropped. There was one draught animal per fourteen persons, one for twelve rural inhabitants, one per 2·7 farms, or one per 6 acres. Comparing this last figure with Europe, the density seems excessive, especially when the small proportion of work actually done by animals is taken into account. The explanation of this underemployment of animals lies in the fact that individual holdings are too small. The pressure of population prevents cultivable land from being used for anything but food production, which is in any case insufficient; this has always presented an insurmountable obstacle to the growing of fodder crops, which, as in India, would permit some replacement of manual labour by animal power. The import of feeding-stuffs from up-river by rafts travelling down with the current might be a partial solution. In the meantime, the rice crop yields both grain and straw, thus feeding man and beast.

88. Returning to the farm at Nam-Xuong, this comprises 2·2 acres of land at an intermediate level, which gives two rice crops a year, and more than 1 acre of paddy on higher land,[1] which in the winter is under dry crops, such as maize, castor, sweet potatoes, beans, and cucumbers. The farm equipment, more varied than in Africa, is indicative of a much older rural civilization and suggests a greater degree of intensiveness. It includes a plough, a harrow, seven hoes of three different types, a shovel, a spade, five sickles, five flails, ten lined wicker baskets, and two scoops and two buckets with ropes for raising water; an assortment of baskets for winnowing and other purposes, sieves, and earthenware pots; also a mortar for polishing rice, with a foot-operated pestle[2] and a hand-mill for husking. Some of these articles, the basket-work in particular, are made in the home; the rest come from neighbouring villages.

Three sows are kept on the farm and four pigs are fattened for market

[1] This description refers to pre-war conditions, and the verbs should be in the past tense.

[2] Blind people are employed for this work for preference; they work at half the standard rates. In the intermediate region one often sees a small fall of water harnessed to operate a primitive rice-mill. The water is led into a trough which swivels down, raising a hammer, as it fills. The water empties as the trough reaches a certain angle, and the hammer falls on to the rice; the process is then repeated over and over again.

and twenty young pigs are sold each year. The average for the whole Delta is hardly one pig per family, and they are mainly reared for sale. The value of the 3·2 acres of the farm in 1934 was the equivalent of 1,800 francs, of the buildings 500 francs, half of which was represented by the paved area for drying the rice; the animals were worth 450 francs, which was far more than the average, and the farm equipment 110 francs. Annual expenses were of the order of 500 francs, but the degree of subsistence in the economy must be borne in mind.

Animal and human excrement, including human urine, are carefully collected; but bovine urine is not generally used, as either a suitable receptacle or an absorbent form of stable litter would be necessary, and neither of these is available. Another contrast with Africa is that the manure is distributed over the whole of the farmed area, and this, combined with the protective covering of water, ensures that soil fertility is maintained in spite of continuous cultivation. In practice, the more exhausting crops—such as tobacco, vegetables, and the mulberry —the nurseries, and the land near the village are manured much more liberally, like the hemp fields of Lorraine until the nineteenth century. Between ½ ton and 1½ tons of manure are often applied per acre.

Green manures are also employed, but to a much smaller extent than in either Japan or India: certain aquatic plants which grow in the flooded rice-fields (*azolla*) or a leguminous crop intertilled with maize in the dry season (*Crotalaria striata*). Before the depression of 1931-6, the farm, which is fairly progressive, used to buy nearly 1 ton of mineral phosphates and 4 cwt. of the waste from the manufacture of *nuoc-mam*, a type of sauce made from fish. There was one full-time labourer on a fixed wage, and seasonal workers were employed for a total of about 135 days in every year: thirty-five days for the two transplantings, about two months for the two periods of weeding, and nearly forty days for the two harvests.

89. An acre of paddy in northern Vietnam necessitates about ninety days of work per crop, rather less in the rainy season and rather more in the winter, when water has to be raised. Yves Coyaud has recorded the extreme figures of forty and 150 days per acre per crop. A typical crop of 11 cwt. to the acre, which represents a very mediocre yield, means that eight days of work are needed to produce 1 cwt. Productivity is thus lower than in Africa in spite of the more advanced techniques. Taking into account the fact that at least a third of the grain is lost in processing, and the amount of time taken in husking, winnowing, sorting and polishing, Gourou estimates that it takes over an hour and a quarter to produce a pound of white husked rice. The Corn Belt

LOW PRODUCTIVITY IN THE UPPER DELTA

farmer can produce up to an average of over ½ ton of maize for every hour and a quarter he spends on the land, though this figure should perhaps be modified to allow for the work not actually performed in the fields.[1]

Low productivity is especially evident in the course of the dry-season operations which are an indispensable part of the economy of this overpopulated region. Their absence in the much less crowded southern part of Vietnam is significant. In Cochin-China, farming practice is more extensive and less attentive to detail, and there is not the same pressure to bring even the poorest and most difficult land into cultivation. Only about two and a half days of work—three times less than in Tonkin—are needed to grow 1 cwt. of rice, which is a good illustration of the inverse relationship between population pressure and agricultural productivity.

In the Delta, fertility cannot be restored merely by waiting—even if one could afford to wait—for Nature to do the work. The soil must be maintained at great cost by man himself. Indeed, it is rash to assume that the *ray* system of shifting agriculture in the bordering hills is necessarily inferior: in the first place, it is associated with very intensive cultivation of intertilled crops in a horticultural belt near the village; and, secondly, although a dense population cannot be supported, because repeated sowings with only short fallows lead to erosion, on the rich soils of southern Annam the productivity of labour—not of the land, of course—often appears to be superior to that in the irrigated rice-fields of the neighbouring lowlands. The difference in the productivity of labour is especially marked where sloping land makes for additional work in the rice-fields in the form of terrace maintenance. Some tribes who grow upland rice and use only spades to cultivate their fields sometimes have food to spare for their neighbours who depend on irrigated paddy and plough animals. The contrast would be even more striking if we compared the Tonkin rice-field with the unirrigated cultivation of French Sudan with its ox-carts and ox-drawn ploughs.

The farm which has been described is situated on fairly fertile land, and 1½ tons of winter paddy are harvested in May and 2 tons of the summer 'tenth-month' crop in November. In addition 1 ton of sweet potatoes is obtained from about ¼ acre, 16 cwt. of taros and 1½ cwt. of beans from a further ⅙ acre each, and finally there are a few castor-oil plants and some vegetables. Obviously, this is a relatively well-to-do family.

[1] Cf. our *Leçons de l'Agriculture Américaine* (Flammarion, 1949).

4. A 'Half-ox' Farm of the Lower Delta: Indigent Farmers and Their Poverty-stricken Labourers

90. Let us now examine a small farm situated in the Nam-Dinh province (Fig. 9). A little less than 2 acres is devoted to double-cropped paddy. In order to obtain the maximum yield, the plough is used in December to turn over the dried sods of earth, which are then piled into low embankments about 2 ft. high and 1 ft. wide, care being taken to space them as far apart as possible and to put the moister sides uppermost. Banked up in this manner, the earth dries very quickly, and after about a month the low walls are demolished and the earth is spread over the ground once more. Whereas the operation takes some twenty-four days per acre, the increase in yield is in the region of $2\frac{1}{2}$ cwt.; this represents ten days' work per hundredweight of grain. Even here the law of decreasing returns is in full play, but where the peasant moves his walls of earth to dig over the sub-soil of the whole field, he may be spending up to fifteen days of extra work for every additional hundredweight of rice.

This farmer, with his 2 acres of paddy, owns 'two hooves'—that is, he owns half an ox, which he buys in partnership with a neighbour before the ploughing season and resells afterwards. Although this saves him from having to feed the animal when it is not working, he is always forced to resell at a loss. If a farmer has a very small holding, he merely hires an animal for a few days, but in January, just before the 'fifth-month' rice is transplanted, animals are in great demand, the rates are high, and the hired ox is therefore used only for ploughing. The farmer himself, with the help of three or four neighbours, pulls the harrow. One man holds it vertical and the rest pull it through the mud. With temperatures around 50° F., the wet earth feels icy cold, for the men get little protection from their tattered clothing. The poorest farmers are forced to dig the whole of their tiny fields by hand.

The value of this farmer's land is about the same as in the preceding case, for though there is less of it, it is more valuable area for area. The farm equipment is also comparable, but the value of the stock in 1934 was only about 100 francs, 50 of which were represented by the 'half ox', and the remainder by poultry and one young pig. The ratio of working capital, about 350 francs, including seed and fertilizers, to the value of the land, which is over 2,100 francs, is only about one in six—a very small proportion indeed.

This same farmer harvests about 2 tons of paddy from his 2 acres of land, but in this province, where large estates are fairly common,[1] half of this goes to pay his rent. Land and capitation taxes reduce the remaining ton by a fifth, and a similar sum is needed for the purchase of necessities, such as clothes and small items of farm equipment, which are less numerous, but almost as varied as in the holding at Nam-Xuong previously described. The remaining 12 cwt. will actually furnish only 8 cwt. of husked grain, and this is not enough to feed the family of six. Thus, one of the sons works in the cotton mill at Nam-Dinh, and his earnings are an essential part of the family income. Two others go to the upper Delta every year and are employed in the harvesting of the 'fifth-month' rice crop, which does not coincide with their own. The farmer's wife peddles a few miserable wares which are themselves the best indication of the abysmally low productivity of her efforts.

It is obvious that this family is financially insecure. It has to resort to borrowing to cover the cost of expensive ceremonies, such as a wedding or a burial, or to make good the slightest degree of crop failure which may result from the season being only a little too wet or too dry. As soon as this happens, its fate is sealed, for, with rates of interest at their current level, it will never be able to clear all its debts. Suggestions have been made in all seriousness that such families should try to accumulate enough money to buy additional land, but though the rich, whose fortunes multiply rapidly without any exertion on their part, can easily put such advice into practice, the poor, who have to scrape and save for years before buying a few hundred square yards, cannot. Indeed, a peasant could afford to enlarge his farm only if he had a run of several years without any unforeseen expenses whatsoever. The chances of this occurring are extremely remote, and even if the farmer were able to buy some extra land, his action would not escape the notice of the mandarin and other influential people; in the event, he would probably find that his taxes had been raised.

91. Nevertheless, such a family is still in a much more fortunate

---

[1] They are really common only in Cochin-China, where nearly half the area is in units of more than 250 acres. In any case, the large properties are rarely associated with farm units of commensurate size, for they are mostly rented by a large number of tenants, each of them with only a very small holding. The following table gives approximate figures for the Tonkin Delta before the recent war:

    900,000 landowners with less than 0·9 acres
    300,000 landowners with 0·9–4·5 acres
    80,000 landowners with 4·5–45 acres
    1,000 landowners with more than 45 acres

position than the landless labourer, who, in a densely populated or badly administered commune, can cultivate for himself only his own tiny share—a few hundred square yards—in the communal rice-fields. Thus his very small wage is none the less his main source of income. His services are required mainly at the seasonal peaks in the work on the land. Under-employment is a problem common to the whole of this overpopulated Delta, and Gourou has estimated that, on average, a peasant works no more than 125 days in the year. As we shall see, this 'hidden' unemployment is rife amongst other land-hungry peasant communities from the Mediterranean to Eastern Europe, from the microfundia of Brittany to those of Belgian Flanders.

If the whole province is short of food owing to a poor harvest, or when the farm labourer owes money to his employer, he is obliged to work in return for the bare price of his food. In the province of Bac-Ninh in 1929, we saw an argument between a large farmer, who also had a business in Hanoi, and his employees, who were working under these very conditions. The men claimed the right to save their evening meal to bring home to their families. Vu-Van-An, the farmer, resisted their claim, for quite rightly he argued that they would not be able to work so hard the following day. He was eventually forced to give way under the pressure of public opinion, for Annamite custom does not allow a man to be forbidden from denying himself for the sake of his family.

The general standard of living of the Tonkin peasant is thus very low. He counts himself lucky if he can eat his fill all the year round, more especially if rice and pulses form 90 per cent. of his diet. When food is short, he eats more tubers, such as taros and sweet potatoes, which are less easily digested; he adds herbs to his rice broth and consumes some of the bran normally fed to pigs and poultry. In the autumn of 1944 the crop was severely affected by sclerotic diseases, which were brought on by the exceptionally heavy rainfall, and the yields of the lower Delta were less than a third of the average. In normal times, rice could have been sent from Cochin-China, but at this period supply by sea was impossible and the railway had been cut. The peasants emigrated *en masse* towards the north of the Delta, and tens of thousands of them perished. In Honan in 1944 and in Bengal in 1943, the number of people who died of starvation has been estimated at 'between 1 and 2 million'. The memory of the children of Nge-An, whom we had seen dying of hunger in September 1931, came back abruptly one day as we were passing a beauty parlour for dogs on New York's Fifth Avenue.

POVERTY IN THE LOWER DELTA

The diet, poor in fats and proteins, is almost completely vegetarian.[1] At night all kinds of insects are caught, and subsequently cooked, as they are attracted by the lights. Fish and other small aquatic creatures are taken even from the smallest ponds. Paddy field rats are much appreciated at harvest-time, and there are various minor sources of animal food, like silk-worm larvae, etc. All these, however, according to Gourou, supply no more than a twentieth of the calories in the diet. Milk is unknown, and most of the eggs are sold at low prices for manufacturing purposes. Only the rich normally eat pork and poultry; more occasionally they may eat young dogs or buffaloes and oxen no longer needed for work in the fields. Ninety-four per cent. of the cereals consumed in the country were for human food, as against 14 per cent. in the United States; the lower figure is an unmistakable sign of a high standard of living.

The overpopulation of the deltas of monsoon Asia poses a problem very different from that of Central Africa, but one which is at least as difficult to resolve. Pierre Gourou has shown that in 1934 a typical poor Tonkinese family of five lived on 450 francs (Poincaré) per year, which was a sixth or a seventh of the average French peasant's income at the time. In our opinion, there is in fact a wider contrast than even these figures suggest. Gourou adds: 'The peasant population lives in stark poverty and on the verge of starvation . . . in penury, but not in despair.' In 1940 he wrote: 'The peasants of Tonkin, taken as a whole, are poor, and will remain so. . . . Any measures which prove effective in preventing the standard of living from falling can be considered to be crowned with success.' Even in 1936 he put forward the following opinion: 'In such an overcrowded country . . . it is too much to hope that plenty will ever be the order of the day.' Then, after suggesting that measures of land reform, which are not specified, should be put into effect 'as necessary', he issues the following warning: 'The moral and social stability of the region, the complex of traditions and customs which enables the peasant to endure his dreadfully wretched material existence, must in no wise be threatened. . . . What would become of a people who meditated upon their own infernal wretchedness? . . .'

[1] Gourou speaks, with some justice, of the 'vegetable civilization' of the Far East. The land provides food, shelter, clothing (cotton, silk, latania leaves for hats and rainproof clothing), and most of the traditional implements. Iron is used only for making teeth for harrows; the point of the ploughshare and the end of the hoe only have a covering of metal. Before the war Indochina consumed a mere 45 lb. of iron per head of the population, and the European community accounted for most of this. In China, consumption per head was only a hundredth of that in Great Britain.

It is fairly easy to resign oneself to the poverty of others. The fact that an eminent person who, far from being either a big business-man or a supporter of a 'firm' colonial policy, is a member of the French intellectual *élite*, could recommend as the principal remedy for their predicament 'the consolations of family and village life—that is to say, in many ways, of religious life', goes far in explaining the reasons for the revolt in Indochina.

5. Priority for Intensification: Water, Fertilizers, Type of Farming

92. The first need in this overcrowded country is to increase the productivity of the rare factor—that is, of the land itself. Every available weapon must be used in the difficult but not impossible struggle against want, and the poorer the region under consideration the more carefully must the order of priorities be determined. For instance, if it was intended to intensify the actual working of the land, the law of diminishing returns would very rapidly begin to operate, as it does in the case of the earth walls of Nam-Dinh. It is imperative, therefore, to discover the techniques which will delay the operation of this law as long as possible. The measures taken so far have rightly aimed at increased water control, and even before the war the diking of the land was satisfactory. In the upper Delta, production has already been raised, thanks to irrigation, by converting areas previously fallowed in the winter into double-cropped paddy land. On the other hand, it is debatable whether progress has really been made when perennial irrigation has been applied to areas which formerly grew dry crops in the cool season, as winter flooding for rice results in a greater degree of leaching. Then, again, in certain irrigation schemes, the dikes are inadequate and there is no network of drainage channels. The result is that only one crop can be taken every year, and even that not under the best conditions, for the water does not circulate freely and becomes stagnant.

A second stage of development was reached just before the war, when a start was made in draining the western part of the Delta. Previously this area was generally flooded throughout the summer, and rice could be grown only in the winter. The damming of the Day, a distributary of the Red, had the salutary effect of permitting the extension of 'tenth-month' rice on some very fertile soils. Other works extended the area available for the double-cropping of rice, notably in the coastal region, by constructing sluice valves and making use of the rise and fall of water with the tide. The greatest difficulties are in the intermediate zone, where draining away the water at the height of the flood, which is a most difficult problem, will have to be assisted by pumping, as in the Camargue.

The population was increasing by 100,000 a year before the war, and the programme of water control which was held up in 1940 was expected, rather optimistically, to keep agricultural production barely abreast of domestic requirements over the course of the next two decades. The pre-war pattern of development, limited as it was to irrigation and drainage schemes, was thus incapable of improving the standard of living to any appreciable extent. Paddy cultivation prevents erosion and lateritization, but it undoubtedly provokes the deterioration of the soil by leaching.

93. In the hope of putting a stop to the complete removal of rice straw and stubble from the fields for use as fuel, a practice which obviously reduces soil fertility, we suggested as long ago as 1934 that coal-dust from the mines near the Delta should be imported in barges and distributed at low prices. With more litter at the farmer's disposal, drainings would no longer be wasted and the amount of manure generally available would be considerably increased.

Sometimes the harvesting of a crop is still associated with three distinct field operations. First the ear and the top half of the stalk, which is used for fodder, are cut with an implement consisting of a curved piece of bamboo armed at one end with a small blade. The small proportion of straw cut in this manner means that the crop can be brought in much more quickly and the likelihood of theft, which is inevitable if food is scarce and sheaves are left out at night, is consequently reduced. After the crop has been brought in, threshed, and dried, the men return to the fields with sickles and cut the lower portion of the stalks about 3 or 4 inches from the ground; these are caked with mud and are used as fuel. Finally, if further supplies of fuel are needed, every tuft of stubble is uprooted by hand.

Unproductive techniques, less efficient even than those of an African collecting economy,[1] are everywhere forced on the peasant by poverty and necessity. His painful search for some means of fertilizing his land is underlined by the high price he is willing to pay for human excrement, often exceeding the value of the corresponding chemical fertilizers. Animal fodder, such as oil-seed residues and sometimes even

[1] It goes without saying that, in a countryside modified so profoundly by the action of man, collecting is entirely absent, although it does play a part in the economy of the interior.

articles of human food, are dug into the ground. We have seen soya beans being mixed with cinders to prevent the man charged with spreading them over the rice land from displaying more common sense than his employer and eating them himself. Vu-Van-An (para. 91, *supra*) acted more intelligently: he paid a hamlet to move, and on the abandoned site, now richly fertilized with every conceivable kind of refuse and offal, he planted his rice nurseries.

This 'fertilizer famine' could be assuaged by the growing of green manures, were it not for the fact that they would oust a similar acreage of food crops. Alternatively, the silt of the Red River, which carries a suspension load of 1-7 lb. per cubic yard, should be spread over the land whenever possible, and this could be done by warping in the summer, or sometimes in the autumn just after the harvest. The method, however, necessitates flooding, and its application is therefore limited by the density of population, but in winter silt could be dug from the dried-up bed of the main stream and taken wherever it was needed by water transport.[1] The main effort, however, must be directed towards the supply of chemical fertilizers. The apatite of Lao Kay appears to be a possible source of phosphates. The important falls of the Da-Nhim in southern Vietnam (24 cu. yds. per second, with a fall of 2,340 ft.) could be harnessed to produce 100,000 tons of calcium cyanamide a year at a low cost. The development of all the water power which could be economically harnessed would enable the whole country's agricultural requirements for nitrates to be satisfied quite easily, and there would, in addition, be an appreciable surplus of electricity for other uses.

As a result of a scheme which was put forward in 1928, we were asked to carry out experiments in the application of nitrates to rice cultivation in Tonkin. The results were positive, though not so marked as in temperate climates. However, as from 1930-1 the financial difficulties attached to the distribution of chemical fertilizers and the dumping of goods by the English and the Germans on the Chinese market resulted in the abandonment of this project. If the scheme was uneconomic by commercial standards, it was indispensable from the point of view of the welfare of the undernourished people of Indochina as a whole. In such circumstances, agriculture is more than ever a public service. Its first duty is to try to provide more food, but it cannot pay for imported fertilizers without depriving the country of much-needed quantities of rice. The shelving of the scheme is a good illustration of the thesis that private commercial interests may differ sharply from the

[1] For other possible solutions see our *La culture du riz dans le delta du Tonkin*.

public good. In 1940, the French Administration again showed interest in the scheme, but circumstances prevented any further progress.

A plan of this kind would have to provide for subsidies so that fertilizers could be distributed at less than cost price, and for credits so as to allow the farmer to wait until the harvest before settling his account, thus making him independent of the moneylender. It would not be worth using less than 25 lb. of nitrogen and about the same amount of phosphoric acid to the acre, and the total requirement for the 5 million acres of the Delta (allowing for double cropping and for an extension of the irrigated area) would be about 120,000 tons of these fertilizers. In this manner yields could be raised by nearly $2\frac{1}{2}$ cwt. per acre, thus adding a good 500,000 tons of paddy to the harvest each year. This would represent a very considerable increment, and an appreciable rise in the standard of living would be bound to follow. Further progress could then be based on this firm foundation.

94. Once irrigation had been extended and improved by more efficient drainage and other similar methods, and once large quantities of chemical fertilizers were available for use, attention could then be directed to the development of varieties of rice which, though more exacting in their requirements, are capable of giving heavier yields. Without a thorough study of plant genetics, the full benefits of the heavy expenses already suggested would never be felt, and a serious beginning had already been made in this field. It should be possible, for instance, to modify the present system of rice monoculture. Transplanted rice is admittedly a hardy crop, well adapted to poor soils, economical in seed, and it can be double-cropped. Also it provides a most valuable food which is in great demand and which can be prepared with much less fuel than would be needed for bread. The latter is an important consideration in countries like this, where fuel is in very short supply.

Rice will long continue to be the best crop in poorly drained, clayey hollows where its only serious rival is the taro. On higher ground with well-drained, light but poor soils it should be possible, after the general level of fertility and particularly the humus content have been raised, to do away with cereal monoculture. This now accounts for 90 per cent. of the cultivated land in Tonkin, but no matter where it is practised the returns are only moderate, although it is only fair to add that rice and maize have greater possibilities than the other grains.

It is not possible to think in terms of the introduction to this region, with its 'horticultural' and man-powered system of farming, of the type of intensification based on fodder crops which has been practised in Western Europe over the course of the last two or three centuries. Assuming for the moment that direct yields of food and fodder crops are comparable in bulk, it takes five to ten times the amount of the latter in the form of animal feeding-stuffs to produce the same number of calories as the former. To obtain the same number of calories from animal food as are already available from cereals, the cultivated area would therefore have to be multiplied between five and ten times. China devotes 85 per cent. of her cultivated land to food for direct human consumption; the Tonkin Delta, 97 per cent.; in the United States 85 per cent. of the land is devoted to various fodder crops. Though they may hanker after meat, the Chinese and the Annamites are equally ignorant when it comes to milk production; they regard the consumption of milk and its derivatives, especially fermented cheeses, or 'rotten milk' as they call them, as degrading. Grasslands on the Dutch model are thus out of the question. Heavily manured row crops, however, analogous to the potatoes and sugar-beet of Flanders and grown for direct consumption, could, under optimum conditions of soil and water supply, give between twice and six times as many calories per unit area as a high-yielding strain of rice. They could thus save the country from the dangerous stranglehold of rice monoculture. The crops which suggest themselves at once are sugar cane, manioc, taro, and sweet potatoes, and the more they are studied the greater will be their value to the country. We have shown in our description of the traditional methods of rice cultivation that, apart from certain modern contributions relating to fertilizers and genetics, they are remarkably appropriate to the conditions: surface sowing after germination, drying of the soil in low walls, transplanting, supply of water to the fields, etc. The techniques are not at present nearly so satisfactory where row crops are concerned.

There are very many varieties of rice adapted to different conditions. They vary in the length of their growing season, in their resistance to diseases, and in their tolerance of salinity and depth of flood water (e.g. floating rice). In contrast, much less attention has been given to the improvement of other crops, with the possible exceptions of tea and mulberry, for French scientists concentrated in the first instance on export crops. About 1930 they turned their attention to rice, but have done little to improve other food plants which were erroneously thought to be of secondary importance.

It has been shown in the United States that there are great possibilities in the improvement of the sweet potato. The great strides which have been made in the improvement of sugar cane since 1880, especially

PRIORITY FOR INTENSIFICATION

as a result of Dutch work at Pasoeroan in Java, are well known. On the other hand, in Indochina before the war, European-owned sugar plantations were so strongly protected that domestic consumption was very much reduced. A large proportion of the cane can be consumed directly, like licorice; or syrup can be made from it by a simple process of evaporation, although costs of transport necessarily confine this product to local markets. The rather crude factories which make this product, however, waste an important fraction of the sugar and also consume the bagasse—from which cellulose could be extracted—as fuel.

As these alternative crops are not so rich as rice in vegetable proteins, their extension could be accompanied by that of various leguminous food crops, such as soya (quick-growing varieties), beans and various species of dolichas, which would make up the deficiency.

These then are the main possibilities for a more varied type of farming. There would be more attention to vegetables and fruits, and rotations of summer rice and irrigated winter roots or pulses could be established on the higher ground. From time to time a whole year would be devoted to sugar cane in the better-drained areas.

95. The Vietnamese peasant's lot could also be improved by growing industrial crops either for export or for reducing the country's dependence on imports. The chances of extending the cultivation of cotton, another 500,000 acres of which would be needed merely to satisfy the home market, appear to be brighter in the interior of Tonkin and in the southern part of the peninsula than in the Delta itself. Enough jute could be grown for local needs. At the request of Lyons industrialists, French agricultural services had concentrated their efforts on silk production, which provides more than twice as much work per acre than rice, but they were not able to arrest its decline.

Tobacco, even more than tea and spices, is the crop of densely populated regions where there is an acute shortage of land. Thus it seems to be particularly appropriate to this region and its cultivation was encouraged in areas of rich soils, but the selected districts were too near the sea and the soil was somewhat saline. Moreover, labour was very wastefully employed, and in one instance a family with two children, who were given outside help every season when the ground had to be prepared, could only look after $\frac{1}{6}$ acre—no wonder when the aphides were picked off the leaves one by one with a sticky ball of rice! As much as 600 days of labour was being devoted to every acre, as compared with forty to 100 in the United States and sixty to 180 in France. In spite of these efforts, the tobacco is of fairly poor quality, as it receives too much human manure and is sometimes spoilt by salinity in the soil. Moreover, it is better suited to the manufacture of pipe rather than cigarette tobacco, an unfortunate coincidence in view of the modern tendency to favour the latter. Notwithstanding these adverse factors, the nature of the problem could be entirely changed by more careful curing, the adoption of improved strains and the use of modern methods generally.[1]

P. Gourou suggested that soil-less cultivation might be tried in cement vats containing plant foods in solution. Such measures, however, would represent too high a degree of intensiveness and cannot be said to merit a very high priority, for they would give too little benefit in return for the large capital outlay required. They must wait until circumstances become more favourable. On the other hand, as a long-term policy, the large-scale export of basic food commodities—cereals and oil seeds especially—from overpopulated Asia to Europe, whose purchasing power has in any case greatly declined, must be brought to an end. The rice which Indochina could not retain before the war for the nourishment of her own people deserved a better fate than to be fed to our calves, our pigs, and our poultry. In the matter of oil-seeds, it is a significant fact that soap is practically unheard of in the villages of northern Vietnam, not because cleanliness is disregarded —quite the contrary—but because of its price.

96. There remains the question of the integration of holdings (which has resulted in a 15 per cent. increase in production in Japan) and that of mechanization, which we have purposely refrained from discussing until now. With regard to the latter, the people could adapt themselves more quickly to the use of mechanical power than the African native. The wholesale introduction of Californian methods of rice cultivation would reduce the number of workdays per acre from eighty to two, but with the present lack of manufacturing industry all the equipment and fuel would have to be imported and most of the rice exported to pay for them. Furthermore, practically the whole population would be left unemployed. To use overpopulation as an excuse for keeping out the machine would, however, be an even more serious mistake. The important principle in the early stages is to propose only those measures which are likely to lead to larger harvests and heavier yields. The most urgent need of all is the pumping station, which would greatly improve the degree of water control by facilitating drainage and by avoiding the need to build irrigation canals so high. The latter

[1] Many other crops also deserve consideration, and we have merely attempted to mark out certain broad lines of possible development. So wide a subject cannot, for obvious reasons, be treated fully in a work of this kind.

INDUSTRIALIZATION, EMIGRATION, BIRTH-CONTROL

would mean that unproductive sections of feeder canals previously required to give a head of water could be dispensed with.

The most convenient source of power, which the Delta is destined to develop sooner or later, would be electricity, which could easily be generated by using the screenings from the coalfields, which are close enough to make power transmission to the densely populated lowlands an economic proposition. An electricity grid would enable the grain to be threshed, husked, and polished with the help of small machines driven by electric motors similar to the ones used in Japan. The region would be mercifully released from its dependence on animal power in its present form. The tendency would be for a drastic reduction in the number of draught animals, which would be used, co-operatively in the case of very small farms,[1] for a much longer season, and they would begin to take their share of other work, especially in transport and the raising of water. The severe pressure of work during the 'fifth-month' harvest could be greatly alleviated by the use of animals or power-driven machinery.

In the next stage of development, electric tractors on the Russian model could render invaluable service, especially where, through lack of animals, the soil had not been thoroughly worked, or where the ground was right for ploughing only during a very short period, as in the clayey districts of the lower Delta, where the soil is now heaped into low walls to dry. The tractors could be worked almost continuously, even at night, to make up for any drastic reduction that might occur in the number of draught animals. They would enable land to be ploughed quickly at the right time, when the soil was dry, and could even be used to break up fallows on really heavy soils. Tractors could be used to make inroads into areas as yet uncleared and to bring back into cultivation land which has been more or less abandoned on the northern margins of the Delta. They would certainly be a factor of the utmost significance in increasing overall production. As in China, mechanization is most urgently needed in the higher areas of low population density. The scythe alone, which we have tried to introduce, would be a great advance on the sickle, but small mechanical reapers will soon be needed where the peak demand for labour in the 'fifth-month' harvest is very pronounced (Chapter XV).

6. Industrialization, Emigration, and Birth-control

97. Modern equipment, such as pumps, tractors, combines, mills,

[1] For an example of this in practice, see Chapter V, section 6.

and driers, will never be generally available in the Delta unless most of it can be manufactured *in situ*—that is, unless manufacturing industry becomes established. The coal and iron resources which are present favour the development of heavy metallurgical works. Everywhere in the world, but more particularly in this region even as compared with Africa, industrialization is an essential factor both in the provision of up-to-date machinery for overcrowded rural areas and in the productive employment of their surplus population. The people of Annam are very adept at acquiring new skills and have already shown a capacity, greater than that of Negroid peoples, for adapting themselves to the conditions of modern industry. Metropolitan industrial interests remained until 1940 an obstacle to progress in this direction, but in the present circumstances the equipping of the region should not be confined to the agricultural sector of the economy. We are not qualified to treat the topic of industrialization at greater length, but it is none the less a basic factor in all questions of economic progress, rural and general.

There are larger possibilities for development and a far greater economic potential outside the Tonkin Delta. This is after all a region of only moderate fertility which is farmed much more intensively than the physical conditions warrant owing to the excessive density of its population. It is, moreover, a region where the law of decreasing returns is already operative. As capital for industrial purposes can be accumulated but slowly from indigenous sources and only in limited quantities from abroad, a rapid movement of people from the Delta towards the south of the country would appear to offer a good prospect of immediate relief. There is room for rice-cultivating settlers in a number of low-lying plains—in western Cochin-China for example—which could be made even more attractive if further efforts were devoted to measures of effective water control. In Cambodia, the soils are generally in an advanced stage of deterioration, but the environs of Lake Tonle are an exception, for they comprise some very fertile but underdeveloped land, and these features are repeated in the lowlands of Laos. Until recently the incursions of Annamite 'invaders', who have been expanding towards the south and west for centuries, have been curbed by officialdom out of consideration for the Cambodians, Laotians, and mountain peoples, who were regarded as being more 'docile'.

Finally, there is a great future for the uplands, from southern Annam to Cambodia, wherever there are basic rocks or where soils on downwash material have been enriched with bases by percolating water from the plateaux above. The prospects here are much more promising than in similar areas in equatorial Africa. Emigration to such new lands with a view to the cultivation of industrial and export crops is the surest way, in spite of the expense and other inherent difficulties, of providing for a rapid increase in the productivity of the now very much under-employed surplus population of the Delta. Indochina, like Siam, has not yet emerged from the 'cereal stage', and exports only rice and a little rubber; these are features which point to economic backwardness. More progress has been made in Malaya, where more equipment is available, and the only exports are rubber, palm oil, and other produce from the large modern plantations. Indonesian agriculture has reached a similarly advanced stage of development under Dutch impetus.

The opening up of the interior of Indochina has so far been the work of plantation companies protected by the French Administration, which, although it took great care to endow the plantations with a transport network, signally failed, unlike the British and the Dutch, to encourage the commercial aspirations of the native peoples. As far as rice is concerned, there is little that one can teach the Annamite peasant, but the high plateaux are more suited to tree-planting than to growing grain, which could be imported from the lowlands to the south. Modern plantations cannot be managed haphazardly and, because of the paramount importance of the fight against pests and disease, the purely native enterprise cannot hope to succeed in growing tung, tea, rubber, or even coffee and cinchona. This seems to warrant the adoption of some form of directed peasant farming, which would ensure that the accepted rules of plant protection are properly observed.

Until now the French have thought only of export crops. A government anxious to raise the standard of living would have tried to stimulate meat production and would have attempted to improve the rearing industry of Cambodia, where cattle are less remarkable for their usefulness than for their numbers. Indeed, the position is reminiscent of India and, as herdsmen, the natives are less painstaking and consequently less efficient than the Annamites and the Chinese. The essential conditions for any development in this direction are in any case the establishment of better communications and effective control of malaria. The transformation of marshy basins into irrigated rice-lands would also rid the area of shifting *ray* cultivation, which often degrades the soil if it remains too long in the same place or if it is practised on steep slopes.

98. The combined effect of all these remedies will be nullified if the

curve of population growth rises too rapidly. We have already seen (Chapter I) that for any given stage of economic development the standard of living seems to have a better chance of improving if an enlightened policy of birth-control is pursued. The aim would be to bring about a lowering of the birth-rate so as to offset the reduction in the mortality rate resulting from more hygienic living conditions. The elimination of a proportion of girls at birth, with which the Chinese have so often been reproached, and the abortion and infanticide which were formerly encouraged in Japan, had this same object of relieving the pressure of population.

The expectation of life in India today is the same as it was in France at the beginning of the eighteenth century—about twenty-six. If a rapid rise in this figure, due to an initial improvement in nutritional standards, were to take place, and this was combined with a lowering of infant mortality (now 20 per cent. in China in the first year) to a rate comparable with that of English-speaking countries, the results would be positively explosive unless there were parallel reductions in the birth-rate. Even if all the measures to increase agricultural production which have been reviewed were put into effect, and whatever the economic structure, there would follow a long period when the food supply was constantly being outstripped by the growth of population. The agricultural scientist cannot be held responsible if this catastrophe, which even now is silently gathering strength, befalls the world.

Before the war the Tonkin Delta had a mean birth-rate of 38 per 1,000 and an annual net increase of 15 per 1,000. At this rate, it could double its population in less than fifty years. Moreover, per head of rural population, there was $\frac{1}{2}$ acre of agricultural land as compared with 7·5 acres (including grassland) in France.

About four-fifths of the population of the Delta are directly dependent on the land. The resources of the land are exploited moderately efficiently and most intensively in terms of human effort. The yields per acre, less than $\frac{3}{5}$ ton of unthreshed grain, or two-thirds of this quantity of white rice, are moderate, but reckoned against hours of work they are extremely low. We invite the conservatives who try by every means in their power, but to no avail, to retain a high proportion of the population of France in agricultural pursuits to compare the standard of living of the work-worn peasant of northern Vietnam with that of the Corn Belt farmer of the United States, where only 15 per cent. of the total population is rural. The latter may not employ many men, but he has an impressive array of mechanical equipment at his disposal.

7. Progress in China More Rapid than in India[1]

99. Even though the population of China is said to have increased by less than 1 per cent. per year since the sixteenth century, there are now only $\frac{3}{10}$ acre of cultivated land per head of the total population in the southern half of the country as compared with $1\frac{1}{2}$ acres 400 years ago. Under Mao Tse-tung, who, for a revolutionary, has an exceptional knowledge of the problems of the peasantry owing to his long sojourn among them in Yunnan, the measures taken by the Government generally conform with Communist doctrine. Rents and rates of interest[2] were brought down first, and then a start was made with land reforms, which actually preceded the collectivization of the factories. The property of the large landowners and some of the land belonging to rich peasants was distributed among the rural population. The Government refrained from dealing too severely with the well-to-do peasant class, who customarily farmed their own land, for fear of aggravating the general state of disorganization which had been brought on by the war.

In the third stage of reform the aim is to get the land farmed communally by setting up producer's co-operatives; so far (early 1953) progress along these lines seems to have been limited to the formation of mutual aid societies.[3] In the U.S.S.R. and eastern Europe the appearance of these generally coincides with the arrival of the tractor, and this tangible evidence of technical progress, which is identified by the people with the general reorganization of production, makes them more acceptable.

Whereas birth-control is condemned with ever-increasing vigour in the U.S.S.R.—a logical enough policy in view of the huge areas still awaiting colonization—we shall be most interested to see where the Chinese Government, whose problems are vastly different, will take its stand in this matter. Admittedly, there are large unsettled areas in the interior. The mediocre quality of their soils and the damage already done by erosion will, however, often prescribe an extensive type of utilization; for afforestation or nomadic stock rearing certainly cannot

---

[1] See *L'homme et la terre en Extrême-Orient*, by P. Gourou, and, for a more general view of present-day conditions, *La Chine du nationalisme au communisme*, by J. J. Brieux, and *L'Inde devant l'orage*, by Tibor Mende.

[2] Interest rates are limited to 10-15 per cent.; where a debtor had already repaid twice as much as the sum originally borrowed, his debt was annulled.

[3] By mid-1952 there were said to be ten collective farms and 317 State farms (forty-one of them mechanized), which together accounted for 95,000 acres of cultivated land.

employ the manpower which the machine will liberate from the older-settled river lowlands. On the other hand, the absorption of labour by manufacturing industry is bound to be fairly gradual.

100. In those parts of Indochina controlled by Vietminh, similar efforts have been made to achieve a more democratic distribution of the land, and the first step was to set aside a basic minimum for peasants who formerly had no land. Rents were lowered by 25 per cent., so that if a peasant previously paid half his harvest he now paid only three-eighths; and old debts were cancelled. At the same time the large concessions of 'stolen' land have, in the absence of legislative measures, been provisionally divided among the poor *métayers* and peasants. Permission has also been given to clear new land without previous reference to the forestry service; this is likely to aggravate the danger from erosion in mountainous districts.

The struggle for 'national unity' has delayed the arrival of a full-scale agrarian reform. Instead, the landowners, animated to some extent by the Government, have made 'voluntary' offers of land. In 1952 for the first time the administration prepared an annual production plan based on the individual plans which each peasant family was asked to draw up for itself. The head of the family then signed a contract undertaking to sow so much rice, to rear, say, a pig and twenty chickens or a sow and her litter in collaboration with two other families, etc. Mutual help in clearing the harvest as quickly as possible, and small water-control schemes, anything more ambitious being out of the question in wartime, were also encouraged.

The direct effects of the fighting in Indochina must also be considered. Draught animals, native farm equipment, and other factors of production appear to be regarded as legitimate military objectives; oxen and buffaloes are killed in the course of air raids and mopping-up operations, rice crops are laid low by amphibious vehicles, irrigation and drainage channels are blocked up. If this kind of thing really did happen, the agronomist is bound to deplore in the strongest possible terms the enlistment of famine as a weapon of war. Already in 1931, as a result of a revolt in Nghe-An, supplies to this province were stopped and the people died of hunger in their thousands.[1] Somewhat tardily the Government of Bao Dai has issued an order reducing the level of rents, but the date of this announcement, May 1953, betrays the influence of the turn of military events.

[1] As we had come to Indochina as agronomists, to help in the fight against hunger—the food position was particularly critical here—we were unable to associate ourselves with such measures, even as tacit onlookers.

101. In the French enclave of Karikal in the south-eastern part of the Deccan lies the commune of Negoundagou, where Ramassamyayar has a farm of 40 acres (7 *vely*, 6 *mas*[1]) on the Cauvery Delta. Of this, 17·5 acres give two crops of rice per year, one grown from September to February and the other from late March to July. A single winter crop is obtained from 22·5 acres and another 5 acres are used for the nursery sowings before being planted to rice themselves. These 45 acres of fertile land—on some farms there are three crops of rice—are generally clayey, and are irrigated direct from the river. There is ½ acre of casuarina coppice which is cut every five or six years, on some sandy ground; ⅔ acre of medium-light/non-rice land is devoted to leguminous crops, like mung beans and dhal (*Cajanus indicus*), which depend entirely on rainfall, and at some distance from the village an area of about the same extent is left uncleared. Along the river and subject to the vagaries of the annual floods there is ½ acre of coconut palms, which provide 800 nuts[2] and 1,000 leaves, which are bound together and used for roofing. Finally, next to the palms there is a vegetable patch which covers ⅙ acre.

For draught purposes there are eight pairs of oxen, which is almost one beast for every 3 acres. In addition to these there are two cows in milk and two female buffaloes; the greater part of the milk is sold and fetches about 1 rupee a day. Stock-rearing is generally based on various forms of arrangement between the owner of the animals and the herdsman. For instance, the calves are often divided between them, each taking a half-share. When there is little work to be done on the land, from the beginning of March to mid-June, the herdsmen often look after the herd for nothing. This is a poor time of the year for forage, and the animals have to survive as best they can on the poor scrub. But the herdsmen are paid by the owners of the rice-fields where they bring the cattle at night, and they spread the manure over the land in the morning before they leave. Naturally, the farmer who manages his herds in this manner reaps no benefit from their manure and chemical fertilizers are debarred by their price.

The equipment comprises a single cart which serves to carry green manures, farmyard manure (180 loads, or about 80 tons, spread over 25 acres), and paddy. In addition, there are sixteen ploughs with their beams, half of them, or one per pair of oxen, for dry ploughing after

---

[1] 1 *vely*=20 *mas*=6·68 acres.

[2] Near the towns, sap is tapped from the trees and, after fermenting, toddy is made from it. When prohibition laws were passed in Madras, the caste which had specialized in this work found itself shorn of its only resource.

the harvest, and the eight others, smaller in size, for working in the flooded rice-fields. Two iron implements for digging ditches and about ten hoes (one per labourer) for levelling comprise the tools for use in the rice-fields, and there are ten hand-barrows for carrying spoil and manure. The preparation of the soil is completed by drawing two planks with a man standing on them, over the ground. They are reminiscent of the Piedmontese *spianone* and perform the work for which a European farmer would employ a roller. Finally, there are about ten sickles, fifteen sacks for paddy, four billhooks, two axes, two buckets, three watering-cans, measures, etc.

102. The personnel includes a driver, a foreman, ten labourers, and twelve women (generally their wives), who may be anything between twenty and sixty years of age, and two young cowherds between ten and fifteen; altogether, a labour force of twenty-six, fourteen of whom work full-time. The men work ten hours a day, from six till twelve and two till six; the women, who bring their husbands' midday meals to the fields, from ten till six. The oxen, however, are incapable of working more than five hours a day. During the course of the year, the men are employed full-time for eight months, not at all for two, and only sporadically with seven hours' work a day for the remainder. There is regular work for the women for only three months in the year: during transplanting and weeding and to some extent during the harvest.

Each worker is paid in kind and receives a bonus of a twelfth of the grain he harvests, making a total for the year of 36 gallons of paddy plus a gratuity of about 40 rupees.[1] If he wants to work overtime, as he must if he has a large family to support, he can earn about another 30 rupees a year by doing a fourteen-hour day at busy times of the year. Taking the most favourable case possible, a family of three will need 20 gallons of paddy a year; the remaining 16 can be sold for 140 rupees. An actual cash income of 176 rupees, which is well above average, is very soon accounted for: clothing, 35; spices and miscellaneous items, 72; doctor, 3; alcoholic liquor made from rice or coconut sap, 60. These expenses bring the family to the brink of penury, and they will have to resort to the moneylender every time there is a feast day.[2]

[1] 1 rupee=1s. 6d. (All prices refer to 1951-2.)

[2] Girod observes that there were still *pannéals*, who were little better than serfs, in Pondicherry in 1937. They were very badly paid, but were at least sure of their food. The coolies, on the other hand, were often in debt and sometimes even on the verge of starvation. He quotes 12 gallons of paddy as the equivalent of the average income per rural inhabitant.

The farmer himself has reaped 2,100 gallons, or 63 tons, of rice from 62 acres (allowing for double-cropping), which is very much more than the average for the region. Moreover, the farm is in the rich, irrigated delta country and is relatively well managed. His family of six consumes 60 gallons, 70 are needed for seed, 160 for wages during cultivation, and 130 under the same item at the harvest. Another 30 go to the keeper and for various dues, and a further 200 are needed to pay the running expenses of the farm. The remaining 1,450 gallons are sold for about 9,000 rupees, animal produce fetches 360 rupees, while dry crops, orchards, gardens, and woods, after the needs of the family have been catered for, are worth about 250 rupees a year.

Of this, Ramassamyayar spends some 400 rupees in gratuities and bonuses to his men, 100 on female labour for transplanting, 850 for cotton seed, oil-cakes, and rice bran for his animals; he pays 400 to herdsmen for manure on his rice land and for carting manure, and 200 for the maintenance and repair of buildings and equipment. The purchase of cattle costs 200 rupees, land taxes account for 350, and loans made to workers who leave before paying them back—a risk he is bound to take —mount up to about 100 rupees a year. To this total bill of 2,600 rupees, the farmer adds 8 per cent. interest on his working capital, estimated at 5,000 rupees, and 5 per cent. on his fixed capital at 90,000 rupees. Taking this into account, he has a narrow margin of profit, but these last two items do not, of course, represent any disbursement of money.[1] The ratio of eighteen to one between these two items reveals both the scarcity of land and the paucity of the equipment. Ramassamyayar and his family spend 500 rupees a year on clothes, 600 for spices and miscellaneous items, 100 in medical expenses, and 200 on amusements— mainly travelling and visits to the cinema. The whole picture is one of a very much greater contrast between the living standards of employer and employees than one would find, say, on a Breton farm of comparable size.

103. The Indian Union is the scene of one of the most dramatic demographic situations in the world today. Its population increase was in the region of 26,000,000 for the quinquennium 1948-52.[2] The population of Bengal alone rose from 36,000,000 in 1881 to 68,000,000 in

[1] This holding is owner-farmed. The same is true of a quarter of the agricultural land in Pondicherry; half of it is farmed by tenants, in which case nearly 50 per cent. of the harvest goes to the owner; under the *métayage* system he receives a full half share unless the *métayer* has to raise water from the well by hand, when he receives only a third.

[2] 304,000,000 inhabitants in 1937, 364,000,000 in 1951—plus 75,000,000 in Pakistan.

1952, in spite of a dreadful famine in 1943 and a civil war when Pakistan was formed. The demise of the Indian craftsmen, intentionally provoked by British industrial interests, has been followed by a most undesirable return to the land. Combined with the very slow rate of industrialization, this has led to a rise in the overall percentage of rural population. This is exactly the reverse of what is happening today in the more prosperous countries of the world, but we shall encounter the same trend in southern Italy, which is another region where economic retrogression is in evidence. In India the average size of holdings is declining rapidly. In a village near Poona, between the eighteenth century and the present day the average acreage has fallen from 40 to 4. In a group of 2,400 Punjab villages, 18 per cent. of the holdings are of less than 1 acre, 26·5 per cent. vary between 1 and 3 acres, 15 per cent. between 3 and 5 acres, and 18 per cent. between 5 and 10 acres. In the United Provinces, Assam and Bihar and Orissa, the mean acreage varies from $2\frac{1}{2}$ to 3 acres, and over half the holdings are actually smaller than the former figure. Seventy-three million Indian peasants cultivate a smaller area than the 8,000,000 farmers of the United States and obtain yields less than half as great. In some provinces the average expectation of life is actually tending to decrease and has in certain cases fallen from thirty to twenty-three during the last fifty years.

As two-thirds of India's peasantry are either completely lacking in land or possess too little of it, they are severely under-employed. In fact, they may be idle for 100 or even up to 200 days, depending on whether they grow two crops a year or not. Apart from a few days of really arduous work, they are even then only partly occupied for the remainder of the year. 'Overpopulation is a paramount factor in the poverty of Pondicherry. Coolies are never employed more than part-time and have no means of subsistence outside the season of farm work.' So writes P. Girod.[1] One can look forward to a better future only if the agrarian situation is changed. A landowning peasantry—practically unknown in Africa, but now growing in strength in the Far East— must be firmly established, and more use must be made of animals— more, for instance, than in southern China—for such purposes as transport, threshing, and raising water.

In fact, the rice yield of $\frac{1}{2}$ ton per acre is barely half the Chinese average, cotton yields are a quarter of those of the United States, and sugar cane yields only a fifth of the Javanese. There is nothing in Indian agriculture that one may even describe as semi-intensive, for human

[1] *L'agriculture et l'hydraulique agricole dans le territoire de Pondicherry* (Pondicherry, 1938).

manure is very little used and oil-cake[1] is used almost as sparingly. Half the cattle dung is employed, as in the Sahara or the marshlands of Poitou, for fuel. And, worst of all, the population is rising while yields of rice and sugar cane are actually falling.

There are 136,000,000 cattle, which represents a fifth of the world total; 40,000,000 buffaloes, or two-thirds of the world total. Though these animals would represent wealth in Western Europe or North America, here they are a liability, and are one of the factors contributing to the economic situation in India today. The immense population of animals furnishes little in the way of power and only provides a very small quantity of milk—perhaps 45 gallons per cow per annum once a calf has been weaned. Religious prejudice forbids both slaughtering and the consumption of meat, and total meat production is consequently less than, for instance, in the United Kingdom. Forage has to be found for millions of useless animals the vast majority of which are either diseased, old, extraordinarily emaciated, and, perhaps worst of all, completely unproductive. The Hindu religion decrees that they must be fed. A man is forbidden to turn them away from his field or from his patch of vegetables, and they are thus in direct competition with the human population for the available food supply. Old men may die on the roads, but old cows are cared for in charitable institutions maintained by the devout. By the same token one finds that the killing of pests is sometimes forbidden: rats, for example, which destroy a large proportion of both standing crops and stored grain; and even monkeys and occasionally, cobras.

Social conditions have been aggravated by the British conquest. The collection of taxes was left to the *zamindars*, who had performed the same services for the Moguls. Now they also received handsome estates, and by virtue of this newly usurped property they were able to extract exorbitant rents as well, without generally effecting any improvements to the land. A farmer must pay a tax even if he wants to dig a well or plant a tree, and he is sure to have to move if he improves his land. When he borrows money at extortionate rates of interest, he has to hand over an ox—in all probability the only draught animal he possesses —as a pledge. If a drought follows and he cannot repay, he becomes an outcast and has little chance of ever rising again in the social scale.

Instead of being reinvested for productive purposes, the majority of the levies on production are spent on gold and precious stone ornaments, which are the accepted marks of social prestige. There are still

[1] It would be better employed as animal feeding-stuffs or even, in the case of ground-nut residues, for human consumption.

large areas awaiting development in the north of the peninsula. More can be done to avert the dangers of drought, although the British have carried through some splendid irrigation schemes. But even these have not enabled food production to keep pace with population growth, and this is a problem which cannot be solved in the absence of an integrated policy of technical progress and economic reform. Most of our conclusions relating to northern Vietnam seem to be applicable here.

104. The future of the world depends partly on the form of government which is destined to undertake fundamental agrarian reforms, not only in Indochina, but in India, where, according to one estimate, the average number of calories in the diet has fallen from 2,200 to 1,600 during the course of a century. In India a prime requisite is that the country should emancipate itself from the religious prejudice which now accounts for the enormous number of livestock constituting such a drag on the economy. Ambitious schemes for irrigation and the like must be remorselessly pursued if the country's future is to be assured, but their full effect will never be felt unless this occurs. Finally, too little attention appears to have been given to the question of fertilizers, which are an indispensable adjunct to the fruition of all programmes of agrarian improvement.

The national income is small and static—only about £20 per head per annum—and from this, taken in conjunction with a virtually feudal social structure, it follows that the accumulation of capital for investment must be extremely slow. The aid provided for in the Colombo Plan, to which the United States also later contributed, is quite inadequate. Quick and impressive results can only be brought about by means which depart entirely from conventional capitalist practices. The better utilization of local resources of fertilizers is already improving the agricultural situation, and is ridding the country of a bottle-neck which has restricted production for many years.

Monsoon Asia's greatest source of wealth is her huge population. The main cause of her backwardness is the inefficient employment of this labour force. Human work is a perishable commodity which cannot be recouped tomorrow if it is not used today. Even without modern equipment, the resumption of certain types of work by the peasants during the seasons of under-employment on the land would represent a net gain and a productive exploitation of a natural source of wealth. Applied to large schemes of irrigation, drainage, and flood control, this work would rapidly raise the level of food production and increase the amount of work which could be performed by a better-fed labour force the following year; the ascending spiral of production would definitely have begun.

Poorer than India in mechanical equipment, China nevertheless mobilized a force of 120,000,000 men and women in this manner between 1950 and 1952 in order to pursue schemes of land improvement. In spite of certain shortcomings in the execution of the various tasks performed, 'the era of great famines in China appears to have come to an end. The floods which used to destroy the crops of whole provinces are apparently now no longer to be feared. The progress of irrigation is reducing the danger from drought. Millions of acres of new land suitable for cultivation have been discovered. Agricultural techniques are being modernized, new lines of communication are linking up the remotest provinces.... Hundreds of millions of men will be able to eat their fill.'[1]

Since these lines were written, the pace of collectivization in the Chinese countryside has greatly increased. During the winter of 1955-6, the proportion of peasants who were members of co-operatives (either 'semi-socialist' co-operatives where land-owners still receive rent payments or 'socialist' co-operatives where only labour is paid) increased from 15 to 92 per cent. In no other country in the world, and certainly not in the East European people's democracies, has collectivization been so rapid. Our impression, however, is that the Chinese peasant accepted this change better than his counterpart in East Europe and he still remained thankful to the Party for ridding him of excessive rent and usury. The average annual rate of increase of agricultural production during the last five years has probably amounted to between 3 and 3·5 per cent. while population has been growing at about 2 per cent. annually (more than one million per month). (See our recent book, *Révolution dans les campagnes chinoises*, Editions du Seuil, Paris, 1957.)

[1] H. Jomin, '*La Chine au seuil de son premier plan quinquennal*' in the March 1953 number of the *Revue de l'Action Populaire*.

V

Sheep and Cereals, Trees and Water in North Africa[1]

1. Mediterranean Aridity and the Dangers of Erosion

105. In the popular imagination, tropical Africa is a land of virgin forest and the Mediterranean is encircled by verdant oases. Admittedly there are quite a number of fresh green lowlands, but the rainfall is mostly concentrated on the upland massifs: Kabylia in Algeria, Kroumirie in Tunisia, the Moroccan Rif, and Middle Atlas. The topography is often too rugged to permit full advantage to be taken of the precipitation, which decreases rapidly towards the south. This is especially true of Tunisia, which is virtually arid beyond the highland backbone terminating at Cape Bon. In Algeria, low rainfall and high altitudes combine, so that agriculture is subjected not only to the danger of summer drought, but also to the rigours of winter cold and high ranges of temperature.

The extensive and luxuriant oases of North Africa are actually found, not in the overcrowded palm-groves of the desert, which are very limited in extent, but in the lowlands along the coast, where they are irrigable or well-watered, or even in sub-littoral plains, although here the climate is already less favourable. Some of these lowlands actually suffer from an excess of water during the heavy winter rains, and for this reason the Mitidja, lower Cheliff, and Bone lowlands in Algeria were developed only after the completion of considerable drainage works. The Moroccan Gharb and lower Medjerda in Tunisia are in

[1] Seven journeys and thirteen months of residence between 1923 and 1949. Throughout this work our attention was focused on the problems involved in the modernization of native agriculture. Our published works include: '*L'agriculture marocaine en péril*' (*Economie contemporaine*, December 1947); Report to Jean Monnet, Commisaire général du Plan (June 1949), portions of which were published in *Economie contemporaine* and *Observation Economique* in June 1949; the chapter '*Les données agricoles*' in *Industrialisation de l'Afrique du Nord*, published in 1952 by Colin for the Centre d'études de politique étrangère. For a general geographical survey, see *L'Afrique du Nord*, by Jean Despois (1949).

process of being drained at the present. The coastal plain reaches an appreciable width only on the Atlantic flank of Morocco; this is also the best-watered lowland, and the only one where the rivers still have an appreciable flow at low water. The Sebou, for example, still has a flow of 18 cu. yds. per second and the Oum er R'bia 48, as compared with a minimum of about 1 cu. yd. per second at the mouth of the Cheliff or of less than 4 on the Medjerda. Morocco appears to have the most promising future, for it has a further advantage in its mineral resources, not to mention the character of its people: 'the Tunisian is a woman, the Algerian a man, the Moroccan a warrior'—so runs a Moroccan proverb! The country certainly kept its independence longer than the others.

There are great variations of fertility among these North African lowlands. At one end of the scale are the poor soils of the dune country of the Algerian Sahel and the sandy country behind Sfax and in the Mamora in the hinterland of Rabat. There are greater possibilities elsewhere, but development is often difficult, and many of the soils, like the clayey *tirs*, whose dark colour is indicative, not of humus, but of iron salts, need plenty of rain. Between these extremes of pure sand and heavy clay there is a whole range of light and medium-light soils, like the *hamri* type, which are better suited to cultivation and better adapted to irrigation.

Not only is the total annual rainfall moderate, becoming very low towards the south, but its incidence is irregular. There is no rain at all in the summer, but even between October and May it is not at all evenly distributed. There is none of the reliability to be found in central Africa, and in some years hardly any rain falls before Christmas. In 1949 Morocco received a large proportion of its rain in April, and in the centre and south it fell quite uselessly on ripening fields of barley. The efficacy of the precipitation from the point of view of plant growth is sometimes very small indeed. Its occurrence on a small number of days in the year emphasizes its torrential character and its destructive violence and erosive power on soils precariously situated on steep slopes where the vegetation has imprudently been removed. The dangers of hydraulic erosion are aggravated by the strong relief and are at least as marked in the lands bordering the Mediterranean as in the western United States. Eolian erosion is fairly strong, especially in central Tunisia, the Moroccan Tadla, and wherever there are drought-ridden, windswept surfaces underlain by soils lacking in the colloidal fraction of clay and humus. Furthermore, there are good reasons for eschewing what have come to be regarded as standard dry-farming practices. The repeated working of the surface, designed to prevent the loss of moisture from below, helps the work of the wind in removing the fine surface material upon which the status of the soil ultimately depends.

Unless special measures are taken, this is not an environment which favours either permanent grassland, the growing of summer fodder crops, or the intensive rearing of cattle. As we shall see, however, animal husbandry is not altogether precluded, and annual crops, mainly cereals, can be grown in the winter, while trees, in virtue of their large root systems, are particularly well suited to the irregular rainfall régime. But the possibilities of a region are also, and perhaps mainly, determined by the nature of the people, which a brief historical review will help us to understand.

2. Nomadic and Sedentary Peoples, Colonization, Demography

106. The country seems to have been relatively prosperous in ancient times. This was no doubt due to the harmonious balance between the two contrasted worlds of nomadism on the one hand and settled agriculture on the other. One economy was concerned with cereals and arboriculture; vines, figs and olives blossomed and vegetables flourished in the gardens which surrounded the smallest town. The areas where the nomads grazed their flocks were roughly limited by the Roman *limes*, and although large-scale seasonal movements were mainly confined to the Sahara, further north transhumant flocks would be taken from the lower plateaux to graze the nearby mountains in the summer.

This balance was not disturbed by the first wave of conquering Mohammedans. On the contrary, they brought with them new crops, such as henna, citrus fruits, rice, and sugar cane, and they made valuable contributions to irrigation. In a second conquest, however, the region was overrun by Hilalian nomads, and they subordinated all else to the quest for pasture. Even today, North Africa has not yet fully recovered from this phase of retrogressive exploitation. Nomadic tents replaced the permanent buildings of settled peoples throughout the Mediterranean and Atlantic lowlands as far as Rabat and Oran. The tree, the garden, the forests and, except sometimes for the environs of large cities, the intensive cultivation retreated everywhere in the plains. The climate changed and the Sahara seems to have spread further towards the north. Everywhere in the south, especially in Morocco, the dilapidated terraces on the hillsides and the thirsty oases, their great olive groves short of water as they never were in the past, are the forlorn remnants of a once more prosperous agriculture more richly blessed with rain. Thanks to irrigation, though its extent was unfortunately limited, intensive cultivation took refuge in the mountains and in the oases of the south, in spite of the less favourable conditions.

European settlers came mostly from the Mediterranean margins, from Italy, Spain, Malta, Provence, Corsica, Languedoc, and also from other parts of France. Mainly by draining the land, they were able to bring settled ways of life back to the lowlands, and re-established the ascendancy of cultivation over nomadic herding. The first wave of settlers was mainly concerned with growing cereals, which gave an immediate return. The Government was anxious at the time to create a veritable French peasantry, working with its own hands, and the holdings taken up by the immigrants were, for the most part, quite small.

Phylloxera in the south of France brought a new wave of colonists who, this time, were mostly vine-growers. The spread of the vine forced those who persisted in growing cereals to seek new land further south. These were mainly men with medium and large holdings—'official' and 'private' settlers respectively. A later start was made in Tunisia and Morocco; hence the absence—except for market-gardens —of small holdings. The core of the European peasantry in the east was Italian, but in the west, where European settlement has always been on a smaller scale, it was Spanish. About 6,800,000 acres are cultivated by 25,000 colonists in Algeria; 1,980,000 acres by 6,000 colonists in Tunisia; and 2,370,000 acres by 4,000 colonists in Morocco, where the average size of farms is well in excess of 500 acres (double the Algerian average), or even 750 acres if market gardens are considered apart.

Irrigation was developed by a third wave of settlers who added horticultural enterprises to the two preceding types. They cultivated early vegetables on the coast and planted citrus groves further inland. They also grew other kinds of fruits, such as olives, especially near Sfax in Tunisia, and apricots and other tree fruits. The hard, physical work was done by Arab rather than French labour. No one can gainsay the courage and the merit of the first pioneers, but the big farmers, who mostly live in Algiers or Oran, arrogate all the glory to themselves. The little that some of them have actually accomplished by their own unaided efforts makes a mockery of their attempts to gain the credit properly due to those who cleared the Mitidja and the Relizane. In the beginning there was much to be gained from the flow of European capital, which helped to curb the extortions of usurers, from efficient management, and even, in the case of the small farmers, from the considerable physical effort which they contributed. Intensive farming was re-established where the conditions were most favourable, a higher degree of water control was achieved, the management of the soil was improved and, all in all, production was greatly increased. Finally, through their contact with the settlers, the native people learned how to apply modern methods and raised their own yields.

107. But all this is the bright side of the picture, known perhaps only to official propaganda, which certainly proclaims it loudly enough. The vine-growers in the 1,100,000-gallon[1] class make blatant use of the 'epic' of the first settlers of Boufarik in their attempt to preserve their abusive privileges. Let us look therefore at the other side of the picture. In the mass, native agriculture has not been modernized, owing to the lack of capital, but even if it were available usury would offer a more profitable investment. Also the extreme fragmentation of property would negative any attempt to equip individual holdings. The best land has been monopolized by the colonists on the Algerian coastal plain, in the lowland of northern Tunisia and, to an even greater degree, in the vineyard country of Oran. The position is not so bad in Morocco, except for El Gharb, the Meknes-Fez region, and to some extent in Chaouia, near Casablanca. Forced back into the hills and mountains, especially in Algeria and Tunisia, the native farmers have been compelled to plough slopes that were far too steep and, until the late war, the French had failed to instruct them in the techniques of soil conservation.

Thus erosion accounts for the loss of 85,000 acres of good land a year in Algeria, while a very much larger area is subject to the less obvious forms of depletion, such as leaching and sheet erosion. At the same time, in 1950 alone the population rose by 200,000. Every day, on average, Algeria suffers a loss of 250 acres of land and yet has another 500 mouths to feed. Pushed towards the south, the Arab-Berber cultivators have had to exploit land which is of poorer value, progressively higher in altitude, as on the High Plains of Algeria, and, above all, less adequately supplied with water. The efficacy of their efforts has in consequence considerably declined, for the maintenance of a reasonable level of productivity would necessitate the application of factors completely beyond the means of all but the colonists themselves. In these southern areas wind erosion has played havoc with the newly ploughed sandy soils.

[1] A settler in Mitidja owns a cellar of this size. By comparison, the co-operative cellar, which serves all the small vine-growers in the village, has only a fifth of this capacity. One of our students, now a Government-employed agronomist, writes: 'Essentially, the worst of the French have shown themselves better than the best of the Tunisians.' He seems not to be conscious of his own racial prejudice.

The vine stocks are often aligned parallel to the steepest slope, an arrangement which accelerates the downward movement of soil, and, as on all steep hillsides in Oran, white patches of denuded rock are rapidly appearing on some of the scarps of Mascara, where yields have fallen from 1,400 to 265 gallons per acre. It would have been almost as easy to plant along the contours, and in this case the mere girdling and root-baring of the vines would have produced the lines of earth necessary to check the free flow of water, which would then have filtered harmlessly through the soil. Even on the frequent occasions when planting has been financed from public funds through the Agricultural Credit Scheme, the layout of the vineyards has not been remedied, and no strong measures were taken even when clear warning of the consequences had been given.[1]

The vine has forced much of the cereal cultivation out of the fertile lowlands in Algeria, and while it has well and truly made fortunes for the settlers, it has also aggravated alcoholism in France, which already held the world record for the consumption of wine and liquor. Moreover, it has seriously compromised the dietetic balance in Algeria. The vine is no doubt well suited to the dry hillsides, but it has also invaded the more humid lowlands. And although it employs more labour and makes larger profits than grain-growing, it is a heavy burden on the balance of payments of the France-North Africa group. Indeed, its development has forced these countries to import both bread cereals and coarse grains, especially in recent years. These purchases, moreover, have not been offset by any notable sales to the outside world of vine products, although one would have thought that markets could have been found for this type of trade.

108. A marked reduction has been apparent in the harm caused by usury, especially between 1937 and 1939, when the Wheat Office stepped in and curbed the activities of the profiteer, who, taking advantage of their very mediocre quality, offered the farmer an advance on his crops and bought them up at absurdly low prices. On the whole, however, French intervention administered a rude shock to the autochthonous subsistence economy by exposing it far too rapidly to the rigours of commercial intercourse.[2] There was no accompanying rise in yields to offset the new costs of distribution and, even worse, there

---

[1] We drew attention to this matter in 1937-8, but without results.

[2] G. Vialas, in the pamphlet *Paysanat algérien* (1951), quotes some of the more important equivalents in this traditional economy, where barter was fairly common: 1 cwt. of wheat=1·3 cwt. of barley=1 cwt. of dates or figs=2 cwt. of grapes or apricots=4·4 gallons of oil=3 cwt. of charcoal.

was none of that stabilization of harvests from one year to another which has been assured in humid, temperate countries by modern science. When the Moroccan or south Algerian *fellah* formerly reaped a good harvest, there was no question of marketing the surplus, and he stored it all in his *matmora*, or underground silo. But he was unaccustomed to the ways of the modern world, and when the railway and the ubiquitous lorry brought the European trader, he sold the grain he had saved from good harvests and bought clothes and jewels or maybe wives. A succeeding year of drought (1937, 1945) often found him with a larger family and devoid of the reserves on which an older generation had relied in such circumstances.

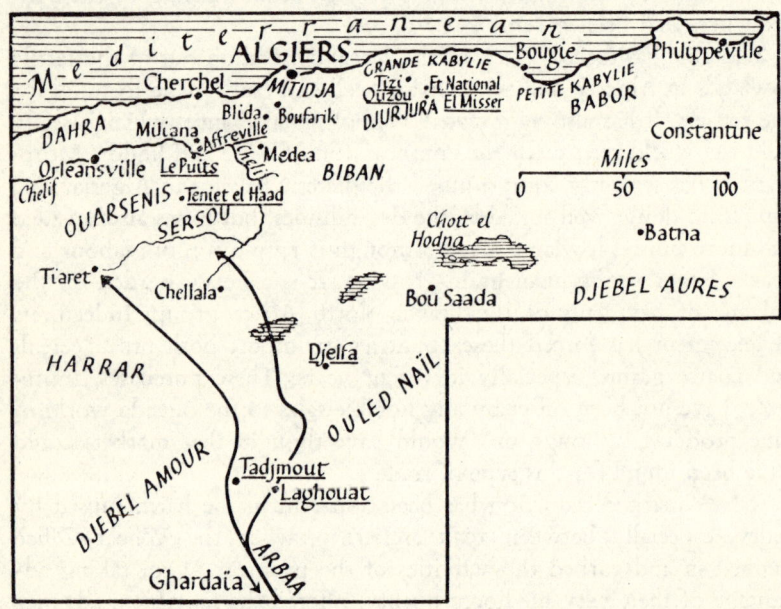

FIG. 10. Algeria.

A biological equilibrium has been disturbed by the sharp fall in mortality. The present situation is ominous: 21,500,000 Mohammedans in the population of 1951 are increasing every year by about 2 per cent. in Morocco and by more than 1·5 per cent. in Algeria and Tunisia. The total increase is more than 400,000 a year. At the same time the output of cereals in Algeria, which reached a maximum of 2,000,000 tons between 1901 and 1914, has barely attained 1,800,000 in recent years. The native population of Algeria, on the other hand, has been well in excess of 8,000,000 since 1950, having, as in the Low Countries,[1] doubled during the first half of this century. If these rates of increase continue, the total population of Algeria will reach 20,000,000 and of North Africa over 50,000,000 by the end of the century.

It is difficult to estimate how much effort would have to be made to quicken the tempo of agricultural production. In Algeria, the area cultivated by the Arab-Berbers, which totalled 5,000,000 acres in 1872 as against 4,500,000 today, has fallen over the same period from 2·1 to 0·6 acres per head of the Mohammedan population. Similarly, the output of cereals shows a drop from 10 to 4 cwt. per head. Unfortunately, a comparable recession, in both absolute and relative terms, has occurred in the case of other essential food products; cattle, sheep and goat rearing, unirrigated vegetables, olives, figs, and dates.

It is true that market gardening and arboriculture, which produce partly for export, viticulture, commerce, and, later, a modicum of industry have compensated to some extent by bringing in new wealth. On the other hand, overpopulation, which has long existed and is so to speak 'traditional' in the Far East, is in North Africa a quite recent phenomenon and one for which European intervention is partly responsible. The pressure is increasing so fast that something must be done about the static condition of native agriculture, but even so the country cannot be saved by agrarian measures alone.

We shall now study in detail some of the traditional aspects of this agrarian civilization and some of the attempts at modernization, in the hope of finding the most practicable ways of increasing production.

3. The Shepherd of the High Algerian Plains and the Fight Against Hunger

109. The confederation of the Arbaa, according to J. Despois, have remained since the seventeenth century in the southern part of Laghouat, where they roam across a plateau region scattered with shallow depressions (Fig. 10). Herbaceous plants flourish on the loams of these *dayas* during the rains. When plenty of rain has fallen, barley and also hard wheat have been cultivated in a few of these *dayas* during the last fifty years. We have actually seen this hazardous form of agriculture carried on in areas where the average rainfall was less than 4 in. a year. The risk involved in such an enterprise, which is nothing more than a mere

[1] In Chapter XIII we shall describe the very rapid increases in production in the Netherlands, which have permitted high dietetic standards to be maintained in conjunction with a large export trade in agricultural commodities.

lottery, is reduced by sowing very lightly, at about 22 lb. to the acre. With favourable weather, the strong tillering may promise a good crop, but it is all too often spoilt at the last moment by the burning heat of the sun.

Sahnoune,[1] a member of the Ouled Salah tribe which forms part of this confederation, is the patriarch[2] of a family of ten, which consists of his wife, five children between the ages of two and fifteen, a married son of twenty-five, and his two children. The family tent is made of four strips or *flidj* of material woven from goat-hair, each measuring 11 yds. by 1, making a total area of 44 sq. yds. Comparable dimensions for the married son's tent are $6\frac{1}{2}$ yds. by $3\frac{1}{4}$. The stock consists in the first place of pack animals and those for personal transport: a mare and five camels, all but one of them male. At the beginning of February 1952 there were a ram and fifty-three ewes, a he-goat, and twenty-five she-goats, and up till then twenty-seven lambs and twelve kids, although more were born later on. Allowing for deaths, the average annual production of such a flock is about forty lambs and twenty kids of both sexes, 150 to 175 lb. of uncleaned wool, and 55 lb. of ewe butter. In addition, there is enough goat hair to weave two *flidj* 11 yds. long and to fill two sacks, or *guerrara*.

The flocks are kept by the owner and his two eldest sons. The women, who often have less to do than the wives of the cattle graziers in Normandy, are only responsible for milking, making butter, and cooking. Some of the produce is consumed by the family, but they are forced to sell thirty sheep or goats every year and a camel every other year in order to buy $2\frac{1}{2}$ tons of wheat and 2 tons of barley for their own, and to some small extent for their animals', consumption. The hundredweight of wool which is sold more or less covers their clothing requirements. As the family budget is very tight, it is supplemented by picking *terfess* mushrooms, a task performed by women and children which in good years is quite a lucrative source of income. The hunting of hares, young partridge, and bustards sometimes makes a welcome addition to the usual fare.

The working capital consists essentially of the animals, but also includes a quite varied but not very impressive assortment of equipment: a pair of shears, two head-ropes made of wool and hair, two *gueddah* of esparto grass for milking, two *chekoua* for churning butter

[1] Details kindly furnished by M. Schaefer, who is the Paysanat's inspector at Algiers.

[2] The breaking up of these patriarchal families is more in evidence in the more 'advanced' communities further north.

and a *borma* for storing it, a *guerba* for water, four grain sacks in camel hair (*guerrara*), four camel pack-saddles, a saddle, a small loom for making the *flidj*, and an instrument for carding wool (*guerah* and *mchatt*). A modern addition is in the form of two galvanized water butts of 11 gallons' capacity. The animal husbandry Sectors, to which we shall have occasion to refer again, lend modern shears and provide facilities for stock dipping.

110. After wintering in the Sahara, where conditions are fairly warm owing to the low altitude in this sector, the caravans, each consisting of five or six families, with perhaps 150 to 250 sheep and goats (Sahnoune's flocks are larger than the average), set out in May, cross the Saharan Atlas, and spread out over the High Plains of Harrar, where there are now water-holes in abundance. They wait until August—that is, until the grain has been brought in—before making for their traditional summer pastures round the Sersou Plateau and on the southern flanks of the Ouarsenis Massif. For though this area was once the summer home of the graziers, both European settlers and Mohammedans have brought it into cultivation since the beginning of the century. This was not achieved without a certain amount of friction, and troops had to be summoned to the region in 1917, for, not without reason, the Arbaa maintained that they had a previous right to the land. The ploughing up of the steppes was, however, compelled by the population increases. Eventually agreement was reached and the nomads were employed at harvest-time, especially for transporting the crop with their pack animals. When the machines came and deprived them of this work they were found alternative employment in harvesting the lentil crop by hand. In the Sersou Plateau near Teniet-el-Haad, Sahnoune sells his animals and buys grain; he purchases more of the latter than he needs for himself and eventually sells the surplus in the oases to the south. In October he returns by stages to his winter quarters.

The first point to be emphasized is that all this work, if one can apply such a term to these peregrinations, is not very productive. Essentially, it is characterized by its extreme irregularity and by its low yields, between 5 and 25 acres, and even more in the extreme south, being required to support one sheep or one goat. These features have become more marked following the annexation of grazing land by the southward extension of cereals, which in their turn have been ousted from the Tell region by the vine. On the cultivated land, improved working of the soil during the fallow period now prevents any natural regrowth of vegetation. The stubble is burnt by many settlers who no longer seem to appreciate its value. Also the number of sheep in Algeria has been falling since the end of the nineteenth century, and the trend has continued, but at a faster rate, since the last war. In the course of a single dry year, as in 1920, more than half the sheep and goats may perish, especially if the winter is unusually rigorous as well (1945-6).

The loss of 3,000,000 animals during the disastrous winter of 1945-6 has been evaluated at 20,000 million francs (1948 value). Even this is without allowing for the emaciation of the remaining animals or for the loss of income due to undergrazing in succeeding years, as, for instance, during the spring of 1949, when the steppe vegetation was particularly rich and there were too few animals to graze it. In the south the proportion of losses was naturally very much higher than the average: from Laghouat to Geryville, and also in eastern Morocco, nine animals perished out of every ten and the flocks of the Ghardaia region were reduced from 60,000 to 1,500. The cereal crop failed, purchasing power fell to zero, circumstances limited the scope of the official famine relief scheme, and the winter also took its toll of the native population. During that winter of 1945-6, many poor nomadic families reverted to their age-old way of dealing with famine. To save the rest, they let the youngest daughter die of hunger.[1]

111. The first step that was taken to remedy the situation was to call in veterinary aid. Also, as the distance from water-holes made large stretches of potential grazing land unusable, wells were dug in these areas for the watering of stock. We studied the problem in March and April 1949,[2] and recommended that first priority should henceforward be given to the fight against hunger. The steppes constitute a free supply of grazing land which flourishes untended, but in a strict economic sense its use can be justified only if the number of animals is large enough to cut the cost of herding down to a minimum per head. Then, again, one can hardly accept a situation where the flocks are decimated once in every five or six years and where, for several months in two years out of three, the animals become emaciated through lack of food.

The Rural Amelioration Sectors (S.A.R.) in Algeria[3] which are mostly concerned with livestock problems are now seeking a better

[1] As in the Far East, this also derives from the anxiety to maintain the balance between production and population.

[2] At the request of the Monnet Plan and of the Comité central de la Laine (Voreux Mission).

[3] See the pamphlet duplicated by the Algerian Government on *Le paysanat algérien* by Vialas and Schaefer (December 1951).

utilization of the steppes by further increasing the number of water-holes. Then they aim at dividing the sheep country into controlled-grazing sectors on the Australian model. The temporary withdrawal from use of overgrazed areas allows the vegetation to recuperate. The process is assisted by planting thornless cactus, a valuable addition to the grazing, and trees for shade in the summer, and shelter from the cold winds in winter.

When this has been done, straw saved from the harvest is collected together, and reserves of fodder, which may belong either to the graziers or to the S.A.R., are thus built up. Alternatively, in the spring the natural grass growth is sometimes vigorous enough to permit cutting and haymaking or storage in silos. Where the water supply is adequate, vetch, barley, and lucerne are cultivated. These forage crops can be grown on a large scale in the wetter north of the Maghreb, but their bulkiness makes them very expensive to transport to the far south. We would suggest, however, that crops such as barley and oats should have priority; the grain could be stored more easily, simply being stacked on a few flat stones or on any swept patch of bare rock. After a few days of soaking and germination, it would supply those very vitamins which are lacking in the desiccated summer pastures.

More forage crops, lucerne especially, could be grown where water has been discovered in the south, as at Tadjmout, near Laghouat, and at Chemorah, near Djelfa, where some 1,500 and 900 acres respectively could be irrigated. Though more expensive to produce than the wild grass of the steppe, such forage crops are essential if the resources of the latter are to be developed to the full. Barley could be grown very economically if it were sown in the depressions, for by cutting it green just as it began to ear, the burning-up which so often destroys ripening grain could be entirely avoided. Unfortunately, the nomads persist in their preference for harvesting ripe grain as an insurance against famine, and the tragic winter of 1945-6 certainly did not help to allay their fears. Vetch-oats mixtures could be cultivated in a similar manner, but as such a crop would need more moisture, it could be reserved for sites which are occasionally watered by the floods of intermittent *wadi* streams.

112. Whenever there are difficult years, many nomads become destitute, and their flocks are bought up by the wealthy few, and the rich are often those who wield some kind of official power. After the disasters of 1945, it was sought to remedy this undesirable tendency by advancing loans, repayable within five years, to destitute families. Each loan constituted a nucleus of twenty ewes and a ram, from which the

flock could be built up again. It seems inadvisable, however, to create a large number of small flocks owing to the waste of manpower involved in herding. The productivity of the nomads of the south will never reach a satisfactory level until a proportion of the people now living in certain overpopulated areas moves northwards. It is true that there are still large areas of potential grazing land the development of which awaits only the arrival of drilling gear and other hydraulic equipment. It is equally true, however, that elsewhere overcrowding is becoming worse, in spite of emigration, and the outer edge of cultivation has reached into sub-marginal areas, where crop yields are subject to dangerously wide fluctuations from year to year.

In the Sersou Plateau some of the grants of land to settlers were too far to the south and have had to be abandoned. But the few years of ploughing were enough to destroy for ever the perennial plants, such as artemisia (*Artemesia herba alba*—it gave the lamb a delectable flavour), which were once the chief element in the summer pastures. The mean decennial grain yield in certain cantons south of Kairouan in Tunisia is less than 1·6 cwt. per acre; obviously such areas should never have been cultivated. Cultivation continues in spite of the adverse conditions, for the density of population is about fifty per square mile, and the people cannot make a living from their flocks alone, even when they supplement their income by collecting esparto grass. So the *fellah* tills the soil, but three years out of five there is nothing to harvest.

When the High Plains which stretch from eastern Morocco and across the whole of southern Algeria to Tunisia have been developed as rationally as the sheep lands of Australia,[1] and when greater efforts have been made to accumulate reserves of fodder, Algeria alone will be able to support about 15,000,000 adult sheep. A third of them could be accommodated in the cultivated zone and would consist of Merino cross-breds with a high yield of wool. Morocco could support a comparable number with a high proportion of the total in the farming areas. Another 3,500,000 could be supported in Tunisia. The total output from North Africa, with its 100,000,000 acres of natural grassland and 22,500,000 acres of crops, might then reach 80,000 to 90,000 tons of greasy wool, or about half this quantity after scouring and cleaning. This would be enough to satisfy the needs of a local textile industry, and there would still be a surplus for export to France.

The French textile industry, both cotton and woollen, is under the constant threat of shortage of raw materials. The world demand for wool is rising all the time, and the possibilities of the natural grasslands

[1] Where the physical conditions are more difficult on the whole.

have been exploited practically to their limit. To 'steppe' wool we most now add 'farmland' wool by the extension of sheep-farming to the cultivated regions of France and North Africa. Finally, production can be increased from 'valorized steppes' by the addition of forage crops to their natural resources.

The shepherds will continue to rely for their income mainly on the sale of meat, and it would be to their advantage to concentrate on the marketing of six-month-old lambs rather than on the full-grown sheep as at present. When drought prevented them from being fattened satisfactorily on the steppes, they would have to be sent to the irrigated lowlands of the north. Such a venture which would imply collaboration between the shepherd, and the settled farmer, might help to abate the age-old hatred which exists between them. But any tendency on the part of the lowland farmer to bide his time until drought on the High Plains permitted him to dictate his own prices would have to be checked right from the beginning.

4. Concentric Belts of Cultivation in the Tunisian Sahel at M'saken, near Susa

113. Owing to the fact that trees thrive much better than annual crops in regions of irregular rainfall, a group of Frenchmen were able to carry through their plan from 1900 onwards for planting the now famous 'forest' of olive groves near Sfax. Where the ground is fairly light and water percolates easily into the soil, the southern boundary of this enormous plantation reaches as far as the 8-in. isohyet. The *m'gharsa* agreement, whereby the fruit was evenly divided between owner and tenants, meant that the return on the European capital invested was most satisfactory, especially as the land had originally cost nothing or next to nothing.[1]

North of these young olive groves in eastern Tunisia, plantations had been established by the Phoenicians as early as the sixth century B.C., but had been devastated during the eleventh century. At the beginning of the seventeenth century the Moors, after their expulsion from Andalusia, settled in this region, bringing with them a number of plants of American origin: agaves, prickly pear, maize, beans, tomatoes, tobacco (*Nicotiana rustica*), and various Cucurbitaceae, peppers,

---

[1] The planting of an olive tree and the attention it needs during the first twenty years cost about 6,000 francs (in 1952); the annual crop from an adult tree (more than twenty-five years old) is worth about 3,000 francs on average, but from this 1,000 francs must be deducted for production costs.

and spices. Whereas in other parts of the Maghreb rural agglomerations are found only in the mountains and the southern oases, and although for the rest the usual type of settlement consists of isolated farms, here the Moors founded a number of 'rural towns' comparable in many respects with those of Andalusia and eastern Hungary. Like urban centres, each has its mosque and market-place, or *souk*. Their single-storey houses, which open on to enclosed courtyards, are very closely spaced and rather remind one of the villages of Lorraine, although these latter are smaller and dunghills are much more in evidence.

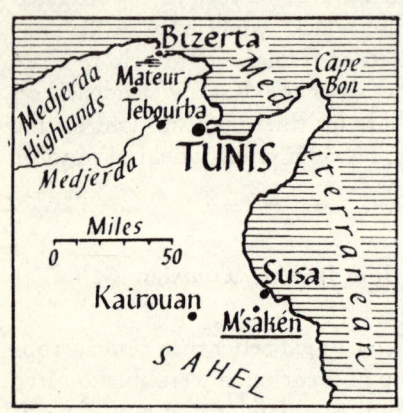

FIG. 11. Tunisia.

About 5,000 families live at M'saken, eight miles south of Susa (Fig. 11). It has an agricultural labour force of perhaps 10,000 workers and a total population of nearly 30,000, or rather more than Susa itself. Moreover, between here and Kairouan, a distance of nearly forty miles, there is not another single nucleus of settlement. The town is surrounded by a number of concentric belts of cultivation, with the intensity of land use decreasing outwards, as in the case of certain settlements in Negro Africa which we have already examined.[1] Immediately around the town is a ring of several hundred yards in depth of gardens and orchards irrigated from wells and supplying vegetables and fruits. Beyond this and stretching for another six miles from the town are the olive groves, with half a million trees covering some 13,000 to 15,000 acres, or a density of about forty trees per acre. As the average rainfall is only 12-14 in. a year and the surface is more clayey than at Sfax, each plantation generally has an *impluvium*, or water cistern—not the only feature which can be traced to Roman times. This cistern, which collects the run-off of rain-water, is invariably sold with the plantation, for the bare limestone, its surface covering of soil completely removed by erosion, is impermeable enough to cause most of the rain to drain away rapidly towards the groves sited on the lower ground.

This continuous belt of olive trees ends abruptly at its outer margin, but beyond this clearly marked boundary there are still a few scattered

[1] Recalling von Thunen's scheme.

plantations, and nowadays one occasionally finds an isolated house among them. Finally, one reaches the open grasslands, where the nomad formerly obtained a precarious livelihood by grazing his flocks. Today cereal cultivation has invaded this sector, and the farmer from M'saken often comes thirty, forty, and even sixty miles to till his fields. These he rents, either from the nomads who often have inalienable rights to the land in this area, or from one of the big landowners at Kairouan. In the latter case he generally pays the owner a quarter of the harvest, for the crop is too uncertain to be relied upon for a fixed rent. The remoteness of these fields is reminiscent of the outlying farms of eastern Kansas, except that, until very recent times, animals were the only form of transport.

Whole expeditions set out three times a year, and the men, with their teams of mules, their small tents, provisions, and equipment, spend weeks at a time away from the town. They leave in the autumn to do their ploughing and sowing; then again at the beginning of the spring for the weeding; and, finally, in the summer for the harvest. If rain is plentiful and yields are exceptionally high, the land may give up to 12 cwt. of grain to the acre. Thus if a man has sown 25 acres, he may have to make fifteen return journeys with his short-shafted, mule-drawn cart to bring in his crop, and if his fields are forty miles from the town this will involve a total journey of 1,200 miles. We were not surprised to find the surface of the tracks leading towards Kairouan badly broken up in the month of October. Nowadays lorries are helping in the work of transport, but the traditional mule-carts are still used.

The last important resource of the inhabitants of M'saken is sheep-rearing. The migrations of the flocks are much less systematic than among the Arbaa. Though they remain for the most part in the third zone of land utilization, the partially cultivated grazing lands, at times they travel long distances—southwards in wet years or northwards during droughts. In spite of the large sums of money spent in rescue work in 1945—animals were even transported long distances in lorries —more than two-thirds of the total flock perished. At the time of our visit in 1949, these losses had not yet been made good. Of all enterprises in which the people here engage, the olive plantations are easily the most important, in spite of their great variations in yields. They also supply the raw material for an oil-mill industry.

114. The social order of M'saken is characterized by several very distinct class groups. Firstly there are six large landowners, each possessing from 4,000 to 10,000 olive trees and an oil-mill, where they also process olives from smaller producers. Each of them employs from six

to ten semi-permanent labourers, who, in years when both cereals and olives do well, may work for up to seven months; otherwise perhaps for barely two or three. In a good year they may engage as many as thirty seasonal workers. Below these large property-owners comes the middle class, which includes about 300 families, each owning between 300 and 1,500 olive trees—that is, between 7 and 40 acres of groves, complete with *impluvia*. Each family cultivates from 25 to 40 acres of cereals and generally possesses two draught animals, a mule and a camel. Before 1945, many of them also had a flock of 100 to 150 ewes.

Finally, more than 1,000 families depend on much smaller resources. They each have from ten to fifty olive trees, and in some cases as many as 100 or 200. They own no draught animals, but generally try to hire one[1] so as to grow enough grain for their own requirements. They cannot make a living except by finding employment with one of the other two classes, but in their search for work they have to compete with the landless labouring class, which, as we have seen, is itself the victim of long periods of unemployment. There is no doubt that the settlement is overcrowded in relation to the area of land from which it ekes out its existence. Leaving the uncultivated grazing land out of account, the density of population is 500 per square mile, and the Tunisian Sahel as a whole exceeds 250 per square mile. As there is little in the way of local crafts and agriculture is of an extensive type,[2] there is a serious shortage of work. This, unfortunately, is a problem which is becoming more and more acute in rural North Africa, although its existence is not always immediately apparent. We shall encounter it again, however, in the Mediterranean coastlands.

The plantations of this area have now been in private ownership for centuries, and the individual holdings are for the most part extremely fragmented, whereas in the rest of the Maghreb until quite recently the land was generally held collectively. According to J. Despois, 'it is only here that one finds peasant communities comparable with those of Europe, strongly attached to their land, their villages, and their trees'.

5. Arboriculture, Overpopulation, and Emigration in Kabylia in Algeria

115. In Kabylian Djurjura east of Algiers (Fig. 10), one finds a very

[1] 300 francs a day in March 1949. Some of the area's olive trees are in young plantations and some are owned by people who do not live at M'saken.

[2] Intensification will be difficult unless allogenic sources of water can be tapped.

different type of landscape, with steep-sided, tree-covered hills in place of the gentle undulations of the Tunisian Sahel. The villages, where families each occupy their own group of houses, are perched on the hill-crests and on the narrow ledges which occur midway up the abrupt escarpments. The houses have dry-stone walls surmounted by three main beams of oak or ash, which are covered with tiles and ash branches, or occasionally with a thatch of wild reed-like grasses, or *diss*. Usually there is only one room, measuring 33 ft. by 15, which is divided into two parts by a low wall. One of these is the stable and the space above it is used for the storage of various tools and equipment. The family use the other part, and here one finds the hand-loom and the huge urns, or *ikoufan*, as tall as the house itself, which are made of unfired earthenware and used for the storage of grain, oil, and figs. A platform covered with mats serves as a bed.

Handicrafts are comparatively highly developed. The women scour, card, spin, and weave the wool. They make saddle cloths and blankets decorated with beautiful regular designs in black, relieved with touches of red and yellow. They also fire and decorate pieces of pottery. In some of the villages there are jewellers who decorate silver bracelets and necklaces with coral set in enamel, coloured in various shades of blue, green, and yellow. Wooden tools, like the three-pronged fork made by bending pieces of oleaster over a fire, and withers yokes for oxen, ropes made of *diss* and Carex, drying screens for figs—all these are made in the villages. The mattocks (*agerzim*), hoes, and hatchets and the shares of the Mediterranean swing-ploughs are all made and repaired by village blacksmiths.

Many of the methods which are still used can be traced back to the days of ancient Rome. The grain is trodden by oxen on small threshing-floors, 20 or 30 ft. in diameter; these are always sited in an exposed position, and when the mixture of grain, clay, and dung is scooped up from the floor with shovels and thrown into the air, the wind carries away the chaff. Crops are reaped with sickles and are brought in from the fields on the backs of mules or sometimes by the women themselves. Similar methods are employed to carry the grain to the bottom of the valley, where a comparatively modern mill, rather similar to those used in France in the nineteenth century, grinds the corn; a waterfall turns a paddle wheel which is connected to the upper of two millstones, the lower one remaining stationary.

116. Chernai Arezki, a landowner at Tala Allem (Tizi-Ouzou), is the head of a family of twelve. His 15 acres of land, and $1\frac{1}{4}$ acres of fig trees, are looked after by a *métayer*, or share-cropper, known here as

a *Khammès*. For supplying all the work, the latter receives only a fifth of the crop, which is, as far as we are aware, the lowest crop share in the world; it is almost as low as the *métayer's* 'sixth' in ancient Greece, and is equalled today only in Egypt. In more advanced countries the worker's portion has risen considerably, and in the south-eastern United States, for instance, even the coloured share-cropper, who supplies none of the seed or equipment himself, is entitled, in theory at least, to half the crop of cotton or tobacco. Unlike their counterparts in the Far East, however, Chernai Arezki and his class are not merely absentee landlords. They farm their own land with the help of labourers, who are paid a share of the harvest. The farmer supplies all the equipment and, as the *métayer* is always extremely poor, he loans him enough food to keep his family until harvest-time, though sometimes at extortionate rates of interest, for usury is still rife.

In the case we have taken, the *métayer's* family consists of ten people, and it is difficult to see how they can possibly make a living. The land follows the two-year rotation of fallow[1] and cereals, either barley or sometimes hard wheat, which is typical of the Mediterranean margins. The $7\frac{1}{2}$ acres cropped each year give an average total yield of 24 cwt., on which two families are dependent, although the *métayer's* share is, of course, only about 5 cwt. The orchard yields about 2 tons of dried figs, and they constitute the farm's principal commercial asset. The stock consists of just a pair of oxen, something between six and ten years old, and a few poultry.

117. The land rises towards El Misser, near Fort National, and as the slopes become more rugged and the resources more limited the density of population actually increases in many places. El Misser, which is perched, like the villages of Corsica, right on the crest of a hill, has 1,200 inhabitants and 750 acres of land. These are divided into 150 separate holdings, varying in size from $\frac{1}{2}$ acre to more than 15. The largest of these holdings form a well-defined group of sixteen farms, fairly adequate in size, with between 10 and 15 acres apiece, and each with a pack-mule and a pair of oxen. The latter, when harnessed to a primitive wooden swing-plough, can scratch the surface of about $\frac{1}{4}$ acre in a day. The mules are bought from Arabs—at Sidi-Aich, for instance—for the Kabyles consider it beneath them to mate an ass with a mare. Owing to the shortage of feeding-stuffs, the oxen are sometimes bought just before the ploughing season—that is, before the autumn rains—and resold immediately afterwards.

[1] The high rainfall would permit the elimination of fallows; indeed, continuous cropping would reduce leaching.

PROBLEMS OF THE KABYLIAN ECONOMY

On these 'large' farms between $\frac{1}{2}$ and $1\frac{1}{2}$ acres of barley, often mixed with lentils, are generally sown, and to this is occasionally added an acre or so of hard wheat. Apart from a few small lots of chick-peas, beans, or sorghum, the rest of the land is fallow, and often remains so long enough to become covered with scrub. On the smaller holdings, the land is ploughed by agreement between the owner and one of the 'large' farms, which alone possess draught animals; the sown areas are obviously very small indeed. The trees which are scattered through the fields may sometimes belong to a third party. A particular tree may be owned by several people in partnership, and sometimes different people each own their particular branch. A lawyer's paradise indeed!

The trees are, however, the basis of the economy. Each of the sixteen farmers owns from 40 to 150 fig-trees—350 in one case—and from 50 to 80 olive trees. Here the latter is very near its altitudinal limit, which is about 3,300 ft. on the south-facing slopes, but the fig-tree rises to over 4,300 ft. Most of the cultivated land is interspersed among the plantations, and the long yokes which are used enable the oxen to turn on the most improbable slopes without toppling sideways. The fig-trees are propagated from cuttings or from shoots from the roots, and as they are never pruned, old trees begin to look like bushes as suckers spring up around them. The fruit is often overripe when picked, and is then dried on flat screens at the mercy of the insects. In the olive groves new trees are obtained by grafting on the wild oleaster. The olives are often left so long in heaps on the bare ground that they begin to ferment, and the oil is very rancid when the fruit is eventually pressed. Although they were once all locally consumed, shortage of money now often compels the Kabyle to sell his olives soon after the picking, and he buys ground-nut oil for his own use.

Trees provide other resources apart from these. The ashes are pruned every two to four years and, together with straw and dried weeds from the fields, they help to eke out the slender supply of fodder during the summer. For three months every year they supply the basic food for the oxen and, more particularly, for the cows. One or two of these are generally kept on each of the 'large' farms, but their numbers are tending to diminish. After the fruit-picking in the autumn, fig leaves are used for the same purpose. According to G. Pelaud,[1] the mulberry would provide a better tree fodder crop than the ash. Finally, the oaks (*Quercus ballota*), which give a sweet acorn, are carefully protected in the fields, as in Sardinia, while the ground surrounding them is regularly ploughed to stimulate growth. The acorns are used for human

[1] See his fine monograph on Tabarout, which has been of great assistance to us.

consumption, as in ancient Gaul, and are either brought home to feed the family or sold in one of the nearby markets.

When food is short, the people even eat the acorns of cork oaks and evergreen oaks, which burn the stomach owing to their high tannin content. They also consume cistus fruits, in spite of the poisonous effects—of which they are painfully aware. Similar practices are to be found in the *sertaos* of north-eastern Brazil, which is a notorious famine area. Goats, however, are gradually replacing the sheep and cows, in spite of their devastating effect on tree growth, and each of the large farms of El Misser has about twenty of them. They cause great damage in the orchards and gardens, most of which are poorly fenced. Finally, because of thefts, due no doubt to the abject poverty of the people, the cultivator is compelled to pick certain fruits before they are ripe—grapes, for instance, while they are still sour.

118. This economy provides the people with only the barest minimum of their requirements, and one may safely say that the fig harvest is virtually the only season when no one goes hungry. The rate of population growth and the fact that the Kabyles were deprived of the use of the neighbouring plains and, after the revolt of 1871,[1] restricted to the mountains, have made the position even more serious. There is little horticulture, and even where the occasional garden bears a small patch of maize[2] the ground is all too often in the shade of a dense thicket of trees.

The water resources, though abundant, are not used to the full because of the incompatibility of competing claims. According to Pelaud, such a situation may last until the local magistrate, or *caid*, intervenes and diverts the whole stream for the exclusive benefit of his own garden. Fertilizers are unknown, the trees are poorly managed, and Kabylia as a whole still has too much fallow and uncleared scrub. Consequently, there is still too much rural unemployment. In 1938 we undertook certain studies, which led us to the conclusion that although in the nearby lowlands the food situation had improved during the two preceding generations, here it had appreciably worsened.

The Kabyle has reacted by emigrating. One finds the men of Tabarout washing cars at night in Parisian garages, crowding into squalid little hovels, and depriving themselves of food so as to be able to send as much money home as possible. Very often victims of tuberculosis,

[1] Which the Kabyles chivalrously postponed until the Franco-Prussian War was over.

[2] Reminiscent of the 'hut' gardens of the Chad on the other side of the Sahara.

they eventually return to find their orchards abandoned and overrun with weeds. Nevertheless, as in Corsica, there are still plenty of men left in these highlands to justify a more intensive utilization of the land. Here too, however, the men are much given to long palavers in the village while the women and children are conscientiously weeding the fields and gardens or tirelessly carrying wood and water up the slopes like beasts of burden. The high density of population makes fuel scarce, and it has to be brought from further and further away.

Cereals are not particularly well suited to the conditions, especially where ploughing increases the danger from erosion. It has long been the practice to cut a few terraces on the steepest slopes and to dig drainage channels on gentler gradients, but these measures have only partly fulfilled their purpose in minimizing the damage done by running water, which is still far too great. For many years technical progress has remained stagnant, largely due to the preoccupation of the Agricultural Service, until as late as 1945, with the needs of the settlers. More recently there has been a strong movement to develop certain areas under the guidance of agricultural scientists. S.A.Rs. specializing in arboriculture, apart from improving the care of trees and the preparation of products—already contributions of the greatest importance—are aiming first of all to protect the soil by encouraging the construction of parallel earth banks across the slopes, spaced at vertical intervals of 13 ft. These check the surface run-off and reduce erosion to negligible proportions.

This highly effective method was applied by the service for the Defence and Restoration of Soils (D.R.S.), a branch of the Water and Forest Service, when certain difficulties were encountered in the work of reafforesting overpopulated mountainous regions, such as at Blida. Obviously, forests alone cannot provide enough work where there are 250 people to the square mile, and methods applicable to the Central Massif or to the southern Alps are quite inappropriate to the Tell Atlas. On the slopes between the banks the tilling of the soil is no longer dangerous. Trees capable of providing animal fodder, such as the carob, and various kinds of fruit trees, such as the fig and the olive, are planted on the banks, in spite of the forestry expert's perfectly justified contention that the modern orchard is better suited to alluvial lowland. It is certainly desirable to encourage the people to descend to the lowlands and establish their orchards there, but the movement will be gradual, and in the meantime the primary objective must be to develop the resources of the highlands to the full. Moreover, it will not be long before the country as a whole will find itself unable to dispense with

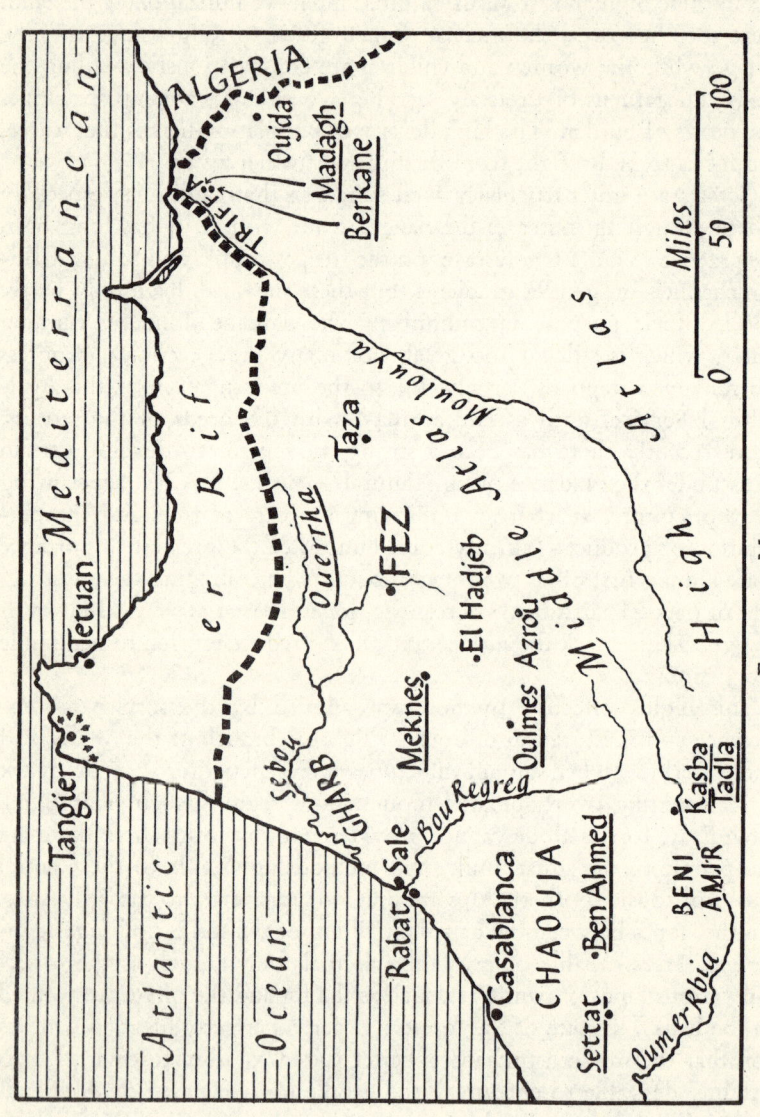

Fig. 12. Morocco.

the production of its highland areas, even though it may prove expensive. The population problem is akin to that in the uplands and mountains of Italy rather than to that in the southern French Alps. Attempts to solve the problem by improving the utilization of the land cannot afford to ignore the human factor in the situation.

Kabylia can be turned into a modern orchard, where the cherry might well be introduced through the agricultural schools to join the traditional fruits, like the fig and the olive. Sericulture would be appropriate to so rugged and densely populated a region, but the prospect for natural silk in the world's markets is distinctly unpromising. The mulberry as a source of fodder, however, is a proposition which deserves serious consideration. Even with all its resources developed to the limit, and even if it became an exporter of high-quality oil and fruit, the region would still be unable to provide full employment for its present population. Inevitably there will have to be emigration, possibly, if the pace of industrialization warrants it, to the interior of the Maghreb.[1]

6. The Traditional Type of Cereal Cultivation in Chaouia in Morocco

119. Before the arrival of Europeans, as in most backward countries mainly dependent on the land, the North African economy was based almost entirely on cereals and pastoralism. In 1923, 97 per cent. of the land under field crops in Morocco was devoted to cereals, and even at the present day the proportion is still over 90 per cent. in both Morocco and Algeria. We shall therefore study an example of cereal cultivation from South Chaouia in western Morocco (Fig. 12). A traditional feature of the cultural landscape in this region is the dispersed nature of settlement, which is in complete contrast with the Kabylian villages and the large agglomerations of the Tunisian Sahel. Si Abdallah, a member of the Ouled Sidi ben Daoud tribe,[2] which inhabits the Settat district, cultivates his land with the help of a *Khammès*, whose duties are to look after the oxen, plough the land, and sow the grain. He also supervises the five women who are employed for a month in the early part of the year for the spring hand-weeding, which is also a feature of Andalusian and Sardinian farming. At harvest-time he brings the sheaves of grain on camel-back to the threshing floor. The owner, or *fellah*,

[1] Cf. *L'industrialisation de l'Afrique du Nord*, by A. Colin (1951).
[2] Details kindly furnished by Ph. Richard, head of the Guisser S.M.P., and also by the heads of the S.M.Ps. at Ben Ahmed, Oulmes, and Berkane.

takes charge of the five men, who are recruited for five days during the harvest, and participates generally in most of the other farm operations. Indeed, contrary to the general rule, and quite unlike his Kabylian counterpart, he appears to work as hard as his *Khammès*. Owners of land, even when the farms are small and their responsibility for general management consequently limited, are often content merely to live on the work of their hired hands, and the large proportion of these semi-parasites is not helping to raise the general level of productivity of North African agriculture.

Si Abdallah has 63 acres of land, 8 of which are fallow. Thus, in spite of the low rainfall, which averages less than 16 in. a year as compared with well over 40 in. in many parts of Kabylia, he has abandoned the two-year rotation of crop and fallow characteristic of native agriculture. In this his farming practice is fairly typical of many small and medium-sized holdings which are short of land, but the traditional rotation persists on the really large native farms, which are often managed somewhat carelessly. The garden, a little over an acre in size, is watered by means of a *noria* turned by animal power, and on Si Abdallah's holding it represents a sector of intensive irrigated farming analogous to the 'hut gardens' of central Africa. A gardener is employed throughout the year and produces crops of beans, onions, potatoes, and turnips, and also fresh mint leaves to mix with green tea and various vegetables; all these are consumed on the farm. In addition, there are fifty fig, ten pomegranate, and ten olive trees.

In 1951 there were 22·5 acres of barley and 10 of hard wheat, the traditional crops; 12·5 of soft wheat, a recent introduction; 2·5 of fenugreek, and a similar area divided between coriander, linseed, and a small patch of lentil, which is a drought-resisting leguminous plant. Camels and donkeys are used for draught purposes, three of the former and five of the latter, but camels are not used for field operations north of the latitude of Casablanca. There are four cows, three calves, and twenty sheep, which are all tended by the young children.[1] On the average, about ten lambs, two of which are generally sold, and one or two calves are born every year.

Even before the arrival of Europeans, Chaouia was one of the best-cultivated parts of the Maghreb, and, as compared with native agriculture elsewhere in North Africa, it still records the highest crop yields. The 45 acres of cereals give an average of 17 tons of barley and wheat, and about another 1·2 tons of grain are obtained from the remaining land. In theory, the *Khammès* receives a fifth of the harvest,

[1] There are nine people in the family; two children attend school.

or a little over 3·5 tons of grain, but in practice he receives enough each week to feed his family, and the balance owing to him is paid at harvest-time. But after a dry year, like 1952, when there were only 11 in. of rain, he may find himself in debt. He is then obliged to remain with the same employer during the following year so as to make up the deficit.

The total capital involved in the undertaking is in the region of 1,000,000 francs (of 1952) or more; two-thirds for the land, about a third for the animals, and a mere 15,000 francs for the equipment. Apart from the traditional swing plough, the latter comprises a harrow, which is shared with a neighbour, and an iron plough. These implements were bought, like one of the camels, on a credit scheme, and are repayable by instalments over three years. They are kept in repair by the Agricultural Service. In 1951 the value of farm output reached 500,000 francs, to which the livestock contributed only an eighth. The importance of the subsistence element in the economy is demonstrated by the fact that only 150,000 francs worth of grain was actually sold. The standard of living is, nevertheless, high—far superior to that of Negro Africa or monsoon Asia and, indeed, well above the general level prevailing among the native peoples of North Africa. Even the Khammès, who works 300 days a year and receives over 3·5 tons of grain valued at 86,500 francs, earns almost 300 francs a day, or more than twice the wage of an agricultural labourer.[1]

In this case, employer and employee are fortunately placed, both cultivated area and yields being well above the average. The *métayer* generally earns very much less, and we have already seen how in Kabylia he sometimes lives in the most abject poverty. In February 1938, after the poor harvest of the previous year, we witnessed a case near Safi of a sheik paying the women employed for weeding his wheat-fields ½ franc a day, hardly the price of 1 lb. of barley, which is the traditional fodder grain—and the poor man's bread cereal. As the women also had to keep their families alive, they had the right to take away half the weeds they pulled up, the remainder being kept to feed the sheik's cattle. In the evening, they sorted out the edible plants and cooked them for their families. In Morocco in 1938, moreover, it was found impossible to find local markets for the whole of the wheat crop, and some of it was disposed of by dumping; in the case of certain consignments to Greece, the price was as low as 14 francs a hundredweight, f.o.b.

[1] After the drought of 1952 he actually received less than a hired hand. In general the Khammès earns less than the permanent labourer employed on a settler's farm.

120. M. Richard has calculated that about 1,000 work-days a year are spent on the running of Si Abdallah's farm. The *fellah* himself and the *Khammès* both give about 300 days, the former perhaps a little less, and seasonal workers account for the remaining 400 days. Nine-tenths of this time is absorbed by the cereal crops, thus giving a ratio of approximately eighteen days per acre, or from two and a half to three days per hundredweight. A less efficient neighbour averages three days of work per hundredweight of cereals. In Kabylia we noted a maximum of twenty-four days per acre and seven and a half days per hundredweight, but these figures were rather exceptional.

Representative figures for typical native holdings are from two and a half to five days per hundredweight of grain, but the number of days increases quickly, first, in mountainous areas because of the extra effort involved and, secondly, towards the south because of the rapid decline in yields. This degree of productivity is attained by methods which make far more use of animal power than, for example, in Tonkin. Animals are used for transport, for raising irrigation water, for threshing, and for many other purposes. The limiting factor on productivity is the aridity of the climate, which effectively depresses the level of agricultural output; yields are only 5 cwt. per acre on the Atlantic seaboard of Morocco, and fall as low as 3 in the drier climate of Tunisia. On the whole, the settlers obtain about 7 cwt. per acre in Morocco and Algeria and 9 in Tunisia, with up to 24 in exceptional cases. The reason for this difference between the European and the native farm is that the former generally occupies the richer land and has more power and better techniques at its disposal.

In this respect, Si Abdallah is certainly more efficient than the great majority of his fellows, who fail to prepare the soil with sufficient care, and who often do not cultivate a large enough area to make full use of the pair of draught animals which are the essential unit in the use of the native plough. The inadequacy of soil-cultivating operations becomes more marked towards the north-east from Settat, in the neighbourhood of Ben Ahmed. M'Ahmed ben Mouhak, a member of the Kouarcha tribe, cultivates 15 acres of land in this region, where the rainfall rises to about 17 in., and is assisted by his wife and two young children. He cannot afford to leave any of his land in fallow, and $8\frac{1}{2}$ acres are under barley, 3 under hard wheat, and a little less than 2 under maize; on the remainder he sows fenugreek, coriander, and linseed. Apart from his two cows and a calf, he has only a donkey, which means that the ground can only be scratched superficially and proper working of the soil is impossible.

The Ben Ahmed Section for Rural Modernization (Secteur de modernisation du Paysanat, or S.M.P.) has provided him with a camel, which he is buying on a three-year instalment plan, and has provided another for his neighbour, Fekek, who, having only $11\frac{1}{2}$ acres to support eight people, lives in even more straitened circumstances. The two camels, harnessed to the iron plough, which is owned in partnership, can now be used to till the fields of both holdings. A proper balance between cultivated area and available animal power is at last being achieved, and at the same time fodder is not being consumed unnecessarily by draught animals at the expense of productive livestock. In the case of very small holdings kept by farm labourers in their spare time, each pair of camels is simply shared between a large number of people. In one example, a pair of animals serves nine different holdings. One of these belongs to Tami ben Mohammed, an employee of the S.M.P., who grows 3 acres of cereals and owns a donkey, a goat, and a cow and her heifer. The S.M.P. has also helped to improve the quality of seeds by supplying them ready cleaned and treated. All in all, average cereal yields have been raised over large regions by about 1·2 cwt. per acre. Similar benefits could doubtless be gained in France if thousands of tiny peasant holdings would band themselves into groups for the co-operative use of tractors. Furthermore, the backwardness of certain rural areas could also be dealt with by the establishment of an organization along the lines of the Paysanat.

7. Mechanization and the Paysanat (S.M.P.)

121. Owing to the continuing growth of the population in Morocco, the appreciable progress which has already been made cannot yet be considered satisfactory. Whereas the Far Eastern river deltas are short of land and western U.S.A. and most of South America and Australia are short of men, here in North Africa the shortage of land is only just beginning to be felt in Algeria and Tunisia, and labour is everywhere more than plentiful. In order to provide enough food for all these workers and their dependants, agriculture must be intensified by concentrating on the two factors which are most seriously deficient—namely, mechanical power and water resources. So long as these are in short supply, the application of other factors of production—fertilizers in particular—will have relatively little effect. By the end of the summer, draught animals are weakened by the scarcity of feedingstuffs, and wherever the terrain is slightly clayey the drought-hardened surface is impossible to plough. The *fellah* awaits the advent of the first

rains for ploughing and the second for seeding. If they arrive a little later than usual, much too small an area is sown and the crops mature too late to give a good harvest, especially as the preparation of the soil leaves much to be desired even at the best of times.

The settler has long appreciated the need for tractors which enable large areas to be ploughed deep and early, and this is the main reason for the high level of his yields. Instead of lying fallow—and providing additional grazing land—the fields are ploughed well in advance of the sowing season. At first, the land used to be worked over during the spring in preparation for autumn-sown crops but later this would begin during the preceding winter. In Tunisia, however, since 1920 ploughing has begun immediately after the June harvest, and this practice has now spread elsewhere. Deep ploughing followed by frequent working of the surface militates against evaporation and weed-infestation, but it sometimes encourages wind and water erosion and it deprives the stock of a certain amount of grazing.

The best method would be to leave the stubble to protect the soil, to sow annually wherever the annual rainfall exceeds 16 in., and to increase the acreage of forage crops. Both traditional and modern dry farming methods rely on mechanization, which is a more pressing and urgent need here in North Africa than in either monsoon Asia or central Africa, capable as it is of raising yields by as much as 3 or 4 cwt. per acre. If the machine could be firmly established in native agriculture, the food problem would be solved for the next twenty-five years.

What Europeans can achieve economically on 750-acre farms obviously remains an impossibility for individual native holdings, three-quarters of which are of less than 25 acres. Some of the settlers have long held the view that their example would suffice to stimulate technical progress among the majority of the Mohammedan peasantry, but their arguments ignore differences of scale and the native's very limited opportunities for the accumulation of capital. Moreover, as they all too frequently occupy the best land, their methods could not be applied universally, which is not altogether regrettable, for their farming practice is not without its faults. Many Algerian citrus-growers, for instance, persist in ignoring modern techniques in their erratic watering and pruning methods.[1] Their attitude towards soil conservation is positively nonchalant. 'After me—the Flood!' replied an Oranian settler—who had no children—when the rapidly growing patches of bare white rock on his land were pointed out to him.

Those responsible for the future of the North African community

[1] In Corsica, citrus trees are treated much less scientifically even than here.

MECHANIZATION AND THE PAYSANAT

cannot afford to be so thoughtless. For a long time it was simply denied that there was a problem at all; some even hoped that all the worthwhile land would gradually be taken over by Europeans. Eventually, in 1945, under the guidance of M. Berque in Morocco and of M. Paye in Algeria, the Paysanat scheme for rural modernization was put into effect. There had been several previous attempts to tackle the problem, notably in Algeria by the technical officers of the Native Provident Societies (1937-9); the name of M. Le Beau deserves special mention in this connexion. In the course of an assignment during this period, we pleaded in vain for an extension of this type of work.

122. In Morocco Berque was of the opinion that 'modernization must either be complete,[1] or never come at all'. His aim was to raise 'islands of prosperity' where a wholesale application of capital would, apart from providing the indispensable schools and hospitals, create an abundance of materials and equipment, and even permit the building of the most up-to-date villages, more or less on the lines of those of Potemkino on the Volga. This was spectacular propaganda, but, as was the current fashion at the time, the economics of this politically conceived project had been entirely overlooked. The limited resources, supplied partly by taxes levied on the *fellahin*, who were sometimes extremely poor, should have engendered a policy of the strictest economy, and the attack should have concentrated on breaking the fetters which were holding back production.

The houses built at Meknes at the S.M.P. should only have been financed by the increased income from better harvests, and these latter should have been the direct and exclusive aim of the initial investment. It would then have been possible to help all those who were willing to build for themselves. In fact, the houses were such that an economic rent would have absorbed the whole of a worker's wages. The stone floors were too cold for people not in the habit of wearing shoes, and the rooms were too large for people who could not afford to furnish them.

When the communally-owned land was taken over from the local tribes, to whom rich rewards were promised before any work began,[2] too little study was devoted in the first instance to the choice of terrain.

---

[1] As if modernization, which is by definition a continuous process, could ever be complete.

[2] Practically every agricultural development project is bound to operate at a loss to begin with, and this was no exception. Money, therefore, had to be paid out of profits which did not exist, after the manner of a fraudulent private company.

Sometimes it almost seemed as if, by a peculiar aberration, difficulties were being deliberately sought: a tract of rock-strewn land was cleared at Ksiba and an attempt was made in the Gharb area to exploit land subject to floods.[1] The first task should have been to classify, according to their quality, the more promising areas of communally-owned land.

Then again, it was the declared objective to mechanize the field operations completely including the harvest. We ourselves have actually seen tribesmen just looking on while the crops on their own land were being harvested by the S.M.P.—surely an indication that the project was begun on a false premise. The desire to copy certain features of the Russian collective was fundamentally unwise, because the economic conditions were simply not suitable for such an experiment, and the result was the establishment of purely administrative units much more akin to the State farm. Moreover, as the policy was to develop these 'islands of prosperity'—which some considered to be thoroughly unhealthy growths—in isolation from the regions around them, the essential task of the State farm was forgotten. The latter, as we shall see, is to forge a link between agricultural research and the co-operative producer; its function is to adapt modern techniques to local conditions and to carry out tasks which call for a high degree of technical skill—producing selected seeds, breeding for stud purposes, nursery cultivation, reafforestation, etc.

We were called in by the Paysanat in 1947, and made certain recommendations which have since been fully adopted. The substance of these was that endeavours should be made to transform native agriculture as a whole and that the S.M.Ps. should be regarded as pilot farms responsible for the diffusion of sound agricultural practices. As the main stumbling block is still poor preparation of the soil, we would also have liked to see more emphasis placed on mechanized gangs equipped with tractors and disc ploughs on the model of the Russian tractor stations. Once the land had been ploughed with the help of the collective tractor, the *fellah* would then have been responsible for the surface workings, which he could easily accomplish with his own animals. He could have paid for the cost of the service when he delivered his crop to the co-operative.

As the factories cannot always absorb the whole of the surplus labour

[1] In Algeria, the cultivation of the Hodna, on the threshold of the Sahara, is a less urgent task than the development of the isolated patches of loamy soil which still remain in the coastal lowlands. In Nurra, in north-west Sardinia, up to 1,000 cu. yds. of stones are removed per acre of newly-cleared land. The pressing overpopulation of Italy and the lack of good land leave less choice than in Morocco.

of the countryside, we would have concentrated on the purchase of tractors and disc ploughs at the expense of combine-harvesters. It seems advisable for the time being to call a halt to any further progress in mechanization beyond the employment of binders and threshing-machines, which, though they do not represent as high a degree of mechanization as the combine, would enable far larger areas to be dealt with for the same capital outlay. Another argument in their favour is that none of the straw and chaff, which are an invaluable adjunct to the development of native animal husbandry, need be wasted.[1] Finally, so far the Paysanat has indulged in a kind of administrative paternalism,[2] and it is high time that the people themselves were allowed to participate in the management of the scheme. There is no other way of guaranteeing them a real measure of economic independence.

123. Higher production could also be achieved by extending the cultivated area. Although in Tunisia and Algeria the farmer has chanced his arm in the dry south and on steep slopes all too often, there are still considerable possibilities for development in the lowlands. This is particularly true of the latifundia, mostly owned by Moslems, of the communal tribal lands, and of the *habous*, which are properties belonging to the mosques. It is doubtful, however, whether even in Tunisia, which is more favoured than Algeria in this respect, any possible increases could do more than to offset the acreage of marginal land which should be abandoned on grounds of soil erosion. The largest areas of as yet undeveloped cultivable land are in Morocco, where a net increase amounting to nearly 7,500,000 acres is possible, according to M. Miège. There are many areas of over-extensive development where the land could be made to yield more abundantly. For example, in the neighbourhood of Oulmes, in the mountains immediately south-east of Rabat, Mohamed ben Mesnaoui owns nearly 1,000 acres. Until 1951 he used to have only 75 to 100 acres ploughed each year, and this land would be sown to barley, wheat, and oats. He followed no set rotations, and the fields often lay fallow for a year or two between crops. Moreover, the high rainfall, about 36 in. annually, made fallowing most unwise, for, instead of recuperating, the soil was actually being subjected to leaching. The work was performed by seasonal labourers, who were paid according to the number of seed measures they sowed; consequently, they were always in a hurry to get rid of one batch of seed before starting on another, and this can hardly have led to conscientious work.

[1] See our *Etude des modalités d'action du Paysanat* (Rabat, 1948).
[2] Professor Knight of the University of California also emphasizes this point.

These farm hands are opposed to the employment of better equipment, and, in spite of the good rainfall, yields are no more than 3-5 cwt. per acre, although it must be admitted that the soil is poor and there might well be a case for using artificial fertilizers. The rest of the land was obviously undergrazed by the fifty cattle and 300 sheep. Half these cattle and a third of the sheep remained in the forest throughout the year, while the remainder were there for five months and grazed the private pastures on the plateau during only part of the other seven months. In the winter they took refuge in the narrow valleys, which dispensed with the need for building shelters.

In the neighbourhood of the Ouerrha Valley, at the foot of the Rif, which is almost as overpopulated as Kabylia, we came across some huge estates belonging to Fassi nobles where the land was used even more extensively. This unhappy juxtaposition of underdeveloped latifundia and rural under-employment is a feature of all the Mediterranean coastlands, from Andalusia to central and southern Italy. In Morocco, the larger landowners must become more alive to their responsibility for rural improvement.[1] At the instigation of the S.M.P. at Oulmes, Mesnaoui has already planted 1,200 trees, which he has begun to prune and care for generally. He has bought a tractor, and in 1951-2 he ploughed 150 acres. It is to be hoped that others will follow his example.

8. Irrigation and Its Difficulties; the Latifundia

124. The comparatively limited scope for improving dry-farming methods is a stimulus to the search for other techniques of intensification, among which the Mediterranean cultivator has for thousands of years given pride of place to irrigation. A recent example can be studied on the tribal land of the Triffas (Fig. 12), near the coast at Madagh, north-west of Oujda, in the narrow strip of Morocco between Algeria and Spanish Morocco. In 1938 the land was divided between the various members of the tribe, who each received between 6 and 8 acres of land. This was irrigated from wells which reached the water table at no great depth. Those who owned the wells and the first pumping equipment quickly exploited their advantage, and in some cases their neighbours found themselves paying as much as half their total harvest for the privilege of drawing water. Today, there are powerful electric pumps, installed by the S.M.P., which provide plenty of water at a moderate

[1] 'In the Bone lowland and the lower Kebir valley, between Djidjelli and El Milia, first-rate loamy soils support only a few goats wherever the land has remained under native ownership' (H. Laforêt).

IRRIGATION AND ITS DIFFICULTIES; THE LATIFUNDIA

price. In the near future, when the Moulouya barrage, now in course of construction, is completed, a far greater proportion of this lowland will have irrigation facilities.

Mustafa bel Hadj, who lives in the *douar*, or encampment, of the Beni Oukil, is married, with a son of sixteen and four young children, who keep his wife fully occupied. All the year long he works with his son on his 6-acre holding. It is instructive to compare his case with that of Mesnaoui at Oulmes, who employs a gardener, three shepherds, and three seasonal workers for 1,000 acres. In addition, for the harvest and for gathering and threshing the beans, Mustafa has to employ casual labour at the rate of 120 man-days a year. In 1950-1 his wage bill was 16,000 francs. A labourer could expect 133 francs a day at busy times and 100 francs during the remainder of the year.

In this area, with its mere 12 in. of rain a year, irrigation makes all the difference between an uncertain harvest one year in two, as in former times, and the reliable yields of the double-cropping system of today. We shall encounter the double-cropping system again, not only in the Spanish and Italian *regadio*, but also in certain areas without irrigation, as in the well-watered country of Brittany and Belgium. One effect of irrigation is that far more labour is needed, in this instance a total of some 600 man-days per year, or 100 days per acre. This is six times as much as in the case of unirrigated cereal farming and twelve times as much as where a biennial rotation of grain and grazed fallow is practised.

In the 1¼-acre orchard there are sixty-two Washington Navel orange trees, twenty-eight clementine, six lemon, four peach, three plum, and four apricot trees. These were planted in 1949 and cost a total of 65,000 francs, which was obtained on loan from the S.M.P. and had to be repaid within three years. In 1950-1, summer beans were planted between the trees, and were followed by early potatoes, thus making the most of the climatic effects of proximity to the sea. Three-quarters of an acre of hard wheat and 2½ of barley were followed by autumn beans, while the acre or so remaining merely gave a single crop of summer beans. Mustafa has devoted considerable attention to these, since the market price of pepper, which he formerly grew in considerable quantities, fell suddenly in 1949. The dried fruits were crushed into a powder and give an ochre-coloured spice. The rapid readaptation to changing prices, which a more predominantly subsistence economy could achieve much less easily, deserves special emphasis.

The 16 cwt. of hard wheat and the 1 ton of barley are consumed on the farm, mostly by Mustafa's family. The 58 cwt. of beans and the

5 tons of potatoes which were obtained in 1951 were almost entirely sold, and fetched a total of 300,000 francs. This compared with a cost of production of 66,000 francs, including water, seed potatoes, labour, and tractor-ploughing. The farm has only a mare, a cow, and ten chickens; the collective tractor is used for tilling the soil. Farmyard manure is made from straw, and, like market gardeners all the world over, Mustafa is always trying to buy more. When the whole of this lowland is converted into irrigated fields, he will be hard put to it to find a source of supply. The following year he was going to grow some mint and some cotton, but he was already beginning to think about acquiring a few more animals and devoting one of his fields to lucerne.

In 1947 and again in 1949 we noticed the unmistakable signs of soil deterioration on these irrigated holdings. Water is applied to the land, often excessively, but although it improves the crops, it quickly harms the soil unless sufficient attention is given to the need for large quantities of organic and chemical fertilizers. The mistake common to all these irrigated sectors is that lucrative cash crops are being grown before the conservation of the soil can be assured by a proper development of animal husbandry.

125. In the area of the Office des Beni-Amir[1] near the foot of the Middle Atlas west of Kasbah Tadla, the first additions to the traditional cereal crops were the olive and cotton; all are exhausting crops. At the same time, both goats, which are the enemies of trees, and sheep were excluded from the area. Whether it was wise to remove their sheep from a people who had always relied mainly on their flocks is a debatable point. On the other hand, this course would have been justified if the growing of fodder crops had been encouraged with a view to the establishment of cattle-rearing. Most of the lucerne, however, which was grown on altogether too limited a scale—less than 2,500 acres out of 38,000 in 1949—was in fact exported. In 1950 there were less than ten head of cattle per 100 acres, and for the most part they grazed the open grasslands and consequently furnished very little manure. Owing to the inadequacy of preparatory surveys, the main canals command some areas which are not well suited to irrigation and others where the conditions are wholly inappropriate. The layout of secondary canals also suffered from the lack of careful planning, and when the water began to flow there was no system of drainage. The result was that in 1947 seepage back to the surface transformed parts of the central area into a veritable morass.

[1] Inspired by the experiments of the Office du Niger.

IRRIGATION AND ITS DIFFICULTIES; THE LATIFUNDIA

The implementation of an irrigation scheme is an extremely delicate operation and involves very heavy capital expenditure. It follows that if errors of this type are to be avoided a thorough campaign of preparatory work must be undertaken. It also follows that if a project is to be economically sound other factors of intensification, some of which in other circumstances can be held in abeyance during the initial stages of development, must be brought into play as soon as water begins to reach the fields. The most important of these are the various forms of fertilization and the unremitting battle against weeds. The latter is facilitated when water can be diverted at will from one field to another and dry crops interpolated in the rotation. The rapidity with which extensive cereal cultivators and semi-nomadic herdsmen are expected to turn themselves into fairly intensive market gardeners begs the question of how they are to acquire the skills necessary to the performance of their novel role. They evidently need to undergo a rigorous course of training under the guidance of agricultural instructors versed in the difficult art of water control. There is certainly no call for sergeant-majors.

126. The Triffas at Madagh rely on pumping water from underground and the Beni-Amir depend on the perennial flow of the Oum er R'bia, which even in the summer has a flow of 1,400 cu. ft. per second. Algeria, however, is not so well endowed with large streams, and has therefore been compelled to construct large dams to store the flood waters which follow the torrential rains. In this case, the volume of investment is even larger and planning should be, but is not always, correspondingly more thorough.[1] Those responsible for building the dams are much too preoccupied with finding favourable sites. They do not think to survey the catchment area and estimate the rate at which their reservoir is likely to become silted up nor do they consider whether the land downstream is either suitable for irrigation or liable to present serious drainage difficulties.

Because these precautions were overlooked, the surface at Relizane is now impregnated with salts, and a lowland which was fertile before the days of irrigation has now been completely sterilized. The Ghrib Reservoir on the upper Cheliff dates from 1937, but it only began to be used in 1949, and even then only for a few hundred acres. At this rate of progress, the distribution canals will not be complete until 1970 and the farmers, when they realize how much more capital they will have to invest, will probably take another ten years to convert all their land to irrigated crops. By the time their trees finally begin to bear

[1] See our article in *Economie contemporaine* for June 1949.

fruit, the reservoir will already be half silted up, the regularization of flow from one year to another, which should permit summer crops to be irrigated even after a dry winter, will no longer be possible, and the efficacy of the whole scheme will be reduced to a mere fraction of what it should have been.

Though completed in 1927, the Oued Beth Barrage in Morocco was in 1953 serving only 25,000 acres, whereas the reserves of water are such that 88,000 could be irrigated. Such instances of the underemployment of resources put the adequacy of the whole economic structure seriously in doubt. Among the engineers there is a tendency to start on new barrages before completing the canal networks of older schemes. This is an extremely short-sighted policy, in view of the rapid deterioration of reservoirs by silting up. In future anti-erosion measures in the catchment areas and the distribution and drainage systems should come first; the barrage itself should not be started until these are approaching completion. If this method is used, as soon as the reservoir comes into being the fullest possible use can be made of it. An appreciable number of years can be added to its short span of life by cutting anti-erosive benches in the catchment area.

127. Corresponding with this fresh approach to the engineering problem there should also be a reorganization of the land in the zone destined for irrigation, and the aim should be to group together some of the very small holdings and to subdivide the latifundia. Whereas in the majority of cases it seems advisable or sometimes even necessary to enlarge the present average size of holding, the opposite is generally true where irrigation is being developed. This is because it necessitates a volume of investment per acre which the large landowner can rarely afford. The degree of intensification is quite likely to make the scale of an undertaking five or even ten times larger than it ever was before. Whereas in a collectivized economy the very large enterprise would still be favoured, in capitalist countries the 'one-man' irrigated holding is generally farmed more intensively and managed more efficiently than the larger unit. The breaking up of the large estates would enable a satisfactory level of productivity to be maintained in spite of the higher density of population.

In most countries of the world a portion of the increased land value due to irrigation is used to defray, in some small measure, the heavy expenditure incurred by public funds. The courageous Martin Act passed in 1942 provided for such payments in the form of surrenders of land from which it was intended to create fresh holdings. The large landowners, both European and Moslem,[1] were the target of this legislation, but they made clever use of its effective date. Under the Fourth Republic the law has not been repealed, but neither has any administration dared to apply it, even in the improved form suggested by that most active body, the Service for Colonization and Hydraulics.[2] One is left with the impression that, in this matter at least, less concern is being shown for the public interest than under the Vichy régime. Finally, water tends to be wasted because it is too cheap. In Algeria, apart from hybrid maize or rice, which give very high yields if heavily manured, cereals still occupy far too large an area, for they are incapable of giving returns sufficient to pay a reasonable water rate; there are even some tracts of uncultivated fallow.[3]

If it is to be an economic proposition, irrigation must be accompanied, not only by heavy applications of fertilizer, but also by an intensification of the crop system. In other words, there must be a transition to enterprises from which high returns can be expected. So far, the main response has been in the form of horticulture, with an emphasis on fruit, mostly citrus, and early vegetables; but whereas North Africa could doubtless share with Italy, Spain, and the Midi their role as Western Europe's winter garden, the market for this type of produce is already showing signs of saturation. Under the present economic conditions, the commercial outlets might well prove unable to cope with further increases in production, and attempts to enter this field should be discouraged in the new irrigated areas. It would be advisable in future to concentrate more on growing fodder crops which could supplement the steppe grazings and become the basis of intensive stock-rearing, thus augmenting the country's resources of meat, milk, and wool.

In the second place, industrial crops must be introduced, and cotton is the obvious choice. In an intensive farming system, it can be grown without damaging the soil, and increased production here would prevent an undesirably large extension of cotton in central Africa, where it is a very real threat to fertility. All three countries of North Africa

[1] For example, the Saïa Estate.

[2] J. Léger has calculated that the existing barrages in Algeria, which in theory would allow 350,000 acres to be irrigated, actually served 187,000 acres at the end of 1945, and only 102,000 of these were cultivated intensively. There has been very little progress since then.

[3] 'Putting the operation of this Martin Act in abeyance was the work of vested interests. . . . The landowners in the irrigable areas have demonstrated by their actions that they do not fully appreciate where their true interests lie' (J. Léger, *Agria*, No. 157).

could also grow sugar-beet in their irrigated zones, or even outside them where the rainfall reaches 18 in. a year. On the Atlantic coast, in the Abda region behind Safi, sugar cane might well be tried, but only with irrigation. There are distinct possibilities even for tea. The main reason for Asia's present supremacy is the cheapness of its labour, but this is an advantage which will not last for ever. It has already been emphasized that tobacco is particularly well suited to overpopulated regions, but the quality of the North African product is still too low.

In its present stage of development the Maghreb is finding that its exports of agricultural produce no longer meet its requirement for manufactured goods and equipment, to say nothing of such commodities as sugar and cotton fibre. The conditions for the cultivation of these last-named crops, however, are ideal, and their production could serve as the basis for new secondary industries nicely related to the needs of the home market. Although the largest possibilities for cotton are in Morocco, they are by no means negligible in Algeria, especially when one considers that the crop has made rapid strides even in Hungary.

9. A Settler combines Stock-rearing and Cereal Cultivation in the Upper Cheliff

128. These two groups of crops, fodder and industrial, can be developed even more fully in the unirrigated areas of adequate rainfall than in the irrigated zones. The average settler is showing a lack of initiative in this direction, and is much too inclined to rely on crops like wheat and the vine, which are either protected or the products of horticulture. The conservation of the soil by the application of humus, the maintenance of fertility, whether the land is irrigated or not, and the raising of both cereal and tree crop production are all, however, dependent on the future of stock-rearing.

At Puits, in the upper Cheliff near Affreville (Fig. 10) which has a mean annual rainfall of 16 in., De Calan farms 9,000 acres of land. Until 1949 there were 3,500 acres of wheat, 1,000 of barley, 125 of unirrigated vegetables, and, a recent innovation, 250 of forage crops. There were also 3,750 acres of cultivated fallow where, in theory at least, a cereal was grown every other year. Immediately after the harvest, when the straw had been gathered up, or even burnt in spite of its value as feed, the ground was ploughed to a depth of 16 in. either with two electric winches drawing turn-about ploughs or with big caterpillar tractors (one type D7 and five D6s) and disc ploughs. On the farm there are also seven machines for breaking up fallow, eighty harrows, fifteen 13-ft.-wide fertilizer-spreaders (used in the spring for spreading 4-9-9[1] at 4 cwt. to the acre), fifteen 16-ft. seed-drills, seven combine-harvesters with a cutting width of 16 ft., three pick-up balers, and four lorries. Finally, five medium-powered tractors, one of them with caterpillars, and fifteen horses and mules complete the impressive list of power resources.

A visitor would have cause for thinking he was on an American farm—although there are few as large as this in the United States or with such an array of equipment—until he saw the crowd of people swarming about the yard and the long lines of labourers busy weeding in the fields. In fact, there are twenty European employees, specialists, and overseers, who account for some 5,000 work days per annum. Then there are 140 'permanent' native labourers who work, according to circumstances, between 115 and 240 days a year, making a total of about 26,000 days in all, and, finally, there are thirty seasonal workers, employed from 15 April until 10 July every year, who supply a further 2,000 work-days.

Thus, in spite of all the modern tractors and equipment, 33,000 days of work are expended on a cultivated area which, if one includes a few olive groves on the hillocks and some market gardens, covers some 5,000 acres in all. Certain 'general expenses in connection with work on the farm' have been left out of account in some of the figures quoted so far, but taking them into consideration one arrives at a figure of 6·6 days of work per year expended on each acre. This figure represents what one would have expected from an up-to-date French farm equipped with a binder in about 1900. The Kansas cereal farmer reckons to spend half a working day on the land for every acre of wheat and only half this time if he is really well equipped; the figures are about doubled if one includes other tasks connected with the farm but not actually performed on the land.

Doubtless the native labourer's zeal for work is less than the American farmer's, who is generally his own master. Besides this, the cheapness of labour makes for a certain inefficiency in its use, a tendency which reappears in the south-eastern part of the United States, where wage-rates are much lower than elsewhere in the country. The presence of combines, moreover, obviously has no effect on the laborious hand-weeding so frequently found in Mediterranean lands. The actual working of the soil is deeper and more thorough than in the U.S.A.; also, the soil is fairly clayey, and more difficult to cultivate on that

[1] 4 per cent. nitrogen, 9 per cent. phosphoric acid, 9 per cent. potash.

account. Programmes of work, however, are not drawn up with the same degree of efficiency.

During the last few years the yields have been 10 cwt. per acre for wheat and 16 for barley: a weighted average of about 12 for cereals as a whole. The number of days needed to produce 1 cwt. varies between 0·5 in good years and 0·85 in bad, as against 0·1 in Kansas. On the whole, therefore, the productivity of labour is midway between that of the native Moslem holding and the North American farm.

The turning-point on this farm came in the autumn of 1948, when the fallow was reduced to 2,750 acres and 1,750 acres of vetch and black gram were sown. In the spring, the latter were cut 8 in. above the ground and used for fodder; the remaining growth was then turned into the soil. In March 1949, 1,800 sheep, cross-breds between Chatillonais merinos and Zemmora ewes, were brought in. Compared with the size of the farm, this is still only a small flock, as it gives barely one sheep for every 5 acres, but since then de Calan has added a herd of eighty dairy cows. We can but hope that he will regard this as no more than a beginning, and that his example will be followed by many other settlers in North Africa. Fallows will then be relegated to the arid regions, and new irrigation schemes like the Ghrib Barrage in the upper Cheliff region will lead to a rapid expansion of the acreage under forage crops.

10. Mechanization, Intensification, and Industrialization in Underdeveloped Countries

129. Irrigation works will not lead to the oft-quoted density of five workers per acre, a figure which can only be attained with a concentration on market-gardening enterprises. Even with only a quarter or a fifth of this density, however, it should be possible to absorb a small proportion of the surplus population of southern Morocco and the highland regions. However, even if irrigation schemes were pushed forward at a much faster rate than at present, unaided they could not hold out the prospect of full employment for the constantly growing rural population.

We have seen that mechanizing cultivation of the soil is the essential factor in raising the yields of dry farming operations. The problem, however, must be tackled on a broader front. So far, the settler has relied on mechanization rather than on intensification; indeed, the arrival of combines in large numbers was the cause of serious rural unemployment in Morocco from 1938 onwards. The Beni M'tir tribe, who had been compelled by the advance of the settlers to leave the plateaux south of Meknes for the high escarpments behind El Hadjeh, complained that they could no longer find work in the country they had previously cultivated on their own account. The accent, therefore, must now be placed on intensification. High-yielding industrial and forage crops must be adopted, there must be better working and cleaning of the soil, and large quantities of chemical fertilizers must be employed on irrigated land and wherever there is adequate rainfall.

These factors of intensification should have priority over the mechanization of harvesting operations, which is costly and does not expand the volume of production. Agrarian mechanization in North America and the U.S.S.R. has as its corollary a rapid expansion of industry which, saving periods of depression in the United States, enables the man forced to leave his field to find employment in the factory. Both in France and North Africa, although the market for the products of secondary industry is still far from saturation point, there is a regrettable tendency to view the absorption of the surplus rural population in 'tertiary' industry with equanimity. The capital needed to open a small shop or a kiosk to sell tickets for the national lottery would not be enough to set up a modern workshop. So large a part of the national revenue, moreover, is committed to negative purposes, such as armaments, that the apparatus of production cannot be renewed quickly enough, nor can the country's competitive power in the markets of the world be maintained. The increasing backwardness thus engendered will have incalculable results on the French economy.

The present rate of growth of the Moslem population is nearly 2 per cent. per annum, and the French must see to it that the food supply increases at least as quickly, for the situation is of their own making, inasmuch as their intervention has contributed to the longer expectation of life. In view of the country's need for equipment and of the necessity for raising the standard of living, agricultural production must be raised by at least 3 per cent. per annum. At present, this figure is still far from being reached, in spite of the greater energy displayed by the authorities since the end of the war.

130. Full employment depends on a rapid development of industry,[1] which the agricultural scientist would doubly welcome if it devoted a considerable part of its energies to the manufacture of the various means

---

[1] In 1950, industry in Algeria, excluding transport, employed 230,000 workers; as against this the settlers employed 100,000 permanent workers on their farms and, in addition, 600,000 native families supplied them with casual labour.

of production on the land, such as fertilizers and all kinds of equipment, and one may hope that even tractors will eventually be made locally. Light industries might include textiles, sugar-refining, preserves, oil and flour mills, wheat pastes, and furniture, and if sufficient capital was forthcoming to give these a start while still leaving enough not only for agricultural investments (including small-, medium-, and large-scale irrigation works), but also for the establishment of heavy industry along the lines of the Erik Labonne plan, everything would indeed be perfect.

Failing this, it would certainly be a great mistake to sacrifice mechanization, irrigation, and soil-conservation works and the establishment of technical cadres—in short, the whole apparatus of rural improvement —for the sake of the essentially military objective of building a huge steelworks in the desert. In fact, the financial resources that would be needed to achieve both these aims concurrently are simply not available. The pursuit of rural improvement need not, on the other hand, militate against the search for oil, nor need it affect the development of other types of mining or of processing industries based on their products. The essential criterion is that such activities must not be encouraged at the expense of agriculture, which, in view of the pressure of population on the land, must receive every possible priority.

In recent years, the amount of money set aside for agricultural development has been insufficient, in view of the difficult natural conditions, to ensure the raising of production by the necessary minimum of 3 per cent. per year. If this unfortunate situation persists, it will become necessary to encourage emigration, though not with the same urgency as in the deltas of the Far East. The countries of Europe generally, in spite of their own population problems, and France in particular, would have to be the reception areas. So far, Kabyles and southern Moroccans, when they have come, have generally taken up the more arduous kinds of industrial occupation, a fact which tends to discourage the modernization of equipment which France needs to give her own workers better conditions. Furthermore, immigration could soon become excessive and lead to unemployment. It is worth remembering that for a given quantity of invested capital, work can be found for more people in a rejuvenated agricultural system than in modern industry.

Here again, in the absence of other effective measures, it might become necessary to consider the possibilities of birth-control. Demographic considerations have already prevented the French system of family allowances from being applied in Algeria, and one hesitates to

THE FUTURE OF THE UNDERDEVELOPED COUNTRIES

condemn this policy, although there are obvious grounds for criticizing it as anti-social.

131. North Africa is the last of the underdeveloped extra-European areas we shall be considering in this work. All these areas are characterized in the main by the prevalence of a retarded agricultural economy of very low productivity, by the undernourishment, qualitative if not actually quantitative, of the greater part of the inhabitants, and by the absence of industrial equipment, which even at best exists only in embryonic form. The whole of Africa uses less than 2,000,000 tons of steel a year: the United States, with a smaller population, consumed five times as much as this in 1951, and her annual increase in consumption is also several times larger. The Negro or Far Eastern peasant produces much less than a tenth of the British farm worker's output, and as his rate of progress is still negligible the gap is widening every day.

The capital investment necessary to achieve a 2 per cent. increase in the yearly production of these areas—the minimum below which differences of productivity would become so wide that difficulties of commercial exchange would lead to an economic impasse—has been estimated by the Gray Report at $14,000 million.[1] This is a cause, therefore, which could be pursued at a fraction of the cost of present-day national defence programmes and one far worthier of the efforts of mankind, but it remains almost entirely neglected. Outside assistance should certainly not absolve the poorer countries—French territories included—from seeking to help themselves by their own efforts, but it can give them fresh heart by freeing them from the overpowering burdens and constraints which oppress them today. Assistance must be given, however, only when there already exists an economic organization capable of administering it efficiently. Finally, Europe herself should seek to provide the necessary investments, for not only is she largely responsible for the present situation, but by now she should realize that with world conditions as they are today her best chance of ensuring her own economic emancipation is by helping the underdeveloped countries.

'Since the war capital has been invested on a fairly large scale. The objectives were to exploit local resources more rationally, to set in motion the process of industrialization by expanding the mining industry and creating new manufacturing industries, to stimulate the flow of equipment into the country and raise its standards of living. In the main the Government has taken the initiative, and between 1945-50 its

[1] Most of these details are taken from *One Way*, the Bevanite pamphlet prepared for the Labour Party Conference at Scarborough in October 1951.

investments totalled 3,500 million francs in gold. But its attempts to attract private capital have been uniformly unsuccessful, except in a very narrow range of enterprises such as in mining. Plans have had to be revised in the light of strategic commitments, and public funds, whether from local or central government sources, have only barely sufficed to maintain the initially determined tempo of investment or even in some cases to provide for the upkeep or completion of works already begun. All are agreed that large investments are still necessary if the countries of L'Union Française Outre-Mer are ever to emerge from their present condition of "underdevelopment".[1]

[1] This is the conclusion reached by J. Dresch in *'Recherches sur les investissements dans l'Union Française Outre-Mer; leur répartition; leurs conséquences'*, which appeared in the *Bulletin de l'Association des géographes français* (January-February 1953).

VI

Arid Plateaux and *Huertas* in Spain[1]

1. Unfavourable Environment, Slow Development

132. On the whole, and with the exception of a few favoured valleys, the Mediterranean coastlands are a poor terrain for agriculture, and the Iberian Peninsula appears to be less favourably endowed than the Italian. Jean Brunhes regards two-thirds of Spain as belonging to 'arid Iberia'; in the vicinity of Almeria[2] the mean annual rainfall is less than 8 in., lower than on some of the esparto grass sheep-lands in southern Algeria. Even well to the north and at some distance from the Mediterranean the rainfall remains low—not exceeding 10 in. per annum, for instance, in the Los Monegros hills near Saragossa.[3] Here, during the five years from 1946 to 1950, the cereal harvest was simply non-existent or very nearly so, and in 1949 the crops did not even break the surface. The mean rainfall figures are unpromisingly low, but the unreliability factor makes the situation even worse than it at first appears.

Rugged masses of upland closely encompass the coastal lowlands, that 'golden fringe' of the Mediterranean with its mild winters, irrigable land and rich-looking countryside. The unwary traveller is readily deceived into thinking that these same features recur in the rest of the peninsula, but erosion creates havoc on the sharp slopes which rise almost everywhere behind the narrow coastal strip. There are few

---

[1] Studied in the field from the end of March until April 1951; prices refer to this period. A provisional edition of this chapter appeared in *Economie contemporaine* for September 1951. A rather milder version appeared in the *Rural Scientist's Bulletin* (Madrid, November 1951), and our Spanish correspondent had promised us some fairly lively replies, 'for', he wrote, 'we ourselves have lost the habit of exercising our critical faculties'. These replies have not materialized, however, the more's the pity.

[2] Where there is a station for the study of desert conditions.

[3] Lom, in central Norway, has the same rainfall and irrigation is necessary.

places in the world, even in the western U.S.A. or Algeria, where the effects of erosion are so striking as in the neighbourhood of Guadix or in the 'lunar landscapes' north of Almeria. In Spain the whole process has been accelerated by deforestation and over-grazing. The latter was the work of transhumant flocks which roamed the great plateaux of the Meseta and for centuries prevented the advance of agriculture and the proper development of the land. The bakers of Lamancha even make use of the sistus and other shrubs, which they uproot in the remaining patches of *maquis*.

FIG. 13. Spain.

In the uplands, the limitations imposed by drought are reinforced by the long cold season. Even the gentler slopes have been dissected and rock is often more in evidence than soil. Seen from the air, Spain gives the impression of vast denuded surfaces dotted here and there with a few luxuriant oases.

As far as agriculture is concerned, to the unfavourable nature of the environment one must add the poverty in materials and equipment. On every side, old-fashioned methods make altogether excessive demands on human labour and coincide with either a scarcity of animal power or more often with its under-employment. The agricultural revolution in Western Europe during the course of the last two centuries has been remarkable chiefly for the growing emphasis on fodder crops, and consequently on animal products, and this has been paralleled by the increased use of animal power in place of human labour, particularly for the harvesting of crops.

The Mediterranean was a less favourable environment for these developments, and in Spain especially, though not, on the contrary, in northern Italy, the new agricultural pattern is far less in evidence than elsewhere in Western Europe. There is therefore a paucity of animal power and an important consequence is that clay soils cannot be deep-ploughed in the dry season, but unfortunately their reserves of moisture cannot be increased in any other way. Finally, machinery has remained beyond the means of the indigent Spanish farmer, and one may travel for many miles on the plateaux of Castille without seeing a single tractor.

2. *Secano* or Dry Cultivation in the Saragossa Steppe

133. After following the Madrid road out of the irrigated Ebro Valley for some seventeen miles and then climbing gradually on to the slopes of the Muela Plateau, one reaches La Muela, the first of the upland villages. The next settlement is La Almunia, another fifteen miles nearer to Madrid (Fig. 14), and the La Muela commune covers an area of over 36,000 acres. There are 1,200 acres of olives sited either near the village or in the small valleys where a little soil remains, 750 acres of vineyards, some of them on terraced slopes, and less than 10,000 under the plough. In theory, there is a two-year rotation of cereal and fallow on the latter: wheat or barley on the better land, oats, barley or rye on the poorer thinner soils. Sometimes the fallow lasts two years, so that cereals, which are the only field crops, cover less than half the cultivated acreage. In addition, there are over 16,000 acres of common grazing land consisting of scarred slopes and rocky screes which make a desolate picture and bear but a very thin covering of sparse vegetation even in the spring. The 7,500 acres of private grazings are sometimes not quite so poor, for they are rented at 3 or 4 pesetas[1] per acre per year!

There are 250 families in the village, a total of 1,040 inhabitants, giving a density of eighteen per square mile. Outside the settlement there are about fifteen large farms with more than 250 acres apiece,

[1] About 123 pesetas to the £1 in 1951.

which have a higher proportion of heath and grazings and an even lower level of land productivity than the average. The other farmhouses are grouped round the village, and each owner generally works his own land, which may be scattered over the whole area in small parcels, some of them up to five or six miles away.

The fifteen 'large' farmers work with four or five mules, and of the others about twenty have two mules and five have only one. Finally, there are eighty labourers who generally have a patch of vines and a few olive trees, the ground being ploughed for them by the farmers in return for labour. These practically landless people are granted hereditary title to between 5 and 15 acres of ground when they marry; on this, they pay a rent or land tax of 2 or 3 pesetas an acre, or twice this amount if they plant vines or olives, the higher rate becoming payable as soon as these begin to bear fruit. The village is not far from industrial Catalonia, and most of the cereals are harvested with reaping machines or binders. The threshing machine, which costs 8 per cent. of the harvest to use, has now replaced the treading of the grain by animals. Yields, however, still remain low: 4 to 6 cwt. of cereals per acre sown; 105 to 130 gallons of wine,[1] and less than 1 cwt. of olive oil per acre. In 1946, an exceptional year, yields of 12 cwt. of wheat and 24 of barley were obtained.

FIG. 14. Saragossa.

134. Thus even when he has a large area at his disposal, the Castillian farmer reaps but little. On one of the larger holdings, which has 210 acres and a complement of five mules, 100 acres are sown in cereals and the farmer counts on between 20 and 35 tons of grain each year.[2] In addition he obtained a total of 8 cwt. of oil, partly from the $2\frac{1}{2}$-acre

[1] Although the acreage under the vine in Spain is comparable with that in France (3,500,000 acres), average yields are only two-fifths of the French (140 gallons per acre).

[2] By law, 75 per cent. must be bread cereals; in practice, at La Muela, wheat, rye, and barley each account for about a third, and small quantities of oats are grown as well. The farm's total harvest has varied between as much as 50 and as little as 10 tons.

plantation which he runs himself, and partly from 15 acres of groves managed by a tenant in return for half the crop. Yet in 1948 and 1949, after he had provided for his household, which includes three sons who work on the farm and a hired hand, his 65 acres of wheat and rye did not even supply enough seed for the following year. His flock of sheep, which browsed the open grazing land and varied in numbers from 100 to 200 head according to the season, had to be sold, and at the end of the drought he therefore found himself with one of his three principal resources gone. In fact, the four dry years which culminated in 1950 cost him about 100,000 pesetas all told, and besides this the value of the land fell from 4,400 to 1,600 pesetas per acre. We need not dwell on the predicament of the hired labourers during this period, nor on that of the small farmers who are short of land at the best of times, but in both cases families sometimes had to go hungry. The medium farmer obtains about 5 tons of cereals and 4 to 6 cwt. of oil a year, and generally has a flock of about 30 sheep.

Admittedly, the drought of the late 1940's was an exceptional one, but the fifty-year rainfall average is only 10 in., and the situation is therefore difficult even in normal years. Taking Spain as a whole, the cereal acreage has decreased from 21 million acres in 1935 to only 17·5 at the present day. Spanish agriculture is only now experiencing the changes which began to be felt towards the end of the nineteenth century in the rest of Western Europe, and the peasant is responding by abandoning the hopelessly sterile areas and the '6-cwt. of grain' holdings. Average wheat yields have actually fallen from about 7 to 6 cwt. per acre since before the Civil War. At La Muela, the wheat acreage has declined to 3,700 acres, as compared with the 1944 level of 5,000, but the vine and the olive together have increased by about the same amount.

From 1946-50 Spain produced an average yearly total of 6,800,000 tons of all types of grain, as against the average of 8,300,000 tons for the ten years preceding the Civil War. As the population has grown from 23,500,000 to 29,000,000 (1951)[1] over the same period and continues to grow at the rate of about 1 per cent. per year, the production of cereals, including forage grains, has fallen from 7 to 4·7 cwt. per head of the population, a decline of one-third in twenty years. We must not forget, however, that the decline in Algeria since 1905 is still greater. Nevertheless, in 1952 Spain was the only European country where agriculture had not yet regained its pre-war levels of production. In 1951 the food shortage was very acute, and we shall long

[1] There were 30,000,000 by the end of 1953.

remember the faces of the children who, peering through the window of our inn, watched us anxiously to see whether we would finish our bread or let them have a crust.[1]

As in Kabylia Morocco, or Sardinia, the ever-present problems on the Castillian plateaux are water supply and fuel. Pine trees yield their branches for the latter, while water is drained off the pathways into cisterns, where the people come to collect it in casks. It would be interesting to know the proportion of agricultural labour—certainly a high one—spent in the quest of these necessities. At Madrilejos in Andalusia water is carried from the storage tank in jugs which are mounted in pairs on a wheelbarrow, and when we passed through on our way to Madrid this seemed to be the major form of activity within the confines of the village.

3. Difficulties Implicit in the Intensification of *Secano* Cultivation

135. Because of the demographic situation, there is a need for the rapid modernization of this type of farming, and it should be carried through in spite of the physical difficulties which would frequently have to be overcome. Wherever irrigation is impossible, the soil, where it has not already completely disappeared, must be retained on the slopes by economically practicable methods. As elsewhere in Mediterranean lands, dry-stone terraces have been known from time immemorial, but they are costly to build and awkward to adapt to the extensive cereal farming for which this region is best suited. Where slopes are not intended for reafforestation, a very useful idea would be to follow the example of the 'Defence and Restoration of Soils' organization in Algeria and build earth banks parallel to the contours at vertical intervals of 13 ft. At the moment, however, modernization is proceeding very slowly indeed, and the result is that even land of very mediocre quality has to be cultivated. After measures of this kind have been taken, the next step will be to raise yields by a more thorough working of the soil. As in North Africa, however, this could never be achieved by the use of animal power alone, for here too draught animals are underfed by the end of the dry season, which is the very time when the need for power reaches its peak.

There remains mechanization, which has successfully revolutionized cereal farming in North Africa, but there are certain obstacles to its

[1] The position has improved since the good harvests of 1951 and 1952, but it had worsened again during the course of 1953.

INTENSIFICATION OF *SECANO* CULTIVATION

introduction here. Spain does not make tractors, possesses scant means for their purchase from abroad, and already has to import all the fuel oil for her present needs. She would in any case be better advised to reserve her foreign credits for importing fertilizers to raise her yields. Finally, as in southern Algeria and Morocco, mechanization would not be worthwhile in the drier areas with yearly totals of, roughly, less than 14 to 16 in.

In the arid areas, wherever the amount of soil justifies a more intensive use than poor grazing, the answer lies in planting drought-resistant trees and shrubs. Already the vineyards are disappearing from the better soils of Catalonia and the east generally and are becoming more and more characteristic of semi-arid La Mancha. This logical trend is reflected in the growing importance of the vine in the province of Ciudad Real, where the acreage increased from 350,000 acres in 1935 to 600,000 in 1949. The same movement is also apparent in Estramadura, an altogether poorer region, where the comparable figures are 125,000 and 150,000 but, as elsewhere in the Mediterranean area, the limit on the expansion of this crop is the export market. In spite of the lowest wine prices in the world, the purchasing power of the home market is such that it could never absorb more than 330 million gallons annually,[1] a limitation which has at least preserved the poorer classes from the alcoholism with which France is so sorely afflicted.

The rational course would be to plant a large proportion of these areas of deficient rainfall with olives. At the same time, much of the land now given over to the olive in more humid regions, especially in Andalusia, which still accounts for three-quarters of total production, could be put to more intensive use. This would also mean the prohibition of fresh planting wherever irrigation schemes were likely to be undertaken in the near future, and it would be logical to apply the same rule to areas of adequate rainfall, with more than 24 or even 20 in. a year, and to encourage planting where the annual rainfall was less than 16 in. Care would have to be taken to avoid planting on submarginal land; at La Muela, which is 2,000 ft. above sea-level, and in the latitude of the middle Ebro, the olive seems to have reached its economic limit.

136. It is easy to outline measures of intensification for the portions of these regions which are less arid and have suffered comparatively little from soil erosion. With the help of tractors, wet-season forage crops such as cereals or cereal-vetch mixtures could be grown and on

---

[1] According to G. Jaltier, in his article, *'Le vignoble espagnol d'aujourd'hui'*, in the May-June 1950 issue of *Bulletin de l'association des géographes français*.

the limestone scarps drought-resisting permanent pastures of *sulla*, or sainfoin, could be established. The cultivation of row crops, such as sugar-beet, potatoes, flax, and cotton, could very well be extended, for they have received too little attention up to the present. The revolution which changed the pattern of Western European agriculture during the nineteenth century is as yet no more in evidence where these crops are concerned than in the matter of fodder crops.

Militating against the possible success of measures such as these, which we discussed with the Director of the Madrid Agricultural Institute, are certain factors in the human situation, the main ones being the sub-division of property and the long distances between fields and village. Intensively farmed land needs frequent attention, and this cannot be given at a range of six or ten miles from the settlement. Sheep- and goat-herding and extensive cereal cultivation where the crops are practically left to their own fate between seed-time and harvest are the only types of farming which can be adapted to such distances. A further handicap is the inadequacy of the road network so that pack animals—donkeys or mules capable of carrying loads of 330 and 550 lb. respectively—are still in common use.

This method of transport applied to bringing 12 tons of manure per acre, which is the normal complement for row crops, to a field six miles away would require a man and a mule to make two journeys a day for sixty days. Only small parcels of the outlying land and irrigated gardens are ever fertilized, and even then only if manure can be brought from some nearby sheepfold. If only pack mules are used, manure cannot be carried much more than about a mile, but with carts this distance may be more than doubled. Oxen, which are not so troublesome to feed, are unfortunately ruled out for journeys over such distances because they are so slow. Even seed and ploughs are still generally transported by pack animals.

4. 'Microfundia' and 'Latifundia'. Agrarian Reform

137. The question of the redistribution of property remains. The problem of the 'latifundia' in southern Spain too often causes that of the 'microfundia' to be ignored.[1] These excessively small holdings consist of tiny parcels of land, some of them less than $\frac{1}{40}$ acre in extent, which are dispersed at very long distances from the settlements. Admittedly the high rainfall enables the Galician peasant to have two harvests a year, the beans being brought in before the maize crop, but he

[1] The term 'minifundium' is also used in Spain to denote the very small holding at the opposite end of the scale from the 'latifundium'.

still cannot make a living out of 2½ acres of land. Furthermore, his animals do not generally produce very much, as their numbers alone prevent them from being fed properly.

In times past the Galician, like the Basque, was free to emigrate to America or, again, he could set out each year with his scythe and follow the harvest from south to north. The rapid increase of population in the south has deprived him of this occupation, and today, in default of enough land of his own, he can only turn to fishing. Even with co-operation and complete reintegration, mechanization would be out of the question for these tiny holdings, and such changes are in any case difficult to imagine when one thinks of the mentality of the Spanish peasantry.

On the large estates mechanization would give rise to a serious social problem, for even in the arid regions few parts of the country are as sparsely peopled as La Muela, and in the areas dominated by latifundia rural unemployment is almost the rule for a good part of the year. We once stopped for a moment along the road between Cordoba and Seville, opposite a field where about sixty women were thinning sugar-beet; even though they took us for tourists, the women immediately pressed round us crying, '*Emigracion!*'

In this particular district, where properties of over 250 acres occupied over three-quarters of the area, the great majority of the people were landless labourers. Very often they did not even possess a small garden of their own,[1] and they gathered each morning in the centre of the village in the hope of being hired for the day. On average, the men would be working for seventy to eighty days a year and the women for twice this time. The reason for the difference was that the men were paid a minimum wage of 20 pesetas for eight hours of work, whereas the women could be hired much more cheaply—for as little as 10 pesetas during the slack season. The female labour was evidently worth more than half the male, for sixty women were able to thin 2½ acres of sugar-beet in a day. At busy times of the year the rates of pay would rise to almost double those which have been quoted.

Mechanization without intensification would thus expose this area to the danger of increasing the amount of unemployment, which is already fairly high, though less obvious than it would be under urban conditions. If crop yields are to be raised, the country must give prior consideration to capital investment; irrigation, mechanized ploughing, and fertilizers must be introduced on a larger scale and measures which

[1] The Institute of Colonization is actually promoting the idea of family gardens, but the pace is still too slow.

would merely reduce the demand for labour, like the mechanizing of harvesting operations, must be deferred. Finally, as in Italy, the comparative absence of industry in the south must be remedied.

138. In the region south of the latitude of Toledo, including La Mancha, Estremadura and Andalusia, farms of over 250 acres occupy more than 40 per cent. of the surface area. The prevalent type of farming varies from place to place, but on the whole the degree of intensiveness is far lower than on the very small holdings. Some large estates are devoted almost entirely to rearing bulls destined for the arena. A cursory examination of the amount of land reserved for hunting and grazing reveals large areas worthy of more intensive development. Even where cultivation is not entirely absent, the farming methods often seem to date from Neolithic times. For instance, a five-year rotation might comprise a cereal crop followed by two or three years of grazing on the stubble and a further year, or two years, of cultivated fallow. Such methods are similar to those of Sardinia—and tropical Africa.[1]

Considering that, side by side with systems of land use as extensive as this, one finds unemployment and malnutrition in the villages, it is fair to conclude that the large landowner is doing less than his duty. Even where technical progress has been made in the use of land, it rarely corresponds with the degree of intensiveness which the pressure of population demands. In the Guadalquivir Valley the olive occupies large tracts of land, especially on the latifundia, which could be completely transformed by irrigation. When, as sometimes happens, the harvest fails, the olive groves provide hardly any work at all. Even the legally imposed minimum of soil cultivation in the olive groves results in very little employment, but it may, on the other hand, accelerate soil erosion if carelessly applied on over-steep slopes. Olives should only be planted on terrain which is useless for other purposes.

139. During the present century, various attempts have been made at agrarian reform, especially by the Republican Government, which sought a middle course between the measures adopted during the periods 1920-5 and 1945-8 in Eastern Europe. The socialists wanted the large estates managed as collectives and were unwilling to pay large sums in compensation, but in 1934 the moderates carried the day, generous scales of compensation were agreed, the tendency towards small owner-managed holdings began to prevail, and the tempo of reform was palpably slowed down. The rise of Franco was probably not unrelated to the exasperation of the peasants with the resulting

[1] Also at Revest-du-Bion (Basses Alpes).

delays and vacillations, and between 1932 and 1935 there were seizures of land similar to those in southern Italy in 1949. This resort to force can easily be understood when viewed against its background of rural under-employment and legitimate impatience with the slow processes of the law.

Since then victory has gone to the party of the landed interests and, as in Western Germany, the present reorganization of property is called 'colonization'—the value of this change of name was impressed on us most particularly. The reorganization depends essentially on the purchase of a number of latifundia by the State. The Government has powers of expropriation, and occasionally uses them, the rate of compensation is an attractive one, and the landowner often prefers to deal with the State than to sell his land privately. Next, as the wide spacing of the nucleated rural settlements is a hindrance to intensification, the second phase in the programme is the rapid construction of new villages at the public expense, complete with churches, schools, and local government buildings. Finally come the measures of land improvement, with an emphasis on irrigation, drainage, sewerage, etc. As the total sum set aside for agricultural investment is strictly limited, particularly as a result of the large police and military budgets, the proportion set aside for these measures of the third phase, which are the only part of the programme capable of raising production, remains unfortunately small.

Spain had 3,750,000 acres of land under irrigation in 1918, 4,500,000 in 1952. In 1934, under the Republican Government, a grandiose scheme was put forward whereby 2,500,000 acres would be added to the irrigated area in twenty-five years, but there would be good cause for satisfaction today if only half this rate of 100,000 acres a year could be achieved. As public funds are inadequate for this purpose, private schemes are encouraged by allowing the sale of produce on the free market, where much higher prices can be obtained. Land improvement is thus partly financed by those who indulge their taste for a more varied diet.

5. 'Colonization'. The New Village of Ontinar del Salz

140. Ontinar del Salz, a completely new village with a pleasant hall and an impressive church, is between Saragossa and Huesca (Fig. 14). The dwelling houses are more spacious than the farm buildings, for the families are generally large, so large in fact that some of the store rooms are already being used as sleeping quarters for children. Apart

from having numerous children, the requisite qualifications for an intending settler are, in the order given in the official questionnaire, favourable recommendations from: the parish priest on religious attitude, non-Catholics thus being excluded; the workers' union on suitability for agricultural employment; the mayor on social activities; the police, etc. The question of a rural upbringing seems to be neglected, and the settler whom we interviewed had been a driver in Saragossa. His shed for four animals and his barn each measured 40 ft. by 15, a total of 600 sq. ft., or 24 sq. ft. per acre of farm land as against the ratio of 60 sq. ft. per acre which is fairly general in France even where farming is more extensive than it is here. The straw-ricks are outside the village, a feature one generally associates with a nucleated settlement hemmed in by fortifications. There would certainly be room for them in the farmyard, where fowl-house, pigsty, and rabbit-hutch are all sited.

Each settler has been allotted about 25 acres in three lots (garden, good land, medium quality land) which will all eventually be levelled and irrigated. He also receives two draught cows, a dairy cow, a small plough, a plough with a turning mould-board, a harrow, and a cart. Stock and equipment are valued at 30,000 pesetas, which the settler must pay back over the course of five years. In the meantime he remains under the authority of the Institute for Colonization, whose technical instructions he is obliged to follow. To all intents and purposes he is a *métayer*, except that part of the harvest pays off a debt instead of rent. He is thus in a better position than the Tuscan *métayer*, who is forced to give up a substantial part of his harvest without the prospect of redemption for many years.[1] The fixed capital, that is land and buildings, is valued at 70,000 pesetas and is repayable over twenty years. It can be inherited by the settler's family, but is not transferable. In 1949 and 1950 serious shortages of water made conditions for the settlers extremely difficult.

At first the compulsory rotation has a basis of cereals, a year of fallow being followed by wheat, then barley, and finally oats. This hardly seems enough to justify the expense of irrigation, but there are already plans for following the fallow year with maize and better-paying industrial crops, like cotton, flax, and sugar-beet. Over $\frac{1}{2}$ acre of lucerne is now compulsory and fruit trees are planted in addition, but it seems evident that more emphasis will have to be placed on industrial, fodder, and tree crops if the heavy outlay on water control is to

[1] A large landowner at Granada told us that he had evaded the legal limitations on rents quite easily by making his tenants *métayers*.

be recouped fairly quickly. Fortunately, however, the ample opportunities which now exist for further intensification mean that a rapidly growing population need not go short of useful employment. The sowing of a catch-crop of maize immediately after the wheat and barley crops have been cut already foreshadows the adoption of more intensive methods.

The intention is that each holding should support a 'two-man family', but everybody goes to the fields, even fairly young children. As irrigation is brought in, the settlers are encouraged to change from sheep- to cattle-rearing, but this is sometimes a difficult transition, as we have seen in Morocco, notably at Beni-Amir. As a temporary measure, the sheep of the whole village are to be herded in common, a plan which will enable each family to keep three or four ewes; the presence of trees fully justifies the ban on goats. The communal tractor has been relegated to the distant future, for, as in Italy, the essential object is to secure useful employment for as many people as possible. Seventy-three families have now been installed on the 2,500 acres of Ontinar del Salz which, except for very occasional and unreliable unirrigated crops, was once almost entirely given over to grazing.[1]

6. Congestion and Falling Productivity in the Murcian *Huerta*

141. We shall now examine the position in certain areas south-west of Valencia and not far from the Mediterranean, where irrigation has long been known. In the area west of Murcia (Fig. 13), one is struck by the great number of houses, each with its garden, large by Mediterranean standards, and at first sight one is reminded of a residential suburb. In fact, however, this is an agricultural region where each family subsists on its own small plot of land, often no more than 1 acre in size. The density of population decreases away from the town, but is still in the region of 3,000 per square mile for the district as a whole, and it is not surprising that most of the young women work in the nearby fruit-preserving factories. The *huertas* of Valencia and Murcia, most of them with 1,500 to 1,750 persons per square mile, qualify for the highest rural densities in Europe, exceeding even those of Belgian Flanders and the Po Delta. Moreover, as is frequently the case with densely populated agricultural areas, the productivity of labour is far too low.

As an example for detailed study, let us take a 'large' farm which extends over 7 *tahullas*, or 2 acres. Two brothers, both of them married, work the farm with occasional help from their father. They have

[1] Compare the agrarian reforms in Italy and East Germany studied in later chapters.

separate dwelling houses, but, with good reason, have refrained from duplicating the farm buildings. The rotations they follow often provide for as many as five crops in two years. For example:

$$\left.\begin{array}{l}\text{Potatoes (spring)}\\ \text{Maize (summer, early autumn)}\end{array}\right\} 1953$$
$$\text{Potatoes (winter of 1953-4)}$$
$$\left.\begin{array}{l}\text{Pumpkins or tomatoes}\\ \text{Maize or potatoes}\end{array}\right\} 1954$$

In addition, some of their land also carries peach and apricot trees, which are planted only 10 ft. apart, and in April potatoes are set between them right up to the boles themselves. When the trees are mature the shade cast by their leaves makes summer cropping impossible, but quite apart from the fruit they still take a crop in the spring and another in the autumn—a total of three harvests a year.

It would be impossible for them to maintain this degree of intensiveness over the whole of their land, and the solitary mule,[1] serving as it does a mere 2 acres, is by no means overworked, for it has little ploughing to do and is used mainly for taking vegetables to market. As every holding has its own mule, it is true to say that these animals are by no means fully employed and yet, in the absence of the labour-saving winch as used in the *huerta* of Vaucluse, there is a shortage of power for such purposes as deep ploughing. The *huertas* have a rich potential, not the least of their assets being the twelve-month growing season, but, as in many other areas where the people are poor and the land is overcrowded, the excessive number of draught animals is a drag on the economy.

Our most vivid recollection of the *huerta* of Valencia is of a group of about ten men double-digging the land to a depth of 16-18 in.—a kind of manual subsoiling operation—while close at hand, harnessed to a small harrow, a horse ambled gently along. Douglas Higgs (Chapter XII) would contrast the leanness of the men with the *embonpoint* of the horses, which he compared with the sleek rotundity of the canons

[1] Productive livestock consists of three sows. The *huerta*, which has a suburban character, supports a large number of dairy cows. Until the beginning of the century a man took his cows on the milk-round and they were milked in front of the customer. A large number of cows are still kept in Barcelona, mostly in cellars, but sometimes also above ground, and the black market has helped to prolong this obsolete and unhygienic practice. Every morning scores of asses bring in the day's ration of fresh lucerne; thus the means of production are transported instead of the finished product.

of Toledo. He affirmed that the weight ratio of priest to peasant was in the region of 1·5 to 1!

The farm mule needs about ¼ acre of lucerne to support it, and about a dozen cuttings can be taken in a year, though evidently the winter yield is less. The shortage of bread grains led the Government to order a third of the market garden land to be turned over to wheat, which occupies the ground twice as long as a crop of vegetables, but necessitates only the minimum of labour. Even with a little cheating, sowing only a quarter of the land to wheat, there remained little more than 1 acre for the intensive rotation.

142. The aim is the maximum possible use of land even at the expense of the productivity of labour. Maize is sown while the potatoes are still in the ground, so that the latter have to be lifted very gently for fear of harming the growing plants. Likewise in the Roscoff market-gardening area in Brittany, where productivity is much higher and the size of holdings may vary from 5 to 50 acres, cauliflower seedlings are planted between the potato ridges a month before lifting begins.[1]

The two brothers spend five days a week working in their garden, but they readily admit that two days would be enough to do the work that really matters and that they merely potter about for the rest of the time, uprooting every tiny weed as soon as it appears. The utility of these supplementary weeding operations is highly questionable, as indeed is much of their labour, more than half of which is sub-marginal. Admittedly, the erection of a shelter of reeds along every row of tomatoes is productive labour inasmuch as it brings on the early crop, but, in comparison with the Vauclusian market-gardeners of Cavaillon, who cultivate their land just as intensively and reckon on one man for every 2·5 to 3·75 acres, the same area here provides employment for three men at least and sometimes four.

This second form of concealed rural unemployment, though less obvious than that of the Andalusian farm labourer, is nevertheless prevalent in many areas, from the Galician microfundia to the *huertas* which succeed each other along the coastlands from the Llobregat Delta near Barcelona[2] to Malaga. The position is rapidly becoming worse. Evidence of this was supplied by the grandfather of the two brothers of Murcia, who, until 1891, had 6½ acres of land irrigated from the rivers, which he cultivated alone. The dry season level of

---

[1] *Voyages en France d'un agronome*, Chapters V and VI.

[2] The story of the reclamation of this delta has been vividly described by our friend, P. Deffontaines, Director of the Institut français at Barcelona, in the *Revue géographique des Pyrénées et du Sud-Ouest*, Nos. 3 and 4, 1950.

the river was too low to allow him to grow summer crops like tomatoes and squashes, which need a lot of water, and apart from wheat and maize he relied on rape and Saint-Jean beans.[1] Moreover, his two mares enabled him to plough more deeply than his grandsons ever do, and not only did they provide an additional source of income when they foaled, but they could also be kept with a smaller percentage of his land under fodder crops than has to be set aside for the mule on the small holding of today. The ratio of two horses per farmer has declined to one mule for two market-gardeners. This is symptomatic of the substitution of human labour for animal power, an unequivocally retrogressive process.

Today, thanks to the barrages, the reserves of water are large enough to make plenty of water available in the summer, except in very dry years like 1945. Indeed, sometimes too much water is used for the good of the soil and leaching is induced. But although the modern irrigation project has brought about a very marked increase in the yield per unit of land, it has been accompanied by a rapid fall in the size of holdings, and the net result is that the productivity of human labour has declined.[2] In the case quoted above, during these last sixty years, which in France have seen the rapid disappearance of microfundia, the size of holdings has fallen from $6\frac{1}{2}$ acres per family to less than 1. The two brothers appreciate the evil consequences of this decline, and would willingly exchange their present holding for one four times as large, which could be cultivated a little less intensively.

143. In this very crowded region, the value of untenanted land—other than for building purposes—is between 12,000 and 60,000 pesetas per *tahulla*, or £320 to £1,600 (1951) per acre. These high prices apply to land with citrus orchards or to gardens devoted mainly to apricots and early vegetables, but these are highly prized, not so much for their intrinsic worth, as for the prospect of employment which they offer. If occupied by a tenant, their market price falls to as little as a tenth of the figures quoted.

[1] When the father began to grow tomatoes at the beginning of the century, exports were out of the question. Murcia was already amply supplied, and so he tried to send his produce to Madrid. At this time the state of the railways was such that it was quicker to send goods by the relays of carts, which took six days to complete the 190 miles to Madrid. By rail the journey took ten or twelve days, which was too long for perishable goods.

[2] The province of Almeria is admittedly the driest in Spain, but, in spite of its large acreage under irrigation and its considerable exports of table grapes, the official estimate was that the value of the harvest per land-worker was less than 1,000 pesetas in 1950.

It must be remembered that the example taken at Murcia was of a farm very much larger than the average. The brothers have several neighbours who have as little as ¼ or ½ acre, and these people naturally have to find work elsewhere, but the supply of casual labourers exceeds the demand. A man who devotes a day per week to his own land generally counts on about 100 days of casual labour a year, but his standard of living is still higher than that of the Andalusian farm worker. Also, he has plenty of wheaten bread, whereas his grandfather was thankful for barley and maize bread, the white loaf at that time being reserved for the sick. The opening up of markets in countries with less favourable winter conditions rather than any improvement in productivity is responsible for this rise in living standards.

Small-scale mechanization—with the use of motor hoes, for instance—would release the small farmer from his present obligation to grow fodder for his mule, and would therefore result in more land being used for market garden crops. Real progress would then depend on finding outlets for the major part of the extra produce in external markets. In fact, of course, Spain lacks the funds to buy this equipment abroad and, although not short of labour, she makes none of it herself. The solution to her rural problems, however, resides in finding the means to relieve the pressure of population on the land, and this end could well be achieved by encouraging the growth of manufacturing industry. Although richer in mineral resources than Italy, her industrial development still lags far behind. A Seville family is reputed to have lived for 400 years on its land revenues, generously supplemented at intervals by drawing on reserves of gold and jewels accumulated during the American conquest. In some of its aspects, the Spanish economy has not yet reached the stage of capitalism.

It would be interesting to know how much of the money paid in compensation to large landowners has been spent on consumer goods and what proportion has been reinvested in productive enterprises. If the latter were considerable, the current rates of compensation might begin to find some justification on grounds of national interest, but one strongly suspects that this is far from the truth. One of Spain's ablest rural economists insists that the excessive rates of compensation simply offer the ex-landowner the means for self-indulgence at the expense of funds ostensibly reserved for land improvement, and that for this reason the development of the latifundia is being held in check.

7. The Guadalquivir. The Future of Southern Spain

144. The Guadalquivir Valley in Andalusia is favoured by its width, by its ease of irrigation, and by the maintenance of the summer level of the river by the melting snows of the Sierra Nevada. In spite of the presence in the upper valley of a reservoir with a capacity of 5,000 million cu. ft.,[1] the water resources are not utilized to the full. The reasons for this are both historical and social, and relate both to the depopulation of the region during the Reconquest and to the prevalence of latifundia. When certain parts of the lower valley near Cadiz were drained, extraordinarily high yields were obtained, and in some cases up to 96 cwt. of paddy per acre were recorded.

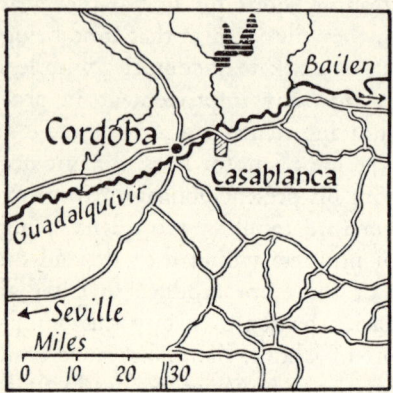

FIG. 15. Cordoba.

The 'Casablanca' estate, not far from Cordoba (Fig. 15), consists of 5,000 acres of undulating land stretching from the banks of the river to the summits of the bordering hills. No special precautions are taken when the land is ploughed, and the scarred hillsides and bare limestone exposures on this 'model' farm, which are reminiscent of Orania, are the visible evidence of the disregard for simple soil-conservation measures which would be inexpensive enough to apply.[2] There are two big caterpillar tractors and two combines. The local agricultural adviser strongly disapproves of the latter because although they save on manpower they are not suited to work on sloping land, and an appreciable quantity of grain is wasted. Too little thought was given to the programme of modernization, for certain types of combine are specially designed for use on sloping terrain.

Even with this equipment the growing of cereals demands twenty to twenty-four days of work per acre per year, or about two days per hundredweight of grain. This compares with two to four days per acre in Soisonnais, which has almost three times the yields; or with 0·4 to

---

[1] The Mediterranean side—the Cartagena region to be precise—has already put in a claim to utilize this water.

[2] They are hardly taught at all at the Agronomic Institute in Madrid; the course lasts five years, and a large place is reserved for political and religious education.

0·8 days in Kansas, where yields per acre are very slightly less. The spring weeding alone, which is performed entirely by hand, takes six to eight days per acre.[1]

Until 1948, the valley lands were exploited on the same rotation as the hill country, and the crops often suffered through lack of water, in spite of the nearby Guadalquivir with its regular régime. This anomaly is now disappearing, thanks to the encouragement which is being given to land improvement. A system of underground irrigation which was copied from California is fed by a pumping station on the river and has now been extended to 425 acres. On this model farm, the two-year rotation typical of Mediterranean lands, with wheat every second year, had already been enriched by the substitution of chick peas or beans and maize or cotton for the traditional fallows. This rotation has been retained on the uplands, but has been replaced on the irrigated lowland by a sequence which is common to many of the irrigated portions of large estates:

Sugar-beet from end of March to end of July.
Wheat from October to end of May, followed the same year by maize or potatoes.

There are thus three harvests in two years as compared with five in the densely populated *huertas*. The climate here is more continental in type and the demographic situation is, of course, very different, so there is some justification for concentrating on bread grains, sugar-beet, and potatoes, which are all in great demand on the home market, and for leaving the intensive market gardening to the overcrowded but climatically favoured *huertas* on the east coast. This argument is reinforced by the fact that the foreign market for vegetables and fruit is limited and that the total area of gardens in Spain shows a progressive increase from 415,000 acres in 1935 to 500,000 today.

8. Intensification and Decongestion in the Rural Areas

145. It would be unfair to belittle the efforts which have been made, notably by the Institute for Colonization, to improve the position of agriculture in Spain. Then again, one must remember the setbacks due to war, the Civil War in the 1930's and the conflagration of 1939-45, which cut off foreign markets and overseas sources of supply. These factors account in part for the shortcomings of the present, but the

[1] Daily rates for casual labour: slack season, 13·5 pesetas; busy season, 35 pesetas; average (for men) about 20. Industrial Catalonia pays its land workers 35-70 pesetas, but the Andalusian cannot go north as often as he would wish.

current programmes of reform, industrial no less than agricultural, are not ambitious enough to make a serious impact on the problems of population and productivity. In this Catholic country, the concepts of time and eternity are closely linked, and the serenity of the Spanish mentality is perhaps incompatible with the urgent action which many present-day problems demand.

As the examples of Orania and the French Midi have already proved, an accelerated rate of progress which aims first at improving the dietetic standards of a long-suffering people depends on the building up of the direct factors of production, that is on intensification, by the injection into the economy of capital on an unprecedented scale. In Spain, the priority tasks are water-control, irrigation and sometimes drainage, and, as soon as the necessary power becomes available, the establishment of a chemical fertilizer industry concentrating on nitrates. The stages which should follow this are, for the present, less clearly definable.

A greater degree of modernization presupposes the use of larger resources of animal and mechanical power. Without these it will be impossible to raise the productivity either of the small farmer or of the agricultural labourer. Large-scale mechanization, however, could not be applied indiscriminately, regardless of its lack of economy, on the microfundia or of its aggravation of rural unemployment on the latifundia. Apart from the establishment of local engineering industries on the largest possible scale, it would have to be preceded by the integration and, what is even more to the point, by the enlargement of uneconomically small holdings. This in turn implies a diminution in the overall percentage of rural population (55 per cent. in Spain today) which is always high in non-industrialized countries and is itself a sign of backwardness.

In short, as in Hungary and Slovakia where in 1948 we found a stage of agricultural development analogous in many respects to that of Spain, a radical improvement in agriculture depends on industrialization which, so far, has been too narrowly confined to the north. The new industries will manufacture the equipment required in ever-increasing quantities by a modernized agriculture and in turn they will process the expanding volume of produce from the land. They will lessen population pressure in country districts, particularly where the maximum development of natural resources would not assure a decent living even for the present population. They will effect a modernization of the country without increasing enforced idleness among farm workers, without worsening the plight—less publicized, but frequently more significant—of the average smallholder; in short, without burdening the countryside with an aggravated problem of unemployment.

VII

Overpopulation and Unemployment in the Italian Countryside[1]

1. Too Many People Living on Too Few Resources

146. Compared with Greece, North Africa, or Spain, Italy seems relatively fertile and verdant. A rapid journey from the north to central Italy, however, generally follows the principal lowlands and gives an altogether too favourable first impression. Comparatively rugged terrain accounts for four-fifths of the peninsula and, apart from the Po Valley and the Tavoliere Plain, the amount of lowland is very small indeed.

The steep slopes of the Alpine region have, in places, been completely denuded, and only a fragmental covering of poor soil remains. In the Apennines the situation is even worse. The richest alluvial soils in the lower valleys and deltas were originally too marshy for cultivation, and some of them were completely under water. Like the Low Countries, therefore, though to a lesser degree, Italy has had to wrest a considerable proportion of her agricultural area from poorly drained lowlands.

The climate is still Mediterranean in character, especially in the islands and the south, but its elements are considerably modified in the zone beyond the limit of the olive, north of the line from Genoa to Ravenna. In the Po Valley the annual rainfall is often high, and an appreciable amount falls in the summer months. On passing through the Mont Cenis or the Simplon, one often finds the Italian side more cloudy than the French or the Swiss; this often deceives the holiday-maker on his first journey towards the land of sunshine.

The summer drought, even in the Po Valley, though not in the

[1] Visited in 1932, 1938, 1951, 1952, and 1953. For further details, see the September 1951 issue of *Economie contemporaine*, which summarizes the results of our visit in the summer of the same year. Prices relate to the year 1952, except for Sardinia (1953) and Tuscany (Section 4, 1951).

Alps, places a severe limit on agricultural production, and maximum yields are attained only with the help of irrigation. As in the Low Countries, water control is the key to intensification, but here the essential aspect is the procuring of water, although the drainage problem is by no means of secondary importance.

147. The landscape bears unmistakable witness to the high density of population. Italy's 120,000 square miles support a population of over 47,000,000, which is increasing by 400,000 a year, a rate which shows hardly any signs of abatement. These inexorable facts dominate the agricultural situation. As in all other advanced countries, the ratio of those employed in agriculture to the total working population began to decline some time ago, and actually fell from 57·6 per cent. in 1871 to 48 per cent. in 1936. Moreover, the total rural population has fallen more rapidly than these figures suggest, for in 1871 rural crafts were in a flourishing condition. Turning our attention now to the regional picture, we find that in Lombardy the figure dropped from 58 per cent. to 28·5 per cent., and fell as low as 10 per cent. in the Turin Province. During the same period, there were actually increases in the south, in Sicily, Basilicata, and most of all in Calabria, where the comparable figures were 45 per cent. and 67 per cent. Here there was no industrialization to compensate for the decline of village crafts.

For the last twenty years, in the country as a whole, the proportion of those employed in agriculture has hardly varied, fluctuating between 48 and 47 per cent., but this in fact corresponds to a very large increase in the actual size of the agricultural population. Drainage works like those undertaken in the Pontine Marshes and the Po Delta have increased the opportunities for employment, but not to the same degree as they have been reduced by the use of modern equipment. The latter has, moreover, been introduced only on a modest scale. In 1929 Italy had more tractors than France, but in 1952 she had only 66,000 as compared with 180,000 in France. Furthermore, of these, 47,000 were concentrated in the northern plain, while the remainder were shared between central Italy with 10,600 and the south and the islands with 8,800.

These factors give substance to the traditional division of Italy into three regions, *les Italies* as Charles VIII of France called them nearly 500 years ago. The general level of industrial activity and rural modernization declines towards the south. In 1950, northern Italy accounted for 5,600,000 cattle out of a total for the whole country of 8,350,000. In contrast, two-thirds of the sheep and three-quarters of the goats, which are usually associated with backward methods and generally absent from irrigated regions, are found in the south and islands. The north produces 57 per cent. of the cereals, 92 per cent. of the sugar-beet, and 60 per cent. of the animal products of the whole country; it accounts for fully half the total agricultural wealth.

To an even greater degree than the Low Countries, where barely a fifth of the total working population is employed on the land, Italy is committed to a policy of intensive agriculture, but this requires capital, which is always more difficult to find when it is destined for investment in the land. In the north, commerce and agriculture provided the initial funds for the establishment of industry, but very soon a much larger volume of investment flowed back from the factories to the land. As one might expect, the land is most intensively used where manufacturing industry is most highly developed—that is, in the Po Valley—and this tendency has been accentuated by the physical conditions which favour high productivity when grafted on to a basis of large-scale investment.

2. Mandatory Labour Laws and High Rents on a *Cascina* in Lombardy

148. From Milan to Cremona and beyond,[1] the landscape is a pattern of rectilinear fields, most of them 5-15 acres in extent, bordered by irrigation and drainage ditches and by earth roads with lines of pollarded poplars, alders, and willows. Although sericulture has died out, the law forbids the uprooting of mulberry trees, and consequently they remain, but are kept very severely trimmed. The law seems unwise in this respect, for even if the industry revived, which seems unlikely, the need would be for dwarf mulberries, which would permit two crops of silk a year. Before irrigation reached its present proportions, the fruit tree was a further element in the landscape, but today farming is dominated by the *cascina* where milk-production, on the basis of irrigated fodder crops, is the main preoccupation. These farms are generally over 90 acres in extent and average about 250 acres. Their name, according to Professor Pagani, derives from the word *casera*, meaning 'cheese farm', for before it became a matter for the dairy factory cheese-making was common to all the large estates.

The traditional *cascina* is a 'fortress-farm', with buildings grouped round a central square or rectangle, part of which was once the drying floor. One side is formed by a handsome house, which very often has a small park stretching behind it. Opposite the house are the barns

[1] See Fig. 16 for all sections in this chapter.

and cart-sheds with hay-lofts. A third side is occupied by stables and cow-sheds with pent-roofs and hay-lofts, facing which is a line of dwellings for the farm workers. The accommodation is the same for every family regardless of size, and consists of two floors, each with an

FIG. 16. Italy

ordinary room, the lower one used as a living-room, and a storeroom which can be used as sleeping quarters in the case of a large family. The dilapidation of these living quarters contrasts all too often with the fine appearance of the farmer's villa. Each worker also has his own tiny outbuildings, hen-roost, wood-store, and pigsty, and his own small garden.

149. The San Antonio *cascina* is situated on the road to Mantua six miles east of Cremona in the commune of Pessina Cremonese. Each worker has a garden of only about 120 sq. yds. Although the wage-earner of the north enjoys his own separate living quarters, his accommodation is generally inferior to that of the average *métayer* family in Tuscany, and his dependence on others and the communal organization of work are inimical to family life. He enjoys a higher income than the average *métayer*, but, on the other hand, we have visited other *cascine* where the pigsties—the smell from which was absolutely unbearable at the height of summer—abutted against the workers' quarters. In 1952 those who were fully employed received a wage of 200,000 lire and, in addition, 24 cwt. of maize, 14 of wheat, 70 of wood, and the right to buy a certain quantity of milk at a reduced price. These payments are made in accordance with collective agreements, and the total of cash and kind came to 330,000 lire.

The number of workers employed by each farmer is determined by law according to the type of farming and the soil fertility, and in this district the mandatory ratio is one man for every 7·5 acres. In one instance near Crema there was one man per 8 acres and one more for every six cows, making a total, for 100 acres, of seventeen employees. At San Antonio there are forty labourers in all, nearly all adherents of the Communist *Federbraccianti*, and together they contribute 12,180 working days in a year. At certain times the legal ratio of employees is increased to a level which varies according to the amount of local unemployment; when we visited the area the addition was equivalent to one man per 50 acres. Finally, about a dozen women, usually labourers' wives, work a total of some 4,000 hours at 85 lire an hour, as compared with the men's rate of 135 lire.

On average, thirty-four days of work per year are expended on each acre, which is three times as many as on the best-equipped farms of the Paris Basin and fifteen or twenty times as many as in the Corn Belt of the U.S.A. By comparison, these two regions have a lower level of production per acre, but their use of labour is much more efficient. San Antonio fulfils its employment obligations with ease, but this is not the case on neighbouring *cascine*, where the farming is less intensive and machinery has to be used sparingly so that the law can be complied with. During our visit in 1951 we were surprised to find how much the scythe was still used on mechanized farms, when its only conceivable advantage is that it cuts closer to the ground than is otherwise possible. We even saw small stones quite needlessly being picked out of the ground. 'We have to keep the men occupied as best we can' was the comment.

The practice of bringing the freshly mown grass to the stalls can be justified on the grounds that it saves the meadows from being harmed by trampling and facilitates the collection of manure; in this respect, methods are more intensive than in France. A great deal of time and care are devoted to the traditional operation of raking over the dunghills, which results in a rich compost, but the amount of labour involved makes the method quite uneconomic. Even this, however, is no doubt preferable to the complete neglect evidenced in Southern Italy, Southern France or Spain. Nevertheless, when the manure is eventually spread on the meadows, the losses of nitrogen which have already taken place as a result of fermentation are considerably increased by exposure to the sun. In any case, the grassland has no great need of humus, and it would be better to fertilize the ploughland. With new manure rapidly turned into the ground, the losses of nitrogen would be minimized and a great deal of labour saved.

In view of the waste of manpower, we examined the possibility of increasing the volume of useful employment, especially by raising the production of forage crops.[1] These already exist in the rotation as catch-crops but if, as quick-growing annuals, they replaced some of the temporary grassland, although more labour would be required than at present and more fertilizers would have to be used, the harvests would be effectively doubled. At San Antonio, fertilizers are used at the rate of 5 cwt. of 16 per cent. superphosphates, 3 cwt. of 16 per cent. nitrates and 130 lb. of 40 per cent. potash to the acre. These figures are far above the average for the whole of Italy, which consumes 120,000 tons of nitrates, 250,000 of phosphoric acid, and only 18,000 of potash for her 32,500,000 acres of arable land, 13,750,000 of grassland, and 6,250,000 of vines and gardens. This is further qualified by the fact that the employment of these fertilizers is concentrated in the north,[2] although even here the rates are still far below those of the Netherlands. Against this, however, is the fact that in Italy, with irrigation, vegetative growth continues right through the year, with hardly any temperature check in the winter.

[1] Technical information bulletin, Ministry of Agriculture (January 1952).

[2] 16·7 lb. of nitrogen and 36 lb. of phosphoric acid per acre of plough-land in the north, as against 7·5 lb. and 13·2 lb. respectively in the rest of the country: these last figures are comparable with the average rate in France for grass and arable land combined.

150. The stock kept at San Antonio is in the ratio of over 600 lb. live weight per acre of land. For draught purposes, in addition to the two tractors (35 and 25 h.p.), there are eighteen horses and four oxen. In addition there are ninety-two cows, thirty heifers in calf, and sixty young stores; two bulls and two stallions . . . and two donkeys. On quite a number of *cascine* near Cremona and Milan, a cow and a store, at the very least, are kept on less than 2½ acres, which is a ratio in the region of 900 lb. live weight per acre, and the figure may be doubled in exceptional cases. The most widely practised rotation has a seven-year course as follows:

1. Maize.
2. Wheat, followed by vetch or maize for fodder or cow-pea (*fagiolini*);[1] followed by rape for fodder, cut at the end of February.
3. Maize.
4. Wheat with temporary ley sowing.
5-7. Mixture of rye grass and white clover, giving four cuttings and one grazing a year.

The dairy cows, which are Friesians, are exclusively stall-fed, so that there are no obvious signs of the intensive stock farming in the landscape of lower Lombardy, for the animals are never taken into the fields. The milk is more remarkable for its quantity (average, over 1,000 gallons per cow) than for its quality, which is not up to the best modern standards, the fat content (32 per 1,000) still being rather too low. The milk is sent to the owner's cheese dairy, which treats about 3½ tons a day in the summer, and from this produces about 150 lb. of butter and 500 lb. of cheese.

The rent of San Antonio is 48 lb. of milk and the same quantity of maize and of wheat per *perche* of ⅙ acre. Expressing the price of milk in terms of cereals, this is the equivalent of over 6 cwt. per acre, or nearly 20,000 lire. The value of the land is in the region of 1,000,000 lire, of the buildings, equipment, and stock about 500,000 lire, and the total annual production can be taken as about 315,000 lire.[2] The net income, after deducting rent and other outside expenses, comes to 220,000 lire, and 150,000 lire are paid out in wages. It will be noticed that the rent is rather less than one-sixth of the gross value of production, but the regional average is rather higher.

In one example observed near Cremona, the rent was 380 lb. of

---

[1] *Vigna sinensis*.

[2] These are average figures for *cascine* in Lombardy in 1949-50; there had been little change by 1952.

wheat and similar amounts of maize and milk per acre. In the unirrigated portion of the province of Piacenza, where lucerne takes the place of clover and rye grass, the Institute of Rural Economy quotes the following rents: 130 to 400 lb. per acre of each of milk, wheat, grapes, and fodder. This is exceptional, but in the worst case the rent, as in China until recently, amounts to nearly half the harvest. In the majority of cases in the Po Valley the figure is still as high as a third or a quarter, and though this is doubtless a stimulus to intensive farming and forces the adoption of efficient techniques,[1] one is tempted to ask whether the money is reinvested in the national interest.

The right bank of the Po has very little irrigation as yet, because the Apennine streams, unlike the glacier-fed torrents from the north, run almost dry in the summer. Nevertheless, barrages are now being constructed and underground supplies are being utilized on a growing scale; irrigation is developing rapidly and the clear-cut contrast between the two sides of the valley is disappearing.

At San Antonio the yields obtained are high. Wheat averages 29 cwt. an acre, maize 36 cwt. It is an enterprise undeniably capitalist in type, open to the economy of exchange, paying rent and wages in kind and engaging exclusively in commercial transactions. As for the impact on such highly organized enterprises of an agrarian reform on socialist lines, Professor Pagani would prefer to see them taken over as collectives rather than fragmented, even as a temporary measure, into tiny holdings in danger of being priced out of the market. The workers themselves are pressing for 'association'; they favour profit-sharing, not the sub-division of estates. As for other countries, Denis Bergmann reminds us that the large dairy farm with a staff of permanent employees is fairly common in England, but less often found in France and the U.S.A.

3. Poverty in Spite of High Yields on the Drained Lands of Ferrara

151. Whereas in Lombardy irrigation has been the instrument of land improvement, enabling two and sometimes three crops to be taken in one year, the marshy alluvia east of Ferrara have had to be reclaimed by a huge and laborious process of drainage. Massive sums of capital had to lend their support to this work, and for the most part

[1] A Flemish agricultural specialist employed in the *pays* d'Ouche in Normandy bemoans the fact that rents are lower than in his native district (2·4 cwt. per acre instead of 5·4 cwt.) because this allows the farmer to be more negligent in his methods.

they were needed long before the land could begin to pay dividends. Hence they were often provided from non-agricultural sources. The following table summarizes progress in the province of Ferrara:

	Millions of acres	
	1875	1941
Arable	302	463
Grassland	108	43
Gardens and orchards	3·3	17·3
Unproductive	235	130
	Thousands	
	1875	1947
Cattle	70	104
Pigs	15	55
Sheep, goats	44	6
Horses	14	8
Total population	215,000	414,000

The increasing number of cattle and pigs at the expense of sheep and goats is a sure sign of progress. But the total population and its agricultural fraction have grown much more rapidly than the cultivated area, and the Emilia-Romagna area has the highest rate of agricultural unemployment in the whole of Italy, higher even than the southern provinces—Sicily, Apulia, Campagna, Calabria, in decreasing order of rates of unemployment. Finally, the size of farms in this recently reclaimed zone is above the average.

The Zenzalino estate covers an area of 3,750 acres in the Copparo commune north-east of Ferrara. Its buildings are impressive in the extreme, and include a private church, a castle and a park, 'which is not open to the workers; they prefer a joint of meat'. The drainage network is adequate, but only a third of the total area has been developed on the Bologna or *cavalletto* system, which is considered to be perfect. It consists of throwing the soil into low ridges about 20 yds. wide, leaving strips of ground about 4 yds. wide between them. These latter are occupied by vines in *filarie*, or rows, and maples, the former, as in Virgil's day, entwining themselves around the latter. This *coltura promiscua* or mixed-crop cultivation is not found in the irrigated areas, which are not suited to the vine, but is commonly practised over the whole of central Italy, where it reaches its greatest development on the holdings of the Tuscan *métayers*.

152. The estate is divided into sixty-five holdings, and there are four different types of land tenure. Even these do not account for all the

possible variations, however, for the Latin mind is not lacking in imagination. Under the first system, a sector which includes a 175-acre vineyard and a 43-acre orchard is worked by wage-earning labourers and the owner retains direct control. It will be noticed that the vineyard is characteristic in this case, whereas on the *métayers'* holdings (see below) the vines are arranged in *filarie*. We find the same contrast between the *jouale* or inter-cultivated vines of the *métayer* of Lot-et-Garonne and the vineyards of the châteaux of Gironde. Where the owner pays the wages himself he demands high productivity of labour and does not tolerate the archaic crop arrangement of the *cavalletto*. Bearing in mind the extremely dense population of the region, the only justification for this crop system would be that it raised production, and that more profitable employment for the labour it absorbed was not available. Provided these conditions were fulfilled, it should therefore be allowed to continue, in spite of any extra work it might involve. Owing to the lack of precise information, we have been unable to make a fair assessment of the actual position here.

A second type of land tenure is 'participation', whereby the worker receives 40 per cent. of the total produce for his labour.[1] Each unit of land consists of just under 5 acres and produces wheat, sugar-beet, and hemp. The crops assure the worker of a reasonable income, for the gross return per acre is in the region of 80,000 lire, and his earnings are thus about 150,000 lire for four to five months' work; in addition, the owner is legally obliged to employ him in the winter on the basis of a minimum of twenty-four hours per acre (twenty-eight hours for rice-fields), and this makes another 150 hours or so at 110 lire an hour. On the Pegola estate, in the Malalbergo commune between Bologna and Ferrara, the units of land are little more than $1\frac{1}{2}$ acres, and payment is reduced to 35 per cent. to 40 per cent. of the gross return; more details of this estate are given below.

In 1951 we visited an area nearer the coast, to the north-west of Comacchio, and here the 'participants' were allowed units of little over $\frac{1}{2}$ acre, plus 0·8 of a unit for a wife and 0·6 for a child between the age of twelve and sixteen. The crops were wheat and sugar-beet, and the worker's share was 38 per cent. With twenty-nine days of work per acre of wheat—the crop was cut with a scythe—and thirty-seven days for sugar-beet, there were only eighteen days of guaranteed work a year. Even if he had a few animals to look after and earned a little

---

[1] In times past the proportion was only a third. M. Estrangin, a farmer at Thorenc (Alpes-Maritimes), confesses that he would be extremely gratified if he had to give his workers no more than 40 per cent. of the harvest.

money by cleaning ditches in the winter or by doing odd jobs from time to time, the participant was rarely employed for more than seventy or eighty days in the year. Plentiful yields and the most modern techniques were thus found side by side with the most abject poverty caused by lack of work. It is worth observing that in the province as a whole under-employment is a far more serious question than unemployment.

153. The 'best' workers on the land under direct control and the 'best' participants—that is, those who show themselves capable and thrifty and have the 'right attitude'—become *métayers*. In all, there are about twenty families who have acceded to this position and another twenty have attained the fourth and final rung in the ladder of promotion and are now 'farmers', each of them responsible for 40-50 acres. The estate provides its *métayers* and farmers with such services as hemp-stripping, wine-making, and, most important of all, mechanized ploughing. Ploughing for sugar-beet costs 4,000 lire an acre. The company which owns the land advances the farmer the greater part of his working capital, which is repayable over fifteen years, and as compared with the traditional *métayer*, the farmer is evidently one step nearer to the capitalist type of economy.

The average 50-acre farm in the hands of a patriarchal family is worked by four or five men and two or three women. They often have about twenty head of cattle of various ages, probably averaging a little over 650 lb. apiece. The stock is worth 2,000,000 lire, and in addition the family has about half this sum in working capital, but machinery represents a mere 200,000 lire. The live weight of stock per acre is well over 350 lb., and at Pegola the *métayers* achieve figures of 530 lb. to the acre.

Gross receipts from 15 acres of wheat at 28 cwt. to the acre are 1,500,000 lire; 7·5 acres of hemp, with yields about 10 cwt., and the same area of sugar-beet, yielding 14 tons to the acre, bring a further 800,000 to 1,000,000 lire; the produce of 2,000 vines in *filarie* and the sale of animals add 600,000 and 500,000 lire respectively, and the gardens, the pigs, and the poultry bring in over 200,000 lire. The gross income of nearly 4,600,000 lire is only 92,000 an acre, and is inferior to the average rate in Lombardy, where far less labour is expended per acre. In fact, nearly fifty days of work are lavished on every acre of the farm. When deductions have been made for the mortgage on capital, for tractor ploughing, and, the heaviest item of all, for the land rent of 1,000,000 lire, each farm worker in the family still earns more money than the participant, but he has worked very much harder for it. By comparison, the *cascina* employee, who supplies no capital whatsoever, earns just as much, although the situation admittedly improves when the farm has paid off all its debts.

The rent is calculated on the basis of 90 lb. of wheat (2,800 lire), 110 lb. of tow (at 130 lire a pound), and 8 cwt. of sugar-beet (3,200 lire) to the acre. The total is thus 20,000 lire per acre, and from this the owner draws a net income of 12,000 lire[1] after the deduction of maintenance expenses, building mortgages, and taxes. In contrast, *métayage* brings him 32,000 lire per acre, and the higher revenues from *métayage* as compared with the farm system deserve special emphasis, for our observations in Italy have repeatedly confirmed this same point.

Naturally, the company admits only to philanthropic motives for its part in the gradual trend towards the farm system. Indeed, 'by a careful process of selection', it is accomplishing 'a measure of agrarian reform from which the most beneficial economic and social results are bound to follow'. Such altruism is bound to be suspect in an economy still governed by the profit motive, and these phrases were doubtless prompted by the fact that 3,000 of the 3,750 acres of San Antonio are scheduled for expropriation in the official programme for agrarian reform. Admittedly, the knowledge that they have a chance of bettering their social position may help to bolster up the morale of the *métayers* and labourers, but the owner is also released from the heavy obligation of finding all the capital needed for his land, and he sets aside only the more outlying parts of the estate for the farm system. Furthermore, the ploughing he does for these favoured tenants and the processing of the farm produce leave him ample scope for financial gain. A wise programme would provide for these communal services to be continued and extended, but the whole enterprise would become co-operative in character.

154. On the Pegola estate, apart from twenty-three permanent labourers of whom fourteen are needed for the orchards, about 150 casual workers are employed on the 500 acres under direct control. The latter work an average of 120 days a year, the permanent employees about 200 days, and this total of 22,600 can be expressed as forty-five man-days per acre.[2] Rice needs 720 and hemp nearly 480 hours

---

[1] This figure was quoted in our presence, but the printed form we were given showed a figure of only 4,000–5,000 lire net.

[2] We had some difficulty in arriving at these figures, and they are quoted only as a general guide. The information sheet we were given for our visit cited 'two work units per hectare of the total area'; there was no indication of the number of days of work per unit during the course of the year.

of work per acre and, on the basis of a seven-and-a-half-hour working day, this means ninety-three days for the former crop and sixty-four for the latter. These figures are almost as high as for rice cultivation in Tonkin, but the yield of paddy, which attains 6 tons an acre, is four times as great. The 73-acre orchard requires sixty-four days of labour per acre, including the time needed for fruit-packing; root crops need half this time, wheat fifty days and lucerne forty, inclusive of sowing.

Here, the first and foremost objective is full productive employment by intensification. Mechanizing the harvest is a less urgent need, especially in view of the present type of economic structure, and it can only serve to reduce employment without helping production in any way. In spite of these considerations, however, it is already fairly well advanced, and we saw, for instance, a recently acquired combine harvesting part of the wheat crop. Its ultimate effect is simply to transfer part of the money previously paid in local wages to the employees of Messrs. MacCormick in Chicago and to the producers, refiners, carriers, and distributors of petroleum products. Locally, mechanization arouses the feelings of the wage-earning class, and the combine is becoming an object of hatred; 'the machines are depriving us of our bread' is a typical comment. The story of the opposition of the weavers of Lyons to the mechanical loom is being re-enacted and carabiniers patrol the countryside to protect the machines should the need arise. 'Last year we had fourteen days of work at harvest time, but this year we had only nine,' complain the women, who have a right to eighty to 120 days of work in the year.

This 'right to work' is jealously guarded, even by force if need be, and a man cannot engage himself for work outside his 'union zone'. A commune like Ravenna has thirty-six such zones which cover a total of 38,000 acres, and 'it is easier to go and find work in France than in the next district'. Wages range from 700 lire for eight hours during the slack season to 220 lire an hour at the harvest. A woman can earn 110,000 lire in 120 days, while her husband, as a '200-day' permanent employee, would receive 240,000 lire. Such a couple would be considered to be really well-off.

155. The two most useful avenues of intensification here seem to be orchard planting and irrigation. Before the war there were more than 70 acres of orchards, and this acreage had been rapidly extended, especially for apple and pear trees. In common with horticulture everywhere in Mediterranean lands—and in the Netherlands too—the ever-present problem is that of markets, and great benefit would accrue to Italy

from a united and prosperous Europe, for a rise in incomes is generally reflected in a rise in the demand for fruit, which is particularly elastic. So far irrigation exists solely for riziculture, and its possibilities for double-cropping have not been exploited as in the Vercellese between Turin and Milan, where wheat is harvested by 10 June and rice is planted out immediately after and harvested in October; here, a hectare (2·5 acres) of land holds the world record of 9 tons 4 cwt. of paddy and 5 tons 10 cwt. of wheat grown in the same year. This is a yield of nearly 118 cwt. per acre. A field of maize in the Corn Belt is said to have approached 112 cwt. per acre, and we have already quoted the 96 cwt. per acre of the lower Guadalquivir south of Seville.

Irrigation is less appropriate to these heavy soils than to those of the upper Po Valley. Nevertheless, it could be applied to many areas provided that certain precautions were taken, and aspersion would probably be necessary in some cases. In 1950, near Lodigoro, a gang of unemployed workmen, on their own initiative, began to construct irrigation canals which the budget had specified for later development. By this kind of 'strike in reverse', peculiar to Italy and a natural consequence of overpopulation, they not only solved their own immediate problem of unemployment, but also ensured an increase in the overall volume of available work. More precisely, they were simply trying, but with little hope of success, to compensate for the declining demand for labour due to mechanization.

If, as we believe, the future of this region lies in the expansion of the orchard acreage and the extension of irrigation, it seems inadvisable to encourage further development of the *cavalletto* system. Inter-cultivation and ridging up of the ground are neither of them favourable for either orchards or irrigation. The agrarian reforms which are to complete the development of the region should aim at preparing the ground for intensification in the future and refrain from applying any stimulus to the traditional system of *filarie*, which only appears to make for unnecessary work.

4. A Well-to-do Owner-farmer and a Poor *Métayer* in Tuscany

156. In France the owner-farmer may cultivate anything from 5 to 2,500 acres, but in Italy the term *coltivatore diretto* is reserved for the small proprietor who works with his own hands, generally without the help of permanent employees. Signor Fabri works his 15-acre farm at Ponte della Chiassa Superiore, a portion of the Arezzo commune, and although he formerly occupied the land as a *métayer* he eventually

succeeded in buying it outright. In Italy, even more so than in France, it is most unusual for a *métayer* to rise in the social scale in this manner.

The *métayage* system still dominates this part of the commune, which counts only twenty-five owner-farmers whose holdings vary between 4 and 15 acres. Fabri's holding is therefore among the largest of its kind, and not only is his daughter continuing with her studies, but he also owns a car, which is a most unusual possession for one of his class. Two hundred and forty olive trees, which are well adapted to the steep, eroded slopes, cover some 2½ acres of hillside and produce an average of 4 cwt. of oil, half of which is destined for use on the farm. They are a sure sign that we have now crossed the Apennines. The 12½-acre stretch of alluvial lowland in the Arno Valley has been thrown into low, parallel ridges and rows of vines, 33 yds. apart and supported by maple trees, trace out the summit of each alternate strip. The vine harvest comes late, from 5 to 10 October, and it gives between 160 and 180 cwt. of grapes which yield 1,300–1,500 gallons of wine of about 12 per cent. alcohol content. Of this, some 900 gallons are normally sold.

A seven-year rotation is often followed on the strips. A row crop, generally maize, but sometimes potatoes or beans for domestic use, is followed by wheat, a three-year ley of lucerne and, finally, another two wheat crops. In 1951 there were 5 acres of wheat, 5¼ of lucerne, and 1¾ of row crops, the remainder of the area being accounted for by the garden, threshing floors, and buildings. In a good year Fabri harvests 7 or 8 tons of wheat. The lucerne can be cut four times a year and, with the aftermath, this enables him to feed two draught cows, a store, a dairy cow, and a pig which, when fattened, will be used by the family.

Two men and a woman work the land. In spite of a certain amount of equipment, such as a mowing machine, this density of one worker per 5 acres is insufficient, even though the olive plantation needs comparatively little attention. Three labourers are taken on therefore for about 100 days a year and are paid 550 lire per day, plus their food. This is somewhat below the official rate, which is adhered to more punctiliously in the north, where the unions are rather more alert. In all, 900 days of labour are devoted to the 15 acres or, more precisely, 850 are expended on the 12½ acres of lowland. This is sixty-eight days per acre, and is even more than in the preceding case, although not quite the same degree of intensiveness is attained.

Here, again, water is the instrument of intensification. There is an artesian well nearly 90 ft. deep, but a certain amount of pumping is necessary to maintain the flow of $1\frac{3}{4}$ gallons a second. Blessed by the priest and armed with a diesel pump, this well is to provide water for the whole of the farm, and this will permit two more cuttings of lucerne and an increase in the proportion of row crops. These will be mainly hybrid maize and Virginia tobacco, for Fabri intends to grow neither vegetables nor sugar-beet. Indeed, in a more rational order of things, tobacco, which is best suited to countries where land is scarce but labour is not, would be sent to the United States from Europe. At present, however, the U.S.A. is certainly not helping Italy to add this item to her list of exports, and a further hindrance is the unreliable quality of the crop.

The buildings themselves form an isolated group in the midst of the countryside. Built originally to accommodate four *métayers* under a single roof, they still house four families. They occupy very little ground, for the only outbuilding is a small stable and the only storage space is beneath the dwelling-house. Thus all the reserves of straw, lucerne hay, chaff, maize spathes and leaves, wood, etc., are kept outside in cone-shaped stacks surrounding the drying floor. The countries of the Mediterranean have fewer buildings than those of Northern Europe.

157. At the top of the scarp slope east of Arezzo is a plateau nearly 2,700 ft. above sea-level, covered with only a sparse vegetation of withered grass and scrub in spite of the mean rainfall of some 32 in. a year. The summer drought is more serious here than in Lombardy or Emilia, especially as the soils are very poor and thin. One of the *métayers* who farms in this region has about 125 acres, and his house stands isolated in the midst of his fields. Thirty-five acres are arable, and only $7\frac{1}{2}$ of these have rows of vines. The latter give 40 cwt. of grapes, which yield 290 gallons of wine, but the *métayer*'s share is hardly enough for the needs of his own family. Lower down, on the scarp, a few olive trees provide about 65 lb. of oil, which represents no more than a three-month supply for the family of three men, three women, and four children.

He has $12\frac{1}{2}$ acres of wheat land under the traditional grain-fallow rotation, and on it he sows 14 cwt. of seed to reap about 80 cwt. in a good year. Again, there is no surplus when he receives his share. Indeed, in drought years, he has to buy back a few sacks of grain to feed his family. During the second course of the rotation, apart from the fallow land, he grows a little over 1 acre of maize and about the same of barley and oats, which altogether provide a further 10–16 cwt.

of grain. In addition, outside this rotation he sows a little red clover and sainfoin, and a few potatoes and beans for domestic use.

His only dependable income is from his three flocks. As in nearby Corsica, each must have a herdsman to ensure that the animals make the most of the sparse grazing. For draught purposes he keeps two cows, which are sold after five or six years of use, and he rears a pair of heifers to replace them. He also sells a milch calf every year. The three pigs are kept for his own table, but the twenty ewes allow him to market 32 lb. of scoured wool, 130 lb. of *pecorino* cheese, fifteen unfattened lambs, and a few of the older sheep from the flock. Whereas by far the greater part of Fabri's income is from his arable land, the only saleable produce here is provided by extensive herding.

Hunger is the immediate result of a poor wheat or vine harvest. As for the building, its roof is sadly in need of repair, and the family still depend on candles or oil-lamps for light. It is not surprising that they want to move. The owner, 'a grasping and unintelligent person', according to Dr Lombardi of the Arezzo Agricultural Inspectorate, lives in Arezzo on the revenue from six similar holdings. It is many a long year since he spent anything on them even for maintenance. On this particular holding the *métayer* has no wheelbarrow, and so the manure is taken from the sheds and sheep-folds on a kind of stretcher carried by two men. As the family obtain so little from their crops, they waste their time gleaning the fields and collecting all kinds of produce for fodder, from oak twigs and reeds to leaves from various plants, including the clematis. Similar use is made of holly leaves on the Lanvaux heathlands in Morbihan.

The agreement reached in 1946 between the landowners and the *métayers* allotted 47 per cent. of the harvest to the farmers, who are also responsible for half the expenses. The *métayer* in question thus retains only 53 per cent. of the crop yields enumerated above, and these are in any case much inferior to those which Fabri could keep entirely for himself. Even when the family have poultry on their table, they have to make a 'compulsory gift' to the proprietor; the Federation of *métayers* is demanding the abolition of this practice. Thus, we have found poverty and plenty within a few miles of each other. A share of 47 per cent. for the owner would be justified under the present economic conditions if it was a question of fertile alluvial terrain where he had procured great improvements by the deployment of a considerable volume of capital, but in this particular situation, where the soil is poor and the investment practically nil, his reward seems to be out of all reasonable proportion. Indeed, considering the capital actually involved and the negligible expenditure on maintenance, the owner's share should not exceed one-fifth, according to a seemingly reasonable estimate made by the Federation of *métayers*.[1]

5. The *Métayage* System in Danger in the Valle di Chiana

158. Continuing southwards towards Lake Trasimeno one follows the Valle di Chiana, which was drained between 1830 and 1840 by Leopold, Grand Duke of Tuscany. The San Caterina estate covers 2,330 acres, 2,000 of them on the lowland and the rest, planted with 4,000 olive trees yielding over 2 lb. of oil a tree, on the undulating hills. It belongs to the 'Company for the Improvement of the Land of the Ferrara District', a limited company founded by industrial interests which already owned 63,000 acres, 50,000 of them in the lower Po Delta, in 1953.[2] The company went bankrupt during the crisis in 1932, but most of the shares were taken up by the Bank of Italy's Superannuation Fund.

San Caterina is divided into fifty-nine *métayer* holdings, two of which are retained under direct control. There are 1,850 acres of arable farmed by fifty-seven families, which account between them for 467 labour units. Including the land under direct control and the employees who provide general services, the estate supports a total of 1,094 people, an agricultural density of 299 per square mile. Rows of vines intertwine their branches with those of the maple on 70 per cent. of the arable land, and the owner's proud boast is that a third of the stocks have been planted since 1946; this system, which we regard as being somewhat outdated, is still regarded here, as it was by the Roman agriculturalist, as an index of intensive farming.

A row crop like maize, tobacco, sugar-beet, or beans comes at the head of the rotation, and is followed by wheat, three years of lucerne, wheat, row crop, and wheat again. In 1952 there were 795 acres of lucerne, 738 of wheat, 135 of beet and maize, 100 of tobacco, 65 of beans, 63 of oats, and 53 under 'miscellaneous' crops. The 682 head of cattle, 487 pigs and 634 sheep give a density of 400 lb. of live weight per acre, a very much higher ratio than the regional average. Twenty-one

[1] From '*Les classes sociales dans les campagnes*', by H. Lefèvre, in *Cahiers internationaux de Sociologie* (Vol. X, 1951). In the opinion of Denis Bergmann, the provision of land is the all-important role in extensive agriculture of this type, and this explains the division of produce in these proportions.

[2] In *Économie contemporaine* for September 1951 we have given details of another estate near Comacchio belonging to the same company.

MÉTAYAGE IN THE VALLE DI CHIANA

people live on the 30 acres of the Vagnoni V[1] *podere* (*métayer* holding); of these, six men are the field workers; $11\frac{1}{4}$ acres of wheat yield at 22 cwt. an acre, worth 3,400 lire a hundredweight; $2\frac{1}{2}$ acres of Kentucky tobacco yield at 10 cwt., worth 12,500 lire a hundredweight; 5 acres of beet yield only 8 tons apiece, for the dry summer is an unfavourable factor and their value per acre is less than that of winter wheat, which is much better suited to the climate. The 4,000 vines produce 9 lb. of fruit apiece, making a total of 320 cwt., worth 3,500 lire a hundredweight. The total value of the crops is thus over 2,000,000 lire.

On the *podere* the cattle, of Chianina breed and carefully bred as dual-purpose meat and draught animals, comprise two oxen, six cows, two heifers, and four calves. Every year the equivalent of 8,800 lb. live weight is sold at 145 lire a pound. Together with about forty piglets, each weighing about 45 lb. and worth 7,000 lire, this makes a gross income from animal products of over 1,500,000 lire. Adding the receipts from poultry- and rabbit-keeping and from a little fruit- and vegetable-growing, the gross value of the produce is nearly 4,000,000 lire.

159. According to Father de Farcy, this money yield is three times as great per unit area as in the interior of Brittany; but it is very much lower per worker. Once the owner's share has been deducted, plus a small sum for running expenses, little more than 250,000 lire remains per worker's family, which generally includes at least one unproductive member, either a child or an old person. This is less than a man may earn in Lombardy without any help from his family, provided that he enjoys the status of permanent worker. It is earned only after many more hours of work and on condition that the *métayer* supplies half the working capital in the form of stock and equipment. Professor Tofani informs us that the low remuneration of the *métayer* as compared with the permanent labourer is the general case. The *métayage* system, in effect, is a type of land tenure which aims primarily at increasing the volume of employment.

Indeed, there is plenty of regular work and there are relatively few unemployed casual labourers The people are in a very much better position than the *métayer* of Arezzo, and this is not entirely due to the richer soils, but also to the deep ploughing, the use of fertilizers, and the selective breeding of animals, which all reflect the greater volume of capital investment. The people have enough to eat,[2] and furniture

---

[1] 35 acres, including the road, ditches, rows of vines, etc.

[2] Number of calories adequate, but the quality of the food leaves much to be desired.

of the 'Levitan' type[1] begins to appear in the homes. But the women still make cloth from a mixture of cotton and locally-grown hemp, a survival from the subsistence economy of the past, while bicycles are still uncommon and motor-scooters are a rarity.

It is significant that foreign visitors are willingly shown over the estate, and the overall picture which emerges is undeniably most impressive. The productivity of the stock farming is well above average for the *métayage* system. San Caterina, furthermore, is reputed for its stock breeding and sells about sixty young bulls every year at a good price. Unlike Parlesca, however (studied in 1951, see note, p. 246), there are few new buildings, and even those which do exist have but a single communal room and have no running water. On the other hand, the living quarters, traditionally situated on the first floor above the stables and the granary, cannot be criticized for any lack of space. In contrast with the workers' dwellings on the *cascina*, which were all crowded together, each house is built on its own holding; but a single communal room for twenty-one people hardly affords the married couples the privacy of a home of their own. As each holding is in the hands of a single family, the system perpetuates the patriarchal tradition and the ultimate authority of the *capocchio* or head of the family.

160. Professor Rossi-Doria shows that this *métayage* system, which is after all a relic from feudal times, is threatened on two sides. First, there is a general tendency to favour the independence of the conjugal family; the patriarchal family is losing its sense of unity and the absolute authority of the *capocchio* is no longer recognized. When the head of a family dies and the moment arrives to choose his successor, it is often found that certain members declare themselves unwilling to submit any longer to patriarchal rule. Married couples are more and more evincing a desire to run their own homes in their own way. In southwest France the holding worked by a farmer and his family is generally larger than one of the farms on San Caterina, but it is cultivated less intensively. Modern equipment, like binders, tractors, and tractor implements, could achieve the same result here, but what would then become of the surplus workers and their dependants?

Secondly, the *métayage* type of land tenure is threatened by an external factor—namely, the incessant battle between owner and tenant. There are interminable arguments about the sale of stock: At what age should the animals be sold? At what time of year? Which is the best market? These waste an enormous amount of time both for the bailiff and the *capoccio*. The respective shares of owner and tenant were

[1] Levitan is a large firm well-known in France for its mass-produced furniture.

determined by the agreement of 1946, although, as we have seen, the merits of fixed percentages are highly questionable. In spite of this, there are still numerous occasions for differences of opinion; prices and the list of products to be shared, which even includes angora rabbit wool, are two cases in point. Farm management is by tradition the responsibility of 'the proprietor, working in agreement with the *métayer*', an ambiguous formula which the latter quotes to suit his own purposes, although no doubt the land would not be manured quite so thoroughly if things were left entirely to him.

Two of the main causes of friction are the duration of contracts and the owner's right to give notice. Until 1946, some *métayer* families had remained on the land for several centuries, whereas others were constantly on the move; but at this time there began endless discussions on the conditions under which an owner could legitimately give notice. The *métayers*, many of whom are Communists, feared lest they might be victimized for their political views. The upshot of the matter is that there has been very little movement since 1946, and the flexibility of the previous system has unfortunately been lost. A family which increases or decreases its numbers can no longer move to a holding of appropriate dimensions; the result is that some now have far too much land and others far too little.

The *métayers*' associations are fighting hard to alter the share percentage in their favour and to force compliance with a clause of the 1946 agreement which has so far largely been ignored, whereby 4 per cent. of receipts must be reinvested by the owner. In Tuscany the association has on occasions paid this 4 per cent. direct to the workers' unions, to which they are politically allied, for the specific purpose of effecting land improvements. More advanced countries like England, Denmark, and the Netherlands have every reason to regard *métayage* as an archaic system. It is appropriate only to regions lacking in both technical knowledge and capital and harassed by a high density of rural population.

The pressure of population makes the search for high yields in terms of both land and labour a matter of the most urgent importance. A senator who owned an estate near San Caterina bequeathed it to his *métayers*, but the yields are said to have dropped steeply after the first few years. The Rumanian measures of agrarian reform between 1920 and 1925 met with similar results. Moreover, according to Professor Rossi-Doria, *métayage* in its present form 'is destined to disappear during the course of the next hundred years'. But an agrarian reform which aims at accelerating the process without any ensuing decline in yields must obviously offer some means of replacing the best landowners in their role of farm managers and as suppliers of workshops and tractors, communal services, and capital. On these clay lands tractors are absolutely necessary for deep ploughing, which increases crop resistance to drought.

Thus the division of the great estates among the *métayers*, although it would present fewer difficulties here than in the *cascine* of Lombardy, does not seem to be the final solution under present circumstances, for there would be a serious risk of technical retrogression. But to condemn the region irrevocably to *métayage* would be equally unwise and would bar the way to future progress.

The present system can no longer be justified in the numerous instances where the owner no longer or only partially fulfils his proper obligations. Such neglect is very frequent in the uplands and almost universal in the south, where, according to Professor Tofani, 'people work from the age of ten until they are eighty for 40 lire an hour'. Finally, this criticism is not valid only for the poorer regions; even at San Caterina great hesitation is being shown at the prospect of spending large sums on irrigation which is none the less the next logical step in land improvement.

6. The Latifundia of the Maremma and Agrarian Reforms[1]

161. Between Leghorn and Rome, where, as in Madrid, extensive farming reaches right to the city boundary, the Roman and Tuscan Maremma encircles Grossetto and Civita-Vecchia and covers 2,500,000 acres of land bordered by the Tyrrhenian Sea and dominated by large estates. Eight hundred of these, all of them over 250 acres, comprise 73·5 per cent. of the total area, whereas 80,000 holdings of less than 25 acres account for less than 11 per cent. Between these extremes, a mere 8 per cent. of the farms, covering 15·6 per cent. of the area, have an acreage larger than 25 but less than 250.[2]

The contrasts are striking. In the vicinity of Pitigliano the tiniest parcels of land, some of them on seemingly impossible slopes, are intensively worked. Elsewhere, on the hills and lowlands nearer the

---

[1] See *Land Reform in the Maremma*, published at Grossetto by Ente Maremma; also the large number of very interesting publications by the Instituto Nazionale di Economia agraria, 36 via Barberini, Rome, and by the eleven Observatories of Rural Economy attached to the Faculties of Agriculture. We only wish there were such sources of material in France.

[2] In the whole of Italy, 2,500,000 *microfundia* cover a total of 5,000,000 acres. As against this the 40,000 absentee landowners with more than 125 acres account for 25,750,000 acres (C.G.I.L. documents).

sea, where relief and climate combine to facilitate the exploitation of the land, the farming is extensive in the extreme; the density of cattle hardly reaches the equivalent of 45 lb. live weight per acre and the animals are of a hardy but ancient breed, the Maremmano, which gives mediocre yields, even of meat.

As in the Hungarian *puszta*, in Andalusia, South America, and other countries where the large estate still predominates, the main resource is still the wild scrub and steppe, and these animals are raised for the most part on natural unimproved grazing land. This is even truer of sheep-rearing, which still follows the age-old Mediterranean pattern of transhumance, in this case between the slopes of the Apennines in summer and the scrub and fallow land near the coast from September to May. In this form the pastoral economy is the most extensive possible type of land utilization; it is little more than a collecting economy, and is strongly reminiscent of the primitive nomadism of the steppes of Central Asia.

The ploughland is seldom threaded by rows of vines, except near the towns, where horticulture generally predominates. The level of intensiveness falls progressively away from the settlements, and their approach is always heralded by a fuller use of the land. The rotation is the traditional one of a year, or sometimes even two, of grazed fallow succeeded by a winter cereal which yields a mere 10 cwt. or so an acre. Modern precautions against soil erosion are ignored, and the consequences are plainly seen wherever the gradient begins to steepen. An indication of the extensive nature of the farming is given by the mean figure of eleven work-days per acre of land, falling to only eight at Grossetto; these figures are low for Italy.

Moreover, these figures are compounded of extremes, for the average on small holdings is eighteen as compared with nine for the latifundia. As a general rule the agricultural worker has a right to about 145 days of work a year, and the labour ratio is one person per 17 acres (one per 20 at Grossetto). The sparseness of population (there are only 146 persons per square mile) is due to the fact that law and order were not firmly established until the beginning of the century,[1] and, furthermore, the region was plagued with malaria until 1930; there are thus certain similarities with the east coast of Corsica. The small development of industry can be judged from the fact that two-thirds of the population are still rural.

162. The large estates are sometimes worked by *métayers*, especially

[1] In the vicinity of Nuoro in Sardinia they could not be said to have been established even by 1953.

near Tuscany, but direct control and wage-earning labour are characteristic in the south towards the Roman Campagna. In a country so densely populated as Italy extensive farming is certainly not in the interest of the nation as a whole, but it pays good dividends for the landowners, who can draw as much as 4,000–6,000 lire net from land worth no more than 40,000 lire an acre. The rate of profit is thus higher than the return on working capital in Lombardy, and this is yet another case where the interests of the *entrepreneur* run counter to those of the nation. The landowner is generally averse to intensification because of the extra trouble it would cause him and because of the heavy expenditure he would be bound to incur. Many of the estates are duchies or principalities, and the feudal-minded owners, although often lacking the ready capital to finance improvements, refuse to sell any part of their land, for in their view this would mean an intolerable loss of prestige.

Those who have considerable means prefer to invest in industry, where the dividends are higher. Indeed, the capital resources and revenues of the rural south have gravitated towards the north, where they have helped to develop industry. But when this industry has reinvested capital in the land it has equally confined its attentions to the north. Thus, from the national point of view, the special credit scheme embodied in the Cazza di Mezzogiorno, analogous to the English 'marginal land scheme', is fully justified, and we have already pleaded for the same kind of facilities to be granted to France's underdeveloped regions. Every winter the shepherd with his transhumant flocks is faced with the fact that, as in Corsica and Sardinia, the available grazing land is owned by a small number of people who are quick to exploit their monopoly. The poorest fallow grazing is let at over 6,000 lire an acre, and the price is sometimes as high as 12,000 lire. Cereal-growing may not give very high yields, but the pastoralist actually pays a higher rent than the cultivator.

The social relationships between the princes of Corsini (owning 50,000 acres) and Torlonia (owning 100,000 acres, twenty-four years of age) and their *métayers* and labourers were still, in the autumn of 1951, virtually medieval in character. When the Prince arrived in his carriage the peasants had to kneel and kiss his hand. For the sake of his own personal safety, he was always closely surrounded by his bodyguard of four armed men on horseback. The existence of rural unemployment (many of the men work only eighty days a year at a rate of 800 lire *per diem*), malnutrition, and underdeveloped land was the best possible justification for State intervention.

THE MAREMMA AND AGRARIAN REFORMS

The situation in the south, in the highlands, and the islands[1] is even more serious. Behind the coastal belt of extremely intensive horticulture, with vines, citrus, and other fruits and early vegetables, there remain large stretches of land exploited on an extensive scale. Latifundia cover 80 per cent. of the area, but the peasant holdings are often cultivated no better. Heavy clay soils predominate and though, in this dry climate, they do not lend themselves easily to intensification, the task is not impossible. Although many types of tree are unsuited to this very heavy land, sown grasses and fodder crops could support sufficient animals to save the region from the tyranny of the extensive cereal-fallow rotation. As in Hungary, the peasants live in huge villages of 10,000–40,000 inhabitants, considerably larger than those in Andalusia. The prerequisites for intensive agriculture are land improvement—soil conservation, drainage or irrigation, and deep-ploughing, which implies mechanization—and the establishment of dispersed settlements where the peasant can live near his fields.

163. It would take too long to give a complete historical account of Italian land improvement and reform. The Serpieri law of 1933 was well intended, but State subsidies for agriculture were often used for other purposes. The large landowners were still very much a law unto themselves; members of the Fascist hierarchy were often invited to their castles to participate in magnificent hunts; the law certainly provided for the expropriation of those who did not improve their estates, but decisions on this question were the responsibility of the 'Corporation', which, in practice, meant the landowners themselves. Between 1938 and 1940 the Government made an example of a few landowners and the land was taken over by the 'National Action for Combatants', but the actual work undertaken was mostly confined to building houses. From our visit in 1938 we well remember the Calabrian labourer who had been chosen as a settler for the Pontine Marshes; he thought the cement stand was so beautifully clean that he obstinately refused to dirty it with manure. Seventy acres and more were sometimes given to men who had too little capital, were given no technical instruction, and who, moreover, had never before managed more than a 5-acre holding.

The present agrarian reform, begun under the Christian Democrat Segni, is concentrating on the lower delta of the Po, the Maremma, and the greater part of the south and the islands. Estates which pay

[1] Which, with the exception of Sardinia (see duplicated report to Monnet Plan dated May 1953), we have not studied in detail. See Professor M. Rossi-Doria's *Riformia agraria e azione meridionalista*.

more than 30,000 lire in land taxes—that is, of more than about 800 to 1,000 acres—are to be broken up, and in the case of the Maremma, 550,000 acres or more than 22 per cent. of the area will be thus affected. The owner will be compensated in State bonds, which are difficult to convert into ready money, and calculations will be based on the declaration he made for the 'progressive surtax on patrimony' and, fortunately for him, on its revision by the tax assessor; he is evidently being treated less generously than in Spain. He has the right to keep a third of his land so long as he conforms with instructions from the Maremma Office for its development, but eventually half the area thus retained for improvement will be distributed among the peasants.

Exceptions will be made only where estates fulfil a series of conditions so severe that they will rarely all be satisfied:

1. Crop yields more than 40 per cent. and density of cattle stock more than 30 per cent. above the regional average.
2. Land farmed by *métayers* living on their holdings.
3. A record of having consistently employed at least 0·24 workers per acre.
4. Heavy expenditure on water control, roads, etc.

Farms like Count Guicciardini's, described in our 1951 article, which are in sight of the necessary minimum requirements, are now issuing attractive pamphlets describing their achievements in glowing terms in the hope of keeping their present status.

164. Of the land acquired by the State in the Maremma, nearly 40 per cent. will be distributed to peasants wishing to enlarge their uneconomically small holdings and to agricultural labourers who want a small plot of land for themselves. The remaining 60 per cent. will be divided into suitably proportioned and independent family farms. Small buildings are erected first of all, with roadways and with drinking water, either piped or from wells. As in the case of the owner-farmer of Arezzo, farms are sometimes grouped together in threes under the same roof. Three of these groups, nine farms in all, form a small hamlet which has a total of some 200 to 250 acres. Another method is to group four individual farms together, each occupying one angle in a cross-roads. Finally, farms are often strung out 150 yds. apart, as, for example, along the Via Aurelia, about twenty-five miles from Rome. But this type of pattern can be severely criticized on the grounds that it adds very considerably to the cost, especially where water and electricity supplies are concerned, and later on the installation of telephones will be subject to the same handicap. Although this

degree of dispersion is preferable to overcrowding, such isolation is obviously not conducive to the development of social life.

At the same time olives and *filarie*, or rows of vine, are planted, the former 15 yds. apart and the latter at 25- or 30-yd. intervals, with the stocks about every 5 ft. A typical farm of 25 acres, which is larger than the average, is intended to support a family of seven and to be worked by four labour units, men counting one, children between 12 and 16, men over sixty, and women counting as a half, old women nothing. In thousands of lire, the house costs about 2,000, roadways 250, water supply installations 70, the vines 450, the olive trees 100, 5 acres of subsoil ploughing 100, and drainage, the initial stage of water control, another 100. The Office sinks some 3,000,000 lire of capital into the typical 25-acre property, which at the outset is worth between 1,000,000 and 1,500,000 lire. In addition, a further 1,800,000 lire of working capital are put at the new farmer's disposal: 1,300,000 for stock, generally about four cows, 300,000 in equipment, and 200,000 in cash to carry the family through the four months which will elapse before it begins to reap the rewards of its labour.

By the beginning of 1952 the Office had received 30,000 applications. The prospective settlers are casual or permanent labourers (43 per cent. of the total in the Maremma), *métayers* (25 per cent.), and owner-farmers with too little land. The majority of them thus have little property of their own, and sometimes furniture and bicycles and even motor-scooters are advanced to them. Half the money for land improvement is a free gift from the State. The remainder is repaid over thirty years at $3\frac{1}{2}$ per cent. interest, and the settler thus repays 5,100 lire per acre per year, far less than the normal rent for such a highly capitalized farm, and at the end of thirty years the land becomes his. Working capital is paid back at 3,600 lire per acre per year. A 25-acre farm thus pays off its debt at 218,000 lire, or about £130, a year (in 1952). The settler is on probation for the first three years, and is not permitted to remain after this trial period unless he achieves a net income, after mortgage repayments, of at least 130,000 lire per work unit.

165. As the prospective settler is generally quite ignorant of modern methods, the intention is to train him by making one out of every ten or twelve holdings a pilot farm run by a progressive small farmer from the north. Also, all will be obliged for the first twenty years to make use of the communal services for cultivating the soil and marketing the produce. Every sector of about 20,000 acres will have a staff of two agricultural scientists, whose task will be to see that bad farming practices are avoided as far as possible, a matter in which they will have

mandatory powers. To start with, there will also be three tractors of 100 h.p., six of 55 h.p., and ten of 25 h.p., a ratio of about 1 h.p. for every 25 acres. At first they will be used only for the heavy work, but eventually all the tillage operations are to be mechanized, leaving the farmer to use his cows for transport purposes only. This stage, as we shall see later, has already been reached in East Germany. Maremmano cattle will be crossed with Chianina, which is a better beef breed. When the settlers, who will tend to think overmuch in terms of cereal crops, have accustomed themselves to the methods of stock-farming, dairying will gradually be introduced, first of all by the loan of dairy cows. This trend is frequently coupled, as in Sardinia, for example, with the development of irrigation.

It is intended to adopt a seven-year rotation on the arable land. As summer row crops suffer from lack of rain (average yield of potatoes, 2 tons an acre), beans, 'the poor man's meat', which are a winter row crop, will be grown. There will follow wheat, fallow, another grain crop, two years of lucerne, and, finally, wheat again or a forage crop for silage. This scheme reflects two important tendencies apparent in Mediterranean lands today—namely, the gradual elimination of fallow and an increasing concentration on forage crops. The natural corollary is the development of intensive cattle- and also sheep-farming, of pig-rearing and poultry-keeping at the expense of extensive pastoralism based on natural grass pastures and scrub.

Special pastoral farms are to be established. They will consist of 75 or 100 acres of land devoted mainly to forage crops. This aspect of the plan is significant in that the division between shepherd and agriculturalist is still recognized and separate provision is being made for the two distinct groups.

The organizers of the reforms have certainly learnt the lesson that similar schemes in the past have failed time and again in Italy and elsewhere, mainly owing to the absence of credit facilities and technical assistance. For the 1,750,000 acres already affected the State will provide at least 2,500,000 million lire. Within fifteen years this should provide employment for another 130,000 units of labour, although in practice it will mean that the casual labourer will be able to earn a wage on 150 days in the year instead of seventy. The latter is still a common figure in the south.

It is true that agricultural investments will not lead to an increase in productivity comparable with what might be achieved in industry with the same capital outlay. The microfundia which it is proposed to establish will find modern techniques difficult to apply. Then, again, one may well question the wisdom of planting these *filarie* of vines in a country which even today cannot find an adequate outlet for the whole of its wine production. The olive should not be grown too near the sea, although, where they are not too clayey, the soils are certainly well adapted to tree and shrub crops. It would be more logical, however, to grow the latter in orchards and, above all, preference should be given to crops which are more likely than the vine to find assured markets abroad.

We realize that this criticism may appear somewhat inappropriate, coming as it does from France, where the same error has already been made with grave consequences. But after all this is a matter for which we are not personally responsible. Those who defend the *filaria* allege that the system helps to combat erosion. It was not, however, invented to serve this end and, unlike the anti-erosive banks of some Algerian hillsides, the lines do not follow the contours and are therefore ineffective against hydraulic erosion. To help against wind erosion, they would have to be aligned at right angles to the prevailing wind, and this is to be done in the Maremma. The traditional *filaria* cannot be held to be the most appropriate soil-conservation measure, for all that. Whatever may be its merits, it is certainly not enough in itself.

7. The Inadequacy of These Reforms; Solutions Outside the Sphere of Agriculture

166. Italian reports give ample evidence of the efforts which are being made to increase the volume of work. Production comes second and productivity comes last. The Maremma Office takes just as much pride in doubling the number of days of work formerly spent on the latifundium on an acre of wheat as it does in raising the yield from 10 to 16 or 20 cwt. per acre. An acre of wheat now occupies ten mandays a year, and comparison of these figures shows that the productivity of work is now significantly lower. In the same way, the subdivision of sheep into smaller flocks will quickly increase the amount of work for shepherds, but will greatly reduce their efficiency. It is generally true of the Italian plans for land development which we have read, that they forecast greater increases in the amount of work than in the volume of production.

In our conversations with leading Italian rural economists, we have generally found them somewhat critical of the reforms. Even Professor Medici, who played one of the principal roles in their inception, confessed that he was rather sceptical. Professor Pagani of Milan denounces what he calls the 'peasant latifundia'—that is, extensive cultivation on small holdings, which he asserts is at least as serious as the problem of the large estates. There are good grounds for his argument that in the Maremma it would have been less costly to establish large, intensively cultivated, and highly mechanized farms capable of keeping up with technical progress than to pursue a policy of fragmentation into tiny holdings. The latter are necessarily subsistence in type and unable to make nearly so large a contribution to the national economy.

In his opinion, the high rate of investment, about 240,000 lire an acre, and the fragmentation of the land will combine to raise the level of wholesale prices in a country which, forced to rely on exchanging her agricultural produce for the raw material she lacks, is already handicapped by her costs of production. Ignoring garden cultivation for the moment, even if only 20 acres were given to every family, half the country's peasantry would still be landless. In the Maremma the ratio is to be fixed at $7\frac{1}{2}$ acres per unit of labour, which is already rather a low figure. But at Ravenna there are 20,000 labourers for 37,500 acres. The inevitable conclusion is that agriculture alone cannot provide the solution. As in the people's democracies, the political motive is often the determining factor in these reforms: in this case, a new class of small landowners is being created in the hope that they will become a strong conservative force.

This is why the settler is eventually to be given the title to his land. But in the absence of further land legislation, the higher nutritional standards of the settlers will result in such rapid population increases that there will very soon be one inhabitant for every 2 or 3 acres, and the holdings will become even smaller and quite uneconomic to work. This tendency could be counteracted if, as in the Dutch *polders*, the settlers were given merely the right to the use of the land. The danger of private property is its alienability, as the Moroccans found to their cost when their common land was divided into individual properties, which the French settlers then immediately began to appropriate. It is freely admitted that the main objective of the reforms is to win over the indigent peasantry from Communism. The success of this policy is not yet completely assured, for the Communists are advising the new settler to take the land and the stock which are offered and are promising that if he continues to vote for them they will annul his financial debt to the State.

Assuming that the vast sums of money which have been voted for them are not misapplied, the reforms will provide less than 10,000 new jobs every year. In spite of their considerable value in some directions, therefore, the reforms will not resolve the problem of rural overpopulation. Forty-eight per cent. of the country's working population is employed on the land, and the proportion has remained fairly constant during recent years. The agricultural labour force is therefore subject to an annual increase of some 200,000 labour units, that is about half the national total. Furthermore, the introduction of tractors and other modern equipment, slow though it undoubtedly is, is more than enough to offset the higher volume of employment foreshadowed by the reforms, even if they accomplish everything they set out to do. The tractor is none the less an essential adjunct to more intensive farming. According to Professor Ciarrocca, intensive mechanization would liberate 3,000,000 to 4,000,000 tons of hay a year for stock farming, and another 100,000 tons of meat and 330,000,000 to 400,000,000 gallons of milk could be produced annually.

167. The political motive behind the reforms, however, makes their real aim to assure as many agricultural labourers and needy small farmers as possible of a minimum standard of living. The size of holdings has been calculated with this in mind rather than in the desire to achieve maximum labour efficiency. The income of the prospective settler will be less than half that of the permanent employee in Piedmont and Lombardy, who appears increasingly to hold a privileged position among Italian agricultural workers. The government is more anxious to provide as many people as possible with the means of subsistence—one might almost say with charitable assistance—than it is to exploit the land to the full. In the absence of employment outside agriculture, the search for the highest productivity of labour, far from being actively pursued, is actually discounted in some quarters.

In a new colony at Pitigliano the land was divided into holdings of 4-5 acres, which were partly devoted to viticulture on terraces where the soil, as in North Africa and near Almeria, 'was brought in baskets carried on the head'. On the level ground rows of vine have been planted at about 5-yd. intervals, and the strips of cereals sown between them could not be cut even by the smallest type of mechanical reaper. Indeed, most of the grain is still cut by hand in many parts of Italy and, in the words of Professor Pagani, 'this is a policy of human weariness, when in fact we should be reducing the amount of toil and raising our production at the same time. At present the latter is too expensive in human work. We could create just as much wealth with only half today's agricultural population'. One may well hesitate in applying the term 'social' to reforms which are to perpetuate and multiply the microfundia; the women and children will necessarily be overburdened with work, as they are already under the *métayage* system, and the education of the rising generation will be broken off at an early age. In contrast, on the *cascina* in Lombardy, the men take a far larger share of the work.

On the credit side it may be said that the land is being improved, especially by the new schemes of irrigation and drainage, although the rate of progress is still too slow. Even though the potential productivity of these new developments is only moderate, the returns are better than those of unemployment. The returns of a project cannot be computed in the same way for an *entrepreneur* as for the nation as a whole. Thus the fairly high net returns of the latifundia are not particularly praiseworthy when, on a wider scale, they are the companions of unemployment and malnutrition.[1] New barrages will create reservoirs capable of adding 500,000 acres to the land irrigated by gravity flow, and 40 per cent. of this area will be affected by the agrarian reform. These schemes and others like them are all admirable examples of land development. Furthermore, the promoters of these reforms are animated by a certain sense of social justice. But they have not always understood that the most effective social reforms are based, not only on a more equitable distribution of wealth, but also on the achievement of the highest possible yields in terms of the labour expended. We have described elsewhere the difficulties with which the pioneer settlements of the Nurra region in north-west Sardinia had to contend. This project should really have been undertaken only after the development of other more easily tamed regions had been completed. But the chronological order of development in different regions depends less on their fertility and the relative costs of improvement than on the legal questions of land tenure and ownership. At all events, agrarian reform in Italy appears as a movement of far greater significance and efficacy than the Spanish 'Colonization', and it shows evidence of greater sincerity in its pursuit of social justice.

168. If she wishes to abolish qualitative malnutrition, Italy cannot afford to neglect a single opportunity of intensifying her utilization of the land. More than two-thirds of the population suffer in varying degrees from a lack of protective foods, such as animal proteins—especially those derived from milk products—mineral salts, and vitamins. After a poor harvest, there is even quantative malnutrition in the uplands, the south, and the islands. There is already a considerable

---

[1] The country should also seek more energetically to raise the productivity of schemes created by public funds: 'Indeed, the word "productivity" has been erased from our vocabulary,' observed an Italian agronomist.

degree of intensification measured in terms of the irrigated acreage and the area devoted to horticulture. There are over 6,000,000 acres of vines, orchards, and market gardens and about the same amount of land under irrigation, and the two only partly coincide. Apart from the north, however, less use has been made of the other factors of intensification than in the Low Countries, which are another overpopulated region.

With 53,000,000 acres of agricultural land and 47,000,000 inhabitants to support, Italy only manages to strike a balance of trade in food products because half her total population works on the land. With a population of more than 10,000,000 and only 6,000,000 acres of farm land, the Netherlands export twice as much food as they import and only a fifth of the population is engaged in agriculture. Better natural conditions do not explain the whole of this difference. In Italy, deep ploughing, the careful husbanding of manure and dung-water, and the use of chemical fertilizers are less in evidence than they might be. Apart from the north, one notices more weeds and fewer signs of carefully tended fields than in the Netherlands. This is a serious criticism in a country where there are idle hands and underfed children.

The lack of capital and of technical instruction are not the only obstacles, for overpopulation hinders the development of mechanization. The low wages of the south discourage purchases of costly equipment. Near Cagliari in March 1953, women cultivating the ground between the rows of beans were earning 300 lire for an eight-hour day. The uneven distribution of incomes means that the market for agricultural produce is much smaller than it would otherwise be. From the health point of view, the families of the *braccianti* in the south eat all too little of the cheese which the *cascine* in the north sometimes find so difficult to market.

Whereas mechanization reduces employment, intensification, of course, multiplies the opportunities; there is more working of the soil, there is a greater percentage of row crops, which need a lot of attention, there are stall-fed cattle to care for, etc. But even developed to its utmost limit, intensive farming cannot yield full employment to the 22,000,000 people, 9,500,000 male and 6,500,000 female workers, who are now dependent on the land. According to Gennari 2,000,000 of these workers are surplus to requirements, and Pagani is no doubt right in his assertion that, with large farms and mechanization, half the present number would suffice. With really modern methods and better farm buildings, the labour force could be reduced even further.

169. For a solution outside the province of agriculture, one naturally

turns as elsewhere to the development of industry. In a country so short of raw materials, this would have to aim at winning a fair share of export markets. But in the present economic framework the chaotic state of the economy and the dearth of capital, which is no less severe than the shortage of land, offer scant hope of developing manufacturing industries to a point where they will afford the necessary relief to the pressure of population on the land.

Emigration, which played so large a part at the beginning of the century, is again showing a slight upward trend. At the time of our visit in 1952, Argentine agreed to receive 500,000 Italian immigrants during the course of the next five years; a stroke of the pen thus guaranteed three times as much employment as the whole programme of reform. But emigration is now subject to quotas and international agreements. In the summer of 1952, for instance, Australia had just reduced her intake of immigrants, and it is extremely doubtful whether Italy could ever provide even for her annual increase in population by means of emigration schemes.

Another partial solution is to ensure a better distribution of the modest sum of employment available, and it is well to remember that even this is dwindling every year as the result of mechanization. The school leaving age would have to be raised, apprenticeships lengthened and earlier retirement encouraged. *Métayer* and *braccienti* alike often continue to work until they die. Reducing the average length of working life is, after all, preferable to the proscription of machinery or to its introduction with police protection. Why should some toil under the afternoon sun while others remain completely idle? Could not these overcrowded countries adopt six- and five-hour days in summer and winter respectively? And could not the working day, apart from irrigation and the care of animals, etc., be mainly concentrated in the mornings?

From now on agricultural intensification will have to contend with constantly increasing difficulties, and one can well imagine that it will be almost impossible for production merely to keep pace with the excessively rapid growth of population. According to a report published in February 1953 by the General Confederation of Italian Labour, agricultural production between 1946 and 1950 exceeded the figure for 1911-15 by only 2 per cent., whereas the population in the meantime had risen by a third. As compared with 1915, the amount of food available per head of the population[1] had risen in respect of milk, poultry, and potatoes; it was the same for wheat and maize, but there

[1] National production plus imports minus exports.

INADEQUACY OF REFORMS; OTHER SOLUTIONS

were serious losses in citrus fruits, wine, oil, and meat. The fall for this last item was from 40 lb. to 30 lb. per head per year. The food position had become worse for the unemployed, who are the living proof of the shortcomings of our economic structure. Finally, therefore, and in spite of the arguments of doctrinaires, we advocate the limitation of births in the belief that, particularly in the context of the present economic anarchy, only thus can a rapid rise in the living standards of the Italian worker take place. In June 1952 we attended a meeting of French and Italian rural economists in Milan. *'Per Baccho!'* cried an Italian when we put forward this opinion, 'A sensible suggestion at last!'

VIII

Pastoralism Dominant in the Val d'Anniviers in the Swiss Alps[1]

Following the Rhône above the Lake of Geneva, past the elbow at Martigny, where it assumes the east-north-east direction which it preserves right to its source, one passes Sion (Fig. 17), the capital of Valais, continues for a short distance beyond Sierre, and then leaves the main valley to climb along the Val d'Anniviers road, which branches to the south. The road, flanked on either side by steep, wooded slopes, twists and turns and occasionally plunges into dark tunnels to avoid the precipitous ravines of the lower Navisance, and soon reaches Vissoie, which was for many years the seat of the only parish in the valley. The convergence of four roads confirms it in its position of small district capital.

1. Age-old Meadows Occupying the Best Land

170. During a dry summer the forests and verdant meadows stand out in vivid relief, for the rest of the landscape is practically devoid of vegetation. The pastures occupy small hollows with richer soils, terraces with average or moderate slopes, and most of the land near the villages. The arable fields, on the other hand, are relegated to land where the soil is often thin, where the slopes are more difficult and sometimes quite incredibly steep,[2] and to the southern faces of

---

[1] Field studies in Switzerland in 1928, 1935, and 1952. Our study of the Val d'Anniviers was made in August 1952, partly inspired by Jean Brunhes' masterly account in *La Géographie humaine*, to which we refer the reader for the position as it was about 1905. We have tried to avoid going over the same ground but, in any case, our approach to the problem is that of the agricultural scientist and necessarily different.

[2] The Anniviards of neighbouring communes assert that at Pinsec, where the arable fields are particularly steep, beans are sown by firing them from the opposite side of the valley with rifles!

AGE-OLD MEADOWS OCCUPYING THE BEST LAND

morainic ridges, which are more favoured by the sun, but for this reason more susceptible to drought.

Any idea that the grasslands are of recent extension, as in Normandy, where so many fields have been put down to grass during the last 10 years, is quickly dispelled by the evidence of oral tradition: the pastures have always been there. Today the old peasant of Anniviers regards the ploughing up of these pastures as sacrilege. 'You are massacring them,' he says. About 1880, in the Pays de Caux, the French peasant had the same opinion of the conversion of his wheat-fields into grassland. Those who reluctantly decided to plough these age-old pastures, which had probably never even felt the blade of a hoe, frequently found that the green sward concealed many shallow inliers of rock which the work of previous generations had succeeded in breaking up in the arable areas.

Visiting the valley at the beginning of the nineteenth century, Dr Schiner[1] recorded the following details: first, in the vicinity of Vercorin, 'a small spring waters the grass which lies in the shadow of several fine firs and larches and always remains fresh and green'. A little further south, nearer the centre of the valley, at Pinsec (which he spells Pain-sec), 'the only wealth of this district is its meadows'. Continuing towards Vissoie, he gives a more graphic description which would still apply today: 'This valley has a few fields of crops, some fine fertile meadows and rich uplands covered with lush pastures where the people graze their flocks during the summer months'.

Dr Erasme Zufferey,[2] in his *Le passé du Val d'Anniviers*,[3] mentions a register of contracts drawn up in this valley between 1298 and 1314, and first studied by Dr Leon Meyer. He quotes from it as follows: 'the fine pastures behind the Castle [of Vissoie]'; 'a pasture next to the Castle garden' (thus adjoining the village); 'the domainal pastures of Paluz, and another pasture of Paluz'; only one field of arable land is mentioned. It speaks of a right to the use on Saturdays of part of the flow of the *bisse* or *traite*[4] (irrigation channel) of Cuiney. Irrigation has

---
[1] *Description du département du Simplon ou de la ci-devant république du Valais*, by Dr Schiner of the Medical Faculty of Montpellier (Sion, 1812).

[2] This name is very common at Chandolin, the only commune in the valley still not served by a road: it was the name given to the stoker of the village bakery.

[3] Printed at Ambilly-Annemasse (Haute Savoie) in 1927. It consists of the first volume of a collection of articles by Abbé Zufferey which originally appeared in the *Bulletin paroissal du Val*.

[4] *Bisse* is from the German *bet*, meaning 'bed'; *traite* is from the Latin *tractus*, meaning 'drawn'. See *Les Bisses*, by Ignace Mariétan (Neuchâtel, 1948).

been practised from time immemorial, and it still bears traces of the influence of the Saracens,[1] who conquered this area, gave their name to one of the *bisses*, and possibly helped to perfect the local techniques. It is certainly a fact that the irrigated land has always been reserved for permanent pastures.

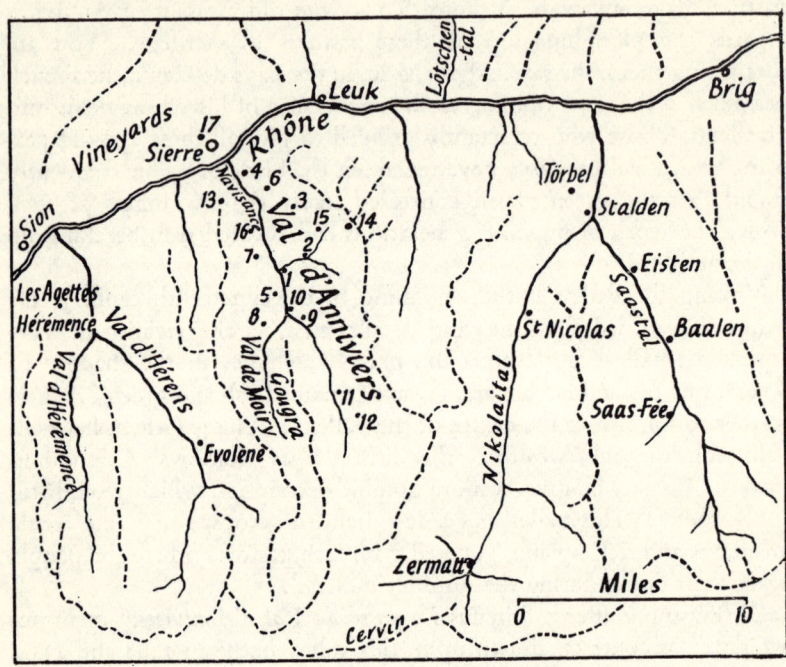

FIG. 17. The Val d'Anniviers and adjacent valleys.

1. Vissoie; 2. Saint-Luc; 3. Chandolin; 4. Niouc; 5. Saint-Jean; 6. Soussillon; 7. Pinsec; 8. Grimentz; 9. Ayer; 10. Mission; 11. Zinal; 12. Alpe de Tracuit; 13. Vercorin; 14 Bella Tolla; 15. Torrent du Moulin; 16. Ziette; 17. Villa (vineyards belonging to Vissoie).

171. The whole livelihood of the region is centred on these grasslands, and the contrast with Briançonnais in the French Alps, which we have described elsewhere,[2] is complete. Saint-Chaffrey (4,470 ft.), at practically the same altitude as Vissoie (4,050 ft.), has a fairly similar

[1] According to the oral tradition of the neighbouring valleys, the Anniviards, who are rather dark-skinned, are descendants of the Saracens: this would perhaps help to explain the survival of pastoralism. It is also noteworthy that the Val is a linguistic island, for the local idiom differs from that of the other valleys.

[2] *Voyages en France d'un agronome*, Chapter I.

climate, also marked by a pronounced summer drought. Irrigation can also be traced back as far as the thirteenth century at least, but is almost exclusively for the benefit of crops: barley, oats, or wheat, and, above all, potatoes. The pastures have only been watered in quite recent times, and they mainly consist of sown species like sainfoin, lucerne, and clover. Whether irrigated or not, the arable land enjoys the *endroit*, or more favourable aspects, the more heavily manured sectors near the village, and the more fertile and gently sloping ground in general. Although, in common with other highland areas, the Hautes-Alpes are beginning to turn to crops other than cereals, the latter, nevertheless, reigned supreme for many centuries. In early times the main animals were sheep and goats, which could make good use of the uncultivable land. Finally, draught animals have long been used for ploughing.

In contrast, in the Val d'Anniviers, most of the manure is destined to enrich the grassland; only the potato crop, a fairly recent innovation, receives any. The valley as a whole does not make use of animals for ploughing; the only exception is Chandolin, which, because its hamlet of Soussillon is so near the Rhône Valley, learned the use of the swing-plough many centuries ago and has adopted the *brabanette*, a small edition of the Belgian plough, since 1927. Nevertheless, in 1952 these implements were employed on barely a third of the arable land; mattocks served for the remainder. Saint-Luc and Chandolin are the only villages which by virtue of their aspect benefit from the sun late in the day. As the setting sun is more conducive to the ripening of grain because temperatures are generally higher at sunset than in the early morning, these villages are distinguished by their greater preoccupation with crop-growing.

Another complete contrast with Saint-Chaffrey is that here the longer axis of the arable fields follows the slope. It is only in recent years, since the very limited introduction of power-operated winches, that they have been worked with implements other than the spade and the mattock. In effect they are simply an extension of the village gardens,[1] and the valley has witnessed a direct transition from manual to machine power without ever having experienced the intermediary stage, where the harnessed animal serves for cultivation. For many years the dominant interest of the valley has been its cattle. Milk, cheese,[2] and salt beef

---

[1] In an article on Corsican agriculture we have spoken of a 'horto-pastoral' economy, an expression which could also be aptly applied here (*Revue du Ministère de l'Agriculture*, December 1952).

[2] The traditional *raclette* of the Valais is made with very fatty melted cheese.

were always the main items in the diet. The place of pork in regions of arable farming was here taken by salt beef.

In the parallel Nikolai-Saas valleys to the east, on the other hand, the typical family was more likely to rely on slaughtering its sheep, and occasionally they would buy a cow from the Hérens Valley. G. Florey, a farmer of Vissoie, tells us that in the past bread was often scarcer in the valley than cheese or meat. Speculators would store two or three years' grain and sell at high prices during periods of shortage. Pigs and poultry are not much in evidence, for they are generally associated with potato- and cereal-growing—that is, with arable land which is not prevalent here. Whereas in Briançonnais meat did not enter into the diet until recently and is something of a luxury, here its consumption is definitely falling.

172. This bias in the farming of the Val d'Anniviers is quite remarkable, and Jean Brunhes had good reason to describe the area as 'an exceptional "island" of the High Alps'. In the Val d'Hérens, immediately to the west, the swing plough has been known throughout the length of the valley as far as Evolène for hundreds of years, and the fields stretch parallel to the contours across the hillsides. Again and again in his description, Schiner mentions 'many fields', 'a great number of fields with grain', 'superb arable land'; his references to arable land are much more frequent than in his comments on Anniviers. He lists four of the communes of Hérens, three of which were sited so as to benefit from the sun late in the day, as bringing grain to market at Sion.

In their *Essai d'histoire de la vallée d'Hérens*,[1] the Abbés Gaspoz and Tamisi write that at Vex 'anyone who in former times cared to climb the slopes around our villages saw great stretches of spring and autumn rye, wheat, barley and oats'. They continue: 'After 1860 when the railways began to bring cheap flour from abroad, the arable land was laid down to grass.' During 1863-5, the commune of Vex obtained a new *bisse* leading from the River Dixence, which facilitated this comparatively recent trend for the conversion of arable to grassland which became typical of the whole area. Except for Niouc, which was once the granary of Saint-Luc and has only recently turned its fields into pastures, the Val d'Anniviers, however, has remained devoted to grassland throughout this period.

In his *Economie rurale*, Dr Laur writes: 'The intermittent clearing of land which characterizes the alpine regions is generally part of a system which utilizes the nearest and best land for meadows and the more

[1] Saint-Maurice, Valais, 1935.

AGE-OLD MEADOWS OCCUPYING THE BEST LAND

distant areas, which periodically revert to natural grassland, for growing cereals.' Our examination of the differences between Hérens and Anniviers has revealed no evidence, in the case of the latter, however, for any alternation of arable and grassland.[1] In recent years, some of the pastures have been abandoned, but that is a very different matter.

In the Saastal, which lies directly east of Anniviers, arable land and field boundaries dominantly parallel with the contours characterize the lower portion of the valley as far as Staldenried, and reappear, though less obviously, opposite Eisten. From Baalen onwards the fields are either square or aligned down the slope, and this change of pattern coincides with the use of hand implements on the land, but in this area large hoes replace the mattocks of the Val d'Anniviers. Cereals, especially spring barley, once occupied a larger area than today. In the upper valley, as at Saas-Fée, potatoes have not long been grown.

Meadows are clearly gaining on the arable land, and the two are closely intermingled. Halfway up the valley, settlement is dispersed, pastures are sited near the chalets, with the crop-land a little further away, a natural consequence of the greater weight per acre of hay as compared with a cereal; but the two zones are less clearly delimited than in Anniviers. The pattern of grasslands in proximity to the settlements with crops on their outer margins is repeated in the villages of the Val d'Hérens, but here the siting of irrigation facilities, which are essential for the meadow land, is another important localizing factor. In the Nikolaital, the plough is rarely seen beyond Torbel, and never at all further upstream towards Saint-Nicholas, where the traditional implements are the *brute Haue*, or broad hoe, for the stone-free garden soils, and the *spitz Haue*, a triangular hoe, for working in the fields, which, unlike the thick glacial silts of Saas-Fée, are everywhere littered with stones.

The explanation for the unique character of farming in the Val d'Anniviers appears to lie in the history of the locality—a factor which is all too often belittled in works on comparative agriculture—rather than in any special character of the natural conditions which are fairly similar to those in adjacent valleys. A comparable situation occurs in the Lötschental, where meadow land, hoe cultivation, and human portage are also characteristic; furthermore, the cart, which was essential to the Anniviards in their journeys to the Rhône, was unknown in this valley right until 1913.

The preponderance of milk and meat in the diet and the absence of animals used for draught are a sure indication of the pastoral nature of

[1] Which we shall find, however, in the Tyrol (*Natur Egarten*).

the Anniviard economy. The deep gorges of the lower Navisance obstructed the early development of transhumance towards the Rhône Valley, which is the nearest approach to a lowland in the area. As compared with the inhabitants of more accessible valleys, therefore, the people here were very soon compelled by the size of their herds and the length of the winter to devise some local means of accumulating large reserves of fodder. This, and the course of history from ancient times, probably explain the paramount importance which has long been attached to the hay from these meadows, which monopolize not only the irrigation water and the best soils, but also the greater part of the manure.

2. The Byre-barn on the Irrigated Meadows

173. In the absence of draught animals, even transport to and from the fields was until recently effected on the backs of men. As the houses were grouped in villages, it would have been too laborious a task to carry hay and manure to and fro between field and settlement. The problem was resolved by building a byre-cum-barn in the middle of each piece of meadow. This became the pivot of the whole system. The abundance of larch, a good constructional timber, the impossibility of floating logs along the Navisance, and the long seasons of leisure were probably all factors which contributed to this solution.

At the Morands, above the path which branches off the road to Ayer and leads to the hamlet of Combas, is a byre-barn of the traditional type, the southern half of which belongs to Guillaume Florey.[1] It is on a slope of one in five and built of larch planks taken, as is the common practice, from older buildings. The hay barn, 6 ft. 6 in. high, is at ground-level on the eastern, upslope side, and is surmounted by the traditional gently sloping roof of wooden shingles; but Florey has 'modernized' his half by covering it with corrugated-iron sheets. Sometimes there is a gallery open to the sun where the drying can be finished if the hay is at all green or damp. To store the hay, a man climbs up a plank to the level of the roof and slides it in through a temporary opening. Florey has $\frac{1}{2}$ acre of grassland, and from this cuts 24 cwt. of hay and aftermath a year, up to 36 cwt. in a good year, to store in his half of the barn.

The first haymaking every year lasts from the end of June until 15

[1] Albert Florey, postman and farmer, who studied at the cantonal agricultural school at Châteauneuf, and his father, Guillaume, who farms at Vissoie, gave us invaluable help in all aspects of our work in the Val.

July, the aftermath is cut during the latter part of August and September, and the regrowth is grazed from 25 October until 10 November.[1] As there are practically no crops other than hay, and this is even truer today than it was in the past, August becomes a month of rest if the summer is at all early, as it was in 1952. The men cut wood and do various odd jobs. Formerly, when there was more arable land, this was the time for preparing the ground for the September sowing. The hay yield varies here between $2\frac{1}{2}$ and nearly $3\frac{1}{2}$ tons an acre, figures which are well above the average, owing to irrigation and manuring. The water comes from the Moulin torrent, whose source is at nearly 10,000 ft. and whose three branches descend from Bella Tola right to the rocky eminence of Budri. The abundance of its summer flow is the good fortune of Vissoie and the envy of the villages of Saint-Jean on the opposite side of the valley, which are compelled to lead their water all the way from the Gougra, ten miles away.

174. The water is brought along *bisses*, or channels, each serving from 25 to 350 acres, which are known to have existed as far back as the twelfth century. They were constructed by *consortages*, or associations, which still ensure their maintenance today. The *Chef du bisse* is elected for four years; he is responsible for keeping the register of water rights, engages workmen when breaks appear in the banks, and sees to it that every user reports for duty in the spring, when the channel is prepared for the year.[2] Each user has the right of access to water once a week, day and time being precisely determined in all cases; Florey's $\frac{1}{2}$ acre, for instance, is watered for two hours every Thursday. In other cases, where the *bisse* is smaller, water may be had only once a fortnight. As at Saint-Nicholas, and even in the *huerta* of Valencia, where the Saracen principle of customary rights survives, the right to water is an integral part of the ownership of land. This is no longer true in the Val d'Hérens, where water rights are often sold separately.

The old type of earth *bisse* and wooden sluice-way leading from the

---

[1] Above Chandolin, at 6,500 ft., the grass is mown and grazed only once during the season. The village is a former *mayen* of Leuk (Loeche), which is in the Rhône Valley upstream of Sierre. Below the village, however, at 6,200 ft., favourable aspect and heavy manuring combine in stimulating grass growth to such good effect that there are two cuttings followed by a period of grazing. In most of the commune of Grimentz there is only one cutting.

[2] Everyone must remain until the work is finished, no matter how modest his right to water. This does not seem particularly fair, but the burden of work is not heavy. Women and youths who have not reached their majority count as 0·8 of a man for this work; two or three people with small water-rights are allowed to delegate their responsibility to a single person.

stream are gradually being replaced by underground cement pipes up to 1 ft. in diameter, and cement take-off channels with sand-traps. These new works are paid for by individuals in exact proportion to the extent of their water rights, but part of the total cost is met by subsidies, and once the channels are completed their maintenance is an easy matter. At Vissoie it is now proposed to follow the example set by Saint-Luc, where a path was built parallel to the new *bisse* so that loads could be hauled along by the small motor-cultivators, which are known here as 'one-axle tractors'.

As in the Saracen system of former times, there is a strict water rota. It covers the period from 5 a.m. to 9 p.m., and the last user may continue beyond this time, but only on the understanding that he must attend to the damage personally if the water bursts its banks. Between the stipulated times, however, the onus for repairs is on the community. Policing is also a collective responsibility, and this avoids the expense of employing channel guards, as in Provence and the Rhône Valley. There are no signs of the virtual anarchy which exists over water rights in Briançonnais, although an individual may at any time interchange his turn on the rota with a neighbour. Florey's meadow is often irrigated for a four-hour period every fortnight, and this is done twice or three times before the haymaking and, on average, about the same number of times before the aftermath is cut. Five turns of irrigation on the $\frac{1}{2}$-acre meadow require about twenty hours of attention, a task which either men, women, or youths may perform. The meadow is twelve minutes' walk from the house, which is less than the average, and so another two hours must be allowed for the five return journeys.

Florey trundles the manure to his meadow in a wheelbarrow and spreads it over a third of the area every year, a task which takes five hours altogether. Elsewhere, on steeper slopes and with larger fields, the flow of water is used to spread the manure below the byre-barn in the spring, while the upper slopes are supplied in the autumn by baskets carried on the back, by pack mules, or by winch-drawn sledges. The mules are kept solely for this purpose. Schiner, in his comments on the Val d'Hérens, mentions the use of horses and mules as pack animals and of sledges for the transport of grain; today hay is carried by the same methods, but in the Val d'Anniviers animals are not used at all for this purpose.

At Chandolin we have seen men carrying loads of hay on their heads from meadows about 300 ft. below the village which were actually crossed by mule tracks. Traditionally, mules serve for carrying wood, for local trade, for the seasonal up- and down-valley movements, and more recently for transporting tourists, but the lorry and the postal van have now largely replaced them. Many of those which remain are owned, as in Nikolaital, in partnership. At Saint-Jean, for example, many of the farmers have 'a third of a mule'. But at Chandolin this does not prevent them from being harnessed to the plough in pairs.

When the snow melts in March, work on the meadows begins again. Any remnants of manure are raked over (three hours' work); the communal *bisse* and the small channels threading through the meadow are cleaned out (two hours and one hour respectively). The haymaking amounts to five hours of work for two people—that is, ten hours in all; the man does the cutting, the woman spreads the grass out to dry. Turning the hay, raking it up, and carrying it back to the byre-barn take another ten hours. The aftermath is lighter and dries more quickly and can be dealt with in about twelve hours.

This makes a total of sixty-five hours of work for rather less than half an acre, a rate of fourteen working days per acre of grassland. The meadow gives between 24 cwt. and 36 cwt. of hay, so that 4 cwt. is produced approximately at the cost of every working day of ten hours, and this is for a meadow which, being on a gentle slope near the village, is easy to tend and gives high yields. In unfavourable conditions, the comparable figure approaches the '2 cwt. of hay per day's work' of Haut-Queyras,[1] and the average for the district is probably in the region of 3 cwt., as compared with 1 ton in the lowlands; a few subsidies are hardly likely to compensate for this seven-fold difference in productivity.

175. The land is covered with snow in the winter, and the store of hay is enough to keep Florey's animals—three cows, three heifers and two goats—for three weeks only. On each of these twenty-one days, morning and evening, the animals, shut away in their partly underground stable under the hayloft, require attention. The door measures 3 ft. 10 in. × 2 ft. 2 in., and is just large enough for the small Hérens cattle. This is a hardy breed, but that is all it has to recommend it. The average milk yield is about 440 gallons a year as compared with over 600 gallons for Schwytz and Simmenthal cattle.

Unlike the barn, the byre is not divided into two separate compartments. By agreement, the whole of it is used in turn by each partner.[2]

---

[1] *Voyages en France d'un agronome*, Chapter II.

[2] Other byre-barns are shared between three and four owners. This is the result of everyone in the family wanting a share in the best meadows on the owner's death—and the buildings which go with them are divided up accordingly. Many *raccards* and even a few houses are also jointly owned.

Two wooden troughs 16 in. wide run along each wall. On one side is the cow-stall which narrows from 5 ft. 8 in. near the entrance to 5 ft. 4 in. at the back, so as to accommodate animals of different sizes. An aisle 1 ft. 10 in. wide runs down the centre of the floor and is bordered by two manure trenches, 1 ft. and 10 in. wide respectively. The narrower one flanks the other stall, which is for goats and heifers and which widens from 4 ft. near the entrance to 4 ft. 6 in. at the back.

So as to keep the animals warm, there are neither windows nor ventilators and the height of the roof—only 5 ft. 4 in. in the middle—falls to 4 ft. 8 in. at the sides; anyone working here, therefore, has to stoop down all the time. The hay could easily be damaged by dampness from the byre, and there is therefore no direct access to the barn. The hay has to be brought out of a side door in the loft and then through the narrow stable entrance—a somewhat difficult manœuvre.

The woman comes from the village morning and afternoon, and her first job is to bring in the hay in a 'hay apron' which is held up by a strap. She cleans out the manure with a fork and a shovel and puts in fresh litter, made in this area, with its dearth of arable land, of spruce and larch needles, which are gathered from the floor of the forests in May and August on days specified by the forester. She curries the animals, feeds them again, this time with aftermath, and milks the cows. The animals are then driven to the wooden drinking trough, which, in this particular case, is close at hand, as there is a spring nearby. In less fortunate circumstances this can entail up to a quarter of an hour's journey across the snow.

Finally, the animals are given another feed of hay, the so-called *après-boire*. When the barn is near the village, a little bran, meal, and beet may be added, but it is customary to reserve this type of feed for when the animals are in the village, as this reduces the labour of transport. All this takes about three hours of work twice a day, whereas in a modern stable, as in some of the large farms of Pouilly (Meuse),[1] a worker can, with the help of machinery, milk twenty-five cows and feed and clean them in about the same time. The disproportion in productivity is again nearly seven to one. Comparison with the open-barn system of the United States would offer a still more striking contrast. At the end of the three weeks the animals will have to be moved elsewhere, and when the snow is deep a path sometimes has to be dug for them.

176. The question of productivity is intimately linked with the size

[1] *Voyages en France d'un agronome*, Chapter XI.

of meadow served by each byre-barn. A building of the usual dimensions, as described above, accommodates 3 tons of hay at the most, which means that it can store the harvest of $\frac{7}{8}$ acres of really good meadow land, or about $1\frac{1}{2}$ acres if the quality of the terrain is about average. This evidently represents a very high density of buildings—the *fourmilière humaine* of Jean Brunhes—and this appears as yet another characteristic feature of the valley as a whole. The Val d'Hérens has fewer of these isolated buildings, especially between Agettes and Hérémence, but their dimensions are appreciably larger. The same is true of Saint-Nicholas. But in the Saas Valley, where the risk of avalanches limits the number of building sites, all the hay is brought into the barns in the village and the cattle divide the year between the village and the alpine pastures.

The new barns are taller (11 ft. 6 in.), and Florey, who has been able to regroup some of his plots of land, owns one which serves $1\frac{3}{8}$ acres. For his seven meadows at Vissoie[1] he has two byre-barns, plus a half, a third, and a quarter share in three others. Moreover, thanks to a convenient path, he brings an ever-increasing proportion of his hay to the village on a small wagon drawn by his cultivator, and here it is stored away with the help of Vissoie's solitary elevator. Already half the crop from Morands is stored in this manner.

This is a promising development, but it is being hindered by the lack of proper roads and of power resources. At Vissoie there is now only 'a mule and a half', as compared with twenty-four of these animals in 1903, and there is but one cultivator-tractor and a single jeep, which is used in the meadows. Another obstacle is the inadequacy of storage accommodation in the village. The *raccards*, or granges formerly used for grain, stand empty today, but their distance from the byres makes them inconvenient to use.[2]

The yields of grass are high, but landslipping sometimes results when water is led on to very steep slopes, especially near the narrow gorges carved out by the Navisance; the flora of certain hollows is indicative of too much water; and though Switzerland prides herself as the most efficient user of manure in the world, dung-water is only very partially retained by the stable litter. Finally, the exposure of manure to the sun

---

[1] Besides the two large ones already mentioned, the other five meadows range in size from a tenth to a little under a third of an acre. Including the *mayen* (see below), he has a total of $5\frac{1}{2}$ acres of irrigable land.

[2] In many parts of Switzerland, even, as in the Gruyère Valley, where the rainfall is higher, the hay is made into conical stacks, but this entails the risk of heavy losses.

throughout the summer leads to the loss of nitrates, while the rain washes out the dunghills near the buildings and the resulting over-enrichment of the ground causes the nearby plant life to deteriorate.

The general deficiency of phosphoric acid, the local incidence of excessive humidity and the over-preoccupation with nitrogenous fertilizers at the expense of others have combined to produce a flora which is lacking in grass and leguminous species and too rich in umbellifers, composites, and ranunculi. Where moss and euphrasy dominate, the yield declines severely. The animals find the geraniums, which are often all too abundant, quite unpalatable. Of late there has been a general decline in the area of watered meadows, due largely to the abandonment of land that was too high or too far from the village, especially if it lacked adequate buildings. Yellow rattle, a species of rhinanthus, known to the Alsatian peasant as the 'hay-eater', quickly supervenes on meadows which no longer benefit from manuring and watering.

The calving time is at the beginning of the winter, between November and January. Until the end of January calves are fattened and pigs are reared on the milk. If there is any left over, a few *tomes*, or cheeses, are made for the family. The village dairy functions between February and May and produces cheese: made from partly skimmed milk, and butter, which are divided between the farmers according to the quantity of milk they supplied. During these four months Florey's four cows bring him about 350 lb. of cheese and 33 lb. of butter. A small quantity of the milk is sold in the village, and this provides the dairyman's salary.

3. Two Types of Land Use in Retreat—Arable Land and *Pacages*

177. The small steeply inclined arable fields[1] are at some distance from the villages. Where the settlements are very high above the valley, like Chandolin, Saint-Luc, and Grimentz, their fields are often below them, and the reverse is generally true of villages which are fairly low-lying. The fields form narrow bands following the slope, and both their small size, which may vary from 36 to 480 sq. yds., and the methods employed on them put one in mind of garden rather than arable cultivation. Florey owns less than $\frac{1}{2}$ acre of fields, divided into ten parcels; the largest is 540 sq. yds., the smallest 55 sq. yds. Only Jules Crettaz at Saint-Jean, Germain Massy at Grimentz, and one

[1] 'At Pinsec even the hens have to wear crampons.'

or two others have recently been able to concentrate their holdings into larger units. On the poorer terrain the usual, and probably traditional, rotation consists of rye year after year. The conditions, which are rather warm and dry, assist the ripening of grain and check the weeds which the frequent repetition of a cereal in conjunction with greater humidity would otherwise favour. Elsewhere the two-year rotation comprises potatoes, or sometimes beans, and rye.

There is a paradox in this situation. At Saint-Chaffrey, where the dependence on these two crops was even more marked, winter rye, which matures early and is therefore drought-resistant, was sown on the drier soils of the *endroit*, but the potato crop was irrigated. In Anniviers, however, cultivation is traditionally on unirrigated land, and one year in two the potato crop suffers severely from lack of water, all the more so because the fields are on the *endroit* so as to promote the ripening of the grain. This applies particularly to the upper portions of the fields, where the soil is thinner. The sowing of beans, which are earlier than potatoes, represents an attempt by some farmers to overcome this difficulty. At Saint-Luc each field is still divided into two portions, one sown to rye and the other to potatoes, the crops being interchanged each year.

On the lower slopes most of the fields are divided thus. This means that the seed potatoes for the following year can be stored in a hole near the top of the field, thus saving a double journey. Naturally, in this dry climate, the non-renewal of seed stock favours the spread of virus diseases, except at high altitudes, as at Chandolin, or where the risk is also reduced by early lifting of the crop.

For detailed study a small field of 120 sq. yds. and situated not too far from the barn was selected. The 6 cwt. of manure needed every year can be brought to it without too much difficulty, but the usual method of transport, in baskets carried on the back, still takes about half a day. The mule and the winch are used but rarely. The ground is dug to a depth of 10 in.[1] with a mattock which has two prongs 8 in. long, and the practice is to work across the slope so as to discourage the downward movement of the soil. Potatoes are set in the ground at the same time, and the whole operation takes a day. The ground is raked over before the shoots begin to sprout through the surface, but this only takes a quarter of an hour; one must add half an hour, however, for the walk to and from the field. The field is later raked again

---

[1] If it was dug any deeper, the head of the mattock would strike the underlying rock and spring back sharply. Opposite the prongs of the mattock there is a small blade for cutting the roots of bushes.

and the rows are ridged at the same time; three hours' work are needed for this. Lifting the crop and transport back to the village occupy a whole day, and, as the soil tends to move downhill all the time,[1] especially with a row crop, another two hours must be spent in loading the soil into baskets and carrying it back up the hill as soon as the crop is out of the ground. Including the journeys to and fro, the field demands three full days of attention. This is the equivalent of 120 days per acre, or rather more than the hand cultivation of early potatoes at Noirmoutiers.

In 1947, a dry year, Albert Florey, on the basis of his work at labourers' wage rates, calculated that the cost price of his potatoes was 90 centimes a pound, when they were selling on the market at 14 centimes. His potato crop was actually worth no more than the price of the manure. He could more easily have sold the latter and bought potatoes with the proceeds. Basile Zufferey at Chandolin now grows only $\frac{1}{10}$ acre of potatoes, just enough for the needs of his family, and fattens his pigs with meal, which he buys. This is notwithstanding the cost of 8 francs per hundredweight for transport from the station in the Rhône Valley to this secluded village. In the case of bran, this almost doubles the price, from 12 francs to 20 francs a hundredweight. No doubt the time will come when all the potatoes needed will be imported from the lowlands, and Chandolin will again become the *mayen*[2] which it once was—a role, moreover, which it should never have relinquished but for the increasing pressure of population on its resources. Today, a fair proportion of the potatoes are already imported, thanks to a subsidy on transport from the excise revenues of the Régie des alcools.

178. Rye is sown directly on the ground from which the potatoes were lifted, and is simply raked into the ground, a task which takes half an hour on a field of 120 sq. yds. The crop is eventually cut with a sickle and bound into small sheaves, which takes a further three hours. The family bring in the harvest in *rètzes* on their backs; this needs about four journeys and may occupy up to two hours if the field is some distance from the village.[3] In former times the sheaves were

[1] Ploughing with winches would prevent this and eliminate all the hard work of carrying the soil back. This laborious task is avoided at Saint-Jean by digging the upper parts with a spade, but this is much more difficult than using a mattock; the net result is that there is no saving in labour whatsoever.

[2] See below.

[3] Children begin to carry the sheaves on their backs—in loads proportioned to their strength—from the age of five or six. 'Bread is hard to earn; nothing but toil can win it.'

dried off in the sun on the *loua*, or gallery round the *raccard*, and they were then stored in this wooden grange, which was secured against rodents by round slabs of gneiss or schist wedged at the top of each upright.[1] The grain was threshed here during the winter with flails. One still finds this traditional system at Chandolin, where—probably for this very reason—cereal cultivation is on the decline.

Elsewhere small co-operatively owned threshing machines driven by electricity have rendered the delightful *raccards* obsolete. The latter were often owned in partnership, and G. Florey still has two *demi-raccards*, one of which has a grain loft. In his younger days he threshed his corn here with a flail, and recalls that the fruits of two weeks' labour were generally about 5 cwt. of grain. In the Val d'Hérens, where the ownership of *raccards* is more fragmented, there are instances of farmers possessing only an eighth share, or even just the balcony. We saw a crop which had been affected by rust being threshed at Vissoie; it was apparent from the lack of firmness in the grain that the ripening process, which depends on the movement of substances contained in the straw towards the ear and which formerly continued during storage in the granary, was by no means complete. This emphasizes the lack of attention given to cereals.

The arable acreage had already begun to dwindle, especially on the steepest land around the *mayens*, as soon as the railway reached Sierre, but the general retreat of cropland has been very rapid since the end of the last war. Hemp and flax have not been grown since 1890, and it is therefore the acreage under cereals which is suffering the heaviest losses, a trend which has been reinforced by the growing disparities in productivity since the mechanization of cereal cultivation in the lowlands. Jules Crettaz at Saint-Jean has had some good results from barley, which is replacing the less reliable spring rye. But conditions in the valley cannot be said to be appropriate for basing an expansion of pig-rearing—which at present is limited by the availability of milk by-products—on the cultivation of barley. On south-facing slopes, maize, which below Chandolin at over 5,000 ft. ripened for the first time in the hot summer of 1952, could be grown at appreciably less disadvantage as compared with the lowlands. The decline of cultivation in general serves to heighten the importance of fodder-growing and stock-rearing in the valley.

Thus even the fields adjoining Chandolin have given nothing but potatoes in the last two years. The same trend was noted at Saint-Chafferey, but it began there over fifty years ago. The reason is not,

[1] They are also found in Scandinavia, but are not placed so high.

as in Briançonnais, the risk of damage to crops by poultry, for the scarcity of grain itself has meant that poultry are few in number and are shut away in the summer. The real reason is the reduced transport of manure.

179. On the precipitous slopes from Saint-Luc down to Vissoie, the meadows are watered and carefully tended near the villages. Further afield one sees occasional fields of crops, but the main impression is of abandoned arable land which actually went out of cultivation between about 1920 and 1950. The old people remember the days when they used to sow this land to rye after clearing the stones and piling them into huge *mourzières*. Their yields were lower than those of the small holdings on the vine-clad scarps of the Plateau de Langres, where the soil had similarly to be cleared. Immediately below Saint-Luc, retaining walls held back the soil on the steepest slopes. Today 'a wall is equivalent to a tax', which only the vineyards of Sierre can afford. Apart from afforestation, a more rational utilization of the land would have been achieved by sowing drought-resistant temporary pastures for sheep-grazing, which would have been more productive than the tall oat grass, which often establishes itself spontaneously.

This has actually been done by a Saint-Luc farmer. The price of land has dropped because of its abandonment, and he has bought 15 acres, a total of about 100 fields, below the Chandolin road for less than 2,000 Swiss francs (but 600 francs had to be paid in legal expenses).[1] Lower down the valley this kind of enterprise would be hampered even more by the extraordinary fragmentation of holdings. Indeed, re-integration (known as *remaniement parcellaire* in Switzerland) is the indispensable condition of progress in the future. In the meantime, the unused fields are being invaded by bushes and thorny shrubs, together with poor fescues and false brome grass which rapidly stifle the rye grass. The land serves no profitable or productive purpose whatsoever, notwithstanding that extensive grazing is the most promising type of enterprise appropriate to this difficult mountain country.

The arable acreage is, however, gaining ground elsewhere. Near the villages there is some encroachment of garden cultivation on the meadow land owing to the increased demand for vegetables, the consumption of which is still rather low, and sometimes owing to minor

[1] Denis Zufferey, a native of Saint-Luc who now deals in cattle, asserts that he is willing to give away the land he still owns in this commune to anyone willing to take it; he would even pay legal costs and treat the recipient to a good supper. The land is a liability, for he has to pay taxes on it; and the commune refuses to accept it as a gift.

extensions of the land under beet, which is always a garden crop. Potatoes can no longer be grown in sufficient quantities on the outlying arable land, and they are slowly appearing on newly-dug meadows, where at last they are benefiting from irrigation. The use of rotating sprinklers now permits even very steep slopes to be watered without loss of time and without the risk of erosion. Vegetables can thus be grown without the fear of drought, and the most recent innovation, the only highly profitable undertaking of the upper valley, is the cultivation of strawberries.

The high altitude prevents the intensive cultivation of most specialized crops which might otherwise alleviate the problem of overpopulation. Fruit trees, which have made the fortune of Agettes in the Val d'Hérens, the vine, and early vegetables are out of the question, but many of the lighter soils could be developed for strawberries. The same applies to the growing of vegetables in season for summer visitors, with the help of glass frames to ensure that the plants were ready in good time. Soft fruits, such as gooseberries, raspberries, and various hybrids, are another possibility. These crops could almost eliminate the differences of productivity between the valley and the Rhône lowland. So far, however, the need to provide employment and likewise the attraction of working in the vineyards at Sierre have hampered the spread of strawberry cultivation at high altitudes. It is more prevalent in valleys where there is not a great deal of vine-growing.

180. The arable land occupies the best of the non-irrigated soils, but of all the land which is exploited directly from the village, the *pacages* or pastures of the lower slopes, are utilised the least intensively. They are rarely watered, difficult or impossible to cut and infrequently manured. The herds are grazed here from mid-May until the beginning of June and again in the autumn, although at this season the aftermath on the lower meadows is also grazed. In the summer the price of milk is 13 or 14 centimes a gallon, as against 9 centimes in the winter. Some farmers keep back one or two cows[1] to make the most of the high prices and these animals graze the *pacages* throughout the period of grass growth. In former times goats were kept in the village to supply milk for the family while the cattle were on the alpine pastures, but their numbers have been greatly reduced since they were no longer allowed to graze the forest clearings and the tracks for glissading the timber down the slopes.

[1] Formerly these cattle were herded in common, but not today. Each small herd of perhaps three cattle and a couple of goats is often looked after by two women—who pass the time knitting.

During a dry summer like 1952 the farmer even has to sacrifice some of his second cutting of hay for grazing. This is unheard of in the Tyrol, but in Anniviers there is a growing trend for the hay crop to be sacrificed for the sake of grazing, especially at Vissoie. This village possesses little in the way of *pacages*, and now that goats are so few in numbers it has to bring in milk from Sierre every day in the summer. Moreover, as M. Genoud, the President of the commune, explained, to concentrate overmuch on summer production would be 'to lose the winter milk for the family'. Some families send all their cattle to the alpine pastures and simply rely on a pair of goats, which they herd themselves on some of the rough grazings nearby, although at Saint-Jean and elsewhere these animals are herded communally. The lower pastures are then cut, where conditions allow, in August, but this is so late in the year that the quality of the hay suffers a good deal. Moreover, it must be emphasized that, like the arable land, many of these pastures are now being abandoned.

4. Encroachment of the Alpine Pastures (Alps) on the *Mayens*; Cheese the Main Product

181. The *mayen* is the *chalet de mai*, the equivalent of the *Voralp* or of the *montagnette* of Tarentaise. It is the intermediate stopping-place between the village and the alp, and has a dwelling-house which is generally separate from the adjacent byre-barn. The cattle are brought up from the beginning of June until the 25th and return in the autumn during the period 25 September to 25 October on their way down the valley. Above Zinal, at nearly 5,900 ft. and not far from the torrent which courses down the Alpe de Cottier, Florey has $1\frac{1}{2}$ acres of irrigated grassland, nearly $\frac{1}{2}$ acre of upland pasture, and a share in the common land, where the cattle graze each morning. But nowadays, since the introduction of fungicides, the men find employment in the vineyards during June, whereas formerly at this time of the year they could relax at the *mayen* before the arduous work of haymaking and harvesting. Mme Florey brings the whole herd up herself, usually three cows, two heifers, a calf, two goats, two ewes and a pig. Every day she makes a tome or cheese weighing $3\frac{1}{2}$ to 4 lb.,[1] described as 'two-thirds fat' because a third of the cream is skimmed off with a wooden *poche* or ladle for making butter. The greater part of the meadow is

---

[1] The quality is often mediocre. We tasted some at Pinsec, and it had fermented so much that it reminded us of very poor 'blue Auvergne'. As it is destined for domestic consumption, little care is taken in its manufacture.

cut for hay at the end of July, but the grazed pasture not until mid-August.

Traditionally the hay was stored in the byre-barn and consumed *in situ* between 25 November and the end of February. Evidently, therefore, the family was compelled to live at this high altitude during the coldest part of the year. This practice has not died out completely even now, but Florey only keeps a small reserve up here as a precaution against rainy days or fog. The remainder is taken down on small wagons drawn by jeeps or motor tractors, with the result that the animals no longer restore the valuable plant nutrients to the soil. Florey compensates for this by bringing up a bag of ready-mixed fertilizer, but the others do not all follow the same example. The chalet is pleasantly situated, has two rooms and a large kitchen, and is let in the summer at 165 francs for three to four weeks. The garden, 120 sq. yds. in extent, faces the gorge of the nearby torrent. The tenant is free to help himself to the few turnips and carrots, cabbages and lettuces he finds there.

Until the turn of the century the *mayens* were also cultivated for crops. Indeed, those of Ziette were reputed to be 'the granary of the valley'. Once or twice in May and June manure was placed in the channels and the water allowed to flow across the meadows, but such practices have long since lapsed. Far less hay is made from the meadows today, and many of the byre-barns are derelict. The Alpe de Cottier, which towers above the *mayens* of Zinal, is beginning slowly to advance on them. These present incursions of upland pasture on meadowland are a rational development only in the least accessible areas, where the grass is most difficult to cut, for the supply of winter fodder has been reduced on so many sides that alternative resources must now be found to make up the loss.

182. From the *mayens* of Zinal a mule track leads south-eastwards to the Alpe de Tracuit, which belongs to an association or *consortage*. In the summer each member has the right to bring up a number of cows proportional to the amount of grassland he owns privately, and the rights embodied in every group of twelve such animals is known as a *huitan*. Two years in ten, every *huitan* involves the task of serving as *procureur*, or steward. The *procureur* has to provide the mule and the bull, carry up straw for the herdsmen's bedding, and, during the first five days on the alp, assist in making preparations for the coming season; finally, he must return to the mountain in the event of snow.

During June every member must work on the alp according to his *fonds d'herbe*—in other words, according to how much grassland he owns. There is maintenance and repair work to be done on the buildings, paths, and *bisses*, and every year a portion of the alp is cleared of stones. The Alpe de Tracuit has five chalets in all; three of them at different levels are used regularly each season, but the remaining two are used every other year in rotation. The middle one, at 6,750 ft., has a small chalet, or *tzijare*, for making cheese, a cellar for storing it, sleeping quarters for the workers, and a paddock for the animals. The latter are put out to pasture at about 5,900 ft. when they arrive at the end of June, and are brought up to the 6,750 level from the beginning until the third week of July. They return here between the third week of August and the third week of September on their way back to the *mayens*, but the descent to lower altitudes is tending to occur earlier nowadays, for there are fewer animals and more hay than in former times, and it is not worth risking the weather for the sake of a few more days of grazing. As recorded by Jean Brunhes, the Tracuit herds used to descend after all the others, between 30 September and 3 October.

The risk of bad weather is naturally greatest at the beginning and again at the end of the period. The paddock is partly covered by two long lean-to's roughly constructed of planks, and as the forests of larch and arolla pine have thinned out very appreciably at this height the animals generally shelter here at night. Modern stables have been built on six of the valley's alps and they are said to have increased milk yields by 25 per cent., but of those who use the upland pastures, the Rhône Valley farmers can afford such buildings more easily than the Anniviards. It is pertinent to ask whether such buildings are really worthwhile and whether the areas which furnish winter fodder near the villages are not more urgently in need of capital development.

At about 4 a.m. the cows are brought to the paddock for milking. The animals graze from 8 a.m. until 1 p.m., following a definite route across the alp. They are brought in for milking at 2 p.m., turned out to pasture about 4 p.m. during cold weather, or about two hours later if the day is warm, and return to the shelter of the woods at about nine or ten in the evening. The dung on the floor of the paddock is washed out by a small stream and thus fertilizes the pastures below. A waterfall some distance away is harnessed to drive the butter churn, but the separator, as it uses a large quantity of milk and whey which would be awkward to transport, is at the chalet and is manually operated.

The high chalet, which is named Composana, is at 8,430 ft. Fuel has to be brought to it for cheese-making, and the wood, in loads of

220-260 lb., is carried by mules from the upper limit of the forest, which is about 6,500 ft. When the cattle remain at this height for a month, the manufacture of Gruyère requires about fifteen of these loads; *sérac* cheese, on the other hand, which is made by coagulating the albumen, needs much more fuel than this, and is therefore not made at all at this level. When the curd has been removed from the coagulated milk, the whey is sent to the separator, and eight Large White pigs are kept on the skimmed whey.

183. In 1952 the Tracuit herd was smaller than the previous year. There were sixty milch cows, ten heifers in calf, and twenty-six heifers of one or two years belonging to thirty different owners. Details of the local decline in the number of cattle are given below, but it should be noted that the *mayens* are suffering in consequence far more noticeably than the alps, which are supporting larger herds from other areas every year. The milk yield is affected by the fact that the cows are nearing the end of the lactation period, and total production from sixty animals drops from 65 gallons a day when the alp is first reached to 50 gallons at the time of our visit on 11 August 1952. The cowman estimated that the figure would have fallen to 35 gallons by mid-September, when the cows, owing to the scarcity of water at this season, are taken down again. The cheese, an extra-fat variety for the traditional *raclette*, is made twice a day at first, but only in the mornings later on. When the herds are based on one of the high-level chalets, the cheese-maker goes down to the middle chalet at about 10.30 a.m., taking the previous days' three cheeses with him on a mule. He returns with a load of wood in the early afternoon.

Five workers are employed altogether. The chief cowman has two assistants to help with the hand milking. In 1951 there were 100 cows, and four assistants were needed. For the three months the cowman and the cheese-maker each earn 1,200 francs as against 400 francs pre-war, made up of 700 francs in wages plus the produce of 3 gallons of milk a day. The two eighteen-year-old assistants receive 700 and 500 francs respectively, the latter being for a boy who is half crippled. There is also a twelve-year-old cowherd who goes up every morning to count the heifers and bring them some salt, and who earns 500 francs. The workers pay nothing for their keep, and the standard of the food has improved noticeably since before the war. Until 1939 they fed on milk products[1] and rye bread, but nowadays they are given *polenta*, or maize flour, potatoes, coffee, and chocolate, which they fetch with

---

[1] They were not allowed anything but milk and *sérac* until 15 August, and had no right either to butter or the better cheese.

the mule from Zinal every fortnight. They are allowed meat on 15 August. The services of two workers could be dispensed with if there were trained dogs and a milking machine. On the other hand, the latter would admittedly be much easier to install in the village for co-operative milking during the winter, while dogs are still a rarity in the valley, which today finds the tax somewhat of a deterrent. In the past there was no surplus food for an animal which was not directly productive.

At Composana there is an open paddock surrounded by a low dry-stone wall where the cows are milked during the first few days. A *bisse* feeds a small pond, which can be drained down-slope to fertilize the alp below. Later on the milking takes place on the pasture in the vicinity of the chalet, where the dung dropped on the ground and the treading of the turf, which is simply a primitive way of using animals to work the soil—still found in Madagascar rice-fields—promotes a most welcome growth of grass. Nowadays, the young herdsman no longer spreads the dung, but this is a task which could be performed admirably by power pumps. These have the advantage that they can pump mixtures of dung and dung-water to higher levels and, sited in the middle of any fair-sized terrace, they would be most effective. This type of intensification is sometimes found on the Tyrolean alps, which are considerably lower (Chapter IX), but on economic grounds the needs of the lower meadow land in Anniviers are more compelling and merit prior consideration.

On this sector of intensive grazing 10 gallons of milk yield 12 lb. of cheese, as compared with 10 lb. elsewhere. Basile Zufferey has an amusing story about a cow which stood out from the rest by its remarkably good condition. Eventually they discovered that it was purloining an extra ration by leaving the paddock every night, and had mastered the technique of surmounting all the obstacles without allowing its bell to ring. Every herd on the alp has its queen, which qualifies for leadership by defeating all its rivals in single combat during the ascent. The fights attract a large number of spectators, and thereafter the queen leads the herd, and remains in excellent condition by reserving the best morsels of pasture for herself. The peasant does not begrudge the price of possible injury to his animals for the prize of owning a queen, even though she may be a poor milker.

On Tracuit the animals are of the Hérens breed, which withstands the arduous climb along the rocky slopes. Arpitetta, further along the valley, also has a number of Simmenthals, which are less sure-footed and always arrive last for the milking. Formerly there was always a flock of 200-300 sheep which roamed the craggy slopes up to nearly 10,000 ft., but only heifers graze at these heights today.

The yield of each cow is measured every week, and on this basis the products are divided between the owners. In 1951, with his three cows, Florey's share of the expenses was 150 francs, of which 30 were allotted for paying off a debt incurred for the construction of *bisses*. His share of the produce was 175 lb. of cheese of high fat content (at 2 francs 50 a pound), and 33 lb. of low fat content (90 centimes a pound), 22 lb. of butter (3 francs 40 a pound), and 6½ lb. of *sérac*. He benefited also from the weight gained by his heifers—at least 65 lb. a head—and by his pig.[1]

184. The Haut-Valais has 16,000 dairy farmers, who own 34,000 cows between them, an average of two per farm, and produce nearly 18,000,000 gallons of milk; another 1,650,000 gallons are obtained from the 25,000 goats. On the very dry alp, an acre of pasture can support one cow for fourteen days, whereas, at the opposite extreme in humid Appenzell, this figure is trebled. Such facts underline two of the basic difficulties which stand in the way of financial investment and modernization—namely, the uneconomically small size of individual farms and the unfavourable nature of the environment, which puts a brake on productivity. In view of its high population density, the Val d'Anniviers is forced to turn to sources of income outside the province of stock-farming. It is now open to trade with the outside world, it imports more and more colonial produce, more flour and potatoes, it buys electricity and has its wirelesses and modern furniture, its people read newspapers, travel abroad, and pay taxes which are very high in relation to productivity; in short, the need for money is growing all the time.

Although there is far too little cultivation to supply local needs, especially for potatoes and cereals, and although the domestic manufacture of cloth and garments has practically ceased, the peasant of Anniviers is forced by the very limited scope of his farming to consume practically the whole of his output of animal products. The Florey family consume the whole of their butter, pork, and poultry, two-thirds of their cheese, a carcase of salt beef every year, and only sell a cow, whose age may vary, once in two years, and one or two calves a season. They are none the less fortunate as compared with some of the families in the mountains of Grisons, who need most of the money they earn by selling one animal a year—practically their sole source of income—to pay their baker's bill in October. The reason is that they have found in the viticulture on the *Coha*, or sunny side of the Rhône

[1] Life on the alps is studied in detail in *L'élevage en Valais*, by Ed. Jacky (Sion).

Valley, a form of commercial agriculture which provides most of the people of Anniviers with the majority of their income from agricultural sources.

5. The Vines of the Rhône Valley Provide the Ready Money

185. Acquisitions of land in the Vallée by the Anniviards are recorded as far back as the twelfth and thirteenth centuries, a period when this region may well have been affected by the surge of population growth which swept over western Europe at this time. These people were thrifty, their farming equipment was not greatly inferior to that of the lowland, which was still half-covered with swamps, and no doubt they made up with zealous effort for any shortcomings in their methods. Before this, according to the legend of Jacquet the dwarf, they only ventured into the Vallée to buy salt and wine. They acquired a taste for wine, but as their numbers grew they found themselves bereft of surplus for exchange, and resolved to grow the vine themselves. Furthermore, they needed more grain and hay, and there was land in the Vallée where these could be grown.

Thus began the nomadism which H. Girard and Jean Brunhes have described. The great seasonal migration took place during Lent, at the end of February or beginning of March, when the village was still buried in snow. The whole population, headed by the curate and the teacher, descended into the Rhône Valley and halted outside the gates of Sierre. The cattle fed on the remainder of the hay until the beginning of April, and then returned to the valley. The men hoed and pruned the vines, planted potatoes and sowed barley, and, later, maize for *polenta* and hemp. In the summer they returned for the disbudding and hay-making and later for the harvest and to tie the vines. The vine harvest followed in the autumn, and was followed, between 5 and 10 November, by the return of the cattle. They grazed the aftermath and were taken back to the valley after the fair at Sierre on 23 November, where any animals which could not be kept through the winter because of the shortage of hay were sold.

At Sierre today, however, one finds the Anniviard peasant in full retreat from his meadows and arable fields, especially the latter. The town has spread to the first scarps and the *montagnards* have done very well from the sale of their plots for building. If a vineyard was displaced in this manner, it was re-established at the expense of meadows at a higher level, but cereal cultivation has been practically abandoned. The people now eat less *polenta* and buy their requirements. Even the meadows are kept mainly as local suppliers of manure for the vineyards, which some local farmers have to buy as far afield as Fribourg.

A kind of secession has taken place. Some of the Anniviards have moved to the villages round Sierre, where it is easier to make a living, and now inhabit their temporary houses of former days. Some tend their vineyards, but the majority have found jobs in the town, and many of the inhabitants of Sierre trace back their origin to Saint-Luc. Furthermore, it has become unusual for whole families to take part in the seasonal migration. At Grimentz, for example, out of twenty-six schoolchildren only five make the journey to the lowland during Lent, whereas thirty years ago practically the whole school went— thirty-seven out of forty, to be precise. At Saint-Jean and Grimentz nearly half the cattle and at Chandolin and Saint-Luc fully half of them still go down, but the proportion decreases at Mission and Ayer. The removal of a household, which used to take place entirely on foot, today requires a lorry and is very expensive. Thus at Vissoie only three out of thirty farming families continue to move. Moreover, the peasant woman of today is no longer content to camp in the open, nor can she afford to keep up three separate places of residence. It is a fact, however, that these seasonal migrations are still much more characteristic of the Val d'Anniviers than of the remainder of the Valais.

Henri Salamin, the postman at Saint-Luc, told us that it cost about 100,000 francs to set up a vineyard today; he himself had given up the idea, as he had no wish to indebt himself to that extent. It is noteworthy that there is more risk attached to borrowing in countries like Switzerland which have stable currencies. Swiss agriculture as a whole borrows about half its capital, and is in consequence one of the most heavily burdened in the world. The vineyards of the Valais are on the whole heavily mortgaged, but the land in the Val d'Anniviers is not.

186. The number of complete households which migrate is smaller than formerly, but many Anniviards have kept their vineyards. Very often the head of the family goes down alone at the reduced tariff offered by the postal bus service. Three or four treatments against mildew and oidium and sometimes against wasps or putrefaction compel more journeys than before. In the past 'after Lent, two-thirds of the labour in the vineyards was complete'. At Villa, west of Sierre, G. Florey owns two meadows—just over ¼ acre—which he rents to a relative who 'remained below' in exchange for manure for his vines. He also has 50 sq. yds. of garden, but his main assets are represented

by nine parcels of vineyard which vary in size from 120 to 640 sq. yds., ⅔ acre in all. The annual yield varies between sixty and 100 *brantées*, or 100-lb. baskets, of grapes a year.

The stocks used to be planted 35 × 28 in. apart and layered, a technique which persists in some of the older vineyards in France. The vineyards of Sierre were slowly attacked by phylloxera, which began its advance up the valley in 1923, but they are now being fully reestablished and, owing to the high lime content in the soil, the new plants are often grafted on American stocks, such as *Riparia* × *Berlandieri 5BB*. Naturally, replanting is expensive and has resulted in some consolidation of ownership into larger holdings. Wine merchants have bought up many of the smaller men who wrote off their scattered holdings when the harvests no longer made their frequent journeys worthwhile. It is none the less true that some of these small farmers still come down to tend as little as 100 *toises*,[1] or about 450 sq. yds.

The mattock is falling into disuse, and the modern tendency is to space the vines further apart, so as to facilitate working with winches: rows 44 in. apart, with stocks every 24 in. White varieties are in the majority, and Ermitage, which gives heavy yields without preventing a reasonable standard of quality to be maintained, has been added to the older varieties such as Humagne, Rèze, and Muscat. Other newcomers are Riesling and Johannisberg and, best known of all, Chasselas, which gives the famous *fendant*. The biggest market for wine is the German-speaking part of Switzerland, where the damp climate is better suited to grassland than to viticulture. In spite of the predominance of white wine in the country—four-fifths of home production, to be exact—this area nevertheless persists in consuming twice as much of the red as of the white variety; the importers seize on this fact to justify their demands.

Thus, apart from Pinot *gris* or Malvoisie, a variety whose excellence puts it in the very highest class, Pinot *noir* or Dôle[2] and even Gamay, which is not quite of the same quality, are now recommended. Here, as in the whole of central Europe, the practice was for the wine-making concerns to buy the pressed grapes in 10-gallon *brantées*. For many years competition between buyers kept prices stable, but at a level which could only have been called 'fair' by medieval standards. Then about 1920 the association of wine merchants brought about an agreement

---

[1] 1 *toise*=4·56 sq. yds. The *fichelin*, or 33 lb. of rye was enough to sow 200 *toises*. 1 *fichelin*=2 *mesures*=4 *quarterons*.

[2] 300,000 stocks planted in the Valais in 1952.

between the buyers which was tantamount to a monopoly of purchase, and the resulting market situation was rapidly exploited to the full.[1] The producers tried to protect themselves by forming the Association of Vine-growers of the Valais, but they soon realized that their only effective defence lay in the co-operative system.

Co-operatives were founded during 1931-2. They intended to sell to the trade, but were boycotted. Following the example of the 'Provins' co-operatives, they then began to work in groups and organized a system of direct sale. In 1951 they were paying 36 centimes a pound for that year's *fendant*, while the trade was offering only 32 centimes, and, furthermore, quality has been improved far more successfully than under the old system. In order to stop the practice of hiding fruit of an inferior variety at the bottom of the *brantée*, they offer higher prices for grapes delivered in flat boxes containing 33 lb. Apart from the differential price scale for grade and variety, the definition of three zones of quality according to altitude[2] is now being undertaken. The lowest slopes, from 1,800 to 2,130 ft., are the best; the least favourable begin at 2,460 and rise to 3,050 ft., the limit of the vine. This upper limit is tending to rise in the Valais, quite the reverse of what is happening in France, and this is the only canton in Switzerland where the area under vines has not shrunk since 1880. At this time the country had 90,000 acres of vineyards, almost treble the present-day figure of 32,500 acres.

At the moment the acreage is slightly on the increase, a fact which is causing some difficulty in finding markets. The Government buys up part of the harvest, but this does not help in stimulating demand. On the other hand, 'Provinor' grape juice is becoming fairly popular, and table grapes, which are bought from the growers at 50 centimes a pound, are retailed throughout Switzerland at 54 centimes, thanks to a subsidy from the *fonds vinicole*. Finally, the new Agricultural Statute, which attempts what has already been tried in France, will confine planting to land unsuited to other types of cultivation. As in France, however, when the Vine Statute was foreshadowed in 1934, some farmers are hurriedly ploughing up their meadows so as to plant fresh areas before the new legislation becomes operative.

187. The 1,300 members of the Sierre co-operative bring in a little

---

[1] 'Large wine concerns have done very good business; on the other hand, until recent years, the quality of Valaisan wine was not satisfactory, and the pressure on prices had been transmitted wholly to the producers.' From a report on agricultural incentives given in the canton of Valais by Dr Howald (1934).

[2] In France, the nature of the underlying rock would also be taken into account.

more than 3,000 tons of grapes in an average year; the total was actually 4,500 tons in 1951, but this was exceptional. Taking 92 cwt. per acre as a typical yield and a mean production of 46 cwt. per member, one arrives at the figure of about ½ acre for the size of the average holding. The smallest is $\frac{1}{10}$ acre and the largest, belonging to a Sierre café proprietor, 7 acres. There are very few, however, who live solely from their vineyards, and the members vary from professional and business people to factory workers, many of whom have not long left the land, and farmers. A vineyard is regarded as a safe investment, and many are owned by associations of townspeople, by *consortages*, chapels, and convents. In short, the small peasant owner is gradually disappearing.

During the war even vineyards affected by phylloxera were bought at 40 francs a *toise*, equivalent to £4,000 an acre, and today prices still fluctuate between 25 and 30 francs, in spite of the restricted market for wine. Those who do not work their own land lease it on the *métayage* system, leaving all the expenses to the tenant, and receive half the harvest in return, an exorbitant share by French standards. Others engage labour at 2 francs a *toise* for the summer work, which includes disbudding, tying, spraying (materials provided), and digging over the ground once or twice.

The vineyards are situated on fairly steep slopes—not so steep, however, as between Saint-Léonard and Sion—and are crossed by dry stone walls, which hold back the soil. The ground is watered once or twice a year from the same narrow channels which Schiner described as long ago as 1812. When the vines were still largely peasant-owned, only about a fifth of the surface was actually irrigated in this manner, but the very deep working of the soil, the so-called *versannage*, kept it very much moister. All the new vineyards are watered *in toto*, and nearly half of them employ revolving sprays, which are less likely to cause gullying than surface-flow irrigation.

For every 100 *toises*, less than $\frac{1}{10}$ acre, G. Florey spends a day and a half for pruning, a day for disbudding, a day or more for three or four sprayings, a day and a half, spread between April and August, for hoeing round the roots. Autumn hoeing is generally effected by means of power winches, which take only about an hour, but cost 10 francs. The women's work is to tie the shoots to the larch vine-props, a task which takes about four days. Finally, men and women share the harvest work, which occupies a further day and a half. This small area thus demands a total of ten and a half days of work during the season, or about 110 days of work per acre, a figure which is only slightly less than for southern Slovakia and Hungary, where methods are much the same.

In contrast, in a quality vineyard at Monbazillac we found a figure of sixty days per acre, while on some of the mechanized estates of Hérault and Orania even this is almost halved. Florey's $\frac{2}{3}$ acre requires some seventy-eight days of work, or ninety-five days with travelling time. Between 1945 and 1947, years when prices were good, the vines accounted for 40-44 per cent. of his agricultural production, which absorbed a total of 700 days of work. The productivity of labour, therefore, is very much higher in the vineyard than in the vicinity of the upland village.

Florey's land is worth 26,000 francs, his buildings are valued at 17,000 francs, his plants, consisting of vines and a few fruit trees, at 4,000 francs, while his working capital comprises 4,200 francs-worth of animals, 1,900 francs-worth of equipment, and 3,200 francs for running expenses. In 1947 gross receipts, including the value of produce consumed at home, were about 10,000 francs. This sum would have to be increased by 15 per cent. to yield 4 per cent. interest on working capital, and at the same time to assure each member of the family of a fair wage. Genoud, however, the President of the commune, who has no vines, would have to increase his gross income by 27 per cent. to achieve this desirable objective.

The value of the land has been estimated conservatively, but it still represents a very large proportion of the total capital involved, and there is little doubt that current prices are not justified by productivity. The cost of maintaining innumerable buildings deserves emphasis. During 1945-6, just before Florey acquired his two-wheel motor tractor, wages accounted for more than two-thirds of the running expenses, whereas on the mechanized but intensive farms of Champagne they account for less than a quarter and are exceeded by the cost of both fertilizers and motor fuel. Finally, although he has a college diploma in agriculture, Albert Florey is also a postman. His rounds do not take long on a motor-scooter, so he can still work on the farm and has enough money to maintain a decent home. Moreover, his young wife thus escapes the life of virtual slavery which is the common lot of the peasant women of the highlands, upon whose shoulders falls the main burden of work on the land.[1]

[1] 'What struck me most of all, and surprises me even to this day, is the lack of consideration for the young mother—or the future mother—and the lack of attention to general health matters . . . overwork and undernourishment' (De Chastonay in *Au Val d'Anniviers*).

6. An Agricultural Economy in Recession[1]

188. In 1946, of the gross receipts of the Florey farm, including domestic consumption, 17 per cent. were represented by the growth of the cattle, 16 per cent. by milk and milk products, 10 per cent. by pig-rearing, and 5 per cent. by sheep- and goat-rearing. Potatoes and cereals provided another 2 per cent., but the latter were insufficient for the needs of the family. A further 3·6 per cent. were derived from a new form of intensive farming—namely, the cultivation of strawberries and other fruits. The insufficiency of income other than from the vine, and the extraordinarily low productivity of work in the valley, apart from the alpine pastures, condemn this type of farming to a slow decline. The retreat of the arable land is clearly discernible in the landscape, more so than in the statistics, which are not always precise.

Until 1918, when the peasants still dug their fields to a depth of 1 ft. or more and piled the stones into *mourzières*, the area under crops continued to expand. There were losses between the wars, but then the acreage remained practically unchanged until 1946. Since then, however, the arable area has shrunk rapidly, as we have already observed, falling from 185 acres of so-called 'open land' in 1939 to less than 125 acres in 1950[2] and to barely over 100 acres in 1952. A contributory factor has been that lorries and subsequently winches and jeeps have replaced the mule for many purposes. These animals are therefore far less numerous than formerly, but the farmer often finds himself with no satisfactory substitute for bringing manure to his fields. In 1914 every family of four or five persons had about ¼ acre or more of crop land. The Floreys, for instance, had ½ acre at this time; about a tenth of this area was sown to rye every year, while the remainder was evenly divided between rye and potatoes, each half following a two-year rotation; at the same time the family consumed the entire milk production of its four cows. Even at this period the valley could not afford to sell much of its potato crop and was forced to import flour.

Only at Saint-Jean and Saint-Luc, where cereals were the dominant crop, and to some extent at Chandolin and Ayer, has the arable acreage ever been important. Its decline has been most rapid at Chandolin,

[1] The head of the agricultural school at Châteauneuf has asked me to alter this to 'slowly developing'. This ostrich-like attitude, the unwillingness to look facts in the face, is thus not only found in France.

[2] 50 acres for grain and 65 for potatoes; as against 1,775 acres of grassland (excluding alpine pastures).

where the potato crop has been particularly severely affected and the total area under crops has fallen from 67 acres in 1929 to only 10 in 1950 and to about 7 in 1952. The same trend is more than ever apparent at Saint-Luc, which is gradually becoming simply a *mayen* for those who have settled permanently in the Rhône lowland. Below Saint-Jean, where the predominance of grassland has always been marked, the lack of resources outside agriculture has tended to check the abandonment of crop land, especially for cereal growing. The opposite is true, however, of the isolated village of Pinsec, and also of Grimentz, where cereals have shown the greatest losses and now account for only about 2 acres. Finally, at Ayer the same trend has been apparent since 1950.

More significant are changes in the number of cattle. Jean Brunhes emphasizes the increase from 1,870 head in 1876 to 2,105 in 1906, but at Grimentz numbers have fallen from 386 in 1901 to 210 at the present, and there have been similar decreases at Saint-Jean (439 to 260), at Ayer (600 to 400), and at Saint-Luc (300 to 175), while at Vissoie the figure has fallen from 223 in 1906 to 160 today. Chandolin alone records an increase over this period, from 133 to 162, but it still has fewer cattle today than in 1916. Taking the valley as a whole, there are thus a third fewer cattle than there were fifty years ago, an overall decrease to 1,367 head. The net decline in production, however, is rather less marked than these figures suggest at first sight, for the yield of meat and milk per animal has shown an upward trend, though this has not really been fast enough.

These upland villages, where the spinning and weaving of wool were once important, are also losing their flocks of sheep. The 600-strong flock owned by Ayer at the turn of the century has now fallen to a mere 100 head, while at Grimentz and Chandolin numbers have dropped from 300 and 143 to fifty and twenty-seven respectively. Until about 1920, every farm had five or six ewes, which were herded communally and grazed the poorest land as long as it remained free of snow, but this practice has been seriously handicapped by legislation for the protection of woodland, which prohibits the grazing of forest borders and clearings. At Saint-Luc and Saint-Jean, however, two flocks, each of over 100 sheep, have recently been added to the reduced numbers, now only two or three per family, of the communal flock. Nevertheless, even this has not prevented the total at Saint-Jean from falling to 200 head, as compared with the former figure of 320. Finally, goats and pigs appear to be declining slowly in numbers, while poultry are on the increase.

189. The first half of the century has witnessed a parallel but even sharper fall in the number of inhabitants. The maximum population of 2,831 inhabitants, as compared with 1,975 in 1870 and 2,238 in 1900, was reached somewhat belatedly in 1910. This date coincides with the first large-scale departures to the factory at Chippis. Previous to this, a few people had left the valley to find employment on the Simplon Tunnel project or on the Zermatt railway: 'on their knees', they begged for work. Mobilization in 1914 accelerated the rate of emigration. Finally, by 1951 the population had fallen to less than 1,600, as compared with 1,743 in 1941. The worst-affected village, Saint-Luc, has fallen from 500 inhabitants at the beginning of the century to a mere 150 today.[1]

In fact, agriculture has suffered more than these figures appear to suggest. An increasing proportion of the people are employed in commerce, crafts of various kinds, public administration, etc., and no longer depend directly on the land. At Vissoie only three full-time farmers remain today, a fact which also demonstrates that agriculture is coming to be regarded as the province of women and children and as a supplementary source of income for the family. The diminutive size of holdings which is likely to persist under these conditions can only lead to a stagnation of techniques, as the example of Saint-Chaffrey in Briançonnais, which has reached further along a similar path of development, shows only too clearly. Any benefit to be derived from modernization would be offset by the uneconomic size of farm units.

The dam project opened at Moiry in the upper Gougra Valley above Grimentz in 1952 will keep 1,000 to 1,500 workers employed for eight to ten years,[2] but it may well serve as a check to progressive farming techniques and as a further deterrent to interest in agriculture, which by comparison will seem more archaic than ever. And what is to happen to the labour force when the scheme is completed? The backwardness of the whole region is epitomized by the tourist, who comes here by car in search of the picturesque. He passes an old peasant woman

---

[1] In 'Val d'Anniviers 49', which appeared in *Annales* (Economies, Sociétés, Civilization) for January-March 1950, M. Et. Juillard writes: 'As for the Val d'Anniviers, the amazing truth is that it has barely changed. . . . A way of life which has lasted a thousand years still shows no sign of extinction.' He speaks of 'a little emigration' and adds: 'It is difficult to conceive of anything but a superficial modernization and development of these methods.' He does not appear to have a full grasp of the problem.

[2] The reservoir will have a capacity of 78,000,000 cu. yds. The scheme will develop 500,000,000 kw.h., two-thirds of it in winter. Cost is estimated at 200,000,000 Swiss francs.

with a load of grass or leaves or even manure on her back, or with a burden of hay on her head or wood in her basket; in all conscience, one would think it was she who had earned a respite from her toil, but the traveller drives on oblivious to the moral.

Switzerland was quicker than most other countries to realize that agriculture in the highland zone needs special assistance. The subsidy on co-operatively owned power-winches was continued after the war, and the new Agricultural Statute even provides for subsidizing their purchase by private individuals. Motor-mowers, however, in spite of their usefulness, are not to be treated likewise, on the grounds that they can play no part in bringing meadows and abandoned arable land back into cultivation, which was the sound principle underlying the wartime Wahlen plan. Furthermore, grants from the Régie des alcools reduce the price of potatoes, apples, and cherries bought in the valley and also, incidentally, reduce the volume of these commodities used for making liquor. This is a scheme which France could imitate to her advantage.

There is a grant for grinding corn for domestic bread-making. For a village at the altitude of Vissoie this is worth 8 francs per hundredweight of grain taken to the mill. The construction on the high pasture of byres with cheese-making equipment is subsidized, and the grants for stock-rearing are slightly more generous for the highlands than for the lowlands. As we have seen, much more could have been made of poultry-keeping in the past, but nowadays selected chicks are made available at reduced prices and eggs are bought from the farmer at 26 centimes each, instead of 25 centimes, to help defray the costs of transport. At the moment poultry contributes only 6 per cent. of the total agricultural income of the country, but Swiss economists would like to see this figure rise to something over 10 per cent., as in the U.S.A. In addition, there are other general provisions, such as grants for fodder cereals, which apply to Swiss agriculture as a whole, while the federal scheme for family allowances is of particular importance for the large families of the Catholic Valais. All in all, these measures provide for an appreciable degree of assistance to agriculture, but they rather give one the impression of an effort that is too dispersed.

190. What changes have in fact taken place in the life of the valley? In 1914 farm equipment was limited to small tools, like mattocks, spades, and picks, sickles for the women to cut the grain, and scythes for the men to work in the meadows. Grass and wood were carried in tall baskets and *rètzes*, more often on the backs of men than on mules. Carts served mainly for the seasonal removal of the household to Sierre,

and but little for transport in the vicinity of the villages. Every family consumed practically all the animal produce of its farm, and generally slaughtered one cow a year, which was salted and cured in the loft. Sometimes one and a half animals would be consumed a year, but this was only when the household included a number of unmarried aunts and uncles who had remained single so as not to aggravate the disequilibrium between population and production.

Boiled in a pot with bacon and potatoes, and with pears in season, this meat was the basic item in the diet. As at Saint-Chaffrey, the vegetable garden grew little other than cabbages, apart from some beet for the pigs. Rye bread and maize *polenta*, which was either grown or obtained from the Rhône Valley in exchange for cheese or ham, provided the cereal food. Local taxes were paid in labour, and 7 or 8 francs was enough to settle the others; 20 or 30 francs in cash for buying salt, sugar, pepper, and a few groceries were enough for a family to survive the winter.

Many of these particulars still apply today, but the way of living has changed more rapidly than farming methods. The consumption of salt meat, cheese, and milk has fallen, and variety has been added to the diet in the form of butter, formerly a luxury, vegetables, oil, wheaten pastes, rice, sugar, chocolate, coffee, and even tea, which is sometimes mixed with wine. Techniques, however, have shown little advance, apart from the development of transport on main roads and the occasional presence of a tractor or a power winch. The latter, moreover, is hired only when nearby construction works have provided more ready money than usual in the village.

Agriculture has become a supplementary source of income, especially at Vissoie, so the farmland has become increasingly concentrated near the villages, while the more outlying areas, and the arable fields in particular, have been progressively abandoned. Consequently, too much work is now lavished on a limited area for the sake of inadequate yields, whereas land beyond, where pastoral enterprises would provide far richer rewards for labour, remains utterly neglected.

7. Extension of Pastures and Intensification on the Meadows

191. Even taking into account the contributions of vegetable- and soft-fruit-growing, assisted by the use of rotating sprays, of ancillary stock-raising enterprises, of poultry-keeping, and even of viticulture, we have no hesitation in concluding that agriculture will never again flourish in the valley unless it reorganizes its cattle-rearing industry and

REMEDIES IN THE USE OF PASTURES AND MEADOWS

its methods of producing fodder. An examination of the various land-utilization sectors today shows that profits and productivity are greatest on the high pastures. Here communal herding economizes on labour, whereas the growing trend near the villages for each family to look after its own cattle has the reverse effect. Furthermore, cheese-making is carried on under favourable conditions, and is much more profitable than on the *mayens*. At Saas-Fée, however, certain rather poor pastures of small extent, capable of carrying only about twenty head, are gradually falling into disuse.

The least efficient sector seems to be that which supplies winter fodder. The system, based as it is on a large number of byre-barns, requires far too much work, both for producing the hay and for tending the animals. The byre-barn is an interesting historical survival, but is inappropriate to modern conditions. It has neither ventilation nor electricity, and is a breeding-place for tuberculosis. In the autumn of 1952 tuberculin testing resulted in the destruction of many animals, Florey's among them. Finally, an enormous amount of time is wasted travelling between village and barn, and at Pinsec, for instance, these journeys sometimes take up to an hour and a half each way across the snow.

In a planned economy, the mountains could be reserved as summer pastures. The Val d'Anniviers would be grazed for six months and winter fodder would be produced, and fed to the stock in the lowlands. Today one sees cattle turned out to pasture in the summer on the Swiss plateau, obviously too extensive a use for such fertile terrain. On the other hand, the alpine villager acrobatically cuts his 'hay from the rocks' and plies his mattock on inaccessible fields which are far too poor ever to repay such intensive labour. In a rational economy such paradoxes would be avoided. The Agricultural Statute, which shows a proper solicitude for the alpine farmer, could profitably be extended to encourage transhumance in reverse—that is, the descent to the lower valleys or to the plateau of upland cattle in the winter. Such a movement would simply complement the summer movement of lowland stock to the uplands, and already in 1947 the wintering of heifers from the Valais in the German-speaking part of Switzerland was in fact subsidized.

Under present economic conditions, such proposals could not be applied immediately on a large scale, and their implementation by isolated individuals who chose, for example, to sell their cattle in the autumn and buy again in the spring might even involve financial losses. The problem of winter employment would also have to be solved.

A compromise more costly than the ideal solution and less logical economically is, however, possible. It would at all events be a decisive step in the right direction. The suggestion is that all land which by reason of ruggedness or inaccessibility is difficult to work should revert to pasture. The upper parts of the *mayens*, the hay from which is now so laboriously brought back to the village, would become part of the alps. The result would be better cheese and more economic herding, while the season spent on the alps would be extended. The more easily reached lower slopes of the *mayens* would continue to provide winter hay, but this would be stored in modern and much larger barns in the village.

The more difficult land near the villages would be given over to summer pastures; neglected fields could be utilized for this purpose without delay. The problem of herding would then arise, but this has several possible solutions. As before, the sheep could be herded, either communally or by *consortages*, on scrubland, fallows, and rough grazing. Spring lambing would reduce to a minimum the need for winter fodder, and would result in the coincidence of maximum feed requirements during the suckling and fattening of lambs with the period of most vigorous grass growth. The calving time for cattle could also be delayed to some extent, and this would meet the ever-growing demand for milk in the summer from tourists. The cows would be kept on enclosed pastures, re-established on the best of the former arable land and rough grazings, just above the level of the *bisses*, from which the animals could be watered. Later in the season they would be taken to the less accessible irrigated meadows. Enclosures of less than about 1 acre are uneconomic, as too much fencing is needed per unit of area. On the other hand, in the interests of control of grazing, this figure should not be greatly exceeded so long as individual herds remain so small.

192. This brings us back once again to the question of the consolidation of holdings. This is the essential condition of the whole operation, for parcels of 100 sq. yds. or so cannot be enclosed. The people of Anniviers, however, have already suffered through a badly organized scheme of land reintegration near Sierre round about 1925. They were more or less obliged to redeem the land they had previously owned in order to retain manageable holdings, and the process is said to have cost them 2 francs 30 a *toise*.[1] Nowadays the Swiss Government undertakes to defray 25 per cent. of the cost of redistribution, and no longer insists, as formerly, on the canton providing a similar sum. By a law

---

[1] £220 per acre!

of 13 May 1937, however, the Valais, which has more fragmented holdings than any other canton, provides 30 per cent. of the costs of consolidation, but will find it a most difficult task to complete its land programme by the target date of 2023. Between 75 per cent. and 80 per cent. of the outlay is for roads, but this expenditure could be avoided in the zone of pastures and meadows if the above suggestions were adopted. As it is capable of effecting such a saving in cost, therefore, the pattern of land utilization should be rationalized before any redistribution of holdings is attempted. In addition, this redistribution should be planned with an eye to the logical development of the region in coming years, not in a spirit fettered by claims for the survival of the anachronisms of today. At the moment, however, as we were informed both at Berne and at Brugg,[1] the existing subsidies aim at retaining a large number of people employed in agriculture in the highlands. Thus conceived, in emotional terms and also in the desire to avoid certain political repercussions, the problem has been met with quite different measures from those we have proposed. Their results are plainly to be seen in the derelict crop land between Saint-Luc and Vissoie.

Generous schemes of financial aid would more logically have aimed at keeping the land in production, with the important proviso that the funds made available were invested in equipment which could really serve to develop the mountainous region and raise the productivity of agricultural labour. To begin with, this would mean, as in France, that the whole cost of land consolidation would have to be borne by the State,[2] and, incidentally, if local men were employed to help the surveyors in this work it would bring a little more ready money into the valley.

Once this task was completed and the pastures had been extended and enclosed with waste wood from the saw-mills, barbed wire, or electric fences (provided they were found to be suitable for Hérens cattle), the next step would be to maintain as far as possible the present production of fodder from the reduced area of meadows. This

---

[1] i.e. by the Ministry of Agriculture and the Swiss Union of Peasants, respectively. 'This class of the population, which has always been considered as one of the main pillars of the State and as one of the richest sources of our national life . . .' (Dr Laur).

[2] Moreover, it would be absurd to envisage a redistribution of land 'to the nearest square yard' in areas which have been abandoned or are in course of being so and which are divided into fields ranging in size from 60 sq. yds. to $\frac{1}{8}$ acre. But local opinion still demands it. For a long time in Ticino, 90 per cent. of the cost of land consolidation was defrayed from public funds, but even so, little progress was made.

could be achieved by intensification on the more readily accessible land, by taking full advantage of the sunny climate and of the irrigation system, and by making equally good use of all the other factors of production.

The most important of these would be the crops of rotation grasses, alternating with root crops and fodder cereals, such as rye and winter barley, which could be cultivated on the old meadows. These would allow the hay to be kept in reserve until late in the autumn without making use of the meadows at Sierre; equally, grass would become available in early spring, and at least three weeks of winter fodder would thus be saved. Oats-vetch mixtures could be grown in the summer and used either directly for milch cows or for making hay. Lucerne does well in the better-drained and more exposed parts of the valley, which have not always been leached of their lime, and might well be established on many a field which has now gone out of cultivation.

On very dry ground a bird's-foot trefoil-cock's-foot mixture (sown at 10 and 16 lb. to the acre respectively) could be tried and might well, with careful grazing—early and methodical—last longer than lucerne. With irrigation, a mixture of cock's-foot (20 lb.) and ladino clover (2 lb.), sometimes mixed with melilot, rye-grass, and yellow oat-grass —the latter especially at great heights—should yield twice as much as the good meadows of the present, and perhaps four times as much as the medium-quality grassland, which is thick with moss, geraniums, and eye-bright. Three early cuttings would have to be taken, followed by grazing, and there would have to be careful fertilizing, especially with phosphates.

193. Cultivation will make the ground more even, and will therefore favour the introduction of motor-mowers. Some of these—the one-wheeled Austrian models, for instance—can be used on slopes steeper than one in two, but some means will have to be found of ensuring that the transport of hay from the fields keeps pace with the greater speed of working. This could be achieved in the intensive zone by constructing tracks like those which nowadays often follow the *bisses*, suitable for two-wheeled tractors. It seems more sensible to aim at equipping the highlands along these lines and so to tackle the problem of low productivity, which is the main cause of their lower living standards, than to subsidize the purchase of consumer goods and attempt by these and similar devices to preserve an utterly outdated agricultural system. It is significant that rural tracks and roads are not always subsidized.

REMEDIES IN THE USE OF PASTURES AND MEADOWS

To lay down as the main principle of development in the highlands that they must first provide sufficient food for their own population is tantamount to advocating the continuance, or in some cases the resumption, of a subsistence, and consequently obsolete, type of economy. It would be better to aim at maximum productivity by exploiting both the natural possibilities of the region and its network of communications, which even as it stands today is an adequate instrument of exchange with the outer world. In his classic *Economie rurale*, Dr Laur writes: 'The greater the difficulties of accessibility, the more the agriculturalist is forced to grow the grain and potatoes needed in the home.' Today there are virtually no communes inaccessible to the jeep, and another precept from the same author is therefore applicable: 'The peasant will be well advised to refrain altogether from cultivating the land to fulfil his own simple needs and to adopt a system based exclusively on grassland.'[1] Self-sufficiency is a justifiable aim when conceived on a national basis as an insurance against international difficulties, but at the domestic or local level it has no place in the modern world. The Government is also beset by the idea of adapting production to the needs of existing markets[2]—for instance, by restricting production from animal husbandry, which is thought to have become overspecialized. The obstacles in the way of inter-European trade admittedly prevent the degree of specialization warranted by the physical environment from being fully attained.

Everyone in the valley is ready to talk about the transformation of the crop land during the war. It was assiduously cultivated, but barely repaid the seed. Even during a war, however, the Wahlen plan, which certainly saved Switzerland from disaster, would have been more effective had it been more flexible and applied with more discretion. In time of war, pasture land can no longer be tolerated in the lowlands, but there are good arguments for retaining it in the highlands. We would advocate that instead of subsidizing only cereals, grants should be made, as in England, for ploughing up permanent pastures, even, or perhaps especially, if they are to be sown with temporary grasses, which are more productive than cereal fodder crops. In this manner the arable land could make a valuable contribution in peacetime, while being easier to convert to bread cereals in case of war.

194. We do not consider that maintaining cereal cultivation on

---

[1] We would have written, 'based on fodder crops', so as to emphasize a preference for these whenever their cultivation is economically possible.

[2] Is this not a sign of a tendency towards restriction, i.e. towards Malthusianism?

unsuitable land by means of subsidies during peacetime is sound political economics. Initial trials at Chandolin by the Mont-Calme Experimental Station have confirmed that there are great possibilities in the valley for the growing of temporary grasses and other fodder crops, but the importance of this veritable agrarian revolution, the lessons from which now remain to be incorporated into local farm practice, have tended to be overshadowed by the official determination to preserve the traditional 'open' fields at all costs. The teachings of the Châteauneuf Agricultural School near Sion have had a salutary effect in the lowlands, but, lacking as they do a specific bias towards the study of intensive fodder crop cultivation at high altitudes,[1] they seem less readily adaptable to the mountain environment. 'The peasant's son has to start earning his living at an early age and rarely continues to study, but, if he does, he is probably training for a calling unrelated to agriculture. As for the few who go to the school at Châteauneuf, they find their outlook very much broadened and begin to understand the inexorable factors in the situation with which they have to contend.'[2]

For the most part, the Swiss mountain peasant regards the present subsidies, which are fairly small and distributed to all farmers, as a form of charity 'incompatible with his dignity'. More help given to those who adopt modern practices would have much to recommend it, and this could take the form, not only of loans for equipment, but also of a reduction in the cost of fertilizers. The latter would be a powerful stimulus to intensification and, moreover, as experience in Lyonais has shown,[3] fertilizers are at their most effective when used on reseeded meadows.

The degree of intensiveness would thus vary with the type of terrain in the different parts of the valley. The intensive zone is now shrunken in size and is tending to retreat towards the villages. This is a natural consequence of the status of agriculture as a subsidiary occupation and of the inconvenience of reaching land which lies further

[1] See the work of the Salize d'Ulzio Station on the Italian side of the Mont Genêvre. The even greater neglect of the mountain environment in agricultural teaching in France should be noted. The head of Châteauneuf informs me that, for forage crops, the school follows the manual of the Swiss schools of agriculture; but on examination it quickly reveals itself to be quite unsuitable for the highland zone. More serious is the fact that Châteauneuf plays the role of agricultural adviser to the Val ... and did not seem to us to be greatly interested in the part.

[2] Quoted from a letter from Albert Florey.

[3] See our analyses of '*la petite exploitation des régions sous-développées*' in the April-May 1953 issue of *Le Journal de la France Agricole*.

afield. It has resulted in the people placing far too much value on the easily accessible land nearby and could be remedied by the construction of pathways. The need to improve local communications appears to be even more urgent than the provision of byres on the alpine pastures, for the working and artificial fertilizing of land thus rendered accessible would double its production of winter fodder.

A more extensive system based on grazing would be best suited to the remaining land. This would not only reduce development costs, but would also avoid the complete abandonment of land, which cannot be justified on economic grounds. It would also be the logical culmination of a process which began when the peasants, who used to ply their sickles on craggy alpine pastures too dangerous for cattle, stopped cutting this *seitiz*, or wild hay, and set their goats to graze it instead. Dr Laur has argued convincingly that, even though intensiveness is desirable in Swiss agriculture as a whole, the same is not necessarily true of the whole of the highland zone. Here as everywhere else in the world the degree of intensiveness must be adjusted as far as possible to the potentialities of the environment.

8. The Size of Farms and Industrialization in the High Valleys

195. A rise in the productivity of labour, especially where it concerns the provision of winter fodder, which is now the main bottleneck in the mountain economy, would pose the problem of optimum size of holdings in a fresh guise. In 1946-7 more than 1,000 days of work were devoted to the upland part—that is, excluding the vine—of the Florey farm. It consists of $5\frac{1}{2}$ acres of meadows cut for hay, just over 1 acre of grazings and $\frac{1}{2}$ acre of arable land, a total of about 7 acres, not counting common land and alpine pastures. At that time the stock comprised three cows, three heifers, two calves, one pig, three goats, and four sheep. A comparison of these figures demonstrates the intolerable waste of human labour, which is consumed especially by the exigencies of transport, herding, and work in the byre-barns.

A similar example in the same locality is quoted by Dr Laur. Here 1,150 days of work are needed for less than 12 acres, and the fruits of this labour are estimated at 2·38 francs a day, whereas workshops in the neighbourhood pay 15 to 20 francs. Already these holdings, with their '8 acres and three cows', are too small, judged by the meagreness of their rewards to the average working family, but when measures of the kind we have advocated above have been given effect their size will prove inadequate even to maintain full employment. The transition towards intensive fodder crop cultivation therefore should be accompanied in its early stages by an expansion of the average family farm towards the goal of '20 acres and ten cows'.[1] There would then be no need for alternative ways of earning a living, and furthermore each farm could afford to equip itself along fairly modern lines, acquiring even a motor-mower and a winch, which could also be used for hauling the milking-machine and other loads.

Unless great efforts are made to provide equipment for highland agriculture—a policy which will be more easily accomplished by dealing individually with each valley—it will soon completely disappear. This opinion is shared by local men, the priest at Chandolin and the guide at Saas-Fée among others. Modernization, however, would necessarily involve a considerable reduction in the number of people now working on the land, and this runs counter to official policy, whose failure to understand simple economic facts would be remarkable even if the commercial economy were a rare phenomenon in the world today. The desire to maintain a high population density is holding back the modernization of equipment. The latter, however, could more surely guarantee the region a significant place in the national economy during the second half of the twentieth century than could the perpetuation of poverty and overpopulation.

Subsidiary occupations are to be regarded as a temporary expedient during the period of transition. The modern tendency in economics, however, is to favour specialization of labour and we would prefer to see a much more clear-cut division of the working population between the various forms of non-agricultural employment than at present. The industrial worker might keep a garden, some poultry, and a few pigs, and might help at first on the family holding. The work he put into his own tiny holding, however, would be poorly rewarded, and it would hardly be wise for him to retain it indefinitely. The Swiss Peasants' Union prefers, however, to subsidize this system of part-time occupations so as to preserve 'a good spirit' in the working population. Moreover, at Vissoie Mme Genoud brought to our notice the 'slavery' of the woman whose husband works all the week on a construction job and who consequently has to cope single-handed with her family of young children and the ill-equipped farm. Because they are needed

[1] Family allowances are given to 'mountain peasants whose holdings yield enough to feed twelve cattle units at the most'. This critical size of holding implicitly recognized by the law should become a minimum; charity could then be dispensed with.

THE SIZE OF FARMS AND INDUSTRIALIZATION

to help on the farm, children go to school for barely six months a year[1] and leave too early. We were assured by the division concerned with agriculture at Berne that the peasant-cum-industrial worker earned his livelihood cheaply; but if the whole family has to be overworked the price in our opinion seems excessive.

196. If, as suggested by H. Roh[2] and Dr Zipfel, industry were decentralized, the smaller numbers engaged in agriculture would not necessarily mean the depopulation of the countryside. In their *Essai d'histoire de la Vallée d'Hérens*, the Abbés Gaspoz and Tamini exhort the people to preserve 'their ancestral simplicity and frugality, which are basic factors in making an honest living ... and the habits of faith, work, and thrift'. Today, fearing lest these traditional attributes of the people should lead them to emigrate to the towns, the Abbé Crétol, who is Rector of the Châteauneuf Agricultural School, joins in the demands for the industrialization of the highland valleys.

Hand-weaving and wood-carving will not suffice to solve the problem. The existence at Saint-Nicholas below Zermatt of a factory employing 400 workers has enabled tracks to be constructed, the school-leaving age to be raised, and rural housing to be improved. In five years thirty-five chalets have been built, but, although they continue to tend the land near the village, the factory employees are abandoning their *mayens*. The risk of agricultural recession attaching to a subsistence economy underpinned by subsidiary occupations is already clearly in evidence at Saint-Chaffrey, and we do not believe that the future of the Val d'Anniviers lies in this direction. Rather does it depend on the resuscitation of the pastoral industry along modern lines, and this goal can only be attained by specialized stock-farming based on summer grazing and intensive crop-growing for winter fodder on holdings larger than at present, combined with a programme of re-equipment generously subsidized by the State. Failing this, the proletarian of the twenty-first century will not be the factory worker, but the highland peasant, notwithstanding his possession of independent means of subsistence.

Calculations made by the Swiss Peasants' Union have clearly shown the economic inferiority of the very small holding. In 1943 fifty-seven working days per acre were spent on farms of $7\frac{1}{2}$ to $12\frac{1}{2}$ acres, as compared with twenty-three for farms over 75 acres. The latter figure is still fairly high in comparison with better equipped countries, like

---

[1] The school is only open for six months; the teacher is only paid for this time, and returns to her father's farm in the summer or works in a hotel.

[2] *Décentralisation et développement industriels* (Sion, 1952).

England and the Netherlands—not to speak of the United States! Statistics for 1949 show that the output of one day's work increases steadily from 8 francs 32 for the first of the above categories—although one could quote very much lower figures from the highlands—to 16 francs 38 for the second. With these facts at our disposal, it is curious to read the Favre declaration of 21 March 1950, which proposes to 'call a halt to the exodus from the countryside and to the declining number of small independent holdings'. This policy was first put forward long ago, but has been signally unsuccessful, as proved by the fact that Switzerland had 206,000 cattle-owners in 1913, 181,200 in 1946, and only 169,400 in 1952. From 36 per cent. in 1888, the percentage of agricultural population has fallen to 19 per cent. today.

197. The small size of farms in Switzerland is hindering the modernization, re-equipment, and intensification of agriculture. In spite of this, official publications are for ever singing the praises of the good old days and thus implying their approval of obsolete methods. Apposite in this context is the beautiful and most interesting book by Dr Laur, 'Le paysan suisse, sa patrie et son œuvre'. Here one finds a great number of illustrations portraying various types of manual work—hoeing, transporting the harvest on the back in *hottes*, hay-making with scythes, etc.—but their obsoleteness and the need for modernization are not stressed.[1]

It is appalling to find writers, whether they be scientists or men of letters, praising the unnecessary toil of an already arduous calling when they are not disposed to wield the scythe or carry the *hotte* themselves. Meanwhile, the traditional exports of cheese and condensed milk have fallen by 70 per cent. and 95 per cent. respectively since 1913. Switzerland's proportion of agricultural population is analogous to that of the Netherlands, but whereas the latter exports twice as much food as she imports, the former in 1939 produced only 52 per cent. of the calories she consumed (but 80 per cent. of the value). The physical background of the two countries is vastly different, but does not wholly explain this contrast; one must also consider that Switzerland has tried to stabilize her peasant population before seeking to raise its productivity.

The problem of the highlands will not be resolved by subsidies 'to

[1] Not having grasped the idea that all forms of modern development lead to a decline in the numbers needed for the production of bare necessities, Laur finds 'the decrease in the population [of Anniviers] alarming'. All the same, in a summary of *L'Agriculture suisse* he observes: 'The use of binders is somewhat limited by the small size of the holdings and of their fields.' A little later he writes: 'The best and most progressive farms are the medium-sized ones' ($12\frac{1}{2}$ to 75 acres).

encourage domestic peasant industries' (Laur); nor by raising a tariff barrier against tropical oil-seeds and substituting butter for them, as the same author proposed immediately after the war, when Europe was still practically starving. On the contrary, it will necessitate study of farming types and of the degree of intensiveness appropriate to different situations; in particular, special provision will have to be made for the supply of equipment, on the lines of the marginal land scheme in England.

The extension of pasture and consequently the lowering of intensiveness on the more difficult land will, like the introduction of more machinery and equipment, lead to a decline in the agricultural population, but only thus can the soil be kept in production, and this, in our opinion, should be the primary objective. Unless greater efforts are made and directed specifically towards the re-equipment of highland agriculture, rendering it better adapted than heretofore to the particularly rigorous physical conditions of this region, the Val d'Anniviers will continue to be invaded by scrub and weeds. The Swiss Government has been at pains to retain too many peasants in the highland zone, and is now in danger of keeping none of them there at all.[1]

[1] Difficulties of modernization appear to be greater in the Val d'Anniviers than in the rest of the Valais. We have purposely chosen a problematic region which is not representative of Switzerland as a whole. On the plateau, the country achieves high yields per acre and a commendable level of labour productivity. The following chapter, on the other hand, describes an example which is typical of the rest of the Tyrol, though not of Austrian agriculture as a whole.

IX

The Stubaital in the Tyrolean Alps. Cultivation Modernized[1]

1. Milk, Butter, and Flour the Basis of Life

198. Coming from the Valais, one traverses practically the whole of Switzerland, crossing the Rhine and then taking the Arlberg Pass, before reaching the Inn Valley, with its *foehn*-ripened maize. From Innsbruck one follows the famous Brenner route along the Wipptal and the River Sill as far as the first valley opening out on the right. This is the Stubaital. The gorges which guard its entrance are not so deep as those of the Navisance, and access is therefore considerably easier. Very soon it widens out and, apart from some short breaks of slope, the gradients near the valley bottom are lower than in the Val d'Anniviers.

The settlement of Fulpmes (Fig. 18) is connected by narrow-gauge railway with Innsbruck. It has an important metallurgical industry, with several factories, and has thus become a small focus of urban life. Between here and the neighbouring settlements of Telfes and Mieders the field boundaries lie parallel to the contours, and a few small terraces signify that this area has known the plough since early times; near the forest, on the other hand, where the gradient steepens, the occasional fields are aligned down the slope, perhaps an indication that here the hoe remained in use much longer.

Potatoes and clover have alternated in these fields, probably since the reign of Marie-Therese; lucerne, which now dominates the *endroit*, has been grown for the past eighty years, whereas maize grown for fodder, which reaches a height of 10 ft., is a recent introduction. A

---

[1] Field studies in the Tyrol as a whole in April 1948 under the guidance of Dr Liebscher of the Chamber of Agriculture. Later, between the end of August and September 1952, we returned to Neustift, where we were helped by a large number of farmers, notably by Vitus Falbesoner, Franz Hofer, and the Stern family.

four- or five-course rotation is generally followed: wheat, potatoes, rye or oats, maize, barley or oats and, from time to time, a long ley under lucerne. At one time the rotation no doubt approximated to that of the Inn Valley, where the field layout is similar and where the rotation typical of north-east France—fallow, wheat, and oats—was practised, and subsequently modified by the substitution of row crops and temporary grasses for fallow.

Nearly all the farms of Fulpmes are situated in either one of the two settlements, Fulpmes itself or Medraz; two-thirds of those of the adjoining commune of Telfes are accounted for by a single but rather scattered agglomeration, and the case of Mieders is similar.

Upstream from Medraz, settlement becomes dispersed, either in straggling hamlets of two or three houses or else in completely isolated farms. The forest, which from Fulpmes onwards generally reaches down to the vicinity of the river on the *Schadenseite*, or shady side, rises again near the hamlet of Kampl, which is the first settlement in the commune of Neustift. On the upstream side an enormous alluvial fan locates a series of hamlets: Herrengasse, Schmieden, Neder. Here in the main valley begins the commune's belt of intensive agriculture, nearly a mile wide and reaching as far as Neustift itself.

Along this stretch of the valley farms also appear on the *endroit*, often on a small terrace 130 to 250 ft. above the valley bottom and separated from it by a steep drop. This slope is under grass opposite Fulpmes, but here it is cultivated, and is divided into square fields which were probably worked with hoes for a very long time. This is not supported, however, by oral tradition, which knows only the swing plough drawn by mules or oxen, which often fell on such precipitous slopes. Since 1930 this has gradually been replaced by the mould-board plough and often by a small type of Brabant plough, which is most in evidence today.

199. Traditionally in these highlands the rotation consisted of alternating crops with grasslands. An example of this system, which Dr Laur calls the 'Celtic system', was observed on the eastern side of the Wipptal, and it consisted of allowing arable land periodically to revert to grassland, a practice locally known as *Natur-Egarten*. At Schirm, 4,750 ft. above sea-level in the upper valley of a right-hand-bank tributary of the Sill, a twelve-year ley, consisting mainly of yellow oat-grass which gives such fine hay, regularly follows a four-course arable rotation of potatoes and three cereal crops. South of Sobald Hall at Rinn, which overlooks a lateral moraine of the Inn and is perched on a terrace at 3,600 ft., temporary grassland, the modern equivalent of the

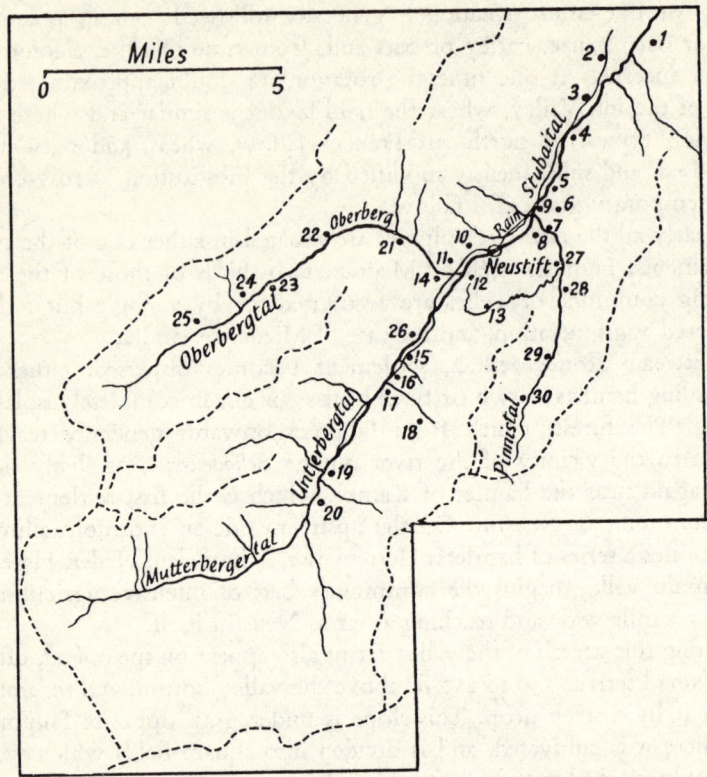

FIG. 18. Neustift, or the Upper Stubaital.

1. Mieders; 2. Telfes; 3. Fulpmes; 4. Medraz; 5. Kampl; 6. Herrengasse; 7. Schmieden; 8. Obergasse; 9. Neder; 10. Kartnall; 11. Forrhach; 12. Auten; 13. Autenalm; 14. Milders; 15. Kröszbach; 16. Gasteig; 17. Volderau; 18. Misbachalm; 19. Falbeson; 20. Ranalt; 21. Barenbad; 22. Seduk; 23. Stocklern; 24. Oberiss-Hütte; 25. Alpeineralm; 26. Oberegg; 27. Herzeben; 28. Iszenalm; 29. Pinnisalm; 30. Karalm.

spontaneous ley, is intercalated between periods of intensive cultivation, and arable and grassland occupy the same acreage.

The alternation of an arable rotation with spontaneous leys is occasionally found at Neustift, where it is still practised on some 5 to 7 acres. Vitus Falbesoner gave the following rotation as traditional on the *Sonnenseite* of the main valley: potatoes and two years of cereals, followed by three or four years under grass. The bad farmers have tended to persist in allowing these leys to revert naturally to grass, but the better ones have been quick to sow their temporary grasslands, which they then call *Kunst-Egarten*.

On the other hand, the *Schadenseite*, like the highland valleys and even like some parts of the *Sonnenseite*, was traditionally characterized, we were told, by an alternation of winter rye and summer barley. That this is a fairly old practice[1] is confirmed by the survey of 1856, which also shows it as being more prevalent during the last century than today. On the maps permanent grassland is indicated in green, dark for hay meadows and light for grazing land; arable land is shown in yellow, the colour of corn. This suggests that there was a clear distinction between grass and arable land and that they did not alternate with each other on the same ground. The valley bottom which was too wet for cultivation and the abundant hay from the mountains, where cutting took place even on precipitous escarpments, were enough to assure supplies of fodder without recourse to the arable land. On the whole, however, the area available for cultivation was fairly restricted, especially in the highland valleys and on the shady sides, where the fields with a favourable aspect were too few to be allowed periodically to revert to grass. In 1772 the population of the commune reached 1,700. The size of the church, which, judging by its beautiful painted ceiling, dates from the same period, tends to confirm this figure.

Unlike the Val d'Anniviers, the Stubaital had considerable areas devoted to crops, often upwards of 2 or 3 acres per family, and these areas were on the land most favoured in point of fertility, aspect, and, wherever possible, gentleness of gradient. Apart from minor invasions of spontaneous grassland, cereals remained the only crops cultivated on this terrain until the beginning of the century. Potatoes were not completely unknown, but they were grown very sparingly. They had long been confined to patches of a few square yards in the small vegetable gardens, and by the end of the nineteenth century they still barely occupied a twentieth of the arable area—that is, between $\frac{1}{8}$ and $\frac{1}{8}$ acre per farm.

200. The diet was based on the two hardy cereals, rye and barley, and on skim milk. By 1914 the peasant was eating more in the way of potatoes, but his diet remained more or less unchanged throughout the year. Soup was the regular meal in the early morning. This was made by diluting flour fried in lard or butter with water and then adding *Musz*, a mixture of flour and skim milk with a little lard. About nine o'clock came the *Vormittag*, a dish of potatoes baked in

---

[1] With the high rainfall, fallows provoke leaching and the degradation of soils; they also lead to erosion on the slopes.

their skins and eaten with skim milk. Then at midday a pot of fresh curds made from skim milk was cooked with flour and a little lard, and at four o'clock there followed a light meal of rye or barley bread, on which the more fortunate families would spread a little butter, dipped in skim milk. Supper consisted of potatoes, this time with *Musz*. On Saturdays it was the custom to bake a pie with fresh curds and pastry made from rye flour mixed with poppy seeds.

The reliance on flour, rather than on bread, as in western Europe, and on fresh milk, often skimmed, forms a link between the cereal régime of the southern Alps in France and the meat and cheese diet of the Val d'Anniviers. Cheese was almost entirely replaced, except for small amounts made from goat's milk, by fresh curds. As for meat, even at Christmas the peasant would not invariably kill a pig. Although a small quantity of castrated goats and sheep were slaughtered from time to time, beef was reserved for the four great annual feasts and otherwise remained extremely rare.

Even though there was a much stronger bias towards cereals than in Anniviers, local farm practice betrayed the influence of pastoralism at every turn. Common rights for grazing sheep and goats on the fields between 15 October and 15 March survive to this day. Although cereals suffer little if at all in consequence and may well survive the snow all the better for having been lightly grazed, the case is different with certain other crops. At Rinn, for example, we noticed that the rape crop had been seriously damaged by this practice, which is a legacy from the time when the region looked to its stock for the basis of its livelihood.

The only vegetables known until the present century were lettuces in the summer and *Sauerkraut* in the winter, both products of the *Krautgarten*, which was analogous to the *choulière* of Briançonnais.[1] Chives were also grown on the lower land and brought up to the alpine pastures in boxes, a custom which prevented serious vitamin deficiencies in the summer. In contrast with the French highland peasant, the people here drink hardly any wine nowadays, and even their consumption of beer is very small. On the other hand, the Tyrolese eat rather more vegetables, more meat, especially pork, and much more in the way of potatoes and butter. The latter is the luxury item in the peasant diet. There is even a certain amount of wastage, for milk is more profitably used for making cheese, as in Anniviers, than in making butter. Today, however, the separator, which first appeared in 1898, is widely used even on the small farms.

[1] *Voyages en France d'un agronome*, Chapter I.

2. The Richest Sector—The Sunny Side of the Main Valley

201. The commune of Neustift embraces the whole of the lower part of the valley and, with its 63,000 acres and 2,000 inhabitants, it is comparable in size with the Val d'Anniviers. The official figure of 252 farmers calls for comment. Sixty-four of them have no cattle, nineteen of them have only one cow, and the individuals in these two groups mostly either practise another trade, have independent means, or have more or less retired. In contrast with the Valais, the real farm here has a minimum of two cows, which are kept both for milking and for draught. There are 125 small farms with between two and four cows, forty of medium size with between five and nine cows, and each with from seven to twenty-seven head of cattle in all, and, finally, five large farms with ten to twelve cows and a total of thirty-five to forty-two head, including calves.

The farms on the *Sonnenseite*, from Rain to Kartnall and Forrhach, are easily the most prosperous in the commune. There are seventeen farms in all, including three small or very small ones with between six and nine head of cattle; but the remainder have between ten and forty-two head apiece. The Census shows that only about 7 per cent. of the farmers live here, but they account for a fifth of the commune's 1,625 cattle, and a quarter of the 1,000 sheep, and for 135 of the 1,000 goats which here can no longer be regarded simply as the 'poor man's cows'. The equipment is comparatively up-to-date. Of the twenty farms in the commune possessing electric motor winches, twelve are here. These were introduced in 1937 and have proved simple and economical to work.[1] In combination with the three-wheeled cart, they have replaced the work of men with baskets for hauling soil back up-slope, and in so doing have removed a cause of early death from cardiac complaints.[2] As the following example shows, they have also permitted the survival, for the time being at any rate, of a form of cultivation which would otherwise have become completely obsolete. In a day, 60-yd. furrows can be cut on $1\frac{2}{3}$ acres of steep land with a cable-drawn plough, and with 100-yd. furrows the area can be increased to 2 acres. The average figure, including time taken to set up the winch, can be taken as $1\frac{1}{4}$ acres a day.

The cable is hauled up at about 30 in. a second, and the operation

[1] 1 schilling—nearly $3\frac{1}{2}d.$ in 1952—per kilowatt-hour.

[2] Witness the stone tablets which one finds on the paths near the scene of an accident and their rather naïve inscriptions asking the passer-by to pray for the victim's soul, in case it should still be in Purgatory.

requires two or three men. One man does the actual ploughing, guides the plough with the wheel, rides on it uphill, and steadies it on the descent; another man works the motor and checks the descent; and a third often watches the pulleys; while a boy with a fork ensures that the tall corn stubble left by the sickle is all thrown back into the furrows. The depth of ploughing is only 4 or 5 in., and the stubble has already been cut a second time[1] with scythes so as to facilitate its burial beneath the thin slice of earth. The more level ground is ploughed with the help of a horse or a cow, whereas the practice in the larger settlements downstream is to use a head yoke and a pair of animals. This job, as in the overpopulated parts of western France, always takes two people, one of them leading the animals.

202. Franz Hofer, who lives in the hamlet of Rain, has a holding which is representative of the fine farms on this side of the valley. He has $6\frac{1}{4}$ acres of arable land and follows a seven- or eight-year rotation. Two or three years of lucerne, which does well on these well-drained slopes, are followed by three years of cereals and two of row crops. He obtains an average of 550 gallons of milk from each of his seven or eight cows. He sells fully 4 cwt. of butter a year, but his household, which comprises ten people in all, consumes half as much again, or about 66 lb. per head per annum, which is as much as in some farms in Thiérache and practically a world record. The farm itself, therefore, which is larger than the average, consumes 60 per cent. of one of its own main products. Similarly, the family drinks between $2\frac{2}{3}$ and $3\frac{1}{3}$ gallons of skim milk each day, and three cows are kept back on the farm every summer mainly to keep the household supplied. The remaining four or five cows, together with calves, and ten goats are taken up to the 70 acres of private alpine pastures in the Oberbergtal between Seduk and Stocklern. The ten sheep are herded as part of a collective flock much higher in the same valley in the vicinity of Alpeineralm.

The farm is very well equipped; there are three electric motors and a stationary petrol engine, three modern ploughs and as many harrows, two potato-lifters, a pounding machine, a grain mill, a mower, a seed drill, a machine for preparing silage, and a threshing machine. In addition there are three winches for ploughing on slopes. There are also two pumps for distributing dung-water through 1,300 ft. of pipes, a very common device on the Swiss plateau, but mostly absent in the

[1] This is common practice in North Vietnam (Chapter IV), where, during a shortage of either fodder or fuel, the field is worked over a third time and every tuft of stubble is pulled up by hand.

THE FAVOURED SUNNY SIDE OF THE MAIN VALLEY

Valais. The land utilization comprises $2\frac{1}{4}$ acres of row crops, nearly 3 of cereals[1] and $1\frac{5}{8}$ of lucerne, the first and last of these items being particularly noteworthy. The type of farming is thus much more intensive and mechanized than in the Val d'Anniviers. After the rye harvest, a catch-crop of vetch-oats mixture is sown and is ready for either hay or grazing by October. The winches do most of the work, and a pair of heifers is harnessed on only about ten days in the year for transport to the village.

Six of the farms in the commune, two of them in the tributary valley of Oberberg, are equipped for pumping a mixture of manure and dung-water to fields and meadows on the up-slope side, while several more have pipes for gravity distribution. Furthermore, Franz Hofer also has a rotating sprinkler with which he can water his potato crop during a dry spring. It will be remembered that at Vissoie this method of irrigation was reserved for strawberries, vegetables, and other garden products; here the technique is extended to field crops. Grain crops, which are sown in rows 6 in. apart, are weeded with Dutch hoes 4 in. wide, an operation which takes nearly four days per acre. At Fisz, 4,600 ft. above sea-level on the right bank of the Inn above Landeck, fields are divided into parallel bands 30 in. wide and 40 ft. long, and alternate bands carry three rows of wheat and two of garlic respectively. The manure is spread twice a year very evenly and yields reach 24 and even 32 cwt. to the acre. These methods are evidently more akin to horticulture than to the usual techniques of field cultivation.

Notwithstanding the importance of crop-growing, apart from 7 or 8 tons of seed potatoes which are here favoured by the climate, the Hofer establishment sells animal products almost exclusively. Apart from the 4 cwt. of butter already mentioned, five to seven cattle are marketed annually. As far as possible these animals are sold between the ages of three and six, when the cows are in calf for the second or third time. In addition to these, fifteen one-month-old kids are sold each year, together with four or five eight-month lambs weighing about 85 lb. apiece. Finally, pig-rearing and poultry-keeping are very

[1] $1\frac{5}{8}$ acres of potatoes, $\frac{3}{8}$ of fodder beet, $\frac{1}{8}$ acre of maize for silage (silo with capacity of nearly 30 cu. yds.), $1\frac{1}{8}$ of winter wheat (reintroduced in 1936 after an initial setback about 1870), $\frac{3}{4}$ of winter rye, $\frac{1}{2}$ of summer barley, $\frac{1}{2}$ of oats; oats are an unusual crop in this commune. Yields of 1 ton an acre are obtained for cereals (more for wheat and less for oats) and 10 tons an acre for potatoes; these are above the average for the commune. The latter has about 310 acres of arable land of which perhaps 125 are under sown grasses, 100 under row crops (potatoes), and 85 under cereals (barley, rye, and wheat in descending order of importance).

strongly established the attraction being that they handsomely repay the cost of foodstuffs and usefully augment the size of a farming concern which has only a limited area at its disposal. The purchase of a dozen tons or so of coarse grain, bran and cake means that Hofer can market ten to twenty pigs a year, either for breeding (240 lb.) or for slaughtering (330 lb.); German-speaking countries like their pork fatter than do the English or even the French. About 100 selected fowls produce a total of some 17,000 eggs a year, 15,000 of which are sold fetching 10,000 schillings (£140).

203. The cattle feed is still based essentially on hay from permanent grasslands which are of two types. In the bottom of the Ruetz Valley, Franz Hofer has $7\frac{1}{2}$ acres of meadow which can be cut twice a year, yielding $2\frac{1}{2}$ to 4 tons of rather mediocre hay, inferior to that of the Valais, per acre. He has six barns, or *Stadel*, here, four new and two old ones for storage, and the largest of them which is sited by the road is connected to the farm by an aerial cable which can take loads of 12 cwt. This device means that hay can be brought up with the minimum of inconvenience for here, as throughout the region, it is wholly consumed on the farm itself.

In the old days it was carried on small carts drawn by horn-yoked[1] oxen. Cows, on the contrary, have long been harnessed with collars like those used for horses, a fact which suggests that they have not been used so long as oxen for draught purposes. Collars are being used more and more nowadays for the oxen as well.[2] Whereas the farm was here only 260 ft. above the bottom meadows and animal transport was perfectly practicable, the case was quite different for Kartnall and even more so for Forrhach,[3] where the highest farms on the *Sonnen-*

[1] Found also at Schirm, but the withers-yoke is used at Fisz.

[2] The commune is recorded as having 28 draught horses including mares, 3 mules, 70 dual-purpose cows (milk and draught), 17 draught oxen and 5 bulls used in harness. These statistics, however, seem to be about 10 per cent. short of the real figures. The small, stocky horses of the Hoflinger breed, which serve equally well as pack animals as in harness, are more numerous than before the war in this Tyrolean 'retreat'. They are fewer in numbers at higher levels, and there are none, for instance, at Schirm.

[3] Forrhach is at 4,575 ft., and its interests are exclusively pastoral; the single farm, unlike the two at Kartnall, has none of the 'agricultural' character of the remainder of the *Sonnenseite*. On the $17\frac{1}{4}$ acres which adjoin the buildings there is now a mere $\frac{1}{4}$ acre of arable land, where potatoes, poppy, and barley-rye mixtures are grown. The farmer does his best to keep his flourishing fields of lucerne (the soil is rather limy) as long as possible—sometimes for as much as eighteen years—without resowing; even at this height they give him three cuttings a year and a grazed aftermath.

seite upstream of Neustift are situated. The differences in level here are 900 ft. and 1,150 ft. respectively, and in the latter case the cable is 1,500 ft. long and can carry 4 cwt. at a time. These cables have eased the transport problem very considerably, and have given greater opportunities for commercial exchange.

On Hofer's newly built farm, the stone house, which faces the sun, and the three-storied wooden byre-barn behind it are both under the same roof. The ground level is occupied by cattle and horses, the pigsty is at a slightly lower level, and the goats are kept separate. Sawdust, for stable litter,[1] and tools are stored on the first floor, and the top storey is used for hay and sheaves of corn which are wheeled up along a ramp. The grain is stored on a platform above the hay. Originally these barns were built mainly for keeping grain and hay was brought from the *Stadel* a little at a time as required.

Each year, in the clearings on the steep, wooded slopes above the farm, Hofer makes hay from half his 19 acres of mountain meadows. The annual yield is about 6 tons, or approximately $1\frac{1}{3}$ cwt. per acre every two years, which is a very good figure for this type of land, and the hay is brought down for consumption on the farm. This crop of mountain hay is a rare feature on the *Schadenseite*, but meadows cover a considerable proportion of the more favoured left flank of each of the three valleys. At the upper limit of the zone, which reaches about 7,500 ft. above Stocklern in the Oberbergtal, the grass is cut once in three or four years, the poorest terrain yielding as little as 45 lb. of hay to the acre.

In contrast with the up-to-date methods employed on some of the arable land this use of mountain meadows is linked with the remote past. The concentration of fertilizing elements on the fields and meadows of the lower slopes and bottom land and the constant depredation of the high mountain sides to this end are features which it shares with the Celtic system.[2] In Anniviers the stock was fed, at considerable inconvenience, in a large number of dispersed byre-barns, but the wide distribution of manure which resulted was a positive achievement. Here, however, most of the farmers use only shovels and wheelbarrows for spreading dung-water, and only manure is actually transported by the cartload.

[1] Elsewhere spruce needles and mosses are used for this purpose; lower down, these are replaced by oak leaves and even by sand from the bed of the Inn. A considerable proportion of the straw has to be chopped up and fed to animals.

[2] Comparable in some aspects with the *ouche* of Morvan and the *terre chaude* of Brittany.

Upstream of Neustift the valley sides steepen, but they have long been divided into small fields surrounded by walls built with stones cleared from the soil. They sometimes show evidence of terracing and extend lengthways down the slopes. These features suggest that hoe cultivation probably persisted until quite recently, and the workers were no doubt part-time farmers who came from nearby Neustift. Tradition has it that, originally, these slopes were communally-owned rough grazings, and today they are, to a small extent, reverting to this type of use. There is, however, very little rough grazing land in the commune, and a more significant change is the increasing number of meadows. Higher up the break of slope remains wooded, and the more continuous nature of the tree cover is directly related to the greater height of the farms at Kartnall and Forrhach, which lie above the forests.

3. The Wet Meadows of the Valley Bottom. Haymaking by Hand

204. The gently sloping lower portion of this glaciated valley has been artificially drained for a very long time, but the scope of the original works was obviously limited by the methods and facilities of the period. The many water seepages at present would, in the absence of an official Works Service, which would be much appreciated here, make a comprehensive drainage scheme rather expensive. 'It is a pity,' remarked Vitus Falbesoner, 'that these 195 acres cannot be ploughed; they could produce grain for the whole commune.' This progressive-minded farmer-cum-hotel-keeper obviously favours cereal cultivation wherever possible, but the broad flood plain of the valley, with its damp, acidic soils, which sometimes favour marsh-loving flora, has remained under grass. The scattered *Stadel*, or barns for storing hay, have long been a feature of this lowland. Here they are devoid of byres, but are still fairly large, some of the oldest being nearly 12 ft. square and averaging about 8 ft. in height. Along the upper part of the walls, where a hungry animal cannot reach, spaces are left between the wooden stakes so as to help the hay, which is often brought in while still damp, to dry. The spaces are generally wider on the side away from the prevailing wind, where there is less chance of the rain beating in.

As the price of timber rose in response to the growing opportunities for export and as the saw-mills, now powered by the same falls which had previously located the primitive mills, got into their stride, the *Stadel* began to be constructed of heavy wooden boards. The new ones, built of planks, often measure over 30 ft. square and 16 to 20 ft. in height. The roof is always of the ridge type, and either tiles or Everit, which are more pleasing to the eye than the corrugated iron of Vissoie, have replaced the wooden shingles of former times. The old type of barn, which was adapted to the transport of hay on the back,[1] had an opening with vertical slots on either side which was gradually boarded up as further supplies of hay were stored away. The modern layout comprises a large door at each end with a central passage between them. The small four-wheeled carts,[2] adapted to the narrow lanes which have been built in this difficult country, come in through one door, are off-loaded, and pass out through the other. The recent inauguration of this type of arrangement emphasizes the late introduction of draught animals for the transport of hay.

The nature of the flora shows evidence of an excess of humidity and nitrogenous manure, whereas calcium and phosphates are always deficient. The rainfall is fairly high, in the region of 45 in. a year. The régime is characterized by a slight minimum in the spring and sometimes again in the autumn, and by a marked July-August period of maximum, which often embraces the months of June and September as well. The contrast with the Valais is self-evident, but although there is no need for irrigation,[3] the heavy summer rain militates against the ripening of grain and hinders the haymaking.

205. In common with Bavaria, Bohemia, and Scandinavia, this region from time immemorial has had to devise means to dry its fodder crops and prevent them from rotting. The basic principle is to keep them clear of the ground during wet weather. A practice which served for many years and which one still finds occasionally in the Kaiser Gebirge west of Berchtesgaden was to make use of conveniently placed lateral tree branches. Young pines and spruces were particularly suitable, as they retained a small proportion of these branches wherever the forest thinned out. For well over a century, however (longer than the Paris Basin), the Tyrol has employed the *Stiefel*. This is a vertical pole, buried to a depth of well over 1 ft. with the help of a heavy iron bar, and stands about 5 ft. high. It has three bars, each about 2 ft. long, forming a horizontal 'H' slightly above ground level. These are placed about 12 ft. apart in low-lying meadows and are loaded with the

---

[1] And not on the head, as in Ötztal.

[2] The same type of cart has been observed as far afield as Hungary and Lorraine, but it is generally larger in the lowlands.

[3] Irrigation is practised in the Upper Inn valley on south-facing slopes where the soil is light (e.g. Grins).

half-dried hay if rain threatens. The first cutting in July or August yields some 13 lb. of hay per *Stiefel*, the second in late August and early September only about 9 lb., as the grass is then shorter.

When the rain stops, the hay is spread over the ground again by hand. When dry it is raked together and pitch-forked into carts. The latter often remain stationary, and the men bring in the hay, held high on their forks, from all corners of the meadow. The animal, therefore, is often used only for drawing the fully loaded cart from the field. It is significant that, although used for cultivation in the remote past, traditionally it played no part in the haymaking, which was carried out by manual labour alone. On small farms, or where the farm is below the meadow, men still bring in the hay themselves, and when the road is uphill they willingly add their weight to help the straining horse or cow.

The tractor-drawn mower and horse-rake are in use at Rinn, but both are unknown in this commune, which boasts only eight horse-drawn mowers and the same number of motor mowers. These machines are employed almost exclusively on the land of the individuals who own them, and even here they are not exploited to the full. The scythe persists, for example, on valley-bottom meadows which are perfectly level and accessible to machinery. Boys learn to handle the scythe from the age of ten, but the women of the region, unlike those of the Valais, are rarely seen with the sickle. Indeed, far from being the province of women and children, agriculture retains a strong labour force of able-bodied men—so much so that outdated practices have tended to survive, although this is more clearly discernible in the management of grassland than in the cultivation of crops. The women follow behind the scythe and carefully spread the grass in a thin, uniform layer with their forks, so as to promote drying. In September, when there is less sunshine than in June, this operation becomes increasingly necessary, especially at the foot of slopes on the shady side of the valley.

4. The Retreat of Arable Land and Cereals on the *Schadenseite*

206. Further downstream, the large alluvial fan formed by the river which emerges from the Pinnistal offers a certain number of favoured locations on the *Schadenseite*. The amount of arable land remains considerable, especially at Herrengasse, which includes some large farms. Both Kampl and Neder, however, have a large proportion of artisans, most of them engaged in the wood industry: sawyers, carpenters, cabinet-makers, and wheelwrights; also masons and merchants of various

kinds. All these people still work part-time on the land. Even those who depend exclusively on farming have smaller holdings and less equipment than farmers on the opposite side of the valley.

Anton Schneider, the 'captain'[1] of the peasants of Neustift, sows only $\frac{5}{8}$ acre of cereals, a little over half this area of row crops, and $\frac{2}{5}$ acre of rotation grasses. The first and second of these items thus represent a smaller proportion of the arable land than on Hofer's farm. There are $6\frac{2}{3}$ acres of meadows giving two crops a year on the valley bottom and adjoining slopes and about 50 acres of mountain meadows. He keeps eight head of cattle, including four cows which average 420 gallons, three pigs, three goats, and eighteen hens, but no sheep. The work is done by the farmer himself, and he occasionally does a few hours of paid work off the farm. He is helped by his wife and three children. They have had thirteen children altogether, but one died young and 'Adolf took two of the others'. The remainder have left home in search of work elsewhere. The farm possesses more equipment than one generally finds in this commune, and has an electric motor, a separator, a mowing machine, a dung-water pump, a winnowing machine, a plough, and a harrow. Two cows suffice to bring in the hay and work the few acres of arable land.

The two farms, Hofer's and Schneider's, have been compared statistically[2] on the basis of 'adjusted productive area' which is given as 44 acres for the former and $15\frac{1}{2}$ for the latter. Taking these somewhat arbitrary figures, the number of cattle and yields of milk per acre appear to be the same in both cases. The smaller farm, however, deploys three times as much manpower per unit area, but, owing to its comparative lack of pigs and poultry, draws a mere 1,724 schillings gross per acre as compared with 2,872 for Hofer's farm. On the latter, one man's work over the course of a year yields some 35,000 schillings gross, but on Schneider's holding this amount falls to 6,860 schillings.

There are worse cases than Schneider's, and the same study reveals similar discrepancies in the productivity of farms in the lowland, where one unmechanized holding produced 25,000 schillings per man per year as against 69,000 for a farm with modern equipment. These figures also reveal the difficulties of the upland farmer and strongly suggest that his days are numbered unless he mechanizes his methods and, to some extent, unless he begins to use the land less intensively. It will never be possible to mechanize haymaking on the mountain meadows, and they will inevitably have to be given over to grazing.

[1] The word *Fuehrer* has been replaced by *Hauptmann*.
[2] *Osterreichische Landtecknik*, No. 5 of 1952.

The *Schadenseite* can be followed upstream, between Neder and Neustift, along the Obergasse terrace. Here the farms, finding themselves short of land, are clearing some of the private forests on the slope above them[1] and converting them into meadows still littered with stumps. A similar extension of grassland is in evidence on the *Sonnenseite*, particularly above Kartnall. The commune had 1,240 inhabitants at the end of the nineteenth century and has over 2,000 today. The rate of increase has slowed down very considerably since 1930 more as a result of emigration—there are seventy local girls in service in Switzerland—than of any slackening in the birth-rate: families with eight or ten children are still common.

About thirty people travel on their bicycles each morning to Fulpmes, where they work in factories. An occupation which can be regarded as ancillary to farming is the wood industry—Austria is often said to have a sylvo-pastoral economy—and there is also a tourist industry. Whereas in Anniviers catering for tourists was kept quite distinct from agriculture, many of the farms here let a few of their rooms in the summer, sometimes providing board as well, and some have virtually added hotel-keeping to their list of activities. Nevertheless, two-thirds of the working population are still employed in agriculture and forestry. The large number of people thus engaged necessitates a high degree of agricultural intensiveness and justifies the clearing of woodland, which provides comparatively little employment, for the establishment of meadows.

207. The valley narrows even more above Neustift, while the forest reaches down almost to the flood-plain meadows and the cultivated area becomes even less. The last farm on this side of the valley which still grows cereals is at Auten, almost opposite Milders. Built in 1414, it has a fine, vaulted porch; at nearby Forrhach even the rooms are still vaulted. As we have seen, the arable fields on this right bank of the valley, with their rotation of rye and barley, were quite distinct from the permanent grassland until about 1900. About this time, Grandfather Stern had a farm on which he kept twelve cows, thirty young cattle, two draught oxen, thirty or forty sheep, eight goats and two pigs. He also employed four farm hands—two women, a cowman and his assistant, and a shepherd in the summer. In addition, one must take into account the work done by the farmer and his family.

The essential differences today are the smaller production of cereals and the concentration on winter wheat, which can now be made to ripen much earlier than before. The latter has been at the expense of

[1] The same tendency is apparent in Scandinavia.

hardier grains. As far as livestock is concerned, cows have replaced the young cattle to some extent, while sheep, after increasing again during the war owing to the shortage of wool, are now rapidly declining in numbers. This trend is characteristic of most of the Alps today. Here, at the downstream end of the upper part of the commune, goats are slightly on the increase. The largest increase, however, is in the number of pigs.

The farm has been divided between the two brothers who did not leave the district. Anton, who has the larger share, grows only about 2 acres of cereals, which is less than a third of the former acreage. He has $2\frac{1}{4}$ acres of potatoes intercalated with maize grown for fodder, $\frac{5}{8}$ acres of fodder beet, the highest total in the commune, and $7\frac{1}{2}$ acres of clover sown with a cereal. Lucerne does not succeed on the humid soil, which is more akin to the bottom land than to the *Schadenseite*. Snow often lies on the ground for 110 days in the year, from 1 December to 20 March. Twelve and a half acres of meadows provide two hay crops a year. On this shady side, which is much more heavily wooded and less devoted to fodder crops than the other, Anton mows 15 acres of mountain meadow in the vicinity of Autenalm, 5,400 ft. above sea-level. He does this each year, but mows a further 25 acres once in two or three years at an even greater altitude and owns about 250 acres of rough grazing land.

208. The mountain hay is brought down in *Taschen*, or bags with a wooden framework, and tied with rope. They contain about 3 cwt. of hay, and men, using their feet as brakes, guide them down the precipitous, snow-clad slopes. A farm hand can complete two journeys from 5,400 ft. to the farm at 3,350 ft. in a day, and brings down the bags two at a time. The farms of the neighbouring hamlet cut some of their hay in the Mutterbergtal above Ranalt, and this not only means a longer descent, but also involves a nine-mile haul to the farm, with a sledge carrying six to eight bags drawn by a horse or a pair of oxen. About 1900 these teams used to set out from Auten in the winter at about 2 a.m. and would not return till very late evening; it was hard work.

On the better parts of the mountain meadows on the *Sonnenseite* a man assisted by a woman cuts the hay, gathers and stores it in the *Stadel* at an average rate of 4 cwt. a day, or about the same rate as in Haut-Queyras in the French Alps. The Autenalm area is representative of the *Schadenseite*, and here 9 acres cut every two years give about 50 cwt. of hay at a cost of a week's work on the part of four men and two women; thus thirty-six days of work each produce 1·4 cwt. of hay, which is only half the output associated with the byre-barns of Anniviers. Adding four days for bringing down the *Taschen* at 12 cwt. a day, one reaches the final figure of 1·25 cwt. per day's work of hay actually stored on the farm. In the winter, on the other hand, the productivity of labour is very much higher, owing to the layout of the byres, where cleaning and milking are easier than in Anniviers and the mangers are conveniently replenished from trap-doors placed above them.

On the poor, rocky terrain of the high Mutterbergtal, where about $2\frac{1}{2}$ cwt. of hay per acre are cut once in three or four years, the fruits of labour are only about half the previous figure. The 70 lb. or so of hay produced per working day approximates to the lowest recorded figure for fodder production, and is incomparably lower than the average for pastoral nomadism. The highlands, however, are forced to accept this method of haymaking as the price of their overpopulation, notwithstanding the fact that it is too intensive a technique under such difficult conditions.

Today Anton Stern keeps a dozen cows—as many as the grandfather had on the whole farm—but he has only twenty-three young cattle, and the sheep have disappeared completely. He used to have about thirty goats, but they are now down to twelve. On the other hand, he sells about twenty pigs a year. The greater concentration of stock is explained partly by the increased acreage of potatoes and partly by the better facilities for buying feeding-stuffs. The labour force is today distinctly smaller than it was fifty or so years ago, but this is not typical of the small and medium-sized holdings which make up the majority of the farms. Although the herd is almost as large as in 1900, there are now only two farm-hands—one woman, an apprentice, and a herdsman in the summer. The farm generates its own electricity, and has a dung-water pump and a motor-mower.

An examination of the maps of the 1856 survey, in default of statistics relating to this period, reveals that the arable acreage has remained constant, or decreased only very slightly, on the *Sonnenseite* between Rain and Milders; the only exceptions are the very high farms at Forrhach on the upstream side. As one travels upstream along the *Schadenseite*, the decrease becomes more marked from about 25 per cent. at Kampl-Neder to fully 50 per cent. at Obergasse-Auten. At the same time, the proportion of cereals grown on the crop land has diminished, and is now barely equal to that of row crops, while rotation grasses cover two or three times the area.

5. The Retreat of Cereals and Arable Land Even More Marked in the Higher Valleys

209. At Milders the valley bifurcates and continues as the Oberberg on the one hand and the Unterberg on the other. At first the former is enclosed by steep, wooded slopes, but it widens upstream of Barenbad,[1] which is at 4,100 ft. In the district known as Oberberg, one finds a number of fine, well-equipped farms, with ploughing winches and dung-water pumps, situated where the southern aspect compensates for the considerable altitude. The old mills, however, no longer function today, and the retreat of the arable land is very much in evidence. Between two-thirds and three-quarters of the arable land have been converted to meadows—the proportion rising upstream—and the second cutting of hay from these is declining steadily.

The hamlet of Zigiduk (which maps now mark as Seduk, from *seductum*), at 5,000 ft., represents the limit of permanent settlement, and has apparently done so for many centuries. The alpine pastures begin immediately behind it and the animals are grazed on them each day. The settlement comprises seven houses, but today there are actually only three households, which account for one medium-sized farm and two small ones. The latter are both in an extremely precarious economic position, with four times as many children as cows in each instance. There were two farms here thirty years ago; later, and until 1950, there were four.

With two cows in the winter, three in the summer, and a total of seven or eight cattle, including a pair of heifers, Joseph Illmer found himself unable to provide for his ten children. Consequently, he took a job at Fulpmes, as did two of his sons, the family allowances being a big attraction. One daughter got work on a farm-cum-hotel at Rain. The eldest son works the farm with the mother, and three children give a certain amount of extra help. The cows are kept in their byre from 15 October until 15 May, pine needles and a small quantity of bought straw serving as litter. Indeed, the farm no longer grows any cereals at all, has no garden, and cultivates a mere $\frac{1}{8}$ acre of potatoes. The goats, being hardier than cattle, are brought in as late as the end of November, when the ground is completely snow-covered, and are put out again at the end of March. Kids are sold when three or four weeks old and, at 11 lb. weight, fetch about 50 schillings (or 14*s*.).

---

[1] There were forty-six children on the school roll in 1946, but only about thirty in 1952.

Goat's milk is hardly drunk at all, except by the poor. It is more often fed to calves and pigs, which is a wasteful practice, especially when the milk is not skimmed.

The greater part of the butter made from cow's milk is consumed on the farm, which, it must be remembered, has to feed the non-farming members of the family, who are in the majority. The quantity which is sold varies from year to year between 20 and 35 lb. In addition, the eleven hens produce about 200 eggs for sale, but the main source of income is the annual sale of two cows, one six and the other four years old, and one store. Hay sledges, their descent checked by the passenger's foot, bring down loads of up to 2 cwt. at a time from the mountain slopes. In the valley below the hamlet, Illmer obtains 6 tons of hay from two cuttings on his 6 acres of meadows. There are another 6 acres of meadow on a level with the farm, and the single cutting from these yields nearly $4\frac{1}{2}$ tons. The $\frac{5}{8}$ acres of mountain meadow 300 ft. higher up, where bare rock outcrops at the surface, furnish another 24 cwt. This hay is used as winter feed for cattle. The hay cut at higher levels is coarser, and is kept for goats: $4\frac{1}{2}$ acres produce 16 cwt. every other year, and the highest meadow, at over 7,200 ft., extends over $2\frac{1}{2}$ acres and yields 8 cwt. of 'rock hay' every three to six years at a cost of fifteen days of work. The farm possesses no plough and very rarely harnesses its two cows, and then only to a small cart. Nearly all the hay is brought in either on men's shoulders or by sledge. On the meadows above the hamlet the aftermath is too scant to be worth making into hay, and herein lies the main cause of poverty in this settlement, which is by far the highest in the commune.

This aftermath, therefore, is cut green and fed to the milch cows when they return from the alpine pastures, which afford poor grazing towards the end of the season. Animals are never grazed, as in Anniviers, on a meadow used for hay. Their trampling or their dung might spoil a blade of grass! They are pastured only on the rocky or scrubby rough grazings at very high altitudes or along the edges of pathways —in short, only where cutting for hay is absolutely impossible. The provision of winter fodder is still the paramount objective. Not until one reaches Saint-Johann away to the east does one find enclosures on grassland cut for hay, not even where mowing machinery is used.

Our irrational economic structure is partly to blame for the contrast between this region, where haymaking persists in virtually inaccessible places, and others, where grass which could easily be cut is used for grazing. Moreover, the ploughing of alpine slopes on gradients of 1 in 1·5, in contrast with the complete neglect or extensive grazing of enormous grassland regions in America, where both relief and climate appear to favour cultivation, presents an even more striking paradox. On the Illmer farm the productivity of labour is one of the lowest for the commune and is possibly less than half that of the Schneider holding.

210. In the main valley, which rises less steeply—hence its name, Unterberg—the *Sonnenseite* is so sheer that it leaves room for only two groups of farms. The other side of the valley, however, benefits from the presence of alluvial fans which have larger tracts of clear land, notably around the hamlets of Kröszbach and Gasteig, where today the very occasional fields of crops give little indication of their great extent in former times. As at Seduk, the potato and the poppy (for the pie on Saturday and also for bread) are the last crops to survive along the retreating edges of the arable land. On the five farms at Gasteig there are about fifteen potato patches and less than 400 sq. yds. of spring barley, which, like the tiny gardens, are protected from the poultry with stout wooden fences.

The periodic floods of the unregulated torrent, which, as in Sardinia, covers the ground with coarse gravel, are a deterrent to cultivation. Satisfactory crops of potatoes are still obtained, however, and these, together with the good-quality rotation grassland of clover and cock's-foot, remain as a testimony to the extensive ploughlands of a bygone era. Twenty old *Stadel* and two new ones are the visual evidence of the pre-eminence of meadow land, which in this high, narrow valley is so abundantly fed with rain and dung-water that it is comparable in its flora with the irrigated and manured grasslands of Anniviers, and similarly infested with crane's-bill and umbellifers.

Kröszbach is a little lower, and has two fields of barley and two of flax. Whereas the poppy is grown on all the farms of the rich valley below, both large and small, flax is a survival from the subsistence economy of the past and is found today only on a few small holdings. The women spin the fibre in winter and take it to one of the local weavers, of whom only two remain. Significantly, one lives at Neder and the other at Milders, both these hamlets having preserved a stronger subsistence element in their economy than has Neustift. At Kröszbach the peasants not only use the *Stiefel* to dry the tops of the potato plants, which in the absence of straw[1] are pressed into service as fodder or as stable litter; they even do the same with chickweed, an obvious sign

---

[1] At Rain the potato tops are spread under the stable litter to save straw. At Rinn they are made into silage and fed to sheep, a practice which is entirely absent from France, except in Alsace and Lorraine, where there has been more contact with Germanic methods.

of the poverty of their resources. The forty-four farms of the Unterberg possess only 228 head of cattle between them, about 100 less than the seventeen farms of Rain.[1]

Higher up the valley, the farm-cum-hotel of Volderau possesses the only agricultural tractor in the commune, and cultivates two enormous fields of potatoes, on one of which maize for silage is sown between the rows. Profits from the tourist trade and the larger amount of space available have both contributed to the introduction of modern equipment, in spite of the somewhat greater altitude of this farm (3,700 ft.). Unlike the Oberberg, this district has witnessed a retreat of permanent habitation from the higher hamlets. Falbeson, a little further up the valley, was once the permanent home of two families, but is now inhabited only in the summer, while Ranalt at 4,100 ft. has seen its population of ten families and seventy people fall to two and ten respectively. And the tourist industry is now its principal resource. Cereals have disappeared completely, and there remain only a few patches of potatoes. The corollary of this trend, however, is the extension of meadow land or occasionally of alpine pasture; the land is never, as in Anniviers, abandoned altogether.

The disappearance of cereals is even more marked in the communes at high altitudes. At Schirm (4,750 ft.), on a farm which today sows $\frac{1}{4}$ acre of barley, less than half this area of rye, and a little more of potatoes, an inscription carved on the barn shows that in 1830 180 bushels of oats, 24 of barley and 4 of rye had been gathered in—a total of some 66 cwt. of grain, as against 8 cwt. today. Oats, well adapted to the wet climate, stood out as the dominant crop at this period, and were mainly grown for food, but they have now entirely disappeared. The peasants of this hamlet, who still wear home-spun linen, have continued to grow barley, however, sometimes even above 5,200 ft.

6. The Alp and *Mayen* Combined—Individual Herding, Butter-production

211. Unlike his Valaisan counterpart, the Stubaital peasant neither engages in seasonal down-valley migrations, nor does he recognize more than a single stage in the summer pastures of the uplands. These

[1] The Oberberg and Unterberg valleys account for 28 per cent. of the farmers in the commune, and they have far less in the way of non-agricultural resources than the main valley; by contrast, they have only 15 per cent. of the sheep and horses and 26 per cent. of the cattle—but 38 per cent. of the goats. But for the few prosperous farms of Oberberg and Schaller, and the one at Volderau, the tragic poverty of the remainder would be immediately apparent from these figures.

pastures always begin at a comparatively low altitude, but there are marked differences between the three valleys of the commune.

The Pinnistal, which reaches the Ruetz at Schmieden, where a mill and a wood factory have taken the place of the old smithies, is approached along a fairly narrow gorge. It appears never to have been cultivated—at least, not for a very long time. Moreover, the first group of privately owned pastures, known as Herzeben, begins just below 4,000 ft., which is about 1,000 ft. lower than Seduk and 2,300 lower than Chandolin. The hamlet is at 4,100 ft., and surrounded by heavily manured hay meadows similar to those of the main valley. It consists of seven well-built houses, each with several rooms, a kitchen, and wooden floored stables, forming a complete contrast with the primitive huts of the Valais, although it must be remembered that the latter are generally at over 6,500 ft. The houses bear a closer resemblance to the Valaisan *mayen*, and indeed in this commune the distinction between *mayen* and alp has never existed, the whole system pivoting on the one building. Nevertheless, both the essential functions are still performed, for the meadows are cut, the hay always being brought down, and the pastures are grazed. Differences of land use are determined not so much by elevation as by the ease with which hay can be cut, and there are many instances of pastures giving way to meadow land on the uphill side.

The hamlet of Herzeben really comprises seven small farms, none of them with more than about ten head of cattle. Iszenalm, on the other hand, which succeeds it along the valley, belongs to a large farm at Neder and, judging by its fine large buildings, it would be logical to call it a 'summer farm'. Hay is cut both on the 15 acres of manured meadow in the valley bottom and, every two years, on the larch-strewn clearings of the west side. As the river, which often disappears underground in the summer, runs from south to north, the latter has no advantage of aspect. The east side, however, is flanked by rocky screes and fit only for grazing goats.

The twenty-six head of cattle, which include seven cows and three bulls, are brought here towards mid-April and, until 10 or 12 May for the young stock and even as late as 8 or 10 June for the cows, they subsist on hay, only half of which is taken down to the main farm. The seven goats are brought mainly to supply whole milk to keep the young bulls in good fettle. The cowman knows full well that it would be better to use this milk for his three children, 'but the boss thinks the fattening of his bulls is more important'. Sometimes goat milk is also used for lambs when the ewes refuse to feed them. The young cowman, who at the height of summer sometimes has to be content with only five hours' sleep, does all the work alone and earns 1,000 schillings (£14) a month, which is more than the average.

The emphasis throughout is on butter. All the milk is skimmed, and even the smallest establishment has its separator. The skim milk is largely fed to the followers and to the pigs. It also forms the basis of the cowman's diet, but is rarely made into cheese. Observing that a waterfall was harnessed to work the churn and provide electric light, we remarked how convenient everything was, but the cowman replied that old-fashioned equipment would need less cleaning.

In contrast with the *consortage* of the Valais, each pasture or 'little mountain', which is enclosed with stone and wood fences, sometimes up to a height of over 5,200 ft., is privately owned and independently managed. The last two sets of farm buildings along the valley bottom, Pinnis and Karalm,[1] provide, not only for their own farmers' beasts, but also for a number of rented cattle. The two daughters of the owner of Pinnis look after sixty cattle in all, but only twenty-seven of them actually belong to the farm. The others are either young cattle, for which the owners pay 80 to 120 schillings apiece for the season, or cows, and in this case the owners receive $1\frac{1}{4}$ lb. butter for the season for every pint of the average daily milk production. The torrent regularly overflows its banks in spring when the snows melt and, like the Drac de Champolion, it carries away all the soil from the lowest parts of the valley. Furthermore, as late as 1952 there was no piped system of manure distribution, and when everything depends on cartage from Pinnis it is not surprising that only a comparatively small area of meadow is manured. Apart from the cattle, these pastures also support twenty goats and thirty sheep, which are left to graze the highest slopes and receive practically no other attention, except that they are given a little salt every three or four weeks.

At 7 a.m. every morning between 15 May and 18 October a fourteen-year-old goatherd leaves Kampl with his flock and makes for Herrengasse and then Schmieden, where more animals from Neder and Obergasse await him. With this combined flock of fifty-eight goats and six kids he climbs for fully two hours to the sparse communal pastures on the right bank upstream of Pinnisalm, and eventually returns at 5.30 in the evening; there are young pines here, but the goats are allowed to graze just the same. By this arrangement, the cows, whose milk production would be severely impaired by such a climb, are assured of a monopoly of the lower grazings; as for the goats, which

[1] Eighty-five head of cattle, thirty of them milch cows, for the latter.

generally come from poor farms, better use is made of their milk than if they were stationed on the mountain for the whole summer. The young goatherd receives 25 schillings per animal for the season.

212. The visitor from Switzerland might well be surprised by what he saw in Pinnistal. He would, however, be astonished by the brand new 'summer farm' at Stocklern, which is over 5,200 ft. above sea-level in the Oberberg Valley and three-quarters of an hours' walk beyond Seduk. The farm was constructed three years ago without subsidies, and took 30 tons of cement to build, although it must be remembered that all these 'valley alps' can be reached by small carts. A mixture of dung-water and manure is distributed by a 15-h.p. triple-barrelled diesel pump through a set of pipes which lead up to the hay meadow 650 yds. above the farm. This hay is partly consumed *in situ* and allows the cattle to be kept here until the end of October, at which season the Valaisan *mayen*, which is often higher than this, is also being abandoned for the winter.

Further upstream in the same valley and favourably located on the *Sonnenseite*, the excellent pastures of Oberiss-Hütte, which extend over 2,500 acres of slopes stretching right into the valley bottom, are grazed in common by cattle belonging to the five co-owners. This kind of arrangement is fairly common in the commune of Neustift, which has sixteen co-operatively-owned blocks of land totalling 8,000 acres, representing therefore a substantial part of the 10,000 acres of valley-slope pastures and 2,025 acres of true upland grazings recorded in official statistics. The land in the former of these official categories, however, is very largely managed as upland pasture, while the rest is grazed during the summer from the home farms. There are also 4,750 acres of mountain meadows, which, in spite of their designation, are no longer wholly cut for hay at the present day. The commune itself owns 10,250 acres of forest, which, according to their needs and in return for a small charge, individuals may exploit for timber and firewood. Likewise, if a farm is gutted by fire or becomes dilapidated with age, the owner may obtain the timber he needs for rebuilding.

Coming back to Oberris, the property is divided into 7·75 'grazing shares', each of them giving the right to pasture fifteen cows. A year-old animal counts as half a cow, a two-year-old as one cow, and a horse counts as two. Two of the graziers each owns two shares, another two own one apiece, and the fifth owns 1·75. Whereas the grazing land is held in common, however, the buildings, equipment, and manured hay meadows are not. Utterly different from an Anniviers *consortage*, this communal enterprise has five separate summer farms, one of which has distribution pipes, but dispenses with the pump, as its meadows are below the buildings.

Each farmer owns an average of fifteen goats and about thirty sheep, but the whole herd, which grazes the highest slopes of the Alpeineralm from 12 May to 29 September, comprises 1,000 head of sheep, 850 of which are kept during the summer for other farmers. This is the only major instance of communal herding, and results in much greater efficiency in the use of labour. In October the sheep graze the manured upland meadows, while in November and until their return to the farm they are moved to the bottom meadows, and, somewhat hopefully, to the arable land. Finally, at the end of March they are driven on to the rough grazings of the *Sonnenseite* above the main valley.

Vitus Falbesoner, who owns two shares, brings up twenty-four head of cattle, including eleven cows, and at the beginning of September the latter were giving enough milk for the manufacture of about 45 lb. of butter a week. The milking, which is performed by two cowmen, one eighteen and the other fifty years old, is always done in the byre, and the cattle return there each evening. This is not the only feature more typical of a high valley farm than of the Valaisan alp, for much of the work is in the hands of women, whereas the mountain pastures in Switzerland provide employment exclusively for men.

The milk obtained from the herd of twenty-three goats, which are milked by a fourteen-year-old boy, is habitually wasted by feeding it to cattle. The goats are brought up as early as 15 or 20 May, whereas the cattle arrive here between 6 and 10 June and return about mid-October, the lower altitude being responsible for the prolongation of the season (which, thanks to the reserves of hay, lasts until the beginning of November at Stocklern). Falbesoner's 15 acres of manured meadows yield some 12 tons of hay, of which 10 tons are taken back to the main farm, the remainder being consumed *in situ*. On the *Sonnenseite*, where haymaking continues far up the slopes, there are fewer *Stadel* than in the Pinnistal, but more hayricks, which are cone-shaped and built around stakes, as in Gruyère in Switzerland.

A young boy of twelve herds the goats of the five partners on the slopes above those reserved for cattle. In contrast, the farmers herd their cattle independently, each on his own 'little mountain'.[1] This greatly increases the number of people needed as compared with Anniviers, and impairs the efficiency of the system very considerably. The small regard for economy of labour is explained by its low cost, wages being much lower than in Switzerland. The two goatherds, for instance,

[1] Communal herding of cattle is found again at Schirm.

each receive 700 schillings for the four months' season and the seventeen-year-old cowherd earns 900 schillings. Furthermore, their diet has a basis of milk and cooked flour, with a lot of curds and butter and small quantities of rice, eggs, noodles, and potatoes, but hardly any meat or vegetables.

213. The spruce forests which clothe the south-east slopes of the Unterbergtal have an undergrowth of fern which is entirely absent from the much drier Val d'Anniviers, and above 5,500 ft. they are mingled with larch and arolla pines. Misbachalm, situated above Volderau at 6,000 ft., is now no more than a 'summer farm', but it has a fine byre built of boards on a stone foundation, to which the cattle return each evening, and shelters made of stout planking for the nineteen-year-old goatherd and his flock. The pasture, being too poor for milch cows, is grazed by twenty-three young cattle from Oberegg on the Unterbergtal *Sonnenseite*. More than half these animals belong to the owner of the pasture, while the remainder are the property of five neighbours, who, for the whole season, which lasts from early June until 26 September, pay 100 schillings (28s.) and 150 schillings respectively for animals aged twelve to eighteen months and over two years.

Apart from his wage of 300 schillings per month, the goatherd is entitled to the milk from six goats, which, with the help of a separator, he makes into 1½ lb. of very white butter each week. In addition, he makes cheese from the skim milk, partly for his own consumption and partly to bring home to eke out his mother's resources during the winter. Whereas cattle are confined almost entirely to the zone below 6,500 ft., the forty sheep which belong to the owner of the land range as far as the upper limit of vegetation, which on these slopes is in the neighbourhood of 7,200 ft., or considerably lower than the chalets of Anniviers. From time to time the shepherd brings them a little salt.

7. Outdated Practices and Intensification in Highland and Lowland Zones

214. At first, and unlike Anniviers, this elevated valley does not give an impression of agricultural decadence, for crop and meadow are both well cared for, and the region is retaining its population fairly well. Indeed, the population is undoubtedly too large, and it is this factor which has led to the retention of old-fashioned methods, especially in the matter of haymaking, which continues today even under the most difficult physical conditions. Similarly, there are survivals of the old subsistence economy in the form of flax- and poppy-growing,

and all these features are the outcome of rural overpopulation.[1] This, at any rate for the time being, is afforded some relief by the industries of the Inn Valley, which are themselves, however, the victims of unemployment. The comparatively low level of wages eliminates any possibility of raising the standard of living, and further improvement in this sphere must await higher productivity, which in its turn depends on increasing the size of holdings. Admittedly, these are considerably larger than in Anniviers, where the agricultural labourer is almost unknown, but the average acreage still needs to be increased. Clearly, this brings us back once again to the crucial problem of emigration from the countryside.

About 1900, at a time when 1 gulden bought over 2 lb. of butter, a good labourer received 170 gulden a year, plus three pairs of shoes and four smocks. In 1937 the agricultural wage rate was 90 schillings a month, and, as the same quantity of butter was now worth 3·5 schillings, this represented a very slight improvement in the real value of the labourer's earnings. It was said that it needed 'a good milch cow to pay a good worker's wages'. In 1952 wages averaged 500 to 800 schillings a month, but, since butter now cost 15 schillings a pound, their real value had somewhat declined. As against this, the worker was generally better housed and enjoyed a higher standard of food, especially as regards the amount of butter consumed. The total number of farm labourers is decreasing, but there are still more than 200 of them in this commune.

There is little incentive, therefore, to seek greater economy in the use of labour, but this obviously does not justify clinging to the wasteful methods of the past. Even the better-equipped valley of the Inn has often one farm worker for every 5 acres, and suffers by comparison with many of the lowlands of western Europe. In the same way, the utilization of upland pastures is much inferior to the system practised in Anniviers, but it is worth remembering that in the main valley of Neustift, especially on the arable land, there were many instances of progressive farming which one may seek in vain in the highlands of the Valais.

215. Between 1938 and 1942 and even until 1943, union with a re-arming or actually warring Germany resulted in large credits being made available for modernization in the Tyrol. At Fisz, and in forty other communes where many chalets were shared by two, three and, at Grins, even six peasant families, the people were given very large

[1] The exodus from the highlands is beginning in other parts of the Tyrol, as at Pfafflar in the Lötchtal.

and splendid new homes. In return, the peasants paid a nominal sum of 100 marks and made a somewhat more substantial contribution in labouring and cartage, but the houses were worth 50,000 marks apiece. Many of the improvements to the byres and many of the dung-water pits and manure pumps date from the same period, as do overhead cables for transport, motor-driven winches for ploughing, and, in some areas, new roads.

As in Switzerland, allowances were granted for peasant families and subsidies were given for young cattle. The provision of farm equipment, however, was the main objective of financial aid, and the beneficial effects of these injections of capital are fortunately still apparent. Impoverished after two world wars and unhappily partitioned until 1955, Austria can no longer offer much financial aid, and most of the subsidies have been stopped, but agriculture is the better able to find fresh investment capital for having had the opportunity to put its house in order under the German régime. With black bread at 1·70 schillings a pound, however, the small farmer has been very awkwardly placed since the fall in the price of butter, which is no longer a scarce commodity. This adverse movement in the price of butter as compared with bread has an analogy in France, where, after the Office du Blé in 1936, the highland peasant also found himself in straitened circumstances.

In Neustift we asked a certain peasant, who was evidently barely making ends meet, what complaints he had against the Government. 'I must first ask the priest what demands to make', was his reply. Nineteen out of twenty peasants in the upper Stubaital, many of whom seem to be on the very edge of insolvency and abject poverty, follow blindly along the way pointed by the Catholic clergy, particularly in matters of politics. Those who rejoice in this trust, however, do not always seem conscious of the manifold responsibilities it places upon them.

As in Anniviers, the family farm is the rule, *métayage* is unknown, and the renting of land is exceptional, an isolated example being that of a young widow compelled to provide for her small children. Whereas nearly all the farms of Anniviers were too small to warrant much capital expenditure and frequently did not give full-time work for the whole family, the existence here of a large number of medium-sized holdings[1]

---

[1] There are larger farms (75-125 acres) in the eastern Tyrol, in the lower part of the Inn Valley, where primogeniture is the rule. The west, however, is characterized by a large majority of uneconomically small farms with, perhaps, 3-5 acres and one or two cows. Neustift falls between these two extremes.

has favoured the utilization of modern equipment, and some progress in this direction has certainly been made. The dispersed pattern of settlement has meant that, for the most part, each farmhouse is surrounded by its own land, and reintegration is not such an urgent necessity as in the Valais. On the other hand, the most rapid advances in the Tyrol as a whole are occurring in the spheres of electrification and ploughing techniques, but the economy of the Stubaital is now quite definitely orientated towards animal husbandry, and many arable farmers who have turned to stock-rearing have not moved quickly enough in improving their methods of fodder production.

Animal manure is collected more thoroughly than in the highlands of the Valais and in this respect the Tyrol is more akin to the German-speaking part of Switzerland. The Stubaital also has the advantage in the intensiveness of its crop cultivation, but fertilizers are too expensive for many farmers and further progress will be hindered as long as they remain so. Then, again, while yields per acre are quite satisfactory, the productivity of labour, apart from a few exceptional cases, like the Hofer farm, is still much too low, a fact which can be attributed to the need for culling winter fodder from difficult and remote terrain and to the persistence of individual herding in the summer.

With so little land at her disposal, Austria cannot afford to neglect her highland agriculture, the fate of which depends on the provision of equipment—that is, on the granting of the right type of assistance. A journey across the country makes it apparent that if highland agriculture were made more extensive for the sake of using labour more efficiently, the lowlands could easily make up the loss in total production by being exploited more intensively. The rural overpopulation of the mountain fastnesses of Europe is a legacy of the past, and it has engendered a type of highland farming where the nature of the terrain does not warrant the effort expended upon it. Meanwhile, the lowlands have contented themselves with a degree of improvement in yields which is far from satisfactory. It will be the task of the next generation to redress this balance, and raise the standard of living in the highlands by increasing the momentum of production.

X

Bavarian Agriculture—Intensive and Mechanized, but Farm Units Too Small[1]

216. On either side of Munich, the broad, level expanse of the Bavarian plateau is composed of highly permeable fluvio-glacial sands and gravels, with a thin veneer of dry sandy loams. Fortunately, the 35 in. or so of rain are concentrated mainly in the summer, with a July maximum and a total fall of 16 in. between May and August. The climate rapidly becomes drier towards northern Bavaria, and the lowest rainfall is recorded in Lower Franconia, where, on the vine-clad scarps of the Main, for instance, the combined total of the four summer months, when water is generally most needed, barely reaches 8 in. During the summer of 1952, even crops of lucerne failed in some districts. The mountainous edges of the region, however, are much wetter, with 25 in. of summer rainfall on the Bavarian and Bohemian forests near the Czechoslovakian frontier in the east, and over 30 in. in the Alps to the south. Conversely, the soils tend to improve towards the north, where loams and even loess are more widely distributed.

Here again agriculture is dominated by the demographic situation. The density of population in Upper Bavaria has moved from 105 per square mile in 1836, a far lower density than in France at this period, to 302 in 1939 and 384 in 1952, almost a fourfold increase. There are almost 2,000,000 refugees in Bavaria, those in the south having emigrated mainly from the Sudetes, those in the north coming also from Silesia, and these people now make up 21 per cent. of the population. Three-fifths of them are in villages of less than 2,000 inhabitants, and

---

[1] Field studies in 1934 and, in more detail, in September 1952, with the extremely valuable help of Herr Lechner, who is an agricultural adviser, of the Weihenstephan Plant Breeding Station, of the agricultural schools at Ebersberg and Pfaffenhofen, and of the agricultural adviser at Miesbach.

they account for 42 per cent. of the population of these small settlements. In consequence, the rural population has risen from 45 per cent. to 53 per cent. of the total. The newcomers have swelled the ranks of the destitute, and sixty-six persons out of every 1,000 are in receipt of assistance from the State.

West Germany has been less successful than the Democratic Republic in solving its unemployment problem. The older refugees include a considerable number of landowners, merchants, and others who once had independent means—people who find it difficult to regain their place in the community. The density of population of the whole country, 492 per square mile, is higher than in Italy, but as against this one must place Germany's vastly superior industrial might and her larger possibilities for future development. Although capital investment is much in evidence and many useful projects have yet to be undertaken, full employment is handicapped by the economic structure. The high density of population, higher than in East Germany and heightened in its significance by the excess of births over deaths (seventeen or eighteen per 1,000 as compared with eleven or twelve), imposes the need for an extremely intensive concentration on agricultural yields and production.

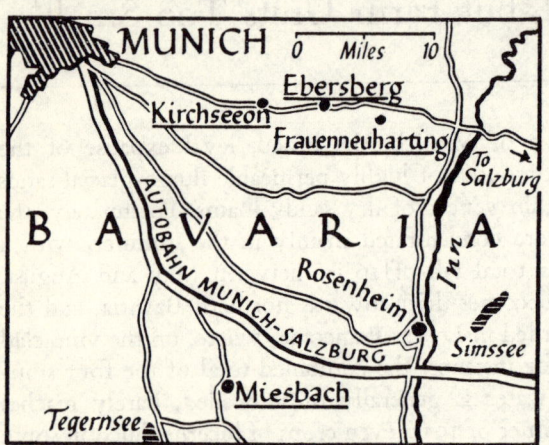

FIG. 19. Bavaria.

1. Old and New Methods East of Munich

217. First of all, at Osterseeon in the commune of Kirchseeon, east of Munich (Fig. 19), we visited a State farm producing seed for the district. Unlike the experimental stations, which are subsidized, this farm has to balance its budget, and in many respects it resembles its counterpart in East Germany, which is discussed in a later chapter. Bavaria has 100 agricultural schools, more than twice the number in France,

and we visited one of them at Ebersberg,[1] where we made our next stop. Much attention is given to research and instruction in both East and West Germany, and in the latter there is an agricultural adviser for approximately every 1,000 farms, which represents more than one for every 25,000 acres of agricultural land.

Unable to boast as many socialized estates as in the East, our guide took us to Steinhöring, where we were shown the 'peasant woman's building', an edifice financed partly from State funds and Marshall Aid and partly by means of an advance from the local branch of the Raiffessen co-operative credit organization. It provides the housewife with a laundry complete with wringers and drying apparatus, with a sewing machine and a machine for repairing sacks, and with a modern cooking range. Not only does this save a lot of work, but by comparison with traditional methods of performing these operations in each individual home it effects very large economies in fuel. In addition there is an efficient plant for pasteurizing apple juice at $77°$ C., a scheme which, if applied in Normandy, might well assist in curbing alcoholism. Finally, there are bathrooms and refrigeration units which maintain a temperature of $-10°$ C. The only fault that can be found is the small number of these establishments. In Bavaria there are only fifteen, which is fewer than in Czechoslovakia, but we know of none in France.

Fully a third of Kreis Ebersberg is covered with forests of spruce, and the remainder is evenly divided between arable and grassland. There are 482 holdings of less than 5 acres, and 576 of 5 to $12\frac{1}{2}$ acres, but most of the men who work these have an alternate means of livelihood. The main group consists of 1,430 units of between $12\frac{1}{2}$ and 50 acres, but there are a further 382 medium-sized farms within the range 50 to 125 acres, although most of these are less than 100 acres. Finally, there are twenty-five of 125 to 250 acres and another seven of over 250 acres; there is evidently little scope for agrarian reform. Of the 50,000 inhabitants of the Kreis, almost a third are refugees, who mostly work in Munich, although many are unemployed, and in all 9 per cent. of the population is assisted by the State.

218. In the eastern part of the Kreis, in the commune of Frauenneuharting, which, with its broad, low roofs and profusion of flowers, is a fairly typical Upper Bavarian village, the distribution of property is much the same. The agricultural land is divided between 126 farms

---

[1] On the walls of its corridors the school displays a number of pictures depicting the old castles of the region, in an attempt to keep the old traditional values alive; in the farms one sees the inscription: 'Religion [Roman Catholic here] and work are the golden blood of the people.'

and accounts for 4,250 acres out of the total of 5,642, there being 2,595 acres of grassland and 1,655 acres of arable land, gardens, and orchards. There are twenty-seven farms of between 50 and 125 acres, but, although this represents a slightly higher proportion than for the whole Kreis, there are none at all in the higher ranges. One still finds that cattle are kept in their stalls all the year round, except in the autumn, when the aftermath, which is difficult to cut, is grazed, but the more typically Western European method of enclosing pasture land and leaving the animals to graze untended is beginning to gain acceptance. These enclosures, which now account for a tenth of the grassland area, are making inroads on the arable land. The ploughing up of permanent pasture was encouraged by grants during the war, but the land quickly reverted to its former use as soon as the subsidies ceased, and today the area under grass is still slowly increasing. The care which is bestowed on grassland, however, makes it a more intensive type of land utilization than in France.

The village is at nearly 2,000 ft. and receives almost 40 in. of rain a year. It is set in a landscape of swelling, morainic ridges crowned with spruce forests and flanked by fields of crops and meadows. The intervening hollows provide stable litter and peat, which is dried in small, open sheds. A fifth of the land under the plough is devoted to row crops, which include potatoes, covering two-thirds of the area, mangolds, and vegetables. Barely a sixth is used for other fodder crops, mainly red clover, which is sometimes sown with a cereal. The remainder, almost two-thirds, is under cereals, the preponderance of which indicates a lesser degree of intensiveness than in Denmark or the Netherlands.

There is, however, a large number of animals, a consideration which may modify one's first impression of the region. Here there are 1,880 head of cattle (1,025 cows, fifty of them used for draught; also seventy draught bullocks), 138 horses, and 650 pigs, which, disregarding the latter, represents a density of one animal for every $2\frac{1}{4}$ acres of agricultural land. This suggests that there is manure in plenty for enriching arable and grassland alike, but it presupposes a good deal of attention to the storage of fodder. Various methods of drying are used, from the simple tripod to the Bohemian hut and the vertical Swedish rack. By 1952 the density of stock in Bavaria was back to its pre-war level, and it should be noted that the average milk yield per cow in Germany is half as high again as in France.

As against about ten tractors before the war, the commune now possesses about fifty, which, at 4·8 h.p. per 100 acres, could provide as much power as the draught animals; that they do not is due to the fact that they are under-utilized. The Kreis had 440 tractors in 1948, but 1,400, together with thirty combine-harvesters, by 1952, Evidently, therefore, the tractor is making its appearance in many farms of less than 50 acres. Having to lead a horse or, even worse, a team of cows or bullocks is no doubt frustrating when not so very long ago one was trained to drive a lorry for the Wehrmacht.

219. At the Wetterstetter farm, which has 30 acres of meadows and 27 acres under the plough and in orchards, the density of stock and the general degree of intensiveness are above the average. More fodder crops and fewer cereals[1] are the recipe for keeping eighteen cows, at least ten stores, two horses, and five pigs. More than half the work is done with a 16-h.p. tractor, which enables the seventy-five journeys needed to empty a dung-water pit with a capacity of 3,360 cu. ft. to be completed in a day and a half. As a general rule, settlement is dispersed so that the fields are near at hand, and on this farm a 290-gallon water tank can be filled with the help of an electric pump, transported to one of the meadows, and emptied, all in the space of ten minutes. The dispersed pattern of hamlets is associated with the traditional rotation, in which grass leys, which were formerly allowed to regenerate spontaneously (*Natur-Egarten*; cf. Chapter IX), predominate, and this relationship becomes even more marked towards the Alps in the south. Conditions are different towards the north, where, as in north-eastern France, the three-year rotation with one year of fallow (*Dreifeldwirtschaft*) was once prevalent, and the farms are grouped in villages to this day.

There is an orchard near each farmhouse, and the one at Wetterstetter consists mainly of apple and plum trees, with a few pears and cherries and even a couple of peach trees. The ground is manured thoroughly and, as 1952 was a good year for orchards, the trees were heavily laden with fruit at the time of our visit. Ploughland and meadows receive 400 lb. of basic slag, 130 lb. of 40 per cent. potash fertilizer, and the same amount of 20 per cent. nitrates per acre per year. The meadows are cut or grazed four times a year, and the effect on the young grass thus obtained is reflected in the average yield per cow of 770 gallons of milk, which is sent to Munich. The farm is fully equipped and has hay and manure rakes, a hay elevator for loading carts, a manure-spreader, and a milking machine.

[1] 5 acres of wheat, $3\frac{1}{4}$ of rye, $3\frac{1}{4}$ of barley, $2\frac{1}{2}$ of oats, $2\frac{1}{2}$ of potatoes, $1\frac{1}{4}$ of beet, $3\frac{3}{4}$ of clover; catch crops are taken as follows: 'liho' (summer rape for fodder) after rye, and turnips after wheat.

The farm is obviously very much superior to the average, but our friendly guide contrived to avoid our seeing any others. The farmer has a car, but again this is not typical in the region: only one person in twenty is a car-owner. Compared with the single room of the majority of farms in Brittany, this one has eleven, and although it dates back 900 years, it also boasts a washing machine and wringer, an electric drier for fruit (pears, plums, and apples), an electric oven, bathroom, etc.

Pork enters largely into the diet—more so than milk and butter. Whereas yields per acre are high—20 cwt. for grain as against the regional average of 16 cwt.—the productivity of labour is lowered by the large number of workers. On this farm, with its 57 acres, there are five male and three female employees, who receive 20 and 15 marks net per week[1] respectively, but the density of workers is even higher on the smaller farms of the village. Milk and animal products are the main sources of income, the sale of grain and potatoes being of secondary importance. Moreover, a considerable number of cattle stalls have been renovated, without the help of State subsidies. Indeed, the Government has succeeded in promoting a great deal of very fine research work, and this, together with the large number of schools and the highly developed advisory services, does far more to help agriculture than could be achieved by more direct forms of assistance.[2]

Side by side with the modern methods, one still sees many workers using scythes, and this prompts the question of how the very small farms can possibly survive. It is true that the more intensive type of farming makes the diesel tractor an economic proposition for a smaller unit than in France; even so, the minimum acreage, as in Switzerland, is in the region of 30 or perhaps even 25 acres, but more than 62 per cent. of farms in the Kreis are below this figure, and their claims do not appear as yet to have compelled the attention of the authorities. The latter are inclined to condemn rather hastily any schemes for the pooling of equipment on the lines of the French C.U.M.A., the similarity of which to the M.A.S. of the East makes it immediately suspect.

The problem is very much more acute in Franconia, where holdings of 5-12½ acres are the rule, while in some areas the typical unit is even

[1] 11·70 to the £1 in 1952.
[2] More than 2,000 students in colleges, more than 1,000 in high schools, and 30,000 in other types of school in the whole of West Germany. By 1949 the number of agricultural advisers and teachers of agriculture in various types of institutions had passed the 5,400 mark. This was an increase of 30 per cent. on 1939. Between 1947 and 1951 more than 2,000 new posts were created. . . . In France, in the meantime, nothing is being done.

smaller and milch cows have to be used for draught. In contrast, there has been an important development of co-operative buying, credit (Raiffessen banks), threshing, and dairies, etc. So far industrial unemployment and the flood of refugees have checked the decline in the number of small holdings, which was already fairly well in evidence before the war, but when other forms of employment become available the effect of mechanization will in all probability make itself felt in the resumption of this trend.

2. Heavily Manured Grassland in the Zone at the Foot of the Alps

220. Towards the south, nearer the buttresses of the Alps, the relief becomes more marked, the soils become heavier, the rainfall increases, and ploughland almost disappears from a landscape dominated by forests, lakes and meadows. In the Kreis of Miesbach thirty miles southeast of Munich, settlement becomes completely dispersed, and the average farm is considerably larger. Only 18 per cent. of the population, however, is classed as agricultural, as against a third in Ebersberg, and, ignoring the many units of less than $1\frac{1}{4}$ acres which are associated with industrial employment in this region of mines, saw-mills, textile and engineering factories, the average size of the remaining 2,500 farms attains 62 acres, one of the highest figures for any part of Bavaria. There is a great deal of mechanization, as evidenced by the 1,080 tractors enumerated in 1952, as against ninety before the war, but it should be remembered that the majority of these are used for the transport of timber rather than for agriculture. The number of horses is declining rapidly, the 1951 figure of 2,500 being 300 less than the preceding year.

There are 94,000 acres of forests, 32,000 of lakes, 45,000 of double-cropped meadows, and 30,000 of upland pastures, rough grazing land, and other grasslands, cut either for stable litter or for a single hay crop. Gardens account for a mere 1,250 acres, and arable land for only double this area. The latter is largely devoted to row crops (30 per cent.), which consist almost exclusively of potatoes grown for human consumption, there being only 3,000 pigs. Cereals account for the remainder, fodder crops and rotation grasses being almost unknown in this realm of permanent grassland. The arable land is concentrated in the north, whereas the large communes of the south are mainly in upland pastures and rough grazings. The specialization of these uplands is the raising of cattle, and there are 29,000 head in all, including 17,400 cows. These are impressive figures when one remembers that the soils are naturally rather infertile and greatly inferior, for example, to those of Normandy.

The number of agricultural workers is fairly high. There are 9,000 permanent workers, half male and half female, and 1,700 part-time workers, 700 of them women, who work an average of 150 days during the summer half of the year. These figures represent a density of one worker for every 5 acres of the intensively farmed arable and double-cropped meadow land. The official figures, which count women as 0·8 of a unit, give 8,500 as the number of permanent workers. Finally, although a large part of the labour force is drawn from the families of the farmers themselves, there are as many as 2,500 permanent wage-earning employees, 900 of whom are women.

221. This, however, is offset by the intensiveness of land utilization. There is a small farm situated in a forest clearing at Rodthal, south of Miesbach, which has no arable land at all save for its 400 sq. yds. of garden, and comprises 11 acres of woodland and only 31 acres of grassland. The latter are subdivided into twenty small meadows, sometimes by fences and sometimes by hedgerows which impart a *bocage* aspect to the countryside. In this region of traditional stock-rearing, the land has long been enclosed, and the fences and hedgerows have none of the appearance of newness which characterized those at Ebersberg. In 1951 farmyard manure and drainings were supplemented by 50 marks-worth of artificial fertilizers to the acre: the equivalent of 88 lb. of nitrates, 120 lb. of phosphoric acid, and ½ ton of lime. Lime and potash are not used every year. In 1952 the outlay was 60 marks to the acre.

The twenty-one cows and the bull, together with a few calves, are kept here all the year round, but the twelve young cattle spend five months in the summer on communal upland pastures. This still means that 80 per cent. of the feed for thirty-three head of cattle, not to speak of ten sheep, two pigs, and twenty-two hens, is produced on the farm itself. Grass is cut for green fodder when it is still rich in proteins, and is stored in two silos, each with a capacity of 1,250 cu. ft. This dispenses entirely with the purchase of concentrates. Indeed, molasses are fed to the animals, as are potatoes in the Netherlands, in order to balance the diet, which is often too rich in nitrogenous matter. The animals are put out to pasture in the summer and autumn and not stall-fed, as in the rest of Bavaria.

Docks, dandelions, and umbellifers show that these meadows are almost over-fertilized, but in spite of the short growing season they yield up to over 5 tons (dry weight) per acre, which puts them on a par with the excellent grasslands of the Netherlands. On average, a cow gives 880 gallons of milk with a fat content of 3·8 per cent.,[1] so that even after allowing for grass consumed by young stock and for milk consumed by the calves and by the family itself, each acre produces 4,000 lb. of saleable milk a year. This small farm has no draught animals at all, but it possesses two tractors, one 22-h.p. and the other 11-h.p., two manure-spreaders, a dung-water pump and a system of distribution pipes, and two 3-h.p. electric motors. There is thus a total of 39 h.p. available for working 31 acres of land, a ratio of nearly 1·3 h.p. per acre, or fifteen to thirty times as much as before mechanization.

It would be unthinkable to provide such a superabundance of power by using draught animals, for, unlike the tractor or the electric motor, they would have to be fed with the produce of the land they helped to cultivate, and so many of them would be needed that they would consume more than the farm could possibly provide. Three men and 2·5 women work here, so that the density of labour is also high, but whereas the example described above was better than average, this farm appears to be quite exceptional. It is true that grassland in Bavaria is more productive than in France, but the majority of farms are far from reaching this standard and, generally speaking, the larger the holding the lower the density of animals and the lower the level of intensiveness.

222. Thus, a little nearer Munich, where, at nearly 2,500 ft., the rainfall averages over 50 in., Herr Lanz farms a total of 345 acres, which include 97 acres of meadow, a number of large pastures totalling 47 acres, 175 acres of his own upland pasture and rough land cut for litter, and about 25 acres of ploughland under cereals, potatoes, and vegetables. His herd consists of forty-two cows and thirty-nine calves and stores of various ages, which, with the exception of the young calves, spend the long summer on upland pastures which are no higher than those at Neustift in the Tyrol. Of the total herd, there are seventy-two adult animals which represent a stock density of one for every 5 acres or, more correctly, of one for every 2 acres of intensively managed grassland as against one per acre in the preceding case. In addition, however, there are 55 acres of forest which play an important part in the economy of the farm which, with the help of an electrically powered saw, exploits the timber itself.

This sizeable farm, with its small castle, also has two tractors, of 22 and 19 h.p. respectively, whereas there are now only two horses, as against five formerly. Machinery can be kept in repair on the farm itself thanks to a very well-equipped workshop adapted for both wood- and metal-work. There is a system of pulleys for loading tanks of

[1] Average age of cows, 5·6 years.

dung-water on to wagons, which avoids having tenders specially built for the purpose and therefore effects a very considerable economy. For the most part, however, the precious drainings are distributed under gravity through a system of pipes. As in the nearby Tyrol, both *Stadel*, or hay-barns,[1] and *Stiefel* for drying the hay are to be seen scattered through the fields. The hay, which has a fine, green colour, is chopped before being blown into the barns so as to save space. Finally, although the land is worked only about half as intensively as on the smaller farm, the density of labour is only about a third and the productivity of work is therefore higher.

3. The Hallertau—Distinguished by Its Hop-gardens

223. There are vineyards in the north of Bavaria, in the Main Valley, but hop-fields replace them further south in the area north of Munich, and especially in the Hallertau in the districts of Mainburg and Pfaffenhofen (Fig. 20). This region is developed on Tertiary sands, molasse, and marls, with superficial deposits of loess and sandy loams. A quarter of the 56,000 inhabitants are refugees and 42 per cent. of the total are employed in agriculture and forestry, a larger proportion than in either of the preceding examples.

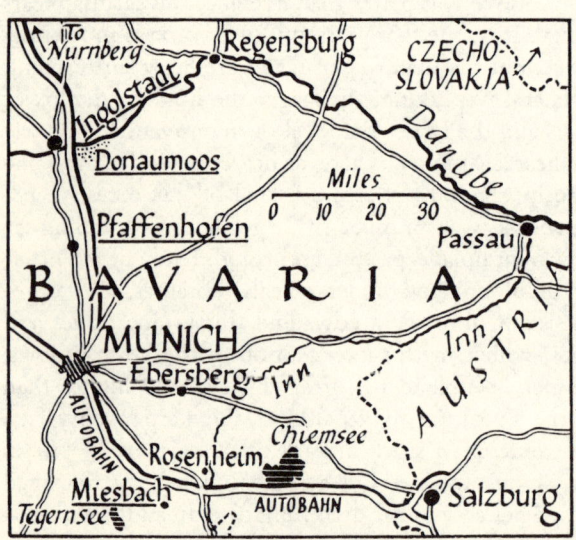

FIG. 20. Bavaria.

In Bavaria as a whole, the percentage of the total population dependent on agriculture and forestry has fallen from 51 in 1882 to 28 in 1939 and 26 in 1946. At the same time, the number of agricultural workers has fallen from 60 per cent. to 38 per cent. and 37 per cent.[2]

[1] One finds them as far as Finnish Bothnia.   [2] 22 per cent. in West Germany.

THE HALLERTAU AND ITS HOP-GARDENS

of the total employed, and these figures demonstrate once again that the proportion of the working population is higher in rural than in industrial areas, for the peasant begins working earlier and retires later than the factory hand. A comparison of overall agricultural and industrial production reveals another fairly general distinction; the figures for 1936 show that the former accounted for a fifth, the latter for two-fifths of the national revenue, and illustrate the lower output per worker of the farming community. In 1949 agriculture's share of total production in Bavaria was 19 per cent.; industry, on the other hand, accounted for 35 per cent. and employed 30 per cent. more people than before the war. Bavaria vehemently repudiates the title of 'The Farming State'.[1]

The majority of the 4,746 farms—2,520 of them, to be exact—lie within the range of 5 to 25 acres, with as many between 5 and $12\frac{1}{2}$ acres as between $12\frac{1}{2}$ and 25. In addition there are about 1,000 between 25 and 50 acres, 500 between 50 and 125 acres, eighty of over 125 acres, and, at the other end of the scale, 651 of between $1\frac{1}{4}$ and 5 acres. The average size of holding is thus even smaller than in Ebersberg. From 200 tractors in 1939 and 300 in 1946, numbers have increased to 600 in 1950 and to 1,200—or more than twice the number of farms exceeding 50 acres—in 1952. In France, where mechanization began rather earlier, there has been a distinct falling off in the number of new tractors in the period 1950-2.

Apart from 39,000 acres of forest in the region, there are 62,000 acres under the plough and 30,000 acres of grassland, as compared with 67,000 and 25,000 acres respectively in 1939. There has thus been a distinct movement in favour of grassland, in spite of the drier climate, which has 26 in. of rain, with 14 in. from May to August. Moreover, at a height of only 1,650 ft., conditions are slightly warmer, and the mean annual temperature of 54·5° F. is about 1° higher than at Miesbach. The encroachment of grassland, however, has taken place at the expense of cereals exclusively, and these have fallen from 41,700 to 35,000 acres, whereas row crops—especially potatoes, which are destined in part for the manufacture of starch—have experienced a slight increase. In Bavaria as a whole the cereal acreage has decreased by 18 per cent. between 1903 and 1948, whereas sown grasses have increased by 2·5 per cent., row crops by 4 per cent., and permanent grassland by 11·4 per cent. The Kreis has 32,000 cattle, including 15,700 cows, and 3,800 of these animals are used for draught, but although this

[1] See *Unser Bayern*, in the volume edited by the Bavarian Chancellery in 1950, pp. 43-8.

represents a lower density than in Piedmont, the number of pigs is comparable, and as for horses, which have hardly yet begun to decline in numbers, there are more than five per 100 acres of agricultural land. In 1950 and 1951 pigs furnished 51·5 per cent. of all the meat consumed in West Germany, and only 5 per cent. of the total was veal. The latter represents a considerable waste of milk,[1] and the fact that it accounts for some 15 per cent. of meat consumption in France is therefore of some significance.

224. Although hop-gardens cover a mere 4,600 acres (3,700 in 1939), or 4 per cent. of the agricultural area, they are none the less the dominant enterprise in the rural economy of the region. The repeated patterns of hop-poles and interlacing wires are a distinctive feature of the landscape. The cultivation of this crop goes back at least to the latter half of the ninth century, when, although the merchants and aristocrats drank wine, each farm grew enough hops to fulfil its own needs and to pay its dues to the Church and the local lord. It was during the sixteenth century, when the vine, which in this area was always very near its natural limit, began to disappear and when brewing began to develop as an industry, that the cultivation of hops received its real impetus. The efforts of the Bavarian Government to stimulate production during the eighteenth century excited the jealousy of Bohemia, which promptly forbade the export of cuttings, but Bavaria herself had begun to export hops in 1768, and it was later proposed to 'bind and seal' the cones according to the various qualities. This had been the practice in Bohemia since 1538, but was not actually adopted in the Hallertau until 1834.

Further expansion of the brewing industry in Bavaria between 1850 and 1880 brought a fresh stimulus to cultivation, and by 1853, with 27,000 acres under the crop and a total harvest of 4,100 tons, this region had taken the leading place among producers of high-quality hops. By 1883 the area had increased to 66,200 acres, and the record harvest of 1889 reached a total of 19,500 tons. Until then the only countries which had supplied the international market were England, Germany, and Austro-Hungary, but after this their ranks were joined by Russia and America, and at the turn of the century production began to out-strip demand. As a result, as from 1908 many hop-gardens were abandoned, and further damage has been suffered by the industry as a consequence of two world wars; the quota system reduced the consumption of beer and prices fell below costs of production.

[1] See our *Problème Agricole Français* (N.E.L. 1946).

THE HALLERTAU AND ITS HOP-GARDENS

The disastrous harvests of 1926-7 followed hard on the appearance of mildew (*Peronospora humuli*) in 1924, but the peasants did not realize the gravity of the danger and hoped that a few propitious seasons would stop the spread of the disease. The federations of brewers and hop merchants therefore took over a garden and put it in charge of specialists so as to demonstrate the efficacy of treatment with a 1 per cent. solution of copper sulphate, repeated a dozen or fifteen times during the growing season. This led to the study of other parasites. Research on methods of working and fertilizing the soil and the development of hybrid species naturally followed. The same kind of sequence is discernible in France, where the Colorado beetle eventually led to the adoption of spraying against mildew.

The region is therefore characterized by a very intensive form of specialized farming, which occupies the best soils and accounts for 1-10 per cent. of the area of most hop-growing farms, although the figure occasionally rises to 15-20 per cent. in districts like Wolnzach and Mainburg, which are renowned for the quality of their crops. According to the experts the ideal is about 5 per cent., for below this figure the crop often suffers from sheer neglect, while above it the farmer finds himself unable to give his gardens the attention they deserve. The largest enterprise of all has 42 acres under hops, but most of the good farms have between about 4 and 8 acres, while the great majority have less than $1\frac{1}{2}$ acres. A great deal of fertilizing is needed: 60 tons of quicklime per acre every three years, plus $5\frac{1}{2}$ cwt. of basic slag, 4 cwt. of 40 per cent. potash, $1\frac{1}{2}$ cwt. of ammonium sulphate, and 3 cwt. of sodium nitrate every year.

No other crop grown on this scale needs so much work, and worst of all in this respect is the picking season, when an army of temporary workers moves into the gardens, even the smallest farms taking their share. A certain farm which devotes $6\frac{1}{4}$ of its 193 acres to hops employed thirty-six pickers from 20 August until the end of the month in 1952. The crop amounted to 60 cwt. of cured hops, rather lower than the average for the year, which was in the region of 12 cwt. an acre. Each worker, on average, picks 130-200 lb. (cured) in the season and can fill six 13-gallon measures, the equivalent of 20 lb. of cured hops, in a good day's work. He receives 90 pfennigs a measure, or about 5·40 marks a day, and pays nothing for board and lodging or travelling.

225. The cones are cured on the farms. Coke is often used for heating, and a modern plant with thermostat, ventilators, and rocking trays, capable of dealing with the produce from $5\frac{1}{2}$ acres of gardens,

costs 9,000 marks. Moreover, an acre of hop-gardens, including the cost of supports, double-trenching, and equipment, represents a long-term investment of some 6,000 marks.[1] Considering the financial risk—illustrated by the fact that in 1930 1 cwt. of hops sold for 90 or 100 marks or even less, but cost 180 marks to produce—it is not surprising that the growers are now clamouring for guaranteed prices.

The low prices of the 'thirties put many hop-growers out of business. At the same time they led to a restriction of production somewhat on the lines of the *Statut viticole* in France, which, by agreement between the farmers and the Government, persists to this day in the form of quotas based on 1929 acreages. The farmers who hold a monopoly of production are thus assured of substantial revenues, a fact which is reflected in the elaborate upkeep of many homes in the fortunate regions concerned. In 1952 Bavaria accounted for 16,300 of the 18,500 acres in West Germany, and in mid-September market prices began at about 620 marks a hundredweight as compared with a cost price, including tax, of 468 marks, as estimated (no doubt generously) by the agricultural organizations.[2]

Hop-growing is also regarded as a useful source of revenue by the State. In one example, a grower with $5\frac{1}{2}$ acres, who harvested 120 cwt. in 1952 and sold it at an average of 460 marks a hundredweight, paid 12,000 marks, or 22 per cent. of gross production, in special taxes, which is a much higher rate than formerly. The same farm also comprises 100 acres of arable land, 25 acres of meadows, and the same of forest, and possesses two tractors and three horses. The farmer paid an additional 5,670 marks in income tax and 835 marks in Church dues

[1] On $2\frac{1}{2}$ acres there would be 4,500 plants, and the following materials, costing 6,500 marks, would be needed: 38 cross poles 29 ft. long and 165 measuring 26 ft., 143 supports 22 ft. long and 36 of 20 ft., 36 stakes. This by no means completes the list; 16 cwt. of strong wire and 11 cwt. of wire for training the bines are but two of the many other items needed. Formerly when vertical poles were employed, they were needed at the rate of 4,500 per $2\frac{1}{2}$ acres, i.e. one per plant, and young plantations of spruce suffered heavily in consequence; on the other hand, hardly any wire was used and once again, therefore, iron is replacing wood.

[2] In 1949 costs of production per hundredweight were given as 350 marks, made up as follows: first, fixed charges: 20·6 per cent. for setting up poles and wire, 18 per cent. for care during growth, 10·5 per cent. for repairs, 10 per cent. for manure, 7·5 per cent. for spraying, 2·5 per cent. for taxes, 2·2 per cent. for insurance and 1·2 per cent. for general expenses; secondly, the following items were subject to variation: 20 per cent. for picking, 6 per cent. for curing and 1·4 per cent. for marketing.

payable to the denomination of his choice (this goes to social work in the case of the few atheists).[1]

The trade in hops has remained entirely in private hands, and the businesses concerned have profited handsomely from the rise in prices favoured by the quota system. In 1949, for instance, prices reached as high as 1,800 marks a hundredweight, whereas the growers had sold most of their crop at 300-600 marks, but in spite of this there has been no move either from the Government or from the farmers' organizations to institute a system of co-operative sale. Wolnzach and Mainburg have broken Nuremberg's former monopoly of sulphur treatment and packing in sealed bales (trade names protected) of 2, 3, or 4 cwt. for export. Between a third and two-fifths of West German production is destined for export, but the ideological frontier which today separates the two Germanys has enabled Bohemia to capture the East German market.

Returning to the 193-acre farm in the commune of Pfaffenhofen, one finds that it consists of 60 acres of woodland, 32 of meadows, $6\frac{1}{4}$ of hops, and 94 of arable land. The farmer adopts a seven-course rotation which, in any one year, gives 55 per cent. of cereals and 20 per cent. of row crops with the remainder in rotation grasses, clover, and even lucerne, which does well here. Power is provided by two tractors and three horses, there is a herd of thirty cattle, including sixteen milch cows, which is stall-fed throughout the summer, and there are fifty pigs. Apart from the hop-pickers, the farm-workers include the farmer himself, his wife, three sons ranging from seventeen to twenty years, a daughter, and three employees, two men and a woman. Considering that the agricultural area of the farm comes to over 130 acres, including the $6\frac{1}{4}$ acres of highly intensive hop-growing, this labour force of six men and three women represents a lower density of workers than was found at Miesbach.

4. The Difficulties of Farming on the Danubian Marshlands

226. Downstream of Ingolstadt, where the road to Nuremberg crosses the Danube, the Donaumoos, which covers some 42,800 acres, long

[1] 'Taxes exceed 40 marks per acre and in some cases represent 15 per cent. of the gross taking of the farm'—from *'L'agriculture de l'Allemagne Occidentale'*, by Weill and Césard, which appeared in *Revue du Ministère de l'Agriculture* for March 1952. In Camargue, the effect of the *Statut viticole* is to subsidize vineyards to the tune of 400,000 francs per acre, on land which, without the vines, was worth 40,000 francs and where the cost of planting did not reach 160,000 francs per acre. How much of the difference is recovered in taxes?

remained an area untouched by agriculture. At the end of the eighteenth century, at a time when the Physiocrats were drawing attention to the merits of agriculture, the Grand Duke Karl Theodor, who came to be known as the 'great farmer', made the first attempts at regulating the river and draining the land, and built a road into the region. A small trial field gave a promising harvest in the first year, and on this evidence it was supposed that a colonist could make a living from $7\frac{1}{2}$ acres. The first colonization began on this assumption, but the available plant foods in the highly organic soils were rapidly exhausted. Moreover, the vagaries of the climate proved a constant source of danger; drought and flood followed in the wake of rainfall variations which ranged from 10 to nearly 40 in. from one year to the next. Above all there were unexpected frosts, and it has since been recognized that only July is regularly frost-free; 23° F. is sometimes recorded in June and, partly owing to air drainage and the resulting temperature inversions, night temperatures over these peat soils fall 7° F. lower than on the small bordering hills, where the soils are not nearly so rich in humus.

In the hope that barge transport would develop to the benefit of the colonists, prisoners-of-war, convicts and soldiers were used to deepen the canals, but the disastrous harvests and the inadequate size of holdings caused the settlers to leave; the canals fell into disrepair and the region became desolate once again. A 9-lb. loaf was worth more than a *tagwerk* (rather less than 1 acre of land), and in spite of the grant of 7 gulden for every couple who were married on the marshland, those who remained were mainly beggars and thieves. Dr L. Scherm, formerly head of the Economic Service in the region, explained its history to us and told us how one of his ancestors used to send his eight children, in pairs, to beg in each of the villages in the neighbouring hills. The marsh-dwellers acquired an unenviable reputation and the priests of the regions round about collected money for them 'on condition that they remained where they were'.

There was some improvement after 1825, when land began to be granted in blocks of 42 acres, but poor harvests continued to force people to emigrate during the winter. It was not until 1860 that trials with potash and phosphatic fertilizers demonstrated how sorely the land needed these minerals, and in order to promote the use of these fertilizers the State, prompted to action by the marshland's record of repeated failure,[1] appointed an Agricultural Commission for the region

---

[1] The State even tried to sell the marshes to a peat merchant; the latter was unable to find the necessary money and the area remained in the hands of the State.

DEVELOPMENT OF THE DANUBIAN MARSHLANDS

in 1890 and created an experimental station in 1898. By this time the pressure of population was becoming a cogent argument in favour of development.

Heavy fertilizing with potash and phosphates to offset the excess of nitrogenous substances, combined with deeper ploughing, helped to establish a paying rotation of rye and potatoes. On the other hand, only spring varieties of rye were sown, for fear that early-maturing winter-sown crops would be spoilt by frost. Unfortunately, this not only meant that yields remained in the region of $5\frac{1}{2}$ cwt. per acre, but also that the crop was often so infested with weeds that, being useless for milling, it had to be put to less profitable use as fodder. Furthermore, the adoption of two crops which both needed to be sown in the spring resulted in excessive concentration of work at certain times of the year.

In recent years the late sowing of certain late-maturing winter varieties has proved successful. Analysis of the potatoes grown here showed that they were deficient in starch, but richer in nitrogen, and that they were therefore more suitable for seed than for starch manufacture. In 1933 there began a process of selecting virus-free stock, and the 'black potatoes', stained by the peat soils of the marshlands, soon commanded the best prices on the market. In 1952, 1,500 farms, covering 6,200 acres and supporting 7,000 people, produced a 50,000-ton crop, the main variety, as always, being Ackersegen.

227. Today every *Strassendorf*, or street-village, of the marshland has about forty tractors. Of extremely varied origin and professing five different religions, the marsh-dwellers have a progressive spirit which is completely opposed to the traditionalism of their once richer neighbours.

One farm near Karlshuld has a total of 32 acres, 25 of them in a 110 by 1,100 yd. rectangle of marshland which, as in the Haarlem *polder* in the Netherlands, abuts against the road at one end and the drainage canal at the other. The biennial rotation of rye, half of it autumn-sown, and potatoes is scrupulously followed. The latter are set 10 in. by 28 in. apart so as to obtain small tubers, and often yield over 12 tons to the acre. Eight workers are taken on for ten days at harvest-time in mid-September and receive 6 marks a day and are 'fed well'. Moreover, with the introduction of silos built above ground, winter rye-vetch mixtures and maize, grown exclusively for fodder, are beginning to appear in the rotation. There are $7\frac{1}{2}$ acres of meadow on the edge of the marshes where the lower peat content favours a good growth of white clover and grasses. This would not be possible on the marshland proper, where the surface opens up in great cracks during the dry summer.

A tractor and a pair of horses suffice to provide the power needed during the busiest times of the year. Potatoes being the main crop, there are often four pigs per 10 acres in the region, and on this farm the stock includes ten pigs, together with four or five cows and three stores. The three men of the family provide the labour and the mother has a woman to help her.

The prosperity of this region, which was still extremely poor at the beginning of the century, finds expression in the construction of silos and the modernization of farmhouses and farm buildings. In the stalls, for instance, the cattle are combed with the help of an electrically-operated suction machine. The fields produce not only food but also, if necessary, fuel; they are, say the local people, 'our forest'. Generally lying near the surface, the peat is cut with a narrow, straight spade with side flanges, 1 acre giving about 400,000 turves. A skilled man can cut them at 1,000 an hour, and they are then stacked up in walls ten turves high, with open spaces left to assist drying.

5. Colonization and the Uncertain Future of the Uneconomically Small Bavarian Farms

228. Many of the Sudeten and Silesian refugees long cherished the hope that they would be able to settle in the country and make a living out of farming, but in Bavaria, as in Spain, the term *Siedlung*, or 'colonization', is preferred to 'agrarian reform', which is not a popular phrase. Indeed, in West Germany reform has not been as far-reaching as in the east. An official document[1] published in Bavaria shows that out of 76,000 applicants who wished to become colonists, 46,000 wished to work full-time on the land and, on the basis of 25 acres per family, which is the generally recognized minimum, this would leave 1,150,000 acres to be found. In this region, however, the prevalence of small and medium-sized farms, together with the lesser severity, as compared with the east, of laws appertaining to the breaking up of large properties, has meant that only 94,800 acres have actually become available out of the 247,000 acres (2·4 per cent. of the agricultural area) in the hands of the State's 410 large landowners.[2] Of these, 13,300 acres have been

[1] *Förderung des Land-und Forst-Wirtschaft, eine Aufgabe des ganzen Volkes* (Bavarian Ministry of Food, Agriculture, and Forests, 1950). See also Dr Alois Schlögl's *Agrar Politik einst und jetzt* (Munich, 1948).

[2] *Unser Bayern* (quoted above) states that, out of half a million farms in Bavaria, 700 exceed 250 acres, covering 342,000 acres. Owner-farmers are in a very large majority, so that properties generally coincide with farm units. The large landowners generally have a larger proportion of their land under forest.

put at the disposal of animal-breeding and seed-propagation establishments owned by the State. Then, again, the future of some of the remaining 81,500 acres is not certain even now, for the owners have delayed the act of expropriation by exploiting every possible device offered by the law.

There are in addition 50,000 acres formerly used for military purposes, 16,000 acres set aside from State forests, and, finally, 26,200 acres of uncultivated land, mostly marshes, which only costly long-term projects can ever make fit for agriculture. By the end of 1949, 960 settlers had been installed on 28,400 acres and a further 5,800 acres had been set aside either for other agricultural purposes of one kind or another or for housing estates. (In 1951, homes were built for 2,500 smallholder families in Western Germany.)

Needless to say, the countryside has suffered little change in consequence. It is nevertheless true that agriculture in Bavaria, which, like the rest of Germany, more than doubled its yields in two generations before the First World War, has shown a more progressive spirit than in France.[1] West Germany as a whole has rapidly expanded her production again, in spite of the ravages of war; she has energetically pursued the dual aim of mechanization and intensification and, with the advantage of superior industrial strength, has quickly outstripped the east in point of mechanical power employed on the land. In 1948-9 she had almost regained her 1938 consumption of fertilizers and was already using three times the quantity of nitrates and potash per acre used in France and twice the amount of phosphates. At the end of 1952 there were 200,000 tractors for 35,000,000 acres of agricultural land, as compared with 180,000 for 80,000,000 acres in France. Nevertheless, in 1950 still only 3·5 per cent. of the farms were mechanized. Finally, although the pace has noticeably slackened more recently, the remarkable expansion of purchasing power until 1950 led to a rapid rise in the demand for agricultural produce from the towns.

229. The greatest obstacle today lies in the prevalence of holdings which are too small, and Franconia, like Alsace, is particularly unfortunate in this respect. The 'minimum living space' of 25 acres has been adopted in the Danube marshlands and by the colonization authorities, but, on poor soils and with mechanization, it seems rather too small. Nevertheless, more than half the farms of Bavaria do not reach this officially recognized minimum and, furthermore, the 2,000,000 farms

---

[1] Ch. Parain informs us that their history shows the Bavarians to be more enterprising than the Alamans who are found from Alsace to Swabia and into Switzerland.

in the whole of West Germany cover no more than 35 million acres, 40 per cent. of which is grassland. The average of 17½ acres per farm is only half the French figure, barely a sixth of the English, and less than an eleventh of the average in the U.S.A. There are twice as many workers per acre as in France, so that in spite of yields being very much higher the productivity per unit of labour remains fractionally lower.

We have searched in vain, however, for evidence of Government plans to deal with the problem of excessively small farms. Moreover, the position is aggravated by the growing use of tractors, and one all too often sees the tractor and the scythe on adjacent holdings, the transition stage, generally represented in France by the horse-drawn binder, being entirely omitted. On the very small holdings, which often drift more and more into debt,[1] there are still far too few mechanical aids, and the upper terraces, although more frequently developed than in France as sources of timber, show signs of reverting to uncultivated waste land. The reintegration of fragmented holdings which it is hoped to complete in thirty years, at 250,000 acres a year, will afford some measure of relief, but will evidently not affect the average size of farms. On the whole, it seems that German agriculture is moving towards a greater degree of social stratification, a trend which frequently goes hand in hand with a capitalist economy, and there are certain elements which would cheerfully exploit the position of the small farmer to the full.

Unser Bayern[2] reiterates the traditional virtues of the small farm, its resistance to economic depression and its association of crop cultivation with animal husbandry; it does not point out that the former is mainly a result of privation and overwork, nor that the latter is not an uncommon feature of other types of farming. It admits that 'the romantic values of a conservative agrarian policy, which were once so widely recognized, no longer have the same appeal either for the younger generation of countrymen or the town-dweller; nevertheless, Bavaria is one of the Germanic regions where these traditional peasant virtues have been upheld most successfully'. H. Haushofen concludes, without offering any convincing evidence: 'It is fair to say that from the modern biological and technical point of view the Bavarian peasant farm offers an absolutely perfect solution to the problem confronting agriculture.'

[1] 'The efforts made by the farmer are handicapped at every turn, especially when he has only a small farm, by the lack of financial means', declare Weill and Césard.

[2] Pp. 61-7.

One may safely assume that when he wrote these words the author had never worked with a team of cows on one of the tiny 7½-acre farms of the Swabian or Franconian Jura. Here in Bavaria the small farm seems not to be regarded, as in the east, as a temporary stage in a process of development, but as a fixed and perfect element in the agrarian structure. We have little doubt that the future will not confirm this opinion, especially if in the context of full employment and economic expansion industry and commerce show themselves capable of absorbing the rural labour surplus which is now being created by rapid mechanization. To our Bavarian friends we commend the thought that to accept the present situation as a 'perfect solution' would be a dangerous error.

XI

The Belgian Farm—Well Kept, but Undersized[1]

230. From the dunes and *polders* of the North Sea littoral to the Luxemburg frontier in the south, Belgium presents a rapid sequence of diverse physical conditions. The sterile sands of the Campine and northern Flanders, the clays derived from the schists of the Ardennes and the rich loams of Hainaut, Brabant, and Hesbaye are at vastly different points along the scale of natural soil fertility. Frosts occur on fifty days a year at Ostend, but on over 160 days on the high plateau of the Ardennes and the rainfall figures show similar variations. As in the Netherlands, however, and in contrast with southern and eastern Europe, scarcity of water is a minor factor in the demarcation of crop lands, and the fodder crop revolution, which faces such heavy odds in the Mediterranean, has here been facilitated by natural conditions.

Belgium even more so than Switzerland is primarily an industrial country, but on the eve of the last war 17 per cent. of the employed and a fifth of the total population were still dependent on agriculture. For many years she was the most densely populated country in Europe, but has recently been surpassed by the Netherlands, whose population increase of fourteen per 1,000 during the last fifteen years compares with only three per 1,000 for Belgium. In 1952 Belgium had only about ½ acre of agricultural land per head, but whereas her population of 8,700,000 represented an overall density of 727 persons per square mile, the Netherlands by this time had risen to well over 750 per square mile. The Belgian peasant is energetic and hard-working; he often enjoys a sound technical education and receives plenty of practical guidance. His farming, nevertheless, does not reach the very high standard set by his northern neighbour. To some extent, Belgian agriculture lacks capital, and this, in conjunction with the generally small

---

[1] Field studies in 1927 and in summer 1950. Prices refer to 1950, when there were 140 Belgian francs to the £1.

size of farms, even more striking here than in Bavaria, is in varying degrees hindering the modernization of techniques.

1. Bouvignies, on the Loess of Hainaut, and the Part-time Farmer[1]

231. North of the industrial town of Ath, the commune of Bouvignies (Fig. 21), which has loess soils overlying sand, comprises a total of 110 acres of agricultural land. Its 143 farmers, however, have also turned their attention to the land of neighbouring villages and actually cultivate a total of 1,190 acres, 695 of which are under permanent grassland. This is better managed than in France, but is still greatly inferior to the grasslands of Holland, and, considering the number of farmers, it is surprising to find so much land given over to a semi-extensive form of utilization. The explanation lies partly in the fact that seventy-one or half the farmers have less than $2\frac{1}{2}$ acres and they devote only part of their time to farming.

Most of the twenty-one farmers with holdings of between $2\frac{1}{2}$ and $7\frac{1}{2}$ acres still have no draught animals, and are therefore partly dependent on other forms of employment. Some of them work in factories, others on the roads, and a few of them own small shops or cafés. Cattle are not used so much for draught purposes as in Flanders, but the larger holding often has its horse, and among the fifty-one farms of over $7\frac{1}{2}$ acres there are fifty-two horses of more than three years of age. Some of the fifteen farmers with between $7\frac{1}{2}$ and $12\frac{1}{2}$ acres still carry on another trade, as we shall see, and only the holdings which exceed this acreage occupy their owners full-time and really deserve to be classed as farms. Altogether there are twenty-one holdings of between $12\frac{1}{2}$ and 25 acres, fourteen of between 25 and 50 acres, and one exceptional case of 65 acres.

For many years this last example comprised more than 200 acres, and its farm buildings are still commensurate with its former size. It was subdivided owing to the pressure of population in the region, but not into quite such small fragments as its nearest rival, which suffered a similar fate. Whereas the average size of farms is on the increase in the depopulated countryside of England and France, in Belgium overpopulation is having the opposite effect, and farms of over 25 acres have decreased from 46,000 in 1836 to 41,000 in 1930 and to barely more than 30,000 in 1952.

[1] Our studies were guided by M. Neerdal, of the Ath Agricultural School.

Overpopulation, moreover, is giving rise to inordinately high rents and land values. In 1950, in spite of price controls, land was selling at 25,000 to 65,000 francs (140 to the £1) an acre and rents were in the region of 6,000 to 7,000 francs, the equivalent of 3 to 4 cwt. of wheat. As in nineteenth-century France, the peasants are willing to slave and starve for the sake of owning a little land, and tenancy is losing ground in consequence. In 1930, 60 per cent. of the agricultural area and 53

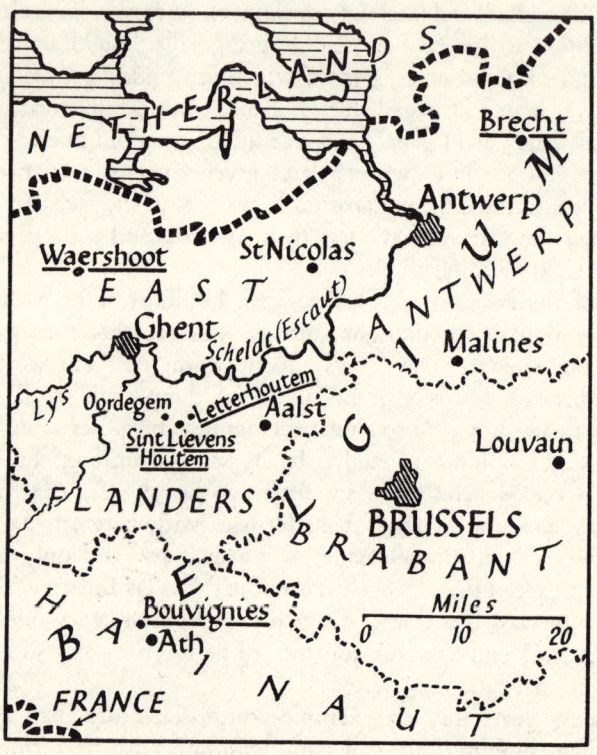

FIG. 21. Belgium.

per cent. of the holdings in Belgium were still farmed by tenants, but these figures are slightly lower today.

232. When he started in 1905, Crispels senior rented 2½ acres of land, on which he managed to keep two cows and a large number of poultry. First and foremost, however, he was a farm labourer. Every year he thinned, hoed, and lifted 2½ acres of mangolds, and for every three days' work he could earn the use of a pair of horses for ploughing his

own land.[1] By dint of a lifetime of privation, he succeeded in buying 7½ acres of land.

The unmarried son, helped by his widowed mother, now works this land and rents another 3¾ acres. Apart from 2½ acres of hay meadow and 3¾ acres of pasture, there are 5 acres of ploughland under the same three-year rotation as on the next farm to be described. There are three cows of the blue Hainaut breed,[2] but they are not often harnessed, as Crispels prefers to hire horses from his brother-in-law at 20 francs an hour per horse.[3] Because of the appreciation in the relative value of property, the son is unable to add to his holding, as his father did, by working on the land. On the contrary, he is unwillingly compelled to work an eight-hour day in a chemical factory, and has to put in another five hours a day on the holding during the summer. Such holdings are too small to mechanize, and they evidently offer little reward for hard work. Indeed, the part-time farmer leads a life of virtual slavery.[4]

The object of farming is self-sufficiency. Only 5 cwt. of butter and two or three fat calves (300 lb. apiece) are sold every year, and a cow is sold for slaughtering from time to time. A little maize has to be bought for the fowls, which are not, however, as numerous as before. Animal products are therefore the mainstay of the enterprise, and this follows the pattern of Belgian agriculture as a whole, which derives three-quarters of its income from animal husbandry. Crispels' eventual aim is to buy another 7½ acres so as to enlarge the holding to the 15 acres, which he considers to be the minimum he needs to make a living. But as he was already forty-five and said nothing about getting married, we refrained from pursuing the subject of how much longer he would have to go on saving on meat before realizing his dream. It would in fact be about another twenty years, always providing that his health, which was already affected, was not ruined before then by the poisonous fumes at the factory.

233. The André family is of Flemish origin, and left its densely peopled homeland about 1880. At first it was regarded with suspicion

[1] At this time, in Dalecarlia, in Sweden, a man gave a day's work in return for two days of work by horses.

[2] This is a dual-purpose breed known in Cambrésis as *Bleue du Nord*. The breed is considered to have originated in Belgium, and it is favoured by the Government; it is tending, however, to give place to the Friesian, which is a more specialized milk breed.

[3] 25 francs 'outside the family'.

[4] Like the Saar miner, who is tending to give up his 'two-cow holding' and content himself with a garden and a patch of potatoes.

by the local inhabitants, and although this attitude has now largely disappeared there is still a certain feeling of jealousy at this 'colonization' of the Walloon-speaking region. Their farm comprises a good 25 acres: $17\frac{1}{2}$ acres of meadows, 5 of which are cut for an early crop of hay, and $7\frac{1}{2}$ acres of arable land, where the standard three-year rotation is scrupulously followed.

The first course in the rotation consists of potatoes, sugar-beet, and mangolds, while wheat remains unchallenged as the second-year crop. The traditional third-year crop is oats, but many progressive-minded farmers are beginning to sow some of their land to spring wheat or winter barley instead. The latter has the advantage that it can be followed more easily by a catch-crop of thousand-headed kale, a common practice, as we shall see, in Flanders. The absence of sown grasses—only 5 acres in the whole commune[1]—is a noteworthy feature.

New high-yielding fodder crops first appeared in 1951, rather later than in Flanders and the Campine: Italian rye-grass, which is sown at the same time as a cereal, and rye grown for fodder, followed by a mixture of oats and vetches. As late as July 1950, although it would have been much simpler to provide grass and nitrogen-rich fodder crops, over 2 lb. of linseed cake per cow and a similar quantity of oats were still being consumed every day, and it was high time that more modern techniques were adopted. The very high density of animals in the region does in fact necessitate the purchase of enormous quantities of concentrates, and on some farms the economic balance of the undertaking suffers in consequence. The André farm has two horses for its $7\frac{1}{2}$ acres of ploughland, and the herd includes eight milch cows, three stores, and the current year's calves. André's aim is to build up his herd to nine cows and six stores of two years or more.

There is also a sow; the piglets are sold at six weeks, and the family consumes some 330 lb. of pork a year. Unlike the Germans and the Flemings, who eat a great deal of pork, the Walloons prefer butcher's meat and poultry whenever they have the choice. In 1880 the André farm began with $7\frac{1}{2}$ acres and three cows, which were also harnessed

[1] Similarly absent in French Flanders. The commune has 475 acres of pastures, 210 of meadows for hay (one cutting), 150 acres of wheat, 102 of oats, 40 of barley, and 5 of rye; also 70 acres of mangolds, 42 of sugar beet, and 37 of potatoes; $2\frac{1}{2}$ acres of tobacco, $12\frac{1}{2}$ of gardens, and 15 of orchards are a sure sign of the beginnings of intensification. As far as animals are concerned, there are 70 horses, 564 cattle, only 232 of which are cows and heifers (31 occasionally used in harness), 38 pigs, and 3,000 head of poultry. These statistics are regarded as military secrets, but they were given to us all the same. We do not think that their publication will constitute a threat to the country's defences.

when needed, 6¼ acres had been added by 1900, and there were 26 acres in all by 1950. Work is provided today for the farmer, his wife, and their twenty-year-old daughter, while the grandmother does most of the housework and the fifteen-year-old daughter helps during the holidays. The result is almost three workers for 26 acres, or one for little less than 10 acres.

The wheat yield, which attained 52 cwt. per acre in 1949, averages about 40 cwt. The crop is partly sold and partly exchanged for flour, and the farm bakes bread, not only for its own requirements, but also for sale to neighbours, 53 lb. a week—that is, 25 cwt. a year—being sold. The main income, however, is from the sale of cattle (four stores and two calves and one or two cows for slaughter every year) and from the sale of butter at the rate of about 44 lb. a week. In addition, over 1 gallon of milk is sold to neighbours each day. As on the North French coalfield and in the suburbs of the Lille-Roubaix-Tourcoing agglomeration, the factory worker here benefits greatly from being able to buy farm produce cheaply almost on his doorstep. As yet there is little in the way of farm equipment, the edges of the fields are still cut with a small scythe, and there are few binders and no tractors in the commune. Mme André considers that their farm is too small, and would prefer to have twice as much land and be able to have a tractor, and a milking-machine, etc.

2. Flanders South of Ghent; Tiny Holdings and 'Satellite Farms'[1]

234. In the sandy region north of Ghent villages are fairly widely spaced, but they cluster together much more closely on the richer sandy loams to the south, where the textile industry is an added resource. Sint Lievens Houtem, for instance, has four cotton mills employing 300 workers, each of whom has his own garden and sometimes a field or two and a pig, a goat, and a cow besides. The same also applies to other workers, to business-men and people of independent means, and this explains the fact that there are 525 holdings of less than 2½ acres out of a total of 1,105 acres of agricultural land.

There are 134 holdings of between 2½ and 12½ acres, and farming is the main source of income of about half their owners, which is a higher proportion than in Hainaut. There are no draught animals on holdings of less than 5 acres, but above this figure and up to about 10 acres milch cows are used for work in the fields much more readily than in

[1] Studied under the guidance of M. Verkinderen, Professor of Rural Economy at the Ghent Agronomic Institute.

Hainaut; there are, however, seventy-one horses in the commune, and one of these is generally harnessed in preference to a cow or a pair of cows. There are a further fourteen farms of $12\frac{1}{2}$-25 acres and three of 25-50 acres. Formerly there were about a dozen large farms, one of them in the region of 125 acres, but only two of these remain, and even the larger one is now down to 75 acres. As for the remainder, they have been replaced by smallholdings mostly in the range of 5-$12\frac{1}{2}$ acres, and today it is farms of this size which account for the greater part of the cultivated area of the commune.

Intensive farming has been practised for very many years. Originally the region was mainly forested, and clearing started to gather momentum in the eleventh century. By the thirteenth century cattle had begun to replace sheep and fallow was already disappearing from the rotation. Rape was introduced in the sixteenth century, flax at the end of the seventeenth, and the potato shortly afterwards. The region had long been overpopulated even at this period, and the effect of the potato was to abolish the famines which had often threatened in the past. About 1810, the Continental blockade favoured the spread of chicory and sugar-beet; the humble mangold had already been grown for many years.

235. Whereas his grandfather, who owned 'two cows and five acres', used to go to France for the harvest and to work on the sugar-beet fields, Serre Deroo now has $12\frac{1}{2}$ acres and a horse, and is one of the 'large' farmers of the district. He keeps four cows ('I really need five'), two stores, two calves for fattening, and two sows. Pig-rearing is particularly important in Flanders because of the association with potatoes and skim-milk. It enables production per acre to be appreciably increased on a smallholding, and so long as grain can be purchased from outside it represents, like poultry-keeping, an invaluable instrument of intensification; cereals are processed on the farm itself as a factory processes its raw materials. On the Deroo farm there are two litters a year, and twenty to twenty-five pigs and a few piglets are sold annually.

The annual yield of milk is about 1,000 gallons per cow. Butter is made from it and, at 30 francs a pound, brings in as much money as if the whole milk were sold direct at 11.40 francs a gallon. In a sense, therefore, the cost price of skim-milk is nil, but in 1950 the most profitable method of using milk was for fattening calves, which fetched nearly 20 francs a pound live weight and gave a return of 18 francs per gallon of milk consumed. When the market price is as high as this, Deroo buys new-born calves in addition to his own, and even includes eggs and half a dozen lumps of sugar in their daily ration.

This waste of food is the direct result of the price of veal, which bears little relation to the nutritive value of the meat.

The 5 acres of permanent grassland[1] represent, even more strikingly than in Hainaut, an anomalous intrusion of semi-extensive land use. The fairly high proportion of inferior grasses—agrostis and feathergrass in particular—and the general standard of management, which is not always above criticism, prevent the attainment of a production level consonant with the high density of rural population. Some of the grasslands of the commune were ploughed during the war, but they have more than regained their 1939 extent. As against this, those who follow the advice of the Agricultural Station at Melle obtain very high yields.

The clearing of woodland, however, which continued in this commune until 1949, reveals a trend in favour of intensification, and techniques of arable farming are superior to those of grassland management. On the Deroo farm, root crops occupy $2\frac{1}{4}$ acres with rather more potatoes than mangolds. The former are used almost entirely for animal feeding, but artichokes would undoubtedly give better yields. Nearly half the $2\frac{3}{4}$ acres of cereals consists of rye, which thrives on sandy soils and helps to feed the pigs. Immediately after cutting, it is stooked alongside the cowshed, and this enables the field to be ploughed, manured, and sown to turnips straight away—sometimes even on the same day.

As in Brittany, the technique of growing catch-crops is highly developed, and as a result 30 per cent. of the ploughland gives two crops a year. Rye would have been much more generally replaced by wheat were it not for its early ripening,[2] which allows an extra crop to be taken. Once fallows are eliminated, catch-crops are the next logical development, and the reliable summer rainfall of this region makes them much more dependable than on the semi-arid chernozems of Anhalt-Saxony in East Germany. As the density of animals on the Deroo farm is so high—it is higher still on several other farms—every field can be manured once a year, or even twice when turnips can be followed by another root crop. There are also $1\frac{1}{8}$ acres of barley (grown

---

[1] The commune has 312 acres of grassland, 35 of vegetables (mainly chicory) and 25 of orchards. There are 720 acres of arable land, the main crops being as follows: 150 acres of wheat, 135 of rye, 72 of oats, 35 of barley, and 116 of potatoes. There are 71 draught horses and 18 foals, 526 head of cattle, including 300 cows, 60 of which are harnessed, nearly 600 pigs, and, finally, 1,100 poultry (far fewer in numbers than in the Campine).

[2] The best answer would be a very early variety of wheat.

THE BELGIAN FARM

as a catch-crop) and the same of wheat, but only $\frac{1}{2}$ acre of oats. The horse may not be overworked, but nor is it fed any too well.

Owing to the pressure of population, land values are about 76,000 francs and rents 960 francs an acre. 'I could not make a living if I were a tenant,' says Deroo, who owns four-fifths of his farm. In addition to himself, his wife and son also work full-time on the holding. His daughter, whose husband works on the railway, lives on the farm and does all the housework. Were he a tenant, Deroo would try to find a larger holding, but the fact that he owns the land prevents him from moving, and he cannot rent any more land where he is.

As far as work is concerned, Deroo admits that he is not unduly hard-pressed, and the general picture of under-employment is in sharp contrast with the situation at Bouvignies, where Crispels, who is both factory hand and farmer and has almost as much land as Deroo, is dreadfully overworked. A neighbouring farm has 53 acres of land and is worked by only seven people, thanks to a jeep and a binder (there are six binders in the whole commune). Admittedly, a larger proportion of the area is devoted to forage crops and less to permanent grass than on the Deroo holding, but the number of animals per acre is comparable. North of Ghent, at Staden, one may find even fewer workers per acre—only four on a 45-acre farm in one instance, but obviously even this ratio would seem absurdly high in the United States. Deroo himself is still very much preoccupied with providing for his own needs, and grows his own pipe tobacco, turnip and mangold seed (this practice encourages the spread of mangold jaundice), and even his own grapes under glass. He goes about without socks in wooden clogs.

236. In the neighbouring commune of Letterhoutem there are only two binders, and the largest farm has no more than 38 acres. M. Eloot has a 20-acre farm, and whereas three of his five sons are students, destined for professional or business careers, most of the very small holdings send their young men out to local factories. The Eloot farm comprises 15 acres of ploughland and 5 of grassland, and has seven cows, seven stores, and three horses. This last figure may appear unduly high at first, but the horses also serve the needs of four satellite farms, ranging in size from $3\frac{3}{4}$ to 5 acres, which have no draught animals of their own.

One of these, which totals $4\frac{1}{4}$ acres, including 1 acre of grass orchard, belongs to a man of fifty. He has $\frac{1}{3}$ acre of potatoes, the same of mangolds and of clover, 1 acre of wheat, $\frac{5}{8}$ acres of rye, and the same of chicory. In comparison with the Deroo farm, the proportion of grass and cereals is lower, the latter occupying less than half the arable acreage. Fodder cereals are entirely absent. The smallholder grows only just enough grain for his own needs, and a relatively large area is devoted to a type of vegetable which demands a very large amount of labour. Rather more than half the chicory plants are forced, and there are four glass frames, each of 18 sq. yds., for this purpose; seventeen days of work are needed in the first stage of growth and a further thirty once the plants are in the frames, but production reaches some 56 cwt. annually. During the last fifty years especially, chicory has steadily usurped the place of flax and rape, and even to some extent of potatoes, in the rotation. It keeps large numbers of smallholders in business, and a sharp fall in price would bring ruin to many.

Having no horses, this particular holding can support two cows and one or two stores, and can fatten from six to eight pigs a year. Nowadays, instead of paying in labour for services, such as ploughing, the smallholder settles his debts in cash. He brings his wheat to the 'parent' farm to be threshed. The farmer, who supplies a labourer for this work and pays for the electric current, receives 75 francs for threshing a cartload, or about $6\frac{1}{2}$ cwt., of wheat. This represents the yield from little more than $\frac{1}{5}$ acre. For clearing the stubble, ploughing, and sowing, the smallholder pays 200 francs an acre. At harvest-time he is employed at 75 francs a day, and on average each satellite holding supplies about a fortnight's work a year.

The father continued with factory work until about the age of forty. By this time his son was fifteen and therefore able to enter the factory in his turn. The father virtually went into semi-retirement and busied himself mainly with growing food for the family and making a few clogs in the winter. The son now helps on the land at busy times of the year. One also finds satellite holdings of as little as $\frac{3}{4}$ acre. These are not invariably run by men who are getting on in years; more generally the smallholders are semi-unemployed labourers of small ambition. Those who have any real pretensions to farming aim at '$12\frac{1}{2}$ acres and a small horse'—not a thoroughbred and not too fond of oats. In Georgia after the Civil War—admittedly it was a less densely populated region than this—the freed slave's dream was of '40 acres and a mule'. The shortage of farms, as in Mayenne, results in later marriages, but causes many young couples to start out with a mere 5 or 10 acres and a horse borrowed from an obliging parent. Unless industry continues to absorb the surplus rural population, the future offers a disquieting prospect.

237. Twenty-five years ago, on the sandier soils north of Ghent, the

willow-lined fields were still separated by stretches of heathland. Buckwheat is no longer grown nowadays, and a fairly common rotation consists of rye followed by potatoes. We visited a one-man farm near Waershoot, and found to our surprise that the owner had no desire to enlarge his holding. In his opinion, where a holding was too large for its owner to manage without assistance, but not large enough to warrant mechanization, the value of additional production accruing from the employment of a farmhand was almost completely offset by the cost of his wages (45,000 francs annually). The employment of labour was thus an economic proposition only in the case of large mechanized farms. If this is true it is certainly a condemnation of the medium-sized holding.

There was a similar kind of social structure in nineteenth-century Lorraine, with some providing the animals and equipment needed for ploughing and others supplying the manual labour. In Lorraine the system has vanished,[1] but it still survives in the overcrowded Flemish countryside. Horses from the larger farms are used for ploughing and for drawing heavy loads, and men digging their fields or drawing their wooden harrows over the land are less common sights than they once were. For the day-to-day work of carting a little manure, green maize, a few beet-tops, or sheaves of rye, the peasant still relies mainly on his wheelbarrow.

The only part of Flanders where there is as yet no rural overcrowding is the *polders*, which were developed later than the other areas and have a larger number of sizeable farms. Some of these, however, have already been subdivided. In one family at Ramskapelle[2] the grandfather has 150 acres, the father 100. In order to provide for both his sons, the father has already built another house so that each of them will have 50 acres, and the next step will be to start planning for the grandchildren. In western Flanders, where the farming population is energetic, enterprising, and progressive by comparison with the east, and possibly, on the whole, more intelligent, at least one member of practically every family has crossed the border into France and settled there.

In this region of high crop yields, rural overpopulation is undoubtedly helping to preserve an anachronistic social structure and preventing the modernization of agriculture. In consequence, the spade and the wheelbarrow are still characteristic items of farm equipment, and the output per worker remains comparatively low. As compared with the Netherlands, Belgium has a somewhat smaller area, but a much larger number

---

[1] *Voyages en France d'un agronome*, Chapter XI.

[2] Near the coast, eight miles south-west of Ostend.

of farm units, and it is of some significance that although the percentage of rural population is similar, the former is a considerable exporter of agricultural produce, whereas the latter always has a large deficit to make up by imports.[1]

Every year the agricultural area loses ground to the advancing tide of town and road, house and factory, stadium and playing-field. Unlike the Netherlands, Belgium has no Yssel Meer for future expansion, but fairly large areas have been reclaimed in the Campine, where physical conditions are similar to the eastern part of the Netherlands.

3. Intensive Farming at Brecht on the Heaths of the Campine

238. The surface of the region consists of friable sands generally overlying clay, and the soils are therefore poor, permeable, excessively dry in the summer, but badly drained in the winter. Birch heath was the dominant vegetation in former times and heather was sometimes cut for use as stable litter. In this case, as in Brittany, it was piled into a hollow in the floor of the stall. Sometimes it was burnt and the ashes used as fertilizer. The first efforts at reclamation began in the second half of the eighteenth century, and were accompanied by the planting of Scots pines and the establishment of meadows, which were sometimes irrigated. Rye, followed by oats and potatoes, was the main crop on the cleared land. There were catch-crops of spurry, and turnips, which were boiled in the same pot as the potatoes, were grown to see the cattle through the winter. Particularly in the vicinity of Antwerp, where city refuse was widely used for enriching the land, the new farms were mostly of less than 8 acres, and 20 acres was exceptional. They generally had a horse or a cow for work in the fields, but some of the cultivation was still done by hand. Lupins came into use as green manure after 1850. Larger farms appeared further east, especially after the end of the nineteenth century and on the recently cleared land around Turnhout and Poppel there are units of up to 175 acres.

At Brecht, fifteen miles north-east of Antwerp, a second wave of settlement, released by the increasing pressure of population in Flanders since 1918, has resulted in the pine plantations being cleared in their turn. Moreover, the dairy cow and the spread of meadows and fodder crops are resulting in encroachments on the fields of rye and other cereals. M. Schoofs, the Government agricultural adviser who con-

[1] Since 1953 increased yields have enabled Belgium to be almost self-sufficient in milk products; she had already reached this position for meat. The lower level of consumption due to unemployment, however, had contributed to this 'equilibrium'.

ducted us, is doing all he can to encourage this trend, and the barns on the Meerstens farm, which were once replete with sheaves of grain, are now filled with hay. Once again therefore the progressiveness of a farm bears an inverse relation to the proportion of its land under cereals.

The new farms are either grouped in hamlets or dispersed in the vicinity of an older settlement. Few of them have less than '$7\frac{1}{2}$ acres and three cows', which is the accepted minimum for supporting a man and his family, and neither the part-time farmer nor the satellite holding plays any significant part in the social structure of these new communities. In the opinion of M. Schoofs, 17 to 20 acres of intensively farmed land are needed to live 'normally'. Nevertheless, M. Meerstens, who owns about 25 acres near the town, would very much like to buy more. Although this region, unlike Flanders, still had land to spare about 1900, there is no room left for expansion today. On the contrary, most of the farms in the commune have been subdivided at one time or another during the last thirty years and many of the young people, and some even who are not so young, are waiting for a farm before getting married. Land was cheap in the nineteenth century, but today it sells at 40,000 to 70,000 francs an acre, and rents are in the neighbourhood of 600 to 800 francs. In other words, land values are as high as in the loess region of Hainaut, which has the only naturally fertile soils in the whole of Belgium. In Hainaut, however, the demand for land is reduced by the greater development of manufacturing industry, which offers an alternative to agricultural employment.

239. Chemical fertilizers have greatly accelerated the process of soil improvement. In the Campine this has compensated for the very late start as compared with Flanders, which has benefited from centuries of careful cultivation, but which, in the north, was once just as sterile as the Campine itself. Indeed, the virtues of chemical fertilizers are so widely recognized that farmers do not have to be encouraged to use them as in France. On the contrary, they have to be restrained from using them too liberally. Meerstens, on his $17\frac{1}{2}$ acres of meadows (of which $6\frac{1}{4}$ are mown for hay) and $7\frac{1}{2}$ acres of ploughland,[1] uses nearly

[1] The proportion of grassland varies between a half and two-thirds of the total area of agricultural land. The Meerstens farm has $2\frac{1}{2}$ acres of oats, $1\frac{1}{4}$ of barley, the same of rye, $\frac{3}{4}$ acres of mangolds, $\frac{5}{8}$ acres of potatoes, $\frac{3}{8}$ acres of rye grass for seed, and $1\frac{3}{8}$ acres which are intensively double-cropped (Italian rye grass, followed by marrow-stemmed kale); in addition, there are catch-crops as listed below. Of the meadows cut for hay, $\frac{5}{8}$ acres are cut three times, once for silage and twice for hay; $1\frac{1}{4}$ acres, comprising a field of permanent grassland some distance from the farm, are cut twice for hay, and the remainder is cut once and then grazed.

7 tons of basic slag (16 per cent. content), 80 cwt. of potash fertilizer (40 per cent.), and 64 cwt. of nitrates (20·5 per cent.) per year. This represents 100 lb. of phosphoric acid, 140 lb. of potassium, and 58 lb. of nitrogen to the acre.[1]

As his father's farm was too small to be divided up among all the children, Meerstens began as a docker in Antwerp, and was thus able to save far more money to buy land of his own than he could have done as an agricultural worker. The peasant today feels that his social position has improved considerably in the last few decades,[2] and although he may still reconcile himself to the idea of his daughter becoming a seamstress, he is no longer so willing for his son to work as a farm hand. Instead, he turns to intensive dairying or to market-gardening and concentrates on crops such as strawberries.

As in Flanders intensification was achieved by planting turnips immediately after the rye harvest. Nowadays, double-cropping with green crops for silage is becoming a common practice. Italian rye-grass follows barley or mangolds, and is succeeded by transplanted marrow-stemmed kale the following summer. This type of double-cropping yields 400 to 500 units of plant food, or the equivalent of 80 to 100 cwt. of cereals, to the acre; and this on soils which as late as 1900 were no better than poor heathland. An acre of old grassland in Normandy, where the soils are naturally more fertile than here, would produce something between 15 per cent. and 20 per cent. of this quantity at the most. The comparison demonstrates that nowadays, thanks to the progress of agricultural science, production depends less on the physical conditions than on the manner in which the land is farmed. The former play a minor part, unless they comprise some intractable adverse factor, which then imposes certain limitations. The local agricultural advisers are encouraging the adoption of this particular rotation on $2\frac{1}{2}$ to 4 acres of each farm. It is very nearly the most intensive technique of fodder production in the world for this type of climate, and in Europe only certain irrigated districts of Lombardy can offer more, but the possibilities of the latter are only occasionally exploited to the full.

The ploughing up of grassland, which is managed in leys of ten to

---

[1] Belgian consumption of fertilizers per acre (grassland and arable land combined) reached its maximum for nitrogen in 1945-7 (41 lb.), for potash in 1947-8 (58 lb.), and for phosphoric acid in 1948-9 ($47\frac{1}{2}$ lb.). In 1952 the figures were slightly lower than in the Netherlands, where consumption was higher than anywhere else in the world; Belgium held second place.

[2] On some farms, several people still eat off the same plate of potatoes. Bread is more often eaten with dripping than with butter. The better times of recent years have not seen the disappearance of all the old habits of frugality.

fifty years, constitutes another advance, but even better results could be obtained by shortening these leys to five to ten years. On his 25 acres, Meerstens can already keep ten cows of the *pie rouge* breed from the eastern part of the Netherlands; and in addition he has two heifers in calf, five one- and two-year-old stores, two calves, a horse, and finally three sows, whose litters are a regular source of income. Before the war Belgium was the third largest exporter of eggs in the world, and poultry-keeping has a larger place in the Campine than in Flanders. The Meerstens farm has 250 pullets and 200 hens. The farm has four full-time workers—the father, two sons, and a daughter; the mother keeps house.

240. Belgian agriculture is often intensive especially in terms of the quantity of fertilizer employed. For the most part, arable land, orchards, and gardens benefit from these, but in spite of marked progress in recent years the standard of grass management still varies considerably. The high crop yields per acre, however, are often very expensive in terms of human effort. The lack of machinery and its corollary, the excessive use of manual labour, bring the law of diminishing returns into full operation and restrict the productivity of labour to a comparatively low level. On the other hand, little can be done about mechanization while farm units remain so small, and this is the main reason why Belgian agriculture does not compare favourably with that of the Netherlands. The higher costs of production in Belgium are an obstacle to the emergence of Benelux as an effective commercial entity and, considered in conjunction with the level of wages, which, owing to greater industrialization, is higher than in the Netherlands, they constitute a threat to the internal economy of the country. The reintegration of holdings on a voluntary basis was the subject of a law passed in 1949, but as compared with French legislation it represents a somewhat diffident approach to the problem. However necessary the regrouping of holdings may be, it has very little bearing on the question of the size of farms.

It is often said that one of the great assets of Belgian industry is the common practice of combining factory work with work on the land. We have seen that when each member of the family is engaged in a single occupation there is generally too little land to keep the farmer fully occupied. On the other hand, if an individual combines both occupations he has to work excessively long hours. In either case, although the factory-owner may often find cause for satisfaction, the worker's position leaves much to be desired.

As we have already seen in the mountains of the northern Cameroons, of Kabylia, and of the Alps, in the deltas and coastal plains of the Mediterranean and the Far East and on the Bavarian plateau, and as we shall see once again in eastern Europe, of all the factors which bar the way to modernization in rural areas, overpopulation is the most ubiquitous. Everywhere industrialization presents itself as the surest remedy. It can rapidly increase production in town and country, drawing population away from the latter, but assuring it of better equipment. At this point in our survey, therefore, it will be of some interest to cross the North Sea and examine the situation in England.

XII

The Recovery of English Agriculture; Rapid Mechanization[1]

With its large area of highland massifs, its relatively cool climate, and its preponderance of heavy soils, the United Kingdom offers an environment which, on the whole, is not particularly favourable for agriculture. The lowlands of the south and east, however, enjoy a comparatively dry climate, with a mean annual rainfall of less than 25 in. in the Fens, and loamy soils well suited to cereals. By way of contrast, the uplands and valleys of the west and north often, as in central Wales, receive as much as 60 in. of rain and are notorious for their cloudy skies; the soils are acidic and relatively poor, and cereals do not ripen well. These conditions favour fodder production, and at its simplest this takes the form of permanent grassland. At least as important as the physical conditions, however, in determining the structure, development, and bias of English agriculture have been the historical factors.

1. From the Disappearance of the Peasantry to the 'Stick and Dog' Farming of the Present Century

241. The three-field system, essentially an arable system, a form of which survives in north-eastern France to this day, was abandoned in England during the course of the seventeenth and eighteenth centuries. The pendulum swung away from communal enterprise, the animals belonging to the village were no longer herded together on the stubble and bare fallow, the people left their nucleated settlements and re-established themselves in the midst of their farmland in small dispersed communities.

The characteristic features of this change were the enclosures, and

[1] Employed as an agricultural worker in south Shropshire in August-September 1950; field studies were undertaken under the guidance of farmers Higgs and Aron. Unless otherwise stated, figures relating to earnings, wages, etc., refer to 1950.

from this time onward every field had its hedgerow or wall. This enabled each farmer to graze his animals separately without having to employ a herdsman; this, unfortunately, is still not true of many parts of France. The grouping of the fields around each farmhouse and the virtual integration which resulted therefrom made for appreciable economies in the costs of production.

At the same time the very small enterprise tended to disappear. Before the enclosures, the cottager was only able to make ends meet by combining the cultivation of his small strips of land with animal husbandry. The latter, however, was based on common land, and only the poorest remnants of this were left over after the enclosures. Moreover, they soon fell into neglect, and served only to keep the animals barely alive or to save them from starvation if all else had failed. Many smallholders simply gave up; they took to the roads, became beggars, and filled the workhouses. The Industrial Revolution was soon to provide work for these unfortunates.

The enclosures may have had certain painful social consequences, but they created a class of independent farmers which quickly emancipated itself from communal obligations and, with a spirit vastly different from that of European peasantry as a whole, rapidly began to improve its farming methods. There was none of the 'land hunger' which was absorbing most of the French peasant's savings at the time, and the farmer did not hesitate to devote all the money he could spare to purchasing equipment, to land improvement, and to selective breeding. Even today 65 per cent. of English farms, covering 70 per cent. of the agricultural land, are worked by tenants; in France these proportions are almost reversed, 70 per cent. of farmers owning their land, which accounts for 60 per cent. of the agricultural area. The prevailing attitude in England was that to buy a farm large enough to be run efficiently was too costly and left too little capital for equipment and improvements. Moreover, the outdated system of *métayage* has completely disappeared; this is another advantage, for the division between *métayer* and landowner of profits accruing either from extra work done by the former or capital improvements undertaken by the latter, is a system which bars every avenue of progress, as can be seen all too clearly in south-western France.[1]

There is thus no equivalent to the intractable and conservative peasantry with which France is still afflicted, and in its absence there has emerged, more clearly than in most countries on the Continent or even in North America, a social grouping into 'farmers' and 'farm

[1] See Chapter VII and our other publications.

workers'. Whereas in France, as in the U.S.A., less than a fifth of the agricultural labour force consists of wage-earning employees, the proportion rises to nearly two-thirds in England. Furthermore, on a medium-sized French or American farm employing two or three men the farmer often does more hard physical work than his employees, but his English equivalent quite often refrains from manual labour except at the busiest times of the year. He certainly keeps abreast of technical developments more effectively than the peasants of less advanced countries, but, all the same, only certain small areas in the south and east reach the standard set by the Netherlands and other countries of extremely intensive agriculture, where the most progressive farmers do not scorn to undertake heavy manual work. England is ninth among the countries of Europe for its gross yields per acre.

242. Changes in conditions of land tenure have been paralleled by the evolution of farming systems. Root crops, which took the place of bare fallows in Flanders about the fourteenth century, began to make their appearance in England during the seventeenth century, and were mainly grown for fodder. The 'turnip revolution', by facilitating the fattening of lambs for the home market, brought about a decline in wool exports and was soon accompanied, especially from 1730 onwards, by the widespread adoption of red clover. Apart from Flanders, the rest of Europe only reached this stage of development between 100 and 300 years later.

After a period of rapid progress which continued until 1825, the repeal of the Corn Laws and the movement towards Free Trade virtually called a halt to further development until about 1850. The acreage under the plough declined for the first time, various improvement schemes—for drainage in particular—were abandoned, and there was a general movement of men and capital—this latter perhaps the more important—away from the land. Capital found more secure and profitable outlets in industry, commerce, and banking, and in land speculation in the vicinity of the rapidly growing towns. This first threatening shadow of agricultural depression did not last very long. The population was increasing at a furious rate; meat and dairy products were needed in larger quantities than ever before.[1] Stimulated by the demands of the home market, agriculture revived after 1850, and there began an era of expansion and rapid technical progress. Poor hill districts were cropped or intensively grazed, and the wave of expansion reached its maximum in 1872 when, for the first time and, so

---

[1] This was before the days of refrigeration; the earliest consignments of frozen meat date from the 1880s.

far, the last, the arable area in England and Wales attained well over 15,000,000 acres.

After this the acreage under the plough declined almost continuously until 1938: 12,500,000 acres in 1897, 11,000,000 in 1915. During the 1914-18 War an increase of 1,125,000 acres was the inadequate response to the German submarine campaign, and by 1917 the country was on the verge of famine. The recession continued through the post-war years, and by 1938 the arable area had fallen to 9,000,000 acres—a low record and only 60 per cent. of the 1872 figure. Of the other 40 per cent., 2,000,000 acres had been abandoned to rough grazings, heath, and moorland, which thus rose from about 3,500,000 to 5,500,000 acres during the period. The agricultural value of these rough grazings is practically negligible, for they consist of self-sown grasses, which gradually became invaded by bracken, gorse, heather, and scrub, and their pastoral economy therefore has not progressed beyond the 'collecting' stage. Most of the remainder of the arable land reverted to permanent grass, which went from 12,500,000 to 16,000,000 acres. Finally, land was being engulfed at a not inconsiderable rate by towns, factories, airfields, and sports grounds; 3 per cent. of the surface of England and Wales was taken up in this way in the twelve years between 1927 and 1939.

These figures, however, do not reveal the full extent of the recession. Tumbledown farm buildings, many of them still dilapidated even in 1950, were part of the visible evidence of its impact, and on marginal land in the west and in Wales many of the farms simply abandoned some of their enclosures. Walls and hedgerows separating one farm from another were kept in repair, as, in theory at least, they prevented animals from straying. Properly manured and tended grassland became a rarity; thorns and thistles were left uncut. Indeed, some of the enclosed land reverted to rough grazing, a process greatly assisted by the spread of bracken, the bane of England's farmland.

This was 'stick and dog' farming. The farmer was almost content to walk his land all the year round, inspecting the herd, which his well-trained dog paraded before him. Closely allied to ranching, an extensive system of this type would not be out of place on the sparsely populated plains of the American West. It is as inappropriate to a densely peopled country like England as it would be to Normandy, more especially as England has lost her world monopoly of manufacturing industry. Her manufactures and coal, her shipping and insurance, bank-loans and brokerage services no longer earn cheap food from the rest of the world. The era of Victorian blessedness was over.

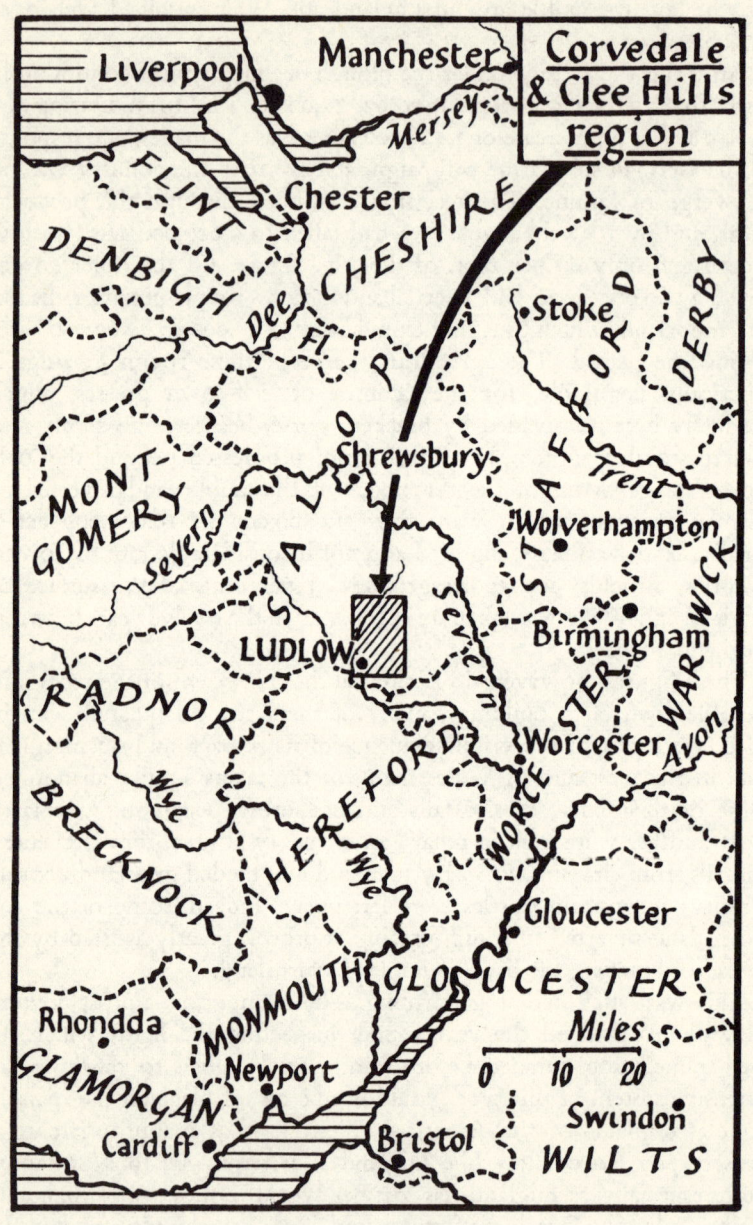

FIG. 22. England.

EFFECTS OF POST-WAR CHANGES IN SOUTH SHROPSHIRE

The task now before her was to bring her land back into production, but whereas her soil is varied and her area extremely limited, she has, if one includes the whole of the United Kingdom, 50,000,000 people to feed, more than twice the number her agriculture can normally support; and this in a world where the terms of trade, which during the nineteenth century favoured the exporter of manufactures, now penalize the buyer of agricultural produce.

2. Arable Cultivation, Grass Leys, and Milk bring Renewed Prosperity to Two Villages in South Shropshire

243. For our detailed study we shall now take a region near the boundary between the dominantly grassland areas of the west and the dominantly arable areas of the east. The neighbouring parishes of Stoke St Milborough and Clee St Margaret lie beyond Corve Dale, at the foot of Brown Clee Hill (1,770 ft.) (Figs. 22, 23). The Welsh uplands rise to the west, and the nearest town, Ludlow, is some six miles to the south-west. 'Around Hereford, Leominster, and Ludlow one discovers a countryside of woodland and hedgerows; it is one of the most verdant and rich-looking landscapes in the whole of western Britain', writes Demangeon in *Les Iles Britanniques*.[1] He is somewhat carried away by his lyrical prose and, moreover, the geographer sometimes confuses verdure and fertility. The climate favours grass and the rainfall exceeds 40 in. The region long remained without roads and remote from outside influences. The soils are naturally somewhat infertile, varying from poor to average, although, as we shall see, modern methods can lead to improved yields.

The mowing machine was introduced in 1880, the hay tedder about 1900. The women, who were thus deprived of a source of employment, hoped that they would prove less satisfactory than their own manual labour. Only in 1905, much later than in eastern England, did the binder begin to come into general use. At this period many families still made their own cheese and bread. Clee village adjoins Brown Clee Hill, a stretch of common land, overgrown with bracken, 1,000 acres in extent and comprising half the area of the parish. The landscape reminds one constantly of Wales. In 1890 the parish had 144 acres of arable land, with 25 acres, or 17 per cent., still in bare fallow; there were, by contrast, 832 acres of grassland, less than a third of which were cut for hay. Next to the south is the parish of Stoke, which has some rather better land; in 1890 it included 850 acres of arable

[1] *Géographie Universelle* Series.

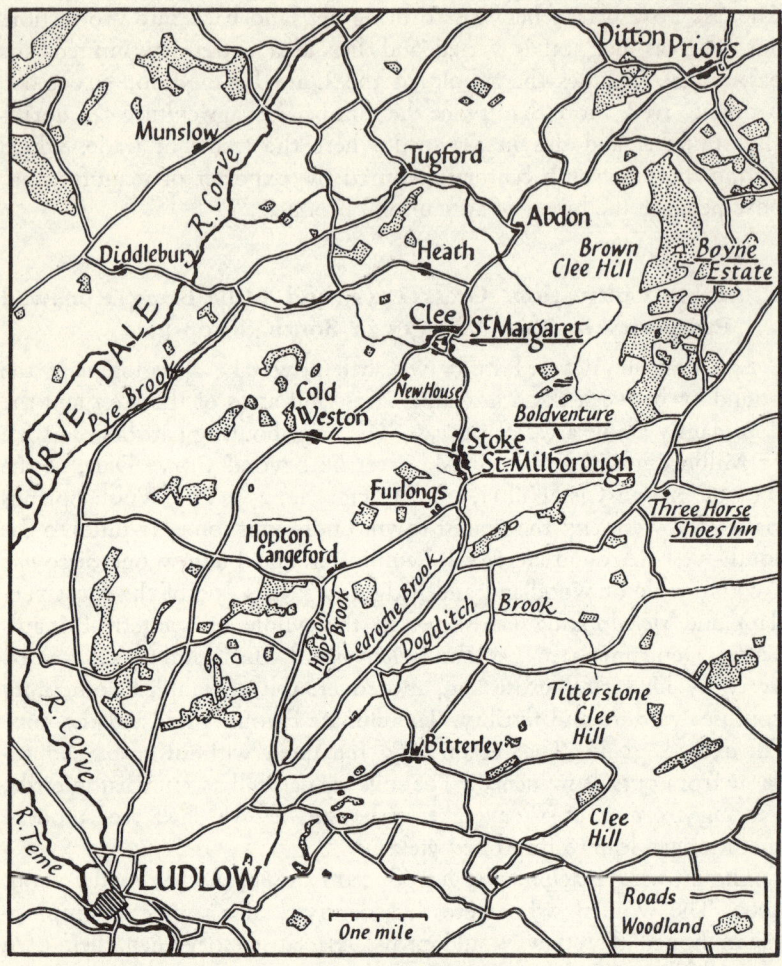

FIG. 23. Shropshire, England.

land, only a tenth of it in fallows, and almost 4,000 acres of grassland, 20 per cent. of which was cut for hay.

By 1900 the arable acreage still showed only a small decline, but the proportion of grassland cut for hay had risen, and at Stoke a further 50 acres or so of heathland had been brought into cultivation. At Clee, however, by 1938 there remained rather less than half the area of arable land which had existed fifty years before. The increase in rough grazing slightly exceeded this decline, which shows that the grassland area had remained more or less stationary. By this time the arable area at Stoke was down to 316 acres; in other words, it had fallen by nearly two-thirds. Nine-tenths of this abandoned area had reverted to heathland, and no longer provided anything of use beyond stable litter and poor grazing. Grassland had made very small gains. The number of cattle had increased by about 40 per cent. (1890, 1,028; 1938, 1,445), but at Clee the gain was barely 20 per cent. In both parishes the number of sheep was almost doubled: 3,060 and 800 in 1890 as against 5,845 and 1,550 in 1938. The methods of providing fodder remained, notwithstanding, extremely extensive.

Settlement is for the most part dispersed, and the centre of Stoke St Milborough, which is a straggling village following the line of an old sheep track, consists of just a few houses clustered round the church and the Vicarage. The region is intricately dissected by valleys, but is less wooded than the Welsh uplands. Moreover, the tree limit is very low: about 1,000 ft. on the slopes exposed to the prevailing wind[1] and not rising above 1,650 to 2,000 ft. even on the sheltered eastern slopes. Brown Clee Hill is wooded only on the leeward side.

244. South-west of the village is Furlongs Farm, 190 acres in extent, and before the war it consisted entirely of old pastures disposed in two groups on either side of the road which passes through the farm. The animals wandered at will over each of these in turn, except that one small area was reserved for hay. In spite of the declining area under the plough, there were more cattle here in 1938 than in 1890, and the explanation lies not so much in the smaller proportion of arable land devoted to bread cereals as in the large purchases of coarse grain and cattle cake, for the latter represented a cheaper supply of feed than could be produced on the farm itself. There was a flock of sheep, the main interest being the sale of three-month-old fat lambs at Easter, and a herd of Hereford cattle. This is the breed which B. Tomkins began to improve in 1760; it is hardier than the Durham and has made a very substantial contribution to cattle-farming in the Americas; it is said, moreover, that Herefords will 'fatten on pastures where Shorthorns would die of hunger'. Young cattle were sold at eighteen or twenty months, when they reached 660 to 770 lb. live weight.

The farmer, who was getting on in years and employed one labourer, was quite content just to keep the farm going and live partly on his capital. Gorse, bracken, and thistles gradually took over more and more of the grassland, which was itself of a rather inferior kind, consisting mainly of agrostis and fescue. The farm buildings were not kept in

[1] The tree line is sometimes lower than 150 ft. in Scotland.

repair. Indeed, about this time, English agriculture as a whole was tending to eat into its capital and new investments were few and far between.

In 1945 Furlongs was bought for £8,000[1] by Tim Aron, the son of an industrialist, who had studied at the agricultural school at Cambridge and expressed a desire to 'go back to the land'. In the summer of 1950 he had one tractor and employed a clerk, an apprentice, and a milkmaid. The last had an Aberystwyth diploma and could have procured an appointment as an agricultural adviser. She had no objection to manual work, and although there was a milking machine, that did not save her from trundling wheelbarrow loads of manure. She had practically complete charge of the dairying side and was responsible for calculating the requirement of supplementary feeding-stuffs and for moving cattle from one pasture to another when she observed a drop in the milk yield, which was weighed every day. It is evident, therefore, that this has now become a recognized career. As yet this is hardly the case in France, but a trend in this direction is becoming apparent.

In 1950 rather less than a third of the farm was under the plough, rather more than a third was in leys, and the remainder consisted of old pastures which are being progressively broken up. Aron was brought to a standstill in his plans for development by lack of capital. He had already spent a little over £10,000, but most of this represented the cost of land and buildings. Only a quarter of it was actually invested in working capital, and as this was evidently not enough,[2] he calculated, quite rightly, that another £2,500 would be needed fairly quickly. His working hours, however, were not particularly long, and he still contrived to take a holiday in Switzerland every year. A French peasant, seeing his way of life, would probably have considered that he was not farming seriously enough.

Reseeded and grazed in rotation, the young leys yielded two or three times as much growth as the old pastures, which had suffered as much from neglect as most of those in Normandy. A few of these old pastures still remained, partly because they were useful for grazing young

---

[1] Furlongs was sold again in 1952, for £11,500—to a 'peasant' who was planning to sow the garden—which was Tim Aron's pride and joy—down to grass.

[2] In 1952, when Furlongs was sold, the cattle were valued at £3,200, the sheep at £1,200 and the equipment at only £700: even then, the working capital represented less than half the value of land and buildings. Equipment, however, was much less expensive than in France.

animals in the winter and partly because the rotational grazing of leys depends on each having a piped water supply, which is quite expensive to install.

245. Development has taken much the same course in the rest of the parish, and in 1949 Stoke had 1,390 acres under the plough, or nearly four and a half times as much as in 1938. Practically the whole of the wartime gains had been maintained, whereas there had already been some slight recession in certain other parts of the country.[1] Imports of feeding-stuffs have remained very much lower than before the war, and in spite of its very real efforts at intensification the parish had thirty-five head of cattle and 400 sheep fewer than in 1939, and only half the number of pigs, which had previously been fed mainly on imported grain.

Ploughland had gained by 64 per cent. since 1890. Rotation grasses had increased in both absolute and relative importance; the acreage was two and a half times as large and accounted for a third instead of a fifth of the arable land. On the other hand, the cereal acreage has fallen from 29 per cent. to 22 per cent. and fallows to a mere 1 per cent. Peas, turnips, and swedes also show losses owing to their partial replacement by mangolds, rape, and kale, which were practically unknown in 1890. These fodder crops, together with potatoes, occupy 17 per cent. of the arable land. The Government insists on a third of the land being ploughed, first- and second-year leys counting towards the total, but there is no reason why the acreage of cereals, which are not well suited to the region, should not be brought down still further, thus making room for more fodder crops. By 1953 official pressure had resulted in the ploughing up of more old pastures.[2]

Another aspect of development has been that milk has taken the place of meat as the farmer's chief interest. Tim Aron had a good herd of Ayrshires,[3] lively, hardy, fine-looking animals; their average yield increased fairly rapidly from 480 gallons in 1945 to 815 in 1950 and 880 in 1952. This changeover to milk production, which is still going on year by year, began about the end of the nineteenth century. The

---

[1] The figure for England and Wales was 14,750,000 acres of arable land in 1944, 13,925,000 acres in 1950.

[2] Between 1949 and 1953 temporary grassland was increasing at the expense of arable land and permanent grass in England and Wales. Oats and potatoes were declining rapidly, the acreage under barley was fairly constant, and wheat and mixed corn were on the increase. The number of cattle showed little change (7·7 million), but pigs had nearly doubled (2·4 million), and poultry showed a decrease.

[3] Also found in Finland.

pace increased after 1920, but south Shropshire remained unaffected until the last war. As far as meat was concerned, the refrigerator ship was bringing overseas competition right into the home market. On the other hand, there was no such competition in the case of milk. On the contrary, its production was very much favoured by the rise in population—especially in the London region, which houses more than a fifth of the people in the United Kingdom—and by the increasing demand per head of the population, which is wisely encouraged by subsidies.

The milk is cooled straight away, and the lorries of the London Co-operative Society collect it every day. Modernizing the stalls and the whole of the dairying side of the farm cost £600.[1] Special precautions are taken to ensure cleanliness,[2] and the whole herd is tuberculin-tested. These expenses find their reward in the extra 4d. a gallon the farm receives for its milk, and, considering that this adds up to some £250 a year, the investment was well worthwhile. An association of producers, the Milk Marketing Board, regulates prices, but it operates under the control of the Government, which watches the interests of the consumers.

Dried fodder grown on the farms is now largely used instead of concentrates. It takes the form of oats—or oats sown with peas—which are cut green before the ears develop; the resulting fodder has a protein content of 14 per cent. The sale of milk, which is the main resource, brought in £1,620 in 1950 (as against £700 in 1945), beef cattle and sheep brought in £860, and cash crops (cereals, potatoes, clover seed, etc.), which are a source of income only on the larger farms of the region, £657.

246. The breaking up of old pastures is the distinctive mark of the new system. A root crop, such as potatoes or swedes, is generally chosen for the first year, or sometimes kale is sown broadcast in the hope that it might thus survive the weeds. A typical rotation would then consist of a cereal, one year of red clover and Italian rye-grass, and then wheat. The ley which then follows is the crux of the whole system. It consists of a mixture of rye-grass or cock's-foot, or sometimes fescue, with white clover, and is often left longer than the two or three years which it should last in theory and, indeed, in 1953 a duration of six or seven years was being officially recommended. In the case of selected rye-grass, grazing ceases between June and August so as to allow the

[1] All these figures refer to 1950.

[2] When we visited one farm, the farmer was milking his herd, and smoking as he did so. 'I'll get fined for this,' he remarked.

seed to be harvested, but in 1950 continuous bad weather resulted in the mown grass rotting in the fields where it lay. Besides the expansion of the arable acreage and the reseeding of old pastures, the other important factor in the intensification of farming practice has been the large-scale use, thanks to subsidies, of lime and phosphatic fertilizers to offset the major deficiencies in the soil. On the other hand, nitrogenous fertilizers and silos, which have both played a decisive role in the Netherlands, appear to be used too sparingly. An appreciable amount of hay is spoilt or lost; sometimes there is too much rain at haymaking time, and then, again, the shortage of buildings due to lack of capital means that all the hay cannot be stored under cover, and it often happens that the seeds near the top of the rick begin to germinate.

Production has risen faster than the numbers employed. This is true for the whole of England, which is the only major country in the world with only 5·5 per cent. of its working population engaged in agriculture. In 1953 there were 644,000 agricultural workers. Elsewhere in the world complaints of manpower shortage often have little basis in fact, but this is emphatically not the case here. The evidence lies in those old pastures still to be seen in 1950, which would offer quick rewards for extra time and labour spent on them.[1] The general effect, however, is mitigated by mechanization. The number of tractors had risen from 60,000 in 1939 to 400,000 in 1953, and by this date there were almost as many motor cultivators. This made agriculture in the United Kingdom the most highly mechanized in the world; one tractor for every 50 acres of ploughland, as compared with 120 acres in the U.S.A., which accounted notwithstanding, for 60 per cent. of the world's tractors. By 1953 the number of draught-horses had fallen to less than half the pre-war figure. Mechanization was stimulated by the low cost of fuel, which was sold to the farmer at the special price of 1s. a gallon. This waiving of taxation on an item of agricultural intensification was an instance of agrarian policy at it best. The tractors themselves, however, are not used to their fullest extent, and a Welsh survey, for instance, revealed an average of only 600 working hours a year.

At Furlongs there is an old Fordson petrol tractor and a milking machine. In the absence of co-operatives, combines are hired from contractors, who are often farmers themselves. Pick-up balers[2] and other

[1] A wave of unemployment in 1953 eased the problem of finding farm workers.

[2] The pick-up baler has been used for practically the whole of the hay crop since 1953.

machinery are sometimes hired in the same way, all at Government-agreed tariffs. The system allows a farmer to operate with comparatively little working capital of his own. Farm hands, who work harder than their employers, do not generally work more than a forty-seven-hour week and receive a weekly wage of £4-£6;[1] the tractor-driver and the milkmaid are generally near the maximum of the scale, and both often earn about the same.

3. The 'Urbanization' of the English Countryside

247. Everyone in Clee St Margaret who owns any land in the parish has unlimited grazing rights on the 1,000 acres of common land on Brown Clee Hill. Although it is very poor grazing land and overgrown with bracken, before the war it enabled many smallholders to keep a few sheep, and in this manner they could earn about £2 a week. They earned another £2 in the local quarries and had enough to live on. Indeed, when the sheep were doing well they were content with £1 a week from the quarry. There are still 2,000 sheep on the hill, but the time they spend there varies greatly, some remaining all the year except during snow, others for only one or two months. Ponies used to be reared for the pits, but there are only about forty of them left today, and they are being replaced by young horses.

The quarries were closed in 1939, and as a source of employment they were replaced during the war by munitions factories. The parish is in one of the most exclusively agricultural districts in the whole of England, but in 1950, out of its population of 115 there were twenty-five farmers, ten farm hands, sixteen industrial workers, a garage-owner, a grocer, a cattle-truck operator, the Vicar, the ageing postmistress, and thirty-eight housewives[2]. More remote than Stoke, Clee still had a large proportion of small farm enterprises: there were thirty-eight in all in 1900 and still thirty-one in 1938. Cottages generally occupied patches of poor land which had continued to be dug by hand right up to the end of the nineteenth century, and after 1910

---

[1] £1 more in 1953.

[2] There is no inn at Clee; the nearest one is right out in the country at Bouldon, a small hamlet one and a half miles to the west and reached by a footpath. We arrived at New House on a Wednesday and invited the two workers to come and drink a pint of beer with us, but they pointed out that Saturday was really the only recognized day for going to the pub, and the only time when all their friends would be there. As in the United States, on this one day of the week, they make up for lost time.

many of those which had not fallen into disrepair were bought by townspeople in search of holiday homes. Thus in 1950 only twenty-five farms remained in this parish, and on average they were smaller than at Stoke. There were five large farms ranging from 75 to 125 acres, eight medium-sized ones of between 40 and 75 acres, and the remainder were smallholdings.

The year 1940 saw a second invasion from the towns, mainly people who, like Mr Pearce, who has since emigrated to Canada, had decided to go back to the land. Whereas before the war there had been only one car—the Vicar's—and not a single tractor, in 1950 there were six tractors[1] and eight cars, while in 1953 the number had risen to nine and fifteen respectively.

248. Tired of his work in a London suburb, where he was employed as an engineer on constructional plans for the Underground, D. Higgs arrived in the parish in 1939. He bought the 125 acres of New House for £2,050, £1,500 of which he borrowed on a mortgage loan. It took him until 1948 to repay this sum, but even so he was fortunate, inasmuch as agricultural prices were beginning to show a downward trend by then. In 1893 the farm, which then covered only 110 acres, was sold for £1,250, and it was mortgaged at the same time for £800. In 1950 it would have easily fetched £6,000. The value of land in this area had doubled since before the war, from £20-35 to £40-70 an acre. Tithe is payable on the farm at £2 per annum, but it would be possible for the farmer at any time to bring his obligation to an end by offering a lump sum equivalent to twenty-one annual payments. In 1953 Higgs had an offer of £7,000 for his property, but, because of the scarcity of country houses in the Birmingham area, it was possible to double this amount by offering the land to local farmers and selling the buildings separately.

Having made his purchase, he was left with a working capital of exactly £63 15s., which enabled him to buy two old horses, a cart, a mowing machine, and a hay-rake; there was nothing left to buy a tedder. Unlike Furlongs, therefore, the available capital was extremely small. Higgs continued to turn his hay by hand until 1947, when he was able to afford an old tractor and a tedder. At first he took in stock from other farms, but later on his farm was classed as marginal land, and he qualified for two development subsidies totalling £900. This enabled him to start clearing the thickets of trees which stood in his fields and the forest of brushwood and bracken which had invaded

[1] A sharp fall in the price of small second-hand tractors in 1947 put them within the reach of the small farmer.

them. Until then they had looked even more neglected than the average meadow in Normandy.

Until 1949 he employed only one man to help him and hired another hand for the harvest. 'Even Rockefeller's money could not persuade me to go through it all again,' he declares. As an engineer before the war, his salary was £1,100 a year; as a farmer he had to be content for a long time with £400 and, of course, the value of money had depreciated. If one considers the six tractor-owners in the parish in 1950, one finds that two of them are from London, one from Birmingham, and a fourth is an ex-schoolmaster; the remaining two have come from farms in predominantly arable regions and regard themselves as being in semi-retirement. None of the local farmers has a tractor, and in many ways they are typically peasant-minded; occasionally, for instance, they still thresh with a flail. Some of them have never travelled by train and others have been to a cinema only once in their lives.

249. The United Kingdom is the most urbanized country in the world, and four-fifths of its people live in urban agglomerations. Country habits obviously cannot help being coloured by what is done in the towns, and the farmer regards taking tea and having guests in the evening as marks of social prestige. Women's Institutes, Young Farmers' Clubs (like the one at Burwarton, where the agent from the Boyne Estate tries to uphold the old way of life), and circulating libraries promote a more lively exchange of ideas than one finds away from the towns in France. The man who has gone back to the land has lost, to a greater degree than his country-bred neighbour, the intimate knowledge of Nature which is characteristic of the peasant. He buys all his food from the shop, and although he may occasionally pick a few blackberries he has little confidence in his ability to recognize any but the commonest varieties of edible fungi. The town is intruding more and more into the country by the very fact of its growth, which in England is a matter of grave concern.

At the same time its food requirements are rapidly increasing, for the town-dweller eats well. In spite of their great efforts, the farmers can only satisfy 40 per cent. of national needs. Even the countryside of the United States, which is more highly urbanized than that of the Continent, shows less evidence of town influence than in England. The English farmer, who has certain lineal ties with the landlord of an earlier age, works less than his French counterpart, but is more greatly concerned with management, planning, and organization. It would not be considered unusual for a farmer to marry a woman qualified in law or medicine. In France, things are quite different.

More than ever one sees children being brought by special buses to better-equipped centralized schools, and now that secondary education is free there is a greater willingness to take advantage of it. Village life had stagnated after the disappearance of the peasant class in the eighteenth century, but today, with its efficient bus service into the nearest town, every parish is tending to assume a new suburban guise, and life is flowing back to the less remote villages.

For many years, and especially between 1825 and 1940, rural capital helped to finance industrial and commercial enterprises. Conversely, the modern reawakening of the countryside could never have occurred but for the injection of non-agricultural capital. A large number of titled people and retired industrialists own very well-kept farms, but they are not solely concerned with making profits.

There has also been an infusion of new ideas. There have been men willing to break with tradition—willing, in fact, to use the plough on permanent pastures.

Although the land and the working capital are for the most part under separate ownership, men like Higgs and Aron, coming from the towns, have generally sought to buy their own farms. Pearce and Aron had sufficient funds to develop their land, but Higgs had been short of money. Being a townsman, he would have found it difficult to make himself acceptable as a tenant. In any case, he is too proud a man ever to submit to a position of social inferiority. For the tenants on the Boyne Estate, however, the bailiff still suggests the feudal authority once embodied in the 'Lord of the Manor'.[1]

4. New House Farm and the Marginal Areas

250. In 1939 New House had only 5 acres of ploughland which had been sown to cereals year after year. In 1950 Higgs had 15 acres of wheat, $7\frac{1}{2}$ of oats, and $2\frac{1}{2}$ of oats and beans mixed; in addition, there were 6 acres of oats-peas-beans mixture for silage, a similar amount of oats for grazing when green, nearly 4 acres of kale, and $2\frac{1}{2}$ of lucerne. There were once doubts as to whether the latter would thrive under these conditions, but 4 tons of crushed lime to the acre—half before and half after ploughing—solved the main problem of soil acidity. There are no mangolds because of the extra work they entail, but a small quantity of potatoes grown for domestic consumption makes up

[1] This is no longer the case in eastern England.

the arable acreage to very nearly a third of the farm, which is the figure officially stipulated.

Higgs thought that he would do better for himself if he was allowed to continue with the old permanent grassland system. Compliance with Government targets during the war was favoured by the so-called 'carrots and stick' system. The carrots consisted of guaranteed prices fixed in advance, loans of equipment, credits and subsidies for lime and fertilizers, for bringing new land into cultivation, and for the ploughing up of grassland (£2 and subsequently £4 per acre).

The stick was, and still is, firmly held by the County Agricultural Committees, which are composed mainly of farmers and agricultural scientists and are empowered to warn and if necessary to evict those who refuse to maintain a certain standard of husbandry.[1] Here and there the system may have been abused; a farm may have been vacated by its tenant under duress and given to a friend of somebody on the Committee. But the expulsion of over 1 per cent. of farmers from their land—there was one case at Clee—had a striking effect on the remainder. Higgs for his part began to look for a Welsh hill farm or for a farm overseas, somewhere at any rate 'where the agricultural adviser does not lay down the rules'. The Liberal Congress of April, 1953, passed a resolution condemning the 'excessive and arbitrary' powers conferred on the Ministry by the Agriculture Act of 1947.

At New House, the steepest of the old pastures and the most difficult to cultivate, a good 25 acres in all, still remain. There are, however, 55 acres of new temporary leys which are sown at 15 lb. of cock's-foot and only 7 oz. of white clover to the acre. The farmer is well aware that too much of the latter is not good for grass growth, but even when a small quantity of seed is employed the white clover sometimes becomes too dominant. The leys are used only for grazing during the first year or two, but after this they provide hay or silage as well and are ploughed again after four or five years. Two years of cereals and, finally, beans or a silage crop then follow, thus giving a seven- or eight-year rotation.

251. Five of Clee's farms have gone over to dairying since the war,[2] but Higgs has remained faithful to his Herefords and restricts his milk

[1] For further details of these measures see our articles in *L'observation Economique* (November 1950) and *Economie contemporaine* (October 1950).

[2] As is often the case in France, these are small or medium-sized farms. In the region as a whole, however, as in the environs of Milan, it is generally the large farms which have revealed a more rapid response to changing conditions and turned over to milk, while the smaller farms continue with their stock-rearing.

production to 3 or 4 pints every morning for use on the farm. He keeps fifteen cows for breeding and in addition buys about twenty one-week-old calves a year. Thus, apart from his cows, in 1950 he had eight stores of two years and more, twelve one-year-olds, and fifteen of less than one year. Each cow can rear two or three calves during its lactation period, and the young beasts are generally sold at eighteen months, the exact moment varying according to the supply of fodder on the farm. They go from here to be fattened on large arable farms, where they are also wanted for treading down straw into manure.

Farms with a certain amount of good grassland reserve it for fattening or for milk production, but those which, like New House, concentrate on rearing are content to rely entirely on pastures of poorer quality. In some cases the cows are left out all winter, and have to manage as best they can on a little straw and whatever pasture may still remain; they are only spared a little hay at calving time in the spring. By 1950 Higgs was obliged by the growing size of his herd,[1] which had long been limited by his lack of financial means, to rent 20 acres of old pastures about four and a half miles (six miles by road) to the east. The rent was only £2 an acre—much less, in other words, than the current rate in France at the time. Here he kept young animals, old cows not in milk, or beasts for fattening.

The sheep at New House consisted of two rams, ten wethers and seventy-five ewes, the latter producing eighty-five lambs between March and May in 1950. He kept his ewes for four years and regularly made up his flock from the lambs; the remainder were auctioned every September at Three Horse Shoes Market, which was near his rented pasture. Sheep give quicker returns than cattle, a fat lamb at eight months often being worth as much as a ewe. They are well suited to the poorer land and will crop down a stretch of pasture after the cattle have finished with it. The sale of animals by auction means in effect that the breeder sells direct to the farmer who wants the beasts for fattening, or even in some cases to the butcher; this does away very simply with the exorbitant profits made by the dealer in France.[2] It is high time that the farmers' unions in France summoned up the courage

---

[1] When he was selling out in 1953, Higgs had another fifty fat pigs and had a total of 200 sheep, half of which were mountain sheep living off the common land all the year round. His cattle were worth at least £1,000, his sheep £1,250. and his pigs £250. He had about £500 worth of equipment.

[2] Cf. Denis Bergmann's analysis of the meat market in *Cahiers Economiques* for December 1952.

to set up similar organizations and resist the abusive privileges of La Villette and the Halles Centrales; in this manner they would be serving agricultural interests far better than by formulating demands, as they sometimes do, with an eye to the popular vote.

Each of the two farm hands, in addition to his wage of £4 10s. a week,[1] was given enough grain, at a fixed price, to fatten five pigs a year and 1 acre of pasture, enough to keep five ewes. One of them has his own small orchard and two small fields. Most farm workers are the sons of small tenants, and sometimes expect to take over the family farm later on. Some of them ask to be paid only once a year, to help them save enough money to start up on their own.

252. A stretch of steeply sloping upland to the south of the farm has been brought into cultivation by the use of Caterpillar D8 tractors and reversible ploughs, thanks to Government subsidies. Unfortunately, the Government, through the Agricultural Committee, insisted on sowing down to rye-grass, as it was holding large stocks of seed from New Zealand at the time. It proved unable to survive, however, on this poor terrain, in spite of the artificials applied; thus suggesting the possible danger of combining a technical advice service with a sales organization, even when both are Government controlled. The steep slopes make the carting of farmyard manure, which is very sorely needed, rather expensive, and lack of water is another handicap.

The battle between man and Nature is at its hardest in the vicinity of Brown Clee Hill. At Black Ford, a hamlet south of the Hill, a man of sixty-five, who has a holding of about 18 acres and works it with the help of his grandson and a twenty-year-old horse, had virtually given up the struggle against the invasions of bracken, gorse, thistles, and brambles, and the depredations of rabbits. In their consumption of pasture, taking the country as a whole, these animals were outdone only by cattle and sheep. They were a particularly serious menace in this region, and we counted nearly 1,000 of them during the course of an afternoon's walk.

A little farther west, however, Boldventure, which is run rather more enterprisingly than New House, has won through. Again the area is about 125 acres, and the young farmer employs three workers. A practically worthless piece of rough grazing land, which consists of a mass of bracken with a few patches of agrostis and fescues, ends abruptly along the line of a hedgerow. Beyond this and on the same kind of terrain there stretches a high-yielding cock's-foot ley in striking

[1] £5 13s. 0d. in 1953; by this time one of them had a car and the other a motor cycle.

contrast. When game coverts of bracken are removed, this marginal land is extremely responsive to scientific management.

Agriculture, however, had fallen to such a low ebb that the flow of capital needed to ensure development, which had never been an easy matter, became quite impossible to provide. It had to come in part from non-agricultural sources. Attention had previously been focused on the fertile regions; marginal lands had been excluded from the compulsory 'plough-up' campaign, but in 1942 it was realized that these areas with their 12,500,000 acres accounted for half the enclosed land in the country. High prices were enabling the fertile regions to finance themselves, but this, as we have seen, did not apply to the poorer districts, and accordingly the Marginal Land Scheme was brought into being. This allowed for 50 per cent. of the cost of improvement schemes, put forward by farmers and approved by technical committees, to be borne by the Treasury. This did not apply to the poorest areas, which came under the Hill Farming Act and were only entitled to limited aid designed to maintain them as regions of extensive farming. The real target of the scheme was land which had a reasonable prospect of eventually giving an economic return, so long as it was given a good start. Since 1951 subsidies under the Livestock Rearing Act are also available to defray half the cost of new buildings and of modernization and repairs to existing buildings, including the installation of hot and cold water, up-to-date kitchens and w.cs. Evidently the aim of this was partly to keep the women on the land. Farm tracks, shelter belts of trees, and piped water supplies for pastures also qualify for grants. Any scheme, however, must embody a comprehensive development plan for the whole farm, and the farmer's portion of the cost is often therefore prohibitive. This was the case at New House, where a scheme was proposed envisaging £545 spent on the house, £750 on farm buildings, £150 for extending the leys, £100 for drainage, and £50 for windbreaks. Higgs would not agree to an item of £500 for bringing water to the farm, with a piped supply to each field of pasture; he argued that he could not afford it and that in any case the proposed source of water was not completely reliable. This led to the rejection of the whole scheme, and to Higgs's departure.

The contribution demanded from the farmers is, of course, designed to avoid the waste of public money, but many of them find themselves unable to raise half the necessary sum. There is also the problem of defining marginal land. Any criterion is bound to be arbitrary, and in the articles referred to above we have analysed the practical difficulties of the scheme and some of its implications. Whatever its demerits, however, it is vastly preferable to the position in France, where the encouragement given to alcohol-producing crops, like sugar-beet, vines and apples, benefits the most fertile regions and favours a type of production which has injurious effects. It is one of the most absurd agricultural policies imaginable.[1]

5. From the Smallholding to the Large Arable Farm

253. A farm is a fairly large enterprise, generally with more than 50 acres, except where market-gardening is concerned. The outward symbols of a farmer, at any rate since 1950, are that he has a car and a tractor. Below him on another social plane and clearly distinguished by a different title comes the smallholder, a kind of cousin to the *manœuvre* of Lorraine; his holding resembles, in type if not in point of size, the *biquetterie* of Mayen or the *penn-ty* of Brittany. He often has another occupation; sometimes he is a craftsman or has a small business or has a salaried job of some kind. Moreover, retired people sometimes lease a smallholding. At all events, he has very little in common with the real French peasant, except perhaps in the case of the smallest farms or largest smallholdings, where the tenant is occupied full-time on his own land.

Mr Weaver, the father of the tractor-driver at Furlongs, owns[2] a 40-acre holding near the sunken and occasionally stream-filled lane leading from Clee to the inn at Bouldon. He rents another 5 acres in addition, and his sum total of eleven fields is enough to keep him busy most of the year, but he needs to hire extra help only occasionally. It is worth remarking that this enterprise, which in England is considered definitely on the small side, is none the less larger than the average in France. Differences of scale would, of course, be even more spectacular as between Belgian Flanders and the Wheat Belt of the United States, while the contrast between a Japanese farm and an Australian ranch strains the conceivable limits of antithesis.

In 1950 the holding was completely under grass, and indeed, being mainly interested in rearing, Weaver rarely has more than 2 or 3 acres under the plough. The standard of farming is none the less greatly superior to that of the Pays d'Auge, which manages its grassland so

---

[1] See *Population*, No. 1, 1953: '*Alcool, lait ou viande, étude technique et économique d'orientation agricole et alimentaire.*' Also *Le Monde*, 15 May 1953.

[2] His father was a tenant. He bought 42 acres (including buildings) in 1921 for £1,100. In 1950 he thought he could get about £3,000 for the 40 acres. Small farms fetch more per acre.

THE SMALLHOLDING AND THE LARGE ARABLE FARM

badly. Near the farm and its outbuildings, which are arranged in two parallel lines, there are 9 acres of grassland which are better cared for than the rest, owing to their accessibility. In the spring they receive the manure made during the previous winter and are mown for hay. The scarcity of fodder on the farm in the winter means that the number of animals varies considerably from one season to another. The cattle herd in the summer consists of six cows plus eight or nine calves (three of them bought at birth); in addition, there are two one-year-old and three two-year-old stores, a total of about twenty head in all. During the autumn about eight beasts, on average, are sold to arable farms, thus reducing the winter total to twelve head or thereabouts. Similarly, the auctioning of lambs in September approximately halves the size of the summer sheep flock, which averages from ninety to 100 head.

A horse serves to bring coal from the village; even this region of hedgerows and woodland scorns to use its own timber for fuel. The horse is also used to fetch bread, which is no longer made on the farm. The sunken track, bordered by hedgerows and reminiscent of western France, is impassable to cars. The farm equipment, which is kept to a minimum, consists of a mowing-machine, a swathe-turner, a two-wheeled and a four-wheeled cart. Before the war, as on the land-hungry farms of Flanders or Bresse, there was a high degree of intensification by the transformation of imported feeding stuffs. Enough grain was bought to keep a sow and a flock of eighty hens; 200 chickens and twenty fat pigs were sold annually. As there was little or no arable land and Weaver had to rely on his ration of grain, he could no longer feed more than thirty-eight hens and thirty chickens, and merely fattened a couple of pigs a year for domestic use. Every farm at this time was entitled to a ration of grain, but had to choose between pigs and poultry; it was not allowed grain for both.

254. The partial cessation of pig- and poultry-keeping curbed the smallholders' independence, and many of them gave up their land after the war. Encouragement was given to the establishment of very small enterprises of 5 acres or so by a law on smallholdings passed in 1908, but in 1948 another law set out to promote the interests, and thereby to increase the number, of 50-acre holdings. It requires that prospective tenants should have sufficient capital and a sound knowledge of agriculture, which are, after all, the indispensable qualifications for any form of land colonization. Weaver opines that 40 acres are the absolute minimum for making a living without recourse to an alternative occupation.

He himself works unaided on an area where one would have found five workers in Bavaria and probably eight in Flanders. Admittedly farming is more intensive in these regions, but the output per worker is very much lower. During the winter he still goes from farm to farm and slaughters a few pigs. In his younger days he used to slaughter 100 to 150 in a season, and therefore his farming was more of a part-time occupation. He used to earn 12s. to 15s. for two hours' work, which included cutting but not the processing of products. He has six daughters and three sons; of the latter, one is in the Army and the other two are farm workers; one of them will carry on with the farm after him. He has been unable to save enough money to buy another holding or even to enlarge this one.

He is fairly well satisfied, however, with his holding as it is, being of the opinion that with 100 acres and one worker he would probably earn very little more than at present. His poor opinion of the medium-sized farm as a business proposition echoes the sentiments we heard expressed north of Ghent. He reckons to earn about £450 a year net from his holding, in which more than £4,000 of capital, including stock, is invested. Higgs earns very little more than this, and the Weavers' son, who works at Furlongs, which is a fairly well-equipped farm, receives £300. Father and son each have a small car,[1] and the son pays a rent equivalent to seven weeks' wages a year for a very trim cottage built by the County Council.

Douglas Higgs's father-in-law, who is a farm worker, has a few fields of his own not far from the parish boundary, which crosses the nearby road between Stoke and Clee at its highest point. He has $7\frac{1}{2}$ acres of pastures, and on them keeps a cow which suckles one or two calves and furnishes his household with enough milk to make its own butter and feed three pigs on the skim-milk. There is also a heifer; this was bought at Shrewsbury Market when one week old, and will be kept for about two and a half years. He keeps ten ewes on Brown Clee Hill from 20 May until the end of November, but brings them down at the end of August to wean and sell the lambs.

He works on a large 500-acre farm nearby. If, however, he cannot spare the time to cut his own hay, he arranges with a contractor to do it; the long-established relationship between the satellite Flemish farm and its large neighbour is completely absent here. The hay is either made into a rick or stored in the tiny hayloft above the equally small cowshed belonging to the cottage. It is carried three or four cocks at a time by two men with a pair of long poles between them. Like the

[1] Which a Bavarian farmer of the same class could not afford as yet.

THE SMALLHOLDING AND THE LARGE ARABLE FARM

hand-flail, this is a rare instance of human energy supervening in the place of mechanical or animal power.

255. We shall now leave grassland farming for a moment and turn our attention to the arable land which dominates the country further east, all the way from Yorkshire to the London Basin. B. G. Ward has a farm of 900 acres at Grindle Shifnal, on the road between Wolverhampton and Shrewsbury in north-east Shropshire. Of this he owns 250 acres and rents the remainder. His rent has been recently reduced from 44s. to 35s. an acre by an arbitration commission; the latter figure is certainly not excessive, for this is better farm land than is found in the Ludlow region. There are 200 acres of temporary grassland, only 100 acres of permanent pasture, and the remainder, some 600 acres, is ploughed every year. The farm is on the edge of the Midlands, its chief interest is in its cropland, and the whole enterprise turns, not on its stalls, but on its fine workshop, where the five tractors and the combine, which cuts an 8-ft. swath, are maintained. The latter is used in September for half the 200 acres of cereals, the remainder still being cut with a binder.

The greater proportion of arable land does not mean that animal husbandry loses in importance; on the contrary, it reaches an even fuller development. Animals are therefore neither absent nor even of secondary importance, as is the case in the Paris Basin. Although, generally speaking, meat-production is giving place to milk, the retreat is not necessarily in evidence on every farm, and here there are only two dairy cows, which suffice for domestic requirements. The flock of 450 ewes produced 670 lambs in the spring of 1950. These were sold during the winter after being fed on mangold tops and then fattened on kale and turnips; the last, of course, were one of the very first levers of progress in English agriculture. There are thirteen sows, their litters being raised on the farm and kept for about six months.

One hundred and twenty 20-month-old heifers in calf are purchased every October or November from grass farms in the south of the county, similar to those we have already described. They calve about February and are resold the following spring, the calves having been weaned in October. They are fattened during the second winter and roam at will in covered yards with mangers running along the sides above the drinking troughs. This method not only saves labour, one man being enough to look after about 100 pigs or up to 140 cattle, but also produces plenty of manure, which, as in Cambrésis about the turn of the century, is really the main purpose in keeping these beasts. About eighty six-month-old heifers are also bought each year, and as the calves born on the farm are retained, the number of cattle rises to between 350 and 450 head, according to the time of year. In other words, there are as many cattle as on a grass farm, but the seasonal rhythm is reversed, the largest numbers being reached in the winter. The density of stock makes for high crop yields, the average for all cereals being about 29 cwt. to the acre.

On the fairly light arable land the first course in the four-year rotation consists of 100 acres of early potatoes. In order to encourage sprouting, the seed, up to 80 tons at a time, is kept in a greenhouse before planting. When the potatoes are lifted, they make room for tomatoes. At the end of June or in early July, shortly after the potato harvest, 40 acres of kale or carrots are sown in rows and, without being thinned, are grazed *in situ*, thus achieving an intensive type of fodder-production while using very little labour. In August $7\frac{1}{2}$ acres of turnips, to finish fattening off the lambs, are sown on the last fields of potatoes. The second course in the rotation is another root crop: 100 acres of sugar-beet and a few mangolds for the pigs and heifers in calf. Next there follows a fodder cereal, mixed with red clover and Italian rye-grass, which constitute the fourth-year crop.

On stronger soils a seven-course rotation is headed by a three-year ley of rye-grass and white clover. Potatoes and a catch-crop follow, and then wheat, sugar-beet, and finally wheat again, together with an admixture of seeds to re-establish the next three-year cycle of grassland.

Ten horses—'Two too many,' says the farmer—still remain, and are used mainly for harrowing.[1] The amount of working capital engaged works out at £50 per acre; the figure is kept comparatively low by the sheer size of the farm, and surveys by the Farm Economics Division of the C.G.A. in France point the same lesson. The splendid house and grounds confirmed the impression of prosperity given by the rest of the farm. In spite of the highly intensive methods of stock-rearing and cultivation, the labour force consists of only thirty-two workers, or one for every 28 acres. This is an unusually low ratio as compared with the Continent generally, but similar or even lower figures are common enough in the Paris Basin; but here farmers make the fundamental error of neglecting animal husbandry altogether and few of them even approach the level of output per worker reached at Grindle Shifnal.

[1] Higgs, who had three horses in 1950, each of them working for less than thirty days a year, said he refused to work out what his car and his horses cost him; he regarded both as luxury items. By 1953 he had only one horse—for riding.

6. The Boyne Estate and Burwarton Castle

256. The largest properties in the United Kingdom are in Scotland, but for the most part they consist of deer forests. The Boyne Estate stretches in a single sweep from the top of Brown Clee Hill to its eastern boundary some four and a half miles away, and covers a total of 10,000 acres, including four whole parishes and portions of three more. During the war the Castle grounds and even the century-old cricket pitch were broken up by the plough, but nowadays the three gardeners—there were thirteen before the war—again cut the lawns with a motor-mower every week. The mowings, which consist of young grass leaves rich in proteins, had never been put to any use, and the agent was astonished at the suggestion that they would be very good for cattle; the lawn is a luxury so far unscathed by the rough and tumble of economic exigencies.

The heather which crowns the Hill is burnt every year to prevent too vigorous a growth of grass, which would spoil the grouse-shooting, a form of the feudal hunt which has survived. Together with stretches of woodland and the 300-acre estate farm, the heath forms a 'reserve' of nearly 2,500 acres. The remainder, about 7,500 acres, is hedgerow country, with fields averaging 5 acres or so in extent. It is divided, in the first instance, among forty-five farms of between 50 and 375 acres, but mostly round about the 120-acre mark. Their tenure often passes from father to son, but a tenant, unlike the French peasant, has little or no chance of ever being able to buy his land. Some families, which were still strongly patriarchal at the time, came here between 1875 and 1880, when they were induced by the collapse in the price of cereals to leave their land in the arable sector of the country and to take up stock-farming, which was not so severely affected. At present many of their descendants are having to bide their time before they can get a farm of their own and marry. Apart from the farmers, there are about forty smallholders, many of whom are also roadmen, postmen, artisans, and tradesmen of various kinds—but not farm workers.

In 1937 for the whole of this area there were 150 horses and four tractors, and 500 acres of ploughland, the whole of the remainder being permanent grassland. In 1950 there remained only twenty-five horses, not a single one of them on any farm of over 125 acres. On the other hand, there was now a tractor on every farm, and the total had risen to fifty-five.[1] There were also two combines and the arable area had

---

[1] 'We have plenty of tractors, but not the men to drive them,' the farmers of Boyne were complaining in 1953.

increased to 2,500 acres, while in addition there were 1,250 acres of new leys. It was hoped, with the fairly safe proviso that agricultural prices should not collapse in the meantime, to add another eighteen combines by 1955. Acre for acre, the estate tenant is better equipped than the owner-farmer at Clee or at Stoke on the other side of the Hill.

257. There is a waiting list of nearly 100 names for farms on the estate. Until recently the Boyne family owned another property which was almost as large, but sold it to provide funds for investment here. Indeed, between 1948 and 1953 they put out £80,000 for development, a rate of £16,000 a year, which is a lot more than they receive in rent. Wiser than its French counterpart, English law allows for the remission of taxes on revenue spent on building and authorizes an increase in rents proportional to 5 per cent. of the cost.

Building contractors are better equipped and less greedy than in France; moreover, they pay higher wages and ask for less money. In 1950 a shed measuring 40 × 50 ft. cost £1,200, and a stall for twenty-four cows with a separate dairy and an annexe for the preparation of feeding-stuffs cost £2,000. At £80 per animal, this is cheaper than the expensive projects put forward by the French Génie Rural, which is the agricultural improvement service of the Ministry of Agriculture.[1] In England, in consequence, the landowner can still keep pace financially with the depreciation on his farm buildings.

The rent on the 120-acre farm where these two buildings had been constructed was raised by £160. Put in another way and taking the prices which were current at the time, this meant an increase in rent from 2 cwt. of grain per acre to about 3. As we have already seen, this is by no means a heavy burden on a farm which concentrates on dairying, especially when the capital investment in question offers an opportunity for the expansion of production. If, by contrast, the main interest was extensive rearing and the predominant breed was the Parthenaise cow of the Marais Poitevin, or even the Charolaise, the only result would be an improvement in amenities. Productive capacity would remain the same and an increase in rent would be hard to meet.

Quite apart from the cost of new construction, the maintenance of existing buildings, including the Castle, costs £6,000 a year, and requires the full-time services of about twenty skilled workmen—masons, plumbers, and painters included; there are also eighteen woodcutters, fifteen workers on the estate farm, five gamekeepers—who serve some

[1] Which proposed cement floors for stables at Saint Véran in the Hautes Alpes, at over 6,500 ft., completely disregarding the fact that it gets very cold in the winter.

purpose if they destroy rats and rabbits—and four clerks in the agent's office. The agent himself has a splendid house, with a domestic staff, a beautiful garden, and two cars, and enjoys a higher standard of living than the local farmer with 250 acres or so. There are still quite distinct traces of feudal traditions; they prompted an American friend to deliver the somewhat hasty judgement that the United States were far more democratic.

The estate, which still operates to some extent in a closed economy, exploits its own woodland and saws the timber in its own mill, which turns out creosoted fence palings, etc. To us the most interesting of all its activities was the way in which land overgrown with gorse or alder thickets was being cleared. With a chain and winch mounted on a Fordson Major, the latter could be cleared at the rate of nearly 4 acres in six hours. Up to 1,150 ft. the cleared land is either used as arable or sown to grass. Above this, 350 acres have already been reafforested; tenants and smaller property-owners, on the contrary, often cut down more timber than they ever replant. As a matter of fact, many stretches of uplands and moorlands could usefully be afforested, but the country's achievements in this direction, although by no means negligible, do not bear comparison with the transformation which has occurred in agriculture.

The survival of such large estates has been favoured by the rule of primogeniture. Death duties, which rise to 40 per cent. of the value of the estate, prevent them from remaining in the hands of those who have no other sources of revenue. The Boyne Estate is something of a model; others often reveal very much less in the way of efforts at improvement. None the less, it is not run for philanthropic motives. Rents ranged from 7s. to 25s. an acre before the war, but they have, to say the least, kept pace with agricultural prices. They do not vary so widely today, but are mostly in the region of 45s. an acre without new buildings or 60s.-80s. an acre where there has been a lot of modernization.

7. A Brave and Difficult Adventure

258. The establishment of good temporary grassland where once heather moorland reigned supreme is an act of courage worthy of the name Boldventure, the farm on the flank of Brown Clee Hill. Moreover, the ploughing, the transport of fertilizers containing lime and phosphates, drainage, the repair of buildings, and the maintenance of stock on improved grazings have all been generously subsidized from

public funds. Agricultural production, which fell so low about 1930, recovered slowly at first and then rapidly during the war; it was a process that required large investments of capital.

The provision of equipment and of tractors in particular has played an important part in compensating for the dearth of manpower, the most serious, in terms of workers per acre, in the whole of Europe. The use of artificial fertilizers has not yet reached the same level as in the Benelux countries, in Denmark, or even in West Germany. In a country which for many years financed the whole world, agriculture still suffers from a shortage of capital; the same point is even more valid in France and her overseas territories. Nitrogenous fertilizers are still not in general use on the grasslands of the west, nor is the silo very much in evidence. There is still plenty of scope for intensifying the cultivation of fodder crops, which would help to reduce the deficit in the balance of payments. The wisest course, surely, is to anticipate the mounting difficulties which will probably face exporters of manufactured goods in the future.

The example of England demonstrates that although industrialization may sometimes appear to be the prerequisite of a progressive agricultural evolution, the opportunity it offers may be either taken or ignored. For a time England saw her future as a country specializing in industry, commerce, and finance, and capable of neglecting her agriculture with impunity. The First War was a warning, the Second a brutal shock which, following on the heels of the inter-war crisis, at last touched off an energetic response. Today we would judge the policy pursued in England to be one of the most enlightened in the world; it is certainly superior to what one finds in France, although unfortunately that is no recommendation. The principle adopted with regard to subsidies is that they are granted to further the employment of factors of intensification. Mechanization, the use of fertilizers, and land improvements, such as the rectification of soil deficiencies, are thus encouraged, and only progress is rewarded.

The United Kingdom also deserves credit for demonstrating the advantages of consumer subsidies. Especially when the demand is elastic, as in the case of animal and horticultural produce, these can effectively widen the market. They are symptomatic of a sounder economic outlook than the doctrine of restricting production to balance supply and demand, which inevitably aggravates a depression. In France, to grow rich while producing less is still the cherished hope of important members of the farming community; and a few of them admit it quite openly. At one time it became the fashion among the bourgeoisie, which ruins its own health by over-eating, to pity *la pauvre Albion*, but for many rationed foods—butter included—consumption per head of the population was actually higher in England. The reason for this is that the working class often enjoys a better standard of nutrition than in France.

259. However remarkable may have been the efforts to stimulate agriculture, in England as in Italy, they still fall short of the mark set by their teeming populations. Here again, therefore, emigration must be resorted to and is encouraged by the powers that be. Agricultural prices—for the more important commodities at least—are controlled either directly or indirectly by the Government, but since 1950 they have not kept pace with either costs of production or the cost of living. In consequence, land values have dropped by about 15 per cent. (though this is also partly due to some tenants paying landlords virtually pegged and uneconomic rents), production is declining, and many farmers are now working their land less intensively in an effort to maintain their earnings. Many of those who went back to the land in the marginal areas are now taking flight: Pearce is already in Canada, Aron is going to New Zealand, and Higgs is proposing to follow him, together with a number of friends from Herefordshire.

It is said that the county committees are tending to become more severe as the Government tries to keep up production without taking the farmers' revenue sufficiently into account. 'More stick and fewer carrots,' 'The more we produce the less we earn' are Higgs's conclusions. The greatest remaining possibilities for production reside in the marginal land, but its working costs are higher. The urban population, however, which dominates the electorate, is accustomed to cheap, subsidized food and is most unwilling to pay more. It will not forgo the pictures or the football pools; it insists on *panem et circenses*. The attitude of the farmer is also typically urban: he is not going to remain on the land and 'get no more money than a peasant'.

England has a tradition of cheap food, but the farmers, remembering the crisis years of 1930-8, prefer controlled prices. The Government pegs the prices, but also wants the development of marginal land to continue and does give special capital grants exclusively for this purpose. Higgs thinks that this conflict of interests could be settled by more price differentials—that is, by paying a higher price for produce from poor land. We, on the contrary, would prefer to see increased subsidies for capital equipment, because these would offer benefits for agricultural intensification exclusively. Though her problem is not a simple one, at least England appears to be tackling it intelligently.

XIII

Intensification in the Low Countries: Its Possibilities and Limitations[1]

1. Overpopulation and the Conquest of the Land, Education and Capital

260. The population of the Netherlands is very nearly a quarter of that of France, but she has less than a sixteenth of the area. Population doubled, rising from 5,000,000 to 10,000,000 during the first half of this century, and the high rate of increase, about fourteen per 1,000 per annum, is due not only to a fairly high birth-rate, but also to a very low mortality rate. This is a sure sign of a country in an advanced stage of development.

The Low Countries are therefore obliged to conquer new land for agriculture and to exploit it to the highest degree. They offer the best example of intensive farming in the world—indeed, the term 'ultra-intensive' sometimes seems more appropriate. The noticeably higher areas in the east are for the most part covered with sandy, podsolized soils of low fertility, which in their natural state support little more than birch woods and heath land. Thus for many centuries new lands have been conquered by draining inland swamps and by progressively diking the coastal warps against the sea. Still more land was needed, and so inland lakes were diked and then drained by pumping. Haarlem Lake was once a constant source of danger to the nearby town, but today cultivated fields 20 ft. below sea-level have been created in its place. This feat was accomplished by building a whole chain of windmills, each one capable of raising water only 3 or 4 ft. Wind power later gave place to steam, and then to electricity.

The draining of the *polders* made available soils which were clayey

[1] Field studies in 1934, 1937, 1950, and 1952. This chapter is based on the last two visits. Cf. *Observation Economique* for September 1950.

and better suited to high-yielding crops. Until the beginning of this century, three-fifths of the agricultural land was on peat or sand, and the former, at all events, is not really suitable for anything other than pasture.[1] The cutting of peat for fuel, however, meant that the sandy sub-soil could be mixed with some of the humus to make an artificial soil. This is cultivated today by the fen colonies, and potatoes, destined for starch manufacture, and rye are the main crops. For a long time the sandy regions produced only a few hardy crops and remained for the most part devoted to rough grazings and poor pastures.

Prompted by the floods of two years before and anxious to extend the area available for crops, the Dutch decided in 1918 to implement the scheme for draining the Zuider Zee which had been formulated by the engineer Lély as early as 1880. The project is destined to produce 550,000 acres of good land, 50,000 of which are already under cultivation in the Wieringenmeer, together with another 120,000 in the North-east Polder. The Netherlands lack the foreign currency to buy huge quantities of feeding-stuffs from abroad—grain and cattle cake in particular. This makes the shortage of arable land all the more serious, for it hinders the adoption of the solution which Denmark and to some extent Switzerland and England have found of virtually becoming factories for the manufacture of animal products from commodities of vegetable origin.

Population pressure is finding relief in the rapid growth of towns, but no special effort is made to save land, as Le Corbusier would do, by building many-storied houses, even where the ground is really firm. Added to the spread of dwelling-houses are the encroachments of roads, railways, canals, aerodromes, factories, and sports grounds; in all, about 10,000 acres of land are lost every year. The completion of the Wieringenmeer drainage scheme in 1930 and the opening up of practically the whole of the North-east Polder in 1953 contributed another 170,000 acres to the agricultural area. During the interval of twenty-three years between them, however, and in spite of the wartime hiatus, an even larger area was appropriated for urban and allied purposes. The last three polders will eventually put another 380,000 acres in three great basins at the country's disposal. Each of them, saving unforeseen complications, will take fifteen years to complete. This rate of reclamation, about 8,500 acres annually, is still no match for the rate of loss, and the agricultural area continues to shrink year by year.

[1] Those who reclaimed the Vanne marshlands near Sens and the Vernier Marsh near the mouth of the Seine may eventually be forced to admit that permanent grassland is the best use for peat soils.

261. The prime necessity, therefore, was for the raising of yields per acre, and this has already been achieved thanks to the combination of physical and human factors, which on the whole have been favourable. Soils vary considerably, from the poorish peats and sands of some areas to the excellent soils of the new polders, which have large reserves of humus, lime, and mineral plant foods. There is a long winter and a fairly short growing season, especially in the east and north, where cattle spend six months in their stalls and large supplies of fodder—far more than in Normandy, for instance—have to be laid in for the winter. On the whole, however, the régime and the incidence of rainfall render the climate favourable for agriculture. Precipitation is regular and comparatively abundant, with a summer maximum,[1] there are heavy dews, and the evaporation rate is low. Water, the essential factor in agricultural production, is everywhere available and supplies can be artificially increased if required.

By any standards, certainly by those of most other countries, the Dutch peasant is extremely hard-working, but above all he is one of the best educated in the world, on a par with the Danish peasant, slightly better than the German, the Swiss, the English, and the Belgian, and far in advance of the French. The State deserves a share of the praise for having opened a large number of schools, some offering general and others specialized courses, but the record of achievement is due to the qualities of the people themselves. There are only a few schools of practical agriculture in France, but even those which do exist are not all full.

Where intensive agriculture is concerned, the Dutch farmer has yet another indispensable asset. By dint of his own strenuous efforts and the hard life he leads, especially in the poorer east, he has appreciable quantities of capital at his disposal. The country having been in the forefront of modern capitalism, funds naturally also came from non-agricultural sources. The importance of the Merchant Navy, which 'tills the seas', and of Dutch commercial activities, and the magnificent way in which the Netherlands East Indies were developed, have for centuries led to an accumulation of wealth and resources which have not—as is the case with France—been mainly invested overseas. One of the results is that the network of communications, as in Belgium, is one of the densest in the world, and the canals provide cheap transport for bulky goods. Manufacturing industry has developed in spite of the rather poor

---

[1] Total rainfall in Friesland is 28 in., and of this 8 in. occurs during the summer months. Spring is rather drier, but there are still reserves of moisture in the soil at this season.

mineral resources, and can supply the farmer with fertilizers and equipment at advantageous prices.

The peasants were themselves responsible for starting a large number of the industries based on agricultural products. Half the sugar refineries and most of the starch factories are peasant-owned. In Friesland four-fifths of the milk output is handled by the seventy-six co-operatives; seventy-two of these collaborate in running a large condensed milk factory which employs 600 workers, deals with 90,000 tons of milk a year, and accounts for 18 per cent. of Dutch condensed milk exports. Fifty-three of them have formed the powerful Frico export organisation, which in 1951 dealt with about 80 per cent. of the province's milk derivatives: 29,000 tons of cheese, 10,000 tons of butter, 3,000 tons of casein, and a quantity of powdered milk, representing altogether 530,000 tons of milk. In 1951 the combine had a turnover of £12,500,000, £7,500,000 of which was for exports. It owns £1,000,000 worth of fixed capital and employs 650 workers, who receive the same wages as they would on one of the farms. In France, for a town the size of Leeuwarden, there would be a considerable difference in wages in favour of the factory employee.

Frico has representatives all over the world who relay information about consumer requirements, however trifling they may seem. The customers are regarded as 'kings of production', which is an extremely sound economic viewpoint. Each week, on the basis of the reports, the Directors decide how the milk supplied by the co-operatives is to be used, whether to increase or decrease the output of this or that product or of this or that type of cheese. Friesland co-operatives own industrial and commercial establishments worth about £10,000,000 all told; their business turnover mounts up to £28,000,000, and they employ 5,500 workers. All this is in a province about the size of an English Midland county or a small French department.

The highly efficient organization of industry and commerce and, even more particularly, of co-operative enterprise is a basic element in the success of Dutch agriculture. In the section which follows we shall study certain aspects of this success, taking as our example a grass polder farm of the type which best illustrates the characteristic features of Holland. These flat, far-stretching polders form a patchwork of fields separated by canals. The farmsteads always stand out alone, each in the shelter of several rows of trees; the large villages are a sure sign of the high density of rural population.

2. The Specialized Grass-milk Farms of North Holland

262. Mr Glas owns a farm in the northern part of North Holland (Fig. 24). The farmhouse, built in 1676, comprises living quarters and accommodation for animals and equipment all under the same roof.

FIG. 24. The Netherlands.

The house itself and the cart-shed face the road, while the long cow-shed with its short stalls and its deep trench for drainings is at the back. The shed is polished in the summer and the floor covered with sand and shells, and with a mat; being unable to remove one's clogs, like the farmer, before entering, one has to wipe one's feet. Hay, the traditional winter fodder, is stored in a loft extending over the whole building. Several farms nearby have been divided between different owners,

SPECIALIZED GRASS-MILK FARMS OF NORTH HOLLAND

but this one, on the contrary, is an amalgamation of two smaller holdings, and it extends over 50 acres which are wholly devoted to permanent grass. The only exceptions are a small lawn and flower garden, a vegetable patch and an orchard, all sited by the house. These together occupy only about ¼ acre. At one time Glas grew his own mangolds. About 50 tons of roots with a 16 per cent. content of dry matter used to be lifted each year from the same 2 acres which had long been subjected to this form of monoculture. Several neighbours still follow this practice. The very small area of ploughland which one sees is given over entirely to row crops, mangolds, potatoes, and vegetables grown as field crops being the main ones. There are no cereals; they are considered to be an extensive crop, and arable land is too scarce to waste.

According to custom, half the grassland on the farm is mown for hay each year, but a 10-acre stretch of pasture next to the house is always reserved for grazing. At the time of our visit in July 1950 none of the grass was as yet ensiled. The haymaking, which lasts from early June until some time in July, depending on the weather, is subject to severe losses during wet summers, in spite of the hay-driers, which are designed rather like a step-ladder with four or five rungs on each side.[1] The cows are put out to pasture from the end of April until 15 November.

He buys about 50 tons of mangolds, or rather less after a good hay year, for winter feed, and 4 tons of mixed feed, consisting of 40 per cent. meal and 60 per cent. cake. There are twenty cows, one for every 2½ acres; six of their calves are kept each year, while of the remainder, bull calves are sold straightaway, and heifer calves after six weeks; six one- to two-year-old heifers make up the herd. In spite of the humid conditions, the farm has thirty-five ewes and forty-four lambs which are kept in good condition by the careful attention they receive; they crop the pastures after the cattle.

263. The main product is, of course, milk. The average annual yield per cow is 8,800 lb. of 3·5 per cent. fat content: 16,500 gallons are sold—at 15 cents in winter, 21 cents in summer; the average price was 18 cents in 1950, but rose to 20·5 cents in 1952. Farms nearer the towns have long concentrated on the liquid milk market, but here until 1933 the round Edam cheeses were made on the farm. Nowadays the milk is

---

[1] There is a general tendency to bring the haymaking season forward. It was almost finished by 10 June in 1952; five days later it was only just starting in Thiérache, where growth is earlier, in spite of its reputation as a region of progressive farming; and had hardly yet begun in Normandy where farming standards are lower and the growing season is even earlier.

sent to the dairy and the farmer's wife has more time for keeping house; the cheese press is the only sign of a once-important domestic activity. Only the great cattle-breeders like Ruyter at Ooster-Blokker continue to make their own cheese, as they thus ensure their own supply of tuberculosis-free whey for young breeding stock. On Glas's farm a calf consumes only 37 gallons of new milk before being weaned, for milk provides 70 per cent. of the revenue.[1] At Ruyter's by contrast, 75 per cent. of the income is derived from the breeding side of the enterprise and calves consume a quarter of the whole milk production.

Each year the farm sells an average of six cows, not all necessarily of the same age, ten bull and four heifer calves, about ten of the older ewes and thirty-four lambs of seven to eight months; it buys a few pigs for its own requirements. There is, therefore, in strong contrast with the purely arable type of polder farm, a high degree of specialization on grass and milk. Specialized production and a commercial economy have gone hand in hand for many years, owing to the presence of large towns and the development of export markets for dairy products. The main item is cheese, which was traditionally exchanged for wine from the Bordeaux region. Indeed, the character of farming in the western Netherlands not only bears the marks of the struggle against the sea and water in every form; it has been powerfully fashioned also by open competition with other provinces and with other nations.

A farmer on the nearby Wieringenmeer who does not need all his draught animals in the spring and early summer lends Mr Glas a horse, free of charge, until the harvest begins on 1 August. In this manner he does not have to waste food on a horse which is not needed for work. Glas employs another man and, not having a milking machine, which some of the younger farmers are beginning to acquire, they milk the herd by hand all the year round. Two more hands are taken on for five or six weeks for the haymaking. This is now a thickly populated agricultural region, but at one time its main resource was the whale-fishing from Medemblik, while the pastures, which were flooded in their lower portions every winter, provided only a minor source of employment. Land reclamation has compensated for the decline of the

[1] On a slightly more intensively cultivated farm in Midden Beemster, with '42 acres and 17 cows', and regularly selling the litters of three sows as well, the average income per acre in 1948 was 586 florins (about 10 florins to the £1 in 1952), made up of 350 florins for milk, 114 for cattle, 78 for pigs and 41 for sheep. Expenses included 112 florins for animal feeding-stuffs, 21 for fertilizers and 46 for rent. If wages had been paid, they would have come to 160 florins. The net profits were 173 florins per acre, or about £17 in 1952, a figure which was above the average.

fishing industry, but without the nearby and recently reclaimed Wieringenmeer, which is still sparsely populated and gives employment to many people from the village, rural unemployment would be a serious menace today. It is, moreover, a sufficiently disturbing national problem for the country to have begun a scheme of agricultural unemployment benefits in 1952; naturally, this has added to the charge on social services.

264. The Glas farm is managed very much more intensively than the average pre-war English grassland under the system of 'stick and dog farming'; very much more so, too, than the present-day pastures in Normandy, where a similar density of stock would be altogether exceptional, and it should be added that the Dutch farms produce by far the greater part of their own winter feed. One of the essential factors in this intensive system is the fairly abundant supply of water, which is assured by controlling the level in the canals. This necessarily involves uniformity of land use within individual polders, as the water-level is kept more than 3 ft. below the surface for ploughland, but is sometimes brought to within a foot for grass. Grass is quite rightly considered in the Netherlands to be a less intensive form of land use than crops, and in the case of the Glas farm, with its permanent pastures of very mixed flora, its neglect of rotational grazing, and its scant use of fertilizers, we have chosen an example rather below the norm. In 1950 he used only $26\frac{1}{2}$ lb. of nitrogen to the acre, which was the average for grassland over the whole country in 1946, an average which it was hoped would reach 106 lb. by 1962. In the arable regions, as in Flanders, the agricultural adviser often has to discourage the over-liberal application of fertilizers, but the reverse is the case on the grass farms, whose owners he considers to be 'a class below' the arable farmer.

In 1950 a neighbour of Glas's kept eighteen cows on 25 acres[1] of grassland, each of which received 176 lb. of nitrogen; grazing was controlled with movable electric fencing so as to give each beast 48 sq. yds. of pasture every half-day. There are pastures in Friesland which receive over 260 lb. of nitrogen and produce 700 to 800 gallons of milk to the acre, giving grass so rich in protein that it has to be supplemented with feed of low nitrogen content in the form of boiled potatoes. Such an excess of nitrogen carries the risk of tetany, especially if potassium is also present in large quantities. Moreover, it leads to the disappearance of white clover, leaving only rye-grass, which is less liable to give

[1] He has comparatively few young cattle and no sheep. The number of cattle per acre is higher in South Holland (often 0·5 to 0·6 cows per acre) than in North Holland and Friesland.

a good summer growth. In 1950 another advance was made in water-control with the adoption of irrigation, a practice which has since spread rapidly. The equipment, complete with motor-driven pump and pipes, costs nearly £1,000, and gives a rate of flow of 52 cu. yds. an hour on rather less than 1 acre, or the equivalent of nearly 1 in. of rain for £1. Such an investment requires first quality grassland to make it pay; on Glas's pastures it would probably be uneconomic.

It is pertinent to ask whether it is worth pushing intensification to this extent, and whether less lavishly fertilized leys with a greater dominance of white clover would not perhaps yield a better product at a lower cost. Experiments at the Haarlem polder Agricultural Station seem to prove that 176 lb. of nitrogen to the acre is the limit beyond which diminishing returns may be expected. It is only natural that the law of diminishing returns should operate in an overcrowded country such as the Netherlands, and along this particular avenue of intensification it seems that the economic limit is being reached.

265. A little further to the east in the same commune, J. De Moel keeps a horse, eight cows, three heifers, three calves, three ewes, and four lambs on $12\frac{1}{2}$ acres of grassland and $3\frac{3}{4}$ acres of ploughland. On the latter a third is for mangolds, a third for temporary grasslands of clover and rye-grass, 1 acre for oats, which are used to fatten five pigs, and the remaining $\frac{1}{4}$ acre is for potatoes and vegetables. In 1949 he produced 9,500 gallons of milk with 15 acres of grassland and fodder crops, more than a quarter of the latter going to feed the horse, the young cattle, and the sheep. When due allowance has been made for purchased feeding-stuffs, an acre of grassland, which here receives 125 lb. of nitrogen[1] on the average, yields almost 700 gallons of milk. The yield per cow reaches the high figure of 1,190 gallons a year, with 38 per mille fat content. He practises rotational grazing, preserves his grass efficiently in a silo,[2] follows—one is almost tempted to say blindly—all the instructions of the agricultural advisers, and is technically far in advance of the run-of-the-mill farm last described. On 27 July he was cutting grass for the second time since 17 May on a field which had been grazed twice in the interval; he was, in other words, reaping a fourth harvest by the time some meadows in France, under a warmer climate, had just been mown for the first time.

De Moel has seven daughters, who, when they leave school, must all

---

[1] And with very little phosphoric acid and potash on these rich virgin soils, which are dressed with carefully collected manure and drainings.

[2] He sows potatoes and beans on the 22 sq. yds. of soil covering his silo, a good indication of the shortage of land.

find employment away from the farm; one is a nurse, another an apprentice dressmaker, while another works in a dairy. His is thus a one-man enterprise; it is poorly equipped,[1] and De Moel is obviously very much overworked in the summer, for he has all the milking to do himself. His wife and daughters give him practically no help at all, whereas in Normandy on a farm of this size the milking, which is the essential part of the business, would doubtless be their responsibility. He would prefer to work 28 acres with the help of a son; to be able to pay a worker from outside the family he would need to have a larger acreage still.

Rents always being higher for the smaller holdings, he pays 840 florins a year for land and buildings. He was given the chance to buy, but would have needed 30,000 florins, or about £3,000 in 1952; this would have involved a mortgage and, what with interest and repayments, would have cost him more than he was paying in rent. He was already finding the rent rather a burden, and consequently refused the offer. It happens only occasionally in this region that the small farmer manages to buy his land. In 1946, when his yield had already reached over 500 gallons an acre and over 1,050 gallons per cow, figures which were very much above the average, the Institute of Rural Economy at Scheveninge, which keeps his accounts, showed that the farm was not paying its way if his work was debited at standard wage rates. In 1949, with production figures as given above, he obtained a return of 3,200 florins on his labour and working capital, which was hardly more than he would have earned as a farm employee.

Even when managed as well as this, such small holdings appear to leave a very uncertain margin of profit. In 1952 the standard of living of large farmers, with, for instance, 80 acres and forty cows, was still, in spite of their trim, well-kept houses, very much lower than that of an American farmer with a herd of a similar size. The Netherlands, as an exporting country, are obliged to keep their prices low. There is, however, more price support than in neighbouring Belgium, which, being a large exporter of industrial goods, must above all keep down the cost of food for its working classes in order to stabilize the level of wages.

3. The Triumph of Selective Breeding in Friesland

266. More remote from the great consuming centres of milk, Friesland has for centuries concentrated its efforts on highly selective breeding.

[1] He has a horse-rake and sometimes hires himself out with it for 3 florins an hour: 1 florin for him, 1 for the horse, and 1 for the equipment.

The Friesian breed, the good farmer's first choice for milk, has spread far and wide all over the world, and has proved successful wherever its essential requirements have been met. Secondly, as we have already shown, the province has responded to marketing difficulties by raising a remarkable structure of co-operation, aimed especially at developing exports.

With a tenth of the area of the Netherlands and a twentieth of the population, Friesland in 1951 produced 1,000,000 tons of milk, an average of 9,570 lb. of 39·5 per mille fat content per cow. This compares with an average of 8,360 lb., with rather less than 36·5 per mille of fats, for the whole country, which long maintained the highest figures in the world, although Denmark has recently sprung into the lead. In the same year Friesland accounted for 18 per cent. of the national output of milk, 20 per cent. of the butter, 43 per cent. of the cheese, and 25 per cent. of the condensed milk. With 680,000 acres of agricultural land—580,000 under grass and 97,000 under crops—the province had 450,000 head of cattle, of which 250,000 were cows. The clayey peat lands of the west are entirely under grass, whereas on the clay soils in the north there is a more varied pattern of pastures and crops.

At Oude Bildtzyl, Den Heer Anema farms part of a marine clay polder which was first diked in 1550 and colonized at that time by people of somewhat diverse origins, who comprised a lower proportion of local Friesian elements than the areas further inland. The soil, which is still comparatively new, has a neutral reaction (pH, 7-7·5), and consists of approximately 30 per cent. clay, 60 per cent. sand, 2 per cent. humus, and 5 per cent. of calcareous material. Shelly limestone commonly occurs 10 in. or so below the surface. The 138-acre Anema farm is thus largely under the plough, and has $107\frac{1}{2}$ acres of arable land, $27\frac{1}{2}$ acres of grassland, and 1 acre of buildings: 35 acres are under potatoes, which are specially selected for the production of disease-free strains.

The Friesian climate favours the cultivation of disease-resisting seed because the relatively low temperatures delay the development of aphides, which carry the viruses, until about mid-July. The diseases are transmitted through the tops of the potato plants, and these are therefore compulsorily pulled out at about the same time. At one time up to 60 per cent. of the ploughland on many farms was given over to this crop, and there were even specialist cultivators who rented 10 or 12 acres, hired the necessary horses and equipment and devoted themselves to it exclusively. Later on, in order to maintain healthy crops (danger of eel worm), and also because market conditions seemed uncertain, each farm was restricted to a maximum of a third of its arable land under potatoes, a quota which they all fulfil. This put the specialists in a difficult position, and they turned their attention to other crops, mostly seeds, which require a great deal of labour. Many of these extremely small holdings are now tending to disappear.

In addition to his potatoes, Anema cultivates about 12 or 13 acres of wheat and about the same of winter barley; cereals thus make up only a quarter of the total acreage under the plough. The low proportion of cereals as a useful index of intensiveness has already been noted particularly in North Holland and in various specialized market-gardening regions, where they are often completely absent. Those who do grow wheat in Friesland have to bring 24 cwt. of their crop per acre cultivated to the official grain storage agencies. Twelve and a half acres of mangolds or sugar-beet and 15 of rape bring up the total acreage of row crops to $62\frac{1}{2}$, or nearly three-fifths of the arable area, another sure sign of intensiveness. Finally, there are 10 acres of flax and the same of two-year leys, with a basis of Italian rye-grass and red and white clovers. The rotation consists essentially of three courses: potatoes followed by either beet, mangolds, flax, or rape, and finally a cereal; leys are fitted into the sequence from time to time.

267. Three-fifths of the farm's receipts come from crops, the remainder from animals, and there is a better balance than in North Holland as between grassland and fodder crops. There are thus twenty or more young cattle and fifteen cows, as compared with eight in 1912; all are descended from the same prize dam. The prize animals of this area have a world-wide reputation, and about three-quarters of the breeding stock exported from the whole country comes from here. Anema sells five or six bulls a year, three of which were brought to England quite recently. The average age of his cows is about four years and three months, and their mean production is about 1,170 gallons of 43 per mille fat content: 4,400 gallons are fed to young breeding stock every year; they are better nursed than the vast majority of the children of Asia, Africa, or South America.[1] Tuberculosis has been eliminated throughout the province since 1951, and both stock and products are guaranteed free from infection. Similarly, war is being waged on foot-and-mouth disease and on Bang's bacillus.

Mechanization in the Netherlands still has a long way to go, and this

[1] Some of his neighbours even give sheep's milk, which is the raw material for making high-quality cheeses of the Roquefort type, to young bulls so as to improve their appearance.

farm has one tractor and four horses. There are about ten workers, which represents more than three times as many per acre as on a well-equipped farm in Brie, where any form of stock is almost unusual and even cultivation is less intensive than it is here. In winter the men are kept busy sorting potatoes and scutching flax by hand.

The farm has been occupied by the Anema family for eighty years, and they pay a rent of 72 florins an acre, plus taxes. With wheat at 12 florins a hundredweight in 1952, this represented a rent of 6 cwt. an acre, but this takes no account of the artificially low price of wheat in the country. A better index therefore is the price of barley, which fetches 18 florins a hundredweight. The rent equivalent is then 4 cwt. per acre, which is lower than current rates in the Nord Department of France, while in Denmark, on poorer land, rents sometimes reach over 8 cwt. to the acre. The cost of land is about 1,600 florins an acre, in the region of £160 in 1952, plus 80,000 florins for a set of farm buildings. The high level of rents is admittedly a stimulus to intensification, but it assures the landowner of gratuitous revenues the application of which is very much open to criticism. With his tenure legally guaranteed,[1] Anema has built at his own expense a double-walled glasshouse for bringing on the germination of seed potatoes. During our visit in 1952 he was erecting a new and better ventilated cattle shed.

268. Crop yields are very high; 16 tons of sugar-beet to the acre, as much of potatoes, or even more if the plants were allowed to mature,[2] 19 cwt. of rape, 30 of wheat, 26 of barley, and 4½ tons of ley grass. The climate is extremely favourable for grass growth, and the idea generally accepted in England that permanent grass is much inferior to rotation leys is not borne out. On the heaviest clay soils near the old dike, which are the least suitable in the district for ploughing, permanent pastures give more hay than the temporary leys, which have been sown mainly to improve the soil. This confirms the idea that permanent grassland is the best response at either end of the scale of intensiveness in grass farming. At one extreme are the alps, on steep slopes, where no other form of land use is possible. At the other, under ideal conditions, are the Friesian grasslands; the soil is fertile and moderately permeable, and the supply of water can be closely regulated so as to avoid extremes of both deficiency and excess. Clayey

---

[1] M. J. Boerendonk, 'La réglementation des fermages et des prix de vente des terres aux Pays-Bas' (*Economie rurale*, the journal of the Société française d'économie rurale, January 1953).

[2] They are lifted before the normal time to avoid infection, and this prevents them from reaching the 'potential' yield figure.

soils, nearness to the sea, and the abundant rainfall with its summer maximum, weaken the case for irrigation, and there are no signs of its being adopted here.

The permanent grasslands yield some 3 tons of hay to the acre at the first cutting, which, in this region where summer comes a full month later than in Normandy, takes place about 1 June. Production ranges between about 200 fodder units in the case of hay to about 240 in the case of alternate grazing and ensiling, which, when carefully carried out, is a better method and subject to smaller losses. As this represents 40 to 48 cwt. of barley, permanent grassland is obviously a more intensive form of land use, in terms of yields per acre, than cereal farming. The reverse is true, however, of many soils in France which are not in fact properly suited to grassland. In Friesland, of course, grass is exceeded by row crops in point of yield, but it still occupies first place in terms of the return on labour. The usual practice with mangolds is to hoe four times by hand, in addition to singling. The French farmer does this only once. At the fourth hoeing the men simply walk through the fields pulling out a few small weeds here and there. Fairly obviously, the employment of this labour offers another instance of diminishing returns forced on a region by the excessive density of rural population. With more land at their disposal, more equipment, and enough living space, these wonderful people in Friesland would soon treble their productivity.

The basic essentials of the farming system are the fodder-rearing-milk association and the seed potato crop. In the latter case Friesian enterprise has triumphed once again by developing the Bintje variety, which is known all the world over, and by perfecting the technique of producing disease-free seed. Although Anema is more concerned with his stock, the other aspect of his farm is by no means neglected. His neighbour, Van den Staag, at St Jacobie Parochiee, on the other hand, specializes in seed selection, but he also has a herd of sixteen cows which keep up an annual average of 1,170 gallons. Nevertheless, he regards his animals as being rather 'ordinary' because of their slight deviations from the pure breed and the fractionally lower fat content of their milk. To make money from breeding in a region where the mean is so very high, one's standards need to be quite exceptional.

With the present-day economic system, the chief factor which prevents this vast agricultural potential from being developed to the full is the difficulty of finding markets. As far as seed selection is concerned, there is still a long way to go before the law of diminishing returns becomes operative. At the Central Bureau of the co-operatives in the middle of the Haarlem polder research is proceeding on potato strains resistant to mildew. Enormous economies in cultivation would result from the success of this project and, moreover, the world's reserves of copper are not inexhaustible. Another result, of course, would be to take away their livelihood from the thousands of Friesian seed-growers, who spend all their time between May and July walking through the fields on the lookout for unhealthy plants, which are immediately pulled up. But for the time being potato viruses still offer many problems, and by the time they are all resolved the Friesian farmer will have found other specialized and productive enterprises to pursue.

4. A State Farm on the North-east Polder

269. Reclamation schemes, like those undertaken by the Dutch in France during the seventeenth century, long remained in the hands of private enterprise. The contractor, anxious to make his profit quickly, would sell the new land to prospective farmers, but the first and even the second wave of colonization, lacking in capital and technical knowledge, generally ended in failure. Labour was treated rather scurvily, and the reclamation of Haarlem Lake, the last private scheme in the Netherlands, was a 'veritable disgrace', accomplished as it was 'under abominable social conditions', according to Den Heer Rijlaarsdam,[1] our remarkable guide in the North-east Polder.

This polder, like the Gezirah irrigation scheme in the Sudan, is a model of scientific achievement. A trial polder of 100 acres was diked near Andijk in 1927, and the principles of cultivation which were later applied on the Wieringenmeer were first established here: the use of plaster of Paris for removing the salt, of winter barley and lucerne. Thereafter the lessons learnt on the trial fields of each new polder were put into practice on the next scheme. Once drained, the land is crisscrossed by a rectangular pattern of ditches (16 ft. wide at ground-level) and canals (20 to 55 ft. wide). The rectangles are 880 × 275 yds. on the Wieringenmeer polder, 880 × 330 yds. on the North-east, and are planned to be 1,100 × 330 yds. in future schemes.

Thorough analysis of the soil and subsoil revealed a slightly higher proportion of poorer quality sands than had previously been suggested by soundings. Several methods of improvement were therefore put into effect. Where the layer of sand is no more than 3 ft. thick, the subsoil is turned over to a depth of over 5 ft., and this increases the clay

[1] Speaking of the Camargue, which he visited on a bicycle in the summer of 1951, he wondered if the predicament of the agricultural workers did not 'make the area a hot-bed of Communism'.

A STATE FARM ON THE NORTH-EAST POLDER

content of the surface layers from 3 per cent. to 30 per cent. Although this operation costs 400 florins an acre and delays cultivation by three years, these disadvantages are fully offset if an extra 3 cwt. of grain to the acre can be obtained annually for ten years. There is, moreover, an enormous difference between the productivity of land treated in this manner, which can be made to grow high-yielding industrial crops, and the grazings which would be the only form of land use possible on the sands.

Elsewhere, hard, lamellar bands of *sluf* impede the drainage, and the drains are then cut at closer intervals after subsoiling. Finally, when the layer of coarse sand is very thick, or when peat, which progressively dries out more and more, is present, the problem is met by laying underground irrigation pipes; this technique had already been developed for market gardens in Vaucluse, and we have described elsewhere[1] a similar scheme for celery cultivation on the sandy soils in Florida. The additional cost is only 200 florins, or about £20 per acre, which is a mere 5 per cent. of the standard cost of reclamation. As future production is thereby doubled, this is obviously money well spent.

The financial outlay is important. If this method proves economically worthwhile, the next century will see the Netherlands undertaking the reclamation of the Wadden Sea between the present dike across Lake Yssel and the Friesian Islands, where the predominance of sand would necessitate some such scheme of irrigation. The same may also apply to part of Lake Yssel itself.[2] As agriculture has been defined as the modification of the environment, it has evidently reached an extremely advanced stage in these polders. Land has been conquered from the sea, and the control of water is complete. Even the soil has been transformed where necessary by digging to a great depth.

270. Four-fifths of the polder consist of fairly clayey soils where it is unnecessary to resort to such methods. Here a special trenching machine similar to an American ditcher is used to dig open ditches 9 to 18 yds. apart, according to the type of soil. The object is to assist drainage during the first phase while soils are still very fresh and not sufficiently permeable. Next, the strips of land are sown to cereals or rape for three successive years, with catch-crops of trefoil, which is turned into the ground. Two or three more years under lucerne then follow, but on these azoic soils the seeds of such leguminous crops have to be inoculated with bacteria before being sown. Earthenware pipes

[1] *Les leçons de l'Agriculture américaine*, Chapter XII.

[2] The Zuider Zee has been renamed Yssel Meer since the dike cutting it off from the sea was completed.

for permanent drainage are then laid at a depth of 3 to 4 ft.; the lines are from 9 to 26 yds. apart, 165 yds. in length, with a fall of 12 in., and drain into the lateral ditches.

At first cultivation is under State direction. Operations are relatively highly mechanized to compensate for the high cost of labour. On an ordinary farm wages are 1 florin an hour for permanent workers, but here the men eat and live in well-planned camps which even have their own gardens, and labour costs as much as 2·50 florins an hour. For the 61,500 acres of cultivated land there are 400 tractors and 60 combines, but there are also 300 horses and 150 binders; average yields per acre are 31 cwt. for wheat, 34 cwt. for oats, 22 cwt. for barley, 20 cwt. for rape, 60 cwt. for dried lucerne,[1] 56 cwt. for raw flax, and 350 cwt. for sugar-beet of 17 per cent. sugar content. The next stage is the erection of farm buildings, which take the form of huge sheds made of pre-fabricated concrete sections in grooved plywood frames, which seven men, with the help of two cranes, can erect in three days. They can be maintained very cheaply, an important consideration from the point of view of the State, which keeps possession, not only of the land, but of the buildings as well.

After this, cultivation is carried out by individual farms. They must have a working capital of 480 florins an acre, a quarter of which they must possess themselves; they may borrow another quarter from their families if they need to and the remainder is loaned by a co-operative bank. Moreover, they must reach a certain standard of proficiency in their knowledge of farming. In so far as the selection of settlers is concerned, the State tries to keep a balance between the different provinces.

Besides the 5,000 acres allocated for woodland, the 6,300 for horticulture, and the 8,800 for villages and factories, the remaining land will carry farms of three types: arable on good soils, grass on sands, and mixed. On the smallest farms, which have 30 acres, the brick-built farm buildings cost 110 per cent. more per acre than on those of 120 acres. On the latter the large shed in six sections costs 50,000 florins (£5,000); a cattle stall adds 27 per cent. to this figure. In France the Reconstruction is spending twice as much and achieving less in the way of practical results.

There are 635 farms of 60 acres, which corresponds to a reclamation unit and is considered to be the optimum size. On the Wieringen

---

[1] When we came here in June 1952, the lucerne had been left rather long before being dried because of a protracted argument between the producer, i.e. the State, and the privately-owned lucerne drying concern which buys the standing crops.

polder the largest farms were of 50 acres, but future plans provide for some of 75. Then there are 206 45-acre and 338 30-acre holdings, the latter being rightly regarded as the minimum acreage possible;[1] these latter are sited on the best soils. Finally, there are another 431 holdings of between 75 and 90 acres and of between 105 and 120 acres and seven large farms of 150 acres apiece. Rents vary from 60 florins for medium-quality grassland to 90 florins, which represents 7 cwt. of wheat, but only 5 of barley, for the best clay soils.

The State is keeping forty-four farms of various sizes totalling 2,950 acres under direct control, and will use them as an index of appropriate rent levels. In 1950 and 1951 the net income of private farms attained 120-200 florins an acre, a fact which prompted some of the officials to ask for holdings of their own; they will now be earning twice as much as they did as agricultural advisers.

271. The landscape around Emmeloord, the regional centre, is somewhat reminiscent of the Middle West. There is the same pattern of modern-looking dispersed farmsteads, there are the same tall cattle sheds and the same concrete roads criss-crossing geometrically; only the silo towers are absent. The countryside, however, is flatter, there are more buildings and gardens, the fields look neater. On State farm No. 65 there is no stock whatsoever, either for production or for draught purposes, except one cow and a few pigs which supply the needs of the farm's personnel. The cultivation of the 180 acres of fields is performed with the help of two tractors, both wheeled, one of 18 and the other of 30 h.p. The manager is assisted by four men and, having no herd to tend,[2] they are kept busy in the winter scutching flax by hand, a method which gives better fibre than a machine could produce, but which none the less seems open to criticism as a waste of labour. Between three and seven extra workers are taken on at busy times of the year. In 1951 an average of ninety-eight hours of work were expended per acre; twenty-eight for wheat, 140 for potatoes, 160 for sugar-beet, and very much more for flax. Tractor use is at the rate of six hours per acre for wheat at one extreme and from twenty-four to twenty-six hours for row crops at the other; it averages 18·8 hours per acre per year.

The use of tractor tools for inter-row cultivation is symptomatic of

[1] This is the final condemnation, by the finest experts in the world today, of the diminutive microfundia which one finds in so many parts of the Continent, from the Mediterranean to Central Europe—not forgetting Flanders, Isère, Béarn, Brittany, etc. See our *Voyages en France d'un agronome*.

[2] 7 per cent. of the farms in Sweden have no livestock.

the relatively low density of workers as compared with the rest of the country. Harvesting machinery on the polder normally includes only the binder and the flax-reaper, for great care is taken to preserve the straw, which is sold for the manufacture of cardboard. In France, by contrast, the combine is used overmuch and the straw is often burnt; then wood pulp has to be imported. The beet are topped by hand (Pommritz method), and the tops are then carefully gathered and sold to neighbouring stock farms. In order to make the most of such by-products, which it would be foolish to neglect in so overcrowded a country, the Dutch have avoided 'bleeding themselves of capital for the sake of mechanized harvesting, which has the dual disadvantage of wasting the earning power of both straw (combines) and beet tops (mechanical lifters)'. The tariff wall against imported sugar in France allows the big Ile-de-France farms to turn beet tops into the ground even when manual lifting has kept them perfectly sound and clean.

Cultivation began either with lucerne or several crops of cereals. The projected rotation extends over nine years: oats, flax, lucerne (one-year), potatoes for culinary use,[1] wheat followed by a catch-crop of trefoil, sugar-beet, peas, caraway, and rape with another catch-crop of trefoil. The two crops grown for green manure and the lucerne will no doubt keep up the humus content. Nitrogen was added at the rate of 35 lb. to the acre for cereals in 1951 and at 88 lb. to the acre in 1953. The high potassium content of the soil dispenses with the need for potash and 35 lb. of phosphoric acid to the acre appears to suffice. Fertilizers count for only 6-7 per cent. in the cost of farming, which averages 440 florins an acre.

One cannot help wondering whether such a farm, with its intensive arable system, would not be well advised to adopt some form of stock-rearing so that the straw, fodder crops, and various by-products might be consumed on the spot. This would certainly save transport costs, especially in the case of beet-tops. In addition, the fertility of the soil could be more easily maintained. Against these arguments, however, one is obliged to consider the inherent advantages of specialization. Finally, we would invite all those responsible for land development, whether it be in the tropics or in mid-latitudes, to come and visit this region before essaying their own projects; and to analyse the reasons for the wonderful success of reclamation in these Dutch polders, where reasoned prudence and calculated risk have been blended to such good effect.

[1] So as to prevent virus infection on this new land only class A or AB seed may be used.

5. The Conquest of the Eastern Heathlands and the Rural Exodus

272. The development of these poor, sandy regions in the eastern part of the country is not so spectacular and has not received the same attention as the reclamation of the Zuider Zee. Nevertheless, during the last three-quarters of a century it has led to economic repercussions of far greater significance. Before this the Celtic system had full sway. The small patches of arable land were fertilized with stable litter culled from the heaths and by the sheep which, as in Sologne and the Landes, browsed the scrub and the heather. The peasants supplied all their own wants; the men shod their own horses and the women spun their own wool and baked their own bread.

From 1880 onwards the import of cheap grain from overseas, the attraction of the towns, and the rise in the price of animal produce brought about a series of changes similar to those which were taking place in Danish Jutland, where conditions were somewhat comparable. The small farms, which predominated, began to produce milk and, more especially, pork and eggs, and as they owned so little land they based this new economy on imports of supplementary feeding-stuffs, among which concentrates such as grain and cake took pride of place.

At the same time the arrival of artificial fertilizers rendered the nearby heathlands, with their poor, sandy podsols and their covering of heather and birch, redundant as a source of manure. These sandy geests, which are found again in north Flanders, in the Belgian Campine, and extend as far east as Poland and the U.S.S.R., then began to be cropped for rye and oats and potatoes. Marshes were drained at the same time and added to the reserves of pasture. About 20,000 acres were cleared annually during the first forty years of the century. The average size of farms thus increased from 16 to 20 acres, but this was merely the net result which conceals the effect of increasing demographic pressure. In fact, the years 1910-47 saw the creation of a quarter of the holdings which can be seen today, and of these half were established on newly cleared land, while the remainder owe their presence to the subdivision of pre-existing holdings; over the same period only 45 per cent. of the farms were actually enlarged by fresh clearings.

This silent re-conquest is practically at an end; the rate of clearing has slowed down since 1948. By 1960 all the cultivable land will have been taken and the remainder given to reafforestation. Nevertheless, even ignoring those of less than $2\frac{1}{2}$ acres, 43 per cent. of holdings even today have less than 12½ acres, and another 30 per cent. range between 12½ and 25 acres. The relative price movements of imported feeding-stuffs and animal products have not been favourable to the region. For the most part, the elusive dollar is needed for the purchase of grain and oil-cake, while the removal of many crushing-mills to the tropics is making oil-seed residues even more difficult to obtain. These problems of supply, combined with the austere mood of the English market, which is narrowing the scope of the export trade, are hindering the stock-farming activities of the small farms in the west, which rely so heavily on purchases of feeding stuffs.

The Institute of Rural Economy at Scheveningue, which kindly supplied these data, also made the point that, whereas some farmers in the sandy eastern region worked up to 3,200 hours a year,[1] others were occupied for only 1,400 hours and were under-employed. It estimated that in 1949 the peasant population was 25 per cent. too large for the existing resources. At that time there were hardly any tractors at all, but since then they have appeared in increasing numbers. The only farms considered to be truly economic units were those of 20 acres and above and, further enlargement being out of the question, the only way in which these could be improved was by increasing the density of stock. The difficulties which confront this line of development have already been outlined. The Institute estimated that increases of no less than 20 per cent., 200 per cent., and 100 per cent. were needed in the numbers of cattle, pigs, and poultry respectively before full employment could be achieved. The prime condition of such expansion was, of course, that feeding-stuffs should be available at economic prices.

Seventy per cent. of holdings were worked by one man and a horse. But, as the Institute emphasized, although this represented the smallest possible unit of labour, it was still too large to be employed rationally on the majority of holdings, and in particular on those of less than 12½ acres. It was recognized as practically impossible to reduce the number of superfluous workers and horses without cutting down the number of farms. Even the ponies and oxen which were once used have now disappeared. As the rise in population continues unabated, the Institute foresees that by 1960 there will be '60,000 prospective farmers without farms' in the sandy regions alone, provided that the proportion of young people leaving the land remains between 30 per cent. and 45 per cent. as at present. Until now the latter figure has been attained only in the vicinity of industrial areas, but, according

---

[1] At Raalte we noted up to 4,000 work-hours per year, which really is overwork.

to the same authority, as many as two-thirds of the children and young people of today will have to find employment outside agriculture if the size of farms is to be restored to a satisfactory level.

273. In 1898 the elder Roest took up a farm west of Amersfoort in the commune of Soest, which forms part of Utrecht Province. He had 12½ acres of what was little better than marsh pasture and kept two cows and about ten pigs in addition to a few chickens. By day, he went out in search of work with his horse and, as on many of the small holdings in north-east France at the time, this provided the only money he ever earned. The farm, on which he worked mainly at night, simply served to feed his family. By the time his son took over, shortly after 1930, he had cut ditches and drained the land and had increased his herd to five cows. It is almost impossible to realize how much this ascent in the social scale had cost in toil and privation.

Like the Antwerp dockers who came to the Campine, workers in the towns enjoyed higher wages than agricultural workers—not that there were ever more than just a few of these on the small farms of the region—and used to find it easier to set up on farms of their own. When we were here in 1950, Roest owned 9 acres and rented another 9 at 40 florins an acre, a rate which he was hoping the Rent Service would reduce. He had enlarged his holding by 2½ acres that same year, but, situated as he is in such proximity to the towns, there is no chance of clearing any new land. On the contrary, the plough is fighting a losing battle against the spread of new buildings.

He has five fields of pasture occupying 10½ acres; there are 6¼ acres of arable land, almost half of it devoted to row crops: nearly 2 acres of potatoes (early and late crops and seed), 1 acre of mangolds, and ¼ acre of maize cultivated as a grain crop. Then there are 2 acres of temporary grass, and finally only just over 1 acre—only a fifth of the arable land—of rye and oats or barley and oats mixed. Moreover, these cereals are nearly always followed, as in Flanders, by a catch-crop of turnips, and they cannot therefore be regarded as a semi-extensive form of land use. The intensiveness of farming is emphasized by the employment of nitrogen at 88 lb. to the acre on both arable land and pastures. When we saw the farm at the end of July 1950—it had been a wet month, admittedly—⅛ acre of young meadow was thus sufficient to graze eight cows for a whole day. The farm supports, according to the time of the year, eight or nine cows together with four stores and four calves. The average yield is only just over 7,000 lb. per beast per annum, but a neighbouring herd attains 8,800 lb., and it is rather unfortunate that productivity should be thus handicapped by poorer than average stock. Roest also keeps two sows, retaining a dozen pigs each year for fattening and selling the remainder.

He has 200 hens and fifty pullets, which at 160 per head give him 40,000 eggs a year. Being classed as a producer of 'quality' eggs, he is not allowed to keep a light in the hen-house during the winter, and his birds therefore reach their peak of production during the spring.

Finally—a typical feature of intensive farming—he grows $\frac{1}{8}$ acre of gooseberries and another $\frac{1}{10}$ acre of strawberries. He also retails a few vegetables in the town, but only what he does not need for himself. A small space between some old gooseberry bushes has been sown down to beans; there are rows of strawberries between lines of newly planted bushes, and indeed at every step one sees similar signs of the oppressive shortage of land.

274. The farm is worked by the man and his son, 'who will have fewer hardships to suffer than his grandfather or even than his father'. The wife is kept busy with her nine children, and only helps on the land very occasionally. The two eldest girls are in domestic service in the nearby town; the younger girls remain at school until they are fifteen and help a little during the holidays. Roest thinks that his 18 acres are enough to keep two men fully occupied, especially during wet years, like 1950, when weeds grow in profusion and the hay crop gives cause for anxiety. The two silos, each with a capacity of 350 cu. ft., are a great asset, especially at times like these. They are used for both grass and potatoes, the inferior tubers being boiled and then ensiled for use as pig food.

Except when Roest makes up a plough-team with his neighbour, the horse works only on this one farm and is seriously under-employed, especially by comparison with the farmer and his son. For equipment, Roest has little more than a small plough, a harrow with wooden teeth, and two small carts. Eight farmers of the locality, whose holdings range from $7\frac{1}{2}$ to $27\frac{1}{2}$ acres, have formed a co-operative for the pooling of horse-drawn equipment analogous to the French C.U.M.As., which are, however, based on the tractor. In 1950 they had at their disposal two mowing machines, a rake, a tedder, a three-row ridger, and a horse hoe. It was intended to acquire a Brabant plough and a grass harrow with the help of the subsidies which are offered to small farms.[1]

There is no binder nor does it figure in plans for the future. The shortage of equipment is illustrated by the frequent use of the scythe

[1] Electric fencing, silos, trenches for drainings, etc., are also subsidized on the very small farms.

for both grass and corn crops, and by the fact that much of the hay-making is still done by hand. Intensive cultivation and the high density of stock, together with this dearth of equipment, explain why Roest regards his 18 acres as sufficient to occupy two men. It must be remembered that even this acreage is above the regional average, and it is evident therefore that a greater degree of mechanization would have to be accompanied by an increase in the size of farms.

His neighbour, who is a member of the co-operative, makes two rounds a day, which take five hours in all, to collect 880 gallons of milk from twenty-eight farms. On his return he starts work on his own 12-acre holding. He does not own a horse, and has to hire one on eight days in the year at 4 florins a day. The milk lorry serves his requirements for the transport of hay and sheaves of corn. He has a herd of only four cows, but as for pigs and poultry, which are less dependent on the dimensions of a holding, he has as many as Roest. On the whole there are many points of comparison with the peasant factory hand of Belgian Flanders or of Isère.

6. Horticulture—Market near the Point of Saturation

275. With its batteries of chimneys overlooking enormous expanses of glass, 'Westland', which stretches just to the south of The Hague, gives the impression of an industrial region. There are the *serres*, each of 380 sq. yds. ($40 \times 9\frac{1}{2}$ yds.), with very steep roofs, and the *warenhuis*, which are larger and have almost vertical side walls. At Poelddijk, Jansens has nine stove houses (six grapes, two peach, one plum) and as many cool houses (two grapes, two plums, four tomatoes, and one French beans). He has in addition one large stove *warenhuis* for tomatoes and a cool one for peaches. Out of a total of $3\frac{1}{4}$ acres, $2\frac{1}{4}$ are under glass. Of the latter, 1 acre is heated from 1 March until mid-May, and 90 tons of coal are burnt in the process. Every year about 300,000 tons are burnt in this manner in the Netherlands and 700,000 tons in England. This is 1,000,000 tons of coal, which the European economy can ill afford.

A house which gives about a ton of early grapes or less burns from 8 to 9 tons of coal. The bunches of fruit look pleasant enough, but in spite of the minimum sugar content of 13 per cent. admissible at the auctions the taste is not always agreeable to the Mediterranean palate. The ground without buildings is worth from 2,800 to 3,200 florins an acre; complete with houses and heating plant, values rise to 128,000 florins, or about £12,800 in 1952. A greenhouse alone, without heating, was worth 4,500 florins in 1950. One man can look after about seven houses, and Jansens manages with two employees,[1] apart from two girls who help for six weeks in the year. During this period, each bunch of grapes is thinned out with scissors, one grape at a time.

Certain types of grape begin to ripen after the end of May or early June, but the black Frankenthal variety is not ready until the beginning of July. This is undeniably a luxury trade, but as 1 lb. of fruit may fetch up to 1·80 florins, as against its production costs of 0·65 florins, the business is very well worth while. On the other hand, prices are falling rapidly and the cost of coal is going up. Already in 1952 some houses with hot-water-pipe installations remained unheated, while in others tomatoes were taking the place of grapes.

On the sunny slopes of Sicily, Andalusia, and North Africa, not to mention Corsica and the Côtière of Bellegarde, in the most favoured situations, early varieties can be ripened in the open from the beginning of July onwards. The cost of coal alone—9 lb. per pound of grapes—exceeds the whole cost of transport from the Mediterranean coast to Covent Garden in London. It is not easy to understand how so artificial a form of production, where the natural temperature and water conditions have to be modified at such great expense, can possibly survive competition from other areas. The greenhouse industry near Paris, for instance, was killed at the end of the nineteenth century by the developments in Vaucluse and Roussillon.[2]

276. The first explanation that comes to mind is the sheer technical prowess of these specialized farmers. They are extremely competent on the practical side and abide closely by the advice of a large band of agricultural experts, each of whom is a specialist. The latter have a research station at their disposal which is financed half-and-half by the State[3] and the 6,000 growers, who pay 10 florins, or about £1 a head. Whenever a new house is built, the soil and subsoil are analysed beforehand, deficiencies to be rectified are noted, and appropriate crops are determined. The choice of varieties, measures to be taken against pests and diseases, and the fertilization needed are all indicated with great precision. Although the ordinary Dutch farmer, with one adviser for every 300 farms, has a comprehensive service of technical assistance at his disposal, the horticulturalist fares even better.

[1] During the part of the year when the houses are heated, he has to get up twice in the night, at 11 p.m. and at 5 a.m.; and he has to work all day Sunday.

[2] *Voyages en France d'un agronome*, Chapters IV and V.

[3] In the same way the magnificent research stations in Java and Sumatra were financed by the planters. The French farmer has not made a comparable effort.

Another reason lies in the highly efficient commercial organization embodied in the splendid *veilings*, or co-operative auctioneering bodies. There was a time when they received all their merchandise by boat, but the lorry is now becoming a serious rival. The buyers sit in an amphitheatre and can keep in touch by telephone with the state of other markets—foreign markets included—throughout the duration of the auction. Sale is by Dutch auction: a needle revolves rapidly on a dial and indicates progressively smaller figures. The first buyer to depress his button stops the needle; his number appears automatically on the dial, and the purchase is thereby made at the price indicated. The officials simply display the goods and record the sales. The seller rather than the buyer seems to be favoured by the system.

Quality is rigorously inspected, and any lot which fails to reach a specified standard is returned to the grower, who is allowed to deal only through his own *veiling*. Here again 'the consumer is king', and the Dutch producer is incessantly seeking to satisfy his requirements. If Covent Garden wants big grapes with rather a sharp flavour, there is no point in trying to send the best French *chasselas*; but it will pay good prices for varieties which resemble the Dutch or Belgian glasshouse grape, so that the natural product, in order to command a good price, must conform with the artificial!

The country is rapidly increasing its horticultural production: 20 per cent. more vegetables and 125 per cent. more fruit than in 1934-8. The expansion of exports, however, may well be confronted with increasing difficulties. There is a battle for foreign import licences at the beginning of every season. On the other hand, a horticultural expert is always called in when trade discussions are being held with other countries, whereas France does not even employ her agricultural experts as Embassy attachés.

When the Mediterranean countries begin to fight with the same weapons of technical and commercial efficiency, they will constitute a real menace to this expensive forcing industry. Italian competition in the German fruit market is already giving rise to anxiety.[1] In response to these dangers, the Dutch have recently founded at Wageningen a remarkable establishment for the study of processing and preserving their produce. The whole question of canning, freezing, etc., is being investigated. When prices at the auctions fall below a certain minimum, the goods are bought by a reserve fund, which is maintained from a commission on sales, and destroyed. It is useless to dwell on the moral

---

[1] We need not dwell on the shortcomings of the French in this particular market; exports of stone fruits, for instance, are in full retreat.

and social aspects of this practice, but it confirms the opinion that Malthusianism is the fatal weakness in our economic structure.

277. Even a brief survey of the Low Countries would be incomplete without a reference to flowers and bulbs. The cultivation of bulbs for export has developed at the foot of the dunes between Leiden and Haarlem, where sand and peat are mingled in judicious proportions. The main nucleus still remains, but the industry now covers 17,500 acres in the whole country and is found as far afield as Enkhuizen and even in Friesland. The area under tulips and daffodils is subject to control, and there is also a reserve fund, as in the glasshouse industry.

A small bulb-grower south of Haarlem cultivates 850 *roede*,[1] which includes 275 of tulips, 170 of daffodils, 120 of crocuses, and eighty of gladioli. The rotation begins with deep digging to a depth of nearly 30 in. Early potatoes are then followed by beans. Tulips, with alternate rows of carrots, are planted in the second year, and another crop of carrots is planted in the spaces when the bulbs have been removed. The other bulbs, following in order, then complete the rotation. Every operation is done by hand, even the digging, for which either a spade or a small hoe is used.

As these same crops have been grown for centuries on the same coveted ground, the soil has become toxic and quite useless for bulb-growing. A special barge is therefore moored in an adjacent canal. It pumps pure sand, mixed with water, from a depth of 16 to 22 ft. below the field itself and discharges it on to the surface. The hard incrustation which commonly develops at a depth of about 6 ft. is thus fragmented by undermining from below and increased pressure from above. The whole process effects an exchange of old soil for subsoil free from toxins and weeds; it can only be described as a truly remarkable modification of the environment. The work occupies two men for five weeks, and in 1950 the cost, including the use of the pumping barge and pipes, came to 1,800 florins per acre. It is doubtful whether this expense can be justified from a national standpoint when it could be dispensed with by growing bulbs on new land elsewhere. From the grower's point of view, however, it allows him to pursue his livelihood without having to move.

278. South-east of Haarlemmermeer at Aalsmeer, 1,000 flower growers, on 750 acres and with mobile glass frames on another 340, produce about 30,000,000 florins' worth of cut flowers, pot-plants, cuttings, and seeds under an even more intensive system. The largest

---

[1] There are 280 *roede* in an acre. The diminutive size of the local unit of area emphasizes the 'garden' character of land use in the region (Hillegom, Fig. 24).

producer has 3¾ acres, and his equipment is worth perhaps 1,500,000 florins. This is fully £40,000 of working capital per acre, and must be very close to a world record. About forty employees, which is almost eleven per acre, attend to the delicate plants, which are grown under completely artificial soil and climatic conditions. Temperature, light, atmospheric humidity, and soil water are all closely controlled. The flowers are conveniently placed on cement platforms[1] and are planted in whatever type of soil they require: pure sand, gravel, peat, or complex mixtures with specific proportions of fertilizers or manure.

The scientific advisory service here reaches its maximum development. For these 1,090 acres alone there are about twenty technical experts, who also teach at the school of floriculture. Sales are again organized through *veilings*, and the co-operative auctions, with their hundreds of flowers of every kind, are a wonderful sight. Here again intensification has practically reached its economic limits. Pot-plants sometimes sell badly; many growers owe money to their co-operatives; some have even gone bankrupt. The Netherlands have only retained a monopoly in the most exclusive specialities—in slips or seeds which are particularly difficult to grow, or in forced plants requiring delicate treatment. Some growers and their families depend on ¼-acre gardens and 240 sq. yds. of glass. Lilacs are allowed to grow in the open for twenty-three months and are then transplanted with all the soil round their roots and forced for a month under glass. Here again there is no permanent guarantee of productive full employment.

7. Lessons to be Learnt from the Netherlands: Technique and Equipment, Austerity and Independence

279. The lessons are as interesting as they are varied. We would strongly recommend the grass farmer in Normandy to go and see how much can be made of grasslands even under unfavourable conditions. In Friesland, the large farms of the Paris Basin would discover how to dovetail stock-farming into an even better arable system. The Breton and Poitevin marshes between the Loire and the Garonne would learn that they could get at least five times as much out of their soils if they fertilized them and fully completed their drainage schemes. In the eastern sandy area, the peasants from the poorer districts of the Atlantic Littoral, from La Vendée to Brittany, would find clear proof that their own underdeveloped and underfertilized lands, with their humid

---

[1] 'The ground is too far down; it ought to be put on a table'—the old man's wish, as he weeded the rows of beet, seems to have come true.

climate, could be made really productive. Even the Basque country would come to realize that modern agriculture has discarded its former dependence on *touyaa*, or heathland, since the advent of chemical fertilizers.

The Netherlands have evolved the best type of intensive farming in the world, and illustrate the two basic principles to perfection: agricultural training for the producers in conjunction with an expert advisory service, and the need for a great deal of working capital. Only countries able to fulfil these requirements fairly quickly are going to win the war against hunger. In the Netherlands additional measures are being planned to forestall the very real danger of overpopulation, and it is hoped to reach a net figure of 50,000 emigrants annually.[1] Investments are pouring into industry even faster than into agriculture, on the premise that a factory 'can utilize more men and capital per acre', as one agricultural expert put it. The industrialization of the poor and overcrowded east, where comparatively little investment has taken place so far, is receiving particular attention from the Government. In France a dangerous policy of industrial concentration in the Paris region is being followed instead of trying to develop the overcrowded west; but industrial firms fear that the incidence of alcoholism in the latter area would lead to too many accidents.

In 1951 the Low Countries invested 14 per cent. of their national revenue, but 20 per cent. is the figure aimed at. With this in mind, firms are being asked to reduce their stocks so as to liberate more funds for boosting production. Concurrently, a 5 per cent. cut in real wages is being sought in order to reduce home consumption. Whether these policies can be carried through or not in the context of a semi-planned economy will largely depend on the overseas market and on the private companies themselves, which still retain a certain liberty of action in the allocation of their funds. Although liberalism no longer rules, there is still no compulsorily enforced national plan.

This policy of austerity, similar to the British and likewise aimed at stimulating investment, is supported by an information service which explains its whys and wherefores. It is also allied with a genuine effort

[1] The Dutch would like, for example, to send fifty farming families a year to France and, in many regions, the influence of such people would be valuable for pointing the way to progress. Such plans do not prevent France from seeking to find better employment for some of the families of the overcrowded Breton countryside by encouraging them to move to the empty parts of the north-eastern limestone plateaux. But Germany and Italy are both spending more on colonizing different parts of France than the country is spending on rural migration schemes of its own.

at social justice and with an effective and reasonably enlightened system of taxation. In consequence, it is fairly generally accepted by the electorate.[1] The progressive outlook of the country is reflected in a fair degree of uniformity in standards of living; agricultural wages are worth considerably more than before the war, in spite of a rise from 250 to 350 in the cost of living index. The Professor of Rural Economics at Wageningen, however, declares, 'We cannot allow ourselves high costs of production', and at this moment there are two laws under consideration which would forbid the subdivision of small farms and call a halt to the rise in land values. It is noteworthy that the average size of farm is none the less larger than in Belgium. For this reason especially, the latter cannot compete with costs of production in the Netherlands, and this is one of the major difficulties confronting an effective Customs union between the Benelux countries.

During the decade before the war, internal prices were kept above world prices so as to subsidize the export trade. In 1937 in Amsterdam we observed that margarine was dearer than Dutch butter in London. For wheat and milk at least[2] the reverse is true today. Domestic prices are in fact subsidized by the exporter of dairy produce, an arrangement which typifies the social conscience of the régime. The consumer, for his part, drinks partly skimmed milk which has a fat content of only 25 per mille, but even this is beneficial from a dietetic point of view.

280. We salute this courageous search for economic independence, and only regret that the same attitude is less apparent in France. Training and capital, the twin bases of rural intensification, are essential to the economic recovery of France, but they are unfortunately lacking in her agriculture. It would not, however, always be advisable to go as far as the Netherlands in intensification. It is important to ensure that the first phase—which is the most highly productive—has everywhere been reached before penetrating at certain points into the zone of diminishing returns.

The advantages of integral holdings, mechanization, efficient handling of seeds, weed-killers, and fertilizers, of specific cultivation techniques, etc., are widely recognized. The Netherlands and England also demonstrate how grassland management and fodder production can be improved. Without going as far as these countries in their costly modifications of the environment for the sake of horticultural produce, let France look to her methods of growing fruit and 'earlies' of various

[1] According to Denis Bergmann.

[2] The State also controls sugar and oilseed prices which are higher than current world prices; bacon is sometimes subsidized.

kinds and to her organization of marketing. She enjoys the benefits of the Mediterranean sun and can therefore grow market-garden produce with the sole help of relatively inexpensive gravity-flow irrigation schemes. Before diking the Baie de l'Aiguillon, she should reclaim the badly drained portions of the Marais Poitevin. Equally, rather than lavishing 180 lb. of nitrogen to the acre on old pastures composed of inferior species (mostly vernal grass, fescues, rushes, etc.), she should break them up to grow fodder crops and leys.

If France refuses to intensify her methods, she can give up all hope of economic independence and resign herself to an even more rapid descent along the road to depression and decadence. If she accepts the challenge, she must proceed cautiously at first, so as to avoid a sudden rise in production costs. The first aim should be to ensure that the productivity of labour everywhere reaches a certain minimum, and in order to achieve this the average size of farms must be increased. To those who quote the Netherlands as an example of the triumph of the small farm, the Dutch economist replies that success has been achieved in spite of the scarcity of land and not because of it. The fact that productivity is by far the lowest on the smallest holding[1] seems to prove the case, and in Nord Brabant farmers with large families, but with less than about 50 acres, are hoping to emigrate, as they see no future for their children otherwise.

If ever the 'green pool' for the unrestricted exchange of agricultural produce comes into being the neglected regions of France will be quite unable to stand up to competition from the Netherlands. At one and the same time they urgently need equipment, schemes of agricultural training, and a service for information about new methods. Generous credit facilities and subsidies along the lines of those granted for marginal land in England should make such innovations possible.

In the chapters which follow we shall study agricultural developments in countries beyond the so-called 'Iron Curtain', and this will lead us finally to attempt a comparison between the efficacy of the two economic systems.

[1] When we arrived at the North-east Polder, our guide, Den Heer Rijlaarsdam, showed us a copy of *Foyer rural*, dated 22 February 1952, which contained the following phrase, written by a Dutchman: 'In our country we live well on $12\frac{1}{2}$ acres.' Our guide informed us that the author of this 'sentimental' declaration has had no agricultural training whatsoever.

XIV

Agrarian Reform in East Germany[1]

1. The Breaking Up of the Large Estates

281. Besides 7,500,000 acres of forests and well over 2,500,000 acres of grassland and rough pasture, much of it of rather poor quality, East Germany has 12,500,000 acres under the plough upon which it relies heavily for its food supply. It was hoped to increase this last figure by 315,000 acres during the first Five Year Plan, due to expire in 1955. The status of her soils, which were classified before the war in accordance with a system of indices ranging from 0 to 100, varies very considerably. At one end of the scale are the rich chernozems of Saxony-Anhalt, which are part of the great belt of steppe soils stretching far into the Ukraine. At the opposite extreme are the barren podsolized sands of Brandenburg and Mecklenburg, which are mainly wooded with Scots pine and birch. Between these extremes, in Saxony, the Thuringian hills and elsewhere, the range includes a variety of loams and sandy loams in various stages of leaching.

The climate is continental in character, with a long and severe winter, short intermediate seasons, and a rather low rainfall, especially in the black earth region. As in the Ukraine, the fertility of certain soils, where evaporation exceeds percolation, and the difficulty of exploiting them to the full are both implicit in the lack of rainfall. Moreover, the 'Stalin Plan for the Transformation of Nature' has been emulated by planting shelter belts of trees similar to those of the lower Volga Valley. Nevertheless, evaporation is not nearly so rapid as along the shores of the Caspian or the Mediterranean. Like the Corn Belt of the United States, this region benefits from a summer maximum of rainfall. Between Leipzig and Dresden, in the centre of Saxony, three-fifths of

---

[1] Field studies in 1939 and 1952. The official name of the country is Deutsche Demokratische Republik, or D.D.R. The statistics, which have been taken from official documents, are given with reserve as we have been unable to examine all the sources to our satisfaction.

the total—namely, 15 in. out of 25—come during the period April to September, when temperatures favour vegetative growth.

It is by no means an easy task to find enough food for 20,000,000 people (including East Berlin) accustomed to better rations of meat, milk, and fats than the rest of eastern Europe, when there are but $\frac{5}{8}$ acre of arable land per head and when half of this consists of poor sands suitable only for rye and potatoes. The high level of investment demanded by rapidly expanding industry makes the task all the more problematic. A great asset, however, is the quality of the people. The German peasant is a worker, and his technical knowledge is fairly good. In addition there is a good advisory service, generously staffed with agricultural experts trained at first-rate schools.

282. Before the war, out of 17,330,000 acres of agricultural land 13,900,000 were privately owned, and of these 5,540,000 were in units of less than 50 acres, 4,930,000 were in medium-sized holdings of 50 to 250 acres, and 3,430,000 were in large farms and estates of over 250 acres. These last also owned 1,595,000 acres of forest, which was more than half the total in private hands. There were also joint properties, property belonging to nobles (*majorats, fidei-commissa*), such as princes, counts, and other gentry, and lands owned by banks and by insurance and industrial companies.

Individual farms are not necessarily devoted wholly to agricultural purposes, and the statistics reveal that in 1939 511,000 units of less than 50 acres accounted for 27 per cent. of the total area, but for 36·5 per cent. of the agricultural land (arable and grass); and that 9,024 farms of over 250 acres covered 45 per cent. of the total, but had only 30 per cent. of the agricultural area. As in France, the large estates were also the domain of the most extensive forms of land utilization. More than a fifth of the whole area was shared between 766 properties of over 2,500 acres, but they had only 3·7 per cent. of the agricultural land.[1] The extensive forests reserved for hunting are the self-evident explanation. Admittedly these large estates were generally on the poorer soils, in the sandy areas of pine forests, but as compared with land of similar quality on the smaller farms the intensiveness of their cultivation and the density of the stock they carried was consistently lower.

Beginning in the autumn of 1945, owners of more than 250 acres were expropriated. Buildings, equipment, stock, and even hives and poultry—or, rather, what remained of the latter—were taken from them: 7,000 farms and 6,048,000 acres were involved. 'War criminals

[1] *Die Bodenreform in Deutschland*, by H. Reuber and B. Skibbe, 1947. Deutscher Bauernverlag, Berlin, has supplied us with the figures quoted in this paragraph.

and Nazis', including in this case those with less than 250 acres, furnished another 250,000 acres, to which were added 1,250,000 acres formerly belonging either to the State or to various provinces and towns. Most of the forests (1,440,000 acres) were distributed among the communes and various other public bodies, among whom research institutes were the main beneficiaries. Only 990,000 acres went to the peasants.

283. The peasants, who received 3,985,000 out of a total of 4,773,000 acres, obtained the lion's share of the agricultural land. In the first instance, 120,000 heads of families, mainly ex-agricultural workers who had no land at all, were each allotted an average of $18\frac{1}{4}$ acres, of which 15 were cultivable. Secondly, 84,000 refugees from eastern areas taken over by Poland or Russia each obtained $20\frac{3}{4}$ acres, $17\frac{1}{2}$ of them cultivable. Then there were 113,000 peasants with very small holdings classed as 'poor in land', who each received an average of nearly $7\frac{1}{2}$ additional acres. Finally, just over $2\frac{1}{2}$ acres apiece went to 49,000 small farmers.

The result was that the number of very small holdings of $1\frac{1}{4}$ to $12\frac{1}{2}$ acres rose from 318,000 to 332,000, but small farms of between $12\frac{1}{2}$ and 50 acres almost doubled, going from 189,000 to 355,000, and from a total acreage of 6,800,000 to 10,400,000. The group of 50 to 250 acres has risen slightly in numbers (56,600 to 58,300), but has declined in total area (6,800,000 to 6,300,000). In 1946 there remained 1,600 properties exceeding 250 acres, but the majority of these were soon to become *Volksgüter*, or people's lands, which were not divided among the peasants, but either run as State farms or given over to research or teaching establishments.[1] The total number of farm units has risen steeply from 570,000 to nearly 750,000, while the percentage of rural

[1] In his extremely interesting article, '*Le rôle de la politique agricole dans l'industrialisation des démocraties populaires*' (to be published at the end of 1953 by the Foundation des Sciences Politiques), which has greatly helped us, Nicolas Plessz expresses the number of properties of specified areas, and the aggregate area of each group, as percentages of the total, as follows:

	$1\frac{1}{2}$-$12\frac{1}{2}$ acres		$12\frac{1}{2}$-50 acres		50-125 acres		125-250 acres		Over 250 acres	
	N	A	N	A	N	A	N	A	N	A
1945	56	9	33	31·8	8·5	22·4	1·4	8·4	1·1	28·4
1950	45·4	10·7	48·5	59·6	5·5	21·5	0·5	4·6	0·1	3·6

N=number as percentage of total.
A=area as percentage of total.

We have underlined the greatest changes, but note also the large reduction in the 125-250-acre group, which, in theory, was not affected (except for war criminals).

population has shown a comparable increase from 15·3 in 1939 to 20·1 in 1946 (totals of 2,324,000 and 3,488,000 respectively).

By far the greater part of the stock which still remained on the large farms (53,000 horses, 132,000 cattle, including 76,000 cows, 54,000 pigs, 200,000 sheep and goats) passed to the new peasants (*Neubauern*). Of special importance were the horses, which were allocated, on average, one to every four farms. Pigs were shared out in the same ratio, and

FIG. 25.   East Germany (D.D.R.)

one farm in three received a cow. Other animals were distributed in like manner. Heavy equipment (tractors, steam traction engines, electric motors, threshing machines) were shared among the co-operatives. Ploughs, harrows, ridging-ploughs, and cultivators were given almost entirely to private farms, whilst mowing machines, potato-lifters, seed-drills, and grading machines were divided between the two groups. Finally, the hay and straw of the 1945 harvest went to the new peasants.

As the stock and the material initially received by the new peasants were quite insufficient for their needs, they were granted long-term credits for buying equipment, and later for building houses. They suffered very hard times at first. Industry was unable to keep up with demand, and everything was in short supply. There was not, however, the abject poverty which marked the early stages of the Russian Revolution, nor did the period of scarcity last so long.

2. A New Peasant in Saxony-Anhalt, Delivery Norms, and the Plan of Production

284. Breitenfeld is a hamlet situated on the border between Saxony and Saxony-Anhalt, six miles north of Leipzig (Fig. 25). It forms part of the commune of Lindental, which stretches as far as the suburbs of the town. Before the war, the 1,250 acres of rich, cultivated chernozems comprised one of several domains belonging to Count Etzdorf. The estate included a castle and its park which are now State property, and rooms have been set aside for the library, the assembly hall,[1] and the kindergarten. Until 1945 the crop rotation was similar to that of many an alcohol-distilling farm in Brie or Vexin, and consisted in the main of sugar-beet alternating with wheat. The harvest was impressive, but, in contrast with the intensive mixed farming of Bavaria, there was a notable absence of cattle and pigs. The buildings have now been taken over by the Fertilizer Co-operative and by the Agricultural Produce Section of the Ministry of Commerce (V.E.A.B.).

Seventy-three new farms each with between 15 and 24 acres are dispersed in a ring all round the park. Each house has five rooms in addition to a kitchen, and has electricity and wireless. There is also a single building for housing cows, stores, and pigs, with a corn loft above. The construction is simple but robust; the buildings are roofed with tiles, but the obviously varied origin of their bricks shows just how scarce materials must have been at the time. The way in which the prevailing shortage of materials was overcome to build 150,000 new farms in the six years between 1946 and 1952 on an area less than a quarter the size of France is an achievement which merits unstinted praise.

The cost of construction ranged from 6,000 to 12,000 marks.[2] The

[1] On the walls, apart from the typical slogans about Germano-Soviet friendship, one reads phrases like 'The traitor Adenauer', 'General treatise on war' (contractual agreements), 'The great Stalin', 'The five-year plan', etc. We quote the following in full: 'Only those who win them every day deserve liberty and life' (Goethe). 'Life seems worthwhile when an idea honoured by humanity wins the day' (L. Uhland). 'Ideas do not live unless given the chance to fight' (Thomas Mann).

[2] It is difficult to estimate the buying power of the East German mark. Taking a loaf of rye bread at 27 pfennig a pound, the mark seemed to be worth about 2s. (100 French francs), and this approximates to the official rate of exchange. But in terms of clothing it is not worth much more than 5d., which is nearer the 'unofficial' rate.

peasants are making insistent demands for a proper domestic supply of water, and work is now in progress, but the rather dispersed pattern of settlement adds to the length of piping needed. Rob. Peters, whom we visited, had a farm of over 100 acres in East Prussia, and feels himself ill at ease on the small plot of ¾ acre where his house is sited. Not afraid of work, he helped build his house to such good effect that it cost him only 6,000 marks, which he was able to borrow from the State. In 1951, 50 per cent. of building loans were remitted by the State, and the balance is repayable, without interest, at 4 per cent. a year. In Peters's case, therefore, this means 120 marks annually.

285. He will have to pay another 260 marks annually for a period of ten years for the 24 acres he received, and at the end of this time the land will be his. The farmhouse is situated in a field which also has a kitchen garden and a young orchard, and there is room for the manure heap and a hen-house as well. When we were there, with the help of a friend from Leipzig who was once a carpenter in Silesia, he was building a pen for his pigs. He was building it to last, in spite of the official policy of economizing on materials by making light wooden structures with thatched roofs.

About half a mile from the house he has another two small fields and a much larger one of 17½ acres. In 1952, 60 per cent. of his land was under cereals and mixed-corn crops: these were about 3 acres of wheat, 3¾ of rye, 2½ of spring oats, nearly 2 of winter barley, 1¼ of mixed barley, oats, and beans, and 1¼ of summer rape. The remaining 40 per cent. is occupied by root and green crops: nearly 2 acres of red clover, just over 3 of potatoes, over ½ acre of vegetables (carrots, cabbage, onions, etc.), over 1½ of mangolds, and 1½ of sugar-beet. The large proportion of row crops, over a third, including rape, is noteworthy. As against this, however, there is little in the way of temporary grassland, and the acreage of permanent pasture (less than ½ acre) is practically negligible. Permanent pasture is not well adapted to these rich but dry soils, and would therefore represent too extensive a type of land utilization.

The importance of catch-cropping, which applies to a quarter of the arable land, is further evidence of intensiveness. The dryness of the summer is more marked here, and the average total rainfall is only 25 in. This favours the cultivation of catch-crops in the winter: white clover is sown with spring cereals and turned into the ground a year later, just before potatoes are due to be planted; or, again, vetches are sown with rye for fodder. This practice represents a distinct advance in the production of feeding-stuffs. Vetches are tending to replace mangolds as cattle food, the latter being rather poor in proteins for a country where oil-seed residues are so scarce.

The farm is thus able to support a large number of animals: four cows, one store, two calves, eleven pigs, two ewes, and seventeen hens. The average in the village for a farm of this size would be two to three cows, three to four stores, and a dozen pigs. By 1952 there were eight times as many pigs as before the war, and the overall density of stock had trebled. Although large farms which had been broken up are now producing more than they ever did before, the difference between the present and pre-war positions reaches its maximum at Breitenfeld. Peters also feeds the co-operative-owned bull and has a horse of his own. Only a third of the new peasants possess one of these noble animals, which do not find much favour with the authorities.

286. The heavy work on the land is done by the Machine Hiring Station (M.A.S.),[1] which at Breitenfeld is housed in one of the old barns. On Peters's farm in 1951 it supplied fifty hours of work in the field (ploughing and harvest) and about twenty hours for transport (beet and building materials) for 500 marks; it takes about an hour and a half to plough 1 acre. Peters's heavy equipment consists essentially of only three small carts and a tun for drainings. If they are to produce more meat and milk, the Germans would be well advised to make more use of cows harnessed in pairs for the lighter work which the farms perform unaided and which will, in any case, be taken over more and more by the M.A.S. as time goes on. Even if the beasts, many of which are Friesians, are not particularly well suited for draught and even if milk yields suffer a little, this is better than giving food which could well support an extra cow to a horse which does only fifty days of work or so in the year.

The other necessary items of expenditure are for fertilizers and seed (800 marks). In 1952 Peters employed 90 cwt. of lime, 32 of 40 per cent. potash fertilizer, 40 of 18-20 per cent. nitrates, and 30 of basic slag with 16-18 per cent. phosphoric acid. The last is the most difficult to obtain, as East Germany no longer imports phosphates from North Africa, and the wartime shortage has therefore continued. It is significant that the Five Year Plan expiring in 1955 proposes to improve the 1950 consumption of nitrogen by 24 per cent., of potash by 18 per cent., but of phosphoric acid, with the help of imports from Russia, by 63 per cent. Social insurance contributions cost Peters 180 marks a year, which is more than he used to pay to his own society before the war, but benefits are also higher than pre-war.

[1] Maschinen Ausleih Stationen.

In 1947 Peters returned from Russia, where he had been a prisoner of war, and today he is a widower with a son of twenty who drove a tractor for a while at the M.A.S. and then went to an agricultural college. The East German Republic, where science reigns supreme, is now seeking all kinds of new ways of keeping its agricultural trainees well informed. The farm is a one-man affair except for busy times of the year, when women from the working-class districts of Leipzig are taken on. Here they earn sugar and fodder and grain for their own pigs and poultry. Their pay is equivalent to 0·69 marks an hour, or rather more than the price of a 2-lb. loaf. Measured in textile goods, this purchasing power would appear much smaller than in the west. Such facts serve to illustrate the general shortage of food, which, following a period of drought and the cutting down of imports, was particularly severe during the winter of 1952-3.

287. Every farm, according to its area and the specific status of its soil, is bound to deliver a certain amount of produce at the low price (*Erfassung*). Peters, for his 24 acres of fertile land, which was classified as 83 (100 is the maximum), has to fulfil a quota as follows: 84 cwt. of cereals (1951 harvest amounted to 230 cwt.), 112 of potatoes, 3·4 of pulses, 6 of rape, 1 of hay, and 12·8 of straw; also 1,408 lb. net of pork, 471 lb. of other meat (beef, mutton, etc.), 5,775 lb. of milk, 862 eggs ... and even $7\frac{3}{4}$ lb. of wool.

The burden of the norm increases disproportionately for larger holdings so as to prevent their owners from becoming rich. Thus in Saxony-Anhalt in 1950 farms smaller than $12\frac{1}{2}$ acres had to supply less than 5 cwt. of grain per acre, but the norm rose to $7\frac{1}{2}$ cwt. for those of $12\frac{1}{2}$ to 25 acres, to 12 cwt. for 25 to 50 acres, to $14\frac{1}{2}$ cwt. for 50 to 125 acres, and to 16 cwt. for those exceeding 125 acres. In Brandenburg, where soils are poorer, figures ranged from 3 to 12 cwt. In Thuringia, for holdings smaller than $12\frac{1}{2}$ acres, norms for various crops were as follows per acre: cereals, 5 cwt.; dried vegetables, 6 cwt.; poppy, 4 cwt.; summer oil-seeds, 5 cwt.; winter oil-seeds, 7 cwt.; potatoes, 32 cwt.; fresh vegetables, 84 cwt.; and for animal products per acre: 17 eggs, 47 lb. net of meat, and 235 lb. of milk. All these norms were lower for the new peasants.[1]

The progress of each farm as compared with its planned norm is posted on the door of the Town Hall. At the beginning of July some had already fulfilled their obligation for the whole year—in eggs particularly. The notice bears the inscription: 'Help the weak and shake up

---

[1] According to Plessz.

the lazy.'[1] Apart from his norm of six pigs, for which he was paid 90 marks a hundredweight, Peters had sold another five the previous year at 320 marks a hundredweight (*Aufkauf*). Milk for the Plan was paid 1 mark a gallon, but even after feeding his calves and his thirty piglets (sold at 2·70 marks a pound, because pig-rearing is profitable and everyone goes in for it), he was able to sell another 880 gallons at 3·65 marks, which was eventually sold on the free market in Leipzig at 10·10 marks. He sells no grain apart from his norm, for it would not even fetch double the low price; instead, he feeds it to his stock and produces more milk and pork. He does, however, supply bread grains for the Plan in excess of his quota, as for every 4 cwt. of surplus he brings he is given 5 cwt. of coarse grains in return, which he needs for his stock.[2]

This system of double prices which is a feature of the people's republics is no doubt a legacy from the black market, but the free price paid by the consumer who wants to improve on his basic ration is a very strong incentive to production and intensification. A bad farmer who merely fulfils his norms can hardly afford to buy anything at all off the farm. On the other hand, the slightest surplus brings in a very good return, and the small farmer seems quite happy that the present seller's market should continue. The large farmer makes very little profit. On units of more than 40 acres or so, the norms are so high that most farmers do not even attempt to exceed them. The traditional type of land-hungry peasant realizes that he can no longer enlarge his holding by purchase, and tends in consequence to be less greedy for money. In any case, there is little to be bought with the money in the way of manufactured goods. The present situation will not last. As in

[1] The small farmers are, to some extent, the 'weak' and the larger men are the 'lazy'.

[2] Prices paid for farm produce in East Germany in 1938 and 1951-2 (after Plessz):

1 cwt. of:	1938-39 (Reich marks)	1951-52 (East marks) Compulsory quota	Free price
Rye	9·60	10	15
Wheat	10·15	10·75	21·5
Potatoes	2·67	3·05	21·5
Sugar beet	1·65	2	3
Beef (category A)	43·20	60·5	151·25
Pork (Category C)	50·8	72	324
Milk	7·5	10	40
100 eggs (category B)	10·50	10	45

the U.S.S.R., the gap between the two prices will gradually narrow as the food position improves. The gap is still large in the case of meat, eggs, butter, and milk, but it has already disappeared entirely for bread. The two prices of sugar are also beginning to move towards each other, and East Germany is believed to be holding large stocks, although considerable quantities are probably being sent eastwards.

288. All farm produce, the compulsory quotas and likewise the surpluses at the free price, is sold to a state organization (V.E.A.B., or Vereinigung der Erfassungs und Aufkauf Betriebe), which has 30,000 employees throughout the country. It was established at the demand of the Soviet military administration in order to try out the system before applying it in the U.S.S.R., where the purchase and sale of produce is still largely in the hands of co-operatives, and even collectives.[1] At the inception of the new organization, all kinds of difficulties appear to have been encountered, and there may have been some corruption; but by all accounts it discharges its functions satisfactorily at the present.

Prices are fairly comprehensively stabilized, and are fixed long in advance. This enables the peasant to judge how he is likely to stand in the future and to plan his production in the framework of the dual-price system. Thus Peters judged it best to build a permanent pig-pen, as he is fairly certain that high prices for pork will continue. He objects, however, to having to grow over $\frac{1}{2}$ acre of vegetables, for although the proximity of the Leipzig market is obviously what the planners have in mind, vegetables are suited neither to the heavy soil nor to the dry climate. His cauliflowers, for instance, had failed completely. The M.A.S. adviser has given him his support in this matter, and is always squabbling with the 'bureaucrats' at the Ministry and telling them that the Plan should be better adapted to local conditions. These, however, are problems of adjustment—inevitable in a transition to a new type of economic structure—which should eventually solve themselves. There is every hope that the situation will improve.

289. At the national level, the Five Year Plan hopes to achieve the following yields and comparative production figures:

	1955/1950 Per cent.	1955/1934–8 Per cent.	Yield forecast, cwt./acres (1955)
Cereals and leguminous crops	125·3	111·1	20
Oil-seeds and fibres	159·7	744	13·6 (oil-seeds)
Sugar-beet	119·5	127	252
Potatoes	119	129	164

[1] Stalin was greatly concerned about this before he died, as we shall see.

The table shows the very considerable expansion of industrial crops (oil-seeds and fibres, especially flax) achieved during the war. It also indicates that, except for cereals, pre-war production had already been surpassed by 1950. In 1951, which was a good year here, cereal production is said to have exceeded the 1934-8 mean. The figures for 1951 given in the note below,[1] however, which are very much higher than for neighbouring countries and greatly in excess of norms, are quoted with considerable reserve. It may well be that no account was taken of harvest losses, which, as we shall see when we study Hungary, were appreciable during the wet summer of that year.

Statistics show that the number of pigs, which is very prone to rapid increases when food is available, had surpassed the pre-war figure by as much as 20 per cent. by 1951, and that breeding sows had increased by 74 per cent. Cattle as a whole have not yet regained their pre-war position. By 1955 the aim was to add 21·7 per cent. to the 1950 figure. It was hoped that there would be 60 per cent. more cows, 66 per cent. more sheep, 111 per cent. more ewes. Even if these targets are reached, however, the density of stock will still remain very much lower than in West Germany. A nation-wide campaign against goats had been launched, and it was hoped to halve the total and replace them with ewes, 'which give richer milk and, with 66 to 110 gallons a year, just as much', according to the official propaganda. The greater difficulty of milking was not mentioned, but the policy is no doubt justified by the shortage of wool and the lack of any market in Germany for cheese made from goat's milk.

At the same time the Plan proposed to raise the average milk yield per cow from 4,576 lb. to 5,720 lb. (32 per mille fat content), the net weight of beef animals to 550 lb. and of pigs to 253 lb. This tendency, which is quite contrary to the West European aim of producing a small, lean pig for the pork butcher, is encouraged by a higher price per pound for the larger pig carcases.[2] Of all stock enterprises, milk- and pork-production are those with the highest yields of animal proteins, and the

[1] Average yields, hundredweights per acre (official figures, but those for 1951 seem too high):

	Rye	Wheat	Fodder cereals	Oil seeds	Potatoes	Sugar beet
1934-8	13·6	19·6	17·6	12	139·2	232
1946	10·4	13·6	12·8	4·8	96	152
1951	18·8	25·6	22·4	11·6	143·2	224

[2] The wisdom of this trend is questionable for, though it is favoured by German taste, the protein yield, for a given quantity of feeding-stuffs, declines as the pig becomes older and the yield of fat is at all times lower than in a good cow.

specific encouragement they receive is therefore a perfectly rational policy.[1] As compared with 1938, the 1955 targets represented an increase of 61 per cent. for meat and poultry, 34 per cent. for milk and 49 per cent. for eggs. The trend in favour of fodder crops and mixed farming began in the west a century or two ago, and the parallel development in the people's republics today might well be described therefore as the 'westernization' of their agriculture.[2]

290. Thus at Breitenfeld the preoccupation with stock-farming is very much more in evidence than before the war, while the attention given to crops remains no less intensive. The population, however, including M.A.S. and other official personnel, has risen to about 300. Many small farmers, even some with only 15 or 16 acres, have the equivalent of two or three full-time workers and support three or four people in all. Although yields per acre compare very favourably with the pre-war years, the output per worker shows every sign of having suffered a definite decline. It was not possible, however, to obtain reliable figures to support this contention. It is none the less the inevitable result of subdivision into small farms, and it was to offset this factor that the M.A.S. was brought in to carry the modern equipment which the individual peasant could not afford. As tractor tools for ridging and inter-row cultivation become available, the overcrowding of most of this land will become increasingly apparent.

Of the seventy-three *Neubauern* in Breitenfeld, twenty-three are refugees from the east, and the remainder are mostly ex-farm labourers. There are also a few former factory workers of rural origin, several of whom came back to the land as a result of the food shortage of the post-war years. As for politics, thirty of them belonged to the Peasants' Democratic Party and fourteen to the United Socialist Party (S.E.D.), which is dominated by the Communists. Peters was once a member of the S.E.D., but later withdrew. Although he now has no party affiliations, he is still the President of the co-operative for mutual aid (which shows very little sign of life), and does not appear to oppose the new régime.

In a country where Thaër and Liebig first laid the foundations of modern agricultural science, and where many other distinguished scientists have followed in their steps, experimental sites and study groups

[1] This is why we pleaded for pig and milk production to be increased so as to bring the post-war period of food shortages to an end as quickly as possible (*Le problème agricole français*, N.E.L., 1946). The figures cited in connection with the Plan are from the official brochure, *Die Landwirtschaft und der Wirtschaftsplan* (1952).

[2] Between 1949 and 1951 the arable acreage rose by 390,000, of which 250,000 were for green crops and 77,000 for fodder row crops.

are now under Russian patronage.[1] The Mitchourine circle has fifteen members who meet nearly every week in the winter, and once a month during the busy summer. Peters farms scientifically. He has, for instance, twenty trial plots each about 1 yd. square, where he sows different varieties of grain and leguminous crops and compares results. With men like this, agriculture in East Germany should be capable of making rapid strides.

Apart from the seventy-three *neu*, there are also twenty-one *alt* peasants. Of these, four have between 2½ and 5 acres, three between 5 and 12½ acres, eleven between 25 and 50 acres, and three between 88 and 125 acres. In 1952 these last three were considered by the officials to be rather mediocre as farmers and positively deficient when it came to fulfilling their norms. They have a lower density of stock than the smaller farms, but then this is true, as a general rule, of the whole of Europe. It does add, however, to their difficulties in reaching the higher norms. The *kulaks* of the future seem already to have been designated.

3. A Machine-hiring Station (M.A.S.) in Brandenburg and Its Differential Tariffs

291. The lack of equipment and, to a lesser extent, of tractive power are the chief handicaps of East German agriculture. The fairly low rate of output of machinery is inadequate to equip all 746,000 of the country's small and medium-sized farms. Such a proposition would in any case be uneconomic. In 1947 existing equipment was shared between 3,427 stations, but at that time only 181 of them had repair workshops. These 181 stations were nationalized in 1949-50, when they were in serious difficulties, and they proved to be the only ones to survive. By 1952 their numbers had reached 550, and it was hoped to raise this figure to 750 by the end of the first Plan.

Thanks to the over-riding priority given to the task—though not until 1951—it was hoped to increase the complement of tractors and ploughs from 12,000[2] in 1950 to 37,500 in 1955; of tractor-drawn

---

[1] In the schools, Russian has taken the place of French as the first foreign language; English is second.

[2] 'In 1949 alone, 1,000 of these complete with tools were supplied through the invaluable help of the Soviet Union, just in time for the spring campaign.' A popular song was written in honour of this gesture. In France it was not until 1948 that agriculture was classed by the economic planning authorities (Plan Monnet) as 'priority' work. Farm machinery and fertilizers had, however, been granted 'priority' status since the inception of the Plan in 1948.

cultivators from 2,300 to 12,000, of drills from 820 to 6,600, of binders from 4,400 to 10,500, but of threshing machines only from 7,000 to 8,350. Combines began to be manufactured in 1952, but they are not mentioned at all in the Plan which was drawn up in 1950. To these figures should be added privately owned equipment, the volume of which remains considerable on medium-sized farms. The great majority of new machinery is destined for the M.A.S. The price which individual farmers have to pay for tractors is almost prohibitive, but, thanks to the profits which can be earned on the free price market, some still succeed in buying them.

The early days of the M.A.Ss., which had to make do with whatever old and broken equipment could be salvaged after the war, make a truly epic story. In default of any other solution, some tractors were even mounted on gun wheels; there were frequent breakdowns; repair shops were inadequate and poorly equipped; the paper binding-string broke on nearly every sheaf. Hindered at every turn in their urgent efforts on the land, the peasants grumbled about the tractor men, who, they said—and sometimes this is still true—'lacked the touch for work on the land'.

Things seem to be improving fast. All the equipment at each station is now of a single make, and this has simplified the spares problem and enabled mechanics to familiarize themselves thoroughly with a small range of machinery. Workshops are constantly being improved; and paper string is now coated with a preparation which strengthens it. The Breitenfeld M.A.S., which included the phrase 'of German-Soviet Friendship'[1] in its title, had fifteen Lanz Diesel tractors with an aggregate horse-power of 490, nine binders, and the same number of threshing machines. It serviced eight communes.

292. Thirty miles south-east of Berlin at Pfaffendorf, the M.A.S. has been taken under the patronage of the *Berliner Zeitung*,[2] whose employees were lending a hand to put up the sheds which were to complete the array of buildings. The M.A.S. for its part was helping to clear up the ruins of Berlin with its lorries. Patronage, however, was mainly in the realm of culture, and representatives from the town

---

[1] As we were looking at the notice-board, a worker assured us that he was also well disposed towards progressive Frenchmen.

[2] With its daily circulation of 600,000 this newspaper is the largest in the whole of Germany, and it kindly lent us a car for the journeys we undertook in the course of our studies. Also we were accompanied by our friend H. Gerstner, the paper's Economic Editor, an 'activist' and an 'officer of the ideological front'. But why was the article we sent at the paper's request falsified when it was translated?

would help to organize lectures and recreational activities. The establishment was very modest to begin with. The offices had to manage with very little accommodation, and the staff slept two to a room and had no sheets on their beds even by 1952. Apart from the cultural director and his assistants, M.A.Ss. are under the management of either an engineer or an agricultural scientist. At Breitenfeld he was an engineer, but here he is an agricultural expert.

The twenty-eight wheel-tractors, with an aggregate of 847 h.p., are divided into three sections. Track-laying vehicles are unknown, and in any case the sandy terrain would be unsuitable for them. The tractors are not particularly modern in type and are rather high, like the Hungarian ones. Nineteen binders are in service, in addition to a variety of cultivators and drills, and, finally, there are fifteen threshing-machines, which make up a fourth section of their own. The M.A.S.'s area extends over twenty-four communes with a total of about 25,000 acres. Rather less than half of this is under the plough, grassland accounts for 2,250 acres, and the remainder is forested. The M.A.S. serves two-thirds of the 1,226 farms. These, however, comprise only 40–45 per cent. of the agricultural land and include practically all the smaller holdings[1] and some of the medium-sized units. Forty per cent. of its contracts are with holdings with less than 25 acres of arable land, 20 per cent. with those with 25–37·5 acres, 10 per cent. with those with 37·5 to 50 acres, and only 2 per cent. with those having more than 50 acres; the *Volksgüter*, or State farms, account for another 12 per cent., and the remainder are for transport and various other services.

Like the norms, the scale of tariffs rises fairly sharply for the larger farms. On average soils of classes 34 to 60, ploughing to 8–10 in. and subsoiling, comes to 10·20 marks an acre for holdings of less than 25 acres and to 21·20 marks, or more than double, for those exceeding 50 acres; there are intermediate rates for 25–37·5 acres and 37·5–50 acres.[2] In fact, however, the cost of the work averages about 30 marks, and since the 30 per cent. cut in tariffs in spring 1952 the State has been subsidizing even the *kulaks*. The work cannot be done as cheaply even with horses, and the use of these animals is on the decline. Consequently, the development of the M.A.S. is permitting a larger number of dairy

[1] 300 of them have neither horses nor oxen, and use their cows in harness.

[2] Three days after the work has been completed the peasant receives a detailed bill which has to be paid within a fortnight. If the account has not been settled by this time, it is sent to the Office for the sale of produce, which credits the M.A.S. with the amount and deducts it from the farmer's first consignment of produce (at 4 per cent. interest).

cattle to be kept[1] and the number of tillage operations to be increased. It is leading, in short, to more intensive farming. In France the protection given to alcohol-producing crops, like sugar beet, cider apples, and the vine, is, on the contrary, limiting the volume of useful production. To stimulate cultivation in some of the underdeveloped *pays* by means of subsidies would be of greater service to the national interest than paying higher prices for the agricultural produce of certain areas.

293. The real cost of ploughing is quite high, for the organization of work programmes does not yet seem to be fully satisfactory. The main stumbling-block in practice is the small size of the fields which have to be worked, many of them not much more than 1 acre in extent. In France the Co-operatives for the Utilization of Agricultural Equipment (C.U.M.A.) have shown that the cost of tractor-ploughing on small parcels of $1\frac{1}{4}$ acres was about twice as much as for fields of 25 acres and, unlike the M.A.S., their prices vary accordingly. Peasants are encouraged to adopt a simple pattern of land use and to block out each crop in units of not less than $2\frac{1}{2}$ acres, as below this the cost of working begins to rise very steeply. From the Peters farm, however, we have seen that this advice has not yet been translated into practice.

It is estimated that each tractor averages 1,500 hours a year on the best M.A.Ss. This is nearly three times as much as in France or the U.S.A. By 18 June in the year of our visit one 40-h.p. tractor had completed its annual target of '700 acres' equivalent', all tractor work being expressed in terms of its equivalent on medium soils. Here again the socialist technique of emulation is fully exploited. Official results are posted, the best workers are declared 'activists', and inventions of various kinds are rewarded. At Pfaffendorf, for instance, there was a device for supporting a small mechanical forge hammer on an old car spring which enabled one man to perform manually and without fatigue in eight minutes what would otherwise have taken two men eighteen minutes. Each tractor has its own official driver—sometimes a young girl and an assistant, the so-called 'peasant friend' who takes over the machine during the second eight-hour shift at busy times of the year—that is, during ploughing and harvesting operations.

[1] In the pamphlet cited above (foot of p. 448) a new Saxon peasant from Bornitz writes: 'Thanks to the help of the M.A.S., I have been able to grow a lot more catch crops (I have a 16-acre farm and a bullock for ploughing), and can now keep three cows instead of two. This has increased my revenue by 1,000 marks and of this, in 1950, the services of the M.A.S. cost me 550. In addition, the better working of the soil has increased my yields.' It is said that the M.A.S. can raise gross production by 25 per cent., and that it allows 'village plans' to be fulfilled easily.

A MACHINE STATION (M.A.S.) AND ITS TARIFFS

The Pfaffendorf M.A.S. has seventy-eight workers, including six workshop mechanics. Most of the personnel are country-bred, but, although they are better off financially than on a farm, their wages are still lower than those in the towns. Generally they do not stay long, but having, as it were, completed their apprenticeship at the station, where they receive a thorough theoretical training as well, they leave to seek employment in the factories. A young man brought up on a farm can thus learn a trade before he presents himself at the factory for the first time. He is no longer just a country bumpkin completely lacking in resources and fit only for employment as unskilled labour. The constant training of new recruits is obviously a source of inconvenience to the station. Efficient organization and the planning of work are bound to suffer.

Another cause of uncertainty at Pfaffendorf is that there have been four different agricultural scientists in two years. Tours of duty as short as this do not facilitate the task of an adviser who needs a very thorough knowledge of local conditions and plenty of opportunity to win over the confidence of the peasants. Given time, he gradually gains both of these by holding meetings at each village in turn about once every two months. For preference, these take the form of a tour across the fields, during which matters of common interest can be profitably discussed. The agricultural advice service is just as comprehensive in West Germany, although it tends to have less of a practical bias, but in France the peasant finds technical guidance of this kind far less accessible. At the M.A.S. the agricultural scientist is responsible for drawing up a plan of work, fixing the best dates for seed-time and harvest, etc. Agriculture has become far too complex an art to be left entirely to the peasants, particularly to those who have received comparatively little training.

294. The region is predominantly one of poor sandy soils which are partly under pine forests, and the acreage of sown grassland is practically negligible; even red clover does not do well. The traditional rotation was based on rye, with a little oats, to which potatoes were added during the eighteenth century. It is now hoped to establish a four-year rotation which includes a green crop as follows:

1. Winter rye.
2. Lupin or bird's-foot trefoil.
3. Potatoes.
4. Oats or spring rye.

In 1952 the shortage of cereals prevented this rotation from being followed. The second course, therefore, alternates with rye, so that the fodder crop appears only every eight years. Catch-crops are exploited to the maximum. On the slightly stronger soils[1] the sheaves are arranged in a long line, and the land is sometimes ploughed immediately after winter barley or rape have been cut. Regardless of the drought, which is becoming marked by this time of the year, the ground is immediately sown again. The proportion of arable land sown to catch-crops fell from 12 per cent. before the war to 4 per cent. in 1945, but rose to 22 per cent. in 1951, and it was hoped to reach 35 per cent. in 1952; but drought took a heavy toll of summer catch-crops.

By giving the small farms an opportunity to use mechanical equipment, the M.A.S. 'is strengthening the bond between the working class and the working peasants with a view to realizing our national objectives and is contributing to the evolution of the peasant masses and bringing them to a better understanding of socialism'. In conservative Brandenburg the process of 'evolution' has had its setbacks. The activists at the Pfaffendorf M.A.S. were accused by the Party of sectarianism when they took down the Iron Cross which surmounted the commune's memorial to its dead. The Soviet star which they wanted to put in its place was not approved, but the Iron Cross did not reappear either.

The M.A.S. is becoming increasingly important as the Plan proceeds as the purveyor of the tractor and the binder to the small farm. Unlike the large estate, the latter was almost unaware of their existence before the war. There are far fewer tractors than in West Germany, and in 1952 one still saw many animals in harness, both on the land and on the roads. The four-wheeled cart drawn, as in Hungary, by a single horse or cow with a collar harness was a frequent sight. In many fields the corn crops had been harvested with a simple reaper or sometimes even with a scythe. Gleaners in considerable numbers were following the harvest, no doubt putting the new régime's slogan into practice: 'Waste not a particle of grain or root or straw.' The Italian habit of sending animals out to glean the fields is seldom observed, pigs and

---

[1] It is proposed to adopt the 'Williams' system (a Russian version of English ley farming, long known in Brittany and Mayenne and practised in Saxony since 1870, but not widely adopted in the east) with a six-year rotation:

    1. Wheat or rye.
    2. Barley or oats, or a mixture of the two.
    3. Row crop—potatoes or sometimes mangolds.
    4. Wheat or rye sown with a clover-timothy mixture.
    5 and 6. Two years of clover-timothy ley.

poultry being let out into the open all too infrequently. The second Five Year Plan is to coincide with the general adoption of combines, 'so as to catch up with America' in the matter of equipment—the oft-repeated aim of the U.S.S.R. before the war.

4. A State Farm in Saxony and Agricultural Research

295. Along the road east of Leipzig, towards Colditz and Leisnig, the Saxon countryside has more of a 'western' look about it. The villages, almost hidden by the green foliage of numerous orchards, sometimes remind one of Lorraine. Quite a lot of children run about barefoot; there is still a fair shortage of leather, but children commonly went about like this, as they did in German-speaking Switzerland, even before the war. We are, moreover, nearing Poland, where, more often than not, the peasant only puts on his shoes to enter the town. Dogs, as in Belgian Flanders, are used in harness for pulling small carts, and then again one may see an invalid drawn along by a pair of goats. No doubt they give him sustenance as well, but one wonders whether the ewe, which is favoured by the authorities, would give such good service in harness. There are far fewer new farms belonging to *Neubauern* and fields are sometimes extremely small, suggesting that some scheme of boundary readjustment is called for. Even before the war there was a very large proportion of small farms, and the majority of the big estates have therefore been taken over *en bloc* as 'properties of the people'. These are intended to play a part similar to that of the State farms in the Soviet Union.

The Volksgut Friedrich Engels at Motterwitz, four miles north-west of Leisnig, between Leipzig and Dresden, has an area of 340 acres, 285 of which are under the plough. Thirty-one and a half acres are under grass, twenty are wooded, and the remainder is taken up by the house, several tracks and a small lake. Thirty-one and a half acres are devoted to seed-selection, especially for grass and other fodder crops: meadow foxtail and timothy for protein content, Italian rye-grass and trifolium for resistance to cold, cock's-foot for leafiness and low silicic acid content, beans for resistance to aphis, perennial rye-grass, etc. The trial plots for seeds and fertilizers of different kinds occupy about twenty farm hands and more than a dozen agricultural students. The 300 acres or so of field cultivation are devoted mainly to the propagation of seed and are worked with the help of two tractors and eleven horses. With all the harness, the yard looks like a farm of comparable size in the Ile de France about twenty years ago.

There are eighty cattle, including forty dairy cows which average 990 gallons a year. There is no milking machine as yet, but it should be remembered that the small dimensions of the average farm would prevent its general adoption for the time being. Even taking the 126 pigs into account, the density of stock is still slightly lower than that of the Peters farm, and there is not the same emphasis on catch-crops (30 acres, or about a tenth of the arable area). The overcomplex pattern of cultivation,[1] the lack of equipment—winter barley is cut with a mowing machine—and the organization of work, which seems to be deficient in some respects, explain the size of the labour force. The total of fifty-five workers is much too large, even when the work of seed-selection is taken into account. There is almost one man for every 5 acres, which is even more than in the overcrowded regions of northern Italy, where farming is intensive to a degree.

296. There were many difficulties on these State farms at the beginning, and even today the official directives are always pressing for better organization of work and more specialization. Unlike the M.A.S., however, this State farm accords its labour a status very little different from that of the pre-war farm employee, and the men do not participate in the management. Another problem is the scale of these undertakings. Many of them are no larger than the private farms which they replaced. In 1952 there were 1,600 large farms which had not been partitioned in the course of land reforms, but on these fully 800 *Volksgüter* had been established (160 in Saxony, including forty-two specialized seed farms). There is, however, evidence from several sources which indicates that in some cases five or six farms have been grouped together to form much larger enterprises. Nevertheless, it is hardly likely that the scale of the 50,000-acre 'Giant' State farm in Soviet Russia, which once had over 250,000 acres, will be reached for many years to come.

Motterwitz itself admirably illustrates the essential functions of these State farms, which is to propagate very high-quality seeds and to produce selected breeding stock. Moreover, they represent the link between the classroom, the laboratory, the research station, and the practical business of farming. In East Germany research projects contributing to the realization of the Plan are assigned to every university professor,

---

[1] In 1952 there were 20 acres of rye, $22\frac{1}{2}$ of wheat, 15 of barley, $17\frac{1}{2}$ of oats, $2\frac{1}{2}$ of maize, 5 of peas, $2\frac{1}{2}$ of gram, $1\frac{1}{2}$ of beans, $12\frac{1}{2}$ of rape, $2\frac{1}{2}$ of flax (for oil and fibre), 24 of sugar-beet, $7\frac{1}{2}$ of mangolds, $27\frac{1}{2}$ of potatoes for human consumption. Also a whole list of crops grown for seed: 4 acres of kale, $1\frac{1}{4}$ of leeks, nearly 2 of cucumbers, $2\frac{1}{2}$ of peas, over $\frac{1}{2}$ of carrots, $2\frac{1}{2}$ of timothy, $9\frac{1}{2}$ of cocksfoot, $30\frac{1}{2}$ of Italian rye grass, etc.

who is expected to keep in close touch with practical work. Finally, there are five large research stations,[1] one for every 2,500,000 acres of arable land.

The one we visited was Bernburg in Saxony-Anhalt, which is sited on a chernozem-covered plateau near the Saale and midway between Halle and Magdeburg. With its laboratories and glasshouses, the establishment has an impressive range of extremely practical equipment. It has a total area of 2,375 acres, and 120 of these consist of trial plots. There are twenty agricultural scientists of 'academic'[2] rank and 600 workers. The annual budget amounts to 3,500,000 marks. Finally, twenty State farms (Motterwitz, specializing in fodder crops, among them) are attached to the station and come under the supervision of one of its agricultural scientists. They function as local sub-stations, the absence of which in France is an unfortunate deficiency.

297. Dr Gunther, who once owned the whole of Motterwitz, has stayed on in the role of a specialist in selection, and shows no signs of harbouring any grudge against the régime. Experts are in great demand, and the celebrated breeder of potatoes, Professor Bohme, who created the world-famous Ackersegen variety, left East Prussia and settled in East Germany, where he continued his work of selection on a State farm. Having one day absent-mindedly taken some asparagus from the collective garden, he was accused of the 'misapplication of State property' by the Party Secretary. Annoyed at having to give an explanation for so trifling a matter, he departed to West Germany. Today the same Secretary is being accused of sectarianism, and is thus having trouble of his own. The Academy of Agricultural Sciences in Berlin is no longer just a debating society; as in Russia, it keeps the whole organization of research under its close control. To some extent it is also responsible for protecting scientists from such petty inconveniences as Bohme

[1] Viz. Quedlinburg, Gross-Lüsewitz, Müncheberg, Klein-Wanzleben, and Bernburg.

[2] The equivalent of doctors of science in agronomy. In 1952 France made severe cuts in the budget for agricultural research, while the reverse was happening in the east. The day will come when France will find it difficult to compete with these countries. In East Germany in 1952 40,000,000 marks were allocated for agricultural teaching and research. Five faculties of agronomic science each received about 100 students every year, and about 300 students completed their studies in 1952, more than in the whole of the Union Française (Institut Agronomique and four National Schools of Agriculture). In June 1952, the President of the third-year students at the Institut Agronomique accused us of being responsible for an 'inflation' in the number of agronomists. Even our young technologists are contracting the Malthusian virus.

suffered and, generally speaking, it does not treat their interests with indifference.[1]

The essential function of Motterwitz, like that of all the *Volksgüter*, is to act as a *Mustergut*, or pilot farm. To this end it receives a large number of visitors each year (1,200 in 1951) and it passes on to the farmer the results of its experiments. It is seeking to establish 30 per cent. of the arable land as the proportion which should bear catch-crops; it recommends that potatoes should be planted in rows aligned from east to west, as this gives better results; and it favours the use of segmented beet seed, the adoption of ploughing at high speed (better for breaking up the soil), subsoiling, etc. Motterwitz seems to be succeeding in its task, for it was cited in the brochure for the Leipzig Agricultural Show for the excellence of its results: 45 cwt./acre for wheat, nearly 46 for oats, 41 for barley and 37 for rye. The year (1951) was a particularly favourable one, but that was not mentioned in the brochure.

The farming system is certainly intensive, and in 1951 440 marks were spent in wages per acre of field crops, and the clear profit per acre amounted to 96 marks. This money is paid over to the Union of State Farms, which was established in June 1949 and has six regional boards. The same organization is responsible for making grants, but so far there is no clear-cut scheme of allocations. The lack of financial autonomy does not seem to be in the best interests of the efficient management of funds. If the individual station makes a profit, the 'director's fund' (similar funds exist in Russia) receives a grant of 4 per cent. of the total salaries, but if the enterprise has operated at a loss the sum is reduced to 1·5 per cent. This money then serves to pay for bonuses, organized outings, sports equipment, etc. The director of Motterwitz, a Silesian by the name of Kube,[2] received a bonus of 300 marks from a second fund (1 per cent. of total wage bill) for having invented a mechanical transplanter.

The scale of bonuses rises so rapidly as to offset by a substantial margin the improvements it is designed to recompense. If a good cow is sold for 2,000 marks, the cowman gets 3 per cent., but if the beast is of exceptional quality and sells for over 6,000 marks, he gets 5 per cent. Over and above his monthly salary of 230 marks he generally receives 120 marks, or more than half again, in bonuses. Dr Gunther, the ex-

[1] 'Our salaries have just been doubled,' Professor Plachy, at the Berlin Academy, informed us. The Academy has published an impressive book, with pictures and details of all the members.

[2] He is very much afraid that his land is not being farmed as well today by the Poles.

owner of Motterwitz, is paid 1,000 marks a month, and on reaching the age of sixty he will be due for a pension amounting to 80 per cent. of his salary. The specialists' emoluments depend on the value of their work. A certain young plant-breeder at Bernburg, who was responsible for developing a variety of sunflower useful for fodder, earns more than many an older administrator. Inventors whose contributions prove particularly valuable, like the recently discovered method of coking lignite, may draw up to 15,000 marks a month. It may be said, therefore, that although unearned income is becoming a thing of the past, the range between salaries at the upper and lower ends of the scale is opening out more than ever.

5. The Old-established Peasants of Saxony-Anhalt

298. The loams which characterize the undulating region near Freckenleben, a village fourteen miles by road south-south-west of Bernburg, are classified as lying between fertility indices 65 and 93. Only a few weathered escarpments are dotted with isolated thickets of birch and there is very little grassland. The commune has, by contrast, 2,323 acres of arable land, slightly more than half of it (52·8 per cent.) under cereals and oil-seeds, and the remainder under green crops, which comprise both row crops (36 per cent.) and sown pastures (11·5 per cent.).[1] The presence of vegetables grown as field crops and of plants grown for seed (chicory) denotes a high level of intensiveness—higher, for instance, than at Breitenfeld.

The commune has sixty-one new-peasant farms,[2] which were formed by enlarging existing holdings considered to be too small. Thirty-one

[1] Areas under various crops in the commune, given as percentages of the total arable land, are as follows:

Winter cereals		Row crops	
Wheat	18	Leguminous crops	2·5
Rye	8	Sugar beet	12·5
Barley	4·3	Mangolds	3·5
Winter rape	3·5	Potatoes	12·4
		Vegetables	4·5
Spring cereals		Sown grasses	
Oats	16	Clover and lucerne	11·5
Barley	0·8		
Spring-sown oil seeds	2		

[2] Three with 5–12½ acres, fifty-three with 12½–25 acres, four with 25–37½ acres, and one with 37½–50 acres. This last holding has grown since the Reform, by renting and also by the purchase of extra land; apparently the farmer does not believe that collectivization will ever come.

farms belonging to 'old' peasants are substantially larger.[1] The stock consists of 467 cattle, including 201 cows (Plan total, 204), 1,233 pigs (Plan total, 1,392), including 124 sows (Plan, 135), and 561 sheep (Plan, 371) in two communal flocks. The horses, 129 in number, do not figure at all in the Plan for the village, but at national level the aim is to maintain their numbers, and throughout Germany the horse is holding its own remarkably well. The Agricultural Secretary[2] of the Kreis of Bernburg, however, is always telling the peasants that 'the horse eats at table, but the cow supplies the table'.

In one instance a holding of $7\frac{1}{2}$ acres with its small yard of 23×40 ft. had belonged to a farmer classed by the Agrarian Reform as 'poor in land'. At that time it was all that remained of a larger farm which, owing to previous ill-health, the owner had been unable to manage. The Reform gave him another $17\frac{1}{2}$ acres, which was more than he would have received in Hungary. Besides $1\frac{1}{4}$ acres of woodland and nearly 2 acres of orchard (apples, cherries, and gooseberries), he now has just over 20 acres under the plough, as follows:

Wheat	$4\frac{1}{4}$
Rye	$2\frac{1}{2}$
Barley and oats	$3\frac{3}{4}$
Potatoes	$2\frac{1}{2}$
Sugar-beet	$2\frac{1}{2}$
Chicory for seed	$2\frac{1}{2}$
Lucerne and clover	$2\frac{1}{2}$

He has a herd of seven cattle: three cows of nondescript breed, but derived from Simmenthal and Friesian, a bull of no great utility, a heifer and two calves. The remainder of the stock includes twenty pigs, six sheep, a goat, and about fifteen hens. Like 60 per cent. of the farmers in the village, he is thus a *Kuhbauer*, or 'cow peasant'.[3] Having neither horses nor bullocks, he harnesses his three cows, but the M.A.S. 'tills my land more cheaply than horses ever could'; and in spite of a fair range of equipment (winnower, potato-sorter, drill, and some small ploughs) he does not possess any form of reaping machine.

[1] Eleven with less than 25 acres, nineteen with 25-50 acres, one with $72\frac{1}{2}$ acres, and another with 110 acres of cultivable land.

[2] Like the Landrat, a kind of sub-Prefect, he is a former labourer who has been to Russia.

[3] He is not very fond of the French—'who disarmed my regiment with such brutality in Austria, when the war had finished, that the Americans had to protect us; and we were only ordinary soldiers'. By contrast, many others told of friendships, especially with French prisoners-of-war.

The holding, which has rather a forlorn aspect, occupies the man and his wife, a daughter of sixteen, and an adopted son of eighteen. This seems rather a lot, even taking account of the extra work in growing chicory for seed, and one recalls a similar situation in Bavaria. The norms are calculated at 1,210 lb. for pork, 418 lb. for beef, 517 gallons for milk, and 835 eggs.

299. In the market-place a travelling shop belonging to the H.O., or State Commercial Organization, supplies cloth in exchange for coupons, and is putting the village shop out of business. Beyond this is a rather larger farm which father and son have divided into two quite separate undertakings of about 25 acres each, sharing only the same yard. Sharing the farm in this manner was preferable to being labelled *kulak*. Between them they have one foal and three plough horses, and apart from their own land they also till the tiny fields owned by factory workers who like to grow their own potatoes and vegetables. They charge more than the M.A.S., but the latter cannot work on these 'pocket-handkerchiefs'.

Father, mother—a vigorous peasant woman—and the son work the farm and enlist the help of three women—war widows or factory hands' wives—who do an eight-hour day on about a hundred days in the year. These women earn 0·60 marks an hour,[1] which is the price of a 2·2-lb. loaf of rye bread, but the equivalent of only 4d. or 5d. worth of manufactured articles. There are now over 3,000,000 old age pensioners in East Germany, and a law passed quite recently now allows them to take a job without losing any benefits. Equally, one may see a girl of no more than fourteen guiding a plough while her young sister leads the team. This is often made up of a horse and a cow or bullock, a custom which persists as far afield as Alsace.

The farmer's wife admits to eating rather better and drinking more beer than before the war. The shortage of food, which lasted longer than in the West, ushered in a prosperous era for the peasants which lasted until 1948. In that year the Kreis Secretary at Bernburg[2] recorded

---

[1] Factory wages in Berlin: 1-2 marks an hour, according to the job. Comparison is difficult, however, for there are all kinds of social benefits.

[2] One has to show an identity card before gaining admittance to any official building, even in the smallest local government offices. The publication of statistics is forbidden officially, but this rule was not applied to us so far as the localities we visited were concerned. Kreis Bernburg complained of having too much bran, for the region is essentially one of cereal cultivation and stock-rearing is only on a modest scale; planning is still experiencing the difficulties which are bound to be encountered in the early stages. In July 1952 there were still coupons for meat, sugar, butter, milk, fats, cloth, and footwear, with a

a transaction of 1 cwt. of flour bought for 1,400 marks of the new currency; 9 marks a pound for wheat was a common price. 'Never,' he confided, 'had German agriculture known such agreeable times.' During the same period, however, manufactured goods were just as scarce. In contrast with a French farm of the same size as this (50 acres), the consumption of wine, as in the whole of Central Europe, was exceptional; and there was no car.[1]

6. Towards Collectivization

300. East Germany in 1952 was the domain of small farms created by the Agrarian Reform, and it is a recognized fact that this is always the first stage in a Communist programme. Politically it corresponds with the existence of several parties and with a 'National Front' type of government. Technical progress, as we have seen on many occasions, raises all kinds of awkward problems on the small farm. For instance, in spite of the unrivalled yield of rape as an oil-seed, other plants are being developed as alternatives, for on very small fields, the myriad parasites which attack the crop cannot be combated with modern methods (spraying from the air). Then, again, the mangold, which is typical of intensive cultivation on a small, overcrowded farm, is still preferred to silage crops, in spite of its lower content of proteins.

After the war, thousands of families had to be housed, but the resources expended in building 150,000 new farms could have been employed more productively elsewhere. Moreover, the efficiency of labour in these diminutive fields and farm buildings is necessarily lower than on the large capitalist enterprises now defunct, and mechanization would obviously be uneconomic. Finally, there is no hope that large families will ever be able to subdivide their holdings among their members, and the effective area is due to shrink even more as the M.A.S. extends its services. In 1945 the country was short of funds, and the solution

---

free market, at high prices, for extra quantities. At this time, in early July, there was still a shortage of vegetables in Berlin, although strawberries had started to arrive from Bulgaria at the end of May and tomatoes at the end of June. Official notices exhorted the public to lay potatoes in store and to beware of 'bicycle thieves'.

[1] Further details of the two farms, taken together, are as follows: twelve head of cattle including five cows and a heifer in calf; summer sales of milk, 11 gallons daily; four sows and twenty-five pigs in all. The very wide range of crops—wider than on the smaller farms—confirms one's impression of the fertility of the loess soils: 10 acres of oats and barley, $6\frac{1}{4}$ of wheat, $3\frac{3}{4}$ of rye, $2\frac{1}{2}$ of peas grown for fodder, $2\frac{1}{2}$ of rape, $\frac{3}{4}$ of poppy, $6\frac{1}{4}$ of sugar beet, $6\frac{1}{4}$ of lucerne, $6\frac{1}{4}$ of potatoes, $\frac{3}{4}$ of vegetables (peas and onions), $\frac{3}{4}$ of mangolds.

arrived at offered a far greater volume of employment than industry could have done with the same amount of capital.

By 1952 there was already an appreciable movement towards the towns, and the Solvay Works in Bernburg, for instance, was attracting a considerable number of young men from 'new peasant' families, and in some cases even the farmers themselves, who would sometimes rent their land to a neighbour. As in Russia during the N.E.P. phase, those who remain on the land are getting a chance to expand and there are signs that the peasant class is emerging as one of men of substance. Moreover, the view that most of the *Neubauern* are anxious to enlarge their holdings is confirmed by the Kreis administration at Bernburg, which regards 35 to 50 acres—considerably more than the Agrarian Reform provided for—as being an appropriate size with the present level of farm equipment. With prices now reverting back to normal, the peasant with less than about 12 acres is having trouble in making ends meet, for his margin of profits is far too small.

East Germany has remained at this stage of development longer than the other countries of Eastern Europe because until 12 July 1952 the overriding political objective was the unification of Germany, so as 'to release the West from the claws of the Atlantic'. It was essential, therefore, to do nothing which would frighten the peasants in the Federal Republic. The possibility of collectivization did not seem to have occurred to the peasants with whom we spoke in the East. Many of them no doubt chose to avoid the issue and preferred to indulge in wishful thinking. At that time the prospect of a reunited Germany did not make socialism seem inevitable, and the future offered a wide range of possibilities.[1]

We were unable, at the beginning of July, to discuss this theme with any of the peasants we met. So as not to worry them unduly, one is not allowed to suggest that 'evolution' might be followed by yet another phase. On 12 July the Thuringian peasant Ernst Grossmann

---

[1] By contrast, 60 per cent. of the industrial structure was already nationalized. The figure was only 30 per cent. for textiles, but banks, mines, metallurgical industries, and key industries in general had been wholly taken over. As for commerce, 20,000 H.O. shops had been started already, and there were co-operatives as well, so that the private trader was being pushed out more and more; there were still 200,000 of these private businesses, however. The trend was not accompanied by any degree of rationalization, for many H.O. shops had simply been put in the place of the previous establishment without being enlarged. Many of them, therefore, were too small, costs of distribution were still too high, and they were less efficient than the supermarkets in the United States.

announced from the platform of the Second Congress of the Party of Socialist Unity that the first co-operative, created by grouping twenty-three farms together, had been formed on 8 June.[1] If only we had delayed a little longer we might have obtained an idea of the peasants' reactions to this turn of events. One of their reactions seems to have been an accelerated exodus to the West during the succeeding winter.

[1] 'Many peasant holdings of small and medium size, though not the large ones, have been amalgamated, so as to raise the efficiency of work and increase incomes. The large fields will allow heavy machinery to be used more easily, so saving labour.' So wrote a colleague of ours at Bernburg in January 1953.

XV

Hungary—Agriculture in a People's Democracy[1]

1. Rural Overpopulation in an Environment of Unevenly Distributed Resources

301. In the popular imagination, the plain of Hungary often evokes a picture of a land blessed with exceptional fertility. Support is lent to this view by the humus- and nitrogen-rich chestnut and black steppe soils of chernozem type which contribute largely to the great agricultural value of the Alfold between the Danube and the Tisza. Elsewhere the plain is covered by shifting sands, which are only now being anchored by the planting of trees in criss-cross patterns similar to those of the Ukraine, but with even closer spacings.[2] Other areas have extremely acid soils or soils consisting of iron, silicon, and aluminium complexes, with a high proportion of unweathered iron and aluminium salts; or, again, sodic alkaline soils, which are by no means easy to improve. Finally, drainage is often poor.[3] On the right bank of the Danube in Transdanubia the brown temperate forest soils predominate.

---

[1] Field studies in March-April 1948. Prices quoted are in florins, which were about 30 to the £1 at that time, 35 to the £1 in 1953. The more recent statistical data are drawn from official documents and from the work of M. Plessz. There are obvious difficulties involved in the study of these countries, and we have done our best to make our analyses objective. As an example of an anti-Communist document, which also has to be treated with reserve, we may quote issue No. 4 of *Romania Muncitoare* (Working Rumania), entitled *Agriculture and the Peasants, from 1945 to 1953*.

[2] The twenty-year Plan (1951-70) proposes to establish forests on 1,850,000 acres of derelict land and tree belts 45-110 yards wide on a further 850,000 acres, thus raising the proportion of woodland in the country from 12 per cent. to 20 per cent. of the total area: 57,000 acres, including 820 miles of shelter belts, were actually planted in 1951.

[3] The 1950-4 Plan provided for the reclamation of 42,000 acres impregnated with sodium salts and 100,000 acres of acidic soils.

These are derived from loess and are leached to some extent; sometimes they are even slightly podsolized.

The continental climate, as in the U.S.S.R., makes the region less favourable for agriculture than Western Europe. Even the duration of the winter is less of a hindrance to vegetative growth than the summer drought, which reaches its greatest intensity in August and September. The lack of summer rain is felt most severely in the eastern part of the lowland, where the well-known Hortobagy Steppes in the vicinity of Debrecen receive less than 20 in. of rain a year. Worse still, and in contrast with Saxony, the minimum here is in the summer, which receives only 6 in. of the annual total. The mean annual total rarely rises to over 28 in. anywhere in the country, and evaporation is accelerated by violent and desiccating winds. Great importance is therefore attached to the large irrigation schemes, which were to cover 125,000 acres (50,000 pre-war) by 1951 and 930,000 acres by 1959. Whereas irrigation was formerly confined to the east, these new projects are developing new areas in Transdanubia.[1] The climatic conditions are thus fairly similar to those in the southern portion of European Russia, though not so extreme.

'Little' Hungary, whose 1945 frontiers stop short of its ethnological boundaries and give it an area of 36,000 square miles, had a population of over 10,000,000 in 1953. This gave a density of nearly 280 per square mile in a country where, before the war, over half the population still depended on agriculture. The proportion fell to below a half for the first time in 1949 and has been decreasing rapidly ever since.[2] There was more evidence of industrialization before the war than in the Balkans, but less than in Czechoslovakia, which was undergoing a similar type of development. The export trade of the latter consisted at one time mostly of cereals and animals and its imports of manufactured goods, but since 1951 this situation has been reversed.

302. In 1944 the agricultural economy was still reaping the consequences of the most half-hearted measures of agrarian reform to be found anywhere in eastern Europe between the wars. More than anywhere else in Europe, Italy and Spain included, it was dominated by

[1] The 1949 Plan aimed to raise the irrigated area to 230,000 acres by 1954; fodder crops were to have first priority, then rice and finally meadows. As in Camargue, rice was the main crop of the first irrigation schemes.

[2] In Poland two-thirds of the working population were employed in agriculture, while in Bulgaria, Rumania and Yugoslavia the figure rose to four-fifths; as against 38 per cent. in Czechoslovakia. In 1949 in Hungary, 2,150,000 were employed in agriculture, as compared with 965,000 in industry and 1,210,000 in other occupations.

huge estates: 1,288 of these still owned 30 per cent. of the country; 300 of them averaged 17,000 acres each; the Esterhazy family, which possessed 1,050,000 acres in 1914, still retained 295,000 acres—the size of a fairly small English county—in Hungary and 145,000 in Austria. As opposed to this, three-quarters of the country's farms had less than $7\frac{1}{4}$ acres (five *holds* each of about $1\frac{1}{2}$ acres). Unless they specialized in viticulture or market gardening, they were too small to be efficient, and they accounted for less than a fifth of the total area.

We have described in detail elsewhere[1] the mechanism of the reforms of 1945-6, which were very similar to those described for East Germany in the preceding chapter. The declared aim was to give 'the land to him that tills it'. It resulted in a fragmentation of land holdings which may seem regrettable from the point of view of efficient development. It seems probable that the reform was guided along these channels by political motives. The destruction of war and the interruption of the flow of investments from abroad, however, placed a severe handicap on attempts to foster the growth of industry. Progress had to rely on local capital, and was thus bound to be slow. It was of great importance, therefore, that for a few years at least the land should continue to support a large number of people.

Before the war Eastern Europe was characterized essentially by its rural overpopulation and by the low level of earnings and of industrial development which went with it. It was to this area that Francis Delaisi applied the term 'draught horse Europe', as distinct from the 'horse power' regions of the West. The Royal Institute of International Affairs in London estimates that 18 per cent. of the agricultural population of Hungary is redundant. Comparable figures for other countries are Rumania, 20 per cent., Poland, 24 per cent., Bulgaria, 28 per cent., Yugoslavia, 35 per cent., Slovakia, 50 per cent., and Ruthenia as much as 86 per cent. The estimate for Hungary seems rather low, especially as compared with Slovakia. From what we saw during our travels in

[1] *Revue du Ministère de l'Agriculture*, December 1948. For the history of these reforms see Fr Fetjö, *Histoire des démocraties populaires* (Seuil edition, pp. 146-8). See also *Les démocraties populaires*, by P. George (Editions Sociales, 1952). M. Plessz summarizes a table from Pikler as follows:

PERCENTAGE OF LAND OCCUPIED BY FARMS OF DIFFERENT SIZES

	Less than $1\frac{1}{2}$ acres	$1\frac{1}{2}$-7 acres	7-14 acres	14-$28\frac{1}{2}$ acres	$28\frac{1}{2}$-70 acres	70-140 acres	Over 140 acres
1935	0.9	9.5	11.6	18.6	20.5	7.6	31.3
1949	0.9	18.6	32.2	28.5	15.9	3.1	0.7

The object was also 'to break the political and economic power of the large landowners, by liquidating them as a class'.

1948 we would not have said that there was very much difference between the two countries. The fact of overpopulation, however, which is the point at issue, is incontrovertible.

When the French representatives at the International Congress of Agriculture in Prague (July 1938) complained of the exodus to the towns, the most conservative-minded of the Polish delegation replied:

FIG. 26. Hungary.

'If only we could relieve the congestion in our rural areas, in southern Galicia especially!' Before the war Morgan asserted[1] that production per head of the agricultural population in eastern Europe was four and a half times less than in Western Europe. The Hungarian output per acre was less than half the German, but even so it exceeded those of Poland and the Balkan countries. The latter was less than a fifth of the Dutch, but the differences would be smaller in comparison with France. Several regional descriptions, based on observations made in 1948, are given in the sections which follow, and will serve as the prelude to a summary of later developments.

2. Mezokovesd, a Poor 'Agricultural Town'

303. Mezokovesd (Fig. 26), at the foot of the volcanic Carpathian foothills, had 22,000 inhabitants in 1948. In spite of its size, however,

[1] *Agricultural Systems of Middle Europe* (New York, 1933).

a rapid journey through its streets gave the impression of a huge village, a vast agglomeration of small farms. Four-fifths of the working population were in agriculture, but the total area of farm land was no more than about 25,000 acres. There were some 1,300 separate holdings, less than a tenth of which exceeded 21 acres (15 *holds*), and the two largest were no more than about 125 acres. The area centred on the town, comprising a total of fourteen communes and 58,000 acres of cultivated land, had 42,000 inhabitants, an even larger proportion of whom were engaged in agriculture.

Before the war the commune of Mezokovesd alone used to send 6,000 to 7,000 seasonal workers for about half the year to various large estates, many of them in Transdanubia, where they would be employed for heavy manual labour. By 1948, as a result of the agrarian reforms, about 750 of these people had been given land, mostly in the Pecs and Mosen region, where the majority of the new colonists seem now to have settled quite happily. By 1948 some of those who began with absolutely nothing had succeeded by dint of really hard work in building up their stock to about three horses and four cows. This the 'judge' who governs the village regarded as wealth indeed! Others took to pilfering to relieve their pitiful poverty, and were sent back fairly quickly from whence they came. About 1,500 people still set out regularly from the town in search of part-time work, which they were finding mainly in the State farms. Finally, a number of families decided to leave the country altogether, and seventy of them had left for Sweden, but later on emigration was banned.

304. One of the town's 'large' farmers has about 25 acres of meadow and a tenth share in 430 acres of common land on the foothills of the Matras, about eleven miles away. On the latter he has the right to graze twelve one-year-old cattle and six two-year-olds. In 1942 the farm had four horses and two foals, eight cows and two stores and twenty-five pigs. In 1948 these numbers had fallen to two and one, four and none and ten respectively. He sells the bull calves at five weeks and keeps the heifers. The reduction in the number of animals has substantially lowered his profits from stock rearing, on which he relied heavily before the war.

The country as a whole lost 39 per cent. of its horses, 44 per cent. of its cattle, and 78 per cent. of its pigs during the war, and it was not until 1951 (?) that the 1938 figures were reached once again. It was intended to attain 2 cwt. of stock per acre of ploughland by the end of 1952, but the plan seems to have been running behind schedule. Mezokovesd, which lost four-fifths of its horses (German and Russian requisitioning, lost in battle, etc.), had to harness men to its ploughs in 1945, after the manner of the Volga boatmen.

As in Slovakia and in contrast with Western Europe, the large and medium-sized farms generally show a wider range of crops than the small. Returning to the example from Mezokovesd, one finds that there are 70 acres of arable land: 56 per cent. of these are devoted to corn crops, with 21 acres under wheat, 14 of barley, $2\frac{1}{2}$ of rye, and $1\frac{1}{2}$ of oats. Then there are 14 acres of maize (grown as a row crop), $2\frac{1}{2}$ of beet, and $1\frac{1}{2}$ of poppy and potatoes, which, taken together, give over a quarter of row crops. Finally, there are nearly 6 acres of vegetables (melons, pumpkins, onions, and tomatoes), $1\frac{1}{2}$ of tobacco, the same of vine, and $4\frac{1}{4}$ of lucerne. The small proportion of temporary grassland is characteristic of eastern Europe, which has not yet completed its 'agricultural revolution' in the sense that fodder crops and row crops have as yet not been widely adopted. The pattern of crops is reminiscent of certain parts of Flanders (Chapter XI), which is another overpopulated region. But the dry summer prevents the cultivation of catch-crops which are so typical a feature of Flanders. Other differences are that the latter region uses enormous quantities of fertilizer and has very high stock densities.

A certain air of affluence was the impression which we gained from a short visit to this well-tended farm. Superficially at least the impression is confirmed by the spectacle of the Corso on a Sunday afternoon, where the young girls and women of the town may be seen parading in their beautiful, embroidered dresses. Before reaching our conclusions on this evidence alone, however, and as hastily as any tourist, let us examine a small farm of the most widespread type.

305. A war widow with two children cultivates six fields located at various distances and in varying directions from the town; one of them is as much as five miles away. A neighbour of hers had calculated that he travelled 940 miles a year with his small single-shafted cart in journeys between his house and his fields. Before the war these carts were often drawn by a pair of pure-bred horses, small creatures which delighted in trotting, but were of little use for deep ploughing. Most of the carts in 1948 were pulled, rather lopsidedly, by a single horse or even by a cow. This, however, was the supreme disgrace, for the peasant tradition of harnessing cattle, though prevalent in Germany, is quite foreign to this region. The horses were very hardy and received hardly any grain except when put to heavy work, such as hauling stone or timber. A ration of straw and $\frac{3}{4}$ acre of good lucerne-clover grassland was quite enough for them. The case is similar in Slovakia, where

all horses without exception are blood animals. In western Hungary one finds a far heavier type of animal used for draught purposes.

In pre-war days this woman had just over 2 acres of land, and her husband used to go off for five or six months at a time, between about May and autumn, to find employment as a seasonal worker. After the war the only property available in this area for subdivision and distribution to the peasants consisted of three estates each of about 500 acres, apart from the common grazings about four miles from the town, which were very poor and partly saline. The widow received $2\frac{1}{4}$ acres, but neither plough nor draught animals. In addition to this, she now rents a further $2\frac{1}{2}$ acres.

Mainly for her own requirements, she grows nearly 3 acres of wheat, $\frac{3}{4}$ of barley, the same of sunflower, and just over 2 of maize with potatoes between the rows. She would have liked to grow some beans as well, but the ground was too dry. The family had owned a horse in her grandfather's time, but neither she nor her father had ever possessed one, and this difference between past and present reflects the decline in the size of holdings which, as in Murcia (Chapter VI), has accompanied the growth of population. Today, therefore, the women have time for embroidery, and the predominance of such activities is not so much a sign of high standards of living as of rural unemployment. Mezokovesd exported the products of this labour before the war, but the embroiderers often earned less than the price of their own food. On this holding the widow pays either for the station tractor to do her ploughing, which costs 30 florins an acre, or for her neighbour to do it with his horse, which costs twice as much.[1] In 1948 the work was also done more satisfactorily in the latter case, but since then the station drivers should have learned their jobs a little better, and the same is probably not true today.

Although she still fattens a pig every year, she lost her only cow during the war, and in spite of her efforts to do so she had not saved up enough to buy another. Indeed, after a series of dry years, like 1947, when she harvested only 6 cwt. of wheat, she was only thankful to have just enough to eat. We saw her three-year-old child eating his *Sauerkraut* on a slice of bread, but she could not afford to give him

[1] Before the war the small farmer was often exploited by his larger neighbour, who hired out his horses at very high rates. Since 1945 everyone who owns a tractor or a pair of animals has had to fulfil a ploughing target of 215 acres in the former, or 27 acres in the latter case, either on his own land or on neighbouring farms; if on someone else's land, there is a low fixed rate of tariffs, but it is sometimes disregarded.

a glass of milk. After we had asked her a few questions, to which her replies revealed the state of her poverty only too clearly, the whole family burst into tears. Their state of penury traced its origin, however, mainly to the devastation of the war and to the régime of the pre-war years.

In *Tardi Helyzett* Zaltan Szabo declared: 'The people of Tard have no possibility of leading lives worthy of human beings. . . . On the surface the village seems gay, the men are likeable and kind, their brightly coloured clothes richly embroidered, but the thick walls of their dwellings hide the poverty of their meals from the eye of the stranger.' No account can be valid if the author has not seen inside these 'thick walls'. We are reminded, in this context, of the nonchalant diplomat who in 1935, at the nadir of the depression, assured us that the Hungarian countryside was remarkably rich—'for I have eaten well there,' he said, 'and cheaply too.' For the sake of those who have such rudimentary ideas about economics, let it be said that this is, on the contrary, the distinguishing feature of poor countries, like Spain in 1953.

A little poultry was all that was sold off the farm: five turkeys at Easter (95 florins for 20 lb.), a dozen chickens, about the same number of ducks, and a couple of hundred eggs. The cash earnings came mainly from the widow's work in a small tobacco factory, where her hours were from 7 a.m. to 4 p.m. and her wages 45 florins a week. As a war widow she also received 63 florins a month for her two children. She was just making ends meet.

In 1948 800 other families in the commune were similarly short of land, victims of this first stage of social evolution. At that time only some of the men had found work in the mines or factories or on the railways, and in these instances, as often happens in the Alps, the women and children did the farm work.[1] The first solution, according to the 'judge' in 1948, was intensification, by concentrating on crops demanding a lot of labour: fruits and the vine, vegetables (tomatoes, cabbages, peas, lentils), industrial crops (hemp, tobacco, sugar-beet, poppy), and fodder crops (lucerne, vetch, clover). The obstacle to development along these lines, however, was the shortage of grain. As in East Germany, the lack of bread would not allow part of the wheat acreage to be abandoned in favour of these other crops.

The emphasis today is on another type of solution. Such towns, with too many people for the amount of land available, are experiencing

[1] According to Plessz, in 1951 the 'miner-peasants', who sometimes worked on their tiny holdings and sometimes in the mines, to the detriment of the effective strength of the labour force, had to choose between the two occupations.

an initial phase of industrialization. The great advantage is that, although factories obviously have to be built, dwelling-houses for the workers exist already, and this economizes a great deal of capital. Many of these towns are thus no longer purely 'agricultural'. Finally, in 1950-1 the presence of many landless workers facilitated the formation of producers' co-operatives on some of the land still available, the object being to set an example for other peasants in the region.

3. Gollo, a Rich Village in Transdanubia

306. This last region, which adjoins the Carpathian foothills, has long been the victim of overpopulation and of the poverty which results from the extreme subdivision of land. More recently it has provided men for the recolonization of the Alfold, that great eastern plain which remained empty after the retreat of the Turks. Further to the south-west and beyond the Danube from Budapest lies the county of Somogy, which reaches out towards Lake Balaton in the north and Kaposvar in the south. The higher parts have a covering of easily worked loess and only a few valley bottoms are characterized by saline crusts. Farms are clustered together in large villages, but not so large that one is tempted to call them towns. Thus Gollo has a mere 2,060 inhabitants, who farm a total of 17,500 acres—above the average for the county—giving a density six times lower than at Mezokovesd.

Before the war the land was distributed among 315 farms, one of which was a large estate belonging to the Order of Pierristes. Large domains belonging to the Church, to nobles, and wealthy merchants made up almost half the area, and were generally exploited wholly under the authority of the owners themselves. Eighty-five per cent. of the 3,500 acres covered by the Pierriste estate had been allocated to its former employees in lots averaging a little under 10 acres, and larger, therefore, than at Mezokovesd. The remaining 15 per cent. went towards enlarging existing holdings of between $1\frac{1}{4}$ and $2\frac{1}{2}$ acres, which were made up to the same size as the others.

The 300 new settlers had to start with a plough, and sometimes even only one horse, between four farms, and at first times were hard indeed. By 1948 many of them had acquired a few simple implements and their circumstances were improving fairly rapidly. One man before the war was a carter and was also the *métayer* of a small farm with two horses and a cow. The land reforms gave him $12\frac{1}{2}$ acres of his own, and he continued to rent a similar area for 26 cwt. of wheat a year. Today he possesses two mares, two foals, two cows and a store, a plough, and a harrow; also 'two-thirds' of a new drill, which he shares with a neighbour. There were many, however, who had not done so well as this in 1948. Half the new settlers ploughed with horses; the remainder with a pair of cows or oxen. Those few who only had a cow borrowed one from their neighbour for cultivating their land, and were doing all they could to become as independent of such assistance as possible.

Lacking any other shelter for their animals, twelve settlers were using the stables of the old house and were preparing to pull them down and build themselves a cowhouse each with the bricks. We tried to dissuade them from their project, which was not only frowned upon by the authorities, but also impracticable, for they were obviously going to be short of bricks. They countered with arguments based on the risk of fire and epidemics and on the distance from their fields, but we soon perceived their underlying motives. Some were demolishing this huge stable with might and main because for them it was a symbol of the old order, which they loathed; but others because it was a possible base for the establishment of a collective, which they feared. No doubt many were motivated both by their hatred of the past and their apprehension for the future.

In 1948 the commune had 700 horses and as many cows and 300 store cattle. This area had not suffered such devastation during the war as the regions further east, and these numbers showed that the 1939 position had been more or less regained; but it must be remembered that when large estates are broken up increases in stock density are the general rule.

307. On his farm of nearly 29 acres one of the 'old' peasants kept three horses and two foals, four cows, a bull and six stores, and about ten pigs. Apart from himself there were three full-time workers, two women and a man, two old men who worked part-time, and four seasonal workers. According to a custom which is still observed, the latter are given a tenth of the grain harvest in return for their help in reaping the corn crops, binding the sheaves, stooking, and loading. Between 1930 and 1945 binders were forbidden in Hungary, as in Yugoslavia, 'so as to give work to the reapers'; as if it was possible to raise the standards of rural life by lowering the productivity of work on the land.

This farm sowed nearly 9 acres to wheat, $4\frac{1}{4}$ to rye and oats, the same to a maize-beans mixture, and a little over $2\frac{1}{2}$ to vegetables, which included potatoes, cabbages and carrots. Finally, there were nearly 9 acres of lucerne and sainfoin, which was a high proportion of the total and therefore typical of these western regions. The farmers of this area, whom the local agricultural adviser describes as 'ambitious', obtain some of the highest yields in the whole of Hungary, for they capitalize the fertility of their soils by means of deep ploughing and fairly heavy manuring. Every year this farm succeeds in producing a substantial surplus for sale, but fundamentally this is still a subsistence economy, for the needs of the farm come first. Nevertheless, 60–80 cwt. of wheat, 16–20 of barley, three or four cattle, five or six fat pigs, a foal of six months or more, and some poultry and eggs, are sold in the course of a normal year.

Maize gives the best yield of all. Although it requires from sixteen to eighteen days of work per acre, it gives a return in exceptionally good years of 32 to 36 cwt. The average for the farm is actually 26 cwt., which is twice the pre-war Hungarian average, itself higher than the French. The nutritional standards are very much better than at Mezokovesd, and seem to be satisfactory on the medium-sized holdings. The ex-farm labourer turned peasant eats a lot more pork in place of the cheaper cereal food to which he was once accustomed, and the amount of food consumed on the farms has increased substantially. The effect of this new factor has been generally underestimated, but in 1948 it was in very large measure responsible for the shortage of food in the towns, more so even than the fall in agricultural production.

For building material, the poor use rammed clay or earth, the more affluent peasant faces his walls with bricks, while the rich build wholly in brick on a stone foundation. Unlike the very long farmhouses of Mezokovesd and Slovakia, where the gable-ended living quarters face towards the road, the buildings here are arranged round a square yard. The dwelling-house at the far end faces a gateway leading onto the tree-lined road with its deep ditches on either side. Adjoining the house are the stables, the awkward-looking cowhouse, and the piggery; the barn is on its right and farm implements are kept along the side of the yard parallel to the road.

4. The Shanty Town of the New Settlers at Eloszallas

308. The Nagykararsom estate, which formerly belonged to the Cistercian Order, covered 2,000 acres of fairly intensively farmed land in this commune, which is fifty miles south of Budapest and near the right bank of the Danube. Maize yields had been particularly heavy, the crop being fed entirely to the pigs. Intermediate in type between a feudal domain and a capitalist enterprise, the undertaking had enjoyed the advantages of its own rail link with the regional network and of

its own sunflower seed crushing mill and soap works. It had also built a huge cowhouse large enough to accommodate eighty beasts. When we saw it, however, the well pump had been dismantled, and two men were permanently employed drawing water by hand for the needs of the nearby village of 600 people. The mill machinery had suffered not only from the destruction and requisitions of war, but also from the activities of the new settlers, who had appropriated whatever they were able to find in the way of building materials.

The estate has been divided into parcels varying in size from 5 to 20 acres. At least eight children was the qualification for one of the latter, and most of the allocations were of between 10 and 12 acres. The first beneficiaries were the former workers on the estate. They retained their living quarters, which comprised two rooms per family, a kitchen between two (elsewhere we noted as many as four families sharing a kitchen), and an oven between ten families. Although they are better housed than the new settlers, they felt bitter, for whereas they regarded themselves as having a prior claim on the land, some of the newcomers had actually received larger grants. It was necessary, however, for this less densely peopled region to make room for others less fortunately placed. Some of the settlers were formerly employed as seasonal workers, and when they came back with their families in 1948 they had nowhere to live apart from their old dormitories. The village has its housing development plan, but so far the schemes existed only on paper.

Their living accommodation is therefore not very satisfactory. The large cowhouse (63 × 11 yds.) consisted of fourteen bays, each $4\frac{1}{2}$ × 11 yds. which have been partitioned to give each family two rather damp compartments, one used for sleeping, the other as a kitchen and living-room. About 100 people lived where there had been only eighty cattle before. 'We would prefer a collective to this co-habitation,' one of the settlers declared. This prompted his neighbour, a Party member, to retort (this was in 1948) that he would leave the Party if they forced him into a producers' co-operative.[1]

The last settlers to arrive had built themselves huts covered with maize stalks reminiscent of the notorious African shanty town. Action

[1] At the 1947 elections, one-third of these settlers voted Communist (15 per cent. for the whole of Hungary); in the main they were the recent arrivals from the north-east (the priest suggested that only a twentieth of the former employees on the estate were Communists). A quarter of them belonged to the National Peasants' Party and a fifth to the Small Landowners' Party, which was strongest among the former peasants. As one might expect, therefore, those who had benefited from the reforms tended to the left.

has since been taken on the question of housing, but the position is still far from satisfactory, and presents a complete contrast with the splendid achievements of East Germany. The settlers are very much alive to their discomfort, for 75 per cent. of them came from the county of Hebres to the north-east, where, as at Mezokovesd, even as agricultural labourers or as 'dwarf' peasants with only 1 acre or 2 of land, they all had pleasant houses of their own. Fifty-two families came together from the single village of Visnec, 'where they were short of food'. The reforms gave them land and the means of earning their bread, but then the State announced that it was taking their houses from them in exchange. Six of the 150 new settlers, when they heard this news, returned to their villages, preferring the comfort of their old homes to the prospect of keeping a better table.

309. The diminutive size of the land grants encourages the concentration on maize, which occupies half the surface area on 17-acre holdings and as much as two-thirds on those between 10 and $12\frac{1}{2}$ acres. There were, in fact, two consecutive years of row crops in the rotation, maize on the one hand and sunflowers grown as an oil-seed, with a little beet and some turnips, on the other. The third year consists mainly of wheat, with smaller quantities of rye, barley, or oats. So lacking in resources were the poorest of the settlers at the outset that they did not possess enough pigs to eat all their maize. On these holdings, therefore, farming was less intensive than on the large estate which preceded them, for they had to sell part of their maize as grain instead of selling it as pork. This early phase, however, soon passed. The average farm of about 10 to $12\frac{1}{2}$ acres supports four or five people, two or three of whom work on the land.

The substitution of peasant farming for the large estate—which, in this case, was competently farmed—has been accompanied, therefore, by a decline in stock-rearing and a greater concentration on row crops.[1] On the other hand, a new pattern of peasant farms, ploughing the land and growing maize and wheat, has been created where formerly the steppes, or *pusztas*, were once the domain of free ranging flocks and herds, as in the Alfold or the Tuscan Maremma or Andalusia. This change has been accompanied by a spectacular rise in production.

---

[1] Maize is more susceptible to summer drought than the autumn-sown cereals, so that although it makes a welcome addition to the resources, it also accentuates the fluctuation in the harvest from year to year. Further east, where the drought becomes more marked, the substitution of maize for other cereals is a questionable policy, as the harvest of 1952 clearly showed and, in the absence of irrigation, autumn-sown cereals are clearly preferable.

Moreover, the peasant holdings build up the density of stock fairly quickly to unprecedented levels.

The Cistercian who used to manage the estate is now the parish priest. He insisted on taking us to the house of the local Communist Party Secretary, who was with us. The house had an even greater profusion of holy images of various kinds than one would expect to find in Brittany. The priest then declared, 'There are no godless Communists,' and from what we could see he was probably right as far as the villages are concerned. He had himself received a land grant of $21\frac{1}{4}$ acres, which was the maximum allowed, but farming was in his blood and, not content with this, in 1948 he was renting twice as much again.[1] Rents per acre, which varied from $3\frac{1}{2}$ cwt. of wheat to 12 cwt. of grain, comprising 5 of wheat and 7 of maize, were excessive at the upper end of the scale, for the land does not compare in fertility with Flanders. Their only explanation is the overcrowding of the land. Some of the new settlers, who showed little anticipation of the future, were actually buying land at between 3,200 and 7,200 florins (nearly 60 to the £1 in 1948) an acre, but already such transactions were subject to certain controls. Unlike those who received land through the pre-war reform measures, the beneficiaries of the post-war reform were generally able to keep their land without running into debt. Although they were told to regard their repayments to the Agricultural Credit Fund as a matter of 'priority', the sums involved were actually very small. Moreover, the absence of restriction on the renting of land until collectivization began to get under way allowed a certain expansion of medium-sized farms—those of the *kulaks*—to take place.

A rather enterprising settler who was granted $12\frac{1}{2}$ acres in two separate parcels, about a third and two-thirds of a mile away respectively, hires another 7 acres about a mile away. Married and with two children (plus his eldest son's family), he has one cow and owns a horse for ploughing. Apart from $11\frac{1}{4}$ acres of row crops, comprising 7 of maize, $1\frac{1}{2}$ of sugar-beet, 2 of poppy (the oil-seed of his native district; but sunflower is probably more suitable here), and $\frac{3}{4}$ of peas, he grows $8\frac{3}{4}$ acres of corn crops as follows: $4\frac{1}{4}$ of wheat and 3 of rye for the household, and $1\frac{1}{2}$ of oats, mainly for the cow. The immigrant from the north-east, who above all else is short of land, finds no room for sown grassland.

He has built a kind of hut with rails from the old railway track and with bricks from demolished buildings. His eldest son is twenty-six

[1] As from 1948, only tenant-farmers' co-operatives, which account for a considerable proportion of producers' co-operatives, were allowed to rent land.

TANYA, PUSZTA, AND 'BULGARIAN' GARDENS

and recently married, but did not qualify for a grant of land, so he rents 4¼ acres, on which he keeps two cows. The two families live in a single room. A plough, allocated to them by the State when the estate was broken up, and a cart, a harrow, and a roller which they have bought since, make up the complement of farm equipment. They had dug a small cellar, about 6 ft. 6 in. by 5 ft., for carrots and potatoes, and had built a store for maize (which served in addition to their share in the communal barn) and an earthen shelter (6 ft. 6 in. × 6 ft. 6 in.), where they proposed to keep three piglets. Near the living quarters there is a place to keep the three cows and the horse; also a lean-to shed where harness and similar tackle are stored.

5. The Isolated *Tanyas* of Kecskemet, the Bugac *Puszta*, and the 'Bulgarian' Gardens

310. Kecskemet has 60,000 inhabitants, three-fifths of whom are dependent on agriculture. About two miles from the administrative and commercial centre, the periphery of the settlement is made up entirely of farms. One of the largest of these was formerly that belonging to the town itself. It had 200 acres of vineyards, which have now been divided between the twenty-five permanent labourers and the forty-five seasonal workers who used to come for the pruning in March, and then again in the summer for the hoeing and for the harvest. Right until 1944 women working in the private vineyards had no right to any of the wine at harvest-time. The men would line up in the evening, and each received a few drops from the owner, who squirted the wine down his throat with a long wooden pipette.[1] One wonders what they would have said in Béziers to such treatment. Worked over and dug entirely by hand, as in France a century ago, the vineyards have about 120 days of work spent on them per acre per year, and the yields often range between 330 and 550 gallons. The product, therefore, has to be sold at luxury prices, and offering a bottle of wine in Hungary is about equivalent to offering champagne in France.

An orchard—of peaches mainly—comparable in size with this vineyard was still the property of the town in 1948. It was rented to a group of fruit merchants, a fact which emphasizes that the evolution towards the people's democracy type of economy was still in its early stages. Orchards which had formed part of large estates also remained

---

[1] The men and the women spooned their food from two communal dishes (according to Dr Szigeti).

under collective ownership, for it was feared that they would be managed incompetently by new settlers, who, generally speaking, knew very little about fruit cultivation.

The inhabitants of the town cultivated a total of 22,500 acres of vines, which often had fruit trees planted amongst them. In addition, another 3,500 acres were devoted exclusively to orchards. Altogether the district had over 1,500,000[1] of Hungary's 40,000,000 fruit trees, and the number was increasing rapidly. The town alone furnished 9 per cent. of Hungarian exports, but, taking the region as a whole—that is, including the three vast adjoining communes—this figure rose to over 40 per cent. The commune of Izsak alone supplied 16 per cent. Three times a week during the season the large market-place seemed to be absolutely full of apricots from three o'clock in the morning onwards.

Though they once lived exclusively in large settlements for the sake of defence, the farmers of the region have long resorted to building crude shelters or huts in the midst of their lands. Later on these tended to become satellite farms, where the owner would keep a permanent employee while dividing his own time between here and his land nearer the town. Finally, many of these *tanyas* became individual farms in their own right.

311. Before the war, while he was out of work a certain shoemaker from Kecskemet built himself a *tanya* on a stretch of shifting sands which, as in Gascony, had been fixed with various types of grasses and with clumps of acacias. He now works $12\frac{1}{2}$ acres of land, including 3 acres of vine. Half the vineyard has fruit trees—cherries especially—planted at intervals. Having no draught animals, he has to pay for his land to be ploughed, which costs him only 14 florins an acre, for a small horse, even if he is not fed properly, is quite strong enough to till the loose, sandy surface with ease. A cow and her calf and one pig are his only stock.

The man lives here permanently, but his wife only comes in the summer, while the eldest of his four children, an agricultural student,[2]

---

[1] In 1942 there were 564,000 apricot trees, 360,000 plum, 290,000 apple, 128,000 morello cherry, 109,000 cherry of other varieties, 52,000 pear and smaller numbers of walnut trees, etc. The famous *Barack-Palinka* was distilled from the fermented apricots.

[2] The growing importance of education is one of the positive aspects of the changes which have occurred. In 1951-2 Hungary is said almost to have doubled the number of pupils undergoing secondary education and to have trebled the number of students attending advanced courses. In 1949 there were 2,100 agricultural courses with 85,000 students, nine-tenths of whom were over twenty.

gives a hand during the holidays. The single-storied house is not very different from the original hut. There is one room and a kitchen, the former being furnished with two beds and the latter functioning also as a stall for the animals. During the summer, when the weather is sometimes oppressively hot, it is better to keep the cow outside under the shelter of a thatched roof, which is made up of two sections and simply propped up on the ground. We have seen similar open-sided shelters on the heathlands of Lanvaux in Brittany. A little further away are the sty and the combined hen-house and wine-store. The water-level in the adjoining well is about 10 ft. down.

To avoid the danger of wind tearing the vines right out of this loose soil, they are planted (there is no grafting on these phylloxera-free sands) at a depth of 28 in. after trenching by hand to a depth of 32 in. Digging the ground thus, a man deals with less than 100 sq. yds. in a day. In March, early potatoes are planted between the rows and lifted at the end of May. The main field crops are rye and maize, which cover $4\frac{1}{4}$ and 3 acres respectively. There are another $1\frac{1}{2}$ acres of late crop potatoes (May to September), and also $\frac{3}{4}$ acre of sugar-beet (an experiment; conditions do not seem suitable), and a similar area under market-garden crops. Besides the famous paprika, which gives an illusion of satisfied hunger to these underfed people, he grows melons, peas, and beans, and various other vegetables.

Remote from medical and veterinary assistance, a long way from schools for the children, with no prospect of an electricity supply or of the telephone for many years to come, the isolated *tanya* can hardly claim to represent a satisfactory type of settlement. On the other hand, the large agglomeration, though conducive to the efficiency of services and utilities, raises such awkward problems for agriculture that it has little to recommend it. Eventually the problem may well be solved by the development of motor transport which would make the farmer-town a feasible base of operations and enable the *tanya* dweller to return to the amenities of the larger settlement.[1] Whether the settlement pattern is reshaped on the lines of the Russian 'agro-town' or on the American model, with city-based 'suitcase farmers', the present arrangement of small fragmented holdings will have to be swept away. Kecskemet itself had been selected by the Plan as one of the thirteen farmer-towns for industrial development, and several factories have appeared since our visit in 1948.

[1] See our *Leçons de l'agriculture américaine*, pp. 145, 198; note also the absence of any trend towards the concentration of farm dwellings into larger nucleations in the pre-motor car era, p. 153.

312. The free-range pastoralism of the celebrated *puszta*, whose delightful costumes and folklore make a strange contrast with their social conditions,[1] extended at one time over the whole region south-west of Kecskemet. In 1911 a village was established in part of the Bugac *puszta* eighteen miles from the town, and it now has 200 farms with between 21½ and 27 acres each, while 1,100 isolated and substantially larger *tanyas* share a far greater area, some of them reaching as much as 55 acres. The transition from steppe pasture to tillage represents a very considerable degree of intensification, and the process has been accelerated by reform measures, but unfortunately the land has had to be allocated in fragments that are pitifully small. As in Brandenburg, a holding of 12½ acres on poor sandy soils is barely enough for a family to live on, and the mistake made in East Germany of not adjusting the size of grants to the fertility of the soil was repeated here. On the famous Hortobagy *puszta* there have been even more spectacular changes. From 1939 onwards the pastoral economy, together with its shelters built of reeds, has retreated in the face of irrigated farming, with an emphasis on rice, lucerne, barley and oats.

Bugac now has only about 2,500 acres of pastures left, half of which belong to the town and half to the State. The pastoral industry, however, is entirely in the hands of the latter, which has developed the region into a breeding-ground for selected stock: thirty Lepidoir horses, forty-five cattle of the old Hungarian breed, about 100 'Cornwall' pigs, 220 Hungarian sheep, and a large number of poultry. State farms have a long history in the country, for they are directly descended from the royal domains, which were also administered as single units and performed functions rather similar to those of the Soviet State farms. The new régime has confirmed this role, and though individual domains have been reduced in size they have greatly increased in numbers. The 1950-4 Plan anticipated 'the development of State properties', those 'great Socialist enterprises, model properties and centres of scientific agriculture . . . examples of a rational farm system which will supply breeding stock and selected seeds to the working peasantry and above all to the co-operatives . . . and will do their utmost to guarantee the non-agricultural population their requirements of food products'. The Plan also made provision for 'the investment of 1,500 million florins in five years for the development and mechanization of State properties and to equip them with breeding stock and with necessary buildings'. In 1952 State farms accounted for 12·7 per cent. of the

[1] See *Ceux de la puszta*, by Illhyès (Paris, 1936), a tragic story, but very near to the truth (cf. *Tobacco Road* and *The Grapes of Wrath*).

arable land, but the Plan had allotted them only 10 per cent. They had inherited the lands belonging to the rich peasants or *kulaks* sooner than had been expected; they had also taken over the holdings of peasants who had opted for factory work. The fluctuations in their yields, however, demonstrated their lack of scientific methods. There is little doubt that Hungarian agricultural science still lags behind Germany and the West, but teaching is rapidly bridging the gap. The objective, 'a tenth of the land in State farms', had been kept in view.

313. The Beni-Amir of Morocco had to be persuaded and even forced to give up their extensive herding and cereal cultivation for irrigated farming (Chapter V). Many of the herdsmen-cereal farmers of the great plains of Eastern Europe, on the other hand, from Rumania and Yugoslavia through Hungary to Slovakia and Southern Poland, do not know the meaning of irrigation, especially in so far as market-garden crops are concerned. Many Rumanians, even today, do almost completely without vegetables of any kind. Elsewhere, jostled into exile by the pressure of population to which his narrow native lowland fell an early victim, the Bulgarian emigrant has settled, and introduced the market garden. The Hungarian rarely utters the word 'garden' without qualifying it as 'Bulgarian'.

Szentes, a farmer-town in the south and the birthplace of Hungarian socialism, is famous chiefly as the leader of one agrarian revolt after another. The Bulgarians are still the market-gardeners of the environs of Budapest, but here, realizing that there was more money in the vegetable trade, they left production to the local people.

One of these local men at Szentes cultivates $8\frac{3}{4}$ acres with the help of six permanent and four to six seasonal workers at various times of the year. On average, therefore, one man looks after no more than 1 acre of this land. Bulgarian traditions, born in a region even more overpopulated than this, persist, and not even an inch of ground is wasted, not even the ridges of the low embankments bordering the irrigation channels. A motor pump which draws its water from the river supplies the latter, and the square garden sections are periodically flooded. Double cropping is the rule except for paprika, which occupies the ground too long. It applies, however, to all the other vegetables—cucumbers and lettuces,[1] which are grown in frames, tomatoes, cabbages, onions, carrots, etc. The second crop may sometimes be maize, which is then sown at the end of August and reaped in mid-October.

The local market for early vegetables is negligible, and the growers

---
[1] Eaten with sugar.

have to dispatch their produce to Budapest or even as far as Vienna. Most of them grow their own wheat ($1\frac{1}{2}$ acres in a garden of $7\frac{1}{2}$ acres in one example) after the fashion of the Spanish *huertas*. In 1948 they were, in any case, compelled to supply the State with 1 cwt. per acre of the total holding, and when food is scarce, as it was then, they try to satisfy their own requirements for bread. Like the gardeners of Vaucluse during the war, they sometimes keep a cow to supply their own families with milk. The land which has now been granted to these people, often in parcels of $7\frac{1}{2}$ acres, formerly belonged to the town, and was managed with hired labour. For the manual work performed in the cultivation of maize and wheat, the men received a third and a tenth of the harvest respectively. It appears, therefore, that the first act of a predominantly Communist government led to a kind of decollectivization and to the furtherance of private enterprise.

6. The Early Days of the Producers' Co-operatives—Recent Developments

314. When we were in Hungary in April 1948 the word *kolkhoz* was banned from the official vocabulary, and it was hardly possible at that stage to give serious consideration to the idea of creating producers' co-operatives. The co-operative principle was applied only to buying and selling and to the tractor and machinery stations. Nevertheless, four experimental co-operatives were discreetly trying out the new formula.[1] Before the war, at Etyek, twenty miles south-west of Budapest, an estate of 11,300 acres was owned by a female member of the Metternich family. In 1948 twelve previously landless families, former employees of the estate and Communists to a man, were voluntarily constituted into a 'pilot co-operative' based on the 245 acres which had already been allocated to them by the land reforms. The region has suffered less than most from shortage of land, and it had been possible to grant $11\frac{1}{4}$ acres per household, $14\frac{1}{4}$ if there were three children, and even $23\frac{3}{4}$ with five children.

The State advanced half the money needed to buy twenty pure-bred heifers on condition that the beasts would not be resold for at least three years. A stockman is in charge of the cow-house and another

---

[1] During a series of lectures we were invited to give at the Agronomic University at Budapest, we informed our audience of their existence for the first time. Some Communist students were actually sent down from their university for having discussed collectivization before the time was ripe, i.e. before 1948. We had some difficulty in being allowed to visit Etyek.

specialist is responsible for the 110 young ewes. About 55 lb. of cheese per animal can be made every year from the sheep's milk—a higher yield than in Corsica—and the price it fetches is equal to the original cost of the ewes. As a general rule, in all countries sheep give quicker returns than cattle.

Two-thirds of the fields were regrouped by exchanges with neighbours, but as far as the quality of the land was concerned the co-operative got slightly the worst of the deal.[1] The work put in by each member is noted at the time, and wages are paid on the basis of 10 florins net a day (nearly 6s. in 1952) after taxes and various other items have been deducted. Forty per cent. of the balance of money was then put aside for financing the next season, and 60 per cent. was divided between the members. The allotments, however, were based not on the amount of work done, as in a collectivist economy, but on the original acreage of land contributed. This was a capitalist principle, and in effect the financial structure was closely akin to capitalism.

There were no horses, and it was not intended to buy any. A motor cultivator had been hired from the State, but it was rather pathetic to see it coupled with the traditional wooden roller. The purchase of a tractor was planned as soon as funds would allow, but all the heavy work was already being done by the State tractor and machinery station, which was actually housed in the co-operative's own buildings.

315. The Cominform resolution of June 1948 condemning Yugoslavia reproached her 'for avoiding the questions of class struggle and of the limitation of capitalist elements in the countryside'. Moreover, at that time 15 per cent. of the cultivated area was in State farms, and with its 774 *zadrugas* the country had advanced further than any other except Bulgaria, along the road to rural collectivization.

The political consequences of this reprimand are well known, but the other people's democracies, where such criticisms would have been much more easily justified, clearly understood the message it contained for them. On 20 August 1948 Rakosi, addressing the peasants of Kecskemet, declared: 'Two roads are open to the Hungarian peasantry. The old order of individual cultivation is ruled by the principle that

[1] When the collective is accorded official status, it will make exchanges advantageous to itself. Rakosi, in May 1953, declared: 'During the advance towards the consolidation of farm units, which is inevitable if the large-scale organization of agricultural production is to be achieved, the authorities have often lost sight of the interests of the working peasantry. On several occasions, during the socialization of a village, we have noticed that, generally speaking, not enough consideration was given to the peasants who worked on their own account, and who, after all, make up the greater part of the rural population.'

"might is right": the *kulaks* are ruining the poorer working peasantry.... We desire that the worker in the countryside should also share in all the rewards of cultivation ... that the differences between town and country should disappear.... With present methods of production on 5 to 20 acres it is not possible to attain that material and cultural standard of living ... the working peasantry chooses the road to co-operation.'[1]

Fifteen months beforehand, the same Rakosi, during an electoral meeting at Pecs on 11 May 1947, had asserted the need 'to guarantee absolutely the small and medium landowner-farmers in their continuing and hereditary right to their property'. In 1949 more than half the farms in Hungary were of less than $7\frac{1}{2}$ acres and more than four-fifths had less than 15 acres.[2] More precisely, there were 630,000 'poor' farms of less than $11\frac{1}{4}$ acres, 400,000 'medium' farms of $11\frac{1}{4}$ to 35 acres, and less than 62,000 farms of over 35 acres, belonging to 'rich' peasants. These are important facts, for Stalin reminded us that the class struggle in rural areas is carried on 'with the poor peasants acting in support of the working class, with the medium peasant as a class ally and the *kulak* as a class enemy'.

Taken in conjunction with the small output of tractors and machinery by local industry, this predominance of excessively small holdings, which is the natural consequence of overpopulation, renders mechanization on an individual basis economically impossible. The pattern evolved in the United States, with its greater industrial development and its comparative freedom from the rural overcrowding common to Europe, is quite inappropriate in this context. Finally, and in contrast with Switzerland or the Low Countries, private peasant enterprise would have been handicapped by the widespread ignorance of efficient agricultural techniques.

316. Following on the experiments in the spring of 1948, by the autumn of the same year there had grown a total of 350 co-operatives, a number which rose to 1,500 by the end of 1949, to 2,272 by 1950, to 4,650 by 1951, and to 5,315 by the end of 1952. By this time they were cultivating 3,200,000 acres of arable land, or 22·8 per cent. of the Hungarian total. They also included 250,000 acres of arable land which was still being farmed privately (1·8 per cent. of the total) and 590,000 acres of collective pastures and vineyards. They embraced 318,500 families with 447,000 workers, and by May 1953 these figures

---

[1] 'The system of small farms is not competent to free humanity from the poverty of the masses' (Lenin).

[2] In Rumania in 1948, out of more than 3 million farm units, well over half had less than $7\frac{1}{4}$ acres and less than a quarter had more than $12\frac{1}{4}$ acres.

had risen to 340,000 and nearly 500,000 respectively. These statistics reveal that in many families some members preferred to remain outside the organization, and continued to farm their own small holdings (average of ½ acre per family) and tend their own livestock. By law they were allowed to keep one cow, one calf, one sow and its litter, a pig for fattening, five sheep or goats, and as many chickens, rabbits, and bees as they wished. Together with the State farms, which comprised 12·7 per cent. of the cultivated land, these co-operatives made up a total of 37·3 per cent. for the socialized portion of the agricultural area (40 per cent. in May 1953).

The co-operatives are favoured, not only by the credits they receive for equipment, but also by tax remissions and by reductions in the volume of cereals to be delivered at low prices. The latter were fixed at $3\frac{1}{4}$ cwt. per acre for private property and $2\frac{1}{2}$ for co-operatives. Some propaganda agents were suggesting that they might even be revoked altogether for the socialized enterprises, and the State seems perfectly justified in encouraging the more efficient forms of production.[1] The French Plan for modernization and mechanization has the same end in view. The greatest difficulty, which was also experienced in the U.S.S.R. in 1929-31,[2] is to persuade the peasant to bring all his equipment and livestock, especially the latter. Plessz reveals that sometimes they join a co-operative only after having 'ceded' their animals and farm implements to relatives outside the organization.[3]

In 1952, 19·6 per cent. of the pigs and 11 per cent. of the cattle in Hungary belonged to the State farms, but they had only attained the density of cattle in the whole country during the course of that same year. The co-operatives, on the other hand, possessed no more than 274,000 sheep, 151,000 cattle, and 522,000 pigs, or 14 per cent., 6 per cent., and 13 per cent. respectively of the pre-war national totals. Thus the *Hungarian Bulletin* had occasion to write: 'On 30 September 1952 in spite of substantial increases in the number of livestock, the density of animals in the co-operatives has not always attained the national average.' According to the Census of 1946, the same situation existed on the medium-sized farms. If a man felt he might be accused of being a *kulak*, he converted his farm investments into cash without delay. The droughts of 1950 and 1952, allied to the fear of collectivization, seem to have

[1] So long as it does not threaten liberty of action and free speech.
[2] In the Ukraine at this time, some peasants are said to have killed themselves by over-eating in an attempt to deprive the collectives of their livestock.
[3] We shall study the different types of co-operative in the section on Czechoslovakia, where there is a scheme of progressive collectivization very similar to the one here.

provoked a certain amount of slaughtering, but no doubt the position is still very different from that in the U.S.S.R. between 1929 and 1931.

317. The picture as revealed in these statistics is quite unlike the Soviet model. The average co-operative had less than 595 acres of crop land, as against 10,000 or more for its Soviet counterpart, and the dimensions of the latter are still tending to increase. Moreover, the average number of members is only eighty-four, whereas in the U.S.S.R. these would hardly make up a 'brigade'. The large number of workers, about one per acre, was another feature, due not so much to the large demand for labour as to the continuing overpopulation of the countryside. The 1950-4 Plan foresaw the absorption of 480,000 workers into industry, and from 1952-4 a contingent of 60,000 a year was to be supplied by agriculture. Most of those concerned were young people, and they were given a period of initial training.[1]

With the shortage of equipment that exists there is sometimes a seasonal shortage of manpower, in spite of the chronic surplus of labour. Part of the 1951 harvest, which came at the end of a very wet season, was lost through shortage of machinery or of seasonal workers.[2] The provision of farm equipment is a matter of priority. At the end of 1951 the 367 stations had 9,500 tractors out of a total of 12,000: the overall total in 1949 had been only 3,500. In 1952, 82 per cent. of the wheat and rye on State farms and 43 per cent. of the wheat on producers' co-operatives were harvested with binders.[3] The proportions were much lower on privately owned land. According to the target set in 1951, which revised

[1] Number of workers in mines and manufacturing industries in Hungary, in thousands:

Year	Workers
1938	330
1943	450
1945	241
1948	383
1951	550

In 1953 Rakosi announced an annual increase of 200,000 in the number of workers in all categories.

[2] In the opinion of Fetjö, the non-participation of the co-operators' wives and families in the harvest, together with the recruitment of labour in industry, was an important contributory cause.

[3] Hungarian machinery and tractor stations:

Year	Number of tractors (average)	Thousands of acres ploughed
1948	700	225
1949	2,800	1,750
1950	6,000	3,375
1951	8,800	5,750

N.B.—Work per tractor is less than in East Germany.

THE PRODUCERS' CO-OPERATIVES

the lower estimates of 1949, by 1954, at the end of the first Plan, there were to be 26,000 tractors, 9,060 binders and even 2,600 combines:[1] also 5,000 large tractor-drawn ploughs and as many large thirty-row drills.

Harvesting machinery had been sorely needed already in 1950, but as a result of the losses in 1951 it was given top priority. Calculations based on the need for agricultural labour for every month in the year show a remarkable maximum in July and again in September-October (maize).[2] Accordingly, Hungary turned out only 1,700 tractors in 1952 (but they were more powerful), as against 3,000 in 1951, but the production of binders was doubled (2,500 and 1,250) and of combines more than doubled (500 and 200).

318. Ever since the depression of 1929, overpopulation and the lack of sale for farm produce in Eastern Europe have stressed the need for industrialization and its corollary, the reorientation of agriculture. The latter must henceforth place its emphasis on satisfying the needs of the home market and on raising the nutritional standards of the new and increasingly productive urban populations. In other words, it must now turn its attention to livestock and forage crops. There is room also for the expansion of industrial crops, which will not only serve as raw materials for developing industries, but also help to cut down imports. The Plan foreshadows increases of between 27 per cent. and 39 per cent. in the production of sugar-beet, sunflower, flax, and hemp. All the people's democracies are showing similar trends, and all are following the route mapped out for them by Western Europe 100 or even 200 years ago.

Of special interest is the development of cotton. Although near its climatic limit (the extreme limit, as we shall see, is in southern Slovakia), its cultivation is forced on Hungary by the restrictions on international trade. Introduced in 1948, it occupied 875 acres in 1949, 14,750 in 1950,

[1] 1,300 in August 1953.

[2] Theoretical farm labour requirements (arable land, gardens, vines and grassland) in millions of days per month:

January	.	.	1·0	July	.	.	42·5
February	.	.	1·7	August	.	.	28·0
March	.	.	10·1	September	.	.	34·0
April	.	.	22·2	October	.	.	30·1
May	.	.	23·2	November	.	.	9·5
June	.	.	32·9	December	.	.	5·6

(After Meszaros, quoted by Plessz.)

The fluctuations would not be so great if animal husbandry, which gives more work in the winter, had been taken into account. But the range would still be far too wide, and this is characteristic of countries dominated by cereal cultivation and still poorly equipped with modern machinery.

70,000 in 1951, and 112,500 in 1952. In 1949 the Plan aimed to reach 144,000 acres by 1954, but in 1952 the targets were revised to 139,000 for 1953 and 277,000 for 1954. Several other crops have also been introduced, including ramie and lemons, the latter grafted on *Citrus trifoliata*. A new crop which is perhaps better suited to the conditions is the groundnut, while rice, which first appeared shortly before the war, already in 1951 occupied 63,000 acres of the 71,000 acres planned for 1954.[1]

Difficulties of food supply have been precipitated, particularly in years of poor harvest, by the growing consumption of the rural areas themselves, the appreciable decline in cereals in favour of industrial crops, and by the movement back to the towns. Rationing was abolished on 2 December 1951, but certain restrictions were reimposed on cereals in June 1952. Sales on the free market were still forbidden until after the official quotas had been fulfilled and handed over to the State.[2]

Although agriculture seems to have made a promising start, it is still lagging a long way behind industry. By 1950-1, given average weather, the farmers could be counted on to equal their pre-war output,[3] but in 1951 the index of industrial production was 150 (250 compared with 1928), and a further 25 per cent. expansion was planned for 1952. The more rapid revival of industry is a feature common to all the people's democracies, and to the U.S.S.R. as well. In 1951 Hungarian industry accounted for 55 per cent. of the national income, agriculture for only 24 per cent. Moreover, the Plan for 1955-9 aims to double the output of coal (to 40-50 million tons), steel (to 3·5-4 million tons), and electricity (to 10,000-12,000 million kw.h.).

To transform Hungary into an industrial country with fully developed agricultural resources is the bedrock of the Government's policy, and is the solution which we have often advocated as the most practicable in areas of rural overpopulation. So long as the manufacture of farm equipment does not continue to be sacrificed in the interests of

[1] According to the Plan, there was to be a reduction of 325,000 acres for bread cereals, of 287,500 acres for oil-seeds, and of 232,500 acres for uncultivated land. The main increases were to be for fodder-beet (86,250), sugar-beet (14,350), maize (144,000), tobacco (86,200), lucerne (70,500 with green crops), vegetables and spices (71,800), leguminous food crops (71,800), rice, and cotton.

[2] Rakosi declared in May 1953: 'We have made errors in our policy towards the peasants. The organization of delivery norms is lacking in simplicity and the changes which have been made almost every year prevent the working peasantry from managing their land with a full knowledge of the situation for they are not aware of their future obligations.'

[3] 1951 was a very good year, and farm production reached 116 per cent. of pre-war; but 1952 was very dry, and the pre-war average was not attained. A record harvest has been reported for 1953.

heavy industry and armaments—the latter especially—the growth of industry should operate as an increasingly favourable factor in the pursuit of agricultural progress. At the moment, however, the rate of investment in the land is insufficient 'to exploit the possibilities offered by the regrouping of property' (Fetjö).

The ailments of the present day are, to some extent, growing pains, but they are also symptoms of resistance to collectivization on the part of considerable numbers of peasants, even of some who subscribe to the Workers' Party. But it would be foolish to regard the Hungarian peasantry as universally and irrevocably opposed to the ideas symbolized by the *kolkhoz*, and it would be an error to believe in the possibility of restoring the *status quo ante*, not only in Hungary, but in the other people's democracies as well. Sentiments of this kind might even contain an element of danger if they led us to underestimate the competition which eastern European agriculture might one day offer to our own. In particular, if she wishes to avoid the kind of retrogression which has occurred in Spain, France must urgently answer the call for equipment from her own countryside.[1]

[1] On 4 July 1953, Imre Nagy, the President of the Council, announced a fundamental change in the country's agricultural policy: 'The aims of the enlarged five-year plans are, in many respects, more than we can hope to reach. Too much industrialization, the over-rapid growth of heavy industry and the large investments that these have entailed have not permitted, with the economic resources at the disposal of the country, the development of agriculture. The help needed by individual peasants has not been given.

'The large number of schemes for land consolidation and the vast scale on which they have been carried out have threatened the security of the peasant undertaking, especially as they have been accompanied by abuses and threats which have violated our peasantry's sense of justice. It is a well-known fact that our agricultural production is firmly based on individual holdings.

'Moreover, the most serious result of the over-rapid development of the co-operative movement has been the great anxiety evinced by the working peasantry as a result of the abuses which have occurred, and the violation of the principle of free consent deserves special mention in this connexion.

'The Government intends to assure the security of production and of peasant ownership by every means in its power. In order to ensure the most absolute regard for the principle of free consent, it will allow members of co-operatives who wish to return to individual production because they consider it offers them better prospects to leave their producers' co-operatives at the end of the current season. It is prepared to go even further and authorize the dissolution of producers' co-operatives where the majority of the members wish it. Meanwhile, the Government will continue to assure the producers' co-operatives of considerable support; it will assist their development and the well-being of their members by means of loans and investments, being convinced that the co-operatives represent the most practicable method of promoting the interests of the peasantry.'

XVI

From the Slovak Peasant to the Czech Co-operative[1] and the Soviet *Kolkhoz*

1. The Slovak Farm, Still Too Small and Overcrowded

319. Where it runs near the foot of the Slovakian Ore Mountains, the River Hornad, a tributary of the Sajo, which in turn joins the Theiss, traverses a wide belt of Tertiary plateaux whose valleys merge into the Hungarian plain. The village of Myslava (Fig. 27), a typical valley settlement which stands astride a tributary of the Hornad, lies nearly four miles west of the splendid Dom, or Cathedral—which has coloured tiles like the one at Dijon—of Kosice,[2] the capital of Eastern Slovakia. The evidence of its little Jewish shops and of the narrow turnings leading away from its main streets places it even further east than Mezokovesd. A mere sixty miles separates it from the Soviet Union, which now engulfs the barren highlands of sub-Carpathian Ruthenia to the east. Its climate is in keeping with its position remote from oceanic influences, and with less than 24 in. of rain this is the driest corner in the whole of Slovakia.

The farms are always sited end-on to the road, where a gate and a slightly wider panel of wooden fencing join on to the porch and mark off the end of a long, narrow yard. Here, in the shade of the fruit trees, is a place for the cart, while behind the spacious house—large families are still the rule—with its freshly limed walls, is the barn with its grain-bins, the reserve of food for man and beast, resting directly on the

---

[1] Field studies in July 1938 and September-October 1948, this section being based on our observations during the latter visit. In 1948 there were 80 crowns to the £1, 110 in 1953. For further details and additional descriptions of farms, see our article, 'L'évolution agraire tchécoslovaque', in *Revue du Ministère de l'Agriculture* (December 1948).

[2] In 1948, in the offices of the agricultural station here, the portrait of Christ still hung on the walls, but on either side were those of Gottwald and Stalin. The latter were found similarly placed in some peasant homes, where they had usurped the places formerly occupied by the Emperor and the Empress.

ground. Each farm bakes its own bread in the oven of its summer kitchen, but sometimes they only knead the dough into a round, stick a number on it, and take it to the baker, who has become, quite literally, a 'baker' of bread and little else. The cellar for storing potatoes is next to the road, and the cart can empty its load directly through an opening. A combined stable and cow-house, a lean-to for storing implements, a sty, and a shed where straw is chaffed complete the farm buildings. At the back, behind the buildings, is the dunghill.

The main object of farming is to grow food for the family and to fill the potato store and the bins. Myslava cultivates 900 acres of cereals[1] and over 290 of potatoes, but only 190 of green fodder crops (clover 75, beet $47\frac{1}{2}$, others, including maize, $67\frac{1}{2}$), $7\frac{1}{2}$ of vegetables (beans, cabbage, garlic), and similar acreages of flax and poppy. Cereals (64 per cent.) and potatoes (21 per cent.) thus occupy by far the greater part of the arable land, as in early nineteenth-century Limousin. There are, however, 125 acres of permanent grassland, the hay from which is almost entirely reserved for the village's 166 horses, which give a density of one horse for every 8 acres of ploughland. From Slovakia to Greece, poor farms—farms that are much too small—have this feature in common: a surplus of draught animals.

320. The official statistics detail eleven holdings of less than $1\frac{1}{4}$ acres, 74 of $1\frac{1}{4}$-5 acres, 81 of 5-$12\frac{1}{2}$ acres, and 37 of $12\frac{1}{2}$-25 acres, of which 30 are between $12\frac{1}{2}$ and 15 acres and 3 between 15 and 20 acres. Between them the four 'large' farms of 20-25 acres have bought the only mowing machine in the village (which they use for cutting hay only) and the only reaper (1948). Out of 203 farms, 185 thus lie in the range $1\frac{1}{4}$-15 acres. The largest area is cultivated by the groups 5-$12\frac{1}{2}$ acres (720 acres) and $12\frac{1}{2}$-25 acres (585 acres). The eighty-five holdings of below 5 acres together cover less than 250 acres.

The livestock in the commune included about 500 pigs, including sixty-three sows and five boars. In the summer most of the 350 head of cattle (including 225 cows, only ten of which are ever harnessed) browse the commons, which are on the poorer and more rugged terrain, and receive a supplementary ration of soilage. In winter they are fed mainly on chaff with some potatoes and a little beet, but never on oil cake and very rarely on 'horse hay'. In spite of its small requirements of protein, the horse, as in Brittany, is accorded the best of the food, and the result of this topsy-turvy régime of rations is that the cows do not always average even 220 gallons a year, and over 330 gallons is unusual. As in the Tyrol, milk whole or skimmed (butter is made from it) is

[1] 230 acres of wheat, 200 of rye, 345 of barley, and 125 of oats.

FROM PEASANT TO CO-OPERATIVE AND KOLKHOZ

one of the main items in the diet, together with flour, including even barley flour, and potatoes. The only dish ever served to us at the inn consisted of a prune garnished with potatoes and undercooked dumplings.

321. The peasant whose farm was described above grew very little other than cereals (wheat and rye, 2½ acres each, barley, 3¾, and oats, nearly 2 acres) and potatoes (nearly 2 acres) on his 12½ acres of arable

FIG. 27. Czechoslovakia.

land. If he had any room to spare, he would sow a little maize for fodder and every now and again, particularly after a dry year, half the acreage normally under barley was sown to lucerne. One and a quarter acres of meadow were kept for the sake of the horses, whose rations were sometimes supplemented from the 6-8 cwt. of oats bought annually for the purpose.

The horses were by no means overworked. They were needed on the farm on about 100 days in the year, and were thus available for carting jobs in the town, especially for journeys between the station and the various factories. There were paper, textile and saw mills, and an engineering works was a recent addition. Their demand for transport was swelled by the requirements of reconstruction schemes, and between May or June and the end of September or November the farmer, with his two horses, hired out his services as a carter on between sixty and seventy days at 450-600 crowns a day. These provided his main source of cash earnings. The household spent about 6,000 crowns a year at the grocer's (salt, sugar, coffee, paprika, soap, etc.) and the butcher's and at the Bulgarian market garden which specialized in irrigated vegetables.

All the peasants in the village, with the sole exception of the man with the largest holding, went out in search of seasonal work, preferably with their horses if they had any. Their land kept them in food, but they had to turn elsewhere to provide themselves with the other necessities of life. Their economy, however, has suffered a severe blow since 1948, as the lorry has increasingly deprived them of the urban market for their services. The arrival of tractor stations and their modern equipment[1] was upsetting the balance even further in this land of violent contrasts, where even the airfield, on which a D.C.3 landed during our visit, was mown with the scythe. The great majority of Slovak peasants were already partially unemployed before modern equipment ever appeared, and our peasant at Myslava, for instance, intimated that he was available with his team of horses for 200 days a year. But he used only to find about seventy days of work.

His stock consisted of two cows, but as there were ten mouths to feed on the farm and only two bread-winners—an abnormally low proportion—there was no surplus milk for sale. In any case, the daily output was never more than 2 or 3 gallons. He occasionally sells off an old cow when he gets a calf worth rearing as a follower. Apart from the cows, there were three pigs, and the Food Supply Service, which had introduced a commercial element into the economy rather abruptly, exacted 202 lb. of pork at the controlled price in addition to 220 lb. of beef (one calf), 16 cwt. of potatoes, and 10 cwt. of bread cereals. The last item is very little more than the quantity of oats which has to be purchased. Little produce was sold at the free price; certainly much less than in the fertile parts of East Germany.

The range of equipment compared favourably with most of the other farms in the village. The more important items were a cart, a drill, a roller, a straw-chopper, a winnower, two ploughs with wheels, and a harrow. Hay and corn crops were still mown with a scythe. The farm had to buy its vegetables, but the people could not afford to buy any kind of cloth material. They had great difficulty in believing that

---

[1] We have recorded elsewhere the disgust shown by Georges Solar of Barca at having waited so long before being able to use a mowing machine (eventually provided by the stations): 'If I had bought it ten years earlier, I would have lived ten years longer, I would feel younger, and I could have drunk enough to quench my thirst properly. . . . And now these youngsters are going to use the machines when I've always had to use my hands—it isn't fair!'

in Western Europe farmers bought their clothes ready-made, but grew their own vegetables.[1] Every day the woman wove a length of hemp (grown on the farm) and cotton (bought as yarn) mixture 13 ft. long and 2 ft. wide. In the Tatra the highlander still uses wood to make his own implements and makes his own shoes during the winter.

322. Larger farms exist in greater numbers away from the towns, where part-time cartage no longer offers a source of income. As in Hungary, their farming systems were more diversified, and they pay more attention to green crops, such as clover and lucerne, to maize, which may or may not be cut green for forage, and to fodder beet, etc. A belt of more intensive cultivation about 100 yds. deep often surrounds such villages as Cecejovce,[2] where soils are warmer and less acid. Here are found most of the commune's sown grassland and a greater concentration on row crops. The land beyond is divided into tiny fields of $\frac{1}{4}$ acre or even less, and entirely devoted to the cultivation of four crops. First in the rotation comes the row crop, which may be potatoes, beet, or maize, and the ground is manured at this stage. Wheat, rye, and barley then follow, in that order, with the most exacting crop first.

In Cecejovce the poor peasants with no more than $4\frac{1}{4}$ acres were little more than farm labourers. As in Belgian Flanders (Chapter XI), they had to borrow horses from their richer neighbours. Four days' work at the peak period of the harvest was the rather heavy price they paid for a teamsman and his two small horses for a day. Human portage—loads being carried either on the back or in wheelbarrows—was still, however, much more important than in Belgium. On holdings of $4\frac{1}{4}$-$8\frac{1}{2}$ acres one generally found that a pair of cows served for drawing loads. Oxen were used on larger holdings of up to $14\frac{1}{4}$ acres, and the more affluent peasant had horses. In the whole commune there were 110 of the latter, about forty oxen, and a similar number of draught cows.

2. A Townsman Wine-grower

323. The people of the area round Turner, twenty miles south-west of Kosice, all speak Hungarian, and the Hungarian frontier, which is

[1] Similarly, a 'modern farmer' in Nebraska, on his return from a course at the Agricultural University at Lincoln, told us, during our visit in 1946, about some new substances which had been invented for putting in the soil. He refused to believe that the fertilizers he was talking about had been used on a large scale in Europe for the past three centuries.

[2] Twelve miles south-west of Kosice.

still quite close today, actually passed north of here during the war. Until 1948 most of the vineyards were owned by absentee landlords from Kosice or Bratislava and managed by hired labour. Their produce was an urban luxury in no way related to local peasant traditions. The vines themselves are trained along poles, and the rows, which follow across the fairly sharp slopes, are heavily earthed up in the winter, while the roots are bared again in the summer. Erosion is thus minimized by ridges of earth lying more or less parallel to the contours throughout the year. As in France at one time, the ground is worked over entirely by hand. Even the hoeing is performed manually, and when we suggested to the officials at the State agricultural station that horses or power-winches might be employed, they were still so haunted by the fear of rural unemployment that they refused even to consider such an idea. At their best, yields may reach 64 cwt. an acre, but they average less than 40 cwt. or about 90 gallons.

Most of the scarp north of Turner, which was clad in vineyards before the onset of phylloxera, was never replanted, in spite of its right to the name 'Tokay'. As on the northern scarps of Burgundy only the piles of stones and a few low terrace walls remain as evidence of the enormous efforts made by previous generations to adapt the terrain to the requirements of the vine. The Austro-Hungarian Empire, which tended towards liberalism in its commercial policies, preferred to import cheap wine from abroad.

One vineyard is owned by the manager of a distillery at Presov, who comes down dressed in his 'city clothes'. At one time it covered $1\frac{1}{4}$ acres and had 5,000 plants, but these had fallen to $\frac{3}{4}$ acre and 2,900 plants respectively, which would have been enough to occupy him for 120 days a year—if he had worked there himself. At the beginning of October 1948 he hired a gang of seven pickers (women, paid 70 crowns a day), one basket-carrier, and three wine-pressers (120 crowns), who harvested the whole crop of 36 cwt. in a single day. This was actually rather lower than the average for this well-kept vineyard. The women carefully parted the leaves of every plant to avoid missing the smallest bunch and picked up any fruit which had fallen to the ground, making sure to keep it clean. One sensed that a most precious crop was being gathered, a liquid which they knew flowed in Prague's exclusive Vinarna. For its owner the vineyard is a pleasant country domain rather than a serious business enterprise. He had brought his wife with him, and the scene might well have been from somewhere in south-west France midway through the nineteenth century.

The grapes were pressed by hand and then poured into a miniature wine-press 30 in. in diameter. The must is loaded straight away on to a lorry in 50-gallon barrels and brought to the owner's house, for fear of thieves. With a certain nostalgia, the owner recalled the good old days when gipsies came to the vine harvests and the wine flowed freely. Today none of the vine-gatherers even tastes the wine, but in western Slovakia, which is the only real vine-growing region in the country, a consumption of $1\frac{3}{4}$ pints a day is not at all unusual. The fixed price for wine is over 27 crowns a pint, but as the grower sometimes sells it even dearer than this he can make a living out of about 3,000 plants, and the number of peasant vine-growers is on the increase. Unfortunately, the management of vineyards was deteriorating in consequence, but nine or ten miles to the west, on the contrary, the standards of peasant viticulture were excellent, and every family had $1\frac{1}{2}$-10 acres of vines. Those with 10 acres were rich indeed.

3. Colonization and the Uphill Movement of Vineyards in Moravia

324. Near the Austrian frontier, south of Brno in Moravia, the vine had once been cultivated by German-speaking settlers of Austrian origin. They were expelled at the same time as the Sudetens in 1945. It was intimated to us by a Czech that they were rather backward and sometimes prone to cretinism as a result of too much inbreeding, but his impartiality was a moot point. Until 1945 there existed three distinct social groups somewhat analogous to those of the villages in Lorraine during the nineteenth century. Firstly, the small vine-grower, who corresponded with the vine-grower-labourer of Pouilly-sur-Meuse,[1] was highly specialized, worked his land entirely by hand and only raised a few other crops, and possibly kept a cow for his own needs. With his small family holding, which included perhaps 1-12 acres of vines and even less of other crops, he represented the intermediate class. Sometimes the holding was too small even to support the whole family. The wealthy class, on the other hand, consisted of farmers who had one or more plough teams, which they would hire out to till the vine-growers' land, and who specialized in the cultivation of field crops. Their farms were often of 25-125 acres, and gave employment to the labourers who made up almost half the total population and constituted the lowest class in the village.

Thus before the war at Dunajovice, which is two miles north-west of the famous Mikulov wine region, there were 700 households, and

[1] *Voyages en France d'un agronome*, Chapter XI.

330 of them had their own holdings. A proportion of the latter had to seek part-time work off their own land, but 45 per cent. of the population consisted of agricultural workers, who were completely dependent on their wages. In 1939 1,940 of the commune's 5,000 acres were under the vine, and this was the highest proportion in the whole of Moravia. By 1948 this acreage had declined by about 25 per cent., and in the whole region the vine did not often surpass an eighth and averaged about a tenth of the agricultural area.

Under these conditions of dry climate and fairly easily worked black soils, a good average farm whose occupants had not fallen victim to the expulsions numbered about two horses, three or four cows, two young cattle, and a few pigs. About 25 acres was a typical size, and of these, 5 were equally divided between the vine on the one hand and fruit and vegetables on the other; 4 acres were devoted to pasture, 6 to row crops (beet, maize, potatoes), and 10 to cereals. The greater intensiveness and the emphasis on livestock and horticulture stand out clearly by comparison with Slovakia. The presence of privately-owned pastures, which is a feature of Western Europe, is another point worthy of attention. The countryside reminds one of the Gironde and the Lot-et-Garonne landscape rather than of the endless vineyards between Narbonne and Montpellier.

The low-lying areas show a variety of crops, but they are liable to frost, and the vineyards, with their scattering of apricot and almond trees, are sited exclusively on the scarps.[1] The vines themselves are trained along wooden stakes and are planted at intervals of just over 1 yd. in rows 4 ft. or more apart. The steeper scarp-tops, which were equally devoted to the vine before the appearance of phylloxera, have since been abandoned in favour of the lower slopes. Here the spread of high-yielding varieties, like Blue Portuguese, and even of a number of hybrids which give deep-coloured wines, has been encouraged by certain sections of the wine trade at the expense of quality.

A hundred and thirty-two work-days are needed per acre when only manual labour is used. The ground has to be hoed five times a year, according to local custom, and soil has to be carried back to the top of all the steep slopes. The first of these operations alone takes sixty days per acre every year. Horses, however, are used on two-thirds of the area, mainly on the gentler gradients, and the total then falls to only eighty days. Methods have progressed further than in Slovakia, but the vine-grower still breaks his back on the sharper slopes and

[1] On 8 and 11 May 1953 all the lowland vineyards of Alsace were severely affected by frost, but those on the scarps were undamaged.

becomes prematurely old and bent. Only the power-winch can save him from this fate.

325. The Slav settlers who replaced the Austrians of Dunajovice came from many different regions. The Moravians and Slovaks from the lowlands are familiar with wheat and vine, on which they base their economy. But these crops are foreign to the men from the highlands, who knew only rye and potatoes and pastures. In the last days of September 1948 we saw some of the results of their ignorance at Perna, where many vines had not been treated against mildew and had shed all their leaves. 'Only the next generation will change this,' remarked Professor Blaha from the Agronomic Institute at Brno. Let us hope, however, that changes will come sooner than the professor thinks. A few of the mountain folk have decided that making wine is a lot more difficult than drinking it and have returned to their homeland in disgust.

The influx of settlers has led to social as well as ethnological changes, for the transformation of the racial character of the region has been accompanied by the emergence of a more egalitarian social structure, the commune now counting only 5 per cent. of agricultural labourers. This has been accomplished by means of agrarian reforms, which followed similar lines to those already described. Holdings were granted according to the size of each family and according to the 'occupational record'. Those who had worked their own land before were favoured as being likely to make better farmers. Every family thus received between $11\frac{1}{4}$ and $21\frac{1}{4}$ acres, part in arable land and part in vineyards ($1\frac{1}{4}$-$3\frac{3}{4}$ acres). Whether they liked it or not, they all became vine-grower-farmers, and the retreat from specialization which this has entailed is a development of dubious merit.

The small farmer harnesses his cows with a collar, singly in the vineyards or in pairs on the ploughland. Before they came here three-fifths of the settlers were farm workers and the remainder had 'dwarf' holdings of 3 or 4 acres, which they had to give up to the local committees for redistribution to their neighbours. They were allowed to bring their livestock and farm implements, and find themselves rather cramped for space in the vine-grower's yards, which had never before accommodated any draught equipment. The low stalls seem very small, and carts have to be dismantled before being brought in. As the village now has only 200 farming families out of its total of 500, most of them have fortunately been able to take over other buildings.

As in the Valais[1] and, for that matter, in the whole of Central Europe, the small Austrian vine-grower used to sell the greater part of his

---
[1] See Chapter VIII.

harvest to the wine-making merchant, who cleared most of the profits. He made a little wine in his own tiny cellar so as to exploit the higher prices which returned some time after the harvest. Only occasionally did he keep the wine for a year or two to let it mature. Today the wine co-operative, which has superseded the merchant, is prepared to treat only 30 per cent. of the harvest. In practice, this is made up by what the poorer vine-growers have to sell straight away. Even if the owners of medium-sized vineyards—there are no large ones left—continue to make and mature their own wine, however, this restriction forces the smaller men to follow suit to some extent, and the high cost of re-equipping the cellars, which were all dismantled and sometimes even demolished, makes life difficult for them. Indeed, it is true to say that by 1948 Communist Moravia was less advanced along the road to co-operative manufacture than was Languedoc in 1938, where the harvest from all but the large vineyards was already being treated in common.

326. Agronomists throughout Czechoslovakia have been assigned to a great task of 'geonomic'—or soil utilization—study which was originally begun about 1930. They proceed from a thorough analysis of each region, examining relief, geology, soil, climatic factors, and present farming systems, each in turn. Finally, taking into account the nation's needs, they determine the most appropriate locations for each individual crop. For every commune a set of twenty-eight maps analysing the relevant factors serves as a basis for recommendations, which are then gradually incorporated in production plans. Finally, sixteen soil samples from every commune have been analysed.

The national drink in Czechoslovakia is beer, and the country therefore only intends to expand current wine production (6,600,000 gallons) to the point where it will make up for the 3·3-4·4 million gallons formerly imported. This means another market lost to the Mediterranean, doubtless for a long time to come. The 'Wine Survey', which records every variety produced in every commune, aims to eliminate all inferior vine stocks and eventually to forbid cultivation on lowlying slopes. Vineyards are thus spreading on to higher ground once again, whereas in France, where this example might be followed with advantage, the reverse has been true for the past 100 years or so. In 1953 various schemes put forward by the vine-growers' unions and the French Ministry of Agriculture suggested that a similar 'survey' might be instituted.[1]

[1] See '*Le problème viticole*' in *Bulletin des transports* (February 1953) and *Population* (No. 1, 1953).

France must beware of the empiricism which is causing her agriculture to lag behind while other countries are minimizing the delays between experimental results and widespread practical application. The uprooting of hybrid vine stocks began in Czechoslovakia in 1948, and Italian Riesling and green Weltwing, which both combine quality and quantity, were being brought in at the same time. In pursuance of its social ideals, however, the Government was hoping to increase the number of producers by allowing no more than a tenth of the cultivated acreage of any farm to be devoted to the vine. We have already questioned the wisdom of this policy, which is now in any case being reversed by the process of collectivization.

4. The Four Types of Producers' Co-operatives

327. The agrarian reforms of 1945 in Hungary and Germany were directed mainly against the landowning aristocracy and middle class. In Czechoslovakia, however, there had already been some fairly drastic reforms in 1920, and the first agrarian measures after the war, in 1945, were essentially of a nationalist character.[1] Some 2,500,000 acres of land belonging to Slovakian or Hungarian 'collaborators' and 6,500,000 acres of German-owned property, much of it in Sudetenland, were confiscated by the State. At the same time 3,000,000 German-speaking people, 700,000 of whom had been making their living from the land, were expelled: 158,000 Czech families took up the land vacated by 250,000 Sudeten farmers and their dependants. Contrary to the usual rules, therefore, this wave of settlement actually resulted in an increase in the average size of farm.

Peasants who had previously subsisted on 'dwarf' holdings of $2\frac{1}{2}$–5 acres gladly accepted their grants of about 25 acres (maximum 43) of new land in a moderately fertile region. The small farmer from the rich loams of Moravia, however, where yields of 32 tons of beet and 32 cwt. of barley to the acre were the rule, was not nearly so anxious to move to areas of rather poor podsolized soils, where he could grow only rye and potatoes or, at best, a few fodder crops. His reluctance was even greater when his new land was well over 1,500 ft. up, and

---

[1] A second reform, in 1948, limited the amount of land a peasant family could own to 125 acres (and to 10 acres for anyone not farming the land himself), thus following the example set by Poland in 1944 and subsequently by Rumania in 1945. In Yugoslavia the maximum varied between 50 and 87 acres from one locality to another; in Albania and Bulgaria it was 50 acres (75 in Dobrudja); and these laws dated from 1945. At that time Czechoslovakia had chosen a more moderate course, therefore.

FOUR TYPES OF PRODUCERS' CO-OPERATIVES

cold and excessive rainfall[1] endangered the harvests. In order to put these areas to some purpose as quickly as possible, and to forestall any criticism by the expropriated Germans on the grounds that the land was lying unused, tillage was often converted to grassland and occasionally reafforested. The process is similar to the extensification which we have proposed for the Alps in the Tyrol and the Valais. Whereas the lower limit for alpine pastures in the latter is about 6,250 ft., however, here they have descended as far as 1,300 ft., which is certainly too low when considered in relation to the density of population.

328. While this type of colonization has been proceeding on an individual basis, elsewhere a few co-operatives were started on large expropriated estates which were handed over to their former employees, or on land granted by the reforms of 1948 which its owners had decided to farm collectively. The State provided most of the working capital in the form of stock and equipment existing on the estates and also of loans for modernization. The contributions which their members brought into the co-operatives remained negligible. East-northeast of Prague, near Trutnov, and not far from the new Polish frontier, the Vicice co-operative in October 1948 comprised 430 acres of ploughland as against 835 acres, or two-thirds of the total area, of grassland. The proportion of the latter compared with only a quarter for the large German farm which had been here before. For five months each year, between May and September, the co-operative took 200 young cattle of eight months to two years from its 210 members. Most of the latter sent no stock at all; those who did sent from two to four animals each. The object of the scheme was to encourage stock-farming among the new settlers from central Bohemia whose previous 'dwarf' holdings had never been large enough to keep more than one or two stall-fed dairy cows.

329. Here too the law on producers' co-operatives[2] which was promulgated on 23 February 1949 was officially justified on the grounds of the country's low productivity of agricultural labour: eight times lower than in industry, 28,000 crowns as against 230,000. The first

[1] 20 in. of rain in the central part of the Bohemian plateau near Prague, but totals reach 40-60 in. in the bordering mountains.

[2] Nearly all our information on this subject comes from various issues of *Interagra* (Prague), the organ of the Czechoslovak Institute for collaboration in agriculture and forestry; and from *The New Road for Czechoslovakian Agriculture*, a pamphlet by J. Kotatko (Orbis, Prague, 1951), from which the quotations which follow have been taken. For a record of the beginnings of producers' co-operatives see 'Czechoslovakian Agrarian Evolution' in the journal quoted above.

plans had concentrated on industry, while agricultural development had remained practically at a standstill, because 'of the out-dated character of individual production on 1,500,000 farms with 33,000,000 separate parcels of land'. The first preparatory committees in the spring of 1949 sometimes devoted their energies to secondary matters, like the establishment of co-operative laundering or poultry-keeping. Perhaps they wished to comply with the letter of the law without raising such controversial issues as the socialization of the land.

The Communist Congress, however, at the end of May 1949 insisted that machines, draught animals, and peasant labour should be pooled for the harvest. This first step towards collectivization needed no new machines or investments. Moreover, it was facilitated by certain traditions of mutual aid which had not entirely disappeared,[1] and was successfully put into effect on about 1,000 co-operatives. The second step was taken in the autumn of the same year, when sowing was organized on a communal basis, and in every village groups of adjacent fields were sown to a single crop. Meanwhile, boundaries between different properties began to be removed for the first time. The harvest was shared, after all expenses had been deducted, on the basis of the amount of land contributed by each individual. The rent principle, in other words, was still respected.

At a Central Committee Party meeting in early 1950 President Gottwald asserted the need to proceed 'neither thoughtlessly nor without due consideration, but rather more quickly all the same'. In order to promote changes without resorting to regimentation ('isolated cases of bureaucratic pressure were dealt with in an energetic fashion'), four types of co-operative, representing four stages along the path to collectivization, were defined for adoption by villages, according to their degree of development. The first type, like the early experiments, was limited to the pooling of labour, machinery, and draught animals for the main farming operations, such as sowing and harvesting. For the most part, production retained its individual character and boundaries remained intact. These symbols of private property were removed, however, in the second type, but although cultivation was thus organized in large units, rents remained in effect, and the harvest was shared on the basis of the land contributed by each individual. Livestock enterprises remained a matter for individuals entirely.

The communal principle was applied to stock-rearing only in the

[1] See '*Les survivances de l'ancien assolement triennal obligatoire dans le Sud de l'Alsace*', by F. Spindler, in *Bulletin technique d'Information du Ministère de l'Agriculture* (68, 1952).

FOUR TYPES OF PRODUCERS' CO-OPERATIVES

third type. Furthermore, most of the produce was now divided according to the amount and quality of work put in by each member and only a small fraction was reserved for payment of rents.[1] Finally, in the last type of co-operative, as in the Russian *kolkhoz*, only work was rewarded. Nevertheless, the land was not taken over by the State as in the U.S.S.R., but remained nominally under private ownership. A similar state of affairs in Yugoslavia allowed land to be given back to those opting out of the co-operatives (1953).

The general adoption of this scheme, and in particular of the second, third, and fourth categories, which alone were recognized as being of the 'superior type', meant that co-operative land had to be regrouped. The same also applied to farms belonging to non-members and to rich peasants, the latter sometimes being regarded as undesirable. The non-co-operators were heavily penalized by being relegated to the outlying and frequently to the less fertile parts of their communes. Out of 7,100 co-operatives and preparatory committees at the end of January 1951, 3,300 were of the superior type; 43 per cent. of the members of these latter owned less than 5 acres, 22 per cent. between 5 and $12\frac{1}{2}$ acres, 17 per cent. between $12\frac{1}{2}$ and 25 acres, 14 per cent. between 25 and $37\frac{1}{2}$ acres, 3 per cent. between $37\frac{1}{2}$ and 50 acres, and only 1 per cent. more than 50 acres. At the same time the co-operatives accounted for 13·6 per cent. of the country's agricultural land. The socialized area, including State farms and various other lands, accounted for 22·3 per cent.

330. Although very much smaller than their Soviet counterparts, the co-operatives averaged over 750 acres each, and they were tending to grow as new members joined. These additions were made with the minimum of inconvenience, for the non-co-operative land in every commune had been consolidated into single blocs of private property. In early 1951 there was one worker per $7\frac{1}{4}$ acres on peasant holdings, but on co-operatives of the superior type the density was almost halved, averaging one per 14 acres. This is still a much smaller acreage per worker than on the large capitalist farms of the Paris Basin, where the figure varies between 25 and 50 acres, while in the United States 125 acres is by no means unusual. The State farms in Czechoslovakia, by virtue of their greater mechanization, attained one worker per $16\frac{3}{4}$ acres. In 1949 their output per worker was estimated at 70,000 crowns, as compared with 29,000 for the small holdings.

The regional differences within the country are significant, and must

[1] In theory only, for 'the poor peasants and workers, who had brought little but their own hands, often opposed the payment of rents, which, as far as they were concerned, perpetuated an intolerable injustice' (Fetjö, op. cit.).

be considered if an accurate picture is to emerge. The density of workers was higher in Slovakia than Bohemia, where mechanization was almost on a par with the West even before the war. Another important criterion is intensiveness, but the co-operatives often publish their better crop yields while glossing over their setbacks. The lack of information concerning livestock, however, is a reminder that enlarging the scale of an enterprise is often, though not necessarily, accompanied by a decline in the density of animals.

In the summer of 1952 the 4,476 co-operatives of the superior type, out of a total of 7,669, cultivated their integrated fields in common; 3,059 of them, accounting for 19 per cent. of the agricultural land in the country, were run on 'truly collective' lines. At that time, the main emphasis was being placed on better organization rather than on further expansion. As on the Soviet *kolkhoz*, special assignments, some relating to cultivation, others to livestock, were given to permanent and properly equipped labour gangs.[1] Every co-operative elects a president to manage its affairs, while all technical matters come under the purview of an agricultural scientist. So as to prevent 'an indolent member profiting unjustly by the work of his diligent colleagues', rewards are based on the amount and quality of work, and norms are laid down for each task on the pattern of the Soviet *trudodyen*.

Co-operative stock-rearing has led to the construction of enormous collective cowhouses,[2] which were subsidized on condition that local materials were employed and used economically, and that the members themselves should supply practically all the labour. Many of the co-operatives are assisted by local workshops and factories, which began by helping to repair machinery and by sending labour sections at peak periods—for the grain harvest and potato-lifting, for instance—which had been rendered acute by the exodus to the towns. This collaboration is more and more extending its range and applies to 'the adaptation of buildings for communal stock-rearing, the elaboration of work plans, the adoption of systems of group work, norms, and units of work'.

A resolution passed by both the Party and the Government on 7 June 1952 recommends that 'back gardens' should be limited to exactly $1\frac{1}{4}$ acres; they might otherwise divert attention overmuch from the communal fields. It advises co-operatives to concentrate on the more fertile regions and to win over 'the "medium" peasant whom Lenin defined

[1] The 'field' gangs have from fifty to eighty members, the others from fifteen to twenty, in the largest co-operatives, as in the State farms. Since 1951, the brigade chiefs have had stronger powers.

[2] Here too, livestock was kept back in some cases, and there was a certain amount of illicit slaughtering.

as the central figure in the village, for his ability, his knowledge and his experience are indispensable to the co-operatives'. This is coupled with the warning that he should not be confused with the rich peasant, the *kulak*, who must be met with firm opposition. But how are they to be distinguished? In Hungary 35 acres was put forward as the criterion, but this takes no account of variations in either fertility or farming systems.[1]

5. Machinery Stations and State Farms

331. Until 1948 tractors and combines were approximately equally divided between the large farms and the agricultural machinery co-operatives, which were 'run by large landowners and rich *kulaks*'. Accordingly, they were transferred from the latter to the producers' co-operatives. From the inception of collective cultivation, however, they were taken over 'by State machinery stations, because the co-operatives eventually realized that large items of equipment which are a heavy charge on the individual village and expensive to maintain would thus be utilized to better advantage and would serve more economically'.

The State stations received a further complement of heavy equipment after the expropriation of large farms in 1949-50, and they absorb nearly all the new tractors and machines which become available. In 1949 they ploughed and harvested 6·7 per cent. of the wheatland in the whole country, but this figure rose to 19 per cent. in the following year. At the beginning they worked mainly for the peasants. Later, however, 'their main political task was to collaborate closely with agricultural co-operatives of the superior type', so as to show the peasants 'the advantages of model cultivation—correctly timed and economical —on large consolidated fields'. A higher tariff for co-operatives of the first type encourages them to develop more rapidly towards collectivization. On the other hand, the removal of boundaries is sometimes a painful task, and has on occasion been opposed by the former owners. It is therefore performed free of charge.

To ensure the best possible work, contracts agreed with the co-operatives stipulate that the payment of station employees will be graded according to the yields from the fields they have cultivated. In the early days, in spite of the protests of the co-operatives' agricultural advisers,

---

[1] In Rumania, the *kulaks* (5·5 per cent. of the peasants, but a quarter of the cultivated area) start at 25 acres; the medium peasants with 7½-25 acres form 34 per cent. of the peasant population. The poor peasants form 57 per cent of the total, but only account for the same area as the *kulaks* (according to *Romania Muncitoare*).

the men used to till the ground much too superficially, so as to reach their acreage norms as quickly as possible. The maintenance of the machines is still not always satisfactory and fuel is often wasted, especially in the cultivation of small, dispersed fields. In 1951 it was announced that 'the political work of tractor-drivers and even of other employees among the co-operatives and the peasantry is not always satisfactory'. A political joint-manager was therefore appointed to each station.

332. Some 190,000 acres of Imperial domains which had been taken over as State enterprises occupied no more than 1 per cent. of the agricultural land in 1945.[1] Like many of the capitalist farms from Saxony to the Paris Basin, they had specialized in cereals and sugar-beet, and kept only a few beef and dairy cattle and hardly any other livestock at all. In 1952 State farms accounted for nearly a tenth of the total area, and thus held a place similar in importance to that of the *sovkhoz* in Russia. Prior to the expropriations of 1945 large farms accounted for comparatively little of the interior of the country, and the Government thus took over a far larger proportion of them as State farms than in East Germany. State farms were also commonly established in frontier areas, where difficulties of colonization were at their greatest. These were the regions which had been largely converted to pasture, and which had been dominated in the first instance by temporary stock-rearing co-operatives, like the one at Vicice.

The specific task of the State farm is somewhat different from usual. It is laid down by the Five Year Plan, which here again shows a bias towards animal products (meat, milk, fats, eggs, wool) and special crops, such as sugar-beet and potatoes, flax, hemp, and tobacco, and fruit and vegetables. While collectivization is still proceeding therefore the State farms are entrusted with making up for the expected decline in peasant production. Secondly, they are to serve as model farms. This is a most important function and, as in East Germany, implies the breeding of quality stock and the propagation of selected seeds.

Unlike the single expanse of 12,000 to 20,000 acres which characterizes the *sovkhoz* or the small unit of 250-750 acres typical of the East German *Volksgut*, the Czechoslovakian State enterprise generally comprises ten or fifteen large and once privately owned farms administered collectively as a unit of about 6,300 acres. Each individual farm is run by a manager, an agricultural specialist, and an accountant;

---

[1] According to Kotatko, State farms date from the end of 1948. However, we visited several in autumn, 1948, which dated from 1945-6. At that time their aggregate area was 235,000 acres, and this had risen to 1,000,000 by autumn, 1949, and to about 1,750,000 by 1952.

each group or State farm by 'a director and his deputy, an agricultural expert, a livestock specialist, a mechanical engineer, an economist, a building specialist, a chief accountant and a whole series of minor officials'. The chain of administration was decentralized in June 1951, and regional directorates were placed under the direct control of 'the regional agencies of the People's Civil Service'.

In order to deal quickly with the shortage of meat, some of the State farms (Smirice, Tremon,[1] and others) have constructed huge installations for pig-fattening, some of which accommodate more than 10,000 animals in feeding-houses, each built for 1,000 head. The preparation and transport of food are mechanized, so that 'three or four men can look after 1,000 pigs and only one man is needed on the whole farm to clean out the dung'. Dairy and market-garden farms have been established in the vicinity of towns and large factories. New crops have been tried, and rice is being grown in southern Slovakia, which is further north than anywhere else in Europe. Ground-nuts and even cotton are also being tried.

In 1951 the State farms were advised 'to eliminate former large landowners, rich peasants, and other enemies of the people from their managements . . . and to replace them with workers and peasants'. The latter were trained at a special school at Pohorelice. They were further enjoined 'to adopt the system of making each individual socialist enterprise pay its own way, like the Soviet State farms, so as to bring about a reduction in costs and an increase in yields; and to concentrate more on livestock and industrial crops'.

Jan Wszelaki,[2] quoted by Fetjö, writes: 'In spite of all the incompetence, all the petty tyranny, and all the bottle-necks which stand revealed, the process of industrialization takes its course.' We incline to the same conclusion for agrarian collectivization and for the final outcome of agricultural development. The labour shortage due to industrialization is still being felt, owing to the lack of capital and the uncertainties of the early years, but the position, according to Poniatowski, is worse in Poland. Finally, with its wealth of qualified specialists, the standard of its agricultural teaching, and the progress of its industrial development, Czechoslovakia appears to be in a better position than the other people's republics. It is ahead of Hungary and has drawn level with Germany.

---

[1] The manure from the latter, which is on the edge of a lagoon, is discharged into the water to promote the development of plankton and so increase the quantity of fish.

[2] 'The Rise of Industrial Middle Europe', *Foreign Affairs* (October 1951).

6. Collective Farms South of Moscow and a Ukrainian *Sovkhoz*[1]

333. The Borietz (the 'Fighter') *kolkhoz* is situated in an area of poor soils forty-five miles south of Moscow and twelve miles beyond the southern edge of the forest zone. Until 1930 the average peasant with about 4 to 8 acres of land, a horse, a cow, and a pig, had to struggle to make a living. The harvests were more dependent upon the weather than they are today, and their irregularity was prone to result in food shortages. The original village numbered 220 families in all, and eighteen of these founded the first nucleus of the *kolkhoz* in April 1931: 85 per cent. of the families had joined by August of the same year, and the forty 'recalcitrants' gradually came in later, the last of them in 1933. The Borietz as it stands today was formed in 1950 by the amalgamation of three neighbouring collective farms, each of which had grown up round a village and each comprising some 2,000 acres. This reflected the trend of the times, for the 254,000 collectives had fallen to only 97,000 by 1951. This meant that the most competent agricultural specialists could be employed to the best advantage. None of this would have been possible, however, without the lorry which enabled labour brigades to be conveyed rapidly even to the outlying areas.[2]

Management is in the hands of a council of nine members, who all work, except the president. The latter is elected for a term of two years and has six clerical assistants, most of whom are accountants. The council has to meet at least twice a month, and must call a meeting of the whole collective once in three months to report progress on the programme laid down by the members. Of the total area of 6,300 acres, 4,300 are under the plough and 1,570 under cereals. The remainder of the arable land is given over mainly to fodder crops and to market-gardening.

Labour is organized in six brigades. The first specializes in cereals and has 120 workers divided into six groups. Next comes the market-gardening brigade with 125-130 workers, and this is followed by the third (thirty-five workers) and fourth (fifty-five workers), which attend to fodder crops and meadows. The fifth (fifty workers) is responsible

---

[1] Together with the Indian holding, this is the only instance where we have analysed farms without visiting them ourselves. The section is based on data collected in 1952.

[2] At this period grandiose schemes were put forward for the concentration of the population in large settlements or farmer-towns. The study of transport and construction costs led to their abandonment.

for orchards, and the sixth, which averages sixty, but has more in the winter, for livestock. A dairymaid looks after eight cows and milks them by hand in the fields, averaging 45 gallons a day. A milking machine was to be installed in the new cow-house for the winter, and the transport of feeding-stuffs for the stalls was also due to be mechanized. Milking is hard work, for it has to be done four times a day, starting at 4 a.m. and finishing at 10 p.m. The pedigree dairy herd of 200 cows gives about 210,000 gallons a year (1,650 gallons for the best milkers).

Each brigade is an independent unit with its own permanent workers and, like a workshop, it has its own complement of equipment. The leader, who is a kind of foreman appointed by the management, does no manual work. The groups which he controls are assigned to specific tasks, and their personnel remains unchanged. Each has a leader, who works with his men. Borietz has eight lorries, two Pobeda cars, and a fire-tender, but possesses no heavy agricultural machinery.

Eighty to ninety per cent. of the field cultivation is effected by the Machine and Tractor Station (M.T.S.). It reserves a team of eight tractors for Borietz, and when these are at work they come under the jurisdiction of the president of the *kolkhoz*. The scale of charges is fixed by the Ministry of Agriculture, and varies according to yields.

334. Each member's work is calculated according to amount and quality, on the basis of norms which are put forward each year by the management, discussed by the labour brigades (counter-norms), and finally fixed by a general meeting. In 1952 lifting $\frac{1}{2}$ ton of potatoes a day, for instance, was equivalent to one and a quarter *trudodnya* or 'work-days'. At the end of the season part of the cereal harvest is sold to the State at a low price. In 1952 this toll, for 1,570 acres of cereals, amounted to 106 tons. The M.T.S. is paid in kind, the members are given their share, and the rest is sold by agreement to the food-supply agencies. In 1951, which was a bad year in this humid region, the net cash revenue was 2,750,000 roubles. The following year was a good one, and it was hoped to surpass 4,000,000 roubles.[1]

A fifth of this income must be invested in machinery, buildings, and livestock. Three-tenths are set aside to finance the following year's operations, and about half (50 per cent. in 1952, subject to variation) is shared between the members. On average in 1951 the latter earned 325 *trudodnya* per head, or 165,000 for the whole farm. The total of 500 workers gives an average of one per 8½ acres of arable land, which includes a significant area under market-garden crops. For cereals, there

[1] 11 to the £1 at the official rate, but real value probably nearer 33 to the £1 in 1953.

is still one worker for 12½ acres. Thus although it is probably no exaggeration to say that the productivity of labour has trebled since 1913, it is still far below North American averages. The reasons for this seem to be inadequate organization and the lack of small-scale equipment.

Two thousand people depending on 6,300 acres of land represents a high rural density of population. In Hungary the absorption of manpower by industry had not yet been compensated by mechanization on the land, but in this more highly developed region the reverse tends to be the case. The demand for labour is therefore kept up by resorting to intensive enterprises, like stock-rearing and market-gardening. Every family supplies from one to five workers. The old people often reserve their energy for the ⅝ acres to which everyone is entitled, and which are intensively cultivated. Everyone has the right to keep one cow, pigs, poultry, and bees.

For each *trudodyen* a member had the right to the following:

	In 1951	*1952 estimate*	
Wheat	4⅕ lb.	5½ lb.	Partly sold on the *kolkhoz* market
Potatoes	8⅘ lb.	17⅗ lb.	
Vegetables	13⅕ lb.	13⅕ lb.	
Forage and straw	6⅗ lb.	6⅗ lb.	
Roubles	5	10	

Each crop is delivered immediately after the harvest; this is, of course, obvious in the case of fresh vegetables. Money is paid out three times a year, on 6 May, on the anniversary of the October Revolution, and on 1 January. Bonuses are granted whenever production surpasses the planned estimates. For example, if milk yields exceed 770 gallons, a third of the surplus goes to the dairymaid; a quarter of the cereals surplus over 15 cwt. per acre is divided among the labour brigade. The higher rate of bonus for stock enterprises, where constant care and attention are so important, is a general rule.

Specialized activities and administration are singled out for high rewards. The woman in charge of the pigs who reared all the litters successfully received twenty-five piglets at the end of the year. The market-garden section responsible for seed-propagation was given a bonus of 7,000 roubles per head. The president earns the equivalent of 150 *trudodnya* a month, and a gratuity of 400 roubles a month if the *kolkhoz* revenue exceeds 1,000,000 roubles. The chief accountant receives 65 per cent. of the president's salary and his assistants a little less. The brigade chiefs are credited with 2 to 2½ *trudodnya* a day. As for social services, medical attention is free, and the development of creches and schools and of the library deserve emphasis. The latter has 9,000 volumes, of which half are fiction, 30 per cent. are on social and political topics, and 20 per cent. are technical and miscellaneous.

335. In an area of forest and peat bogs twenty miles south of Moscow, the 'Memorial to Lenin' collective extends over some 1,750 acres. It has 175 acres of orchards and a considerable area of soft fruit in addition: 30 acres of black-currants and 15 of gooseberries. There are three large glasshouses, 6,000 glass frames, and 38 acres of field crops of vegetables. Livestock comprises 210 cattle, including 125 cows, 255 pigs, sixty sheep, and fifty hives. The fact that mechanization is still incomplete is emphasized by the presence of 105 horses, but ten lorries fulfil the majority of transport requirements. Four hundred and thirty-one workers from 362 families are divided into nine brigades: two for vegetables and the rest for orchard and soft fruit, frames and glasshouses, fodder crops, horses, other animals, transport, and, finally, for workshops and auxiliary services. The division of labour is thus carried further than in the preceding case and, with its special sections for transport and workshop, the organization approaches that of a factory.

Production is more specialized, and only 40 per cent. of the crops are distributed among the members. The *trudodyen* (which corresponds, for instance, to picking 66 lb. of strawberries) represented 6 roubles and 11 lb. of potatoes or vegetables in 1951. The individual lots of ⅝ acres, like the rest of the enterprise, supply the collective farm market which furnishes a quarter of the food requirements of Moscow. The library has 5,000 books and, in 1951, 21,000 loans were made to its 370 members, an average of fifty-six volumes per family per year. Every morning two doctors are available at the clinic; the club has a television set, and there are daily film showings.

In a very significant article which appeared in the *Bolshevik* of September 1952, Stalin wrote: 'The group property of the collectives and the collective market are beginning to hinder the mighty development of our productive forces, inasmuch as they are raising barriers against the extension of State planning to the whole national economy and to agriculture in particular.' According to J. Armel,[1] this condemnation 'reflects the torpor of Soviet agricultural production, where progress is slow as compared with industry'. The collective market still permits a certain amount of speculation, and the present organization continues to favour co-operatives situated in fertile regions at the expense of the rest. In other words, a form of rent differentials still remains.

336. In the Ukraine, further south, a *sovkhoz* of 16,500 acres which

[1] *L'observateur*, 28 October 1952.

specializes in livestock and bases its cultivation on cereals and fodder crops gives employment to 550 workers[1] and owns 1,350 cattle, including 650 pedigree cows whose average yield it is hoped to raise to 1,320 gallons a year. In addition there are 2,500 pigs, 4,000 sheep, about 1,000 goats, and 5,500 head of poultry, and there are still 250 horses. The figures not only reveal a higher productivity of labour than on the *kolkhoz*, but also suggest a more rapid rate of progress. State farms possess their own equipment, which in this case includes forty tractors and thirty lorries and cars. Mechanization has gone further than on the collectives, and the tractors account for 98 per cent. of field cultivation. Milking, shearing, and the preparation of feed have long been mechanized. All the evidence points to these enterprises being specially favoured by the powers that be.

For a long time the *sovkhoz* worker was no more than a wage-earner. When food was scarce during the war, however, his colleagues in the collectives made a lot of money with their individual plots of land, and this led him to demand similar privileges for himself. Here in the Ukraine he is now allowed ⅜ acre of land and a cow. There is a seven-and-a-half-hour working day, and cash earnings rise to about 700-800 roubles a month, with a two-month bonus each year. A fifth of the profits is taken by the State, 30 per cent. is reinvested for productive purposes, and a half goes to 'raising the standard of living'. About 40 per cent. of overall production is consumed by the workers themselves. Pedigree animals are sold by the State to the regional collective organizations.

Apart from the 250 acres of gardens, in 1952 there were 780 acres of oak and acacia tree belts, which constitute a useful reserve of timber. The general layout is determined by the State, and consists of two sets of parallel belts forming a pattern of squares sixty miles across. Each band of forest is composed of three strips 330 yds. apart, and the double row of land between them is filled with orchards and market gardens. The ground is first trenched to a depth of 16 in., and seeds are then sown in planting holes five at a time, only one shoot being eventually allowed to mature. Unlike the Mediterranean and the south-east of the United States, wind rather than hydraulic erosion is the greatest danger on these semi-arid steppes, and its incidence was greatly aggravated by the mechanized farming of the decade 1930-40. It was time to act.

As rainfall is the most uncertain factor, the greatest importance is attached to plans for irrigating a total of 15,000,000 acres, 'which will be able to feed 100,000,000 people—Indians, for example' and which

[1] Twenty of them are taking advanced courses in agriculture.

will facilitate the fulfilment of the final objective, 'the transition to Communism', everyone receiving 'according to his needs'. Naturally, these plans need to be more rigidly defined. It would be difficult to attain North American standards of nutrition if 100,000,000 people had to rely on 15,000,000 acres of irrigated land. None the less, this southern region of the U.S.S.R. is evidently advancing much more rapidly than French North Africa.

Peasant opposition to collectivization has since shown itself more clearly. Agrarian policies in the people's democracies adhered much more rigidly to the Soviet model than in China and, while imitating their great neighbour, the East European countries have failed to make allowances for differences in social conditions and, in particular, for their own problems of overpopulation.

In consequence, agricultural co-operatives decreased in numbers, not only in Yugoslavia (from 10,000 in 1950 to 700 at the end of 1956), but also in Poland (from 10,000 to 2,500) and in Hungary. In February 1957 the situation appeared unchanged in Czechoslovakia and Rumania.

CONCLUSION

Malthusian Economics Responsible for the World's Hunger

1. Small Farms and Collectives—the Archers *versus* the Tanks[1]

337. Elsewhere we have described some of the French *pays*, discussing at some length the areas of uneconomically small farms and demonstrating their fundamental inefficiency. And now we have found the same disability common to Africa and Asia and to the greater part of Europe. The tractor is for agriculture what the steam engine was for the Industrial Revolution. Mechanical energy, allied with the discoveries of chemical and biological research, is initiating an agricultural revolution which calls for profound changes of structure—in those countries, at least, who want to keep up with the modern world.

For so-called 'social'[2] reasons, certain idealists and a number of politicians wishing to curry popular favour are demanding special measures to assist these microfundia. They are mistaken, for the survival of an agrarian structure which hinders productivity is as effective a barrier to social progress as an unjust distribution of incomes. Progress demands a rapid expansion of production, and it is by their aptitude for serving this end that the various kinds of economic system will be finally judged. The average figures for the department of Haut-Rhin show 25,000 farms of 20 acres, each divided into fifty-six fields of $\frac{1}{3}$ acre. The average size falls to a mere 15 acres if the 1,000 largest farms are ignored. Even so, in spite of rural overpopulation, land is going out of cultivation, as at Hirsingue, and the same is happening in the

---

[1] In June 1925, with the 28th Dragoons, we were taught that the way to deal with a machine-gun concealed in the edge of a wood was to charge it at full speed and decapitate the firer with our swords. In November 1939 we were given an old Gras rifle and taught to aim at the slits in a tank so as to kill the crew. The opportunity of performing such an exploit, however, never presented itself to us.

[2] In fact, the reasons are more often political, or sometimes even religious.

fertile Limagne of central France. Some think that the problem can be solved by glossing over the inefficiency of the small farm, as if it were a shameful disease. In March 1952 we were officially requested to stop teaching that the number of farms in France was declining. We have since estimated that during the year ending May 1953 at least 100 farms disappeared from every department between Haut-Rhin and Isère, between Basses-Alpes and Basses-Pyrénées, and from Corsica; and this by no means exhausts the list. It is useless to deny these facts. Far better is it to examine their causes, their nature, and their consequences. Only thus can remedies be found to prevent the French economy from drifting any further along the road to bankruptcy—a road which has little to offer in the way of social improvements.

Mechanical power is the chief instrument of modern agriculture, and its use must correspond with enlarged fields and bigger farms. The very small farm affiliated to a co-operative often avails itself of the tractor for only 5-10 per cent. of its cultivation, while for more than 90 per cent. of its operations it continues to rely on the work of men and animals. It is therefore obsolete. According to Klatzmann, more than 800,000, or over a third, of French farms produce too little to support, even frugally, the families who live on them. Unless they seek other forms of gainful employment, therefore, these people are condemned to a miserable existence which the protagonist of the microfundia, who is not always disinterested, would accept only with the greatest reluctance. These criticisms evidently do not apply to the whole of French agriculture, but the burden of the small units is a handicap to progress elsewhere, and restricts the full employment of soils, equipment, and men. For the last thirty years the interests of about 1,000 distillers and large sugar-beet growers, who are alone responsible for France's large surplus production of alcohol, have taken precedence over those of the farming community as a whole, and agricultural policies have been dictated by this infinitesimal minority.[1] A miracle will be needed before the archers can halt the tanks. Is there enough social justice in France to hold out the hope that they ever will?

338. Planned agriculture, by reason of its comparative novelty and of the complexity of the problems it raises, deserves a much fuller treatment than could be given in a series of short summaries. We have,

---

[1] We are thus proving ourselves incapable of putting the most flagrant errors in our economic system to rights, which may well mean that its days are numbered and, in their excesses, the Malthusians, the Gribouilles of the modern world, are hastening its end.

however, established a basis for comparing it with the economy of the very small-scale enterprise.

The large undertaking can plan for huge farm buildings where all operations can be simplified. Field dimensions place no limit on the degree of mechanization nor on the use of heavy tractors and large items of highly specialized equipment. All these improvements, however, depend on the existence of a fund of technical skill, which is essential to the 'building of the socialist state'.

Greater attention to the adaptation of arable systems, and also of stock-rearing, to the physical and economic conditions would allow large areas to specialize in a particular type of activity.[1] Quicker and wider application of basic geonomic principles would have the same result. This would narrow the range of equipment required, and mechanization would become an even more attractive proposition. On a 'one-ox farm' in the Ile de Ré the mowing machine which cuts $2\frac{1}{2}$ acres a year was a much higher charge per acre than the very modern equipment (tractor, combine, pick-up baler) on a 2,000-acre farm in Soissonnais. There are, of course, economic limits to this type of specialization, the main factor being the cost of transport.[2] Thus commodities with a high price/weight ratio, such as cotton, are at an advantage. Furthermore, diversification also leads to a better use of manpower.

In general, planned agriculture makes better use of agricultural science. Farming tends to be more scientific and decisions are arrived at on the basis of technical data. The small peasant holding, on the other hand, is ruled by tradition and modifies its obsolete practices all too slowly. Teams of highly qualified experts, who combine theory with a wide and varied experience, thus have an important part to play. Finally, schemes of agricultural training are essential to the success of the new type of structure.

In the summer of 1952 we flew over the Bohemian plateau, which is mostly farmed by the co-operatives (seen from the air, the old and the new types of agrarian structure stand out very well), and a few

---

[1] In the 'wet' Marais Poitevin (see *Voyages en France d'un agronome*, Chapter XVII), poplars logically find their place in low-lying areas very much subject to flooding, the grasslands at intermediate levels, and beans on the higher patches of land. But those whose fields do not stretch beyond the lowest levels are forced to grow beans under quite unsuitable conditions, and the crop is spoilt by late floods every other year.

[2] See our article '*L'adaptation et la spécialisation regionales en agriculture*' in *Bulletin des Transports* for February 1952.

hours later we were looking down on the limestone plateaux of northeast France. The patches of abandoned land which wove an intricate pattern across strips of woodland and through the narrow fields that were still cultivated, the neglected orchards, the poorly managed pastures invaded by reeds and brambles confirmed our poor opinion of the very small farm. Dramatically revealed by the comparison was the manner in which agriculture can be fettered by the rights of private property. The rational utilization of the land cannot be ensured, best areas cannot be reserved for crops, and large homogeneous units of forest, pasture, and arable land cannot be established.[1]

We have already[2] directed attention to the many illogicalities of French farming, which cultivates poor soils too intensively in some places (interior of Brittany, the highland zone generally) and fertile soils too extensively in others (grasslands of Normandy and Charolais). A comparison of techniques as between Bohemia on the one hand and Flanders or the Netherlands on the other would still be in favour of the latter. But it would be idle to suggest that these would not benefit from having larger farms, provided that the redundant rural population could be absorbed by further expansions in industry.

339. At the start, the new type of agrarian structure is subject to trial and error, and above all it needs specialized staffs and equipment.[3] Furthermore, for us, collectivization would be politically acceptable and true to socialist traditions only if it remained genuinely voluntary. One of the main drawbacks, with human nature such as it is, seems to be the removal of the spur of personal interest. The profit incentive is the key to peasant agriculture, and it is the main motive behind the care which is lavished on livestock and crop alike, especially on the former. Even so, the argument applies only when the farm unit is not uneconomically small, and it loses some of its force in the case of the large capitalist undertaking. In the latter, the majority of the employees may justifiably be supposed to take less care over their work and to be less concerned about the overall progress of the enterprise than the member of a producers' co-operative in eastern Europe. Another

---

[1] Cf. *Le problème agricole français*, Chapters XI and XII. When the land is owned by individuals, too much has to be sacrificed for its purchase, at the expense of productive investment.

[2] *Voyages en France d'un agronome* and *Annales de l'Institut Agronomique* (1949).

[3] To call co-operatives into being will not of itself produce the right conditions for the operation of large modern undertakings; it is but the first step. On all points, the peasant holding is preferable to a co-operative lacking in power and machinery. (Plessz.)

danger of the new structure is bureaucracy. The emergence of a swollen and barely competent administration and the rise of a parasitic and privileged class are dangers which will have to be constantly guarded against. The former seems to have been largely responsible for the failure of a number of projects, such as Tanganyika ground-nuts and the cattle and grain scheme in Queensland, initiated by Labour governments.

We have already observed[1] that the Soviet model does not hold a monopoly of socialism in agriculture. The kibutz and other similar co-operative organizations in Palestine are of particular interest in this connexion, as are certain developments in the Yugoslavian *zadrugas*, from which the peasant is now free to withdraw, although in 1953 he was still encouraged not to do so.[2] Even the very limited experiments in pooling peasant labour in France are worthy of mention in this context.

The choice is not only between the microfundia and the planned economies of various kinds. In North America,[3] which we have not chosen to examine in detail in this work, one finds the most modern techniques and a high level of mechanization in the context of an agrarian structure which is more capitalist in type. Moreover, according to Colin Clark, North America ties with Australia for the highest agricultural production per worker in the world. This superiority is related in the first instance to the large area which each farmer has at his disposal and to the fact that the land is often fertile because it has only recently been settled.[4] Secondly, it results from the great wealth in natural resources of every kind per inhabitant in a continent which hardly knows the meaning of rural overpopulation. The latter is a great hindrance to agricultural progress in its final phase of mechanization, which is today the essential factor in the productivity of labour. This

---

[1] Particularly in *Voyages en France d'un agronome*, Chapter XII.

[2] '*Paysans d'hier, Agriculteurs de demain*' (*Economie et Humanisme*, 1951). It should be made clear that the *zadrugas* are farmers' co-operatives which resemble the old patriarchal farm units in name only. In May 1953 the law permitting people to withdraw from the *zadrugas* led to the departure of the *kulaks*, and the Government thereupon imposed a maximum of 25 acres per family of cultivated land (37 acres for large families).

[3] Cf. our *Leçons de l'Agriculture américaine* (Flammarion, 1949).

[4] 'Commercially-run family farms of adequate size are eminently profitable', says the University of Oklahoma. The term 'profitable' occurs more frequently than the term 'productive' in the United States, thus emphasizing that, even more so than in Europe, theirs is an economy based on profit.

effect is a modern phenomenon, as in the past in Flanders, the Po Valley, China, and elsewhere overpopulation had for centuries operated in favour of increasing yields per acre.

American productivity is also the result of the abundance of equipment. The present high level has been helped by injections of capital from outside, whereas in Europe the process was one of slow and laborious accumulation, partly from rural sources. Industry is so highly developed that agricultural equipment can be produced with comparatively little labour, while the scarcity and high cost of the latter are, in turn, a stimulus to mechanization. Productivity can also be referred, in some degree, to destructive exploitation of the land. Almost a century of recurrent 'soil-mining' has therefore led to a reduction in costs and to more capital being available for equipment.

In native Asian and African agriculture from two and a half to seven and a half days (in exceptional cases, ten) of work are always needed to produce 1 cwt. of grain. In eastern Slovakia from twelve to sixteen days of work per acre produce from $9\frac{1}{2}$ to 12 cwt. Six days give $14\frac{1}{2}$ cwt. on the rather poorly equipped farms in western France. In 1946, however, in the heart of the American Corn Belt (Indiana, Iowa), we noted a figure of five hours' work per acre of hybrid maize, giving a return of from 24 to 48 cwt. of grain.[1] Neither the collectives nor even the State farms in the U.S.S.R. as yet possess enough equipment to be capable of attaining a comparable level of productivity.

For exact measurements, it would evidently be necessary to count the time spent off the land, at the farm, at the factory and the shop, and the addition would naturally be much larger for the more advanced type of economy. The manufacture, distribution, and maintenance of the new factors of production (machinery, fertilizers, fuel, insecticides, etc.) employed by the modern farm take more time than the work on the land. Nevertheless, even allowing for this, there would still be an enormous range of productivity.

These spectacular contrasts between one economy and another did not exist about 1820, when a tenfold difference roughly represented the maximum range as between three-quarters and seven and a half days of work per hundredweight. The Asian and African systems have hardly progressed at all since then, while modern agriculture, in the context of rapidly improving transport facilities, has made enormous strides.

[1] On some farms in 1952, the figure fell as low as four hours of work on the land per acre, from the initial ploughing until the maize cobs had been put in the crib.

340. Small-scale peasant agriculture, with its traditional, pre-capitalist structure, thus appears to be in the gravest danger. The most vulnerable countries are those which, like France, also suffer from intensification based overmuch on work alone, and from the effects of a very late start in the spread of technical knowledge. In France every family is responsible for its own holding, and agricultural education must in consequence reach out to 2,400,000 individual farmers. It is too much to hope that they will all be receptive to new ideas. The final choice, therefore, seems to lie either between the various types of socialist structure capable of using the whole range of necessary farm equipment; or between these and a system which combines a high degree of mechanization and a large area per unit with a 'family' basis and which can operate only where the rural population is fairly sparse.

These alternatives invite a comparison between the United States and Russia, which is a difficult task because the two economies are not developed to the same degree. Its percentage of rural population, which is still high, and its less abundant supplies of equipment prevent the Soviet Union from competing with the United States in point of efficiency. Any valid comparison, however, must take account of the future, and must therefore be dynamic in character. Thus the real criterion is how fast the rate of output can be expected to rise.

American propaganda emphasizes the level of current production, which is evidently in her favour, whereas Russia points to her speed of development and to the prospect of great projects in the future. The complexity of pattern makes it impossible to separate the effects of the economic system from those of the current level of mechanization, the standard of agricultural training, the natural resources, international trade, etc. Unless a trend appears in favour of co-operative socialism, the use of increasingly heavy and specialized equipment in the capitalist countries must lead to some kind of amalgamation of enterprises. The trend is not very apparent as yet even in the United States, but, as we have already seen, the employees would in any case be less interested in the undertaking than the members of a co-operative, and another threat would be the risk of bureaucracy.[1]

The fundamental danger of the present-day political economy of the West has been clearly diagnosed by Alfred Sauvy: 'The essential point is not the absolute level of current consumption, but its annual rate of increase. Thus in France the consumption of steel per head is hardly

[1] Cf. *Motorisation et Avenir rural*, by René Colson (Paris, 1950).

more than in 1929, but over the same period it has experienced a fivefold increase in Russia.[1] ... The mere existence of Communism, by a kind of repellent effect, makes us turn away from novel solutions and condemns us to the *status quo*, or in some spheres even to retrogression: this is a most unfortunate reaction, for no system can develop except by changing its techniques.

'The systematic refusal to go courageously forward favours the enemy, who, fearing more than anything a slow social evolution keyed to technical progress and at variance with his political objectives, is happy to observe conservative tendencies which, in fact, spring directly from the desire to avoid his example. The conservative class has fallen into the snare, and noisily celebrates its victories, which are fêted more discreetly but with equal fervour in the opposite camp. ... Everyone has a perfect right to believe that the capitalist engine is more powerful and efficient than its collective counterpart, but such an opinion becomes untenable if the capitalist engine is voluntarily set at half speed.'[2] If, as appears likely, the war is to be waged on social and economic grounds, it would be as well to choose better weapons than microfundia and Malthusianism. We must invest in the land and re-equip ourselves with all speed.

To defer judgement on the merits of the two systems is the wisest course for the present. Beyond this we can only express the hope that peace may continue, and that by their results men of goodwill may judge them. Every agricultural scientist alive to his social responsibilities and aware of the impotence of technique alone in the face of hunger will choose the system which proves best able to raise the production of agricultural commodities—of food especially—and to distribute them equitably. For although we have discussed the problem purely from an economic point of view, we do not underestimate the importance of psychological and political factors, which are bound to play a decisive part in the efficiency of the two systems and in the choice between them. We are not qualified, however, to treat of these matters, and they are in any case beyond the scope of this book. In conclusion, we shall see that the superiority of the planned economy resides not only on the technical plane, where it manifests itself chiefly in the matter of equipment and specialist services. Most important of all, in our opinion,

[1] It is worth emphasizing the slower progress in agriculture than in industry, especially in the first phase of the economy of the Soviet Union or of the people's republics.

[2] *Cahiers économiques* (formerly *Economie contemporaine*), August-September 1952.

is that it permits a larger expansion of production concurrently with a wider extension of markets.[1]

2. Priority for 'Real' and not Simply 'Economic' Food Requirements

341. Since the great depression of 1929-38, the great danger of free enterprise[2] has been its inability to find markets sufficient to absorb the volume of production offered. The philosophy of liberalism, which is to satisfy only economic needs, armed with purchasing power, is not worthy of the dignity of man. Modern schemes of social security, social insurance, and family allowances have already departed from its principles. Admittedly, in France they are too half-hearted to set in motion the full development of potential resources, but they are none the less designed to satisfy the real needs of the whole population, even of the families of the unemployed.

Essentially, for many years the restriction of production was the conventional answer to economic crises. In the sphere of agriculture this is a particularly inhuman response for, as Cépède and Lengellé have reminded us,[3] according to work carried out by the F.A.O., more than two-thirds of mankind is inadequately fed. Moreover, the curb on production is partially ineffective, for it engenders a parallel decline in demand.

The structure of a planned economy appears to be better adapted to the distribution of wealth, for purchasing power and the volume of demand can be continually adjusted to keep pace with expanding production.[4] Instead of being regulated indirectly, purchasing power becomes subject to the specific control of central planning organizations. In a capitalist economy, the profit motive exercises an indirect influence on production, but as the planned economy is perfected its direct form of control appears by comparison to become increasingly efficient. In the words of Malassis, 'the office replaces the market'.

---

[1] See also the conclusions of our last three books, cited in notes 1, p. 519, 1 and 3, p. 520.

[2] 'Free' for those who have the capital, but not for anyone else.

[3] *Economie alimentaire du globe*, edited by Th. Genin (1953).

[4] But the demand on the producer is not always orientated in such a way as to correspond with the wants of the consumers, which the planned economy will have to seek unremittingly to assess accurately. It is not without its faults, and there is no guarantee that the future will rectify them all: there will have to be a continuous process of readaptation.

PRIORITY FOR 'REAL' RATHER THAN 'ECONOMIC' DEMAND

The aims of production and the orders of priority are in any case at variance with the social good in a free economy.[1] Thus, to return to our own ground, the low nutritional levels of the majority of the human race should force acceptance of the principle (even in well-equipped countries, for their resources are more abundant) that first priority must be given to agricultural investments in the widest sense of the term. These would comprise, first, direct investments, such as the conservation and improvement of the soil (anti-erosive measures, drainage, consolidation of fragmented holdings, etc.) and agricultural research, training, and advisory work. Secondly, but just as important, comes indirect investment in the factors of production. This includes fertilizers and soil-rectifiers, tractors and other machinery, electricity, equipment for preventing crop and animal diseases, fuel oils, and even factories for the processing of agricultural produce. The paltry sums expended in France since the war have been spent on grand and ambitious schemes or else on water-supply installations. The craze for stone and concrete, which is a dangerous obsession at the Génie Rural, has led to the erection of farm buildings which are always too expensive and sometimes unpractical, and which will prove difficult to adapt to the rapidly evolving techniques and crops of the future. Reclamation on the Vanne Marshes near Sens was followed by crop failures, for the peat soils should never have been used for anything but permanent grassland. In Haute-Alsace, on the other hand, on the extremely porous sands of the Hardt a preposterous irrigation scheme supplies the equivalent of 600-800 in. of rain a year—a quantity unparalleled anywhere else in the world. The soils have been ruined by leaching and bear only the most degraded type of meadow flora, in the form of upright brome grass. Any kind of cultivated fodder crop would give better returns, without irrigation. The original 1,750 acres were first irrigated in 1904, and now, in default of any fieldwork by agricultural experts, £500,000 have been spent to perpetrate the scheme on another 7,500 acres. Near Lyons the Marcilly d'Azergues fruit co-operative indulged in some splendid buildings, only to find that it had no money left to buy sorting and packing machinery. At Arles there are silos of

[1] Without wishing to dwell on the point, we would draw attention to the enormous waste of paper and energy in advertising. There is not enough paper to teach illiterates to read or to make the results of agronomic research as widely known as they should be, and yet, as Sauvy remarks, the American Sunday paper can afford to be extravagant in its consumption of newsprint. In France, 600 million francs is the reported cost of the advertising campaign which launched the detergent Omo on the market. Half the price of a tablet of Monsavon Soap is for advertising and distribution costs.

concrete and steel which turn the local rice crop yellow; timber would have been cheaper and better....

Practically all the financial loans for equipment are offered to the rich regions of northern France. According to the law of diminishing returns, however, and provided that the necessary advisory services are made available, these sums could be better employed in the underdeveloped regions (excluding the very poor areas), which cover almost the whole of the rest of the country. It is not surprising, therefore, that in 1952 the agricultural exports of France, 'the sick man of Europe', totalled only 53 per cent. of the imports. The exporting nations would be perfectly justified in withholding their food consignments from a country whose potential production per head greatly surpasses the average in Europe and the world.

342. Because agriculture is comparatively unremunerative and wealth is unevenly distributed in a capitalist system, the satisfaction of economic wants, whatever their nature, is given first priority. Luxury goods for the privileged take precedence over basic necessities. There are, for instance, many more cars in the world than tractors, and the young man at the wheel passes shamelessly by as the old woman plods wearily home, weighed down by her bundle of firewood. Refrigerators and television are less important than the war against hunger. Since 1945 more money has been poured into bars and night-clubs than into the fight against erosion.[1] Methods of soil conservation are common knowledge, but the inadequacy of their application is threatening the future of mankind. In the U.S.A. in 1946 we developed this theme at a meeting attended by rural economists serving in Government and university posts, and some of them readily agreed with us.[2]

But there is still hope. There is room for a dynamic form of capitalism so long as it shows that it can rapidly increase the production of real utilities for peaceful purposes and, by subsidizing consumption, raise the demand at the same rate. The Food Stamp Plan during the American crisis and the milk scheme in Britain during the war achieved this objective. Capitalism in the faint-hearted mood which pervades it in Europe, however, is doomed in the long run, as must be any system

[1] 'Francisco Pignatari, the latest of Sao Paulo's millionaires, is building his fiancée a house which will have two Turkish baths, a firing range, a bowling green, one open-air and one enclosed swimming pool, the latter 45 yards long and with an artificial waterfall 30 ft. wide and 20 ft. high at one end ... a neon-lit grotto equipped with a bar.' Quoted from Tibor Mende in *L'Amérique latine entre en scène*.

[2] They asked me not to publish their names as they feared that their hesitation in endorsing the merits of free enterprise might lead to their dismissal.

which has become inefficient. Its profits are too often neglected as a source of capital, and above all they are maintained by restricting production. 'We mean to preserve the profits of the capitalist régime, but without respecting its first law—free competition', Paul Reynaud reminds us.

It is not here, however, that the great mass of unproductive expenditure is to be found. The powerful North American economy certainly seems better equipped for combating a depression than it was between 1929 and 1939. Today the United States have the protection of a better knowledge of economic problems and of their dominating position in the 'free enterprise' camp. Moreover, the administration does not hesitate to play 'out of character' when the need arises. During the last twenty-five years, for instance, agricultural prices have been insulated more and more effectively against the 'free' play of supply and demand.[1] Then, again, it was only when the Americans set aside their liberal principles that they were able to begin saving their farm land. Examples such as these bring to light an element of hypocrisy in the propaganda which extols free enterprise as the only path to salvation.

The Marshall Plan was the antithesis of economic liberalism and the first example of a 'distributive' economy on an international scale, even though political motives were not entirely absent. Nevertheless, in the United States at the moment it seems that the surpluses accumulated by the capitalist economy, but for which no commercial outlet can be found, are being diverted through the safety valve of the armaments industry.

3. Symptoms of European and French Decadence. The Revival of Malthusianism

343. Though its existence may be acceptable in a country where production attains such high levels, the armaments industry will rapidly become an intolerable burden in Europe. Impoverished by two fratricidal wars and burdened by a legacy of overpopulation from its short-lived era of industrial monopoly, this small continent should be devoting a larger part of its resources to agricultural investment, both in the east and in the west, but more especially in the latter. Its capacity to buy abroad is declining in measure with the contraction of its overseas markets for manufactured goods. The weakening of its political

[1] Jacques Rueff believes that any attempt to curb the free play of economic factors is 'a step towards Communism'. We mentioned these facts to him during the course of a meeting and asked him whether the United States were on the road to Bolshevism; we are still awaiting his reply.

power has set a term to the centuries-old tradition of depriving the tropics of their necessities of life in order to improve its own standards of nutrition. In Western Europe at least the greatest reserves of latent agricultural productivity lie today in the underdeveloped regions of France.

Unfortunately, there are no signs of a rapidly quickening tempo of development in these regions. In 1953 the agricultural trade deficit was still the main reason for balance of payments difficulties. The leaders of trade and industry are often more affluent than before the war, due to the partly unearned increment in their share of the national revenue. These gratuitous benefits have accrued to them at the expense of the working class, which in some cases has not regained its food standards of the pre-war era, which were qualitatively deficient even then. Finally, between 1950 and 1953 agricultural production stagnated at a level 6-8 per cent. above that of 1934-8.

Allowing for the worthless surpluses of wine and alcohol,[1] the rise in production has not surpassed the increase in population. It seems probable, therefore, that whereas in industry output per head of the population has risen by 45 per cent., in agriculture it has remained static. The situation is showing little sign of improvement, for the sale of tractors and other modern material was on the decline, and although the Renault tractors, for instance, were admittedly inferior to Fergusson's the factories in Le Mans were running short of room for their unsold stocks. In 1951-2 the consumption of fertilizers was 17-30 per cent. less than in the preceding year, the decrease being especially marked in areas of small farms, where the difficulties of making a decent livelihood are at their greatest. Finally, in Alsace there was unemployment in the potash mines, and machinery was lying idle.

To maintain the number of agricultural workers, raise their output and lower costs of production were the declared objectives of a section of those concerned with agricultural policy when confronted with this situation. They did not fully appreciate the incompatibility of these ends, which, in effect, were an indirect way of saying that production should be reduced. The resuscitation of Malthusianism, to which reference has already been made (Chapter I), does not seem to be the best way of giving fresh life to the French economy. It can do nothing to encourage the flow of oil, pyrites, copper sulphate, cotton, and sisal from abroad, but all these are indispensable both to a modernized agriculture and to an improved standard of living in the countryside.

[1] See our article, '*Alcool, ou lait et viande*', in *Population* (No. 1 of 1953). Cf. '*Une politique agricole*', in *Le Monde*, 15 May 1953.

344. The necessary rise in production must certainly not be achieved at the expense of peasant earnings. The most 'liberal' sections of the farming community are demanding in no uncertain terms guaranteed markets and fixed prices. Many of them do not realize that these would represent a step towards a planned economy. They would not, however, absolve the farmer from seeking to raise the efficiency of his labour, and to promise him a better standard of living without this proviso would be politically dishonest.

Once again this raises the question of the more glaring irrationalities of land utilization, such as the use of rich soils for low-yielding permanent grasslands. The small vine-growers want a 'social price' for their wine, but what would have happened to the country if the guilds of the eighteenth century had held back the development of modern industry by demanding a 'social price' for their wares?

The land must be used to better purpose by the rapid extension of improvements—drainage and consolidation of property particularly. Secondly, there must be better equipment and more credit facilities, and the whole approach to research, advisory services, and training must be revolutionized so as to place the farming community on equal terms with those of other countries. These questions have already been studied —notably during the discussions on the Agricultural Plan for 1953-7[1] —but it is to be feared that in mid-1953, at the time of writing, the means put at the disposal of French agriculture are still very much inferior to those granted to the other rural communities of north-west Europe, from England to Denmark and from the two Germanies to Czechoslovakia and Switzerland. This is the inevitable consequence of a defence policy which, limited as it is to the military sphere, absorbs a significant fraction of the nation's resources for unproductive purposes. The fact that the struggle is taking place mainly on social and economic grounds is ignored.

Too many people in France refuse to recognize the peril and prefer to overestimate the country's economic strength. Their ostrich-like attitude is the most dangerous of all. Others, fully aware of the issues involved, are apprehensive lest rapid progress should make the need for changes in the economic system blatantly apparent. This they fear above all else. Even more serious than the low level of production,

[1] Which, in the first place, proposed to reduce the 'parasitic' production of alcohol (from sugar-beet, vines, and apples), to hasten the reintegration of holdings and the spread of modern techniques (pilot areas), to intensify fodder production and stock-rearing. But what miserable resources are to be put at its disposal, in view of the magnitude of the need! Will its rate of progress be any quicker than that of the first plan?

however, is its feeble rate of growth, its general lack of momentum. Coupled with this is the absence, among many influential politicians and agriculturalists, of any genuine belief in the great possibilities—which do in actual fact exist—of French agriculture. It looks as if the nation is bent on exemplifying a decadent form of capitalism.

4. Food Production Lagging Behind Population Increases

345. In the under-equipped and underdeveloped countries of Africa and Asia the situation is even more dramatic. Declining production is a feature of an increasing number of areas, and stagnation is the rule. In the highlands of North Cameroons and Kabylia, in the majority of the Asian deltas, and in many of the lowlands of Africa agricultural production is already failing to keep pace with population. Utterly inadequate food standards, pregnant with disastrous consequences, are beginning to decline still further, and confront the world with the possibility of a dreadful catastrophe.

Alfred Sauvy has shown that in Europe medicine was in some ways a by-product of economic progress, and that the former kept pace with the latter or more usually lagged slightly behind. Thus lower death-rates were accompanied or even preceded by increases in production. The latter were extremely large in the case of industry, and very considerable—though perhaps still inadequate—in agriculture. Today in Asia and Africa the introduction of medical techniques, on a massive scale, but at no great cost, is effecting a decline in mortality which is far more abrupt than was ever experienced in Europe. In the fight against malaria, the death-rate in Ceylon has been cut by 40 per cent. at a cost of half a dollar a head. On the other hand, the F.A.O. has calculated that $500 per agricultural worker in India or about $250 per head of the population would be needed to achieve 'a modest improvement in cultivation conditions'. Twice this sum would be needed to make any substantial difference. On this reckoning, the flow of agricultural investment should be about 1,000 times as large as for medicine, when in fact it is no more than a trickle.

Some seek comfort in the anticipation that birth-rates also will eventually fall, but the history of Europe shows that the population may treble before this factor becomes fully operative. The population density of the deltas of Asia is infinitely higher than in Europe at the turn of the nineteenth century, while their endowment of material equipment is very much less substantial. The dangers therefore are incomparably greater. Agricultural science can evidently bring immensely powerful forces into play, but it would be foolish to underestimate the financial resources it needs to do so. Furthermore, these under-equipped countries are, by definition, poor and would be unable to find the necessary capital from local resources, especially in the initial phase of development. In India, for instance, it is impossible to find $500 per head for investment over a short space of time when individual earnings average only $100 a year. Even if labour, her greatest asset, were employed less wastefully, how could the peasant be asked to part with a substantial amount of this pittance for the sake of capital investments? Later on equipment would no doubt accumulate more quickly, and production would correspondingly rise, but under these conditions progress would be dreadfully slow at the start. In the meantime, the world is witnessing an explosive surge of population increase, running at the unprecedented rate of 1 per cent. per year. Never before has mankind had the doctor—the sorcerer's apprentice of the contemporary world—and the tools of his trade at its command.

346. From Asia to tropical Africa and from Egypt to Morocco the curve of population growth has steepened swiftly. For Egypt, on the basis of the present rate of increase (viz. 43−28=15 per 1,000), Cépède and Lengellé have calculated that numbers will have risen from 16,500,000 in 1940 and 19,000,000 in 1950 to 38,500,000 by 2000. By then, 232 per cent. of the agricultural production of 1940 would thus be required in order to maintain the present inadequate nutritional standard. To bring it nearer to European standards, but without actually attaining them by the year 2000, the consumption per head of 'original' calories[1] would have to be raised by 125 per cent. This, however, would bring the death-rate down to 13 per 1,000. Taking this into account and assuming a constant birth-rate, the 1940 population would in fact be trebled by the end of the century. On this basis, a modest improvement in the food position would necessitate an increase of 630 per cent. in production from an extremely limited agricultural area where there is little scope for bringing more land under irrigation. The vast majority of statesmen, and even of intellectuals, underestimate the magnitude of the problem, and this is one of the main obstacles to its successful solution.

The anti-malarial campaign in Ceylon reduced the death-rate from 21 per 1,000 to 12 per 1,000.[2] over the course of a few years. The birth-rate

---

[1] i.e. taking into account calorie losses in the conversion of seed into food of animal origin.

[2] Death-rate now down to 14 per 1,000 in Algeria; the birth-rate is only slightly lower than in Ceylon.

oscillates between 35 per 1,000 and 40 per 1,000. On the other hand, so far there is not a single precedent to suggest that, under the present economic system, agricultural production can be increased by more than 3 per cent. per year. The highest known rate of increase is in the United States between the crisis years 1932-4 and the boom of 1950-2. Over the period it reached 2½ per cent. per year, but was achieved under conditions very much more favourable than in Ceylon: better soils, low density of population, and, most important of all, a basis of enormous industrial resources.

Those who oppose a Malthusian policy with regard to births do not always realize that they are *ipso facto* morally committed to promoting, at the very least, corresponding increases in production, particularly with regard to food. The Catholic farmers' leaders, who at one and the same time advocate the application of various Malthusian devices to agriculture, direct and indirect, and the raising of the birth-rate by means of special grants, are taking upon themselves a responsibility which we do not wish to share.

Aid to the underdeveloped countries is an inescapable moral obligation on the richer nations of the world. According to a report presented to President Truman,[1] the 1,075,000,000 inhabitants of backward countries (non-Communist) produce only a third as much wealth as the 150,000,000 people of the United States. The latter represent 7 per cent. of the world's population and enjoy 42 per cent. of the world's income—a proportion which is rapidly increasing. The 54 per cent. of mankind at the lower end of the scale enjoy only 13 per cent. of the world's income. The range between the wealthiest and the poorest, reflecting as it does differences in productivity, widens every year. Half the children of the poorest regions die before the age of six.

347. To speak, like Truman, of assuring these less fortunate people of 'three good meals a day' with Point Four aid and then, in 1951, to vote $227,000,000 for the purpose, or a quarter of a dollar per head, does not betoken a very serious approach to the problem.[2] Evidently the world is not governed by altruism, but James Warburg reminds us that the American economy creates a yearly surplus of at least $6,000,000,000 to $7,000,000,000 which the imperfections of its structure make it impossible to absorb. Moreover, the enormous and ever-increasing range of agricultural productivity, not to speak of industry where the range is still greater, aggravates the difficulty of re-establishing

[1] Quoted in *One Way*, by Bevan, Wilson, and Freeman (published by *Tribune*).

[2] In May 1953, the figure of $428,000,000 was proposed.

normal trade relationships and of returning to the 'good old days'. The latter, of course, were also an era of exploitation of colonial peoples.

According to the report quoted above, Point Four, which followed logically from the Marshall Plan, would need at least $14,000,000,000 a year to augment the national revenues of these backward regions by 2 per cent. But the United States has preferred to undertake the far larger financial commitment of military preparation, and the future will doubtless impugn her choice as a political error. Meanwhile, the failure of Chiang Kai-shek demonstrates that outside help does not suffice for the development of an economy in default of the willing co-operation of the mass of the people concerned. The effectiveness of such assistance is also minimized if large sums are diverted from productive channels for military preparation, or if they are simply misapplied.[1] Finally, there is little hope of promoting economic progress when the aim of financial aid, as in colonial Africa and, more recently, in various parts of Europe, is partly to set up or maintain certain forms of political organization.

Speaking of financial aid programmes, the Bevanites ask, 'Does it involve an association for the fight against want or a plan for buying mercenaries in another kind of war? Does it involve destroying malaria and furnishing tractors or protecting landowners and bolstering up feudal régimes? ... The foreigner can only remain in Asia or in Africa if, in the metropolis, his government has the wisdom to offer a true association in place of the old imperialism and an alliance to help in the pursuit of a true social revolution, which these countries need even more than foreign capital.'[2]

5. The Fight Against Hunger, the Categorical Imperative of Modern Times

348. From collecting and hoe cultivation to the Cantonese ricefield, the Flemish holding, and the 'combine farms' of the Ukraine and the Far West, the crux of the history of mankind has been its fight against hunger—the most noble—indeed, the only noble—battle in all its wars. At first, Nature guarded her secrets inscrutably and man confronted her unarmed or with only primitive tools. Today the elimination of

[1] What has been the effect on the Greek economy of the $2,000 million (according to Fetjö), exclusive of military expenses, poured into the country by Britain and the United States between 1944 and 1951? How much are the efforts of French agronomists really worth in the face of the yawning chasm which the war in Indochina opened up in the French economy?

[2] *One Way*, op. cit.

irrational processes and the accelerating tempo of advance in agricultural techniques seem to offer humanity an unlimited range of action. Indeed, they do, but the inception of new schemes and their subsequent rates of development are the all-important factors. If standards of living are to be bettered, increases in production must overtake the growth of population, which has a fair start and has already gathered momentum. Potential cannot, however, be translated into fact if economic—that is, political—obstacles bar the way.

As obstacles to progress, these latter have largely replaced the technical deficiencies of former times. The pace of agricultural development will remain too slow to save European civilization from disaster so long as the imperfections of the economic system continue, and the producer who improves his yields is faced with the threat of ruin; and so long as throughout the world—particularly in France—productive investment is sacrificed to armaments, economic welfare to sterile military preparation, life to death.

For the first time in its history humanity has the power to win the fight against famine on all fronts. The essential condition of success is that vast resources should be devoted to this end and not foolishly wasted in the unworthy cause of 'cold war' or open conflict. What final conclusion can we draw? Cépède and Lengellé have indicated the extent of the changes needed: 'The problem of feeding humanity can thus be solved by a technical revolution, but this implies an economic and, by extension, a social and political revolution.'[1] Alfred Sauvy warns us: 'The insufficiency of investment in underdeveloped countries threatens to end in disaster if the cold war continues.'[2]

349. Human dignity demands more than free speech[3] and the right

---

[1] They continue: 'The present-day system, which has produced poverty in the midst of relative abundance by preventing essential needs from being translated into effective demands, has created a network of far-reaching monopolies —of sale, of property, and of means of production in the widest sense of the term—and the existence of these monopolies and property rights is threatened by a technical transformation as profound as the one we have envisaged.'

[2] *L'Observateur* (6 November 1952). He adds: 'The two men, one in the East the other in the West, who hold our destiny in their hands, should have no difficulty in recognizing the need for a massive transfer of allocations from arms production to the creation of utilities if they are not (or either of them is not) one day to be faced with an Asian surge that will be difficult to control. If we are merely to join in a pact against a third party, the pact must be aimed at none other than the monstrous enemy of rising poverty.'

[3] The quest for which was nevertheless the most precious contribution of the nineteenth century. Restricted in the East, it is becoming more and more threatened in the West. McCarthy has been trying to combat evil with evil.

to vote, which are worthless to the famished. Above all, it demands the right to a normal life and, first and foremost, to 'three good meals a day'. At the opening of the international F.A.O. Conference at Hot Springs, President Roosevelt declared: 'No obstacle must be allowed to prevent a nation or a group of citizens within a nation from obtaining the quantity of food necessary to their well-being.'

Ten years later the obstacles are still with us. The determination to overcome them has wavered, but the demographic explosion has already begun, and world population bids fair to reach nearly 4,000,000,000 by the year 2000 and 23,000,000,000 by 2350. Everywhere, however, agricultural expansion is proving difficult to set in motion, and production is failing to keep pace. Aldous Huxley concludes:[1] 'Meanwhile, every day brings its quota of some 55,000 new human beings to a planet which in the same period of time has lost through erosion almost the same number of acres of productive land and goodness knows how many irreplaceable tons of minerals. Whatever may be happening to superficial crises, to the crisis on the political or industrial or financial levels, that which underlies it persists and deepens.

'The current almost explosive growth in world population began about two centuries ago and will continue, in all probability, for at least another 100 years. So far as we know, nothing quite like it has ever happened before. We are faced by a problem which has no earlier precedent. To discover—and, having discovered, to apply the remedial measures—is going to be exceedingly difficult. And the longer we delay the greater the difficulty will be.' The emigration of the teeming millions of Asia to Australia, Siberia, and the Americas, however desirable it may seem, is in the present state of the world beset with insurmountable difficulties.

350. The moment has come to dissociate ourselves from those whose actions are slowly but surely bringing the world to disaster. Is it moral to hinder the widespread adoption of birth-control and to let young people die of starvation? Many changes must inevitably follow this unprecedented drama in our history. The food standards of the most distressed nations and social classes are being eroded by destruction and waste, prerogatives of the rich and of wealthy nations, and by the Malthusianism which paralyses our creative potentialities. This lowering of standards is inimical to health and, as Cépède and Lengellé have shown, is directly related to rising mortality rates. It therefore

[1] 'Food and People', *Current Affairs*, April 1949. The world's population is now said to be increasing at a rate of over 60,000 a day. And how many agricultural scientists are being trained?

constitutes an assassination, in the most literal sense of the term, and those mainly responsible are still at large.[1] Because they hold back the production of food, the arms race and economic Malthusianism[2] are more lethal than war. By preventing the battle against erosion from being waged with adequate means, they are jeopardizing the soil resources which future generations must depend on for their sustenance. The agricultural scientist who passes over such crimes in silence is not worthy of his noble calling.

To provide more or less adequate nourishment for everyone in the world today, without attempting to achieve anything like North American standards, agricultural production would have to be instantly more than doubled. Furthermore, as the example of Egypt shows, the necessary increase will have to be far greater than this in the long run. In spite of all the propaganda, there will come a day when world opinion will no longer tolerate the waste of every kind of resource by the wealthy nations. Every animal calorie consumed by a North American reduces the pitiable ration of a Mexican peasant or of a dweller of the Brazilian *sertaos* by eight calories of vegetable origin. Every lavish meal of a French bourgeois means short commons for a needy working-class family, a peasant of the highland zone, a Kabylian, or for some old person somewhere in the world, stricken with age and 'economically weak'. The Australian robs the Indian, the New Zealander the Chinese. The fatting calf in Gâtine or Limousin destined for our table thrives on milk which would reduce the mortality of weaned Negro infants in the sparsely peopled region south-east of Lake Chad. The young bulls of Charolais, the rams of the Ile de France, and even our Leghorn hens, are more adequately fed than the children of the poorer suburbs. They lack nothing in the way of health-giving proteins, vitamins, or minerals . . . because they pay. Every spring a certain co-operative dairy on the outskirts of Dieppe tips its surplus of skim-milk, the ideal protective food, into the sea because it is an economic proposition to do so. We know that some of our readers will smile at such considerations. Their children will nevertheless be compelled to devote themselves more seriously to the problem. An economy based on profit, bolstered up by an armaments programme—so

---

[1] Funds allocated in France to agricultural research, which is running the 'risk' of increasing production overmuch, thus creating marketing difficulties, were cut down to a mere pittance in 1952-3, and the productivity of both staff and equipment has been reduced in consequence.

[2] 'Malthusianism, public enemy No. 1,' declared Paul Reynaud—better late than never—in the speech he made at his investiture on 27 July 1953.

much so that peace almost becomes a threat—will have to give place to an economy based on the fight against hunger.[1]

Paris, January 1952-July 1953.

POSTSCRIPT
(February 1957)

This judgement on a planned economic system was written by a pacifist who had no wish to increase world tension. At that time, the personal contacts we had had with Communist countries were insufficient for us to form a final and considered judgement and we still hoped to see a 'liberalised' Communism of the type which seemed to be emerging during the summer of 1956. These hopes were shattered by the tragic events in Budapest and, at best, they must now be deferred to a very distant future.

More recently, the author was able to contrast the relative flexibility of Chinese agrarian policy with the servile way in which the Rumanians imitated the Soviet programmes—even though economic and demographic conditions were quite different. This is why our latest book, *Révolution dans les campagnes chinoises*, strikes a somewhat different note.

---

[1] We repeat once again: we certainly do not think that agricultural progress in France is impossible under the present economic system, although it is now twenty years since we began to fight for the adoption of progressive ideas regarding equipment and modernization. But the money available is still ridiculously inadequate. Progress is too slow, the economy is ailing and the country is being overtaken by all and sundry. If those who uphold the country's economic organization as it stands today succeed in making it work, we shall be the first to applaud their success.

Index

Figures in italics refer to maps

AALSMEER, *410*, 432-3
Abroma, 39
Aboudeya, 73
Accessibility of land, 397
Acorns, 183
Advisory services, agricultural, 344, 373, 414, 430, 433, 434, 438, 448, 449
Aerial cable, 318-19
Affreville, *170*
Age brotherhoods, 21, 91
Agricultural area, decreases in, 371, 379, 407, 427
  education, 522
  labour, efficiency of, 11
  population, decline in, 309
  production, rate of increase in, 532
  recession, 379
  revolution, 211, 216, 470, 516
  schools, 340, 408, 509
  science, 2
  scientists, 453, 518
  system, 10
  techniques, advance in, 534
  training, 434, 457, 518
Agriculture, commercial, 7, 47
  definition of, 1
  incomes supplemented by, 296, 298, 306-9, 322-3, 327
Agrostis, 383
Agro-town, 481
Alcohol, 41
Alfold, the, 465
Algeria, *170*, 164-77, 180-7
Algerian High Plains, 171
Alpine pastures, 282-8
Alps, 282-8, 300, 330
  the, 264-309
Amersfoort, *410*, 427-9
Am-Timan, 73
Andalusia, 218-6

Animal husbandry, 54, 86, 363, 399
  sectors, 173
  products, 508
Annam, 152
Annamite Commune, 133
Anniviers, Val d', 264-309, *266*
  alps, 283-8
  arable land, 276-81
  general, 294-8
  industrialization, 305-9
  mayens, 282-3
  meadows, 264-76
  pacages, 281-2
  possible lines of development, 298-305
  vineyards, 288-93
Anti-erosive benches, 200
Arable land, 268, 276-81, 294, 303, 313, 345, 399-400, 470
Arbaa, *170*, 171-7
Archaean basement, 19
Armaments, 527, 533, 534
Arms race, the, 536
Arrezzo, *232*, 242
Ash trees, 183
Asses, 87
Aubergines, 85
Auction, Dutch, 431
  sale by, 393
Auctioneering, co-operative, 431, 433
Austria, 310-38

BABOUA, 44 et seq.
Bac-Giang, 135, *136*
Bac-Ninh, 142
Bagasse, 149
Balanites egyptiaca, 72
Bambesa, *24*, 43 et seq.
Bambaras, 104
Bananas, 26, 33, 37, 38, 39, 46, 49
Bang's bacillus, 417

539

INDEX

Bantu system, 34
  improved, 36
Barley, 172, 175, 183, 188, 190, 197, 313, 330, 373
Barrages, 260
Basilicata, 230
Bavaria, 339-59, *340*, *348*
  land problems, 356-9
  population, 339-40, 348-9
  soils and rainfall, 339
Be, *24*, 83
Beans, 85, 91, 137, 139, 183, 188, 197, 246, 277
Bebedjia, *25*, 75
Beef, salt, 267-8
Belgian Congo, 18-60, *24*
  climate, 18
  communications, 20
  density of population, 23-4
  education, 21
  land ownership, 21
  language, 22
  local handicrafts, 20
  natives, 22
  racial segregation, 23
  soils, 19
  vegetation, 18-19
Belgian textile industry, 51
Belgium, 360-75, *362*
  climate, 360
  economy, 360-1
  soils, 360
Ben Ahmed, *186*, 190
Benelux, 374, 435
Beni-Amir, *186*, 199
Bent grass, 80
Berlin Academy of Agricultural Sciences, the, 457
Bernburg, *440*, 457
Beverage, alcoholic, 70
Bicycles, 47, 73, 108
Binders, 103, 368
Bintje seed potatoes, 419
Bird's-foot trefoil, 453
Birth control, 16, 154, 155, 206, 263, 532, 535
Bisse, 265, 268, 271-2, 273, 284
Black-arm, 110, 112
Black gram, 204

Blind people, 137
Boldventure Farm, *382*, 394-5
Bologna system, 237
Bongor, 99
Bonuses, scale of, 458-9, 512, 514
Borietz *kolkhoz*, the, 510-13
Boudy-Bougou, 94
Bourgou, 96
Bouvignies, *362*, 361-5
  land use, 361
  overpopulation, 361-2
  size of farms, 361
Boval, 63
Boyne Estate, the, *382*, 391, 401-3
Bozoum-Bocaranga, 79
Brabanette plough, 267
Brabant plough, 311
Bracken, 379, 388, 394
Brantées, 290-1
Bread grains, 227
Brecht, *362*, 371-4
  land use, 372
Breeding, selective, 8, 377, 456, 508
Breitenfeld, *440*, 441-9
Brewing, 350
Brewing, native, 31
Brigades, labour, 510-11, 513
Brown Clee Hill, *382*, 381, 383, 388, 394, 398, 401
Buffalo, 135, 137
Bugac, *468*, 482
Building loans, 442
Bulbs, 432
'Bulgarian' gardens, 483
Bullocks, 87
Bulls, 331, 417
Bureaucracy, 519-20
Burnt-over land, 51
'Bush fields', 68-71
Butter, 235, 276, 316, 328, 332, 365, 366
Butyrospermum parkii, 72
By-products, agricultural, 424
Byre-barn, 270-276, 299

Cacao, 54
Calabash, 89, 104
Calabria, 230
Calcium, 35

540

INDEX

Calories, 14, 143, 148
Calving, 276
Cambodia, 152
Camels, 172, 188
Cameroons, 74
Campine, the, 371-4
Capital, 289, 377, 378, 384, 391, 398, 408
    accumulation of, 152
    equipment, 405
    European, 167
    fixed, 159
    investment, 124, 161, 207-8, 225, 231, 252, 256, 258, 402
    lack of, 261
    working, 140, 159, 172, 239, 255, 293, 384, 388, 389, 391, 400, 422, 433, 434, 503
Capitalism, decadent form of, 530
    dynamic form of, 526
Capitalist type of economy, 520, 523, 524
Capsicum, 26, 90, 104
Carrots, 400
Carts, 91, 157, 179
Casablanca, *226*, 226
Casamance, 115 et seq.
Cascina, 231-6
Castor, 137, 139
Castor oil, 66
Casuarina, 157
Catch-crops, 317, 364, 367, 371, 400, 427, 442, 443, 452, 454
Cattle, 80, 85, 91, 93, 96, 102, 107, 113, 161, 230, 237, 246, 270-6, 281-8, 295, 298, 300, 315, 317, 326, 327, 331, 335, 342, 345, 353, 365, 383, 397, 447, 456, 460, 474, 493, 513, 514
Cattle, breeding of, 412, 415-20
Cattle, breeds of:
    Ayrshire, 385
    Bleue du Nord, 363
    Chianina, 247
    Dahomey, 27
    Friesian, 416-19
    Hainaut, 363
    Hereford, 383, 392
    Hérens, 273, 286
    Lagoon, 27
    Maremmano, 251
    N'dama, 27
    Pie rouge, 374
    Schwytz, 273
    Simmenthal, 273, 286
    Zebu, 70
    fattening of, 393, 399
    rearing, 393, 396
Cauvery Delta, 157
Cavalletto system, 237-42
Cecejovce, 496
Cellulose, 51
Celtic system, 425
Cereal cultivation, 169, 179, 182, 187, 211-13, 220, 226-7, 279, 287, 294-5, 303-4, 314, 316, 325, 345, 353, 385, 386, 417, 442, 451, 493
    extensive, 216
Ceylon, reduced death rate in, 531
Chad 'Mesopotamia', 82, 112, 113
Chain pump, 135
Chalets, 283-4
Chandolin, 267
Chaouia, *186*, 187
Chasselas, 290
Châteauneuf Agricultural School, 304
Cheese, 235, 245, 267 et seq., 284, 286, 412
Cheliff, *170*, 202-4
Chemical fertilizer industry, 228
Chiana, Val di, *232*, 246-50
Chickens, 397
Chick-peas, 183
Chicory, 366, 368-9
China, 155-6, 515, 537
    agrarian policy, 537
    birth control, 155
    collectivization, 163
    co-operatives, 155
    land improvement, 163
    reforms, 155
Chinese civilization, 125-8
Chives, 314
Cistus, 184
Citrus trees, 43
City refuse, 371
Ciudad Real, 215

INDEX

Clearing, intermittent, 268
Clee Hills, *380, 382*
Clee St Margaret, 381-2, *382*, 388-99
  occupations, 388
  size of farms, 388-9
Clementines, 197
Climate, artificial, 433
Clover, 235, 310, 325, 329, 342, 378, 386, 392, 400, 417
Cochin-China, 152
Cock's-foot, 392, 394
Coconut palm, 26, 157
Coffee, 43, 54
Coha, 287
Cold War, the, 534
Collecting, 1, 34, 52, 72
Collective market, the, 513
  type of economy, 523
Collectives, 510-13
Collectivization, 163, 459, 462-4, 485, 487, 491, 502, 508, 509, 519
  opposition to, 515
Colocasia, 32
Colombo Plan, 162
'Colonization' (Bavaria), 356-9
  (Spain), 219-21
  schemes, 354-5
Coltivatore diretto, 242-4
Coltura promiscua, 237
Combine-harvester, 103, 203, 226, 241, 343, 387, 401, 402
Common land, 211, 377, 469
Communications, 408
Communism, 'liberalised', 537
Compagnie générale des Oléagineux tropicaux, 115
Compensation, rates of, 225
Composana, 284-6
Composites, 276
Consortages, 271, 283, 292, 332, 333
Co-operative buying, 345
  credit, 345
  organization, 520
Co-operatives, 120, 291-2, 409, 416, 428, 518
  producer's, 155, 163, 473, 484-91, 502-7, 515
Copparo, *232*, 237-42
Copper sulphate treatment, 351

'Cord' of cotton, 75
Coriander, 188-90
Corn Laws, repeal of, 378
Corve Dale, *380, 382,* 381
Corvée, 45
Costs, farming, 412, 424
Cotonco, 44 et seq.
Cotton, 44 et seq., 50, 65, 68, 74 et seq., 85, 89, 90, 91, 92, 93, 100, 104, 106, 107, 108, 110, 111, 149, 201, 202, 489
  manufactures, 58
  strips, woven, 92
  ginning companies, 80, 81
  seed cake, 81
  oil, 81
County Agricultural Committees, 392, 405
Cow-pea, 90, 235
Cows, 188, 235, 243, 245, 346, 347, 364, 368, 369, 393, 411-15, 427, 443, 495, 511
  dairy, 204, 243, 366, 371
Crane's-bill, 329
Credit schemes, 132, 189, 191, 220, 255, 478, 487, 503
Cropping, continuous, 60, 95
Cucumbers, 137
Cucurbitacea, 65, 85
Cultivation, continuous, 52, 55
  temporary, 34
Czechoslovakia, 492-509, 494
  agrarian reforms, 502
  geonomic surveys, 501
  producer's co-operatives, 502-7

Dablaka, 79
Dairying, 386, 392
Dams, 199, 296
Danubian Marshlands. *See* Donaumoos.
Daughters, exchange of, 108
Day, R., 144
Dayas, 171-2
Death duties, 403
Defence expenditure, 124
Demographic problems, 530-3
Development plans, 113
Dhal, 157

INDEX

Dia, 96
Diaka, R., 95
Diet, 143, 298, 313, 493-4
  qualitative deficiencies of, 13
Dietetic standards, 228
Diminishing returns, 140, 144, 152, 374, 414, 419
Direct control, land farmed under, 238
Directed peasant farming, 43 et seq., 153
Distributive economy, 527
Diversification, 518
Djelfa, *170*, 175
Djurjura, *170*, 180-7
Dokhone, 68
Dolo, 70
Donaumoos, *348*, 353-6
  colonization, 353-5
  economy, 355-6
Donkeys, 69, 91, 188
Double cropping, 55, 112, 134, 137, 140, 144, 197, 373, 483
Drainage, 103, 105, 107, 110, 144, 145, 198, 228, 230, 236-42
Draught animals, 73, 91, 104, 121, 135, 137, 151, 157, 183, 190, 222, 267, 269, 318, 342, 347, 365-6, 387, 412, 428, 443, 451, 496, 500
  under-employment of, 137
Drought, 213
  resistant crops, 215
'Dry' cultivation, 134, 139, 144, 211-16
  farming, 165, 192, 204
Dual price system, 444, 445-6, 495, 511
Dunajovice, *494*, 498-501
Dung, cattle, 86
  water, 319, 333
    pit, 343
    pumps, 286, 316-17, 323, 326, 327, 333, 347
Dust storms, 94

EAST GERMANY, 437-64, *440*
  agrarian reform, 438-41, 462-4
  cattle, 447
  climate, 437-8
  exodus to the West, 464
  farm equipment, 449, 450
  Five Year Plan, 446, 447
  food problem, 438
  goats, 447
  land use, 437
  milk yields, 447-8
  pigs, 447
  sheep, 447
  soils, 437
  stock density, 447
Ebersberg, *340*, *348*, 341-5
  agricultural school at, 340
Economic structure, type of, 16, 518-24, 537
Economy, commercial, 5
  directed, 60
  pastoral, 2
  planned, 38 et seq.
  primitive, 1
  rural, 2, 9
Edam cheese, 411
Education, 391, 408
Educational system, 5, 109
Efficiency of organization, 409, 453
  technical, 430-1
Eggs, 374, 428
Egypt, population problem in, 531
Egyptian thorn, 66
El Misser, *170*, 182
Electricity, generation of, 151
Elephant grass, 63
Eloszallas, *468*, 475-9
Embroidery, 471
Emigration, 142, 153, 184, 187, 206, 262, 296, 405, 469
  from countryside, 336
  to towns, 122, 378, 426-7, 463
Emmeloord, *410*, 423
Enclosures, 376-7
Endroit, 277
English agriculture, 376-405
  development of, 376-81
  environment, 376
  See also United Kingdom.
Environment, natural, 1, 3
  physical, 1
Equatorial rain forest, 18-60
Erfassung. *See* Dual price system.

543

Estramadura, 215, 218
Etyek, *468*, 484-5
Euphrasy, 276
Europe, declining role in world affairs, 527-8
  overpopulation in, 123
Ewes, 92, 398, 399, 411, 443
Experimental station in the Chad, need for, 113
Export crops, 77, 153

Faidherbia albida, 122
Fallow, elimination of, 256
  period cultivation, 173
  productive, 49
Fallows, 87, 93, 94
Family allowances, 206, 297, 327, 337
Famine, 14, 15, 89, 174
Farm buildings (*see also* Byre-barn, Stadel, Raccard), 220, 231-2, 237, 284, 319, 331, 333, 335, 383, 384, 402, 409, 410, 422, 441, 474, 475, 478, 479, 481, 492-3, 500
  maintenance costs, 402-3
  equipment (*see also* Binders, Tractors, Combines), 103, 202, 244, 254-5, 262, 297, 298, 315, 316, 323, 343, 347-8, 356, 377, 397, 399, 404, 409, 422, 423-4, 428, 448, 451, 455, 460, 473, 474, 479, 488, 489, 495, 514, 521
  range of, 518
  incomes, 159, 239-40, 247, 287, 293, 294, 344, 390, 398, 415, 498, 511
  units, 4
  wages, 158, 217, 227, 233, 241, 247, 285-6, 292, 332, 333, 335, 336, 344, 388, 394, 421, 444, 458, 461, 474, 484, 497, 511, 513, 514
  worker/land ratio, 243, 306-8, 336, 344, 346, 347, 348, 365, 368, 418, 433, 456, 461, 505-6, 511-12
Farming, efficiency of, 9
  intensive, 8, 366, 406, 434, 458, 512
  mixed. *See* Mixed farming.

subsistence, 7
tropical, 17
types of, 7
Feeding-stuffs, purchased, 8, 318, 326, 364, 383, 385, 397, 411, 425
  rationed, 397
Fellah, 187-191
Fen colonies, 407
Fenugreek, 188-90
Ferrara, *232*, 236-42
Fertilization, 3, 6, 26, 94, 99, 102, 199
Fertilizers, 42, 51, 86, 112, 338
  chemical, 6, 41, 56, 138, 146, 147, 234, 283, 343, 346, 351, 355, 357, 372, 373, 387, 404, 409, 413, 414, 424, 425, 427, 443
  natural, 56
Feudal system, 97
Fianga lakes, 79
Fig trees, 183
Figs, 182, 184, 188
Financial aid, 301
  incentives, 87
Fishing, 54
Five Year Plans, 446-7, 455, 460, 482, 488, 489, 490, 508
Flanders, 365-71, *362*
Flax, 329, 366, 417
Flocks, size of, 176
Floods, 329
Flowers, 432-3
Fodder, 136, 145, 301, 346
  cereals, 400
  crops, 8, 231-6, 325, 342, 371, 448, 493
  intensive cultivation of, 306, 307
  dried, 386
  production, 373, 376, 435
  winter, 299, 305, 307
Fonds d'herbe, 283-4
Food production, 535-6
  shortage, 122
Foot-and-mouth disease, 417
Forage crops, 112, 175, 215, 234, 256, 385, 489
Forest, clearing of, 32, 38, 39, 42, 48, 49
  fallows, 35, 36, 52, 56
  secondary, 31, 39, 52

INDEX

Forestry, 324, 347
Fort National, *170*, 182
Foulbes, 83
Fragmentation of holdings, 168, 180, 280, 301, 358
France, agricultural investment criticized, 425-6
  agricultural possibilities, 435-6, 529, 537
  decrease in number of farms, 517
  irrational use of land, 529
  liberalism and planning, 529
  production and population, 528
  underdeveloped regions, 528
  vested interests, 517
Francis-Bougou, 94
Franconia, 344-5
Frauenneuharting, *340*, 341-5
  size of farm units and land use, 341-2
Freckenleben, *440*, 459-61
Free enterprise, 524
  modifications in practice (U.S.A.), 527
Free Trade, 378
French Equatorial Africa, *24*. See Chapter III.
  West Africa, *24*. See Chapter III.
Frico, 409
Friesland, *410*, 409, 415-20
Fuel, 214
Fulpmes, *312*, 310, 311
Furlongs Farm, *382*, 383-5

Gabac, 65, 72, 87
Game, 41, 70
Gardens, 345
Garlic, 104
Geonomic studies, 501
Geonomy, 10
Geraniums, 276
German unification, 463
Ghrib Reservoir, 199
  Barrage, 204
Glasshouses, 429-30, 513
  heating of, 429
Gleaning, 245, 454
Goats, 66, 70, 83, 85, 87, 89, 92, 96, 107, 172-6, 184, 230, 281, 287, 315, 326, 327, 331, 332-3, 334, 447, 514
Gollo, *468*, 473-5
Gourds, 26, 49
Government interference, 13
Grain, shortage of, 472
  storage, 181, 319
Grape juice, 'Provinor', 291
Grapes, 429-30
Grass fallow, 42, 52
  mown, 234
Grassland, 342, 397
  management, 374, 435
  natural, 2
  permanent, 2, 8, 313, 318, 367, 376, 411
  ploughing of, 373, 392
  temporary, 303, 304, 311, 313, 399, 403, 414, 427, 459. *See also* Leys.
Grass-milk farms, 410-15
Grazing, 62, 251, 411
  controlled, 413
  extensive, 305
  rotational, 384-5, 414
Green crops, 373, 442, 496
'Green pool', 436
Grindle Shifnal, 399-400
Grosseto, *232*, 250
Ground-nut oil, 82
Ground-nuts, 35, 37, 39, 49, 54, 66, 83, 85, 86, 87, 89, 92, 93, 114 et seq., 490
Gruyère cheese, 285
Guadalquivir Valley, *210*, *226*, 218, 226-7
Guaranteed prices, 352, 392
Guidder, 86
Gullies, 94
Gumbo, 66, 85, 89, 107

HAARLEM, *410*, 432
  Lake, 406
Hainaut, *362*, 360
Hallertau, 348-53
  hops, 348-53
  land utilization, 349
  livestock, 349-50
  size of farms, 349

INDEX

Handicrafts, 71, 86, 120, 181, 496
Hard pan, 63
Hardwood trees, 51
Harmattan, 94
Harvesting, mechanized, 121, 424
Haut-Valais, 287
Hay, 270-6, 283, 302, 313, 318, 319, 328, 331, 348, 387, 392, 398, 410, 411
   driers, 411
   mountain, 325-6, 328. See also Mountain meadows.
   ricks, 334, 387
   sledges, 328
   yields, 328
Haymaking, 321-2, 323, 334, 411, 414
Heather, 401
Heathlands in the Netherlands, 425-9
   reclamation, 425-6
Hemp, ambaria, 87, 90, 104
Hens, 328, 428
Herding, communal, 299, 334
Herdsmen, nomadic, 8, 70
Hérémence, Val d', *266*, 275
Hérens, Val d', *266*, 268, 269
Hevea, 52, 54
Highland agriculture, 306-9, 338
Hill Farming Act, 395
Hillegom, *410*, 432
Hives, 513
Holland, *410*
'Home' field, 46
Horses, 107, 342, 400, 401, 460, 470, 471, 474, 493, 494, 513, 514
   hire of, 363
Horticulture, 251, 429-33, 499
Huerta, 221-5
Huitan, 283
Humus, 114
Hungary, 465-91, *468*
   agrarian reform, 466-7
   agricultural policies, 485-6, 489-91
   climate, 466
   irrigation, 466
   overpopulation, 467-8
   population, 466
   reclamation, 465
   soils, 465

Hunger, 13
   war against, 434, 533-7
Hunting, 41, 54, 63
Hydro-electric power, 58, 146

IJELIJ, 72
Immigration, 111
Indian civilization, 125-8
Indian Union, 159-63
   cattle, 161
   crop yields, 160
   future development, 162
   industrialization, 160
   population, 159
   religious taboos, 161
   size of holdings, 160
   social conditions, 161
   under-employment, 160
Indigo, 65
Indochina. See Vietnam, Northern.
Indonesia, 153
Industrial crops, 149, 201, 489, 509
Industrial revolution, the, 377
Industrialization, 5, 57, 59, 122, 151-2, 160, 205-6, 228, 262, 307, 309, 359, 375, 404, 434, 466, 473, 488, 489, 490-1
Ingolstadt, *348*
Institute for Colonization, 227
Integration of holdings, 150, 280, 300-1, 358, 374, 377
Intensification, 2, 3, 11, 56, 199, 205, 221, 230, 241, 261, 308, 373, 397, 414, 472
Intensiveness, degree of, 304, 305
Investment in industry, 434
Investments in agriculture, types of, 525
Iron, consumption of, 143
Irrigation, 85, 105, 110, 118, 135, 144-5, 150, 167, 188, 196-202, 204, 219, 221-4, 226-7, 228, 230, 231-6, 241-4, 265-6, 271-3, 292, 414, 483, 514-15
   basin, 97, 100 et seq., 134, 157
   economics of, 200-1
Italian rye-grass, 364, 373, 386, 400, 417

INDEX

Italy, *232*, 229-63
   agricultural labour force, 230
   balance of trade, 261
   capital, 231, 261
   climate, 229
   divisions, 230-1
   drainage, 230
   emigration, 262
   industry, 262
   irrigation, 230
   land reform, 253-62
   malnutrition, 260-1
   population growth, 262
      problems, 230
   reclamation, 229
   soil erosion, 229
   technical instruction, 261
   topography, 229
   under-employment, 262

JEEPS, 275, 294, 368
Jute, 149

KABYLIA, *170*, 180-7
Kale, 385, 391, 400
Karikal, 157
Kasba Tadla, *186*, 198
Kecskemet, *468*, 479-81
   orchards, 479-80
   vineyards, 479-80
Khammès, 182, 187-90
Kids, 317, 327
Kirchseeon, *340*, 340
Kirdis, 86
Kokry, 103, 106
Kola, 26, 86
Kolkhoz. See Co-operatives, producer's, and Collectives.
Kosice, *494*, 492, 496
Kouia, 107
Kouroumari zone, 110, 111
Krautgarten, 314
Kuhbauer, 460
Kulaks, 449, 461, 486, 507
Kunst-Egarten, 313

LA MANCHA, 218
Labour, cheapness of, 203
Labour laws, 231-6, 243

Labour, peak demand, 61, 71
Laghouat, *170*, 171
Laissez-faire policy, 13, 16
Lambs, 317
Land chief, 92
   concessions, 129-30
'Land hunger', 377
   improvement, economics of, 260, 377
   ownership, 64, 96, 129-30, 391
   purchase, 415
   reform, 155, 156, 162, 218-19, 236, 240, 249-60, 356-9, 438-40, 455, 460, 462-4, 466-7, 469, 471, 473, 476, 479-80, 500, 502 et seq.
   political motives for, 258-9
   tenure, 45, 237-8, 401, 418
   utilization, 7
   values, 131, 140, 224, 292, 293, 362, 368, 384, 389, 405, 415, 418, 429-30, 435, 478
Landless labourers, 142, 180, 212
Landowning class, 131, 141
Languages of communication, 22.
Laos, 152
Large estates, 438, 454, 455, 467, 473, 474, 475
   undertaking, the, 518
Latifundia, 195, 196, 200, 217-18, 226, 250-7
Leaching, 62, 114, 145
Legal system, the, 4
Leguminous crops, 37, 157
   food crops, 149
Leiden, *410*, 432
Leipzig, *440*, 441
Leisnig, *440*, 455
Lentils, 183, 188
Leo-M'boro, 78
Lere, 78
Letterhoutem, *362*, 368-9
Leys, 311, 312, 343, 373-4, 384, 386, 392, 394, 400, 417. See also Grassland, temporary.
Liberalism, philosophy of, 524
Lilacs, 433
Lime, 391
Lindental, *440*, 441

INDEX

Linseed, 188, 190
Livestock Rearing Act, 395
    rearing, sentimental, 85, 89
Locusts, 67
Loincloth, 47, 76
Lombardy, 230-6, *232*
Lorries, 179, 495, 513
Loua, 279
Low Countries, 406-36
    capital, 408-9
    climate, 408
    co-operation, 409
    education, 408
    land reclamation, 406-7
    lessons to be learnt from, 433-6
    market research, 409
    political and economic factors, 434-5
    population, 406
        pressure, 407
    soils, 408
Lubilash sandstones, 19
Lucerne, 175, 198, 220, 243, 244, 246, 302, 310, 311, 316, 318, 391, 421, 474
Ludlow, *380*, 381, *382*
Lupins, 453
Lycopersicum, 26

MACHINE HIRING SERVICES, 443, 449-54, 461, 471, 485, 488, 507-8
Macina Canal, 106
Madagh, *186*, 199
Mainburg, 348, 351, 353
Maize, 32, 35, 38, 39, 49, 83, 85, 89, 90, 91, 104, 107, 137, 190, 235, 244, 246, 310, 311, 325, 330, 475, 477, 481
Malaya, 153
Malnutrition, 13, 260
Malthusianism, 11, 16, 528, 532, 535, 536
Mandarins, 130
Mangoes, 46, 89
Mangolds, 342, 364, 366, 373, 385, 411, 414, 417
Manioc, 33, 35, 37, 39, 49, 67, 83
Manpower shortage, 387, 488

Manufacturing industry, 57, 231, 372, 408
Manure, 65, 83, 85, 90, 93, 101, 105, 138, 145, 157, 216, 234, 267, 270, 272, 273, 275, 276, 277, 283, 284, 286, 289, 317, 319, 332, 333, 338, 342, 346, 475
Manures, green, 86, 116, 138, 146, 371
Maremma, *232*, 250-7
    land use, 250-1
    size of units, 250
    Office, 254
Marginal land, 379, 389, 395-6, 405
    Land Scheme, 395
Market for agricultural produce, 11, 16, 419, 524
    fruit, 227
    grapes, 290, 291
    hops, 352
    liquid milk, 411
    meat, 112, 113
    vegetables, 227, 446, 483-4
    wheat, 189
    wine, 501
    gardening, 85, 483-4, 512, 513
    prices, 461-2
    research, 409, 431
Marrow-stemmed kale, 373
Marshall Plan, 527
Martin Act, the, 200
Mayens, 279, 282-5, 300, 330-1
Mayumba Massif, 24
Meadows, 234, 264-76, 320-2, 331, 343, 345, 347, 371
    irrigated, 300
Mechanical power, 228, 517
Mechanization, 2, 3, 6, 11, 42, 44, 55, 56, 102, 115, 116, 118 et seq., 150, 151, 191-6, 204, 214-15, 217-18, 225, 241, 259, 261, 374, 387, 509, 520-1
    partial, 120
Medemblick, *410*, 412
Medical techniques, effects of (in Asia and Africa), 530
Mediterranean coastlands, 209
Medraz, *312*, 311
Meknes, *186*, 193
Melfi, 73

INDEX

'Memorial to Lenin' collective, 513
Métayage, 220, 238-40, 244-52, 292, 377
Mezokovesd, *468*, 468-73, 492
  seasonal workers, 469
  size of farms, 469
  working population, 469
Microfundia, 216, 250, 516-17
Micro-region, 11
Mieders, 310, 311, *312*
Miesbach, *340*, *348*, 345-8
Migration, 11, 55
Mikulov, *494*, 498
Mildew, 351
Milk, 148, 231-6, 267 et seq., 287, 316, 385, 410-15, 416-19
  derivatives, 123, 148
  fat content, 347, 411, 414, 416, 417, 447
  increasing production of, 385-6
  Marketing Board, 386
  yields, 273, 284, 285, 287, 342, 343, 347, 366, 384, 385, 411, 413, 414, 415, 416, 417, 427, 447, 456, 493, 511, 514
Milkmaid, 384
Millet, 69, 85, 86, 87, 91, 104
  great, 68, 90
  pearl, 86
  red, 83
  spiked, 66, 68
Miniankas, 102, 107
Mint, 188
Mixed farming, 42, 89, 448
  in tropical Africa, 119
Modernization, kinds of, 121
  of agriculture, 168, 214, 375
Mohammedanism, 64
Mohammedans, 166-7
Molodo, 103
  Channel, 108
Moneylending, 101, 131, 132, 140, 158, 161, 167, 169
Mongo, 74
Monoculture, 147, 148
Monsoon Asia, 162
Moors, 177-8
Moravia, *494*, 498
Morio, *24*, 65 et seq.

Morocco, 164-71, 187-202, *186*
  modernization, 191-6
Mortars, 47, 94, 137
Mossi region, 111
Mossis, 108
Motor cultivators, 387
  transport, 481
Motterwitz, *440*, 455-9
Moulouya Barrage, 197
Mountain meadows, 319, 333. *See also* Hay, mountain.
Mowers, horse-drawn, 322
  motor, 302, 306, 322, 326
M'Pesoba, *24*, 89 et seq.
M'saken, 177-80
Muela, 211-13, *212*
Mulberry, 231
Mules, 182, 212, 222-3, 272, 294
Multiple cropping, 222, 227
Mung beans, 157
Murcia, 221-5, *210*
Mustergut, 458
Musz, 313-14
Mutterbergtal, *312*, 325
Myslava, *494*, 492-6

NAM-DINH, *136*, 140
Nam-Xuong, 135 et seq.
Nara, 104
Native Agricultural Association, 109
'Native' shortcomings, 22-3
Natives in Africa, status of, 123
Natur-Egarten, 311-12
Navisance, R., *266*, 264, 270
Negoundagou, 157
Neo-Malthusians, 13
Netherlands, the. *See* Low Countries.
Neubauern. *See* New peasants.
Neustift, 311, *312*, 315-35
New countries, 3
  House Farm, *382*, 389-94, 395
  peasants, 440-9
Niémina, 102
Nikolaital, *266*, 268, 269
Niono, 106, 107
Nitrates, 146
Nitrogen in the soil, excess of, 413, 414
Nomadic grazing, 73
Nomadism, 166-77

INDEX

Noria, 188
Norms, 506, 511. (*See also* Production no. ms.)
North Africa, 164-208
  agricultural types, 166
  climate, 164
  colonization, 166-7
  present trends, 171
  demography, 170-1
  erosion, 165, 168
  native agriculture, 168
    economy, 169-70
  peoples, 165
  rainfall, 165
  soils, 165
  topography, 164
  usury, 169
  vine, 169
North Cameroons, 83
  Holland, 410-15, *410*
North-east Polder, *410*, 407, 420-4
Nuoc-mam, 138
Nutrition, 16, 54
Nutritional standards, 14, 475, 525, 535

OAK TREES, 183, 184
Oases, 164
Oats, 246, 371, 391, 453
Oberberg, *312*, 327-9, 330
Oberbergtal, *312*
Office des Beni-Amir, 198
Office du Niger, 97, 99 et seq.
Oil mills, 81, 115, 179
Oil-palm, 26, 35, 43, 46, 52, 53, 118
  collective plantations, 29
  compulsory plantations, 29
  voluntary plantations, 29
Oil-seed residues, 145
Oil-seeds, vegetable, 117
Old-fashioned methods, 335
Olives, 177-80, 183, 188, 211-13, 215, 218, 243, 244, 246
Onions, 104, 107, 188
Ontinar del Salz, 212, 219-221
Orange, 26, 89, 197
Orchards, 185, 187, 241-2, 343, 479-80, 513
Ouarsenis Massif, *170*, 173
Oubangui, 79

Oude Bildtzyl, *410*, 416-20
Oued Beth Barrage, 200
Ouerrha Valley, *186*, 196
Ouled Salah, 172
Ouled Sidi ben Daoud, 187
Oulmes, *186*
Oum er R'bia, 199
Overpopulation, 2, 143, 160, 171, 242, 336, 338, 361-2, 370, 375, 419, 434, 467, 478, 486, 488, 515
Owner-farmers, 242-4
Oxen, 137, 140, 182

Pacages, 281-2
Pack animals, 172, 216
Pacte colonial, 58
Paddy. *See* Rice.
Pala, 79
Pannéals, 158
Papayas, 46
Paprika, 481, 483
'Participation' system, land farmed under, 238-9
Part-time agricultural employment, 361, 363, 369, 374
  employment, 427
  non-agricultural employment, 324, 388, 398, 401, 429, 472, 494, 495, 499, 517
Pastoral farms, 256
Pastoralism, 187, 482-3
Pastures, communal, 346, 388
  co-ownership of, 333, 334, 335
  enclosed, 300, 342
  permanent, 383, 384, 399, 418
  ploughing of, 342, 384, 385, 386
  summer, 299, 300, 330-5
  unimproved, 8
  upland, 345, 347
Patriarchal family, 21
Paysanat dirigé, 38 et seq.
Peach, 197
Pears, native, 43
  avocado, 43
Peasant agriculture, 522
Peasant, Swiss, 304
'Peasant woman's buildings', 341
Peat, 342, 356, 407, 421
Pegola, *232*, 240-1

INDEX

Pene Niolo, *24*, 24 et seq.
Penga, 95
Pennisetum subangustum, 116
People's democracies, 489, 490, 515
Pessina Cremonese, *232*, 233-6
Pestle, 47, 94, 137
Peuhl nomads, 93
Peuhls, 96
Pfaffendorf, *440*, 450-4
Pfaffenhofen, *348*, 348
Photo-oxidation, solar, 19
    chemical, 37
Phylloxera, 167, 290, 292, 497, 499
Pick-up balers, 387
Pigs, 41, 137, 140, 237, 246, 285, 317, 325, 326, 342, 345, 350, 356, 366, 369, 397, 443, 447, 460, 475, 495, 509, 513, 514
Pilot farms, 194, 255
Pimento, 33
Pineapples, 26, 33, 46
Pinnistal, *312*, 331-5
Pinsec, 265
Pisciculture, 27, 54
Planned agriculture, 517-18
    economy, 524, 537
Plans, production, 501
Plant genetics, 147
Plantains, 26, 48
Plantation system, 52 et seq.
Plantations, 19-20, 43, 127, 153
Ploughing, cost of, 452
Plough, ox-drawn, 89, 93, 157
Po Valley, *232*, 229, 231-42
Poelddijk, *410*, 429-30
Point Four Aid, 532-3
Polders, 406-7, 409, 410-24
    in Flanders, 370
Poll-tax, 31
Polygamy, 64, 75
Pomegranate, 188
Ponies, 388
Ponte della Chiassa Superiore, 242
Poppy, 329
Population, declining, 296
    density of, 5, 230, 466
    growth of, 14, 154, 159, 170, 230, 258, 262, 339, 378, 406, 530-3
    migrations, 11, 55
    pressure of, 55, 137, 228, 249, 407, 425-7
    redistribution of, 121
    surplus, 110, 205
Pork, 143, 318, 364
Postal van, 273
Potatoes, 188, 197, 227, 267, 277-8, 281, 287, 294, 295, 310-14, 325, 329, 330, 342, 345, 364, 366, 369, 371, 385, 386, 400, 453, 481, 493, 508
    disease-free strains of, 416-20
    seed, 317, 355-6
Poultry, 89, 140, 143, 295, 297, 317, 472, 514
Power/land ratio, 347, 387
Price control, 405, 435
    supports, 415
Primogeniture, 403
Priorities, order of, 525
    scheme of, 57, 113, 144, 260
Private property, 258, 519
Production costs, 374, 377, 435
    norms, 444-5, 487, 490, 495. (*See also* Norms.)
Production, techniques of, 13
Productivity, agricultural, 2, 9, 107, 139, 144, 190, 203, 204, 207, 221, 223, 228, 233, 241, 248, 273, 274, 275, 278, 281, 287, 293, 294, 302, 305-9, 323, 325-6, 329, 336, 338, 344, 374, 464, 468, 514, 520, 521
    differences in, 532
    of labour, 138
Profit incentive, 519
    motive, 524, 536
Progress, obstacles to, 534
Protective foods, 13
Proteins, 35
Puits, *170*, 202-4
Pumping, 145, 150
Purchasing power, 13, 14
Puszta, 482-3

RABBITS, 394
Raccards, 275, 279
Raiffessen co-operative credit organization, 341, 345

INDEX

Rain, *312*, 316-19
Rainfall, efficacy of, 165
 reliability, 165
Rambutans, 43
Ramskapelle, 370
Ranching, 73
Ranunculi, 276
Rape, 123, 235, 366, 385, 417
Ray system, 139, 153
Reafforestation, 403
'Real' as opposed to 'economic' requirements, 526-7
Rearing. *See* Stock-rearing.
Reclamation, 236-42, 255, 371, 403, 420-4, 425-6
Red Delta. *See* Vietnam, Northern.
Refrigerator ships, 386
Refugees, German, 339-40, 439-41, 448
Re-grouping of land in Czechoslovakia, 505
Religious taboos, 91, 161
Remaniement parcellaire, 280
Rent differentials, 513
Rents, 130-1, 179, 235-6, 240, 362, 368, 392, 399, 402, 403, 415, 418, 423, 427, 478
 for grazing and herding, 332
Research, 16, 344, 351, 420, 455-9
Reservoirs, 199-200, 226
Restriction of production, 524
Rètzes, 278
Rhône Valley, 287-93
Rice, 54, 82, 83, 87, 90, 92, 95 et seq., 107, 108, 128-60, 226, 490
 floating, 98
 harvesting, 145
 straw, 136
 transplanted, 98
 upland, 37, 38, 54, 139
 wild, 96, 97, 104, 105, 106
Rice-fields, communal, 142
Rice-mills, 98, 137
Rickshaw, 59
Rimaibe, 96
Riziam, 106
Rodthal, 346-7
Root crops, 367, 442

Rotation, crop, 7
 grasses, 302, 303, 326, 329, 355, 385
Rotations, annual, 52
Rough grazing, 328, 345, 379, 394
Row crops, 148, 216, 243, 311, 316, 342, 345, 353, 427, 459, 477
Rubber, natural, 54
 synthetic, 54
 wild, 53
Rural Amelioration Sectors, 174-5
 housing, 307, 336-7, 476-7
 population, 228, 230, 237, 340, 345, 349, 387, 466
Russia compared with United States, 522
Rye, 277, 278, 294, 355, 367, 369, 371, 373, 453, 481
 grass, 235, 313, 386, 400

SAASTAL, *266*, 268, 269
Sahel, 98, 110
 Canal, 106, 108
Sainfoin, 474
Saint-Luc, 267
San Antonio estate, 233-6
 Caterina, *232*, 246-50
Sansanding Barrage, 100
Saragossa, *210*, 211, *212*
Saré field, the, 83, 85, 86
Satellite farms, 368-9, 370
Sauerkraut, 314
Savanna fires, 62, 78, 94
 tree, 63, 78
 clearing of, 115, 116
Schadenseite, 313, 322-6
Seasonal agricultural inactivity, 122
 food shortages, 112
 labour demands, 489
 migration, 8, 166, 173-6, 288-9, 299, 366, 469, 471
Secano, 211-16
Section for Rural Modernization, 191-6
Seduk, *312*, 327
Seed selection, 455, 508
Sefa, 115
Segou, 89
Seitiz, 305

INDEX

Semi-planned economy, 434
Senegal, 114 et seq.
Sérac (cheese), 285
Sericulture, 187, 231
Serpieri Law, 253
Serres, 429
Sersou Plateau, *170*, 173, 176
Sesamum, 68
Settat, *186*, 190
Settlement pattern, dispersed, 46
Settlers in N. Africa, 202-4
Sewing machines, 47, 73
Shanty town, 476
Shari, 82
Shea tree, 72, 92
Sheep, 27, 96, 172, 177, 179, 188, 204, 213, 221, 230, 245, 246, 251, 295, 300, 315, 332, 334, 335, 383, 388, 393, 447, 460, 513
Shelter belts of trees, 437, 514
Shropshire, south, *380*, 381-403
    agricultural development, 381-3
    climate and soils, 381
Sicily, 230
Siedlung, 356-9
Sierre, *266*, 288-9
Silage, 373, 391-2
Silk, 149
Silos, 355, 428
Sint Lievens Houtem, *362*, 365-8
    crops, 366
    land use, 367
    occupations, 365
    size of farms, 365-6
Sisal, 120
Size of fields, 452, 455, 462, 517, 518
    undertaking, 4, 250-1, 287, 296, 305-9, 336, 341, 345, 365-6, 372, 374, 388-9, 401, 422-3, 425-7, 429, 433, 435, 438-40, 441, 451, 463, 466-7, 469, 493, 517
Skim milk, 313, 332, 435
Slaughter houses, 112
Slav settlers in Moravia, 500-1
Slovakia, 492-8, *494*
Sluf, 421
Small farms, 516-19
Smallholdings, 388, 396-9, 401

Social insurance, 443
    position of farmers, 373
    services, 413, 512-13
    structure, 64, 87, 100, 108-9, 179-80, 212, 252, 377-8, 396, 498, 500
Soest, *410*, 427
Soft fruit, 281, 428
Soil, 1, 2, 3
    artificial, 407, 433
    azoic, 421
    classification, 110
    conservation, 4, 15, 57, 94, 185, 192-3, 226, 525
    Conservation Programme (U.S.A.), 11, 15
    correctives, 15
    destruction of, 14
    deterioration, 36, 45, 49, 63, 78, 114 et seq., 198
    drying of, 140
    erosion, 4, 15, 54, 79, 95, 110, 165, 168, 185, 229
    exchange of, 432
    impoverishment, 82
    improvement of, 525
    structure, 101
    toxic, 432
    utilization studies, 501
Soil-less cultivation, 150
'Soil-mining', 521
Somogy, 473
Sonnenseite, 312-13, 315-20, 333, 334
Sorghum, 66, 67, 68, 77, 80, 83, 86, 89, 90, 91, 93, 107
Sovkhoz. See State farms.
Sows, 364, 460, 493
Soya beans, 54
Spain, 209-28, *210*
    climate, 209
    erosion, 209-10
    industrial development, 225
    lack of mechanical power, 211
    poverty, 210
    topography, 209
Specialization, 424, 518
Spices, 104
Spinning, 63, 91
Sprinklers, rotating, 281, 317
Stable litter, 319, 327, 329, 342

INDEX

Stadel, 318, 320-1, 329, 334, 348
Stalin Plan for the Transformation of Nature, 15
Standard of living, 142, 154, 415, 534
State farms, 194, 340, 420-4, 455-9, 487, 488, 505, 508-9, 513-14
State shop, 461
'Stick and dog' farming, 379 et seq.
Stiefel, 321-2, 329, 348
Stock-breeding, 248, 482
Stock ratio, 235, 239, 246, 251, 287, 342, 343, 347, 400, 411, 447, 449, 456, 469, 478, 487
Stock-rearing, 8, 63, 73, 153, 157, 202, 469, 504-5, 512
   co-operatives, 506
Stoke St Milborough, 381-8, *382*
Stone ground-nut, 67, 83
Strawberries, 281, 294
Striga, 90, 93
Stubaital, *312*, 310-38
   clergy, 337
   diet, 313-14
   family farms, 338
   intensiveness of farming, 338
   land use, 310-13
   settlement pattern, 338
Subdivision of farms, 370, 372, 425, 435, 448
Subsidies, 11, 147, 253, 278, 291, 297, 302, 303, 304, 307, 308, 309, 337, 344, 387, 389, 392, 394, 395, 404, 405, 452
   consumer, 404
Subsistence economy, 303, 329, 335, 363, 475, 493
   farming, 7
Sugar-beet, 227, 246, 364-6, 400, 417, 441, 508
Sugar cane, 33, 54, 149, 202
Sunflower, 477
Surpluses created by the American economy, 532
   destruction of, 431-2, 536
Sweet potatoes, 83, 85, 90, 104, 137, 139, 148
Swing-plough, 182, 189, 267, 268, 311
Switzerland, 264-309
Szentes, *468*, 483-4

TABOURIS, 79
Tala Allem, 181
Tanyas, 480-1
Taro, 32, 46, 139, 147
Tariffs for machinery hire, 388, 451-2, 461, 471, 507-8, 511
Tax remissions, 487
Tea, 202
Technical adviser, 109
   education, 109
   instruction, 261
   knowledge, 95
Techniques, farming, 298, 519
Telfes, 310, *312*
Tenant system, 131, 377
Tenkedogo, 108
Terraces, 86, 89, 139, 185, 214
Terracing, 320
Three-field system, 376
Tikem, Lake, 79
Tilapia macrochir, 27
Timber, 51, 110
Tizi Ouzou, *170*, 181
Tobacco, 76, 87, 104, 107, 149, 202, 244, 246
Tomatoes, 46, 89, 104, 107
Tomes (cheese), 276, 288
Tonkin. *See* Vietnam, Northern.
Tonle, Lake, 152
Tourists, 296-7, 324, 330
Towns, growth of, 407
Tractor stations, 495, 511
   tools, 423, 424
Tractors, 103, 104, 119, 121, 192, 198, 256, 342, 343, 347, 353, 355, 357, 387, 389, 390, 401, 423, 452, 516
   electric, 151
Tracuit, Alpe de, 283-7
Trade, terms of, 381, 426
   with underdeveloped countries, 532-3
Trading, profits from, 65
'Trading economy', 64
Traite, 265
Transdanubia, 465-6, 473
Transhumance, 251
Transport difficulties, 43
   revolution in, 10, 59

554

INDEX

Trefoil, 421
Trial plots, 449, 457
Triffas, *186*, 196, 199
Tropical savanna of Africa, 61-124
 climate, 61
 European influence, 64
 fires, 62
 handicrafts, 63
 native economy, 64
 peoples, 63
 soils, 62
 vegetation, 63
Trudodyen, 506, 511-13
Tuberculosis, 417
Tunisia, 164-71, 177-80, *178*
 cereals, 179-80
 olive groves, 177-80
Turner, *494*, 496-8
'Turnip revolution', 378
Turnips, 188, 373
Turumbu, 37 et seq.
Tuscany, *232*, 242-50
Tyrol, the, 309
 modernization, 336
Tyrolean Alps, 310-38

UMBELLIFERS, 276, 329
Underdeveloped countries, 14, 207, 530-3
 aid to, 532-3
 difficulties of establishing trade with, 532-3
Under-employment, 142, 160, 162, 239, 261, 262, 368, 426, 495
Undeveloped land, 16
Unemployment, rural, 184, 217, 218, 223, 228, 237, 252, 340, 413, 471
Urena lobata, 35
Union Française Outre-Mer, 208
United Kingdom, 376-405
 agricultural policies, 404-5
 capital, 391
 education, 391
 urbanization, 390
 See also English agriculture.
United States compared with Russia, 522
Unterberg, 329, 330

Unterbergtal, *312*
Utrecht, *410*, 427

VEAL, 350, 367
Vegetables, 139, 178, 281, 342
Veilings, 431, 433
Vereinigung der Erfassungs und Aufkauf Betriebe (V.E.A.B.), 446
Versannage, 292
Vetch, 175, 204, 235
Vietnam, Northern, 125-56, *136*
 agricultural systems, 127
 Chinese merchants, 133
 climate, 125-6
 effects of war, 156
 flood protection, 126
 historical, 127-8
 import duties, 133
 irrigation, 127-8
 land reforms, 156
 maize exports, 133
 population density, 125
 regional differences, 126
 rice exports, 133
 social organization, 128-9
 soils, 126-7
 use of animals, 128
 vegetation, 125
Vietnamese village, 134
Vine, 167, 169, 211-12, 215, 237-45, 246-7, 257, 281, 287, 293, 479-80, 481, 497-8
Virus diseases, 277
Vissoie, 264 et seq., *266*
Volksgüter, 439
Volksgut Friedrich Engels, 455-9

WADDEN SEA, 421
Waershoot, *362*, 369-70
Wahlen plan, 297, 303
Walls, retaining, 280, 292
War of 1914-18, effects of, 379, 404
 1939-45, effects of, 404, 467, 469-70, 472, 476
Warenhuis, 429
Warping, 146
Waste of resources by wealthy nations, 535-6

INDEX

Water control, 105, 144, 228, 413, 418-19
  power, 137, 284, 332
  resources, 191
  rights, 271-2
  supply, 184, 214
  tax, 105
Weaving, 63, 72, 91
Weeding, 69, 71, 199, 223
Wells, 196
West Germany, agricultural progress in, 357-8
Westland, *410*, 429-32
Wetterstetter farm, 343-4
Wheat, 67, 172, 183, 188, 190, 197, 235, 243, 246, 311, 365, 386, 391, 441, 474, 484
Wheat, winter, 324
Wieringenmeer, 407, *410*, 413, 420
'Williams' system, 454
Winches, 267, 290, 294, 306, 315-16, 327
Wind erosion, 114, 514
Windmills, 406
Wine, 215
  merchants, 290
  Survey, 501

Witch-doctor, 92
Wolnzach, 351, 353
Wood pulp, 52
Wool, 172
  production, 176-7
Work per acre, 251, 257, 259, 273, 292, 293, 305-6, 323, 423, 475, 499
World population, increases in, 535

Yam, 32
Yangambi, *24*, 36 et seq., 48
Yellow rattle, 276
Yield per working day, 9
Yields, crop, 9, 11, 160, 292, 373, 378, 400, 408, 418, 419, 422, 447, 458, 475, 497
  record, 242
Yssel, Lake, 421, *410*

Zamindars, 161
Zenzalino, 237-40
Zeriba, 101, 102
Zinal, 282-3
Zuider Zee, 407

Printed in Great Britain by
Lowe & Brydone (Printers) Ltd., London, NW10

WITHDRAWN
UTSA LIBRARIES

HALF-LENGTHS

HALF-LENGTHS

BY

GEORGE W. E. RUSSELL

"The Figures are less than Life, and about Half-Lengths."
HORACE WALPOLE.

Essay Index Reprint Series

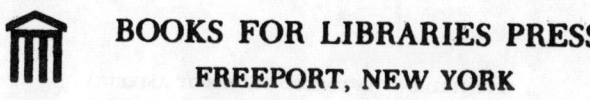

BOOKS FOR LIBRARIES PRESS
FREEPORT, NEW YORK

First Published 1913
Reprinted 1970

INTERNATIONAL STANDARD BOOK NUMBER:
0-8369-1849-5

LIBRARY OF CONGRESS CATALOG CARD NUMBER:
71-128309

PRINTED IN THE UNITED STATES OF AMERICA

TO
THOMAS WILLIAM LUMSDEN, M.D.
WHO
EXCELLING AS A PHYSICIAN
EXCELS NOT LESS AS
A FRIEND

CONTENTS

		PAGE
I.	"Sense and Sensibility"	11
II.	The Last of the Whigs	38
III.	The First Lord Coleridge	70
IV.	Henry Labouchere	82
V.	A Cabinet of Miniatures:	
	The Duchess of Buccleuch	96
	Lady Lindsay	99
	Mrs Pascoe Glyn	103
	Mrs Vaughan	106
	Adelaide Procter	108
	Lord Kimberley	115
	Lord Gladstone	118
	Lord Wolverhampton	122
	Thomas Ellis	126
	Walter Wren	128
	Westcott and Lee	131
	Henry Kingsley	143

CONTENTS

		PAGE
Baron Ferdinand Rothschild	. . .	151
The Wilberforces .	. . .	154
Joseph Hume .	. . .	168
VI. A FORGOTTEN PANIC .	. . .	175
VII. THE INNER SIDE OF A TRANSACTION .		191
VIII. OXFORD	. .	200
IX. CAMBRIDGE	. .	234
X. THE JUBILEE GARDEN-PARTY	. .	242
XI. AN ODOROUS TASK . .	. .	247
XII. FLOWERS	. .	254
XIII. SOME USES OF WEALTH	. .	260
XIV. "JOHN INGLESANT" . .	. .	268
XV. A GREEK REQUIEM . .	. .	275
XVI. A CLUSTER OF ADVERTISEMENTS	.	278
XVII. "BOTTLES"	. .	286
XVIII. RELATIONSHIPS :		
Mothers and Sons .	. . .	294
"More, Please" .	. . .	300
"Tender and True"	. . .	307
Fathers and Sons .	. . .	313

CONTENTS

		PAGE
Fathers and Daughters	. . . .	320
Brothers	. . . . .	327
Home	. . . . . .	334
XIX. FRIENDSHIP	. . . . . .	342
XX. A SILVER WEDDING	. . . .	349

I

"SENSE AND SENSIBILITY"

OR, THE TWO CARDINALS

I CRAVE Miss Austen's pardon for borrowing her title. My excuse must be that no other would so exactly fit my purpose, which is to analyse Mr Wilfrid Ward's Life of Cardinal Newman. "Exhaustive" and "monumental" are the consecrated epithets for books of this type—books of great bulk, containing an immense amount of matter carefully arranged, and including within their scope everything in heaven and earth which can illustrate their theme. It is whispered that, in addition to all public records collated in England and on the Continent, Mr Ward has read 50,000 letters—

A thing imagination boggles at.

But he has his reward. Here at last is the story, never henceforth to be denied or gainsaid, of the Man to whom, more than to any other one person, must be attributed both the "Second Spring" of the English Church and the present position of the Roman Church in England. Large as the book is, it would have been much larger. if Mr Ward had retraced in detail the story of Newman's Anglican life; but he has wisely realized the fact that nothing can be advantageously added to, or substracted from, the *Apologia*, and he has left that spiritual and literary masterpiece to tell its own tale. By the time we reach the 94th page of the first volume, Newman has been received into the Roman Church. Henceforward the Church of England disappears; and our concern is with Rome and Romanists and Romanism.

John Henry Newman was now in his forty-fifth year, at the height of his influence, and in the full perfection of his powers. Not often, surely, has Providence fashioned such an intellect—so piercing, so swift, so pliant, so subtle. The intellect expressed itself in the style—flexible and sinuous, yet sharply pointed, natural, easy, unforced, as a bird's song; clear as the thought which it expressed; simple as the Bible and Shakespeare are simple, and withal rich as they are rich. Life, light, colour, and movement are the notes of Newman's style; and, though he gave it later a more sumptuous turn, it was, at the moment of his secession, as near perfection as genius and care could make it. In that very year he wrote: "Perhaps one gets over-sensitive even about style as one gets on in life." " I have not written a sentence, I suppose, which will stand, or hardly so." " Besides rewriting, every part has to be worked out and defined as in moulding a statue." As we read Newman, his style seems the easiest, most natural, most inevitable, in the world; and yet those extracts show that, even in the throes of the spiritual crisis which cut his life in half, he worked at his manuscript like a sculptor working at his clay.

The intellect and the style were enough to have made Newman famous; but they were joined in him with a keen sanctity "which the world cannot tame," and were used with sedulous care and the most consummate skill for the furtherance of one great end. "After hearing those sermons you might come away still not believing the tenets peculiar to the High Church system; but you would be harder than most men, if you did not feel more than ever ashamed of coarseness, selfishness, worldliness; if you did not feel the things of faith brought closer to the soul." Genius and holiness together had made Newman master of the young and generous world which thronged round the pulpit of St Mary's. As Mr Ward says, "he exercised a Kingship in Oxford, extending far beyond the ranks of a party, an influence so extraordinary that the tradition of it is now no longer realized and only half believed." The extent of that influence can never be measured. Some notion of its force may be gathered from the list of those who rose up and followed him without delay into the Roman fold. In his fall, as some esteemed it, he drew after him, as Mr Gladstone said, "a third part of the stars of Heaven," and what we lost Rome gained. Surely, since her final breach with us in 1570, Rome had won no such convert as Newman. He had already dissipated ignorance concerning her, and allayed suspicion, and made her seem interesting and beautiful and attractive where before she had been abhorred and dreaded, or at best despised. Surely, if guided only by a human instinct, she must realize the magnitude of the boon which Newman brought her; must welcome him with open arms, and crown him with her choicest honours. That was the ideal. What really happened Mr Ward tells us, and a sorry tale it is. The story of Newman's experience in the Church of Rome, from 1845 to 1879, is a story of disillusionments, rebuffs, frustrations, disappointments; a story of unjust suspicions and calculated insults, with here and there disagreeable symptoms of treachery and double-dealing. When I write the word "disillusionments," I do not mean the gravest disillusion of all. His religious faith never failed nor wavered. He had deliberately accepted the religion of the Papacy with all that it involves; and faith in that religion carried him, if not serene, yet patient and dutiful, through all experiences of earthly sorrow. His "disillusionments" did not touch the Truth. They touched systems and methods and hopes and plans and efforts, and often they touched human characters, and saintly reputations which masked ambition and emulation and some worse faults. He had long believed that "to follow the lead of Rome was to prosper"; but that belief was now shattered by harsh realities. We may take them, very briefly, point by point :—

(1) In 1850 an ex-Dominican called Giacinto

Achilli came to England and delivered a course of lectures against the Inquisition. Cardinal Wiseman, then the head of the Roman Church in England, replied by an article in the *Dublin Review,* in which he charged Achilli with shameful immoralities. Newman, in an evil moment, took Wiseman's allegations as facts, and repeated them, with emphasis, in a public lecture. Achilli prosecuted Newman for libel, and Newman naturally applied to Wiseman for his authorities; but Wiseman gave only half his mind to the business; looked for the documents, could not find them, or, as Newman thought, did not try to find them; and eventually found them when the trial was over, and Newman had been found guilty of libel, heavily fined, and publicly rebuked by the judge. It was a disillusioning experience, and Newman, who never forgot anything, remembered it.

(2) In 1851 Newman was requested by the Hierarchy to undertake the formation of a Catholic University in Ireland, and to be its "Rector." The difficulties which surrounded the enterprise were many and immense, and Newman saw them all. But the Pope had given a special sanction to the scheme, and this fact made Newman look upon the request of the Bishops as a Divine call. Here was to be the work of his life. He was to be the means of spreading the highest education among the untaught, or half-taught, Catholics of Ireland, and was to show them that perfect harmony between, or rather identity of, Faith and Philosophy, which Oxford was always

trying to establish. It was a worthy ambition; but it came to nothing. Newman had no organizing skill, no talent for creating new systems. He knew nothing about business. He did not understand the Irish, nor they him. The best authorities on Irish Education differed about his curriculum. The Irish gentry looked askance at the undertaking; and—worst of all—the Irish Primate distrusted Newman, and showed his distrust by thwarting and snubbing him. Through these clouds there suddenly burst a ray of light and encouragement. Cardinal Wiseman suggested that the Pope should confer on Newman the Episcopal dignity, as a suitable recognition of his gifts and labours, and with a view to strengthening his position in Ireland. Somehow or another, Newman's opponents got wind of the Pope's intention, and it never was fulfilled. This is Newman's own note on the transaction: "The Cardinal never wrote to me a single word, or sent any kind of message to me, in explanation of the change of intention about me, till the day of his death."

The clouds, pierced for a moment by this ray of encouragement, were now as black as ever; and in 1858 he resigned the Rectorship of the University, and returned in profound dejection to England.

(3) Newman's pen was now idle; idleness of such an instrument could not long continue; but in resuming literary activity Newman only prepared for himself fresh disappointments. The Roman Hierarchy asked him to edit the New English Version of the

Scriptures which the Roman Synod in England had recommended. Newman saw in the invitation another sign of God's leading, and he accepted the task with reverent and joyous thankfulness. But more than a year passed before he heard anything more on the subject. Opposition to the scheme came from America, where a Roman Archbishop was engaged on a similar work. Newman was ready to abide by the decision of his ecclesiastical superiors. But time went by; nothing was done; and it became evident that Wiseman, if not hostile, was apathetic. "I found," says Newman, "that the Cardinal was washing his hands of the whole affair, and throwing the responsibility on me. . . . That there is some mystery about it, I know, though what it is I have not a dream. Father Faber, on his deathbed, told me that he knew how badly I had been treated in the matter."

Newman abandoned the task, and the Bishops never asked him to resume it. Another great plan had been projected; "and yet another time the ecclesiastical rulers, after words of most flattering recognition, had seemed absolutely indifferent to the reality of his work."

(4) Newman's next attempt to serve the Church was made in the way of journalism. He was profoundly convinced that, if the Church of Rome was to retain her ascendancy in Europe, and regain it where she had lost it, she must put herself right with the intellectual world. She must no longer ignore history,

or criticism, or physical science. She must no longer rely on unassisted logic to establish her fundamental positions. Still less must she depend for her authority on terror and ignorance and superstition. With the hope of disseminating higher views, he allied himself in turn with such publications as the *Atlantis*, the *Rambler*, the *Home and Foreign Review*. Those papers and the men who conducted them fought a gallant fight for mental freedom; but Newman only received further injury from his connexion with them. Rome disapproved, the publications came to an end, and Newman emerged with damaged reputation as a "bad Catholic"—a Liberal theologian, only the more dangerous because his loyalty to the Church could not be gainsaid—and was delated to Rome for heresy. He was now thoroughly sick at heart. "I am treated," he said, "like some wild incomprehensible beast, a spectacle for Dr Wiseman to exhibit to strangers, as himself being the hunter who captured it." And again—"God has marked my course with almost unintermittent mortifications. Few, indeed, successes has it been His Blessed Will to give me through life . . . but since I have been a Catholic, I seem to myself to have had nothing but failure."

(5) The string of disappointments is not yet complete, but, as Mr Ward says, "the years 1859 to 1864 may be called the low-water mark of Newman's life-history." His health was bad; he thought the end was near. His spirits were at their lowest. His books had ceased to sell, and he had ceased to write.

"His name was hardly known to the rising generation"; and it seemed as though his life was closing in the saddest of failures. The resuscitation of his fortunes came from an unexpected quarter. At the beginning of 1864 Charles Kingsley, then at the height of his vogue as Muscular Christian and Broad Churchman, made a sudden and unprovoked attack on Newman's veracity. Newman replied with alacrity, demanding the grounds of the attack. And then Kingsley, instead of frankly apologizing for his ill-mannered rashness, proceeded to entangle himself in discreditable endeavours to run away from what he had said, and yet leave the imputation of falsehood unrevoked. He struggled in contortions of baffled anger, "like a wild bull in a net," while Newman wove that mesh of logic, sarcasm, and contemptuous humour which formed the Introduction to the *Apologia pro vita sua*.

Never was a controversial victory more signal or more complete. Kingsley, all unwitting, had given Newman the opportunity for which he had longed, of "vindicating his character and conduct." Henceforward, whatever might be said about Newman, all England knew him for an honest man.

(6) The triumph over Kingsley, and the accession of public respect which had followed it, made a bright interval in Newman's darkened life; but disappointment was again at hand. He had long wished to establish a Hall for Roman Catholic students at Oxford, feeling sure that the University would not

wean them from the Faith, but would open their eyes to aspects of life and thought which are not revealed to Seminarists. He believed that all the forces in Oxford which made for Faith would tend to come together, and that thereby the resistance to Rationalism among young men would be immeasurably strengthened. He felt that the establishment of a House of the Oratory at Oxford, with a suitable Church and imposing services, would serve the Catholic cause, which, as far as its material setting was concerned, was very poorly represented there; and, as he was human, he must have recalled his former ascendancy over undergraduate hearts, and hoped to reassert it. So he drew his plans and arranged his schemes, and actually bought the site for a house in Oxford. His intention was welcomed even by academical authorities. The English gentry rejoiced that their long exclusion from the University was drawing to an end; and everything looked prosperous for the new venture, when suddenly the usual blow fell. The English Hierarchy, acting under influence from Rome, forbade the scheme, and again Newman had to sit down beaten. "And now," he wrote from his house at Birmingham, "I am thrown back again on my do-nothing life here—how marvellous!" Marvellous indeed it was; but yet one more rebuff remained to be administered.

(7) Newman has told us that, as a matter of personal conviction, he had always, after his submission to Rome, held the doctrine of the Papal

Infallibility; but he held it subject to all the conditions and qualifications which history required and theologians had admitted. In 1867 he wrote thus: "I hold the Pope's Infallibility, not as a dogma, but as a theological opinion; that is, not as a certainty, but as a probability." This was a view of the matter which was intolerable to the "Ultramontane" school of ecclesiastical politicians.

The social and political aspect of Europe was threatening. The historic princedom of the Popes was dangerously undermined. There was a feeling of revolution in the air, and a tendency to fall away from the faith was visible whichever way one looked. Men's hearts were failing them for fear and for looking after those things that were coming on the earth. At this crisis the confidential advisers of the Papacy conceived a strange way of escape from gathering perils. They thought that an Œcumenical Council, meeting at Rome, would awe the world into submission. Pius IX. had spoken of such a council in 1864, intending it to discuss and counteract the evils which beset an age of apostasy. In 1867 he announced that it would be definitely summoned for the winter of 1869; and forthwith the wire-pullers at the Vatican, acting with their allies in England and elsewhere, determined that the Council, when it assembled, should define the Papal Infallibility as an article of faith. "They seemed," says Mr Ward, "to conceive of such a definition as a protest against an apostate world, and a crown of honour for the persecuted

Pontiff." The years 1867-8-9 were years of great controversial stress, as the Roman Catholic world was sharply divided into those who welcomed, and those who deprecated, the prospect of the Definition. Among those who deprecated it was Newman, and once again he had to pass through the fire. "If ever he acted against his inclinations, and from a stern sense of duty, it was at this crisis. He had a full consciousness that many good but not far-seeing people, whom he respected, would condemn his attitude.... But throughout he believed himself to be defending the interests of Catholic theology against extremists who were—without realizing the effects of their action—setting it aside." He expected "untold good" from the Council, if only as bringing into formal acquaintance men from the most distant parts of the world; but he was anxious lest the assembled Bishops should treat such subjects as the Inspiration of the Bible, and the Intellectual Apprehension of God, with insufficient skill; while the prospect of the Definition filled him with dismay. The Council assembled in due course, and soon after it began its work he wrote his fears to his bishop, Dr Ullathorne, concluding his letter thus: "With these thoughts before me, I am continually asking myself whether I ought not to make my feelings public; but all I can do is to pray those great early Doctors of the Church, whose intercession would decide the matter —Augustine and the rest—to avert so great a calamity. If it is God's will that the Pope's Infallibility should be defined, then it is His Blessed Will to throw back the times and the moments of that triumph He has destined for His Kingdom; and I shall feel that I have but to bow my head to His Adorable Inscrutable Providence."

This letter was private; but, by some means never disclosed, it made its way into the public press, and naturally redoubled the wrath of the extremists against a man whom they regarded as at best a half-hearted Papalist, at worst a secret traitor to the Holy See. Once again that man was defeated, and his enemies triumphed. The dogma of the Infallibility was "defined" on the 18th of July 1870. Newman wrote to a friend, "Our good God is trying all of us with disappointment and sorrow just now; I allude to what has taken place at Rome. . . . It looks as if our Great Lord were in some way displeased with us."

(8) Newman "bowed his head," as he had promised, beneath this final blow; and for the next nine years he remained buried in his Oratorian home, emerging only to cross swords with Gladstone over the question of the Civil Allegiance of Catholics. During this period of what looked like final retirement he wrote a solemn testament for the use of his friends after his death; from it I quote these words: "I have before now said, in writing to Cardinals . . . when I considered myself treated with slight and unfairness, 'So this is the return made to me for working in the Catholic cause for so many years'—*i.e.* to that effect.

I feel it still, and ever shall—but it was not a disappointed ambition which I was then expressing in words, but a scorn and wonder at the injustice shown me, and at the demand of toadyism on my part if I was to get their favour and the favour of Rome."

Those words, and others revealing "the real state of my mind, and what my cross has been," were written in 1876: but now a startling change was at hand. Pius IX. died in 1878, and Leo XIII. succeeded him. Newman had loved Pius personally, but had notoriously deplored his policy, and had suffered accordingly. The sentiments of Leo were believed to differ materially from those of his predecessor; and "the natural reaction of opinion—the swing of the pendulum from one Pontificate to another—seemed to some of Newman's friends a golden opportunity for securing for his great work for the Church the formal approval from Rome itself, which had been so long delayed."

So says Mr Ward, and the Duke of Norfolk adds: "It appeared to me that in the cause both of justice and of truth it was of the utmost importance that the Church should put her seal on Newman's work." That "seal" could only take one form—the Cardinal's Hat. The Duke of Norfolk, in a private interview with the Pope, made the suggestion; it was graciously received. After various delays, some of which bore a suspicious resemblance to former frustrations, Newman received the supreme honour in May 1879. To the journal of 1876, from which the foregoing confession of disappointment is cited, he now appended this significant note: "Since writing the above I have been made a Cardinal!"

When John Henry Newman was seven years old, an event occurred of which he had then no cognizance, but which was destined in the long run to exercise a decisive influence over his working life. This was the birth of Henry Edward Manning. In 1808 the Mannings were a wealthy family, though afterwards they lost their fortune; and "Harry Manning" began life with some single advantages. He was educated at Harrow (where he was Captain of the Cricket Eleven) and at Balliol; and, after obtaining his First, became a Fellow of Merton. He was exceptionally good-looking, beautifully dressed; full of self-confidence, and loving to have the pre-eminence. The circumstances which determined him to enter Holy Orders need not now be recapitulated; it is more important for my present purpose to note that, once ordained, he at once began to rise in his profession. At twenty-five he was a Rector; at twenty-nine Rural Dean; at thirty-two Archdeacon; at thirty-four Select Preacher at Oxford. From 1840 to 1850 he was one of the most considerable figures among the English clergy; and during the last five years of that time, after Newman had seceded, he was commonly regarded as the main strength and stay of those earnest churchmen who had been scandalized by Newman's fall, and had no confidence in Pusey's leadership.

We now know, what at the time was never suspected, that during these latter years he was tormented by grave doubts about the position and claims of the Church of England. He yearned for "authority," and could not find it in Anglicanism. His misgivings came to a head when the Judicial Committee pronounced in favour of the Rev. G. C. Gorham, who seemed to have committed himself to a denial of the Catholic doctrine of Baptism. Suddenly, as it appeared to the world, but deliberately, as we now know from his writings, he resigned his preferments in the Church of England, and was received into the Church of Rome in April 1851. Three years later he wrote in his journal, "I am conscious of a desire to be in such a position as I had in time past"; and his heart's desire was not long denied him. Nothing can be more instructive than the difference between the treatment accorded to Newman and the treatment accorded to Manning by the Church to which they submitted themselves. What Rome did for Newman the first section of this chapter has already set forth. Manning's career was strikingly dissimilar.

Newman was received into the Church of Rome in October 1845, and was not ordained Priest till May 1847. Manning was received in April 1851, and was ordained Priest on the Trinity Sunday next ensuing. He was made D.D. by the Pope in 1854; Superior of the Oblates of St Charles at Bayswater in 1857, and Provost of the Chapter of Westminster in the same year; Domestic Prelate to the Pope, Protonotary Apostolic, and "Monsignor" in 1860; and in 1865, in spite of the fact that he had not been elected by the Chapter, he was made Archbishop of Westminster by the sole act of Pius IX.—"Searle and a hundred other poor devils," pleasantly said Herbert Vaughan, afterwards Cardinal, "will think you are come to torment them before the time."[1] Perhaps they did; but their thoughts could not impede Manning's progress. He was Archbishop in spite of them, and ten years later he was raised to the Purple. It is matter of common knowledge that Manning's early and conspicuous ascendancy in the counsels of the Papacy rested on the intimacy of his personal relations with Pius IX.; though it is not necessary to give literal credence to that account of those relations which Bishop Wilberforce, in his diary, repeated from Mr Odo Russell. Manning was, indeed, a man after the Pope's own heart. There never lived a stronger Papalist. He was more Ultramontane than the Ultramontanes. Everything Roman was to him divine. Rightly or wrongly, he conceived that English Romanism was practically Gallicanism; that it minimized Papal Infallibility, was disloyal to the Temporal Power, and was prone to accommodate itself to its Protestant and secular environment. Against this temporizing policy he set his face as a flint. He believed that he had been divinely

[1] Monsignor Searle was a member of the Westminster Chapter, and a staunch foe of Manning.

appointed to Papalize England. In Cardinal Wiseman he found a chief like-minded with himself, and they worked in perfect accord for an end equally dear to both. Here comes in the tragedy of Newman's life. Manning thought him a half-hearted Papalist. He dreaded alike his way of stating religious truth and his practical policy, and he regarded it as a sacred duty to frustrate his designs.

To Newman, with his abnormal sensitiveness, the situation must have been galling beyond endurance. Here was Manning, seven years his junior, in every gift of intellect immeasurably his inferior, and a convert of five years later date than himself; and yet Manning, through his relations with Rome and his ascendancy over the aged and decrepit Wiseman, was in a position where he could bring all Newman's best-laid plans to naught. They had begun as good friends, though never intimate; for Manning, in his Anglican days, had kept clear of Tractarianism. Newman offered Manning the post of Vice-Rector in the Irish University, and Manning declined it, as he was at the moment entering on his three years' residence at Rome. When he came to live in London, he passed instinctively into that innermost circle of Ultramontane sentiment which surrounded Wiseman, preached by the mouth of Faber, intrigued at the Vatican through Monsignor Talbot, and wrote with the powerful pen of W. G. Ward.

The time, as we have already seen, was full of stress and strain; and some controversies, which had hitherto belonged to the region of theory, were forced into practical action by the developments of European politics. Manning thus summed up the points at issue—" During these years three subjects were uppermost:—(1) The Temporal Power; (2) The Oxford Question; and (3) The Infallibility. On all these Newman was not in accordance with the Holy See. I am nobody, but I spoke as the Holy See speaks." When Manning spoke he also acted, and through his instrumentality Newman was forced to resign the editorship of the *Rambler*, which had taken a line hostile to the Temporal Power. It was easy to offend Newman, and Newman did not readily forget. It is significant that in the *Apologia*, as originally published, though it contains such generous references to friends both Roman and Anglican, Manning's name never appears; and Manning actually denounced "this Kingsley affair," as he called the *Apologia*, as tending to "make Anglicans remain where they are." This was written on the eve of Manning's elevation to the Archiepiscopate, and from thenceforward his power of frustrating Newman was of course increased tenfold. Newman wrote this in the following year: " I think this of Manning: he wishes me no ill, but he is determined to bend or break all opposition. He has an iron will and resolves to have his own way. . . . He has never offered me any place or office. The only one I am fit for, the only one I would accept, he is doing all he can to keep me from."

The other side of the case is thus stated by

Manning: "I was and am convinced that no Catholic parents ought to send their sons to the National Universities; and that no Catholic can be there without danger to faith and morals."

But it was an unequal contest. Manning was all-powerful at the Vatican, and Newman was defeated. When the contest was over, Manning suggested an interview and explanations, but Newman icily declined—"I do not trust him, and his new words would be the cause of fresh distrust. . . . I could not in my heart accept his explanations."

Anyone who wishes to know what Manning could be and do when his heart was set on a great object, should study those chapters in his Life which describe the supersession of Archbishop Errington, his own elevation to the Archiepiscopate, and the Vatican Council. With reference to this last, his biographer says: "It was the event of his life. . . . For years he had made the question of Papal Infallibility his own. He was identified, whether for good or for evil, with the mysterious dogma, by the popular mind of England. He had preached about it, had worked for it, and in tones and terms of infallible certitude had predicted its definition." He went into the Council under a solemn vow to do all in his power to obtain the Definition. He used all conceivable means to secure his end. He wrote, and talked, and plotted, and canvassed. He avoided argument, and appealed to passion and terror. The Church, he said, was in her last struggle with the powers of darkness, and here was the opportunity of striking the blow which should make her victorious. His intensity, his rhetorical skill, his inexhaustible activity, inspired his friends and produced a palpable effect upon the waverers; but all the time there was the other side, and on it were ranged Darboy and Dupanloup, Strossmayer and Haynald, Ketteler and Hefele and Deschamps; "and a greater name by far than theirs was on their other side and in sympathy with them— John Henry Newman." When the battle was over and Newman again defeated, Manning wrote, with unmistakable reference: "They were wise and we were fools. But, strange to say, it has turned out that the wise men were always blundering and the fools were always right. At last the wise men have had to hold their tongues, and in a way not glorious to them, to submit and to be silent." To compare this passage with Newman's words about the "Adorable Inscrutable Providence" is to gain some notion of the two men.

Eight years passed. Pius IX. died, and Leo XIII., acting on suggestions from England, made Newman a Cardinal, and so affixed the seal of Infallibility to principles and methods against which Manning had waged a thirty years' war. In 1883 he said to me, pointing to two pictures on the wall, "That is Pio— history will pronounce him to be a very great Pontiff. Yes, and that is Leo—*hum, hm, h—,*" but I find it impossible to express in letters the curious *diminuendo* of depreciatory sound.

Seven years later Newman was in his grave, and

his brother-Cardinal talked of him and of their mutual relations with impressive candour. One saying must be recorded: "I suppose you have heard that I tried to prevent Newman from being made a Cardinal. Yes, of course you have. Everyone has. But it is not true. Indeed it is the reverse of the truth. The Duke of Norfolk and Lord Ripon came to me and said: 'We have been to Rome. We have urged Newman's claim to the Cardinalate. We have done as much as laymen can do—and we have made no impression. We come back, having accomplished nothing.' I said, 'Leave it to me.' I wrote to Rome, and it was done in three weeks. *Very few people know that.*" Very few indeed!

Why, in the long duel which I have now described, was Newman always defeated and Manning (except in the last tussle about the Cardinalate) always successful? Something may, no doubt, be ascribed to training and environment. Manning had all the advantages for mind and body (though they may sometimes be disadvantages for the soul) which belong to an opulent home and a great Public School. Newman was brought up in a Calvinistic seclusion, varied by eight years at a private school, where he never played a game. At Oxford Manning was popular and fashionable: Newman lived, from first to last, like a Seminarist, hampered, as he himself says, by "extreme shyness" and "vivid self-consciousness." Manning, as soon as he had got his degree, quitted Oxford, took a clerkship in the Colonial

Office, went freely into society, more than once fell in love, and married early. Newman went from his Scholarship at Trinity to his Fellowship at Oriel, regarded himself as divinely called to celibacy, and seems to have had no ambition beyond a curacy in a suburb of Oxford.

Temperament co-operated with environment. Manning, already a man of the world and knowing how to deal with men, may stand for Sense: Newman, the shrinking and ascetic student, for Sensibility. He said of himself that he had a "morbidly sensitive skin," and that is about as bad an equipment for active life in a world of struggle as nature can bestow. That a pre-eminently sensitive man tastes more keenly than others the choice delights of life is probably true, but it is certain that he suffers a thousand miseries which tougher natures never feel. An acute sensitiveness may be allied with, though it is by no means a synonym for, keen sympathy with the sorrows of others, and so may gather round a man a band of grateful admirers; but it will never disarm an opponent, or turn a foe into a friend. Still less will it enable a man to force his way through clenched antagonisms, or to crush resistance as he marches towards his end. Then again a sensitive nature is

Wax to receive, and marble to retain.

It may forgive, but it cannot forget, slights and injuries, buffets and bruises. Forgetfulness of injuries is the blessed lot of those who have inflicted them.

"Poor Newman!" said Manning in a moment of genial expansion—"he was a great hater"; and though the phrase had something of controversial rancour, it expressed a kind of truth. When Newman had been injured, he did not expose himself to a repetition of the injury. When he had been deceived, he did not give the deceiver a second opportunity. When he had been offended, he kept the offender at arm's length. There are curious traditions of personal estrangements, lasting through years, between him and members of his own house; and there is on record a letter in which he told Archbishop Whately, with agreeable frankness, that though he had not purposely kept out of his way when Whately lately was paying a visit to Oxford, he was glad of the accident which prevented them from meeting.

I question if Manning was very sensitive. No doubt he felt a knock, as we all feel it, but with him it was only a reason for hitting back again, and when he hit he showed both strength and science.

And, yet once more, Newman was too much of an Idealist. He idealized the Calvinism in which he had been brought up, but soon found that it was hopelessly inadequate to the demands of the intellect and the broad facts of human life; and in his reaction from it he went perilously near the ways of thought which a few years later were stigmatized as Liberalism. When he had adopted the Tractarian position, he idealized the Anglican Bishops; and the dissipation of that ideal by contact with Episcopal realities,

"SENSE AND SENSIBILITY" 35

is the history of his submission to Rome. As a Roman Catholic he found even larger and more promising scope for Idealism, and disillusionments even profounder and more grievous. That to the end he idealized the Church of Rome—"the one oracle of truth and the one ark of salvation"—I cannot doubt, but he soon ceased to idealize Roman Bishops as he had before ceased to idealize their Anglican brethren; and to these must be added Cardinals, and Jesuits, and politicians, and editors, and in short, all the agents by whom the Church of Rome does its practical work. To say that he was ever disillusioned about the Pope would be offensive and might be misleading, so let his own words stand. "I had been accustomed to believe that, over and above that attribute of infallibility which attached to the doctrinal decisions of the Holy See, a gift of sagacity had in every age characterized its occupants. . . . I am obliged to say that a sentiment which history has impressed upon me, and impresses still, has been very considerably weakened as far as the present Pope (Pius IX.) is concerned, by the experience of the result of the policy which his chosen councillors led him to pursue." From first to last Newman idealized the systems to which for the time he belonged, and when, in their working, they proved to be quite different from what he dreamed, the blow fell with a disabling force, and the people who wished ill to his schemes "grinned demnebly."

Of Manning it may, I think, be said without breach

of charity, that, willing the end intensely, he also willed the means; that he was entirely free from what Bishop Wilson called "the *offendiculum* of scrupulosity"; and that, where a cause was at stake, he did not shrink from crushing an opponent.

In a contest with this kind of temper Newman was hopelessly handicapped. The sensitiveness which pervaded his nature all through was at its tenderest in the domain of conscience. To him conscience was "a Prophet in its predictions, a King in its imperiousness, a Priest in its benedictions and anathemas." Its faintest whisper was to him as certainly the Voice of God as though it had spoken amid the thunders of Sinai, and it taught him that, though the object which we seek may be the most important on earth, it must be sought with an incessant, scrupulous, almost morbid, regard for the ethical considerations which the search involves. His feelings, hopes, desires, prejudices, personal opinions, schemes of usefulness—all these Newman was ready and eager to sacrifice for the cause which absorbed his life. The one thing which he would not sacrifice was Conscience, and he who declines to sacrifice his conscience must look for his reward in a better world than this.

In a passage of vivid self-portraiture Newman described himself as "one whose natural impulse it has ever been to speak out; who has ever spoken too much rather than too little; who would have saved himself many a scrape if he had been wise enough to hold his tongue; who has ever been fair to the doctrines and arguments of his opponents; who has never slurred over facts and reasonings which told against himself; who has never shrunk from confessing a fault when he felt that he had committed one; who has ever consulted for others more than for himself; who has given up much that he loved and prized and could have retained, but that he loved honesty better than name, and Truth better than dear friends."

In 1894 Archbishop Benson wrote in his diary, "I never find any Oxford man realize how weak a man was Newman." Perhaps the passage which I have just quoted may help to explain our dulness.

II

THE LAST OF THE WHIGS[1]

LORD BEACONSFIELD was fond of talking about "The Great Revolution Families"; and in his day the phrase still meant a good deal. It was another way of saying the Whig Party; and, as Lord Russell —the "Lord John" of the first Reform Bill—observed, "'Whig' says in one syllable what 'Liberal Conservative' says in seven." On the 11th of May 1694 William and Mary created the Dukedom of Bedford and on the following day that of Devonshire. The second Duke of Devonshire married a sister of the second Duke of Bedford, and the alliance thus originated lasted for close on two centuries. Lord Russell, reverting in old age to his early days at the University of Edinburgh, said: "A public dinner was held in 1810 to commemorate the birthday of Mr Fox, and the following toast was given: 'The Houses of Russell and Cavendish—may they ever be united in the cause of freedom!'" This pious aspiration was fulfilled, and the union between the two Houses was maintained at least down to 1880. On the 20th of

[1] Reprinted from *The Contemporary Review*.

THE LAST OF THE WHIGS

March in that year I received the following letter from Lord Hartington, then titular leader of the Liberal Party:—

> I write a line to express my sincere wishes for your success in your contest at Aylesbury. The names of Russell and Cavendish have been so long associated together in the political history of the country that I cannot help feeling something more than a common interest in your success.

I need not quote the rest of the letter; but it was interesting as showing the durability of political association between the "Great Revolution Families" —or, in more scientific phrase, the "solidarity" of the Whig Party. But it was the last word of that "solidarity." The "Great Revolution Families" were nearing the crisis which destroyed them as a political party, merged the great mass of them in Toryism, and turned the small residuum into Radicals. During and after that time of transition, I always regarded the late Duke of Devonshire with the interest which belongs to a survival. In him I saw embodied all the attributes that made the Whig, and thereby had made a distinct part of our history; and, as far as I could see, he was the sole survivor of the breed to which he belonged. "Breed" is, I believe, the right word, for the essence of Whiggery was relationship. All the Whigs were cousins; all descended from the first Earl Gower. Beresford-Hope, who like all true Tories hated the Whigs, poked fun at "the sacred circle of the Great Grandmotherhood," which, according to him, included them all; and Mr Gladstone, who never poked fun, stated the same case in his own more serious way: "As a rule, a man not born a Liberal may become a Liberal; but to be a Whig he must be a born Whig." A born Whig, if ever there was such a creature, was Spencer Compton, eighth Duke of Devonshire, who was a Whig in all the qualities which make the character. For Whiggery, though primarily a matter of blood, is scarcely less a matter of belief; and all the beliefs—and unbeliefs—which characterize the true Whig flourished in the Duke's mind with extraordinary vigour.

When the third Duke of Devonshire built Devonshire House in Piccadilly, Horace Walpole wrote that the house was "like himself, plain and good." And the epithets apply to Mr Bernard Holland's Life of the Eighth Duke. It fills two volumes, each as large as an ordinary biography of the present day; and both are stuffed with closely printed matter. They tell a plain tale of a consistent and honourable, but uninspiring, career, and in telling it they give a political history of England from 1857 to 1907. The history is not marked by that absolute impartiality which Bishop Creighton commended and practised; nor must it be relied on in the minutiæ of names, dates, and allusions. But it is a bold, clear, and effective narration, written from what may be called the anti-Gladstonian standpoint. It is enlivened here and there by passages of political and philosophical reflection which, whether one agrees with them or not, set one thinking; and the author displays the personal knowledge of, and feeling for, his hero, without which biographical writing is the driest of remainder-biscuits.

If anyone takes up this biography in the hope of finding secret things, whether of character or of life, unveiled, he or she will be disappointed. Mr Holland has made his book not the study of a soul, but the record of a career, and in so doing he has acted wisely. To have explored, even if it had been possible, the inner recesses of the Duke's natural temperament, or to have estimated the forces which really swayed his life, would, indeed, have been a work well pleasing to the vulgar, but it would have served no high or useful end. It is better, as Mr Holland has done, to tell a plain story of public service, and to imitate, even when telling it, something of that tremendous reticence which in life distinguished the hero of the story.

William, Earl of Burlington, and eventually seventh Duke of Devonshire, who was Second Wrangler in 1829, married in the same year Lady Blanche Howard, daughter of Lord Carlisle, and had three sons and one daughter.[1] The eldest son was the subject of Mr Holland's memoir. Lord Burlington had been unhappy at school and resolved to educate his sons at home. In the case of the eldest this was a signal misfortune. For the heir-apparent to a great title and corresponding wealth to be educated among

---

[1] With reference to this union, Sydney Smith wrote, "Euclid leads Blanche to the altar—a strange choice for him, as she has not an angle about her."

his father's dependents is the most spoiling of experiences. The son of a Southern planter, reared among the slaves who will soon be his own property, could scarcely be more unfortunately placed than an English boy of vigorous body and imperious will, brought up among grooms and game-keepers, and fed from the cradle on the thick flattery which is the appointed diet of an eldest son. If the youthful Cavendish had been sent to Eton, and surrounded from his twelfth year to his eighteenth by boys of equal importance, and for some portion of that time subjected to the rule of a vigorous fag-master, he would not have grown up in the calm assumption that all the world was made to give way to him, and that, while his own convenience mattered a great deal, the convenience of other people was a negligible quantity. Mr Holland puts the case very delicately when he says that "Lord Hartington established early in life the principle that little was to be expected of him in the way of etiquette." Some people thought him "rude" and "spoilt"; and this was not wonderful, for his way of staring blankly when he was addressed, and presently uttering a half-formed "What?" was not a little disconcerting. "He might arrive very late for dinner, or possibly not at all. . . . Life is certainly rather spoiling in these minor respects to a young man of great position." And the "spoiling" effect produced on the young man is not obliterated, but rather deepened, by years. When the Cabinet decided to drop an Education Bill at

THE LAST OF THE WHIGS 43

which Sir John Gorst as Vice-President of the Committee of Council had been toiling, the Duke of Devonshire, then Gorst's official chief, strolled into his room, and, after standing some time in silence with his back to the fire, said: "Well, Gorst, your damned Bill's dead." These are the less desirable fruits of a domestic education.

In October 1851 Lord Cavendish went up to Trinity College, Cambridge; and I have heard, from quarters wholly untainted by academic snobbery, that his mathematical faculty was unmistakable, and that, if only he had chosen to read, he might have attained to something like his father's distinction. However, as Lord Burlington noted in his diary, "Cavendish is certainly fond of amusement"; and he took his fill of it, as in after-life, so also at Cambridge. In 1854 he graduated in the Second Class of the Mathematical Tripos, and now his future was a little uncertain. That he must some day be Duke of Devonshire was plain enough; but what he was going to do with his life in the meantime was not so clear. He was fond of sport in all its forms, of racing, and of gambling. He made the social round in town and country, and occasionally went abroad. But Lord Burlington was not satisfied with this rather desultory programme, and he took counsel with some old and intimate friends—one of them a Russell—as to the fitting career for a young man of great possessions. It was decided that in this case the young man's character required the force of a strong excitement to divert it from unworthy pursuits, and stimulate it to activity. The friends in council agreed with Lord Roehampton in *Endymion* that there was "no gambling like politics," and it was decided that Lord Cavendish should stand at the next election for North Lancashire, which returned two members. The dissolution came in March 1857, and Cavendish was returned unopposed as a Liberal, with a Conservative colleague. Next year he changed his name; for Lord Burlington succeeded his cousin as Duke of Devonshire, and Cavendish became Lord Hartington.

Now begins half a century of political life, which Mr Holland has narrated with scrupulous fidelity. I propose to point out how perfectly in all its parts and aspects it illustrates the ideal of Whiggery.

The most important point should be taken first. A leading characteristic of the Whig mind was its irreligiousness. Charles Buller's plea for the Established Church, "Why, it's the only thing that stands between us and religion," sufficiently indicates the Whig view. But even Whigs sometimes—very rarely—deviated from their type; and Lord Burlington, himself one of the best of men, wrote on his son's seventeenth birthday: "I trust he has strong religious feelings." The rest is silence. Of those "feelings" and their effect on his life, not a word is said. We are told that when Hartington became Duke of Devonshire, "he did not appoint extreme men to livings"; and "there is nothing to show that at any

THE LAST OF THE WHIGS

time he took the slightest interest in any purely ecclesiastical questions." Once when such questions were invading the political area, he said to his Private Secretary: "Can you explain to me what 'Transubstantiation' means that they are talking about?" His biographer says that, as to the relations of Church and State, and the ideal of a Church, "his views were not very different from those of Sir William Harcourt." I cannot improve on that compendious and conclusive judgment.

The finest characteristic of Whiggery was its devotion to civil freedom. Whether tyranny was attempted by the Crown or by the mob, by a corrupt Parliament or by a high-handed executive, the Whigs were its implacable foes. They believed that in a free country Government can only rest on the consent of the governed; and they supported, though not all of them with equal zeal, successive extensions of the suffrage. In this respect Hartington was worthy of his Whig traditions. He supported, and was indeed partly responsible for, the Reform Bill brought in by Russell and Gladstone in 1866. He supported the larger measure introduced by Derby and Disraeli in the following year. He was stirred to unusual activity by the Franchise Bill of 1884, and even mastered his prepossessions sufficiently to concur in its extension to Ireland. It appears that in early manhood he had sympathized with the Southern States of America in their conflict with the North; but Mr Holland seems to hint that his sentiments on this head changed as he grew older. On the Eastern Question his constitutional hatred of enthusiasm, emotion, and rhetoric made him seem more indifferent to the sufferings of the Sultan's victims than in truth he was; and in the question of Home Rule he based his action in great part on his conviction that under a Nationalist Parliament individual liberty would not be safe. No statesman's career is absolutely consistent, but of Lord Hartington one might truly say what is inscribed on the place where his kinsman and mine was beheaded: "He was a sincere lover of a temperate freedom."[1]

Liberty, Fraternity, Equality—Liberalism loves all three equally: not so Whiggery. The Whigs believed in Liberty, and served her with blood and brains and money; but they were the most confirmed inequalitarians. Lord Lyndhurst, who hated them with his whole heart, said: "Whiggery is a real and selfish aristocracy"; and the close ties of kinship which bound the Whigs together intensified the conviction that they were, socially as well as politically, the chosen people. Hartington held his creed not the less tenaciously because he never uttered it; but everyone who can remember his demeanour in Parliament must have seen it in his manner and heard it in his voice. It was said, with much semblance of truth, that when some would-be fine people were lamenting the presence of a "mob"

[1] William Lord Russell, whose daughter Rachel married the second Duke of Devonshire, was beheaded in Lincoln's Inn Fields.

THE LAST OF THE WHIGS 47

in Hyde Park at some political demonstration, Hartington remarked, with his characteristic growl or grunt: "But there always is a mob in the Park; only some of the mobs are better dressed than others." Because he dressed anyhow,[1] travelled by the 'bus or the Underground, or whatever came handiest, and devoured with good appetite the hunches of bread and cheese and the mutton-chops which constitute an office-luncheon, people nurtured in the faith of Ouida fondly imagined that he did not realize his position. If they could have seen him doing the honours of Chatsworth or Hardwicke—a rare experience—they would have judged differently. "As he had an evident deep pride of race, so he had in equal measure a legitimate pride of possession, mitigated by his strong sense of responsibility." When Lord Salisbury offered him the Lord-Lieutenancy of Derbyshire, in succession to his father, he replied that he "could not even go through the form of demurring. My father told me that he believed the office had been held by one of our family for over two hundred years, and I know that he hoped that I might succeed him."

"A deep pride of race; a legitimate pride of possession." In that conjunction you have the essential notes of an aristocracy, exhibited by no section of men more conspicuously than by the Whigs. Whiggery has always been on the side of property; and it was only natural that

[1] Cf. *Lothair*, vol. i., c. 28.

when Mr Chamberlain launched his "Unauthorized Programme," Hartington should have begun to smell mischief. "He defended Feudalism against Socialism; that is, the administration of land by land-owners against the proposed gradual transfer of administration to local authorities." To Whig eyes, if Liberty was sacred, so also was Property; and Equality must not lift its hand against the rights of ownership. The circumstances which took Hartington into Parliament have already been indicated; and, indeed, the life of an idle M.P., turning up now and then for a critical division, but spending the greater part of his time in sport, or racing, or society, might have fitted in well enough with his temperament and habits. That Palmerston, the craftiest of Parliamentarians, should have wished to annex so great a name to the support of his Administration was only natural. It is not so easy to understand why Hartington consented to join. It certainly could not be that the eldest son of the Duke of Devonshire hoped to gain social consideration or needful emolument by becoming Under-Secretary for War. A Radical M.P. once said to the present writer, in a tone of snuffling admiration, "Hartington can't be bought," and grace restrained me from the too-obvious retort, "Can you?" All the minor incidents of office were disagreeable to Hartington. He disliked spending his days and nights in the House; he disliked the drudgery of departmental work, though, when he had undertaken

THE LAST OF THE WHIGS 49

it, " his sense of *noblesse oblige* made him do his best." He disliked the constant interference with leisure, society, and country life which office demands; he disliked speaking in the House, and he loathed the platform.

What then could tempt him on those stormy seas?

It may have been that the counsels of family and feminine friends prevailed. It may be that already the whisper of ambition had reached his ear, pointing out the supreme prize which, in the event, he thrice grasped and thrice surrendered. But, on the whole, the most creditable explanation is also the simplest. He wished to use his position and his powers in the professed service of the State. In making the offer, Palmerston had said: "I feel very strongly that it is of great importance to the country, and is highly conducive to the working of our Constitution, that young men of high aristocratical positions should take part in the administration of public affairs, and should not leave the working of our political machine to classes whose pursuits and interests are of a different kind."

In accepting this view of civil duty, Hartington acted in close compliance with Whig tradition. After their long exclusion from power under Pitt and Liverpool, the Whigs took office with a relish. Indeed, between 1830 and 1885, the only difficulty was to make them believe that the great offices of the State were not theirs by right. Once, when an extremely incompetent Whig had been appointed to an extremely important office, I ventured to suggest that he would have done better as Lord President of the Duchy; whereupon came the swift reply, "Not at all; he has a right to one of the £5000 a year places."

Lord Hartington became Under-Secretary for War in April 1863, and spent the next three years in the creditable, but unexciting, discharge of official duty. Lord Palmerston died in October 1865, and was succeeded by Lord Russell, who thus resumed the Premiership after thirteen years. Early in the Session of 1866 he promoted Hartington to be Secretary of State for War. "He thus, at the age of thirty-three, entered the Cabinet as one of the chief officers of State." So it fell out that the Edinburgh student who, in 1810, had responded to the toast of "The Houses of Russell and Cavendish—may they ever be united in the cause of Freedom," was now able to unite them by the closest of political bonds. The chief business of the Session of 1866 was the Reform Bill, which, by lowering the franchise in towns, would have added 400,000 new voters to the electoral body. Hartington, as in duty bound, spoke in favour of the Bill, and amazed his friends by making a poetical allusion. But, in spite of this unwonted effort, the Bill was defeated, and the Government resigned. "Hartington now found himself, much to his pleasure, free for all too short a space from official duties."

The Tory Reform Bill of 1867, which had for its

THE LAST OF THE WHIGS

avowed object to "dish the Whigs," did not "dish" Hartington, who was a convinced supporter of the extension of the franchise to the artisans. In 1868 he spoke and voted for Gladstone's Resolution in favour of disestablishing and disendowing the Irish Church, and in the following autumn he had to pay the penalty. Hitherto he had never been forced to contest his seat, but had simply walked in. Now Gladstone's attack upon the Irish Church had aroused bitter hostility in Lancashire, and Hartington had to fight for his life. His cousin, Lord Granville, wrote, with the characteristic cheerfulness of the onlooker, "This contest is the best thing that could have happened to you. It stirs your blood, airs your vocabulary, and adds much to your popularity in the country at large." But it ended in defeat—a new sensation to Hartington, who admitted that he "didn't like it."

The result of the appeal to the country was a majority of a hundred for Gladstone and Disestablishment. Disraeli resigned and Gladstone became Prime Minister for the first time. He desired to reinstate Hartington in his old place as Secretary of State for War; but Hartington had no seat in the new Parliament, and there was an awkward hitch. Hartington declined to be made Lord Lieutenant of Ireland, but accepted the office of Postmaster-General, which was offered to him on the condition that he obtained a seat in Parliament. A Welsh member obligingly retired, and Hartington got in after a contest. But still he was not happy. To be Postmaster-General after being Secretary of State for War was a descent in official dignity, and the transfer had not been very flatteringly effected. "I am not quite pleased about it," he wrote to his father, "and don't feel sure that I have done right."

The office thus rather grudgingly accepted was exchanged two years later for the Chief Secretaryship for Ireland, which was held by Hartington till the Liberal Government came to an end in 1874. He thus was party to all the great reforms which signalized that memorable period—the Disestablishment of the Irish Church, the first Irish Land Act, the abolition of Purchase in the Army, the arbitration on the Alabama, Compulsory Education, the Establishment of the Ballot, and the abortive attempt to create an Irish University which was to reconcile all religious creeds by the singular device of not teaching metaphysics, ethics, or modern history.

It is impossible to suppose that all these reforms were congenial to Hartington. Indeed, his biographer tells us that he was "a reluctant convert" to the Ballot. He himself says that he found the Irish Land Act "a hard morsel to swallow"; and his correspondence, all through those five years, shows frequent signs of unrest, coming to a head, now and then, in a hint of resignation. Nor was he on very happy terms with his chief. "This plain-minded Whig nobleman, educated at Cambridge University,

THE LAST OF THE WHIGS 53

honestly endeavoured to follow this great man through the bewildering phases of his strange career; but there was not much sympathy between the two men." In one respect, and that an important one, they were, fortunately, in complete harmony. Hartington, as became a Whig, was a tenacious supporter of the rights of property; and there was no stauncher opponent of "collective ownership" than the son of the corn-merchant of Leith and Liverpool. Gladstone was always inclined to pay an even exaggerated homage to the claims of rank; he held that a young aristocrat who forsook (even partially) the amusements proper to his age and class, in order to devote himself to the public service, was entitled to the warmest admiration; and he had, from first to last, a sincere respect for Hartington's capacity and character. But the two men could never get on together. Again and again, as this record shows, Hartington misunderstood his chief's language, misconstrued his motives, misapprehended his designs. The two men had little enough in common, even in the sphere of opinion, but nothing in the sphere of policy and method. Hartington had the plainest, simplest, most direct mind in the world; governed his life by common sense, and was wholly impervious to sentiment, emotion, and rhetoric. Gladstone's intellect, rapid and piercing, was dominated by passion; all his opinions were articles of faith; he always believed that words, if sufficiently multiplied, could undo facts; and he had an unbounded power of self-deception. Mr Holland applies to him the saying of St Augustine: *Quod vult, non quod est, credit qui cupit errare.*

That with temperaments so contrariant, and opinions, in many respects, so dissimilar, the two men worked together without open rupture for ten years, proves in Gladstone a certain magnanimity with which he was not always credited; and it shows in Hartington the truly Whiggish habit of sticking, at any cost, to the Party. By slow degrees, the Whigs had come to admit that the Party included some Radicals; but they considered themselves by very much the most important part of it, and it was sacred in their eyes. To "keep the Party together," to avoid ruptures, to compose dissensions, and to present an unbroken front to the Tories, had always been the Whig policy; and Hartington, a Whig to the backbone, stuck to his Party and to the Government, through endless vicissitudes; not indeed without secret qualms and timely threats, but without a word or deed which would give the Tories occasion to exult. To a man of his nature and habits, retirement into private life would at any moment have been an unspeakable relief; but he took office, and held it almost to his life's close, because he "felt the true feudal doctrine that great property and social position are only rightly held on tenure by public service."

The Liberal Government had for some time been visibly declining in public favour, when, in January 1874, Gladstone announced a dissolution.

The result was a Conservative majority. Gladstone and his colleagues resigned, and Disraeli became Prime Minister. All this had been to some extent expected, though not by Gladstone; but what had not been expected—what now upset everyone's calculations—was that Gladstone announced that he could not continue to lead the Liberal Party. He would appear occasionally during the approaching session, but beyond that he would not pledge himself. His own account of the arrangement was: "For 1874 there was a sort of compromise, without prejudice. As having a title to some rest, I was not a very regular attendant, but did not formally abdicate." The formal abdication came in January 1875, and then the Liberal Party, amid much heart-burning and confusion, approached the election of a leader in the House of Commons. The last words are important, for Gladstone always insisted that he resigned his trust to Lord Granville, and that therefore Granville was the leader of the Liberal Party as a whole. But the leadership in the Commons was a much more vital matter. Practically the choice lay between Hartington and Forster; and the real difficulty was to induce Hartington, if the choice should fall on him, to accept the post. He "did not think he could endure the toleration he would have to put up with from the Radicals," and "nothing would induce him to have his name put up in opposition to Forster." Eventually Forster declined to be nominated, and at a meeting of Liberal Members of Parliament Hartington was chosen without a division. So his fate had found him, and there was no escape.

The new Leader was now forty-two years old. He had sat in the House for eighteen years; and no man of a corresponding age and Parliamentary position had made so few speeches. He regarded his future with something less than his habitual equanimity. He wrote to his father: "How I shall get on, Heaven only knows"; but a strong word of encouragement came from the quarter best qualified to give it. "Those," wrote Gladstone, "who are now choosing you will be perhaps surprised—certainly pleased—when they come to know by experience the quantity of available material, pith, and manhood that is in you."

To lead the Liberal Party in the House of Commons, with Gladstone sitting as an independent member at one's side and prepared to chip into the debate at any moment, was indeed an alarming task; but Hartington was sustained by the consciousness that every Whig, in or out of Parliament, wished him well, and relied on him to overrule the extreme men, such as Fawcett and Dilke, and their frequent allies, the Irish Home Rulers. During the sessions of 1875 and 1876, he found his task rather easier than he expected. He conducted the regular business of opposition with moderation and good sense; the Radicals, though they murmured, did not rebel; and Gladstone kept silence even from good words, though

THE LAST OF THE WHIGS 57

we cannot doubt that it was pain and grief to him. But this halcyon calm did not last more than two years, and then it was interrupted by a tempest which completely broke up the weather.

In the autumn of 1875 an insurrection of the Christian subjects of the Porte had broken out in Bulgaria. The Turkish Government had suppressed the insurrection, and had then indulged in a hideous orgy of massacre and outrage. When the rumour of these reached England, public indignation woke spontaneously; but Hartington was not the man for the emergency. His mind worked very slowly, and he had a morbid dread of enthusiasm and exaggeration. His sympathies were on the right side, but he seemed unwilling to avow them. The feeling of the Liberal Party demanded prompter action and more emphatic speech; and what it demanded Gladstone supplied. He flung himself into the crusade against Turkey with a vigour which, even in his prime, he had never displayed. In Parliament, on the platform, in the public Press, in private correspondence—wherever he could make his voice heard—he thundered against the Turk, the Tory, and the *Times*. "He believed that he was leading the sound-hearted people of this country to fight in the cause of freedom against the allied powers of darkness—the spirit of Judaism incarnate in Disraeli, the spirit of ancient Rome acting through the Vatican, the spirit of Islam embodied in the Sultan, and the spirit of Imperialism latent in the English aristocracy. He believed himself to be God's instrument." So says Mr Holland, and shows us that Hartington and the Whigs generally did not share that belief. With excellent self-command, Hartington jogged along; but as 1877 and 1878 went by, he felt increasingly that he was being brushed aside from his titular leadership. A few Whigs doggedly supported him, but three-fourths of the Liberal Party, and all its fighting and adventurous element, were sworn to Gladstone's standard. Hartington's discomfiture reached its height in the winter of 1879, when Gladstone made that celebrated progress through Midlothian which marked the climax of his career. Gladstone had now, whether he intended it or not, resumed the actual leadership of the Liberal Party; and Hartington, who never encouraged himself in illusions, thought that the time had come to resign an office which had ceased to be a reality. Had he been left to his own devices he would certainly have taken this step, but his Whig allies and his Party-whips implored him to hold his hand. It was felt that the Liberal Party would have a better chance of victory at the General Election, which was impending, if it were united under one flag, than if it approached the polls with the rival cries of "Gladstone" and "Hartington." The Chief Whip sagaciously observed that "those who follow Mr Gladstone will all join him in following Hartington, whereas there are many who call themselves Moderate Liberals, but who would not move a finger to support

THE LAST OF THE WHIGS

Mr Gladstone." These counsels prevailed, and Hartington, true as usual to the Party, consented to remain at his post of thankless duty.

Parliament was dissolved on the 24th of March 1880, and at Easter the Liberals returned with a majority of 100 over Tories and Home Rulers combined. Lord Beaconsfield resigned without meeting the new Parliament, and on the 22nd of April Hartington, in obedience to Queen Victoria's command, went down to Windsor. As controversy has sometimes arisen about what actually ensued, it is best to cite Hartington's own account of it, given to the present writer in 1892.

> The advice which Lord Hartington gave to the Queen from first to last was that H.M. should send for Mr Gladstone, and consult him as to the formation of a Government, and that, if he should be willing to undertake the task, she should call upon him to form an Administration. Lord H. had, up to that time, had no communication with Mr G. on the subject, and did not know what his views as to returning to office might be. With the Queen's permission, Lord H., on his return from Windsor, informed Mr Gladstone and Lord Granville, but no other person, of what had passed between H.M. and himself, and neither Lord H. nor any other person is at liberty now to make those communications public. From the time when Lord H. was first sent for to Windsor to the time when Mr G. was sent for by the Queen, Lord H. neither saw nor communicated with any of his friends or former colleagues, except Lord Granville and Mr Gladstone.

Since those words were written, a full account of what passed between the Queen and Hartington has been given, on Hartington's relation, in Gladstone's *Life*. We now know the Queen desired him to ascertain whether he was right in his belief that Gladstone would not act in a Ministry except as Prime Minister. The answer was exactly what Hartington foresaw, and next day he returned to Windsor, this time accompanied by Granville. They reported Gladstone's reply to the Queen's enquiry, and jointly advised that she should send for Gladstone and ask him to form a Government. Her Majesty consented; the statesmen returned to London, and before dinner that evening Gladstone had kissed hands and was for the second time Prime Minister of England. In describing these events to the present writer, twelve years after they occurred, the Duke of Devonshire said: "I declined what I felt was an impossible task, with Gladstone occupying an irresponsible position outside the Government. But, if I had consented, I should have had no difficulty in forming a Cabinet. Harcourt was very anxious to join." Mr Holland says: "Hartington, who had a real distaste for leadership, was forced to undertake it in 1875, because Gladstone then had persuaded himself that he no longer desired to lead. He was deprived of the rewarding honour, to which no man can be absolutely indifferent, of being Prime Minister, because Gladstone had recovered from his illusion."

In the Administration now formed, Granville took the Foreign Office and Hartington the India Office, though he would have preferred the Governor-Generalship of India. On the 2nd of May 1880, Archbishop Tait, describing the annual dinner of

THE LAST OF THE WHIGS 61

the Royal Academy, says: "Gladstone was sitting between his two tame elephants, Granville and Hartington." One of the two was tame indeed; but the other had reserves of resistance in his nature which before long were roused into activity.

"Lord Hartington," says his biographer, "began his new term of administration in a mood neither joyous nor sanguine"; and yet for the next three years things went tolerably well. The Afghan War was brought to an end, and Hartington defended the evacuation of Kandahar in one of the most powerful speeches which he ever made. "We go away now because we do not want Kandahar, and because we have no right to be there." That was the Whig all over. No sympathy with glittering policies, no false shame about imaginary loss of "Prestige"; but simply reason and justice. We do not want Kandahar; therefore it is foolish to stay. We have no right to be there; therefore we ought to go. On the 6th of May 1882, the long tragedy of Irish discontent culminated in the murders in the Phœnix Park. Hartington had stoutly supported Forster, the Chief Secretary, in his demand for coercive powers; and, since the Act of 1881, which gave those powers, was soon to expire, he was anxious for a new and stronger Crimes Act. But he felt that it was time to release the political suspects, including Parnell, whom Forster had summarily imprisoned under the expiring Act. He took very much the same line as he had taken about Kandahar. "When the moment arrived when we could no longer say that their continued detention was required for the safety of the country, at that moment we were not only justified, but absolutely compelled, to agree to their release." Forster resigned; and two days after this speech was delivered, Lord Frederick Cavendish, who had been appointed to succeed Forster as Chief Secretary, was foully murdered when attempting to save the Permanent Under-Secretary, Mr Burke, from a gang of assassins armed with surgical knives. All England sickened and shuddered at the crime; but the stoicism of Hartington's nature stood him in good stead. His brother had been murdered, his father's old age rendered desolate, and a united family shattered; but these things made no difference to public policy. After his brother's murder he was no more hostile to Ireland than before. He had always believed that the abolition of known grievances and the firm administration of law were our main duties in Ireland; and the tragedy of the 6th of May was powerless to dislodge him from that position.

At the end of 1882 there was a rearrangement of ministerial places, and Hartington went back to his old seat at the War Office. So began the least successful, and, one would think, the least agreeable period of his life. Alexandria had been occupied by our forces in the previous July; and now Hartington became responsible for that long series of perversities, blunders, and self-contradictions which was called our military policy in Egypt. For the crowning

THE LAST OF THE WHIGS 63

and most tragical folly of all—the despatch of General Gordon—Hartington, as Secretary of State for War, had, of course, a special responsibility. But it was a venture so extraordinarily unlike the prosaic and businesslike methods in which his soul delighted, that his part in it is inexplicable. When it was done, and repentance was all too late, one of the Ministers who had concurred in it said: "We were proud of ourselves yesterday—are you sure that we did not commit a gigantic folly?" Gordon left England for Khartoum on the 18th of January 1884. He was killed on the 26th of January 1885. The whole of the intervening year was spent by Hartington in fruitless and belated endeavours to mend the error; to accomplish the purpose for which Gordon had been sent, and to save the hero's life. But his mental slowness, his extreme deliberation in making decisions, and the fact that he was working in a divided Cabinet, hampered him at every step. It is a miserable history as regards all concerned; but Hartington emerges from it with neither less nor greater credit than can be claimed for Gladstone or the rest of his colleagues.

Gladstone's second Administration was terminated by a defeat on an amendment to the Budget, on the 8th of June, 1885. "Probably no man in the Liberal Government was more relieved by its termination than was Lord Hartington, and he must have enjoyed more than usually, this same week of June, the Ascot races. . . . Ascot Week is a good moment for release."

True, and horse-racing is a truly Whiggish recreation. He had now left behind him for ever the embarrassments which attend on the effort to "ride two horses at once," *i.e.* to serve in a Whig-Radical combination. From this point on events may be hastily summarized. Parliament was dissolved in November, and the General Election resulted in a tie between Liberals (of all shades) and Tories *plus* Parnellites. In December, Mr Gladstone's conversion to Home Rule was announced. When Parliament met in January 1886, Gladstone promptly defeated the Tory Government by the aid of the Irish vote; and on the 1st of February he became Prime Minister for the third time, and addressed himself to the task of framing a plan of Home Rule. Of course, he asked Hartington to join him, and, equally of course, Hartington declined. It was useless to press him with abstract considerations about the greater or lesser amounts of local self-government which can be allowed to exist under central control. All those pribbles and prabbles, though they delight theorists and constitution-mongers, and sedentary persons who look at politics through study-windows, failed signally to touch the realities of the situation. "We do not mean the same thing," said Hartington to a busybody, who pleaded the merits of "Autonomy"; and he decided to remain outside. "No Risks" had ever been the motto of the Whigs; and Hartington had no mind to face the enormous risk which fascinated Gladstone. There can be no need to recapitulate the events of

THE LAST OF THE WHIGS 65

the summer of 1886. Their concrete result is known to all men. Gladstone appealed to the country for its judgment on Home Rule, and received an answer which he did not expect. He said to the present writer: "I was assured by the experts that we should sweep the country." But, in spite of the experts, the result of the election gave a majority of 110 against Home Rule. Gladstone retired; and Lord Salisbury, gracefully recognizing the enormous part which Hartington had played in the defeat of Gladstone's policy, recommended that he should become Prime Minister at the head of a Coalition Government. But here, again, the Whig stepped in. Hartington saw that, if he became head of a Government which must rely for its main support on Tory votes, those Unionists who remained Liberals would probably fall away from him. The Liberal resistance to Home Rule would devolve on Mr Chamberlain and his friends, whose position would shortly become untenable, and the Liberal Party as a whole would soon become identified with Home Rule. Thus, for the second time, Hartington declined the crown of a statesman's reasonable ambition. Yet one more such chance remained. At the end of 1886 Lord Randolph Churchill's sudden resignation threw the Unionist Party into most perplexing confusion. Lord Salisbury offered to surrender the Premiership, and wished Hartington to take it. The Queen wrote strongly in the same sense; but the considerations which governed his refusal in the previous summer governed it again. After it was settled, he doubted if he had "done right." His biographer has no doubt that he did wrong, and closes the episode with this question: "Has any other Englishman refused three times to be First Minister of the Crown, or is this a 'record'?"

The next few years were uneventful. Hartington continued to offer an opposition of rock-like solidity to the policy of Home Rule, which monopolized Gladstone's later years; but the controversy became, year by year, less exciting. In 1891, he succeeded his father in the Dukedom of Devonshire, and in the following year he married "his most intimate friend of nearly thirty years," the Dowager Duchess of Manchester. In 1893, he made a powerful speech in moving the rejection of Gladstone's second Home Rule Bill. The Bill was thrown out by 419 votes to 41, and, as Cromwell said, "not a dog barked." Gladstone, who had become Prime Minister for the fourth time in 1892, retired finally in 1894, and was succeeded by Lord Rosebery, whose Administration lasted for fifteen months. In June 1895, he was beaten on a snap-division in the House of Commons, and was succeeded by Lord Salisbury. "Now from even the most sanguine breast had vanished the hope of a reunion of the Liberal Party on the basis which had existed before Home Rule came up"; and Hartington accepted the post of Lord President of the Council in the new Administration. That Administration lasted through all the miseries of the

South African War and the Khaki Election of 1900, and was still in full vigour when, in 1903, Mr Chamberlain startled England by proclaiming the revival of a Protectionist policy. The controversy is still with us, and its leading incidents are fresh in remembrance. For our present purpose, it is only necessary to say that Hartington, Whig in all things, was pre-eminently Whig in his loyalty to Free Trade. He was no dogmatist. He rather distrusted abstract speculation in Political Economy, as in every other department of thought; and, at the insistent bidding of his colleague—for Mr Chamberlain had joined the Tory Government at the same time as himself—he honestly re-examined the old arguments for and against the new policy, and came to the definite conclusion that it was bad. His judgment was shared by some of his colleagues. For defending Free Trade, Mr Ritchie, Lord Balfour of Burleigh, and Lord George Hamilton were made to resign, and the Duke ought to have followed them. But here again his fatal slowness intervened. "Both merits and defects of the original character tell more decidedly towards the end of a man's career, like the bias in a bowl, as the dynamic force decreases." The Duke's innate slowness became a "lethargic habit," and made it increasingly difficult for him to keep pace with the movements of other minds. He was also, on his own showing, rather deaf; and it is not unnatural to surmise that, during Cabinet discussions, his thoughts sometimes travelled from the arid regions of finance and commerce to the more cheerful scenes of sport and society. Perhaps, when his body was in Downing Street, his mind was at Newmarket. But, whatever was the cause of his delay, the Duke did not resign when those who held with him resigned or were driven. The situation was further complicated by the fact that Mr Chamberlain also resigned, in order that he might have full liberty to prosecute the policy of "Fiscal Reform," and the Duke judged it best to remain; but his decision "left him in a tormenting state of mind." "He felt that the Ministers who had resigned must think that he had not stood by them, for his explanations did not satisfy his own keen sense of honour and loyalty." On the 1st of October Mr Balfour made a public speech, which so defined his attitude towards Tariff Reform that the Duke perceived at last the parting of the ways. He resigned on the 2nd of October, and his resignation probably did as much to secure the victory of Free Trade as any single action throughout the whole campaign.

Thus ended the Duke's career; and surely it was an ending which well became "The Last of the Whigs." He lived to see the triumph of Free Trade at the General Election of 1906, but it was accompanied by other incidents less pleasing to him. "Campbell-Bannerman," he wrote, "seems prepared to go any lengths, and Asquith, Haldane, and Co. will do nothing effectual to stop him." *Tempus abire.* The end came suddenly, though not without some previous signs of failing health, on the 24th of March 1908. His last words were: "Well, the game is over, and I am not sorry."

"Throughout his political career his attitude was that of a man refusing to be hurried." Such is Mr Holland's epitome of the Duke's record, and it strikes the distinctive note of Whiggery. In 1883 the late Lord Cowper, himself a graceful ornament of the Whig Party, wrote in the *Nineteenth Century*: "I am not much in favour of Democracy, and I particularly dislike the feeling that we are doing anything very rapidly." Exactly so. He who refuses to be hurried gets left behind; and the dislike of doing anything, however excellent it may be, very rapidly, leaves the doing of it to other and less timid hands. It fared thus with the Whigs. "Until 1886 the word 'Whig' was still in common use to denote a connexion loosely bound together—the moderate Liberals, led by the chiefs of certain families of long standing. Since 1886 the word has been used in a purely historical sense, while 'Tory' has still a living meaning." The Whig Party, as a concrete reality, "had a history of as nearly as possible 200 years"; and the last survivor of it was the eighth Duke of Devonshire.

III

THE FIRST LORD COLERIDGE

THIS is a pleasant book,[1] but, if the Stars and Stripes will forgive me, I am going to use Mr Yarnall merely as the recipient of Lord Coleridge's confidences. It is of Coleridge that I wish to write, and my wish is prompted by considerations partly personal and partly general. On general grounds, it is good to praise famous men, and to revive their memory when it seems to be fading: on personal grounds, I have often wished to say a word about Lord Coleridge, whom I greatly admired, and who, when I was a young man, treated me with distinguished kindness. His opinions I did not always share, and his actions I sometimes regretted; but on some great issues of Freedom and Humanity we were in close sympathy, and his mental gifts attained, in my judgment, to the altitude of genius.

The correspondence which supplies me with my text begins on "St Mark's Day, 1856." John Duke Coleridge was now thirty-five years old, and was still —as his way of dating his letter shows—under the influence of the Tractarian Movement. From that

[1] *Forty Years of Friendship* (Macmillan & Co.).

influence, as the years went on, he passed into a kind of misty Latitudinarianism, except in so far as a personal devotion to Cardinal Newman and "dear Mr Keble" kept him loyal to his earlier ideals. "To me," he wrote in 1891, "Newman remains, on the whole, far the greatest man I ever knew, and I have known Wordsworth and Mr Gladstone."

In Coleridge's case the usual law of political development was suspended. Trained in Tory traditions, and beginning life as a Liberal-Conservative of the Gladstonian type, he developed, with increasing years and accumulated honours, into a hardened Radical. From first to last, through all phases and permutations, he retained a singular independence of judgment; he saw a good deal more in the world to decry than to extol; and when the critical mood was on him, he spoke his mind with an engaging freedom. When he trounced the early poems of his intimate friend, Matthew Arnold, the aggrieved poet wrote: "My love to J. D. C., and tell him that the limited circulation of the *Christian Remembrancer* makes the unquestionable viciousness of his article of little importance. I am sure he will be gratified to think that this is so." Faithful are the wounds of a friend; and, when Coleridge's critical judgment was offended, no mawkish tenderness stayed his hand. Thus, when this correspondence begins, his mood was to rebuke Ruskin. "I have been," he said, "and still am, a great admirer of his. My life has been made more happy and more interesting in many ways by him." But, in spite of that circumstance, candour compels the following sentence: "I was at Oxford with him, and I know what sort of a scholar he was. I am very fond of Greek and Latin, and have kept up my acquaintance with them as well as I can, and *I am sure* that, on all matters of classical literature, he is as ignorant as he is arrogant. In England we are so ignorant of Art and Nature too, and so apt to be led after any man who is a bold self-assertor, that it is more important than perhaps appears to examine with some severity the claims of any man who sets up to guide us." That task of severe examination was one from which Coleridge never weakly shrank, whether the subject was art, or literature, or politics. "Bismarck is a thorough blackguard," and Carlyle "an ill-conditioned man." Forster's speeches "did not raise his character." The great Lord Derby "was not an honourable man." "The base idolatry of such a man as Lord Palmerston disgusts and disheartens me." Macaulay he considered "a grossly overrated man, and, as a *poet*, really not to be named." He "knew too many distinctly unhandsome things" of Bishop Wilberforce to be "tolerant" of him. Bunsen's books "were naught, and his conversation most unattractive." Lord Campbell "lied, no doubt, and malignantly," about his rival Lyndhurst. Coleridge's "old friend Salisbury" was debauched by Disraeli, "till he took to imitating the worst Dizzy qualities, with none of the wit and *bonhomie* that made one like Dizzy in spite of oneself." As to Froude, Coleridge was even more vigorous. "I know that the truth is not in him. I do really believe him to be physically incapable of speaking it. . . . I cannot even like his style, which seems to me like himself—*i.e.* false and affected." "Browning almost always, and not seldom the great Alfred himself," gave us, instead of poetry, "rough notes and embryos of thought." "*Locrine*, I am told, was telegraphed to America in its entirety, and it must be very unlike anything I ever read of Swinburne's if a line of it was worth such trouble." Coleridge had moved much in ecclesiastical circles, and affirmed that "perfect integrity of thought and expression was a very rare thing in a Bishop"; while an American prelate, mercifully unnamed, struck him as being "a poor, vain snob as ever I came across." Lowe "took his eloquence wholesale from De Tocqueville, and in office was a failure." Gladstone was the one man in the political world whom Coleridge honoured and followed; yet even here he could perceive defects. "I have known him since 1847, and have long been aware of the *fault*—in geological phrase—which runs through his character. He is one of the greatest, and, at the same time, one of the strangest, men I ever knew. . . . He does not like strong men, and, like many Kings of Men, he is a little the worse for flattery."

Coleridge's Radicalism, to which I referred above, consisted in great part of hostility to existing institutions. He was the only man in great station whom I ever found bold enough to criticize "The Fountain of Honour." To Prince Albert he attributed "a sordid love of money"; and I have heard him draw comparisons between George IV. and a later Prince, enormously to the advantage of the former. If Coleridge thought little of kings, even lower was his estimate of aristocracy. The vulgarity of a northern duke who filled a Gothic castle with the fittings of an Italian palace moved his eloquent disgust. "The dominant class in England I thoroughly dislike." A general depreciation of property was no great mischief "if it brought down the high looks of the proud a little." No American, he said, could "tell to what an extent it emasculates and deadens us—this aristocratic influence and the snobbishness which it engenders." In 1858 he writes: "I want to see property divided and entails destroyed, hereditary privileges — not hereditary honours — abolished." Twenty-eight years later he writes: "I do think that Feudalism is at last doomed, and that the sham splendours, and real miseries, which always follow in its train, are doomed with it, and that is some comfort for the future."

At the period when the correspondence with Yarnall begins, the controversy about American Slavery was nearing its final and decisive stage. Coleridge writes with becoming indignation against the "Peculiar Institution" and all its works and ways. Of an American clergyman who justified it he says:—

> This wretched man has, I suppose, all his life asserted that he really believes that God Incarnate sanctioned fathers selling

THE FIRST LORD COLERIDGE 75

their children into prostitution, and masters considering their fellow men and women as beasts to breed from.

When John Brown, of Harper's Ferry, was put to death, Coleridge writes :—

> I cannot measure words about this matter. The execution of that gallant old man was an act of utterly unnecessary, and therefore of wicked and disgraceful, cruelty, and . . . shows that slavery is bringing the slave-holding gentlemen of America to the level of barbarous and savage tribes.

But here again Aristocracy rears its detested head. In 1862, he writes :—

> If anything could deepen the detestation I feel for the character and influence of our English aristocrats, it would be the shameless manner in which they have rejoiced at the misfortunes of America. . . . But I am apt to lose my temper and my judgment when I think of this magnificent country and this grand people, dominated by squires and peers who can be, and are daily, guilty of just so much insolence to us all as they think it safe to exhibit.

After this indignant outburst against the system under which he lived, Coleridge goes straight to a characteristic confession. "Of course, all this vehement democracy is for home consumption (where, by the way, it sometimes rather disconcerts my dear, good old father) and will not be put forward in public." He was just preparing to enter Parliament, and he did so, under Palmerston's leadership, in 1865. He was re-elected as a Gladstonian in 1868, and became, in rapid succession, Solicitor-General, Attorney-General, Chief Justice of the Common Pleas, and Lord Chief Justice of England. Of his own professional qualifications he always spoke disparagingly, and he said that the profession itself, "except the actual excitement of conflict," was "thoroughly uncongenial" to him. He accused himself of "want of law, indolence, and merely surface discharge of duties which did not interest him." He "always worked with a melancholy sense of inadequacy and inferiority." When he was made Solicitor-General, he said, "I don't like office at all, but a man cannot do in these things as he likes"; but when he was promoted to the Attorney-Generalship, he remarked philosophically, "One may as well be on the top round as the top but one, and I am glad to lead the profession before I am fifty." When he ascended to the Bench he pronounced that he was "a very poor performer," and when he became Lord Chief Justice of England, he "had a feeling of unfitness for his great office, which was at times almost disabling." And yet, again, in 1886:—

> I have never liked my profession; and the practice of it, which, even with the excitement of advocacy, was barely interesting, is now positively repulsive. I am eager to get away, and be replaced by someone who will do it better.

But he died Lord Chief Justice eight years later.

In 1883 Coleridge wrote to Yarnall: "Gladstone, I believe, will give up public life before many months are over." Other Liberals thought the same, and were always suggesting the precise moment at which their leader's retirement might most conveniently be effected; but they little knew their man. In 1885

THE FIRST LORD COLERIDGE 77

Gladstone was returned for Midlothian by an enormous majority of the newly-enfranchised voters, and in December the world knew that he had become a convert to Home Rule. Coleridge was one of the many whom this disclosure seriously perturbed. All his antecedent sympathies were with Ireland. In 1868 and 1869, in the debates on Irish Disestablishment, he had depicted the horrors of English tyranny in Ireland in his most successful orations. In 1886 he wrote, "Centuries of wicked misrule cannot be undone in twenty years," and he hoped that Home Rule might be a way out of difficulties; but he denounced "the detestable cruelties which the Irish are guilty of towards anyone who in any way exercises any right displeasing to them," and "was thankful he was not in the Ministry which had to deal with these things." After the Home Rule Bill had been defeated in the House of Commons, and the Home Rule policy rejected by the nation at the General Election, he wrote, with reference to Gladstone, who was now driven into Opposition: "I believe he is right; but I also believe that the deep distrust and dislike he has inspired into some of the leading men of his own Party will make his policy impossible till he has left the stage of politics."

In 1887 there is a slight change of tone:—

> I believe Gladstone will win, and what is just and right will be done by the British democracy. Whether in this or that particular Gladstone is wise, I will not say—very likely not; but in substance he is perfectly right. I do think that the Party

have a good deal to complain of at his hands. His change—at least the declaration of it—was far too sudden, and he was too unbending at first in his refusal to listen to compromise.

In 1893 he voted for the second Home Rule Bill, and his conclusion on the whole matter was this:—

> I have been a Home Ruler long; but it was to me always a counsel of despair. We were well thrashed the other night in the House of Lords. But there is such a thing as *overdoing*, and it is a tolerable proof that the House of Lords cannot claim to represent the country, when the majority is ten to one.

The complete independence of judgment which Coleridge manifested at a time when the Liberal Party, as a whole, was hypnotized by Gladstone's influence, is the more remarkable because he had long been a Gladstonian. When Gladstone first contested the University of Oxford, Coleridge had been secretary to his Committee. In Parliament Coleridge was a zealous supporter of Gladstone's policy. From Gladstone he received the four great offices which he successively held, and in 1874 Gladstone made him a peer. After the Liberal defeat of that year Coleridge wrote of him as "the greatest, noblest, purest, and sincerest public man of the century," and was so much disgusted by the "lightness and ingratitude" of the Liberal Party that, "except for Gladstone's sake, I would have declined the peerage, and turned my back on public life for ever."

This is a hard saying. When Coleridge wrote it he was only fifty-two years old. If I read him aright, the *in honoribus complacentia* (which some great saints have noted in themselves) was not absent from his character. Nor can I conceive that a man so keenly interested in human life and action would have been happy in complete withdrawal from the world. It is true that he repeatedly accuses himself of "laziness" and "indolence"; and I can well believe that it needed some strong stimulus to make him a hard worker. But that stimulus was supplied, partly by the honourable desire to provide for his own household, and partly by an ambition of which he seems to have been scarcely conscious. His intellect was the most flexible and adaptable of implements, and he used it with a consummate ease which must have made even "drudgery," if not "divine," at any rate enjoyable. What he may have wanted in law and logic was made good by rhetoric and persuasiveness; and the arts and graces of the Bar were not discarded when he mounted the Bench.

The correspondence before us deals very lightly with the professional side of Coleridge's life, and leaves absolutely untouched his gift of oratory; yet in the great debates of 1866 and 1867, 1868 and 1869, he held his own with the foremost speakers in Parliament; his voice was pure music, and his voice-production so perfect that he seemed to be speaking in one's ear.

I have been struck by the frequency with which in the correspondence Coleridge dwells on his "bad spirits" and "desponding" temper. That he felt acutely the pressure of great sorrows is only to say that he was human; and, when life was going well, he seemed to live in perpetual sunshine. He had good health and great position; an assured place among the most eminent men of his generation; a circle of friends not numerous indeed, but devotedly attached; and a never-failing source of enjoyment in the follies and foibles of mankind at large. The duties of his office did not seem to sit heavily on him, and the moment they were laid aside he passed instinctively into a kind of σχολή such as an Athenian citizen would have enjoyed. The brutal sports of the field were repulsive to a nature which shrank from pain; and, like the Apostle, he held that bodily exercise "profiteth little." But Literature and Society, Nature and Art, all appealed to him with equal force; and he could turn from one to the other with equal enjoyment. First and foremost, he was a man of letters; saturated in the scholarship which Eton taught, but keenly alive to all that is beautiful in modern literature. His special devotion was to Wordsworth, whom he read, continuously and systematically, year in, year out. "He is *the* poet of English literature since Milton, and κατ' ἐξοχήν *the* poet for busy men." Coleridge delighted in "tuney" music; loved literature and understood it; knew all the best pictures in Europe, and held Turner to be "the greatest landscape-painter who ever lived." To the study of Nature he brought, as became Wordsworth's disciple and Arnold's friend,

> A heart
> That watches and receives.

THE FIRST LORD COLERIDGE 81

The subject invites expansion, but considerations of space, if of nothing else, forbid. A single word will suffice for my summing-up. It has been my fortune to know many great men, in various senses of the word "great"; but of all that distinguished company the most interesting was Lord Coleridge.

IV

HENRY LABOUCHERE[1]

"WHEN the Grand Old Man goes, our leader must be Le-bowcher." This fervent utterance of a convinced Radical, somewhere about the year 1882, supplies me with a fitting text.

My task, undertaken at the Editor's bidding, is not easy. The account of Mr Labouchere which appeared in *Truth* immediately after his death was so clear, so full, and so well-informed, that it puts subsequent writers at a disadvantage. I cannot pretend to write Mr Labouchere's early history, or to describe his habits in private life; nor can I even profess to have ever been an intimate friend. My connexion with him was purely fortuitous; it was confined to the House of Commons, and began with the new Parliament of 1880. The saying which I have inscribed at the head of this chapter sufficiently indicates the position which, quite early in the life of that Parliament, he acquired in Radical circles out of doors. Inside the House we saw a different side of him, and the contrast between the Labouchere of the

[1] Reprinted from the *Cornhill Magazine*.

House and the Labouchere of the platform was at once amusing and instructive.

As a Harrow boy of fifteen, I had admired the gay audacity with which, at the General Election of 1868, the democratic Labouchere upset the apple-cart of official Whiggery in Middlesex, though he lost his own seat by doing so; and it may be that some allusion of mine to that "unchartered freedom" first commended me to his kindly regard. At any rate it is certain that from April 1880 onwards he always showed himself to me in his most accessible and obliging aspect. I will speak first of some slighter traits, and will then pass on to matters more important.

"The Christian Member for Northampton" (as he delighted to call himself in contrast to his colleague Mr Bradlaugh) was not, at the time of which I speak, much known in general society. His social day was over, and I cannot suppose that he regretted it.

He was the oracle of an initiated circle, and the smoking-room of the House of Commons was his shrine. There, poised in an American rocking-chair and delicately toying with a cigarette, he unlocked the varied treasures of his well-stored memory, and threw over the changing scenes of life the mild light of his genial philosophy. It was a chequered experience that made him what he was. He had known men and cities; had probed in turn the mysteries of the Caucus, the Green-room, and the Stock Exchange; had been a diplomatist, a financier, a journalist, and a politician. Under these circumstances it was not surprising that his faith—no doubt originally robust—in the rectitude of human nature and the purity of human motive should have undergone some process of degeneration. Still, it may be questioned whether, after all that he had seen and done, he really was the absolute and all-round cynic that he seemed to be. The palpable endeavour to make out the worst of everyone—including himself—gave a certain flavour of unreality to his conversation; but, in spite of this drawback, he was an engaging talker. His language was racy and incisive, and he spoke as neatly as he wrote. His voice was pleasant, and his utterance deliberate and effective. He had a keen eye for absurdities and incongruities, a shrewd insight into affectation and bombast, and an admirable impatience of all the moral and intellectual qualities which constitute the Bore. He was by no means inclined to bow the knee too slavishly to an exalted reputation, and he analysed with agreeable frankness the personal and political qualities of great and good men, even they that sat on the Liberal Front Bench. As an unmasker of political humbug he was supreme, but his dislike of that vice often led him into unreasonable depreciations. I well remember the peroration of Mr Gladstone's speech in introducing the Irish Land Bill of 1881 ; and I think it deserves to be reproduced :—

As it has been said that Love is stronger than Death, even so Justice is stronger than popular excitement, stronger than the passions of the moment, stronger even than the grudges, the resentments, and the sad traditions of the past. Walking in that light we cannot err. Guided by that light—that Divine light—we are safe. Every step that we take upon our road is a step that brings us nearer to the goal, and every obstacle, even although for the moment it may seem insurmountable, can only for a little while retard, and never can defeat, the final triumph.

When the orator sat down we streamed into the Lobby, each man saying to his neighbour: "Wasn't that splendid?" "The finest thing he ever did!" "What a thrilling peroration!" "Yes" (in a drawl from Labouchere), "but I call it d——d copybook-y."

I have spoken of the flavour of unreality which was imparted to Labouchere's conversation by his affected cynicism. A similar effect was produced by his manner of personal narrative. Ethics apart, I have no quarrel with the man who romances to amuse his friends; but the romance should be so conceived and so uttered as to convey a decent sense of probability, or at least possibility. Labouchere's narratives conveyed no such sense. Though amusingly told, they were so outrageously and palpably impossible that his only object in telling them must have been to test one's credulity. I do not mind having my leg pulled, but I dislike to feel the process too distinctly.

These arts of romantic narrative, only partially successful in the smoking-room, were, I believe, practised with great effect on the electors of Northampton. Labouchere was never happier than in describing the methods by which he had fobbed off some inconvenient enthusiast, or thrown dust in the eyes of a too curious enquirer. His accounts of his dealings with his constituents had, I suppose, a good deal in common with his experiences as President of a South American Republic or Commander of a Revolutionary force; but they were extremely entertaining. He used to declare that he had originated the honorific title of "Grand Old Man," and his setting of the scene was as follows: Mr Bradlaugh had been expelled from the House, and straightway went down to Northampton for re-election, his colleague, "the Christian Member" for the borough, accompanying him. What ensued at the first meeting may be told as Labouchere used to tell it. "I said to our enthusiastic supporters: 'Men of Northampton, I come to you with a message from the Grand Old Man (cheers). I went to see him before I left London; I told him of my errand here; and he laid his hand on my shoulder, saying, in his most solemn tone: 'Bring him back with you, Henry; bring him back.' That carried the election." I daresay it did; and the picture of Mr Gladstone fondling Labouchere and calling him "Henry" can never be obliterated from the mental gaze of anyone who knew the two men.

There was a good deal of impishness in Labouchere's nature. He was of the family of Puck, and "Lord! what fools these mortals be!" probably expressed his attitude towards his fellow-creatures. But it was noticeable that his impishness never degenerated into rudeness. There is as clear a difference between gentlemanlike fun and vulgar fun as between champagne and swipes. Labouchere was a gentleman to the backbone, and had all the courtesy which one would have expected from his antecedents. I remember that, in the stormy days of January 1881, when the Prime Minister and the authorities of the House were obliged to extemporize rules against disorder, I happened to be crossing New Palace Yard in company with Mr Herbert Gladstone. We met Labouchere, who chirped, in his cheeriest manner: "Well, has the tyrant made any fresh attack on free speech to-day?" Herbert Gladstone passed on, and Labouchere said to me, with genuine concern: " He can't have thought I meant his father, can he? Of course, I was thinking of the Speaker." It was interesting to see that he seemed to shudder at the bare notion of having been unintentionally rude.

I remember Mr Gladstone, in one of his odd fits of political speculation, asking if I thought that there was even one man in the House of Commons, however Radical he might be, who would vote for unwigging the Speaker. I, rather obviously, suggested Labouchere, and Mr Gladstone replied: "Yes, possibly; but that would be from freakishness, not from conviction." No powers of divination could have ascertained what Labouchere really believed; but I think it was easier to know what he really enjoyed. I suppose he enjoyed his wealth—most people who have it do so—but chiefly, I should think, on rather impish grounds. It was an acute delight to him in early days to know that he was bound to inherit the wealth of his uncle, Lord Taunton, a high-dried Whig who detested his eccentricities. He took pleasure in saying to casual acquaintances, "You know that my sister married the Bishop of Rochester," for he felt the incongruity of the fate which had made him brother-in-law to Bishop Thorold, the primmest, correctest, and most stiffly starched of all the Anglican episcopate. Litigation always seemed to delight him, less for the objects contested than for the opportunity which it gave him of scoring and surprising; and I am sure that I do him no wrong when I say that he found a peculiar zest in buying a freehold house in Old Palace Yard, and thereby impeding the schemes of Mr H. Y. Thompson for creating a National Valhalla. I feel certain that he thoroughly enjoyed the proprietorship of *Truth*, and not less the reputation (which we are now told was erroneous) of being its editor. I myself believe, though some of his obituarists deny, that he had a genuine sympathy with all victims of cruelty, fraud, and injustice, and found a real pleasure in the immense service which *Truth* did in unmasking impostors and bringing torturers to justice.

Labouchere made *Truth*, and, in one most important respect, *Truth* made Labouchere. I do not refer to anything in the way of profit or of consideration which it may have brought him: he was placed by the circumstances of his birth in a position where

HENRY LABOUCHERE

such things neither make nor mar. I refer to his political career. I do not know whether, when, as a young man, he flitted in and out of Parliament, he cherished any serious ambitions. I doubt if he had them even when he became M.P. for Northampton. But the events of the Parliament of 1880 brought him rapidly to the front. His valorous championship of Bradlaugh gave him a peculiar position at a moment when the public mind was violently agitated by panic-fears of Atheism. He stood for religious freedom when many of its sworn adherents ran away; and on all the points of old-fashioned Radicalism (before Socialism affected it) he was as sound as a bell. Hence the cry of the London democrat: "Our leader must be Le-bowcher." Before that desirable consummation could be reached, the Liberal majority of Easter 1880 melted like last year's snow. The Tories took office. The General Election of 1885 did not displace them, but in February 1886 Mr Gladstone, having squared the Irish members, came back to office.

Labouchere's position was now difficult and tantalizing. His party was in power, and the way seemed clear for some radical reforms on which Liberals had long set their hearts. But Mr Chamberlain, and some of the Radical group with whom Labouchere had acted, declined to accept Home Rule, left the Government, and created Radical Unionism. If they voted against the Second Reading of the Home Rule Bill, it would almost certainly be thrown out, and the

Government would follow it into retirement. Here was, indeed, a perplexing situation, and it forced Labouchere into action which must certainly have been uncongenial to him. Four days before the vital division, when argument on either side was exhausted and everyone had decided on his course, Labouchere, writing on behalf of a large body of Liberal M.P.'s, addressed to Mr Chamberlain an earnest appeal, imploring him either to vote for the second reading or at least to abstain. He pointed out that a second General Election within seven months would be a serious matter for Liberals, and he remarked that a General Election without Mr. Chamberlain (then at the height of his popularity) on the Liberal side might lead to a Whig-Tory or Tory-Whig Government, which "would relegate to the dim and distant future" those measures which they had so long and so ardently desired. To this appeal Mr Chamberlain naturally replied that he and his friends would be stultifying themselves if, after all they had said and done, they were at the last moment to abstain from giving effect to their convictions. "I admit," said Mr Chamberlain, "the dangers of a General Election at the present time; but I think the responsibility must in fairness rest upon those who have brought in, and forced to a division, a Bill which, in the words of Mr Bright, 'not twenty members outside the Irish Party would support if Mr Gladstone's great authority were withdrawn from it.'"

I must believe that, when Labouchere penned the

appealing document, he had his tongue in his cheek. The simple souls in the constituencies, and the not much wiser ones who had just entered Parliament, may have dreamed that Mr Chamberlain, having staked his whole career on a decisive act, would shrink from it at the last moment for fear he should embarrass the Liberal Party; but Labouchere, I feel certain, had no such illusions. Yet the incident was not without its effect. The championship of Bradlaugh was now over, for Bradlaugh was in the House to look after himself. Henceforward Labouchere was one of the most persistent, and, through *Truth*, one of the most powerful, advocates of Home Rule, and a highly resourceful counsellor in all the plots and stratagems which made the political history of 1886-92.

It was at this period of storm and stress that Sir Frederick Bridge, who was one of Labouchere's neighbours in Westminster, was moved to utter his thought in song. The poem appeared in *Punch*, and is reprinted here by the special permission of the proprietors of that journal:—

LABBY IN OUR ABBEY

Tune—" Sally in our Ally"

Of all the boys that are so smart
There's none like crafty Labby;
He learns the secrets of each heart,
And he lives near our Abbey;[1]

---

[1] Mr L. resided in Old Palace Yard, Westminster.

> There is no lawyer in the land
>   That's half so sharp as Labby;
> He is a demon in the art,
>   And guileless as a babby.
>
> For Arthur Balfour, of the week
>   By far the very worst day
> Is that dread day that comes betwixt
>   A Tuesday and a Thursday;[1]
> For then he reads his vile misdeeds
>   ("Unmanly, mean, and shabby")
> Exposed to view in type so true
>   By penetrating Labby.
>
> Our Ministers and Members all
>   Make game of truthful Labby,
> Tho' but for him 'tis said they'd be
>   A sleepy lot and flabby;
> But ere their seven long years are out[2]
>   They hope to bury Labby;
> Ah! then how peacefully he'll lie,
>   But *not* in our Abbey.

What Sir Frederick Bridge wrote jestingly, Labouchere—for once in his life—took seriously. There can be no doubt that by this time he had formed a definite ambition of political office. During the six years of Tory ascendancy he fought incessantly, with tongue and pen, for the Liberal cause, and he reckoned confidently on being included in the next Liberal Cabinet. But he had reckoned without his host. The Parliament which had been elected in July 1886 was dissolved in June 1892. The General Election gave Gladstone a majority of 40 all told. He became Prime Minister for the fourth time, and formed

[1] Mr Balfour was Chief Secretary for Ireland, and *Truth* was published on Wednesday.
[2] A reference to the Septennial Act.

HENRY LABOUCHERE

his last Cabinet. But he did not find a place in it for Labouchere. Before he submitted his list to the Queen, he had received a direct intimation that he had better not include in it the name of the editor of *Truth*. On this point her Majesty was reported to be "very stiff." Whether that stiffness encountered any corresponding, or conflicting, stiffness in the Prime Minister I do not know; but for my own part I believe that "the Grand Old Man" acquiesced in the exclusion of "Henry" without a sigh or struggle.

Displeased by the issue of events, Labouchere took a mild revenge. He printed in *Truth* some severe strictures on Mr Gladstone's new Administration—partly because it was too Whiggish—and illustrated them with a hideous cartoon, in which all we who had accepted office were caricatured. Participating in these rebuffs, and surprised by my friend's lapse from amenity, I wrote Labouchere a letter of remonstrance, which proved about as efficacious as his own appeal to Mr Chamberlain six years before. This was his answer:—

Aug. 24, 1892.

MY DEAR RUSSELL,—Never be drawn. Let a licentious and scurrilous Press say what it likes, and sit tight. . . . My Radicalism goes to the utter destruction of the aristocracy. So, of course, I call attention to young patricians, and compare them with those children of the people, Cobb and Channing.[1] This is involved in being on the side of destruction.

Yours sincerely,

H. LABOUCHERE.

---

[1] H. P. Cobb, M.P. for South-East Warwickshire, and F. A. Channing, M.P. for East Northamptonshire (afterwards Lord Channing).

Thus Labouchere's political ambitions came to an end, unsung indeed, but, I fear, not unwept. Very soon he developed a new scheme for the employment of his powers, and pursued it with the most untiring industry. He wished to be made Ambassador at Washington, and he wished it with an insistence which people who knew him superficially would scarcely have expected. Lord Rosebery was at the time Foreign Secretary; and, if it be true, as I have seen it stated, that he was one of the very few people whom Labouchere hated, I think the reason might be found in the correspondence of 1892-94.

In later years my communications with Labouchere were few and far between. It happened that towards the end of the year 1906 I had occasion to write to him for some information about a foreign question. He immediately replied, and then turned to current politics:—

I find it very comfortable being out of Parliament, and reading in the papers what they do—or don't do—in the H. of C. Our pawky friend C. B. seems to be very popular. I am a Radical, but it strikes me that he will . . . create a reaction if he yields so much to the ultra-Labour men of the —— type on social issues, particularly if "Joe" remains an invalid, and the Conservative Party can free itself of his fiscal "reforms." As for the Education Bill, I do not love Bishops, but I hate far more the Noncon. Popes. Either you must have pure Secularism in public schools, or teach religion of some sort; and, altho' I personally am an Agnostic, I don't see how Xtianity is to be taught free from all dogma, and entirely creedless, by teachers who do not believe in it. This is the play of Hamlet without Hamlet, and acted by persons of his philosophic doubt.

So, at least for once in his life, Labouchere was on

the same side as the Bishops, and in that good company we may leave him.

P.S.—If in one passage of this chapter I have borrowed from my former self, let me plead Lord Morley's excuse: " A man may once say a thing as he would have it said, δὶς δὲ οὐκ ἐνδέχεται—he cannot say it twice."

V

A CABINET OF MINIATURES

THE DUCHESS OF BUCCLEUCH [1]

THE Duchess was Lady Louisa Jane Hamilton, the third daughter of the first Duke of Abercorn and sister of the present Duke and of Lord Claud Hamilton, M.P., Lord George, Lord Frederic, and Lord Ernest Hamilton, Harriet Lady Lichfield, the late Lady Durham, the late Lady Mount-Edgcumbe, Lady Winterton, Lady Blandford, and Lady Lansdowne. She married the Duke of Buccleuch (then Lord Dalkeith) on 22nd November 1859, and had six sons and two daughters. Her eldest son was accidentally killed while deer-stalking in 1886. Her other sons were Lord Dalkeith, Major Lord George Scott, Colonel Lord Henry Scott, Lieutenant-Colonel Lord Herbert Scott, D.S.O., and Captain Lord Francis Scott, and her daughters were Lady Hampden and Lady Constance Cairns.

The Duchess of Buccleuch had the charm of perpetual youth, and it was difficult for those who only a few years ago mourned the death of her wonderful

[1] Louisa, Duchess of Buccleuch, died on the 16th of March 1912.

mother, the Dowager-Duchess of Abercorn, to realize that "Tiny" (to use the Duchess of Buccleuch's pet-name) had passed the ordinary bounds of human life. Lord Beaconsfield drew in *Lothair* a portrait of the daughters of the house of Hamilton, in which their external and superficial characteristics were cleverly depicted. It was true of more than one of them that, in Lord Beaconsfield's phrase, "the bright maiden woke one morning and found herself famous," for the world welcomed each successive daughter as she entered society with a warmth which was due in part to the popularity of her parents, but in greater part to her own gifts and gràces. Few sets of sisters have been so universally liked and admired, and none have better deserved the good fortune which awaited them, or were more perfectly fitted to the positions which they were called to fill.

This was peculiarly true of the Duchess of Buccleuch, who, in spite of the youthfulness which in her case was so wonderfully prolonged, was, in the best sense of the phrase, a "lady"—and a very great lady—"of the old school." Her habits and way of life, her modes of thinking and acting, were those of a more dignified age than our own. She abhorred all the friskiness and riskiness, all the craving for notoriety, all the disregard of convention, which in later years had become fashionable. She knew instinctively the wisdom of the principle which bids an aristocracy "hide its life"; and, though she was ready on fit occasion to display the splendour and stateliness which her position demanded, the life which she loved was the life of home and family and friendship. But, with the dignity which came natural to her, and with the social reserve which commended itself to her taste, she combined that bright humour, that love of fun and pleasantry and innocent mirth, which she had inherited, through her mother, from Georgiana, Duchess of Bedford, and more remotely still, from Jane, Duchess of Gordon.

In one respect, and in one only, Louisa Duchess of Buccleuch departed from the traditions of her youth. She had been reared in a school of Evangelical religion which impinged on Presbyterianism; and in her parents' pew at Dr Cumming's church in Crown Court she was accustomed in early youth to hear the end of the world predicted and the wickedness of the Papacy exposed with alarming eloquence. But the lively oracles of "the Kirk and Covenant" made no permanent impression on Louisa Hamilton; and, first as Lady Dalkeith and afterwards as Duchess of Buccleuch, she was a loyal and consistent member of the Scottish Episcopal Church.

No notice of the Duchess, however brief, would be complete without a reference to the tragic death of her beloved son, the late Lord Dalkeith, which, though it could not avail to darken or depress so fine a spirit, yet left a trace of pensive tenderness which gave the crowning beauty to her character.

It remains to add that the Duchess was an intimate friend of the Royal family, particularly of Queen

A CABINET OF MINIATURES

Victoria. She was Mistress of the Robes in Lord Salisbury's and Mr Balfour's Administrations from 1885 to 1886, from 1886 to 1892, and again from 1895 to 1901. She was retained in office by Queen Alexandra on the accession of King Edward, and she remained as Mistress of the Robes to Queen Alexandra in the present reign. She was extremely fond of children, taking, even down to the last few days of her life, a great delight in giving them pleasure. She was also widely charitable, and she will be greatly missed by philanthropic agencies at Dalkeith and Edinburgh.

LADY LINDSAY

A few words are due to the memory of this much-loved friend, who died on 4th August 1912. Blanche FitzRoy was the only surviving child of the Right Honourable Henry FitzRoy, M.P., First Commissioner of Works in Lord Palmerston's Administration, by his marriage with Hannah Meyer, sister of Baron Lionel de Rothschild. She married in 1864 Sir Coutts Lindsay, Bart., of Balcarres, by whom she leaves two daughters.

From her father, a man of great ability and culture, Lady Lindsay inherited the power of writing good English; from her mother, the taste for music. She speedily became a very proficient pianist, and had a light and delicate touch and a great charm of execution. She was a favourite accompanist of Joachim and Mme. Norman Neruda. It was, perhaps, a dangerous experiment to desert the piano for the violin, but the latter instrument gave her unfailing delight, and she spent long hours in learning to master its difficulties. She not only became a very fair executant, but also a composer, and worked with indefatigable energy at harmony and counterpoint. From her earliest years she had illustrated her stories and poems by the aid of her facile pencil, and showed an extraordinary neatness and delicacy in her designs. As she grew older she began to paint in water-colours, and acquired great skill in copying the fine work of some of the Italian masters. Her colouring was beautiful and her rendering always thoroughly artistic. She was untiring with her brush, and devoted to her art.

When the Grosvenor Gallery was first started under the auspices of her husband, Sir Coutts Lindsay, she gave it the best of her powers, and by her social gifts as well as her artistic taste she helped to make it a success both in the world of fashion and art. She lived in a circle of artistic and literary activity. She cared little for the ordinary amusements of what is called society, but delighted to surround herself with men and women distinguished by genius and accomplishments. Matthew Arnold, Robert Browning, Watts, Burne-Jones, and Leighton were among her intimate friends, and her acquaintance with artists was unusually wide. Indeed, every artist recognized in her a kindred spirit, for a love of beauty and a knowledge of its manifestations were among her most conspicuous gifts. She was a true "æsthete" before the word "æstheticism" became fashionable, and was one of the first women in London to dress, or drape, herself after artistic models in form and colour, and to make her rooms unconventionally beautiful. She had an intimate knowledge of Italian painting, and a passionate love of Italy, more especially of Venice, which she was never tired of revisiting. Her little book of verses, called *From a Venetian Balcony*, is sold at Venice almost as a guide-book. In later years she gradually abandoned both music and painting, and devoted herself to literature. She wrote short stories, novels, essays, addresses, and several volumes of poetry. Her verse was marked by fluency, facility, a sensitive ear for melody and cadence, and a wistful sadness. A poem of hers, called "The Christmas of the Sorrowful," struck an absolutely fresh note in the concert of Christmas song, and attained a wide popularity.

For a long series of years she issued every quarter a booklet of meditations enriched with extracts from prose and verse, which she called *Green Leaves*. These "Leaves," gathered from the wide field of her literary knowledge and skilfully adapted to various phases of human sorrow, travelled far and wide, and reached from the hospitals of London and the provinces to India and the Antipodes. The many sorrows that had assailed the bright spirit of the writer had given her a key to saddened hearts.

Although essentially an artist by temperament,

Lady Lindsay had a great capacity for practical affairs; indeed, she was most thorough in every work that she undertook. Both in Scotland and in England she interested herself in the arrangement of her gardens, and acquired a great deal of information about practical horticulture. She loved colour and beauty, and was formed for enjoyment. Her power of repartee, her sense of humour, her love of pure fun had, in the old days, made her the centre of a joyous and distinguished circle. She delighted in entertaining her friends, to whom she was an excellent hostess, and, in spite of delicate health, she was unflagging in her efforts to amuse and interest her guests. A long illness, following upon an accident, withdrew her for some time from all social life, and made it difficult for her to resume her former occupations; but, in spite of physical weakness and much discomfort, she continued to work untiringly for many years, until of late ill-health, bravely endured, began to tell upon her spirit more heavily than she would own. To the last she was deeply interested in a beloved little grandson, and clung to the care of her devoted daughters, who came as ministering spirits to comfort and sustain the mother whom they worshipped.

Keenly as she could suffer, she could also look forward with hope, as she tells us in the pages of her *Green Leaves*:—

And if everything about us and concerning us seems black and sad, let Hope enter into our hearts and cheer our sadness. The darker the night, the brighter shines the beacon. Yet sometimes the night is unutterably dark; we cannot see a step forward; we are altogether hopeless. Then let Patience hold up Hope's lamp for a few moments; Hope is probably close behind her, and will come back to us at the very first word, the very first entreaty.—*Green Leaves*, Christmas, 1909.

One of her oldest friends—" C. B. "—writes thus :—

Her love of truth, her hatred of all shams and pretences, her high sense of honour, and her strong and determined will, all conduced to a very remarkable personality. But, knowing her as I did, I feel that she would love best to be remembered for the constancy and warmth of her affections, even more than for the gifts with which she had been so richly endowed.

Her own words may aptly close this notice :—

OF REMEMBRANCE

Methinks that you'll remember, when I die,
Not some brave action, nor yet stately speech—
Though sheltered lives to these sometimes may reach—
But just a turn of lip, a glance of eye,
A trivial jest, a laughing word, a sigh,
A trick too strong to cure, too slight to teach,
Scarce noticed, haply mocked by all and each—
Now a full source of tears you'd fain defy.

Ah, do not weep ! The traveller, having come
From mountain heights, cares naught for drifted snow,
Nor rock, nor branch, as record of the day :
But plucks a gentian blue and bears it home,
Safe in his bosom—I would have you so
Keep one sweet speck of love at heart alway.

MRS PASCOE GLYN

On 22nd August 1912 there passed away, at the age of seventy, Mrs Pascoe Glyn, who for many years worshipped at St Barnabas', Pimlico, and gave to that parish a full measure of devoted service. Mrs

Glyn was the daughter of Captain William Amherst Hale, and was born in Canada, where her father was at that time serving with his regiment. In 1861 Mrs Glyn became the second wife of the Hon. Pascoe Charles Glyn, sixth son of the first Lord Wolverton and uncle of the present peer. He was a partner in the banking house of Glyn, Mills, Currie & Co., and a member of the Council of the English Church Union, and sat as a Liberal for East Dorset.

Though educated in the rigid Protestantism of Canada, Mrs Glyn soon found her way, by a kind of natural affinity, into the ranks of the High Anglican party, then passing from its Tractarian to its Ritualistic phase. In this matter she was entirely at one with her husband, who, from his Oxford days, had been a staunch adherent of the Movement, and was closely allied with St Barnabas', Pimlico. In the riots of 1850 Pascoe Glyn was one of the laymen who defended St Barnabas' Church, by physical force, against the Protestant mob; throughout his life it was his favourite place of worship, and he was one of its most generous benefactors. It was, therefore, with a peculiar pleasure that he saw his young and beautiful wife throw herself, with self-sacrificing ardour, into the active work of the parish. Under the supervision of the Rev. Malcolm MacColl, then a curate of St Barnabas', Mrs Glyn took a district in a slum which is now abolished, and worked in it with excellent judgment as well as zeal, until she and Mr Glyn moved their home into the country. Through this early association with St Barnabas', Mrs Glyn was brought, at the very beginning of her married life, into close relations with the Rev. G. Cosby White, and those relations continued to the end.

Feeling a keen interest in the work of reclamation, she early attached herself to the House of Mercy at Clewer, and her associateship dated from 1865. As years went on she became interested in the higher education of Church women, and she was a hardworking member of the Council of Lady Margaret Hall. One of her last acts of generosity was to give a large sum towards the provision of a Chapel for the Hall; and among "the almsdeeds which she did," her liberality to the London house of the Cowley Fathers, and more recently to the Sisterhood of Reparation in St Alphege's Parish, Southwark, should not be forgotten.

Some sixteen years ago, Mr and Mrs Glyn, who had for some time been living in the country, returned to London, and established themselves at No. 14 Eaton Square, thus renewing their old familiarity with St Barnabas'; but by this time Mr Glyn's health had begun to fail, and for several years all Mrs Glyn's energies were absorbed in the task of attending to his wants till he died in 1904. Admirable as she was in all the relations of life, it was as the ministering wife of a suffering husband that she excelled.

Her own health had been by nature remarkable; but it began to give way about twelve months ago. When she passed away, one who knew her most intimately wrote, "a beautiful soul was transferred to Paradise." A *Requiem* Eucharist was celebrated at St Barnabas' on Monday morning, 26th August, and the interment took place at Brookwood.—R.I.P.

Mrs Vaughan

Catherine Vaughan, daughter of Edward Stanley, Bishop of Norwich, and wife of the Master of the Temple, was one of the most original women of her time. In personal appearance she closely resembled her brother Dean Stanley, to whom she was devotedly attached, though she always loudly professed her detestation of his theology. The resemblance between brother and sister was not merely physical; they had the same intellectual vivacity, the same wide range of interests, the same literary taste, the same faculty of graphic and picturesque expression. But Mrs Vaughan had certain qualities which her brother did not share. She had an exceedingly keen sense of humour, a perception of the ridiculous in other people which she was at no pains to conceal, and a startling emphasis and vehemence of speech. Dr Vaughan, on the other hand, masked a mordant satire under the guise of more than feminine delicacy; and nothing could be more entertaining than the conflicts of wit which not seldom took place between this truly eminent husband and wife—each of whom, be it remembered, had with good reason a most genuine respect for the other's powers. Mrs Vaughan, whose birth and education had accustomed her to a society at once aristocratic and intellectual, never acquired the apostolic art of suffering fools—or snobs—gladly; and her palpable contempt for commonplace and pretention prevented her from being popular with those among whom her husband's official duties threw her. Her famous gatherings "under the pear tree" in the Temple were, it must be admitted, rather curiously assorted; and she used to describe with infinite glee how a bluff Yorkshire servant whom she brought with her from Doncaster repelled some Indian princes from the tea-party to which she had invited them, saying, "I wasn't going to let any of them black musicians come here when they wasn't wanted." But in spite of undeniable peculiarities, Mrs Vaughan was deeply loved by a narrow circle of intimate friends who had in their own experience proved her essential kindness, her keen sympathy, and the depth and fervour of her spiritual life. She always had wretched health, which compelled her to live a rather wandering life, but her delicacy of constitution was counterbalanced by untiring energy. She was exemplary in the discharge of parochial and extra-parochial works of mercy, and only last year fulfilled what she called "the dream of her life" in a first visit to Rome and Pompeii. Mrs Vaughan was fond of music, and was certainly above the average of amateurs in water-colour drawing; but her real delight was in books. She was an indefatigable letter-writer, and her letters, cherished by many friends, will be her best memorial. I am not aware that she ever published anything with her name, but she compiled a book of religious extracts called *Rays of Sunlight for Dark Days*, a volume of selections called *Words from the Poets*, and an excellent abridgement of Stanley's *Sinai and Palestine*, under the title of *The Bible in the Holy Land*.

Adelaide Procter

A quotation which I lately made from "a poetess whom no one in the present day remembers" brought me a shower of questions. "Do you mean Mrs Hemans, or Mrs Sigourney, or Mrs Browning? Are you quoting Miss Jean Ingelow or Miss Emma Tatham? Or are you inventing, as Scott and George Eliot invented; forging a rhyme to suit your purpose and then crediting it to 'Anon' or 'Old Song'?" But one or two correspondents have shown themselves more faithful to early loves, and have said, "Do let us hear a little more about Miss Procter." With all my heart; and we will begin with her beginnings.

Bryan Waller Procter was born in 1787 and died in 1874. He was a schoolfellow of Byron at Harrow, and Byron described him as "Euphues" in *Don Juan*—

> Then there's my gentle Euphues, who, they say,
> Sets up for being a sort of moral Me—
> He'll find it rather difficult some day
> To turn out both, or either, it may be.

A CABINET OF MINIATURES

To be a Byron is a fate not conceded to two men in a generation; but to be moral is, happily, an easier ambition, and Bryan Procter, under his pen-name of "Barry Cornwall," contributed two hundred intensely moral poems in the *Literary Gazette*, edited Shakespeare, expurgated Jonson, biographized Lamb, and "selected" Browning. I should imagine that his tragedy of *Mirandola*, his tale of *Marcian Colonna*, and his description of *The Flood of Thessaly* have long since perished; but most people remember his buoyant verses on the sea—

> The sea! the sea! I love the sea,
> For I was born on the open sea.

As a matter of fact, he was born at Leeds, and his wife was inhuman enough to murmur this mendacious ditty in his ears when he lay tossing in livid agony between Dover and Calais. Mrs Procter was, as may be inferred from this incident, a woman of much sprightliness and vigour. She was born in 1799, was a friend of Keats and Shelley, visited Harrow Speeches in Byron's company, kept a Sunday *Salon* for half a century, and lived till 1888.

The literary tastes of this remarkable couple were not transmitted to their only son, who became an Indian general, but were bestowed in double measure on their daughter, Adelaide Anne Procter, who was born in 1825 and died in 1864. Her love of poetry was so precocious that, before she could write, she made her mother copy her favourite pieces into a tiny album, concerning which Dickens said: "It looked as if she had carried it about as another little girl might have carried a doll." This love of poetry increased with increasing years, but she concealed her ambition in the way of authorship even from her nearest relations. Like most young writers of that period, she began by contributing, anonymously, to the *Book of Beauty*; and in 1853 she made a bolder plunge. *Household Words*, afterwards re-named *All the Year Round*, was then edited by Dickens; and, as Dickens was an intimate friend and a frequent guest of Mr and Mrs Procter, it might have been natural for Adelaide Procter to base her appeal to the editor on grounds of friendship. But she chose a more independent line. "If," she said, "I send him, in my own name, verses that he does not honestly like, either it will be very painful to him to return them, or he will print them for papa's sake, and not for their own. So I have made up my mind to take my chance fairly with the unknown volunteers." She therefore assumed the pen-name of Miss Mary Berwick, addressed her letters from a circulating library, and sent a poem to *Household Words*. It was accepted, published, and praised; Miss Berwick was asked to send some more, and soon became a regular contributor, showing herself "remarkably business-like, punctual, self-reliant, and reliable." In December 1854, Dickens, going to dine with Mr and Mrs Procter, took with him an early proof of his Christmas number, and remarked, as he laid it on the drawing-room table, that it contained a very pretty poem by a Miss Berwick. Next day he learned that his unknown correspondent "Miss Berwick" was his young friend Adelaide Procter; and thenceforward she published in her own name. The total body of her work is small, and it is almost entirely comprehended in *Legends and Lyrics* and *A Chaplet of Verses*. She had, beyond question, a sincere vein of poetic feeling. She saw life and nature in their beautiful and pathetic aspects, and she had the gift of fluency and the knack of easy metre and satisfying rhyme. Her poetry is perhaps slight, and certainly not profound; but it is wholly free from formality, priggishness, and pedantry; it is always pretty, even when it does not quite rise to the height of beauty; and it never torments the ear with a rhyme which is only true to the eye. The prevalent tone of her writing is pensive, and often melancholy; and she was, in the best sense of a word too often used as censure, a sentimentalist. It is, I suppose, through this quality of sentimentalism that so many of her poems became popular songs. "The Lost Chord" has, perhaps, had its day, but when sung by Antoinette Sterling to a popular audience, it used to stir a deep and wholesome emotion. Of the same type were "Three Roses," from which I quoted, "Sent to Heaven," "Angels' Bidding," "In the Wood," and a dozen more. "Sentimentality" is a synonym for affectation; but sentiment is one of the great realities of life, and, when it is uttered in fluent and harmonious verse, it takes men captive even in spite of themselves. Sentimental Adelaide Procter certainly was, but Dickens has left it on record that to imagine her gloomy or despondent would be a curious mistake. "She was exceedingly humorous, and had a great delight in humour. Cheerfulness was habitual with her; she was very ready at a sally or a reply, and in her laugh there was an unusual vivacity, enjoyment, and sense of drollery. . . . She was a friend who inspired the strongest attachments; she was a finely sympathetic woman, with a great accordant heart and a sterling, noble nature."

Some poets there have been, and poetesses too, who made their divine vocation an excuse for neglecting, and even despising all human duties. Not of that loathsome crew was Adelaide Procter. Her bright and tender spirit was the joy of her home; and out of doors she laboured even beyond the limits of her strength in the social service of humanity. "Now it was the visitation of the sick that had possession of her; now it was the sheltering of the homeless; now it was the elementary teaching of the densely ignorant; now it was the raising up of those who had wandered and got trodden underfoot; now it was the wider employment of her own sex in the general business of life; now it was all these things at once." She spent her health and her earnings in establishing and tending a "Night Refuge for the Homeless Poor," and commended it in words of burning sympathy. "We have all known that in this country, in this town, many of our miserable fellow-creatures were pacing the streets through the long, weary nights, without a roof to shelter them, without food to eat, with their poor rags soaked in rain, and only the bitter winds of heaven for companions. . . . It is a marvel that we could sleep in peace in our warm, comfortable homes with this horror at our very door."

Poverty and privation were not the only forms of suffering which appealed to Adelaide Procter. Her experience in works of rescue and reclamation taught her to look back from the evil to its cause, and she saw this cause, or a great part of it, in the unemployment of women. Lord Brougham's favourite creation, " The British Association for the Promotion of Social Science," made her a member of a committee to enquire into this subject, and she joined herself to Miss Emily Faithfull in promoting the employment of women as compositors, and edited the first-fruits of that movement—a volume of prose and verse set up in type by women, and called in honour of the First Woman in England, *Victoria Regia*.

The briefest notice of Adelaide Procter must take account of her religion, for every line she wrote was steeped in it. She had fallen early under the influence of the Oxford Movement, and the deeds of martyrs, the ministries of saints, the fruits and flowers of the cloistered life, were themes on which she always loved to dwell. She wrote several hymns which found wide acceptance, and, with regard to one of these—

> My God, I thank Thee, who hast made
> The earth so bright;
> So full of splendour and of joy,
> Beauty and light,—

a staunch Evangelical, Bishop Bickersteth, said: "This most beautiful hymn touches the chord of thankfulness in trial as perhaps no other hymn does, and is thus most useful for the visitation of the sick." She was one of the distressed Anglicans who followed Manning and Dodsworth in the exodus of 1851, and for the remainder of her life she was a devoted daughter of the Church of Rome. Much of her most effective poetry is inspired by the devotional practices with which she now became familiar; and the only note of strong indignation which I can recall in all her writings was evoked by the doings — or what she believed to be the doings—of "The Irish Church Mission for Converting the Catholics." She heard that, at a time of famine, the Irish peasants were bribed with doles to change their religion, and she bursts into indignant protest. The Protestant Church, securely, as it seemed, established and richly endowed, ministered only to a handful of the population; and in this passionate outburst we feel the working of the spirit which, not ten years later, delivered Catholic Ireland from the yoke of an unjust ascendancy. The poet is addressing England—

> Partakers of thy glory
> We do not ask to be,
> Nor bid thee share with Ireland
> The empire of the sea.

· · · ·

A CABINET OF MINIATURES

> Take, if thou wilt, the earnings
> Of the poor peasant's toil,
> Take all the scanty produce
> That grows on Irish soil,
> To pay the alien preachers
> Whom Ireland will not hear,
> To pay the scoffers at a creed
> Which Irish hearts hold dear.

All this England may do, and yet leave Ireland not mortally wounded; but to attack her spiritual faith through her bodily privations, this is, indeed, to deal a felon-blow.

> Curs'd is the food and raiment
> For which a soul is sold;
> Tempt not another Judas
> To barter God for gold.

LORD KIMBERLEY

Time out of mind the Wodehouses of Kimberley had been the leaders of the Tory Party in Norfolk, waging an age-long conflict with the Cokes of Holkam, who headed the Whigs. For these services Sir John Wodehouse, Bart., M.P., was created a peer, as Lord Wodehouse, in 1797, and he carried on the campaign till his ninety-fourth year. His son, the second Lord Wodehouse, died in 1846, and was succeeded by his grandson, John Wodehouse, who lived to become Lord Kimberley. This John Wodehouse was born in 1826, and educated at Eton and Christ Church, where he obtained a First Class in Classics. Succeeding to his grandfather's title and estates in his twentieth year, he horrified the Tory world by announcing that he was a Liberal, and from that time till the day of his death the Liberal Party counted no stronger, more loyal, or more active adherent. Such a recruit to the Liberal army was not likely to be neglected, and Lord Wodehouse was soon made Under Secretary of State for Foreign Affairs. Before he was thirty he was sent by Lord Palmerston as Envoy Extraordinary and Minister Plenipotentiary to St Petersburg. In 1864 he became Lord-Lieutenant of Ireland, and, as a recognition of the skill and courage with which he administered that country during the first outbreak of Fenianism, he was created Earl of Kimberley in 1866. When Mr Gladstone formed his first Administration in 1868, Lord Kimberley became Lord Privy Seal, and he was a member of each Liberal Administration till his death, filling successively the offices of Secretary of State for the Colonies, Secretary of State for India, Lord President of the Council, and Secretary of State for Foreign Affairs. It was a rare record of official experience.

The ignorant always spoke of Lord Kimberley as "an old Whig." He was essentially a Utilitarian Radical of the Benthamite type; a convinced believer in popular institutions, a genuine lover of political and religious freedom, and a zealous Free Trader. Wherever the Liberal Party marched he was in the van, and increase of years brought no abatement of his reforming zeal. As an administrator he was exceptionally vigorous and decisive, always courteously receptive of advice, but essentially a man of his own counsel; weighing all arguments, but deciding for himself. He was thoroughly convinced of his own opinions, and incapable of doubt, uncertainty, or conflicting views. He was a wonderfully rapid worker, yet withal extremely thorough—overlooking nothing, neglecting nothing, scamping nothing; but always master of his own time, and never hurried, preoccupied, or overweighted. He was a sound scholar of the old Eton type, and thoroughly well read; but perhaps his most remarkable accomplishments were in the direction of modern languages, which he spoke with a fluency which rivalled that of his English speaking—and that was not saying a little. Fluency was, indeed, one of his most remarkable attributes, whether on the platform or in society. At a public dinner, he would eat, drink, and talk with the best, till the moment when the chairman called upon him; and then he would break off in a sentence, dash off a speech without an instant's hesitation; and when the speech was ended, would drop down into his chair and resume his truncated conversation. He never made use of notes, and was, stenographically tested, the most rapid speaker of his time.

Though Lord Kimberley liked society and enjoyed it, and had of necessity lived much in London, he was essentially a country gentleman — profoundly versed in all that pertained to the management of rural property, a good horseman, a brilliant shot, and in his younger days one of the finest tennis-players in England. In private life he was one of the most generous, kindest, and most affectionate of men, incapable of meanness or rancour, eagerly active in all benevolent work, singularly happy in his home, and rejoicing in the happiness of others. In his twenty-second year he married a beautiful and charming wife, and her death (in 1895) was a blow from which even his buoyant nature never recovered. He died on the 8th of April 1902.

Lord Gladstone

Anyone who should stumble on an Eton photograph book filled between 1866 and 1872 would very likely notice the picture of a pretty little boy, with wide, surprised eyes, curly hair, and a very open cricket-shirt — a kind of "Infant Samuel" of the Playing Fields. The child there depicted is Herbert John Gladstone, born in 1854, and named after his father's friend, the illustrious Sidney Herbert. He was a very strong and a very unprecocious boy—at once the pet and the provocation of his brilliant tutor, "Billy Johnson." "Tuppence Gladstone" was his nickname, in playful allusion to an additional impost recently levied by his father; and "Tuppence, you're bird-witted," was the remonstrant outcry of the impatient Tutor when the boy's large eyes wandered through the pupil-room window, and his chirpy but irrelevant answers showed that his thoughts had sped their flight to the practice-nets or the "Wall."

At eighteen Herbert Gladstone left Eton — a pleasant-looking lad, a man in strength, a child in heart, walking the plain path of duty

> With conscious step of purity and pride.

He had already made one decision which showed that under an almost babyish exterior he concealed a manly power of self-discipline. The example of his father and two elder brothers would have naturally disposed him to Christ Church, but he deliberately avoided that "favoured school of learning and larking," and entered University College, because he believed that he would be able to read more steadily at a small and quiet college than amid the manifold distractions of "The House." As an undergraduate Herbert Gladstone led a retired and regular life. His character and conduct were always above reproach, and he was loved by intimate friends; but he did not lay himself out for general popularity. His favourite amusements were cricket, shooting (when he could get a day in Bagley Wood), and music. He was not demonstrative of his opinions, but was understood to be, as became his name, a Liberal in politics, and "a moderate High Churchman." He read steadily but, as he did everything, unostentatiously, and it is no disparagement to his excellent abilities to say that when, in the summer of 1876, he obtained a First Class in History most people were surprised. It was rumoured at the time that he had made a great impression on the examiners by an essay on the Moral Obligation of Treaties, and that this paper was the result of some conversation with his father about the diplomatic aspects of the Eastern Question, just then bursting into prominence.

Immediately after taking his degree, Herbert Gladstone was appointed Lecturer in History at Keble College by the Warden (afterwards Bishop of Winchester), who had married his cousin, Lavinia Lyttelton. And now all looked as if he had settled down to the uneventful life of an Oxford don. He worked hard at his lectures and was an active and useful tutor, but he lived very much the same sort of retired life which he had lived as an undergraduate, and took no prominent part in the contests and interests of the University. Those years, 1876-79, were eventful years. The Bulgarian Atrocities came to a head, and were followed by the Russo-Turkish War (in which Lord Beaconsfield endeavoured to enlist England on the wrong side), the reign of Jingoism and Imperialism, the Congress of Berlin, and the shoddy triumph of "Peace with Honour." The 16th of July 1878 was the culmination and the catastrophe of Lord Beaconsfield's career. Two years before, Mr Gladstone had emerged from his retirement and had become the protagonist in the great controversy between Turk and Christian — barbarism and civilization—and now he became candidate for Midlothian, and threw all his amazing energies into the task, as he said, "of counter-working the purposes of Lord Beaconsfield." Never was the Liberal host so splendidly led. No one could live through those years without feeling the *certaminis ardor*—the glow and rush of battle—and a son of Mr Gladstone who remained unmoved by the all-pervading passion would indeed have been a moral miracle, or even a "moral monster." So the fascination of the Eastern Question touched Herbert Gladstone in his quiet rooms at Keble, and drew him out on to the stormy sea of politics.

At the General Election in 1880 he stood as Liberal candidate for the undivided county of Middlesex. His appearance in the field was late and sudden. He had no time for special preparation or equipment. He had never made a speech in his life. Not in "Pop" at Eton, not at the Union at Oxford, not even at a wedding breakfast or a cricket-supper had he ever opened his lips; yet it was the deliberate opinion of a critic so little disposed to eulogy as Robert Lowe that, as regarded form and style and manner, Herbert Gladstone spoke as well as his father at the same age. He had an unlimited fluency and a voice of music. Mr Gladstone's feeling about his son's candidature was deliciously expressed in a letter to Sir Algernon West :—

Tell Herbert, if you see him, he is constantly in my mind, and I am so delighted, though not surprised, to hear that he has done well in speaking. . . . Experience has shown that you judged well and wisely in encouraging him to stand. Had I been on the ground my heart might have failed me, but I would not have stood in his way. The accounts of him give me intense joy but no surprise. *I think his face is worth a thousand votes.*

In spite of that advantage Herbert Gladstone was beaten by something over 3000. But his performance had made a most favourable impression, and he was the son of the new Prime Minister, just then at the very zenith of his fame and power. Mr Gladstone had been doubly returned for Leeds and Midlothian. He elected to sit for Midlothian, and on the 8th of May 1880 his place at Leeds was filled by the election of his son Herbert, who continued to represent that place until he was raised to the Peerage in 1910.

Lord Gladstone's political career is too recent and too well known to need recapitulation. Nor is this the occasion for an estimate of his character and gifts. It is enough to say that he is one of those rare spirits who have learned to "bring those dispositions which are amiable and lovely in private life into the service and conduct of the commonwealth, and so to be politicians as never to forget that they are gentlemen."

Lord Wolverhampton [1]

When Mr Gladstone (who was not quite at his happiest on a social occasion) was laying the foundation-stone of the National Liberal Club, he damped the ardour of his audience with this depreciatory comment on clubs at large: "Speaking generally, I should say there could not be a less interesting occasion than the laying of a foundation-stone of a club in London. For, after all, what are the clubs

[1] Henry Hartley, first Viscount Wolverhampton, died on the 25th of February 1911.

of London? I am afraid little else than temples of luxury and ease." No doubt those words, though they have a disparaging sound, fairly describe the prime purpose of a club. For "luxury" read "comfort" with efficiency and moderate prices; and you have the first use of a club. Add "ease"—freedom from the worries of home or family, and liberty to say what one thinks—and you have the second. A third, and certainly not less important, is the exchange of gossip. This is what Pennialinus means, when writing his London letter in the *Drumble Dictator*, he says that "the clubs to-night are full of excitement about Mr Popkin's rumoured resignation"; or, "The report that the German Emperor, disguised as a nigger minstrel, has been found spying on the beach at Brighton, is widely discredited at the clubs." A fourth use of, at any rate, some clubs is study; and at the Athenæum or the Reform Club, the library is as much frequented as the billiard-room or the dining-room.

Now, it happens that Mr Fowler, Sir Henry Fowler, Lord Wolverhampton — to give him his successive designations—and I belonged to the same club, and I am asked to describe his club-life. This forces me to consider him in relation to all these foregoing points, and, after a careful survey, I am bound to say that he did not seem to touch life at any of them. I will take them one by one. Luxury certainly did not appeal to him, though "comfort," "efficiency" and "moderate prices" may have done so. He liked, if I remember aright, the kind of food which

Sir Henry Thomson considered to be the root of all our national evils—"plain roast and boiled." Temperate to a fault, he drank one glass of sherry in a bottle of soda-water, and looked none the more cheerful for it. But "efficiency," as meaning a joint in good cut and a punctual waiter, suited him, and "moderate prices" suit us all. Of "ease" in a club he had no notion. Perhaps he had enough or too much of it at home. Anyhow, he bustled into the club as a solicitor might bustle into his office, or a stockbroker into "the House," looking as if he were oppressed by a thousand cares and as if every moment were precious. I don't think he ever lounged, or sat back in a deep arm-chair, or fell into that fitful slumber which so irritates the man who is on the watch for the sleeper's paper. No—he came to the club with definite objects in view—to get his luncheon, to read the evening paper, or to look up something in a book of reference. There seemed to be nothing superficial about his reading: whatever he read, he read it with concentration and thoroughness and for a practical purpose. The lively oracles of Hansard, and the bound volumes of the *Times* were objects of his fervent study, for in them he could find material for those crushing reminders in which political speakers delight: "What did Mr Balfour say in 1885?" "Such sentiments come strangely from the Duke of Devonshire, who, when Lord Hartington, etc., etc." He neither smoked nor played billiards, nor took a hand at the whist-table. My memory does not connect him with the library, but I feel sure that, if he ever went there, it was to read a political memoir, or Mr Herbert Paul's *History of Modern England*. Again, he never came to the club for gossip. If he chanced to meet a friend, he was willing enough to talk; but his talk could not be called gossip. It was substantial, business-like, and serious. Of private and personal matters he never spoke, except to announce that his health required the window to be shut, or to whisper a word of honest pleasure in some recent performance of his gifted family. But the bulk of his talk was political, and then indeed it was not serious only but lugubrious. According to Fowler, everything was for the worst in this worst of all possible worlds. If the Liberals were out of office, they would remain out for a long time to come. " The extreme men were playing the mischief. Compromise" (which he himself adored) "was out of fashion, and common sense had fled to Jupiter and Saturn." If, by way of a change, the Liberals were in office, disaster was always impending. " The by-elections were going against us. The majority on the last division was alarmingly small. The *Skibbereen Eagle* had a most mischievous leader, and its effects would spread far beyond Skibbereen. The whole thing was rotten " (this with indescribable emphasis), "and when we went to the country, some of us would be unpleasantly surprised." If there were any elements of joy in the political situation, Fowler, when addressing his fellow-clubmen, kept them locked in his own bosom. In general society, in his own house, or even in the House of Commons, he would be cheerful and chatty, but he left those qualities behind him (perhaps as feeling they would be out of place) when he crossed the threshold of the "Sarcophagus." To him a club was no "temple of luxury and ease," no bureau for the exchange of jokes and rumours. Dr Johnson defined a club as "an assembly of good fellows meeting under certain conditions." He would have pronounced Fowler not a "clubable" man, and would, I fear, have detested his typically Nonconformist virtues of seriousness, strenuousness, and unremitting industry.

THOMAS ELLIS[1]

Dear Tom Ellis! Even at this sad moment it seems impossible to call him by any more formal name. Of him it was true, if it ever was true of any human being, that to know him was to love him. His appearance, expression, voice, manner, address—all were attractive. Everyone who met him, even seldom and casually, felt kindly towards him, and if circumstances brought one more closely into contact with him kindness became affection. He was in a supreme degree one of nature's gentlemen. Delicacy, refinement, consideration for the feelings of others, absolute freedom from "pushfulness" and self-assertion, perfect courtesy which knew nothing of

[1] Thomas Edward Ellis, M.P. for Merionethshire, died April 5, 1899, in his 40th year.

social distinctions—all these qualities were congenial in Tom Ellis. His warmth of heart, his generous temper, his eager, lively sympathy with his friends and their concerns, could be neither simulated nor mistaken. He had all the "picturesque sensibility" of the Celtic temperament and that inborn love of natural and literary beauty which Matthew Arnold long ago indicated as the characteristic of the true Welshman. Patriotism was with Ellis a passion. He never was so thoroughly happy, so completely at home, as when he was handling some political or social theme which touched the national aspirations of his beloved Principality. But with the loftiest ideals of patriotism he combined in an unusual degree a sane and sober judgment of practical possibilities. Indeed, nothing was more remarkable than this practical bent in a mind so finely attuned to the poetry and romance of racial idealism. Politics, as Bacon said, is of all studies the one most immersed in matter, and when Mr Ellis became Chief Whip of the Liberal Party there were some of his friends who doubted whether so exalted and so imaginative a mind could be chained to the commonplace and tedious mechanism of a laborious, and in some respects, a sordid office. Never were doubts more completely dispelled by the event. Ellis threw himself into the work of his new duties with a wholehearted devotion which really left him no proper leisure for rest or recreation, and the nervous energy which often accompanies a frail organization enabled him to work at a level of speed and of thoroughness which might well have broken down a man of ten times greater strength. And now the end has come with startling suddenness. The sun has gone down at midday, with every circumstance of domestic pathos to deepen the gloom. Ever since I heard of my friend's death two hours ago there have been ringing in my ears those exquisite words of Divine eulogy: " Thou hast a little strength, and hast kept My word and hast not denied My name. Him that overcometh will I make a pillar in the Temple of My God, and he shall go no more out, and I will write upon him My new name."

Walter Wren

Mr Walter Wren, widely known by his success in preparing candidates for the Indian Civil Service, died at his residence in Powis Square on the 5th of August 1898, in his sixty-fifth year. Mr Wren was educated at the Grammar School of his native place, Buntingford, in Hertfordshire; at Elizabeth College, Guernsey ; and at Christ's College, Cambridge, where he was a contemporary of Sir Walter Besant and of " C. S. C." His career was a conspicuous and almost unequalled instance of triumph over physical difficulties. An accidental injury in his school-days resulted, while he was an undergraduate, in spinal disease. He was obliged to leave off reading for honours and to content himself with a pass-degree. The disease made rapid progress, and he became permanently

A CABINET OF MINIATURES

crippled. For many years of his life he lived night and day on an inclined couch, being wheeled from one room to another and never going up or down stairs. To the end of his days he could not walk without the aid of two sticks, and the spinal disease set up a variety of internal mischiefs. Yet in spite of a physical condition which would have seemed to most men an absolute bar to effort, he set himself resolutely to make his fortune. He established himself in London and took pupils for all examinations. It was soon recognized that he had some special qualifications for a teacher. He excelled in discerning a boy's capacity, in forcing him to concentrate on the particular subject for which he was fitted, and in making him master thoroughly whatever he professed to learn. Superficiality and pretension were Mr Wren's special aversions. The *minimum* of subjects and an absolute knowledge of them were the principles which he instilled into his pupils. Thus he was the exact opposite of what is commonly known as a "crammer." It was his well-founded boast that whatever a pupil of his professed to know he knew. His methods of preparing for examinations, whether for the Universities, the Army, or the Civil Service, were soon justified by results, and before long he had so firmly established his reputation that he was able to "specialize" in preparing for the Indian Civil Service, and in that particular branch of his business he had practically no rival. In 1869 he passed sixteen men into the Indian Civil Service, and this rate of success was maintained to the end. Of late years increasing infirmity had made it impossible for him to do more than give a general superintendence to his business; but he had the satisfaction of knowing that his personal efforts and absolute knowledge of what was required for the Indian Civil Service examination had made "Wren's" one of the most permanent institutions of the educational world. Apart from education, Mr Wren's keenest interest was in politics. He was a Radical of the most uncompromising type, and a vigorous speaker and writer on behalf of the causes in which he believed. He was returned for the Borough of Wallingford at the General Election of 1880, but was unseated on petition. He afterwards contested Wigan and North Lambeth; but it became evident to his friends that the amount of exertion required by public life was more than he could safely make. His own extraordinary pluck made him the last to realize this truth, and, failing to re-enter the House of Commons, he became representative of Bethnal Green on the first London County Council. During the last few years of his life he was obliged to spend the greater part of his time on the south coast, and in spite of all that could be done by medical skill and the devotion of his family, his strength ebbed away under a combination of maladies. The end came tragically, for he was seized by a paralytic attack just as he was starting from his house to attend the marriage of his daughter to his colleague and successor, Mr T. M. Taylor. He lived only eight days after the seizure. He will be sincerely regretted by the friends who knew his sterling merits, and not least by his former pupils, in whose fortunes he took a fatherly interest. Far beyond the circle of friendship, his career will be remembered as a standing proof that no amount of infirmity and disease can prevent a clear intelligence and a strong will from making life honourable, prosperous, and useful to the world.

WESTCOTT AND LEE

When that exceedingly weak-kneed Seeker after Truth, Robert Elsmere, found his faith shaken by his sceptical squire, he said in his most lachrymose tone: "It often seems to me that I might have got through, but for the men whose books I used to read and respect most in old days. The point of view is generally so extraordinary limited. Westcott, for instance, who means so much nowadays to the English religious world, first isolates Christianity from all the other religious phenomena of the world, and then argues upon its details."

Perhaps the truth was that poor Robert had never understood his former oracle—and to that extent I can sympathize with him. When Liddon was Canon of St Paul's and Westcott Canon of Westminster, the former, writing to a friend at Christmas, said: "London is just now buried under a dense fog; this is commonly attributed to Dr Westcott having opened his study-window at Westminster"; and, when an admiring disciple inscribed a book of vague divinity to Westcott, Liddon remarked: "This is the kind of book which a little fog writes and dedicates to the Great Fog." If anyone wishes to test the aptness of the nickname, let him consult one of Westcott's Commentaries for the interpretation of some difficult or disputed passage, and then he will assuredly find himself in the thick of "darkness visible." It has been well said that "the effect of Westcott's style is to make you feel that it does not matter where you begin or where you leave off." You wander on interminably, through a beautiful but bewildering haze. But the obscurity of his style was even more perplexing in speech than in printed words. After all, when one is puzzled in reading, one can turn back and read again, and weigh, and ponder, and faintly discern a possible sense. But in the rapidity of spoken utterance there is no chance of such return, and one's mind keeps panting after the elusive thought, if indeed there is any thought to pursue. There is a story, so life-like that it must be true, of a pupil who came to Westcott with an exceedingly difficult passage from St John. Westcott, who had made the Fourth Gospel the subject of a very special study, poured out words of explanation mystical and beautiful even beyond his wont. When he had made an end of speaking, the pupil gratefully exclaimed: "Thank you very much, Dr Westcott; you have made it perfectly clear to me." But the Professor recoiled with a shudder from the unwelcome praise, pressed his hands over his eyes and murmured, " Oh, I hope not ! I hope not ! "

Westcott had, in early life, been touched by the social enthusiasms of the Chartists, and he lived to become President of the Christian Social Union. His Inaugural Address to that society has been thus described :—

> None of us who were present can ever forget it. Yet none of us can ever recall, in the least, what was said. No one knows. Only we know that we were lifted, kindled, transformed. We pledged ourselves ; we committed ourselves ; we were ready to die for the Cause ; but, if you asked us why, and for what, we could not tell you. There he was ; there he spoke ; the prophetic fire was breaking from him ; the martyr-spirit glowed through him. We, too, were caught up. There was nothing verbal to report or to repeat. We could remember nothing except the spirit which was in the words, and that was enough.

Westcott was a pupil of the famous Prince Lee at Birmingham, Senior Classic in 1848, Fellow of Trinity, and from 1852 to 1870 an Assistant Master at Harrow. He was an exquisite scholar, to whom not merely every word, but every inflection and every accent, was vocal with delicacies of meaning. Thus in supervising the composition—Greek, Latin, and English—of the Sixth Form he was peculiarly at home ; but in the rough-and-tumble of daily contact with a herd of unscholarly boys he was conspicuously and even painfully ill at ease. His friends rejoiced when he was transferred from these uncongenial surroundings to a Canonry at Peterborough and a Professorship at Cambridge ; yet at each of these turns his habitual vagueness dogged his steps. At Harrow he had preached a sermon imploring us boys, when we grew older, to revive the ascetic life in the Church of England, and enforcing his appeal by reference to St Benedict, St Antony, and St Francis. From later discourses it appeared that these prospective monks were to be married, and to live with their wives and families in a "Cœnobium." At Cambridge, as Professor of Divinity, Westcott seemed unable to arrive at any direct decisions; no resolution or manifesto could ever quite satisfy the fastidiousness of his judgment. As one of the greatest authorities on the text of the New Testament, he was of course a member of the Company of Revisers; but, when arguments were closely balanced on a question of a reading or a version, he never could be induced to vote, but ran into the corner and hid his eyes till the decision was attained. In every relation and transaction of life, he was hampered by that intellectual idiosyncrasy of which his obscure style was the outward expression.

But towards the end of his life his character seemed to receive, almost in an instant, an absolutely new direction. In 1890 he was unexpectedly called to the strenuous See of Durham. All his friends were filled with misgiving. How would the frail and pensive student, the fastidious scholar, the rapt prophet, the mystical dreamer, bear himself amid the rough and practical realities of the great industrial district of which he was to be Chief Pastor? Amid crowding and urgent problems, the clash of capital and labour, and "the strife of tongues," would he ever be able to make up his mind, or, having made it up, to express it intelligibly? These questions soon answered themselves, as much to the amazement as to the delight of his friends. "The scholar's indecision was flung away, and he proved to have convictions that could be put into direct and practical shape on every kind of matter, and with the utmost rapidity. He proved perfectly able to handle all the immediate problems with surprising efficiency." Nothing could have been better than the way in which he timed his action in the great Coal-Strike. He refused to prescribe a solution, for that would have been obviously out of his range as Bishop; but he got the opposing parties into separate rooms at Auckland Castle, and mediated between the two camps till peace was secured.

Personal asceticism had always been one of Westcott's most marked characteristics. Even at Harrow, his pupils realized that he practised the most rigid self-denial, eschewed all forms of indulgence and display, and spent his whole time at his desk or on his knees. Asceticism—its efficacy and its beauty—had been the inspiring idea of his sermons on the Monastic Life, and on that strange "Cœnobium." "We used to be told," said one of his children, "that in the Cœnobium no one would have two helps of pudding, and we dreaded it accordingly." Westcott lived as he taught; he ate sparingly; he wore his clothes till they were threadbare; and, when he became a Bishop and the unwilling owner of a carriage, "he crept into it as if it was a hearse." The feudal splendours of Auckland Castle fairly appalled him; but "his misery at its splendour yielded, as he discovered how great were the possibilities of making that splendour a public possession." It was typical of his Episcopate over the coal-pits that the famous park of Bishop Auckland, which once held its deer and its hounds, was used by him as a resting-home for exhausted pit-ponies, against whose hard usage in the pit he constantly pleaded. The whole story of Westcott's life in Durham illustrates the magical power of practical responsibility to rouse dreamers and theorists from speculative reverie, to clarify obscurity, and to transmute vagueness into decision.

After so much that is excellent has been recorded, it is sad to remember that, just at the close of life, Westcott lapsed again into a condition of mental obscurity, in which black seemed to assume the character of white, and darkness to be a synonym for light. There was no subject on which he had been more intense, more eloquent, or more impressive than International Peace.

None who heard him on that high theme can ever forget it. He felt that Christianity, with its prophetic conception of the variety of Nations building up the body of the one complete Humanity, had laid the true grounds for universal Peace. It had carried the ideal of Nationality forward into the fulness of a complex Internationalism, in which all Nations suffered by the wounding of any one Nation, and for which the weakest and smallest Nationality had its proper contribution to make.

That is vastly fine; but, when, two years before Westcott's death, Mr Chamberlain and Lord Milner

A CABINET OF MINIATURES

and the capitalists who manipulated them, plunged England into the South African War and crushed two small Republics, the Prophet of Peace was foremost to bless the unhallowed enterprise. Strangest of all the inconsistencies in a long, and in some ways beautiful, career was this concluding negation of International Righteousness and Christian Ethic.

Having spoken so far of the pupil, I am led to add a word about the master.

James Prince Lee was the son of Stephen Lee, Secretary and Librarian of the Royal Society, and was born in London in 1804. He was educated at St Paul's School and at Trinity College, Cambridge, of which he became a Fellow in 1829. By common consent he was among the best Greek scholars of his time—some said he was the very best; and to scholarship, at once profound and graceful, he added a singular gift for teaching such boys as were willing to learn. From 1830–38 he was an Assistant Master at Rugby under Dr Arnold, and in the latter year he was elected to the Head Mastership of King Edward's School. To have trained Westcott, Lightfoot, and Benson, even if no other names were added, was such a distinction as few schoolmasters attain.

As a Head Master he was very great, though by no means faultless. His temper was wayward, his discipline was severe, and he had no mercy for idlers or dunces; but over his more intelligent pupils he exercised a peculiar fascination. Archbishop Benson wrote: "We recognized magnificent power, wide interests, large sympathy, inexhaustible freshness, stern justice, and, above all, invincible faith in the laws of thought and in the laws of language." Bishop Westcott said: "He enabled us to see that scholarship is nothing less than one method of dealing with the whole problem of human existence, in which Art and Truth and Goodness are inextricably combined." That saying savours of Westcott's characteristic mysticism; but Lightfoot, a man of plainer mind, wrote more intelligibly: "I have sometimes thought that, if I were allowed to live one hour only of my past life over again, I should choose a Butler lesson under Lee." A school-master who could interest a boy in the *Analogy* must indeed have had a genius for teaching. Well might another pupil write: "It is, I think, quite impossible for a stranger, or perhaps for anyone except a Birmingham pupil, to understand the complete devotion and affection which some of us felt towards him."

The See of Manchester was created by Act of Parliament in 1847, and the old Collegiate Church became the Cathedral of the new See. Who was to be its first Bishop? Lord John Russell had become Prime Minister in 1846. He was one of the best of men, but he was a Whig all over in his dislike of active churchmanship; and, now that the Church, aroused by the Oxford Movement, had woke from her long slumber, and was beginning to reassert her spiritual claims, he was seriously, and rather quaintly, alarmed. The appointment to the new

See of Manchester gave him an opportunity of showing his quality, and he was not slow to use it. In October 1847 Lancashire heard with astonishment and indignation that its first Bishop was to be a Birmingham school-master, who had never done a stroke of parochial work, whose views of religious truth were completely unknown, and who was reported to be a favourite of Prince Albert—no recommendation in orthodox eyes. A useless resistance to the appointment was set on foot, and some of the opponents, in their eagerness to discredit the Prime Minister and his nominee, roundly accused Dr Lee of habitual intemperance. The Bishop-designate was forced to vindicate his character in a court of law, where it was proved that what had been represented as inebriety was really the result of laudanum taken as a remedy for neuralgia. It was an unfortunate beginning to an episcopate likely, on other grounds, to be unpopular; and it may very well be that a sense of injustice warped the new Bishop's mind and contracted his sympathies. "As a school-master," wrote Dean Vaughan, "he was wonderful. As a Bishop he attempted despotism, and the despotism of Bishops is incongruous and out of date." One of his clergy says: "He kept us at a distance, and treated us like schoolboys; an autocrat he certainly was." And in 1858 Bishop Wilberforce wrote, after a visit to Lancashire: "Lay defence organizing against the oppression of the Bishop of Manchester."

The Bishop lived in state and bounty at Mauldeth Hall. He was surrounded by a splendid library, and a great collection of works of art illustrating the classical studies which were his real life. Daily he rolled into Manchester in his carriage, with servants in purple liveries, and transacted his business and received the clergy at a dismal office in St James's Square. At his palace he exercised a most splendid hospitality (which the clergy seldom shared), and his whole way of living and ruling was such as would have become a Cardinal of the Renaissance. "In stature he was a little above the middle height. His head was shapely and intellectual, covered with crisp, curly hair, giving him the appearance of an old Roman patrician. If anything could give dignity to the 'magpie' costume of Victorian Bishops, it would be the way in which Bishop Lee put it on, or rather, had it put on for him by his valet, and the way he wore it over his full silk cassock, and his shoes and silver buckles." He very seldom preached, but when he did his sermons were remembered; for he was an accomplished orator, though less at home in the pulpit than on the platform. In speaking he planted himself firmly on his feet, and advanced or receded a step or two when he emphasized a word or a sentence, his action being limited to his right hand. His mouth was firm and finely shaped, with lips which curved, sarcastically or approvingly, according to the mood of the moment; and his strict observance of the rule—" Take care of the consonants, and the vowels will take care of themselves"—made his voice audible in the largest buildings. One of his characteristics was an intolerance of anything short of perfection, and this extreme fastidiousness of taste restrained him, in spite of his wealth of learning and accomplishment, from publishing anything beyond two Charges and two Sermons. To a friend who remonstrated on this waste of power, he said with a fine dignity: "I do not think that my thoughts will perish with me, for there are some who will not, I believe, forget what they have learnt from me."

Lee's health was always unsound, and he bore an increasing burden of painful illness "more like a Stoic than a Martyr." Yet he laboured incessantly at the duties of his office; not rushing about the diocese like Bishop Wilberforce, but ruling it from his library like the bishops of an older day. If he ruled with a rod rather than with a Pastoral Staff, it was because he was still at heart a school-master. The most noted memorial of his episcopate was the number of new churches which were erected while he was Bishop. He consecrated the first of these on the day on which he was enthroned, and the last, the 130th, within a week of his death. He was a scholar, a humanist, and a profound student of the text of the New Testament; but he was not a theologian; nor, in spite of his episcopal character, did he regard men or things from an ecclesiastical point of view. He exerted his organizing and oratorical powers to the utmost in helping to establish the Manchester Free Library, and he bequeathed his own magnificent collection of books to Owens College. He was sorely displeased when both his daughters married clergymen, and the only reason that could be assigned for his displeasure was his dislike of clergymen as such. "Of one thing we clerics were fully aware, and that was that we had no chance of an interview as long as any laymen were waiting."

Throughout life Lee was, partly by his own fault, misunderstood, and often cruelly misrepresented. He seemed a student, a pedagogue, a secular prince, —anything rather than a Christian clergyman. Yet those who knew him most intimately bore the most strenuous testimony to his spiritual earnestness. When someone disparaged him, Archbishop Benson said: "To him I owe all that I was or am or ever shall be. He was the greatest man I have ever come within the influence of—the greatest and the best. You see how people are misunderstood." There, perhaps, spoke the exuberant devotion of the grateful pupil, but, nevertheless, the testimony is impressive. When the Bishop was nearing his latter end, he said to an intimate friend: "There is only one word which I should wish to have upon my gravestone," and he added, with a smile, "It is a Greek word, of course." It was the one word which the Authorized Version expands into the victorious saying, "The trumpet shall sound."

The Bishop died on Christmas Eve 1869, and was buried in the churchyard of Heaton Mersey. The friend who suggested this sketch writes:

> This morning I observed the excellent condition of the granite block which covers the Bishop's grave. It bears in addition to his name and dates and mitre the one word from 1 Cor. xv. 52, engraven in Greek capitals. Although the grave is close to the principal entrance to the church, I was surprised to find that neither an elderly woman placing flowers on an adjacent tomb, nor the school-children, knew the Bishop's resting-place.

I do not think there was much occasion for surprise.

A friend has disinterred from an old scrap-book the following lines, which appeared in the *Manchester Examiner and Times*, shortly after the death of Bishop Prince Lee. They were cautiously prefaced by the statement that the writer was neither a Radical nor a Dissenter:

> Here lies a Right Reverend Father in God,
> Who ne'er spoiled his children by sparing the rod,
> Who took not his pattern from Him who, when living,
> Was merciful, large-hearted, meek, and forgiving;
> But, preferring in strife to work out his salvation,
> Made quarrels and scolding his Christian vocation;
> And, in mind of the pedagogue's narrowest span,
> Held the birch the sole nostrum for governing man.
> Would you edit a book, without learning or brains?
> You have only to study his "Barrow's Remains."
> Are you seeking your posthumous venom to spill?
> You cannot do better than copy his will.

HENRY KINGSLEY

A lady writes: "I do not remember that you have ever told us anything about Henry Kingsley; although, from references to characters in his books,

I think you must be a lover of this delightful and almost forgotten novelist. Do tell us something about him. . . . One can hardly know too much about the Kingsleys." To this challenge I respond with great goodwill; for Charles, George, and Henry Kingsley were indeed a noteworthy trio of brothers, and with two of them I had enough of personal acquaintance to give me a special interest in their writings. "We are," said Charles Kingsley in 1865, "the *disjecta membra* of a most remarkable pair of parents. Our talent, such as it is, is altogether hereditary. My father was a magnificent man in body and mind, and was said to possess every talent except that of using his talents. My mother, on the contrary, had a quite extraordinary practical and administrative power; and she combines with it, even at the age of seventy-nine, my father's passion for knowledge, and the sentiment and fancy of a young girl."

In this distribution of hereditary gifts, it is not difficult to see which fell to the lot of the third son—Henry—who was born in 1839 and died in 1876. Of "practical and administrative power" he had absolutely none; but he had a wiry and active body, unbounded energy and pluck, and a keen love of romantic adventure. His early home was the Rectory House of Chelsea, close to that wonderful old church which all Americans but not all English people know, "where the great flood of change beats round the walls, and shakes the door in vain, but never enters." When living at Chelsea Rectory, he went, as a day-boy, to

King's College School, and from thence he was transferred in 1850 to Worcester College, Oxford. "At the University," writes his contemporary, Sir Edwin Arnold, "he did nothing commensurate with his great natural abilities (for I consider him quite the equal in genius of his eldest brother Charles). He gave himself to athletics and social life; being always generous, manly, and of an inner temper nobler than his external manners. He was one of the best scullers on the river, and, for a wager, ran a mile, rowed a mile, and trotted a mile within fifteen minutes."

In 1853 he went down from Oxford without a degree, and set out for the Australian gold-fields in search of fortune. But fortune did not come, and he enlisted in the Mounted Police—a service for which his pluck, activity, light weight, and love of horses exactly fitted him. Unfortunately, however, he was obliged, in the way of official duty, to attend a public execution, and he left the police in disgust; but not without having accumulated a mass of material which he afterwards turned to excellent account. During this expatriation he ceased to communicate with home; but in 1858 he suddenly reappeared in England, settled himself in a cottage at Eversley, where his brother Charles was Rector, and, to the astonishment of his family, became a novelist. Twelve volumes of his work face me as I write. In 1864 he married, and moved to Wargrave, in the Valley of the Thames. "He was the kindest and most chivalrous of men," said one of his neighbours. "Perhaps more emphatic in conversation than I could comfortably respond to," adds a lady. "A bright-eyed, pleasant-looking fellow," says a contemporary, "a trifle under the medium height, with the carriage of an athlete, a light-weight champion, or a crack rider in an artillery regiment." In 1869 he went to Edinburgh, and undertook the editorship of the *Daily Review*. The experiment was disastrous, and in the following year he abandoned the editorial chair to act as war-correspondent in the Franco-German campaign. He was present at the Battle of Sedan, and is said to have been the first Englishman to enter Metz. In 1872 he returned to England, and resumed his literary work; but his health soon failed, and he died in his forty-seventh year at Cuckfield, in Sussex, where he lies buried.

So much for Henry Kingsley's history. What of his writings? It is easy enough to criticize them. As Dryden said of Elkanah Settle, "his style was boisterous, and his prose incorrigibly lewd." Half his books were pot-boilers. He did not always write grammar, and he was constantly "mugging to the gallery," taking liberties with his reader, and obtruding his own personality. All this, and more, may be urged in disparagement, and yet, when all is said and done, he had the one essential gift for novel-writing —he could make a plot. As soon as we have got into his stories, we want to know how they will end. His heroes and heroines are real men and women, and we follow their fortunes with eager interest till the last chapter lifts us into triumph, or (and this more frequently) abandons us to dejection.

Let us take the principal stories one by one. *Geoffrey Hamlyn* made Henry Kingsley's fame. When he wrote it he was still reeking of Australia —indeed, the ground-work of it had been laid before he set sail for England. " Alone among our novelists he has focussed for us the early life of a new country, the first building-up of a great commonwealth." *Geoffrey Hamlyn* describes the loves and fortunes and lives and deaths of a company of neighbours who emigrated from Devonshire and established themselves three hundred miles south of Sydney, when Van Diemen's Land was still a penal settlement. Bush-ranging plays a leading part in the narrative of their adventures; and the escape of Sam Buckley and his sweetheart from the bush-rangers' gang is one of the most thrilling episodes in fiction. One cannot read it without holding one's breath, and hearing the tramp of the marauders' horses as they near the spot where the fugitives are concealed. With this fine tale one may link some portion of *Ravenshoe*, and the whole of *The Hillyars and the Burtons* which begins with a Dickens-like account of life in Chelsea in the forties, and then transfers itself to New South Wales. In both hemispheres Kingsley is writing his autobiography, and this book is to me the most interesting that he ever wrote.

The main interest of *Ravenshoe* is altogether

different, and, in some of its mysterious involutions, it seems infected with the morbid fear of Romanism which Henry Kingsley may have imbibed from his brother Charles. The glory of the book is the description of the Battle of the Alma, and I have heard soldiers say that Charles Ravenshoe's memory of the charge is exactly true to life in similar conditions.

> Charles was sixth man from the right of the rear rank of the third troop. He could see the tails of the horses immediately before him, and could remark that his front-rank man had a great patch of oil on the right shoulder of his uniform. . . . Charles would have given ten years of his life to know what was going on on the other side of the hill. But no. There they sate, and he had to look at the back of the man before him; and at this time he came to the conclusion that the patch of grease on his right shoulder was the same shape as the map of Sweden. A long, weary two hours was spent like this, and then the word was given to go forward. . . . Charles saw only the back of the man before him, and the patch of grease on his shoulder; but ever after, when the battle of the Alma was mentioned before him, Charles at once began thinking of the map of Sweden.

In *Austin Elliot* Henry Kingsley lapsed into the didactic vein, and the book is principally an exposure of the misery and shame which grew up under "the accursed system of the Duello." In *The Harveys* he deals similarly with Spiritualism. In *Silcote of Silcotes* he conducts us lovingly through the Valley of the Thames and the sands of Bagshot, to unexpected conclusions at Turin and Genestrello. *Stretton* is a fine tale of schoolboy-friendship and woman's love, culminating splendidly in the Indian Mutiny.

Valentin is the story of Sedan, told from a strongly anti-French point of view.

In all these books Kingsley was more or less describing what he had seen and known. In *Mademoiselle Mathilde* he makes a sudden plunge into French history, and gives a good picture of expiring Feudalism and the part which it played in preparing the Revolution. His friends ought to love this book, if only because he loved it. "Of all the ghosts," he said, "which I have called up in this quaint trade of writing fiction only two remain with me, and never quit me. The others come and go, and I love them well enough; but the two who are with me always are the peak-faced man Charles Ravenshoe and the lame French girl Mathilde."

What is the charm of Henry Kingsley's writing? As I said before, he had the power without which style, dialogue, analysis of character, description of scenery, and all the rest are nothing worth—the power of constructing a plot. Then, again, though his writing was almost insolently careless and faulty, yet here and there it burst into passages of vivid eloquence. He had a rich though unregulated humour, and a closely observant eye for Nature, both in her softer and in her stormier aspects. The loss of the *Titanic* sent me back to the description of a storm in *Our Brown Passenger*; and, when I collated that description with the loss of the *Wainoora* in *The Hillyars and the Burtons*, I felt that the tragedy of the sea had seldom been more powerfully presented than by Henry Kingsley.

> Where was the *Wainoora*? ... From the wild shore, from the wilder sea, from the coral reef and sandbank, from the storm-tossed sailor, or from the lonely shepherd on the forest-lands above the cruel ocean, no answer but this—she had sailed out of port, and she never made port again. A missing ship, with the history of her last agony unwritten for ever.

Another charm of Henry Kingsley's writing is to be found in its actuality. I do not mean that his characters are always lifelike, or his situations always probable; but one feels, as one reads, that he wrote what he felt. Lady Ritchie, than whom there is no more delicate critic, notes this characteristic. "He seems to have lived his own books, battered them out, and forced them into their living shapes; to have felt them and been them all: writing not so much from imagination as from personal experience and struggle."

Although Kingsley lived what is called a wild life, and knocked about the world in all sorts of rough company, his writing from first to last is unstained by a moral blot. Everything that he wrote is pure and upright and manly; and where he handles a distinctly religious theme, as in the scene in the Rajah's dungeon where Jem Mordaunt is preparing himself for death, we feel the touch of personal conviction. Lady Ritchie, who visited him in his last illness, has described the naturalness and simplicity and courage with which he faced the end.

A CABINET OF MINIATURES

Perhaps in those last days he remembered his own premonitory words in *Ravenshoe*.

> In the long watches of the winter night, when one has awoke from some evil dream, and lies sleepless and terrified with the solemn pall of darkness around one—in such still dead times only, lying as in the silence of the tomb, one realizes that some day we shall lie in that bed and not think at all : that the time will soon come when we must die.
>
> Our preachers remind us of this often enough, but we cannot realize it in a pew in broad daylight. You must wake in the middle of the night to do that, and face the thought like a man—that it will come, and come to ninety-nine in a hundred of us, not in a maddening clatter of musketry as the day is won ; or in carrying a line to a stranded ship, or in such glorious times, when the soul has mastery over the body : but in bed, by slow degrees. It is in darkness and silence only that we realize this ; and then let us hope that we humbly remember that death has been conquered for us, and that, in spite of our unworthiness, we may defy him. And, after that, sometimes will come the thought—Are there no evils worse even than death?

BARON FERDINAND ROTHSCHILD [1]

Everyone who has ever stayed at Waddesdon will agree that Baron Ferdinand Rothschild excelled as a host, had a true delight in entertaining, and cultivated a special attention to each guest's tastes and wishes. The present writer once had a slight but significant experience of this attention. The first time he stayed at Waddesdon he had some difficulty in sleeping, owing to the early incursion of the morning sun. The host discovered this, and when next the sleepless guest visited Waddesdon every bedroom in the huge house

[1] Baron Ferdinand James Rothschild died on the 17th December, 1898.

had been furnished with shutters. Waddesdon Manor, though not very beautiful, is an astonishing creation. Twenty-five years ago it was a bare hill rising almost perpendicularly out of the great grass vale of Aylesbury.

Hunting in the vale with his cousin's staghounds, Baron Ferdinand Rothschild took it into his head to ride to the top of this hill, which was almost precipitous, and survey the scene. Once at the top he found a wonderful view, extending in all directions as far as the eye could reach. The pastures of Buckinghamshire lay on one side. On another the woodlands of Oxfordshire clustered round cornfields. The white chalk range of the Chilterns bounded the view in one direction; in the other the eye could faintly discern the spires of Oxford. It was a case of love at first sight. The estate belonged to the Duke of Marlborough, who was very willing to sell, and in 1874 it passed into Baron Ferdinand's hands. He immediately began engineering works on a gigantic scale, levelling the summit till its hollows and hummocks became a wide and even plateau, drawing corkscrew roads round the hill so as to make the approach possible for horses, and carrying stone and wood from the bottom to the top of the precipice for the construction of the "lordly pleasure-house" which was to be. In due time it arose, a vast French château, with a central tower and turrets at the four corners, all carved out of a dazzlingly white stone. The most astonishing work, however, was not the building but

A CABINET OF MINIATURES 153

the planting; £40,000 a year was laid out for several years in bringing full-grown timber trees from distant parks and woodlands and drawing them to the top of Waddesdon Hill. Each tree travelled upright in a separate cart, and the sight of this arboreal procession moving at a foot's pace along the lanes of Buckinghamshire recalled irresistibly the Scripture vision of "men as trees walking." When bantered by his friends on the enormous expense of thus transplanting full-grown forestry, the Baron used to say that he had bought a bare hill because at the moment when he wanted a country house there were no ready-made places in the market. If he had waited two years the bad times would have set in and he would have been able to buy a wooded estate and plant his new house among old trees.

As it was, he was forced to make a new place look old—a difficult task even for skill and capital. The contents of the house were of fabulous value, and unusual luck, combined with prodigious wealth, had enabled Baron Ferdinand to form an unsurpassed collection of Gainsboroughs, together with several Romneys and Sir Joshuas of great merit. The fountains, gardens, and glass-houses were also of unusual scale and beauty, and elicited a well-deserved compliment from Queen Victoria, who was induced by Princess Louise to make a day's excursion from Windsor to Waddesdon.

Baron Ferdinand was not a great talker, but he loved good conversation, and, like Lord St Jerome in *Lothair*, he supplied the audience for his more loquacious guests. He had great knowledge of art and of that borderland between art and furniture which our fathers called *virtu*. He was also an accomplished linguist and had a special knowledge of French memoirs. He was a most public-spirited landlord, and by the exercise of a paternal despotism transformed a squalid village into an earthly paradise of health and beauty. Better than all, he was a warm, faithful, and generous friend. He is sincerely mourned, and will be long remembered.

THE WILBERFORCES

The Wilberforces spring from a place called Wilberforce, or Wilberfoss, in the East Riding. In the eighteenth century they were established in business at Hull, and there William Wilberforce, famous as the Emancipator, was born. Having inherited ample wealth, he parted with his father's business as soon as he was twenty-one, and made his choice for politics. As an undergraduate at Cambridge he had been famous for the beauty of his singing voice, and the same organ stood him in good stead when he abandoned singing for speech-making. In 1780 he was elected M.P. for Hull; and though his body was so small and frail that "he looked as if a breath could blow him away," he was at once recognized as a power in politics. His melodious voice, his grace of gesture, and his expressive play of features, make him a most attractive speaker, whether on the hustings or in the House; and these qualifications, added to the fact that he was the intimate friend of Pitt, seemed to mark him out for a great political career. In 1784 he was returned for Yorkshire, as a staunch supporter of his Prime Minister-friend, and his political advancement seemed more than ever a certainty; but there was a change at hand which altered the whole complexion of his life. Let it be told in his own words. Down to this time, his life had been "not licentious, but gay," and yet something was amiss.

> Often while in the full enjoyment of all that the world could bestow, my conscience told me that in the true sense of the word I was not a Christian. I laughed, I sang, I was apparently gay and happy, but the thought would steal across me—" What madness is all this, to continue easy in a state in which a sudden call out of the world would consign me to everlasting misery, and that when eternal happiness was within my grasp!"

In brief, he underwent an old-fashioned conversion; and, as a result of it, he "devoted himself, for whatever might be the term of his future life, to the service of his God and Saviour."

His conversion showed itself in very practical forms. He gave up card-playing, of which he had been very fond. He took to early rising, and did his best to fast, but found it difficult on account of his physical frailty. He stripped himself of luxuries; spent a great deal of his time in prayer, and in the study of the Bible; and was a regular and most devout communicant.

For a brief space he thought of abandoning politics and seeking Holy Orders, but was dissuaded from that course by the famous Evangelical, John Newton, who insisted that Parliament was the appointed sphere of action for a man so conspicuously endowed with Parliamentary gifts and opportunities. He therefore returned to his work in the House of Commons with greater zeal and a more determined purpose than before; and, foreseeing the offers which his intimacy with Pitt made almost inevitable, he resolved within himself never to accept either office or a peerage. Henceforward his life was dedicated to the unrewarded service of humanity.

In 1797 he published a book which at once became famous. It is called "A Practical View of the Prevailing Religious Systems of Professed Christians in the Higher and Middle Classes in this Country, contrasted with Real Christianity." It is a grave and tender appeal to consciences deadened by conventionality. It reminds them of the great realities of life and death, sin and repentance; it insists that a faith, where genuine, always supposes repentance, and abhorrence of sin; and it calls on them "faithfully to adore that undeserved goodness which has awakened them from the sleep of death, and to prostrate themselves before the cross of Christ with humble penitence and deep self-abhorrence." The book from first to last is eloquent of personal experience. It won the warm admiration of Edmund Burke. It ran through fifty editions, and it established its writer as the lay leader of Evangelical Religion. Wilberforce was evangelical in the best and highest sense. He was no Calvinist, but proclaimed universal redemption. He appealed throughout to "the Holy Scriptures, and with them, the Church of England." He believed in baptismal regeneration, and loved a cheerful Sunday. Above all, his religion was essentially practical. He worked the causes which were then most unfashionable—Christian missions, the circulation of the Bible, the suppression of vice, the mitigation of the criminal code, and popular education; above all—and on this achievement his fame eternally rests—the abolition of the slave trade.

The horrors of the "Middle Passage" had already been brought before public notice by Granville Sharp; and in 1787 a group of men whose hearts were touched by divine indignation formed the first committee for the suppression of the slave trade. Wilberforce became the parliamentary leader of the movement, and in 1788 he induced Pitt to espouse the cause—a notable triumph of persuasive power. In 1789 Pitt moved his resolution in favour of abolition; but the moment was not propitious for humanitarian reform. France was in the throes of revolution; men's minds were fixed on the dangers which impended over England; and all the energy of the Prime Minister's majestic mind was absorbed in the task of safeguarding the kingdom against foreign and domestic foes. At such times of crisis, moral causes fare badly, but Wilberforce and his friends were men not easily daunted. In 1792, in 1796, and again in 1804, they carried a bill for abolition through the House of Commons, and in each year it was defeated in the Lords. But no disappointments and no delays could damp the ardour or slacken the efforts of the abolitionists. Throughout all those dark years Wilberforce's motto was: "This one thing I do." He worked for the cause nine hours a day, scarcely stopping for his meals. Sometimes he was writing all night. He roused a spirit of intercessory prayer for his object among all his evangelical connexion, and at the same time conducted a public agitation up and down the country. Almost the last written words of the great John Wesley were addressed to the young reformer :—

My Dear Sir,—Unless the Divine Power has raised you up to be an *Athanasius contra mundum*, I see not how you can go through your glorious enterprise, in opposing that execrable villainy which is the scandal of religion, of England, and of human nature. Unless God has raised you up for this very thing, you will be worn out by the opposition of men and devils; but, if God be for you, who can be against you? Oh, be not weary of well-doing. Go on, in the name of God and in the power of His might, till even American slavery, the vilest that ever saw the sun, shall vanish away before you. That He, who has guided you from your youth up, may continue to strengthen you in this and in all things, is the prayer of, dear sir, your affectionate servant,   John Wesley.

These words were written in 1791, but sixteen years of arduous fighting and diligent labour and uncomplaining endurance had to pass before the consummation of Wesley's hopes. The Act abolishing the slave trade passed into law in 1807, and "the whole House of Commons rose to cheer the member for Yorkshire, by whose devoted toil this great triumph of mercy had been achieved."

It is interesting to enquire, rather more particularly, the nature of the gifts which enabled William Wilberforce thus to inscribe his name on the roll of the benefactors of humanity. Pitt said that of all the men he knew, Wilberforce had the greatest power of natural eloquence. Burke said the same, though he had only known him in the early stages of his career. Lord Brougham testified to "the inspiration which deep feeling alone can breathe into spoken thought." In Wilberforce the gift of persuasion was blended with a turn for sarcasm, which, as a rule, was sedulously controlled, but those who heard it long remembered his reply to a scoffing opponent who had taunted him with a facetiousness not in keeping with his religious profession: "I submit that a religious man may sometimes be facetious; and I would remind the Hon. Member that the irreligious do not necessarily escape being dull." To these gifts he added another not less valuable to a Parliamentarian. "If there is anyone," said Canning, "who thoroughly understands the tactics of debate and knows exactly what will carry the House along with him, it is certainly my Honourable friend." His high character and absolute freedom from self-seeking gave his words a moral weight more impressive than even eloquence; and, in his later years, Sydney Smith declared roundly that he "could do anything he liked with the House." Such as he was in public life, such also he was in private. Madame de Staël, after making his acquaintance, said that she had always heard that Mr Wilberforce was the "most religious man in England," but she had never before known that he was also the most agreeable. "No one," said another admirer, "touched life at so many points." "He always," said a third, "had the charm of youth." When once the slave trade was abolished, the friends of humanity determined to abolish slavery itself. After moving, in 1824, for total abolition, Wilberforce said, "I have delivered my soul." Age and infirmity were increasing on him, and he retired from Parliament, leaving what remained of the fight to younger and stronger men. At a public meeting of his supporters in 1830 he said: "The object is bright before us; the light of Heaven beams on it, and is an earnest of success." The anticipation was justified. In the session of 1833 the first Reformed Parliament passed the Act which abolished slavery, and "the Father of the movement lived just long enough to bless God that the object of his life had been attained." He died on 29th July 1833, and the two Houses of Parliament followed his body to its resting-place in the Abbey. This is the inscription on his monument:—

For nearly half a century a member of the House of Commons, and, for six Parliaments during that period, one of the two representatives for Yorkshire. In an age and country fertile in great and good men, he was among the foremost of those who fixed the character of their times; because, to high and various talents, to warm benevolence, and to universal candour, he added the abiding eloquence of a Christian life.

Eminent as he was in every department of public labour, and a leader in every work of charity, whether to relieve the temporal or the spiritual wants of his fellow-men, his name will be ever specially identified with those exertions which, by the blessing of God, removed from England the guilt of the African slave trade, and prepared the way for the abolition of slavery in every colony of the Empire : in the prosecution of these objects he relied, not in vain, on God ; but in the progress he was called to endure great obloquy and great opposition. He outlived, however, all enmity, and in the evening of his days withdrew from public life and public observation to the bosom of his family. Yet he died not unnoticed or forgotten by his country ; the peers and commons of England, in solemn procession from their respective Houses, carried him to his fitting place among the mighty dead around, here to repose, till, through the merits of Jesus Christ, his only Redeemer and Saviour (Whom in his life and in his writings he had desired to glorify), he shall rise in the resurrection of the just.

William Wilberforce the Emancipator had four sons—a second William, M.P. for Hull; Robert, a philosophical theologian of high repute; Henry, an accomplished man of letters; and Samuel, 1805–73, successively Dean of Westminster, Bishop of Oxford, and Bishop of Winchester, who has been called "the Remodeller of the Episcopate." It was said of the Emancipator that he was the only man in England who had three sons first-class men at Oxford, and of those three incomparably the most brilliant was Samuel. It was in him that his father's special gifts of persuasive oratory and social charm were most conspicuously reproduced; and it was through him that the genius of the Emancipator was transmitted to the third generation. Speaking in the House of Lords in 1853, Bishop Samuel Wilberforce paid this filial tribute:—

> I deem it to be my greatest boast to be sprung from one who, gifted with the vastest opportunities, with the friendship—the close friendship—of England's greatest Minister, the highest powers, the most commanding social position, used them all for no personal aggrandizement, and died a poor commoner—a poorer man than when he entered public life; and leaving to his children no high rank or dignity, according to the notions of the world, but bequeathing to them the perilous inheritance of a name which the Christian world venerates.

A great name is indeed a "perilous inheritance"; but assuredly it suffered no disparagement in the person of Samuel Wilberforce. "He was one," said Mr Gladstone, "of the three men I have ever known who had the greatest faculty for public speaking. Who can count the numbers — they are not in hundreds, they are not in thousands, they are in hundreds of thousands—who in every part of this country listened from time to time to the tones of that silvery voice, sometimes like a murmuring brook, sometimes like a trumpet-call?" "In society," said Lord Carnarvon, "he shone and sparkled beyond anyone I have ever known; but, even in that respect, he was not so remarkable as he was for devotion to his work." Archbishop Tait, who had constantly been brought into collision with him, spoke enthusiastically of his "social and irresistibly fascinating side, as displayed in his dealings with society"; and paid this noble tribute to his public virtues:—

If it be ambition to be conscious of great powers and talents, carrying a heavier responsibility than is borne by many, and to have a great desire to use those powers and improve those talents for the service of Him who gave them, then I doubt not that he was ambitious; but it is a noble and holy ambition, which deserves no censure and needs no defence.

The statesman Lord Carlisle thus described his eloquence: "He made a speech of two hours, combining the qualities of his father, Macaulay, and Ezekiel, which produced immense effect. His voice and delivery are exceedingly good." Lady Lyttelton, who was governess to Queen Victoria's elder children, wrote in her diary: "I never saw a more agreeable man; and, if such a Hindoo were to be found, I think he would go far to convert me, and lead me to Juggernaut; so it is hard if all those who know him are not altogether Christians sooner or later. He never parades, or forces forward his religious feelings. They are only the *climate* of his mind—talents, knowledge, eloquence, liveliness, all evidently Christian." "No one," wrote the late Canon Overton, "no one can ever forget the magical effect of his presence—like the coming of spring to a winter landscape; his thrilling confirmation addresses; the brilliant wit of his conversation; the inimitable tones of his wonderfully modulated voice; the fascination of his look and manner." Dean Burgon wrote thus about his friend's grave amid the Surrey downs: "None but those who knew him will have the faintest conception what an exquisite orator, what a persuasive preacher, what a faithful bishop—in every private relation of life what a truly delightful person is commemorated by the stone which covers the grave of Samuel Wilberforce."

These quotations read in connexion with what goes before will have shown the transmission of exactly the same qualities from the first to the second generation. I now approach the third. Bishop Samuel Wilberforce had four sons. The fourth, his "Benoni," as he loved to call him—for Mrs Wilberforce died when the boy was born,—is the present Archdeacon of Westminster and Chaplain to the Speaker. In his case the intimacy of a close friendship seals my lips; and I turn to his next elder brother. Ernest Roland Wilberforce, sometime Vicar of Seaforth and successively Bishop of Newcastle and of Chichester, was born in 1840 and died in 1907. Of his character, perhaps the most salient feature was strenuousness, but this was combined with a full share of the qualities which had been so conspicuous in his father and grandfather. Before he had been two years in Holy Orders he was preaching sermons of which a competent critic said: "They were some of the very best I ever heard, and the good material was coupled with a perfect delivery." Five years later, Mr Gladstone, whose father had built and endowed St Thomas's, Seaforth, wrote thus to Ernest Wilberforce: "If you would take this church, it would be a true delight to me to present you to it; first, as the son of your great and dear father, who seems even now at my hand (nor should I exclude the still more venerable memory of your grandfather).

Secondly, from all that I have heard of you in the work of the Holy Ministry." The offer was accepted, and Wilberforce's work at Seaforth is not yet forgotten. He was seen at his best in a house where bereavement, sorrow, or anxiety had crossed the threshold—there the hereditary gifts of sympathy and compassion came into play,—but he was also excellent in the pulpit, and super-excellent on the platform. "I can hardly say," wrote one of his hearers, "what was his greater power. Sympathy was *strong*—very evidently strong. His earnestness was a great point. His clear ringing tones carried conviction of his sincerity; and there were beautiful strains of eloquence, particularly in description of those natural beauties in which his soul delighted."

"The familiar Wilberforcian tones" were promptly recognized by those who remembered his father, and also "the true Wilberforce well of feeling." "A chip of the old block" was the homely comment of Bishop Jacobson. "The Queen told me that you reminded her of your father in voice, only less studied," was the report of Dean Wellesley after a sermon at Windsor. From Seaforth Ernest Wilberforce was summoned to take charge of a mission among the great towns of the Winchester diocese, which had been established in memory of his father; and Bishop Harold Browne, in offering the post, claimed "a Wilberforce for the Wilberforce Mission, with the zeal and tongue of a Wilberforce." "Inspiration," said another, "will come from your father's dear memory, sympathy from troops of your own friends."

The call to Winchester was dutifully accepted, but a more momentous change was at hand. The see of Newcastle was created in 1882, and Mr Gladstone invited Ernest Wilberforce to be its first bishop. "I earnestly hope that you may carry far onwards into a second century the unbroken association of your honoured name with the history of the Church of England, and that you may add largely to the records of the noble services of your father and your grandfather."

Northumberland unlocked its strong and loving heart to what it called "the open sesame of your father's name." "That name was in itself enough to secure a hearty welcome in the North of England, where his father's untiring labours and magnetic eloquence were still fresh in the memories of churchmen, and where his grandfather's devotion to the cause of the slave was unforgotten by Englishmen of every creed and party." Of his purely spiritual power, as evinced at ordinations, confirmations, and in more private ministries, this is not the place to speak, but his magnificent work for the cause of Temperance can never be forgotten. The Treasurer of the Church of England Temperance Society wrote:—

> There will always remain with me the memory of his charming personality, and his eloquent efforts for the promotion of habits of temperance, for the reformation of the intemperate, and for the removal of the causes which lead to intemperance.

A CABINET OF MINIATURES   167

The present Duke of Northumberland said, "You have completely mastered the peculiarities of us Northerners." The present Lord Grey referred with relish to the "episcopal tobacco and good company" which, when the day's work was done, he had enjoyed in the Bishop's company; and Bishop Creighton, then vicar of Embleton, described him (though a staunch teetotaler) as "a born boon-companion— his father's son."

After thirteen years of extraordinary labour in Northumberland, the Bishop's constitution, originally of abnormal vigour, began to show sign of wear and tear; and in 1895 he accepted from Lord Salisbury translation to the see of Chichester. There exactly the same qualities of energy, éloquence, and practical sagacity manifested themselves in his diocesan administration; and some unfortunate disputes about the anise and cumin of ritual gave peculiar scope for the exercise of his great gift of sympathy. One of the clergy wrote, after a visit to the Palace at Chichester: "Your kindness to me personally this last week will not be readily forgotten." Another said: "I can never tell you all that your sympathy and kindness have been to me and to my wife. I had no idea that it was possible to be on such delightful terms with one's diocesan." After the Conference of Anglican Bishops in 1907, one of the American prelates wrote: "No bishop of the Anglican communion treated me with more consideration and gracious hospitality." One of the doctors who attended him in a sudden and dangerous illness wrote: "He was so patient, so grateful for the little we were able to do for him. He seemed to me to have such a very great personal charm. I shouldn't think that a man like him could ever have had a single enemy."

It is time to end. We have traced through three generations the marked qualities of eloquence, sympathy, social pleasantness, and spiritual devotion—surely a notable illustration of heredity; and perhaps the hereditary gifts are not yet exhausted. Bishop Ernest Wilberforce left a numerous family; and of them the present Dean of York once wrote: "They are dear children, and I only wish that their good and honoured grandfather could have seen them."[1] That grandfather was the Emancipator's son; so here we touch the fourth generation of a family which for a hundred and thirty continuous years has served England with soul and speech.

Joseph Hume

One must go to the provinces for news of what is happening in London. In this bewildering city no one knows his next-door neighbour. One may wake up any morning to discover that Professor Dingo, of European reputation, has lived and died in one's own street, or that the most colossal crime has been hatched in the mews just round the corner. The

[1] One of these "dear children," Mr Victor Wilberforce, is now a chief light of the motor-cycling world.

A CABINET OF MINIATURES 169

provincial papers disclose these secrets; and great was my astonishment when I lately read an announcement that Mr A. O. Hume, the leader of the Liberal Party in Dulwich, who has presented South London with a herbarium at Norwood, is a son of Joseph Hume, the famous reformer. What excited my interest in this announcement was not the "herbarium," for I must confess that collections of dried flowers leave me cold; but the discovery that I am living within three miles of a son of a man whose political achievements began when George III. was King, and who had laid the foundations of his fortunes before the eighteenth century had ended.

Joseph Hume was born in 1777 and died in 1855. His father was a tradesman at Montrose; but the son preferred science to shopkeeping, and qualified as a surgeon. In 1796 he obtained an appointment in the service of the East India Company, and sailed for India. On the voyage the purser fell sick; Hume took over his duties, and discharged them so well that the Company transferred him from marine to civil employment. He threw himself with ardour into the study of Oriental languages, and acquired them so thoroughly that he was made an interpreter, and in that capacity transacted a good deal of delicate and important business between the Company and the native powers. Those were the grand old days when proconsuls became nabobs, and the humblest officials in the service of the Company had frequent opportunities of indulging in the pastime of "shaking the pagoda tree." By 1808 Hume, who, no doubt, like Clive, was astounded at his own moderation, had put by £40,000—no great sum indeed, but enough for his immediate object, which was to enter the House of Commons. Willing the end, he willed the means, and, returning to England, he proceeded to buy one of the two seats which the borough of Weymouth then possessed. The transaction was perfectly deliberate, straightforward, and business-like. Hume drew his cheque, and the Free and Independent Electors of Weymouth undertook to return him for two Parliaments. He was duly elected at a by-election in January 1812, but, a dissolution occurring in the following November, the vendors of the seat declined to fulfil their bargain, whereupon he brought an action for breach of contract, and recovered half his money. In 1818 he regained a seat in Parliament, this time for the Montrose Burghs, and he represented in turn Middlesex, Kilkenny, and again Montrose. He was a Radical of the deepest dye, and for thirty years was the recognized leader of the Radical group in Parliament. Charles Greville, surveying the first Reformed Parliament from the point of view of the cultivated worldling, thus analyses the composition of the new House: "There exists no *party* but that of the Government; the Irish act in a body under O'Connell, to the number of about forty; the Radicals are numerous, restless, turbulent, and bold—Hume and Cobbett and Roebuck, bent upon doing all the mischief they can, and incessantly active; the Tories without a head, frightened, angry, and sulky; Peel without a party, prudent, cautious, and dexterous, playing a deep waiting game of scrutiny and observation"—as one reads the analysis it strikes one that 1832 was not so very unlike 1912.

Through all this time of storm and stress Hume worked hand and glove with O'Connell, who provided him with the seat at Kilkenny when Middlesex turned him out; and the alliance of English Radicalism with Irish Nationalism evoked, then as now, sarcastic comments. To Sydney Smith, who was a Whig to the backbone, the combination of "Joseph and Daniel," as he called them, seemed fraught with mischief, and he repeatedly implored his leader, Lord John Russell, to offer a more vigorous resistance to "Joseph and his brethren" of the Radical persuasion.

It has always been the portion of Radicals to be dreaded and dispraised by the bigwigs of the Liberal Party, and yet all the while to be tracing the path of advance along which, a few years later, the whole party advanced to victory. This was as true of Joseph Hume as in later days of Bright and Cobden, of Mr Chamberlain and Mr Lloyd George. In 1834, amid universal derision, he attacked the Corn Laws as producing artificial starvation, and declared for repeal. In 1835 he forced the attention of the House to the treasonable conspiracy which was masquerading under the name of Orangeism. He laboured for the extension of the suffrage, for the establishment of the ballot, and for the reform of the ecclesiastical revenues. He moved for the abolition of sinecures and of flogging in the army. In the queer slang of the day (for which see the second chapter of *Nicholas Nickleby*) he "went the extreme animal" with Tom Duncombe and J. T. Leader, but his special devotion was reserved for financial reform. It was at his suggestion that the word "Retrenchment" was inserted between "Peace" and "Reform" in the official motto or war-cry of the Liberal Party; and on all questions pertaining to finance, revenue, expediture, and the like, he was the most pertinacious and unsparing of critics. So thorough-going and business-like was his criticism that he kept a private staff of clerks entirely occupied in watching, even in its minutest details, the financial conduct of each successive Government; and whenever a vulnerable point was detected Hume swooped down on it like a hawk on a partridge. He was commonly reported to have served on more Committees than anyone else who ever sat in Parliament, and to speak "longer and oftener and worse" than any one of his contemporaries. His marked peculiarities of diction, tone, and pronunciation gave abundant cause for merriment among those who disliked his reforming zeal, and one of his most frequent phrases—"the tottle of the whole"— became a stock-instance of Parliamentary humour. It was characteristic of him that he was the first man to open his lips in the first Reformed Parliament, and by his discourse on that occasion drew from his ally O'Connell the friendly criticism that he " would have been an excellent speaker if only he would finish a sentence before beginning the next but one after it."

Hume's pertinacity in debate is well illustrated by his behaviour to Macaulay on the second reading of the India Bill of 1853 (signalized by Bright's great oration—No. I. in his *Collected Speeches*). It had been arranged that Macaulay, who was then in failing health, should speak early in the debate, but Hume moved the adjournment of the debate and so got Macaulay's place. "Everyone who could venture to remonstrate with the Member for Montrose on so delicate a subject entreated him not to stand between Macaulay and his audience; but Hume replied that his own chest was weak, and that his health was as important as that of any other person, that he knew just as much about India as Macaulay, and, in short, that speak he would. The House had very little compassion on an invalid who had been on his legs six times within the last ten days and who now spoke from the resumption of the debate till dinner-time."

To one of Hume's innumerable Committees on financial abuses a curious sequel was attached. This particular Committee was to enquire into the salaries of Ministers of State, which, in Hume's opinion, were grossly excessive. The first witness called was the Prime Minister, Lord John Russell, and when Hume put the question, "Do you think that the First Lord of the Treasury is overpaid?" Lord John replied, "Well, all I can say is that I am not at all a rich man, but, till I was Prime Minister, I never was in debt." This reply created some sensation, and Lord John's eldest brother, the Duke of Bedford, immediately placed £10,000 to his credit at Messrs Vere's bank (I choose that noble name from the British peerage because I mean to convey that Lord John's bank had social connexions of the highest). At the following Christmas Lord John was paying a visit to his brother at Woburn Abbey, and the Duke, who had received no acknowledgment of his gift, asked, "Well, Johnny, does your account look any better this quarter?" And Johnny replied, "I never look at it. Messrs Vere's clerks are all young gentlemen, and they make so many mistakes in their arithmetic that it is no good looking at their figures." This has always struck me as one of the quaintest instances of *non sequitur*.

VI

A FORGOTTEN PANIC[1]

FRIDAY, 13th September 1867, was the last day of the Harrow holidays, and I was returning to the Hill from a visit to some friends in Scotland. During the first part of the journey I was alone in the carriage, occupied with an unlearnt holiday-task; but at Carlisle I acquired a fellow-traveller. He jumped into the carriage just as the train was beginning to move, and to the porter who breathlessly enquired about his luggage he shouted, "This is all," and flung a small leathern case on to the seat. As he settled himself into his place, his eye fell upon the pile of baggage which I had bribed the station-master to establish in my corner of the carriage—a portmanteau, a hat-box, a rug wrapped round an umbrella, and one or two smaller parcels—all legibly labelled

G. W. E. RUSSELL,
Woodside,
Harrow-on-the-Hill.

After a glance at my property, the stranger turned to me and exclaimed, "When you have travelled as

[1] Reprinted from the *Cornhill Magazine*.

much as I have, young sir, you will know that, the less the luggage, the greater the ease." Youth, I think, as a rule resents overtures from strangers, but there was something in my fellow-traveller's address so pleasant as to disarm resentment. His voice, his smile, his appearance, were alike prepossessing. He drew from his pocket the *Daily News*, in those days a famous organ for foreign intelligence, and, as he composed himself to read, I had a full opportunity ot studying his appearance. He seemed to be somewhere between thirty and forty; of the middle height, lean and sinewy, and, as his jump into the train had shown, as lissom as a cat. His skin was so much tanned that it was difficult to guess his natural complexion; but his closely cropped hair was jet-black, and his clean-shaved face showed the roots of a very dark beard. In those days it was fashionable to wear one's hair rather long, and to cultivate whiskers and a moustache. Priests and actors were the only people who shaved clean, and I decided in my mind that my friend was an actor. Presently he laid down his paper; and, turning to me with that grave courtesy which when one is very young one appreciates, he said: "I hope, sir, that my abrupt entry did not disturb you. I had a rush for it, and nearly lost my train as it was. And I hope what I said about luggage did not seem impertinent. I was only thinking that, if I had been obliged to look after portmanteaus, I should probably still be on the platform at Carlisle." I hastened to say, with my best air, that I had not been the least offended, and rather apologized for my own encumbrances by saying that I was going South for three months, and had to take all my possessions with me. I am not sure that I was pleased when my friend said: "Ah, yes; the end of the vacation. You are returning to college at Harrow, I see." It was humiliating to confess that Harrow was a school, and I a schoolboy; but my friend took it with great composure. Perfectly, he said; it was his error. He should have said " school," not "college." He had a great admiration for the English Public Schools. It was his misfortune to have been educated abroad. A French lycée, or a German gymnasium, was not such a pleasant place as Eton or Harrow. This was exactly the best way of starting a conversation, and, my boyish reserve being once broken, we chatted away merrily. Very soon I had told him everything about myself, my home, my kinsfolk, my amusements, my favourite authors, and all the rest of it; but presently it dawned upon me that, though I had disclosed everything to him, he had disclosed nothing to me, and that the actor, if I rightly deemed him so, was not very proud of his profession. His nationality, too, perplexed me. He spoke English as fluently as I did, but not quite idiomatically; and there was just a trace of an accent which was not English. Sometimes it sounded French, but then again there was a tinge of American. On the whole, I came to the conclusion that my friend was an Englishman who had lived a great deal abroad, or else an American who had lived in Paris. As the day advanced, the American theory gained upon me; for, though my friend told me nothing about himself, he told me a great deal about every place which we passed. He knew the industries of the various towns, and the events connected with them, and the names of the people who owned the castles and great country-houses. I had been told that this habit of endless exposition was characteristic of the cultured American. But, whatever was the nationality of my companion, I enjoyed his company very much. He talked to me, not as a man to a boy, but as an elder to a younger man; paid me the courtesy of asking my opinion and listening to my answers; and, by all the little arts of the practised converser, made me feel on good terms with myself and the world. Yankee or Frenchman, my actor was a very jolly fellow; and I only wished that he would tell me a little about himself.

When, late in the afternoon, we passed Bletchley Station, I bethought me that we should soon be separated, for the London and North-Western train, though an express, was to be stopped at Harrow in order to disgorge its load of returning boys. I began to collect my goods and to prepare myself for the stop, when my friend said, to my great joy, "I see you are alighting. I am going on to Euston. I shall be in London for the next few weeks. I should very much like to pay a visit to Harrow one day and see

A FORGOTTEN PANIC

your 'lions.'" This was exactly what I wished, but had been too modest to suggest; so I joyfully acceded to his proposal, only venturing to add that, though we had been travelling together all day, I did not know my friend's name. He tore a leaf out of a pocket-book, scrawled on it in a backward-sloping hand, "H. Aulif," and handed it to me, saying, "I do not add an address, for I shall be moving about. But I will write you a line very soon, and fix a day for my visit." Just then the train stopped at the foot of the Hill, and, as I was fighting my way through the welter of boys and luggage on the platform, I caught sight of a smiling face and a waved hand at the window of the carriage which I had just quitted.

The beginning of a new School-Quarter, the crowd of fresh faces, the greetings of old friends, and a remove into a much more difficult Form, rather distracted my mind from the incidents of my journey; to which it was recalled by the receipt of a note from Mr Aulif, saying that he would be at Harrow by 2.30 on Saturday afternoon, 21st September. I met him at the station, and found him even pleasanter than I expected. He extolled Public Schools to the skies, and was sure that our English virtues were in great part due to them. Of Harrow he spoke with peculiar admiration as the school of Sheridan, of Peel, of Palmerston. What was our course of study? What our system of discipline? What were our amusements? The last question I was able to answer by showing him both the end of cricket and the beginning of football, for both were being played; and, as we mounted the Hill towards the School and the Spire, he asked me if we had any other amusements. Fives or racquets he did not seem to count. Did we run races? Had we any gymnastics? (In those days we had not.) Did we practise rifle-shooting? Every boy ought to learn to use a rifle. The Volunteer movement was a national glory. Had we any part in it?

The last question touched me on the point of honour. In those days Harrow was the best school in England for rifle-shooting. In the Public Schools' contest at Wimbledon we carried off the Ashburton Challenge Shield five times in succession, and in 1865 and 1866 we added to it Lord Spencer's Cup for the best marksman in the school-teams. All this, and a good deal more to the same effect, I told Mr Aulif with becoming spirit, and proudly led the way to our "armoury." This grandly named apartment was in truth a dingy cellar under the Old Schools, and held only a scanty store of rifles (for the corps, though keen, was not numerous). Boyhood is sensitive to sarcasm, and I felt an uncomfortable twinge as Mr Aulif glanced round our place of arms and said, "a gallant corps, I am sure, if not numerically strong. But this is your school corps only. Doubtless the citizens of the place also have their corps?" Rather wishing to get my friend away from a scene where he obviously was not impressed, and fearing that perhaps he might speak lightly of the Fourth Form Room,

A FORGOTTEN PANIC

even though its panels bear the carved name of BYRON, I seized the opening afforded by the mention of the local corps, and proposed a walk towards the drill-shed. This was a barn, very roughly adapted to military purposes, and standing, remote from houses, in a field at Roxeth, a hamlet of Harrow on the way to Northolt. It served both as drill-shed and as armoury, and, as the local corps (the 18th Middlesex) was a large one, it contained a good supply of arms and ammunition. The custodian, who lived in a cottage at Roxeth, was a Crimean veteran, who kept everything in apple-pie order, and on this Saturday afternoon was just putting the finishing touches of tidiness to the properties in his charge. Mr Aulif made friends with him at once, spoke enthusiastically of the Crimea, talked of improvements in guns and gunnery since those days, praised the Anglo-French alliance, and said how sad it was that England now had to be on her guard against her former allies across the Channel. As the discourse proceeded, I began to question my theory that Aulif was an actor. Perhaps he was a soldier. Could he be a Jesuit in disguise? Jesuits were clean-shaved and well-informed. Or was it only his faculty of general agreeableness that enabled him to attract the old caretaker at the drill-shed as he had attracted the schoolboy in the train? As we walked back to the station, my desire to know what my friend really was, increased momentarily; but I no more dared to ask him than I should have dared to shake hands with

Queen Victoria; for, to say the truth, Mr Aulif, while he fascinated, awed me. He told me that he was just going abroad, and we parted at the station with mutual regrets.

. . . . . .

The year 1867 was conspicuously a year of Fenian activity. The termination of the Civil War in America had thrown out of employment a great many seasoned soldiers of various nationalities, who had served for five years in the American armies. Among these were General Cluseret, educated at Saint-Cyr, trained by Garibaldi, and by some good critics esteemed "the most consummate soldier of the day." The Fenians now began to dream not merely of isolated outrages, but of an armed rising in Ireland; and, after consultation with the Fenian leaders in New York, Cluseret came to England with a view to organizing the insurrection. What then befell can be read in *Lothair*, where Cluseret is thinly disguised as "Captain Bruges," and also in his own narrative, published in *Fraser's Magazine* for 1872. He arrived in London in January 1867; and startling events began to happen in quick succession. On 11th February an armed party of Fenians attacked Chester Castle, and were not repulsed without some difficulty. There was an armed rising at Killarney. The police barracks at Tallaght were besieged, and at Glencullen the insurgents captured the police force and their weapons. At Kilmallock there was an encounter between the Fenians and the constabulary, and life was lost on both sides. There was a design of concentrating all the Fenian forces on Mallow Junction, but the rapid movement of the Queen's troops frustrated the design, and the general rising was postponed. Presently two vagrants were arrested on suspicion at Liverpool, and proved to be two of the most notorious of the Fenian leaders, "Colonel" Kelly and "Captain" Deasy. It was when these prisoners, remanded for further enquiry, were being driven under a strong escort to gaol, that the prison-van was attacked by a rescue-party, and Sergeant Brett, who was in charge of the prisoners, was shot. The rescuers, Allen, Larkin, and Gould, were executed on 2nd November, and on 1st December Clerkenwell Prison was blown up in an ineffectual attempt to liberate the Fenian prisoners confined in it. On 20th December Matthew Arnold wrote to his mother, "We are in a strange uneasy state in London, and the profound sense I have long had of the hollowness and insufficiency of our whole system of administration does not inspire me with much confidence." The "strange uneasy state" was not confined to London, but prevailed everywhere. Obviously England was threatened by a mysterious and desperate enemy, and no one seemed to know that enemy's headquarters or base of operations. The secret societies were actively at work in England, Ireland, France, and Italy. It was suspected then—it is known now, and chiefly through Cluseret's revelations

—that the isolated attacks on barracks and police-stations were designed for the purpose of securing arms and ammunition; and, if only there had been a competent general to command the rebel forces, Ireland would have risen in open war. But a competent general was exactly what the insurgents lacked; for Cluseret, having surveyed the whole situation with eyes trained by a lifelong experience of warfare, decided that the scheme was hopeless, and returned to Paris.

Such were some—for I have only mentioned a few—of the incidents which made 1867 a memorable year. On my own memory it is stamped with a peculiar clearness.

On Wednesday morning, 2nd October 1867, as we were going up to First School at Harrow, a rumour flew from mouth to mouth that the drill-shed had been attacked by Fenians. Sure enough it had. The caretaker (as I said before) lived some way from the building, and, when he went to open it in the morning, he found that the door had been forced and the place swept clean of arms and ammunition. Here was a real sensation, and we felt for a few hours "the joy of eventful living"; but later in the day the evening papers, coming down from London, quenched our excitement with a greater. It appeared that, during the night of 1st October, drill-sheds and armouries belonging to the Volunteer regiments had been simultaneously raided, north, south, east, and west of London, and all munitions of war spirited

A FORGOTTEN PANIC 185

away, for a purpose which was not hard to guess. Commenting on this startling occurrence, the papers said : " We have reason to believe that one of the ablest of the Fenian agents has been for some time operating secretly in the United Kingdom. He has been traced to Liverpool, Glasgow, Edinburgh, and London. It is believed at Scotland Yard that he organized these attacks on Volunteer headquarters, arranged for the arms and ammunition to be transferred by a sure hand to Ireland, and has himself returned to Paris." A friend of mine who had gone up to London to see a dentist brought back a *Globe* with him, and, as he handed it to me, he pointed out the passage which I have just cited. As I read it, my heart gave a jump—a sudden thrill of delicious excitement. My friend Mr Aulif must be the Fenian agent who had organized these raids, and I, who had always dreamed romance, had now been brought into actual contact with it. The idea of communicating my suspicions to anyone never crossed my mind. I felt instinctively that this was a case where silence was golden. Fortunately, none of my schoolfellows had seen Mr Aulif or heard of his visit; and the old caretaker of the drill-shed had been too much gratified by talk and tip to entertain an unworthy thought of "that pleasant-spoken gentleman."

Soon the story of these raids had been fogotten in the far more exhilarating occurrences at Manchester and Clerkenwell which closed the year; and the execution of Michael Barrett on 26th May 1868 (the last public execution in this country), brought the history of Fenianism in England to an end.

As I looked back on my journey from Scotland, and my walk round Harrow with Mr Aulif, I thought that the reason why he did not arrange for our school-armoury to be attacked was that he would not abuse the confidence of a boy who had trusted him. Perhaps it really was that the rifles were too few and the risks too many.

.   .   .   .   .   .

The year 1870 found me still a Harrow boy, though a tall one; and I spent the Easter holidays with my cousins, the Brentfords, in Paris. They were a remarkable couple, and, if I were to mention their real name, they would be immediately recognized. They had social position and abundant means and hosts of friends; but, acting under irresistible impulse, they had severed themselves from their natural surroundings, and had plunged into democratic politics. It was commonly believed that Brentford would not have committed himself so deeply if it had not been for his wife's influence; and, indeed, she was one of those women whom it is difficult to withstand. Her enthusiasm was contagious; and, when one was in her company, one felt that "the Cause," as she always called it without qualifying epithet, was the one thing worth thinking of and living for. As a girl, she had caught from Mrs Browning, and Swinburne, and Jessie White-Mario, and the authoress of *Aspro-*

monte, a passionate zeal for Italian unity and freedom, and, when she married, her enthusiasm fired her husband. They became sworn allies both of Garibaldi and of Mazzini, and through them were brought into close, though mysterious, relations with the revolutionary party in Italy and also in France. They witnessed the last great act of the Papacy at the Vatican Council; and then, early in 1870, they established themselves in Paris. French society was at that moment in a strange state of tension and unrest. The impending calamity of the Franco-German War was not foreseen; but everyone knew that the Imperial throne was rocking; that the soil was primed by Secret Societies; and that all the elements of revolution were at hand, and needed only some sudden concussion to stir them into activity. This was a condition which exactly suited my cousin Evelyn Brentford. She was "at the height of the circumstances," and she gathered round her, at her villa on the outskirts of Paris, a society partly political, partly Bohemian, and wholly Red. "Do come," she wrote, "and stay with us at Easter. I can't promise you a Revolution; but it's quite on the cards that you may come in for one. Anyhow, you will see some fun." I had some difficulty in inducing my parents (sound Whigs) to give the necessary permission; but they admitted that at seventeen a son must be trusted, and I went off rejoicing to join the Brentfords at Paris. Those three weeks, 12th April to 4th May 1870, gave me, as the boys now say, "the time of my life." I met a great many people whose names I already knew, and some more of whom we heard next year in the history of the Commune. The air was full of the most sensational rumours, and those who hoped "to see the last King strangled in the bowels of the last priest" enjoyed themselves thoroughly. My cousin Evelyn was always at home to her friends on Sunday and Wednesday evenings, and her rooms were thronged by a miscellaneous crowd in which the Parisian accent mingled with the tongues of America and Italy, and the French of the southern provinces.

At one of these parties I was talking to a delightful lady who lived only in the hope of seeing "the devil come for that dog" (indicating by this term a Crowned Head), and who, when exhausted by regicidal eloquence, demanded coffee. As we approached the buffet, a man who had just put down his cup turned round and met my companion and me face to face. Two years and a half had made no difference in him. He was Mr Aulif, as active and fresh as ever, and, before I had time to reflect on my course, I had impulsively seized him by the hand. "Don't you remember me?" I cried. He only stared. "My name is George Russell, and you visited me at Harrow." "I fear, sir, you have made a mistake," said Aulif; bowed rather stiffly to my companion, and hurried back into the drawing-room. My companion looked surprised. "The General seems put out—I wonder why. He and I are the greatest allies. Let me tell you my friend, that he is the man that the Revolution will have to rely on when the time comes for rising. Ask them at Saint-Cyr. Ask Garibaldi. Ask McClellan. Ask General Grant. He is the greatest general in the world, and has sacrificed his career for Freedom." "Is his name Aulif?" "No, his name is Cluseret."

. . . .

Next day at *déjeuner* I was full of my evening's adventure; but my host and hostess received it with mortifying composure. "Nothing could be more likely," said my cousin Evelyn. "General Cluseret was here, though he did not stay long. Perhaps he really did not remember you. When he saw you before, you were a boy, and now you look like a young man. Or perhaps he did not wish to be cross-examined. He is pretty busy here just now, but in 1867 he was constantly backwards and forwards between Paris and London, trying to organize that Irish insurrection which never came off. England is not the only country he has visited on business of that kind, and he has many travelling names. He thinks it safer, for obvious reasons, to travel without luggage. If you had been able to open that leather case in the train, you would probably have found nothing in it except some maps, a toothbrush, and a spare revolver. Certainly that Irish affair was a *fiasco*; but depend upon it you will hear of General Cluseret again."

And so indeed I did, and so did the whole civilized world, and that within twelve months of the time of speaking; but there is no need to rewrite in this place the history of the Commune.

[The personal part of this narrative is fictitious; the rest is historical.]

VII

THE INNER SIDE OF A TRANSACTION

MR PERCY THORNTON, sometime M.P. for Clapham, has, like the rest of us, published a volume of reminiscences.[1] It is a very pleasant, chatty, and discursive book, ranging over genealogy, sport, athletics, naval history, Harrow, Cambridge, and the House of Commons. I am not attempting to review it, but I am impelled to reveal the inner side of a Parliamentary transaction, which, in its outward manifestations, made an indelible impression on Mr Thornton's mind.

I carefully observed Mr Gladstone during the increasing efforts he made to defy old age and rule over the House of Commons. They said that the Irish question somewhat circumscribed the field of his energies; but one remarkable exception must remain in the memory of everyone present when, on an evening devoted to private members' motions during the 1893 Session, the Prime Minister had undertaken to urge patience and moderation upon those of his supporters who demanded an immediate extinction of the opium traffic between India and China. The reason for the extra exertion was that Mr G. Russell was Under-Secretary for India, and also officially connected with the Anti-Opium Society.

---

[1] *Some Things we have Remembered* (Longmans).

I only pause to say that I was not connected, officially or otherwise, with the Anti-Opium Society, and I pass on to my narrative.

In fulfilment of a pledge to Ireland, Mr Gladstone devoted the Session of 1893 to the foredoomed Home Rule Bill. The summer was hot; the debates were exciting; the proceedings in Committee engrossed sixty-three sittings, and everybody was more or less exhausted and dispirited. On Thursday, 29th June, the House sat all through the night, discussing Gladstone's motion for closure by compartments, and adjourned at 3.45 on Friday morning. At 12 on Friday we met again for a morning sitting, concluded the debate, and carried the resolution. According to the practice of those days, the House rose at 7, to meet again at 9.

The subject for the evening's debate was, as Mr Thornton says, " The Opium Traffic between India and China." Mr Alfred Webb, M.P. for West Waterford, a Quaker and a Nationalist, had given notice of a motion condemning the traffic, root and branch, and reaffirming a resolution carried in 1891, to the effect that "the system by which the opium revenue is raised is morally indefensible." Mr Webb was, in general politics, a staunch supporter of the Government, but this was a matter of conscience, which overrode all questions of party allegiance. He might, very reasonably, have been allowed to make his motion without opposition from the Government. If he had carried it, nothing very serious would have

INNER SIDE OF A TRANSACTION 193

happened, for he proposed that a Commission should be sent to India to enquire into methods of repairing the loss to the revenue which the stoppage of the opium-traffic would cause, and things would soon have adjusted themselves. But this view did not commend itself to the Secretary of State for India, Lord Kimberley. That remarkable man was not, as the newspapers always dubbed him, a Whig, but a Utilitarian Radical of the toughest fibre. His mind was clear, direct, and logical in a high degree. Commonsense was his most conspicuous attribute, and with sentiment he could make no terms. His view of the opium question was this: India draws a revenue from the traffic. India is a poor country, and it would be a crime to make her poorer. If anyone can show me a way of raising a fresh revenue equal to that now produced by opium, well and good. But I must know for certain what that alternate revenue is to be, before I consent to sacrifice what we now possess. "A bird in the hand," etc. Of the considerations that weigh with missionaries, preachers, humanitarians, and members of the Society of Friends, he took no account.

As the duty of opposing Mr Webb and his friends would officially fall to me, I urged on Lord Kimberley what I knew of the views of the Liberal Party on the subject; for it seemed likely that, with a majority of forty all told, the Government might be beaten by a combination of Tories and Humanitarians. However, Lord Kimberley, who had never sat in the

House of Commons and was always inclined to hold it cheap, insisted that Webb's motion must be opposed, so far as condemnation of the traffic was concerned, though he was willing that the traffic should be "reduced" and that a Commission should be sent to enquire into the whole question of opium, its uses and abuses, production, and sale. Accordingly, on 28th June, I put down an amendment on these lines to Webb's motion (which was, technically, an amendment to the formal motion, "that the Speaker do now leave the chair,") but I very soon became aware that the proposals of the Government would not satisfy the anti-opium party, and that we must be prepared for a sharp tussle. All Thursday, and the morning session of Friday, were, as I have just stated, engrossed by the fierce debate on Mr Gladstone's motion for closure by compartments, commonly called "the guillotine"; but, during the afternoon of Friday, the Whips reported that the Government would probably be beaten if they opposed Webb's motion at the evening sitting. I held a brief consultation with Mr Gladstone, who, on surveying all the circumstances, came to the conclusion that we had better accept Webb's motion.

But this could not be done without Lord Kimberley's consent. "Will you," said Gladstone, "go across to the House of Lords, explain matters to Kimberley, and ask him to come to my room and talk it over?" So to the House of Lords I went, and Lord Kimberley came down to me at the Bar. When I had delivered my message, he said, with characteristic directness: "I can't possibly leave the House. We are discussing Home Rule for Scotland, on a motion of Camperdown's, and I am just going to speak. But there is no reason for my seeing Gladstone. Nothing would be gained by discussion. If he accepts Webb's motion, I resign. Pray tell him so, with my kind regards," and bustled back to his seat. Returning to the House of Commons, I delivered my message. Gladstone was not much disturbed. "So," he said, "Kimberley holds a pistol to our heads—in the kindest and most gentlemanlike manner possible, but still a pistol. Well, never mind, we must just fight it. I will come down to the evening sitting, and speak; and now, please bring me any papers or books on the subject which you think I ought to read." Ten minutes afterwards, I left him in his private room behind the chair, poring over blue-books and reports and memoranda, like an undergraduate "mugging-up" for *viva voce*.

Just at seven we carried our "guillotine," and dispersed in search of dinner. Sharp on the stroke of nine, when the House resumed, Mr Gladstone reappeared on the Treasury Bench, with a flower in his button-hole, fresh and cheerful, and evidently full of fight. The question, "That Mr Speaker do now leave the chair," was put, and up rose good Mr Webb to move his amendment. He referred to the Resolution of 1891; he quoted Gladstone's famous speech on opium in 1840; and he dwelt, earnestly and long, on the moral considerations involved in the traffic.

It was a very good speech, and evidently made an impression on the House; but it was marred by one defect. Mr Webb resembled that orator whom the mob at the Eatanswill election recommended to "send a boy home to ask whether he hadn't left his voice under the pillow," and Mr Gladstone, who was extremely deaf, tried in vain to follow the speech. "What is this fellow saying? I can't hear a word —I can't hear a syllable," and gave up the attempt in despair.

Then followed the seconder of the amendment, Sir Joseph Pease, head of a family long and honourably distinguished by its hostility to the opium-traffic, and, if ever there was one, "a man weighted with piety." There was no difficulty about hearing Sir Joseph, who roundly and resonantly backed his brother-Quaker. "We attack to-day, as we have attacked before, the entire revenue derived by India from opium."

Then rose Mr Gladstone, full of candour, amenity, and the desire to make things easy all round. The best plan would be to withdraw the technical motion for getting the Speaker out of the chair. Then Mr Webb's amendment would become a substantive motion, and "My honourable friend near me" (G. W. E. R.) could move his amendment. Then came compliments to Mr Webb. The Prime Minister regretted the physical infirmity which had precluded him from following the honourable member's argument in detail. "I sympathize wholly with the general tone of his remarks, which, I think, tended

INNER SIDE OF A TRANSACTION

to elevate and purify the atmosphere of the House." But some points were vulnerable. Mr Webb had relied on the Resolution of 1891, but that Resolution was founded in great part on the testimony of "experts"; and it was a regrettable fact that "experts" were nearly always wrong, and had been so in various instances, which were now recited with scornful emphasis. As to the question now immediately before the House, the Prime Minister was no partisan. "I do not wish to bind the House. I do not say that the opium-traffic ought not to be extinguished. I wish to keep a perfectly free mind. Before I commit myself to the policy of extinction, I must know how it is to be done." Now he turned to Pease. He respected the honourable baronet's zeal, but questioned his methods. To demand the abolition of a source of revenue, and yet to put nothing in its place, might be an agreeable exercise of philanthrophy but it was not business-like—nay, it was even immoral. Again, we were prescribing for India without ascertaining the wishes of the people prescribed for. Opium had great value as a febrifuge, and it would be wrong to withhold it from those who needed it; though no one would deny that the trade with China had in times past been attended by enormous wrong-doing.

At this point let Mr Thornton resume his tale.

As an effort of denunciatory oratory, shaded by sorrowful regretfulness at the grasping un-Christian conduct of British statesmen in the past, those who were present declared with one accord that they had never heard any forensic effort comparable. To myself, I must own a revelation was there and then vouchsafed of the foundation whereon was built the immense reputation of the Premier as an orator. . . . Let the reader then judge of the horror and dismay which visibly affected anti-opium enthusiasts when it was discovered that the orator's theme had led him gradually to disclose another side of the shield, or, in modern slang, gradually to climb down. . . . All this time, Sir Joseph Pease kept rising partially in his seat, and declaiming in deprecatory dumb-show with his hands, even once venturing upon a passing ejaculation of an indignant character; whereupon those near the Government benches were astonished to hear a *sotto voce* aside from Mr Gladstone of a simple and unparliamentary character: "Shut up, shut up." This has not found its way into Hansard; but, to such a rebuke, with some addition, had one of the most faithful of Mr Gladstone's supporters to submit.

I cannot vouch for the "simple and unparliamentary" aside, but my mind's eye retains a vivid picture of good Sir Joseph bobbing up and down in impotent wrath while Mr Gladstone emphasized his points with menacing forefinger. I think it was the accusation of immorality that most painfully affected Sir Joseph's conscience.

The obligation of strictness in financial proceedings belongs to a very high morality; and political morals cannot be upheld if financial laxity be allowed to come in and obscure the relationship between liabilities undertaken, and the means proposed for meeting them.

Turning at length from the discomfited Pease, the Prime Minister resumed his most moderate and conciliatory mood. After all, everyone in the House was, to a great extent, agreed. Mr Webb proposed a Commission to India. The Government proposed

INNER SIDE OF A TRANSACTION 199

the same thing. They desired as keenly as anyone to "reduce" the opium-traffic, but they were trustees for the revenue of India, and they felt that it would be to the advantage of all concerned if there were a full, exhaustive, and scientific enquiry into all the difficult problems with which the question of opium was so closely intertwined. He proposed, therefore, to adopt the amendment of which his honourable friend, the under-secretary, had given notice, and he now begged leave to move it.

When Mr Gladstone sat down Mr George Curzon, who had been Under-Secretary for India in the Tory Government, congratulated him, with evident sincerity, on the forcible argument and wide grasp of a difficult subject which he had displayed in the last hours of a week of tremendous labour. To Mr Curzon succeeded Mr Channing, Mr Naoroji, and Sir James Fergusson; but Mr Gladstone did not stay to listen. "I think," he said to me, "the bottom is knocked out of this; the division will be all right. I shall go to bed"—which he promptly did. When the division came, Mr Webb was beaten by seventy-nine votes; and the victory had been won, single-handed, by a man in his eighty-fourth year. Well might Mr Thornton be lost in admiration.

VIII

OXFORD

I

It is a terrible prerogative of genius to create permanent libels. For the libelled there is no question of damages, nor for any redress at law. Genius has, by some happy but perhaps unconsidered phrase, attached a particular character to a man, a place, or a thing; and, as long as the language is spoken, the character will stick. It is thus with the months. May is no "merrier" than any other month; nay, for gardeners and flower-lovers much less so, for it brings endless disappointments in the way of bitter east winds, parched soil, night-frosts, and ruined gardens. So May acquires from its proverbial epithet a character which it does not deserve; but, on the other hand, October has a grievance. The finest landscape of the Victorian age was labelled "Chill October"; and the epithet bestowed by genius became indelible. No doubt, in those northern regions where Millais loved to stalk and sketch, it was appropriate enough; but, for men of the Midlands and the South, October has always worn a friendlier guise, and seems to deserve a more exhilarating epithet.

"Bright October" would seem to me a good deal nearer the mark than "chill." Our fathers called October "The Painter's Month." Gamboge and Indian yellow and burnt sienna will supply the prevailing tints, with a splash of vermilion here and there for the mountain ash, and lake for the Virginia creeper; and—above all—cobalt for the sky, which arches over us like a dome of sapphire melting into turquoise. The grass under our feet is still green, and, even after six months' drought, is beginning to be soft. The hedgerows and the woodlands seem decked with amber and topaz and ruby, and the heavy drops of last night's dew flash like a diamond necklace. The south wind blows gently, and to all the sweet smells of earth and vegetation there is added, when we near the abode of men, the winsome odour of brewing. But here memory makes no long stay, pressing on towards the forest of Scotch firs, where the pink bark gives off, under the joint influence of dew and sun, its fascinating fragrance. All round are picturesque scraps of heather and common, the blackberry-bushes all red and yellow in the hedges, and the bilberry bushes underfoot. And presently, through the aisles of the fir-wood, we emerge into a genuine bit of virgin forest, where beech and birch and the gaudy rowan display their strong rivalry of colour. Here come the hounds, winding through the dingle which lies between the forest and the road. The Master is evidently in high spirits. "Plenty of the animal about, I hope?" "Ah! that's all right." "The hedges must be fearfully blind." "Pretty bad going in some places still," and so on, with seasonable pribbles and prabbles, as we move slowly homeward towards the distant kennels.

. . . . . .

Hark! that horrid crash. The Duke of Omnium, no friend either to Reynard or to his pursuers, is shooting his covers.

Slides the bird o'er lustrous woodland,

and a much better bird than what the rather maudlin young man in "Locksley Hall" was dreaming of. Well! well! The Duke may be sending me some pheasants later on; so I will keep my opinion of cover-shooting to myself, and will close my ears to the death-shriek of a wounded hare.

All this (barring the hare) is gay enough; but, though October is a month of exquisite beauty, it is wholly free from languor and *dolce far niente*. It does not invite to repose on grass and heather, nor encourage us to lie supine and watch the sailing clouds through the sun-pierced roof of the "nemorous temple." Its peculiar charm is that its very air breathes energy. It inspires even the lazy and the lethargic to bestir themselves, and "lift up their eyes unto the hills." October is at this moment exercising this wholesome spell on every school in England. Cricket, though unduly prolonged by an unnatural season, has ingloriously dribbled out; and football, the rightful king of the schoolboy's winter, has come to claim his own. The present writer, though trained to play with a "hassock," under all sorts of erroneous rules about "three yards" and "off-side," and taught to call a goal a "base," is not ashamed to say that he would rather see a stoutly-contested fight at Rugby football than any other athletic contest in the world.

But King Football brings with him, I must confess, a suspicion of that quality which Millais expressed in "chill"; and Edward Bowen fixed it in a Harrow song:—

> October brings the cold weather down,
>   When the wind and the rain continue :
> He nerves the limbs that are lazy grown,
>   And braces the languid sinew ;
> So, while we have voices and lungs to cheer,
>   And the winter frost before us,
> Come chant to the King of the mortal year
>   And thunder him out in chorus.

But the frost is not yet, and before it sets in there is time to visit yet another scene where October shows its highest beauty. At Oxford, the blood-red creeper incarnadines towers and cloisters, "making the grey, one red"; and a new generation of "young barbarians," the very flower of English manhood, is entering on its four years of play. As I write, I seem to hear a shriek of angry protest from the villa-dotted "Parks," where the University Reformers mainly have their habitation. "Four years of play?" they cry. "Four years of work, you mean. Four years of anxious toil in the pursuit of culture, or at the least in practical preparation for careers of active utility. People who talk of 'play' are living in the past. To-day in Oxford we worship the great goddess, 'Efficiency.'" It may be so, and the people who say it ought to know. But as long as Oxford remains what she is, and hundreds of young Englishmen flow into her every October from the Public Schools, I shrewdly suspect that play will make a good stand against efficiency. No less do I suspect that the plausible defenders of ancient abuses will continue to suggest, as they have done from the beginning, that a due attention to the one by no means precludes just participation in the other; and that, in effect, play is the strongest ally of efficiency.

In October 1836 Dr Arnold wrote thus to his favourite pupil, Arthur Stanley, then just returning to Oxford for the autumn Term:—

> Some of my most delightful remembrances of Oxford and its neighbourhood are connected with the scenery of the late autumn; Bagley Wood in its golden decline, and the green of the meadows reviving for a while under the influence of the Martinmas summer, and then fading finally off into its winter brown.

To Oxford-bred ears the name of Bagley Wood suggests something more substantial than the pleasures of landscape. For there the landowners— even the President and Fellows of St John's College— tenderly nurture the helpless youth of the timid pheasant; and, now that he has reached maturity and undergone a worthy death, no doubt they are sending him far and wide to members and friends of their opulent society. "I presume," wrote Matthew Arnold to his friend Wyndham Slade, "I presume you are blazing away in your ancestral woods. Need I say that I am passionately fond of the Colchic bird? As for me, I shall never look along the deadly tube again, I expect; however, this will be no great blessing for the brute creation, as I never used to hit them." That was very becoming in a poet, who certainly ought to eschew blood-sports; but the majority of one's friends are not poetic; and manly prose is ever prone to pheasant-shooting. George IV., esteemed a great authority on the pleasures of sense, would not have shared Matthew Arnold's devotion to "the Colchic bird"; for he used to say that, if only a barndoor fowl cost as much as a pheasant, everyone would pronounce it a better thing. However, George IV. had impaired a naturally fine palate by the inconsiderate use of Curaçoa and punch; and I am by no means displeased when the Duke of Omnium shows that he has not forgotten old times.

With the Duke of Omnium's Compliments.
Gatherum Castle, Loamshire.
2 Brace of Pheasants. Killed on 6th October.

I detach the label thoughtfully, and lapse into meditation. Simply roasted? A little monotonous, and, if they are artificially fed, likely to be hard. Boiled, with celery sauce? No, that must be kept for February. *En casserole*—well, there is a great deal to be said for that process, because it combines animal with vegetable food; but, before I commit myself, let me see what Dr Hunter says :—

> Stuff the inside of a cock pheasant with the lean part of a sirloin of beef minced small, and season with pepper and salt. The gravy coming from the beef diffuses itself through the flesh of the pheasant, thereby rendering it more juicy and tender.

This, when compared with the same author's recipe for partridges, sounds rather vapid; so I turn to Dr Hunter's rival oracle, the happily-named Dr Kitchener. But Kitchener apparently sided with his King :—

> The rarity of this bird is its best recommendation. Its flesh is naturally tough, and owes all its tenderness and succulence to the long time it is kept before it is cooked. Until it is *bien mortifiée* it is uneatable. Therefore suspend it by one of its long tail-feathers, and the pheasant's falling from it is the signal of its ripeness and readiness for the spit.

But to eat putrescent food, even when disguised under a French participle, is sheer savagery; so the casserole carries the day.

II

The ugly cry of "efficiency" (which, though it has been adopted by persons so eminently graceful as Lord Rosebery and Lord Curzon, must surely have originated with Mr Gradgrind) reaches me from every corner of Oxford. Not only from the strongholds of Balliol and New College, but from the remotest Parks, from the heights of Headington and Boar's Hill, from the agreeable suburb of Summertown, come the clamant voices. "We are efficient in philosophy." "We are efficient in science." "We are efficient in empire-building." "We are efficient as a school of statesmen." "We are, or are becoming, efficient as a school of medicine." "We train efficient Territorials, who will some day be efficient soldiers; and, if it must be admitted that we are efficient at athletics, that efficiency rather heightens than impairs our efficiency in other departments."

Now I dispute none of these claims. As far as I know they may all be perfectly sound; but I regret to hear them urged. Somehow, to my ear, Oxford and efficiency go ill together. Manchester and efficiency, if you like, or Birmingham and efficiency; or Leeds, or Cardiff. But the name of Oxford suggests to those who love her a more winning idea. To those who love her, I say; for I am well aware that she has her enemies, who murmur against the "Oxford sniff," "the Oxford snigger," and "the Oxford manner" generally; even as I once heard Mr W. E. Forster, that Philistine indeed, say in his wrath about a Fellow of Trinity College, Cambridge, "One could have sworn without knowing it, that he was an Oxford Don." This dislike, though often, as in the instance quoted, based on imperfect knowledge, may yet perhaps point to some peculiarity in the sons of Oxford which marks them off from their fellow-men. What is that peculiarity? Henry Kingsley, himself an Oxford man, had his own idea of it, and also insisted that Chaucer had the same, and that the type had not changed since the fourteenth century. What, he asked, are the popular opinions about Oxford and Cambridge now? The ideal Cambridge man is plodding, thrifty, quiet, diligent, solemn, wise. The ideal Oxford man is fantastic, noisy, extravagant, and given to practical jokes. Most of the "Joe Millers" for many years were laid at the door of "Oxford students." And then he turns back to the *Canterbury Tales* to show that the types are unchanged. "Compare Allan and John, the Cambridge lads who carried the wheat to Trumpington, with Hendy Nicholas and Soloman, the Oxford lads. . . . Was there ever such a perfect Oxford man as Soloman, with his love for gaudry, and his taste for private theatricals with an easy part and a fine dress?"

Henry Kingsley was a man of genius, and, in my judgment, a great writer of fiction; but surely he missed the mark in his description of the typical Oxford man. (On Cambridge I do not presume to dogmatize.) Let us take the epithets one by one. Is the Oxford man fantastic? Well, perhaps, in some of his opinions, Yes. He lives in a "home," not, as was said in a famous passage, "of lost causes," but of causes which have again and again emerged victorious, when Philistinism and Convention had rejoiced over their discomfiture. But "noisy"? Surely no, except at a bump-supper; and boating conviviality is not confined to Oxford. Noisiness is quite inconsistent with the "Oxford sniff," and the "Oxford snigger," and the "Oxford manner" generally. They require for their display an icy calm, and an air which says, as plainly as words could say it, that nothing is really worth much fuss, but, if anything were, it would be the ignorance displayed by the last speaker. Extravagant? If Kingsley was thinking of pecuniary extravagance, his remark would have applied just as well to any other society of men not obliged to work for their living. If he meant literary extravagance— the Corinthian style of utterance,—the memories of Newman and Church and Arnold and Jowett would rise up to contradict him. Yet again, practical joking? Some colour is lent to the allegation by a passage in the first chapter of *Kenilworth* as well as in more modern fiction; but the most successful instances of that abominable pleasantry in our time were perpetrated, one at Cambridge and the other on board a man-of-war. And then, again, "Gaudry" and private theatricals? As to "Gaudry," it is a fact even painfully notorious that the pride of the Oxford undergraduate at the present day is to be dressed as shabbily, as untidily, and as incongruously as possible; and, as to theatricals, why Cambridge had her "A.D.C." and her Frank Burnand forty years before the Oxford University Dramatic Society made the first fame of that admirable comedian who is now Father Adderley.

No. The offence of the "Oxford manner" is not in extravagance or boisterousness, or love of finery, or of showing-off. It is of quite a different kind. It consists, if I know it, in a calm assurance, a quiet but immovable conviction, never expressed but never forgotten, that Oxford is by far the greatest thing of its kind in the Universe, and that to belong to it, however feeble one's powers, however petty one's attainments, lifts one—

> Above the smoke and stir of this dim spot
> Which men call Earth.

Even an Oxford man can conceive that this manner may not be wholly acceptable to those who were reared in other shades; but, if it offend us, let us not reason of it, but regard it, and pass on.

Dismissing manner, and turning to more essential characteristics, what is the idea which Oxford suggests? Is it grace? Is it amenity? Is it the sense for beauty, the hatred for rawness and valgarity? Is it a disinterested zeal for truth, a real desire to see things as they are? Is it a chivalrous devotion to the weaker side? Is it a generous tolerance of opinions which we do not share?

I protest that my ideal of Oxford, and of the typical Oxford man, includes all these attributes; and, where these are present, the character is fairly near perfection, and there is no crying need for efficiency. Not that I would unduly disparage that useful but pedestrian quality. If the Oxford man, as I conceive of him and have tried to describe him—the true Euphues,—can superadd efficiency to his other virtues, he will perhaps be a more valuable citizen; but he will not be a more agreeable member of society. And, if he puts efficiency first among his aims, and takes it for granted that the more spiritual graces will be added to him, he will find—or rather, perhaps I should say, his friends will find—that Oxford does not impart her richest gifts to those who serve her with a divided devotion.

I suppose there is something impalpable and elusive about the true spirit of Oxford—something which, like the rainbow, one can see, but not grasp. For not otherwise can I account for the fact that, when so many authors have set out to describe undergraduate life at Oxford, not one has succeeded. Henry Kingsley, whom I have already quoted, tried his hand in *Stretton* and *Ravenshoe*, and seems, as I have just said, to miss the mark. Tom Hughes endeavoured to make Tom Brown the schoolboy grow naturally into Tom Brown the undergraduate, but failed through his undue tendency to preach. *Loss and Gain* is a work of genius, but theology never mixes well with fiction. *Hugh Heron* and *Fawcit of Balliol* are perhaps nearer the mark. *Downy V. Green*, which depicts the adventures of a Rhodes Scholar, is excruciatingly funny. *Keddy* dealt with a seamier side of Oxford life; and *The Compleat Oxford Man*, just published, has been described as a "cinema-show" of Oxford up to date. In discussing this theme Sir Arthur Quiller-Couch drops, for once, into what seems like paradox, and affirms that, after all is said and done, "*Verdant Green* marks the nearest approach yet made to a representative Oxford novel." If asked to give reasons for this judgment, he will reply that, in the first place, *Verdant Green* is youthful and high-spirited—essential qualities in a book which would describe what Lord Houghton called "our favoured school of learning and larking"; and, in the second, because it conveys some sense of the "glamour" of Oxford. "You may argue that glamour is an illusion which will wear off in time. To this I answer that, while it lasts, this glamour is just as much a fact as the *Times* newspaper or St Paul's Cathedral, and until you recognize it for a fact and feature of the place, and allow for it, you have not the faintest prospect of realizing Oxford. Her glamour is for him to catch who can, whether in prose or rhyme."

Most Oxford men would, I think, agree that the man who taught that "glamour" most effectively in prose was Matthew Arnold; and Sir Arthur himself—the beloved "Q" of *The Oxford Magazine*—has done the same in verse. To those names I must add that of Mr St John Lucas, who, in *The Return*, has given us a poem about Oxford, which is truly interpretative. Space forbids to quote it in full, and to choose one's favourite verses seems to disparage the rest, but it must be done:—

      I will go up on Cumnor height
        Amid the early mist,
    And watch the city change to white
        Her spires of amethyst.

      Easy and beautiful the path
        That leads to her below;
    O short and beautiful the path,
        But yet I will not go.

OXFORD

O Men who tread the ancient ways
   About the lovely town,
Fair be your sojourn, long your days!
But my Men have gone down.

The elms are bare, the creepers die
   In scarlet on the wall:
It is a place of ghosts, and I
   Am ghostlier than all.

III

You have given us so admirably Oxford as the gownsman sees it, that even a Manchester man can feel something of its glamour. But what is Oxford to the *townsman*? Is it a glamorous place to him?—Yours, etc.,   A SON OF THE DIOCESE.

Before I attempt to answer the question — so agreeably put, — I ponder on the signature. It certainly is wide enough. The Diocese of Oxford— for that, I presume, is "the Diocese" to which my friend refers — covers the three large counties of Oxon, Bucks, and Berks. My friend may therefore spring from the fat pastures of the Vale of Aylesbury, or the woodlands of Whaddon Chase, or the beech-clad recesses of the Chilterns; from the "distant Wychwood bowers" or the "warm, green-muffled Cumnor Hills"; from the slopes of the White Horse, or the breezy uplands of the Ridgeway, upon which Mr Chesterton, in his latest ballad, has conferred a fresh immortality. Something, though perhaps not much, depends on these alternatives. If the "Son of the Diocese" belonged by birth to its remoter districts, Oxford may be little more than a name to him; for a Bishop, unless he be a Wilberforce, is a rather flimsy bond between three counties, and there is nothing beyond this diocesan unity to make a son of North Bucks or South Berks feel at home in Oxford. But, if a man was born somewhere within sight of the "Dreaming Spires," or even near enough to know by report the fairyland out of which they spring, he must perforce feel something of that "glamour" which the poet and the essayists extol. "His father had told him that, just beyond those darking wolds, lay the most beautiful city in the whole world. 'How far off?' asked the boy. 'Fifteen mile, across through Ipsden. A matter of eight and twenty by Benson and Dorchester.' 'It isn't Seville, is it? Of course it is not. Seville is the finest town in the world.' 'Oxford beats it hollow.'" Henry Kingsley, who knew the district and its inhabitants, puts this dialogue into the mouths of two peasants looking out on the wolds of Oxfordshire from the towering summit of Boisey Hill, near Maidenhead; my experience leads me to think that he was right, and that the "glamour" of Oxford extends, from its centre at Carfax, to a wide circumference.

But the "Son of the Diocese" may urge that he asked me not about the county, but about the city, of Oxford. "What is Oxford to the *townsman*? Is it a glamorous place to him?" Here my answer is quite positive. *Yes*—and yes a hundred times. I have known Oxford and the people who dwell there for forty years, and I should say that the townsman loves his town with a passionate love. Broadly speaking, no one willingly leaves Oxford. Those who are born there know their blessings, and remain, all their life long, in the delicious surroundings where Providence placed them. If by exigencies of trade or profession they are driven away for a space, they return like homing pigeons. They have indeed heard of London, and many of them have seen it; but they all dislike it. Perhaps Oxford has bewitched them with her "glamour," or entangled them in her mesh. Anyhow, she has made them hers. The "townsman" loves his town, or rather the citizen his city. But the relations of the City to the University, of the Town to the Gown, are rather more complicated. Some fifty years ago, Dr Jeune, then Vice-Chancellor, and afterwards Bishop of Peterborough, speaking at the Mayor's banquet, tried to draw a moral from the city's name. "Just consider its derivation. If *Ox-ford*, or *Oxen-ford*, had not become the site of a university, what would it probably still have been but a resting-place for a few cattle-drovers? But, under the influence of the university, it has become a city of palaces, of towers, and trees, and pleasant waters."

The relations between the City and the University resemble the relations between Labour and Capital. Neither could do much without the other; but which of the two contributes most to the alliance is a highly contentious question. The gownsmen may say, with perfect truth, that the university made Magdalen Tower and the Radcliffe Dome, the Lime Walk at Trinity, and the gardens of Wadham. But the townsman may reply that the Parish Churches which dominate the peerless High Street are to the full as beautiful as Oriel or Brasenose; that the proud Isis and the lilied Cherwell owe nothing to Doctors and Proctors; and that "Tom" sent his melodious note across the fields from Osney Abbey long before Wren built his belfry at Christ Church.

Whether in the eyes of the townsman the actual presence of the gownsman adds to, or detracts from, the amenities of the place is also a disputable point. Everyone who knows Oxford through fiction knows all about the Fifth of November as celebrated there, and the strange outbreaks of chartered barbarism which, in the old days of "town-and-gown rows," used to signalize that night. I well remember that a worthy citizen with whom I lodged once said to me, "Our mob"—that is, the townsmen's mob—"is a very savage one," and certainly there was a good deal to justify his verdict. It was permissible to imagine that, in these annual outbreaks of senseless violence, the young citizens were, all unconsciously, exacting vengeance for long-forgotten insults inflicted in darker ages by the alien youths who frequented the university on the artificers and merchants of the town. That, of course, is conjectural; but what is certain is that an undergraduate always found it very difficult to make friends with a townsman. It was the constant teaching of Ruskin and Tom Hughes and the two Kingsleys that difference of station and occupation ought to be no bar to a genuine friendship. Under their guidance many an undergraduate has tried to establish such a friendship as subsisted between Lancelot Smith and Tregarva, or between "Egerton's Brother" and Egerton himself. But again and again the effort has been frustrated by some strange survival from the old tradition of natural enmities; and the undergraduate has learnt that the townsman regards with a profound, and perhaps not unreasonable, suspicion the advances of rich and idle youths, who use his city as a play-place, and, when their four years' fun is over, disappear to whence they came. This mistrustful estrangement of class from class, always and everywhere deplorable, is specially to be deplored in a university; and I rejoice to know that at this moment Oxford is making one more effort in the direction of brotherhood. There lies before me as I write a strong statement of the mischief of estrangement and a suggestion for remedying it. "To set class against class is imputed as the greatest of crimes to a politician — to bridge the gulf between classes is certainly the greatest of social duties." It is admitted on all hands that we are now confronted by social problems of formidable urgency; and some of those who observe the signs of the times believe that among the privileged classes there is "a quickened conscience and a livelier feeling of responsibility." Of this I am not so very sure. I should have said that, under the poisonous influence of the South African War, with its combined evils of jingoism and money-worship, our zeal for social reform had palpably declined. "The Christian Social Union," asserting the Gospel as the rule of social life, was a natural product of forces at work between 1880 and 1890; but would scarcely have sprung from the mental soil of to-day. If it be true that zeal for social service is reviving, I pray that Oxford may once again bear her part in that highest of endeavours. "Oxford by itself tends to be something of a hothouse. It provides unlimited opportunity for theory, but a very limited range of experience. Such theory is apt to be abstract, thin, and inadequate to life; and, perhaps, this is why the Oxford man, 'who only Oxford knows,' so often makes an unfavourable impression on the outsider, and why the term, 'Oxford manner,' is not always used in a complimentary sense."

All this is terribly true; but is it remediable, and, if so, what is the remedy? It might seem that the most obvious course would be for men, while they are undergraduates at Oxford, to make themselves acquainted with the lives and homes of the mean streets and hidden slums which lurk behind the manifest glories of "the High" and "the Broad." But beyond question this is difficult. In the first place, the Term only lasts eight weeks, and it is a bad plan to be always dropping work and taking it up again. Then the undergraduate has to contend with the suspiciousness of which I have already spoken; or he meets, to his disgust, that parasitical spirit which regards a gownsman as its lawful prey. Then, again, there is the difficulty of combining social work with fixed studies and the requirements of examinations. A man who by "slumming" loses his First and gets a Third, ultimately injures the cause which he is trying to serve. And yet, once more, work among the poor tends to separate a man from the companions of his own class and type, and, by interfering with friendship, robs him of the richest boon which Oxford has to give. Men who have passed the undergraduate stage, and have settled themselves for good in the service of the university, can indeed take their part, with excellent result, in the life of the city. Let the names of T. H. Green in the past, and the Rev. L. R. Phelps in the present, illustrate what I mean. But for the undergraduate who wishes to know the life of the poor as it really is, and so to train himself for good citizenship, the university "Settlements" in London and other great towns offer the readiest opportunity. "The university Settlements are organizations specially contrived to create in the university a knowledge of the facts of the social problem, and to establish that permanent and active connexion between the university and the poorer classes, without which such knowledge is fruitless, if not impossible."

From a term of residence at a "Settlement" men come back to Oxford "triumphantly certain of the enormous good which they have gained." They have acquired an insight into the facts of life which not all the blue-books in the world could convey. It is now more than twenty years since a desire to acquire this insight, and to impart in return some of the blessings which Oxford's sons have received from her, led to the foundation of Oxford House in Bethnal Green. It has had its followers and imitators all over London, and together they have rendered glorious service. Yet, we are told, the Oxford men of to-day take less interest than their predecessors took in these characteristic products of Oxford; and for that reason men whose hearts are in the social question are making a special appeal to the better mind of the undergraduate world.

To bridge the social gulf is a work to which Oxford is definitely committed. She has been so closely connected with the origin of Settlements in the past that on her lies a special duty of maintaining them in the present. For those to whom her continuous corporate life is a real thing, the task of continuing and extending their work is not optional but obligatory. This generation inherits both the privilege and the duty.

The appeal is clinched by the bold suggestion that some personal experience of life at a Settlement should be regarded as a normal part of an Oxford education. "The true question which everyone should ask himself is not, Have I any clear reason for going? but, Have I any clear reason for staying away?"

IV

A correspondent says that "Oxford as an institution has its dark side"; and apparently he thinks that its bright side has been too exclusively considered.

"Age after age," he says, "men have been rearing this thing of emotional power, and I would that you showed your numberless audience something of the stern realities of consequences of youthful tendencies. How easy it is to give way in our likes to the 'glamour' of things! *But real men don't.*" And then my friend makes this startling request: "Please tell us what Oxford is to the man who is in earnest; *say, to General Booth*, or any other man you may be able to interpret."

This passage really teems with suggestiveness, and the area of discussion which it opens is wide indeed. "The man who is in earnest" either has, or has not, been connected with Oxford. If he has, we can trace the softening and beautifying effects of the university on his already strenuous character; if not, we can speculate on what he would have been if Oxford rather than Homerton or Cheshunt had been his nursing mother. In the former case we can illustrate our theme by reference to concrete examples, such as Dr Horton, of Hampstead. In the latter, we can fall back upon the pleasures of imagination. "William Booth, of Balliol," would make a capital companion story to "Hugh Heron, of Christ Church"; and for more serious-minded readers the enquiry might take the form of dissertation—"What would have been the effect of Loder's on the Life and Ministry of C. H. Spurgeon?" or "Hugh Price Hughes considered in relation to the Oxford Movement."

It certainly is not news to me, and I should scarcely

think it is news to my readers, that "Oxford as an institution has its dark side." That side is perceptible in everything that has been written about Oxford, prose and verse, theology and fiction, though Memory dwells more willingly on the brighter side, and Hope naturally looks towards the sunrise. Oxford is an enchanted and inspiring world; but the darker side is always there; and at Oxford, as elsewhere, experience reveals the hidden tragedy which waits upon the brightest aspects of human life.

"Age after age," says the critic, "men have been rearing this thing of emotional power," and the context seems to mean that this "emotional power" may have some injurious effect on the hearts which feel it. Probably this is true, and the ethical Dryasdust (own brother to the famous antiquary of the same name) is never tired of telling us that the emotions, untempered by reason and unregulated by will, are dangerous guides. From eighteen to twenty-two, I suppose, our emotions are in their most excitable state; our reason is blinded by passion, and our will is only half-developed. Coming from the restraints of home or school to the almost complete liberty of Oxford, it is easy enough for a lad to make shipwreck. Liberty is the most exhilarating draught that the soul can drink; but, unless it is swallowed with due care and preparation, it may bewilder and even intoxicate. A man deeply versed in the knowledge of young hearts, alike at Public Schools and at the Universities, once spoke thus, at Oxford, to the typical undergraduate who, meaning everything that is good and upright, has failed through mere weakness—perhaps an uncontrolled emotionalism:—

> Unawares, under influence, through mere thoughtlessness, for want of one grain of firmness, you have wasted your time, you have failed in your examination, you have run into debt, you have secrets which you cannot tell, your life is a spoilt life, you talk sometimes as if you wished it gone. Death, death literal and self-inflicted, has sometimes been the stream from this spring.

The "dark side" of Oxford, on which my friend insists, is sufficiently indicated in the words just quoted; but they do not exhaust the possibilities of Tragedy. Oxford holds, for all who belong to her, those trials which St Paul taught his Corinthian friends to reckon as "human"—incidental to the common lot of man,—and, besides these, some special trials of her own.

> Bright visions of glory, that vanished too soon,
> Bright day-dreams that departed ere manhood's noon;
> Attachments, by fate or by falsehood reft,
> Companions of early days, lost or left—

these are the everyday topics of pensive retrospection. But, in addition to all these, Oxford has the tragedies which belong to her specially as a place of thinking —tragedies of mental darkness and the eclipse of faith; tragedies of comradeship perverted into enmity; tragedies of changed sides and lost leadership; tragedies of conviction, which have reversed the whole purpose and meaning of a life.

Even in these tragedies of the intellect and the

conscience, emotionalism may have its part. If we have been passionately in love with our beliefs, it is agony to part with them. If we have sworn ourselves to a particular standard we cannot unmoved see it go down; if we have built our hopes upon a friend we resent his conversion to the other side as a personal injury. But I cannot see—as the critic seems to think—that "Oxford without the glamour" would be a more valuable possession to the nation than Oxford as she is. Surely it makes for the elevation of national life that there should be a place where English citizens learn, while they are quite young, to cultivate romance, to believe in ideals, to cherish dreams, which, though they may be illusory, are golden while they last; or to give themselves with self-forgetting ardour even to causes which later life may show to have been mistaken. "Oxford without the glamour"—an Oxford of red brick and straight avenues, electric trams and overhead wires — an Oxford snorting efficiency and boycotting the emotions—would have tragedies of its own, and would, I firmly believe, have infinitely less influence for good upon the life of England.

"How easy," says the critic, "how easy it is to give way in our likes to the 'glamour' of things! *But real men don't.*" Don't they? I respectfully dissent. It is "the glamour" of things that inspires great discoverers, like Livingstone and Sturt and Eyre, to wring Nature's secrets from her at the peril of their own lives. It is "glamour" that enlists such warriors of the Cross as St Francis Xavier and Henry Martyn and John Coleridge Patteson. It is the glamour of a glorious though mistaken patriotism which draws young Englishmen, by an irresistible attraction, from the sanctities and the serenities of home to the living hell of war. The discoverer and the missionary and the soldier may, indeed, be victims of a strong delusion, but, in spite of the critic, I hold them to be "real men."

"Please tell us what Oxford is to the man who is in earnest?" Let the Methodist Revival of the eighteenth century and the Oxford Movement of the nineteenth—which have between them changed the face of English-speaking Christendom — be the first to answer. Let the incessant stream of vigorous intellects and stout hearts which year by year pours out of Oxford into the active service of the State make reply, telling what each of those heads and hearts has owed to Oxford. "What Oxford is to the man who is in earnest" Whitefield and the Wesleys, Keble, Pusey, Newman, and Liddon have told us. "The man who is in earnest"—do we forget Thomas Arnold and Arthur Stanley and Frederick Maurice and Tom Hughes? "The man who is in earnest"—to whom, in these later days, does that title so rightly belong as to Gladstone, with whom every belief was a religious faith and every act of life a work for God? And this is what Gladstone said of Oxford even when she had abandoned him: "I have loved her with a passionate love." A quarter of a century later his loyalty was still undimmed: "There is not a man who has passed through that great and famous university that can say with more truth than I can say—'I love her from the bottom of my heart.'" From his deathbed this "man who was in earnest" sent this final benediction: "There is no expression of Christian sympathy which I value more than that of the God-fearing and God-sustaining University of Oxford. I served her, perhaps mistakenly, but to the best of my ability. My most earnest prayers are hers, to the uttermost and to the last."

V

A friendly reader, not tired of this inexhaustible theme, makes a suggestion—Oxford from the point of view of the outside struggler—*e.g.* "Jude the Obscure," *i.e.* the case of self-taught men, with a thirst for culture, who feel that their spirits' true home is Oxford, and yet never can force their way through her doors.

"It is a city of light," said Jude to himself.
"The tree of knowledge grows there," he added a few steps further on.
"It is a place that teachers of men spring from and go to."
"It is what we call a castle, manned by scholarship and religion."
After this figure he was silent a long while, till he added:
"It would just suit me."

I am grateful to my friend, if only for sending me back to this remarkable though saddening book. My

"Commentary on Jude" and his experiences shall be my answer to my friend's enquiry.

The longings of an impecunious youth for the blessings of a University Education have often been treated in fiction. Farrar and Charles Kingsley and Tom Hughes have all tried their hands on the theme, which indeed makes a potent appeal to all generous natures. The love of Oxford in particular, as it might affect a shepherd's boy on the Berkshire wolds, was pictured by Henry Kingsley, whose more famous brother had laid the scene of his story at Cambridge. There are some points in which Mr Hardy's book recalls both *Alton Locke* and *Silcote*, but the essential pathos of his story is all his own.

Jude Fawley was self-taught—self-taught in the intervals of a laborious trade, and self-taught to a point of familiarity with the classics which was, to say the least of it, unusual. He has set his heart on being a clergyman, some day perhaps a Bishop, "living a pure, energetic, wise, Christian life," and giving away £4500 out of his £5000 a year. With this end in view he resolves to settle in Oxford (which Mr Hardy perversely calls by another name), work at his trade there, save money, and then—"One of those colleges *shall* open its doors to me—*shall* welcome whom it now would spurn; if I wait twenty years for the welcome." And so, with his stone-cutting tools in his bag, he marches, through his native Wessex, into Oxford—"a species of Dick Whittington, whose spirit was touched to finer issues than a mere material gain." He soon obtained employment at his craft, and in his leisure wandered about the quadrangles and lanes and cloisters of which he had read so much, evoking as he went the spirits of the men who had long ago made Oxford famous. What Mr Hardy calls the "sentiment" of Oxford and what others call her glamour, "ate further and further into him; till he probably knew more about those buildings, materially, artistically, and historically, than any one of their inmates. But now, when he found himself actually on the spot of his enthusiasm, Jude perceived how far away from the object of that enthusiasm he really was. Only a wall divided him from those happy young contemporaries of his with whom he shared a common mental life; men who had nothing to do from morning till night but to read, mark, learn and inwardly digest. Only a wall—but what a wall!" How to surmount, or pierce, or undermine the wall became now the object of poor Jude's life. As he gazed into the space beyond, he said: " Let me only get there, and the rest is but a matter of time and energy." But how to get there? He soon came to see quite clearly that to obtain entrance to a college by open scholarships or exhibitions was impossible for a man who had only the fag-ends of hard-working days for study, competing with "those who had passed their lives under trained teachers and had worked on ordained lines." The alternative plan was to save money enough to cover all his expenses, and enter a college by simple matriculation, for which his equipment of scholarship was adequate; but he soon realized that, at the rate at which, with the best of fortune, he would be able to save money, fifteen years must elapse before he would be able to matriculate. "The undertaking was hopeless." By degrees he came to the conclusion that "this hovering outside the walls of the colleges, as if expecting some arm to be stretched out from them to lift him inside, wouldn't do." His next step was to choose five of the most appreciative and far-seeing men among the Heads of Colleges, to whom he wrote letters, "briefly stating his difficulties, and asking their opinion on his stranded situation." Four of the Heads took no notice of his letters. The master of Biblioll College wrote as follows:—

SIR,—I have read your letter with interest, and, judging from your description of yourself as a working man, I venture to think that you will have a much better chance of success in life by remaining in your own sphere and sticking to your trade than by adopting any other course. That, therefore, is what I advise you to do.—Yours faithfully,   T. TETUPHENAY.

To Mr J. Fawley, stonemason.

With the rest of poor Jude's frustrated and hapless life this chapter has no concern. Let me turn back to the questions which started it:—"What is Oxford from the point of view of the outside struggler, such as 'Jude the Obscure?' Is the attitude of Dr Tetuphenay a typical one?"

(1) What Oxford is to the "outside struggler," who wishes to belong to the university, is, I suppose,

pretty well known to many of my readers. The struggler feels as Jude felt, that, once inside the wall, he could fulfil all his ambitions—perhaps ambitions of service, perhaps of mere fame and opulence. Sometimes the struggler obtains what he desires. The "educational ladder" has long been a favourite ideal with social reformers, and boys are climbing it every day. When a more fortunate Jude has made his way, by scholarship or exhibition, into a college, I believe that he is always received with open arms. Oxford is a place alive with generous emotions, and undergraduates who have had their way made for them regard with genuine admiration the cleverness and energy and perseverance which have carried Jude over the wall into the desired enclosure.

But how does an unsuccessful Jude—a Jude who has had no particular schooling and is therefore hopelessly disqualified for competition with highly-taught boys—how does he regard Oxford? I fear rather bitterly. He sees these large endowments, and beautiful buildings, and generous institutes of all kinds, designed long ago by religion or patriotism for the service of the poor. He knows that from these advantages he is hopelessly excluded; and there is gall in the thought that three-fourths of the lucky youths who now enjoy what was meant for his birthright are absolutely indifferent to their intellectual opportunities, and regard Oxford as a glorious play-place—only that, and nothing more. The Bishop of Oxford seemed to have this thought in mind when on the 30th of April 1912 he addressed the League of Young Liberals on " Industrial Unrest." Surely there can be no more disturbing reflection for the young and ardent minds of an industrial population than that educational advantages for which they vainly long are daily squandered in waste and idleness. When we hear of a millionaire's son who leaves the university owing forty thousand pounds, it is natural to say that he might as well have done his squandering elsewhere, and left Oxford for such as would know how to make use of her gifts. The annals of Ruskin College would, I fancy, teach the same lesson.

(2) "Is the attitude of Dr Tetuphenay a typical one?" I should say that it is characteristic rather than typical. I mean that the letter is precisely what the Head, who is nicknamed Tetuphenay, would, under the circumstances, have written; but a good many Heads would have answered differently.

The real Tetuphenay worshipped success. He had a most unevangelical hatred and contempt for failure. To succeed, to attain, to "come off"—this was, in Tetuphenay's mind, the real good of human life. Failure, in whatever line, was to be scorned, not pitied. He was, according to his lights, sincerely benevolent; and, if a half-educated stonemason, already older than the general run of freshmen, had proposed to enter Biblioll College with a view to success in one of what are called "the learned professions," the Master would certainly have discouraged him. He would have felt that such an undergraduate would not be sufficiently successful in the schools to secure a Fellowship; would have, after leaving Oxford, to starve at the Bar or slave at Journalism; and would never come near the front rank in anything (the idea of Holy Orders Tetuphenay would have disregarded). Whereas, if the stonemason stuck to his stonemasonry, he might make money enough to live comfortably, and buy a few books, and perhaps might attain a leading position in his trade, become a Trades Union official, or even some day an M.P. The advice would have been honestly given, and not unkindly meant. Of course, if Jude had been a really remarkable scholar, or metaphysician, or mathematician, or scientist, Tetuphenay would have welcomed him with ardour; would have watched his career at every point, and have trained him for the highest honours; but Tetuphenay had no use for mediocrity.

Other Heads would have behaved differently. They would all have been alike in welcoming first-rate ability, whether it came from the pit or the ploughtail; but mediocrity would have been handled differently by different men. Some would have enjoyed the sense of patronage; would have made the entrance examination as easy as possible, would very likely have found money for college fees; and would have revelled in the knowledge that they had a sentient creature bound and helpless in their grasp. To establish a kind of property in a penniless student, and to make him the subject of fads and experiments, is to some minds a keen delight. Others would have persuaded themselves that Jude was something quite out of the common. They would have been, as indeed I should be, amazed by his range of knowledge acquired under such profound disadvantages, and they would have clung to the belief that they had discovered a genius, "in a white blouse, with stone-dust in the creases of his clothes," until the genius turned out to be nothing superhuman, and then they would have been disappointed and disagreeable. Yet, again, there are some—but the excellent must always be the few—who would have combined the commonsense of Dr Tetuphenay with intellectual insight and the spirit of Christian brotherhood. I could fancy such an one saying to Jude: "It is a serious thing to change one's profession, even though it be the humblest. Therefore, weigh well the step which you are contemplating. If, on full reflection, you decide to become an undergraduate, I will take all your disadvantages into account, and if I see the signs of a mind at work in your papers, I will try to get you admitted. As to expenses, I have access to a fund out of which some small grant might be made; and perhaps by working at your trade in the vacations you might make a little for yourself. Anyhow, you apply to us in the name of Brotherhood,

> And our free latch-string never was drawn in
> Against the poorest child of Adam's kin."

IX

CAMBRIDGE

A YOUNG man of great possessions but less intelligence once heard in casual conversation some reference to "The Isis." Being not the least ashamed of ignorance, he cheerfully enquired: "The Isis; what is that? Is it a river?" "Oh, yes; don't you know? It's what the Thames is called at Oxford." "Really? What is it called at Cambridge?"

That artless youth, with his pardonable vagueness about the universities—pardonable, for he was not a university man but a Hussar—was recalled to my memory by the following letter:—

> After Oxford, may I ask if you will tell us something about Cambridge, especially with regard to its influence on the Liberal thought and action of the nation?

This request makes me feel rather like the Hussar. My friends have a right to whatever I can give them; so I comply, but not without misgiving. If this volume chances to fall into the hands of a Cambridge man, he will snort defiance and contempt. Probably he will remind me that the Hussar was at least conscious of his own ignorance, and, instead of attempting to impart knowledge, sought humbly to acquire it. "Ignorance," said Mr Gladstone, "is often pardonable, but pretension is always despicable."

The thesis propounded by my friend divides itself naturally into two parts—(1) "Something about Cambridge," and (2) "It's influence on Liberal thought and action." In attempting to discuss the first part, I must avow myself frankly a partisan, and a partisan whose prejudices were contracted some forty years ago. On my lips, "Something about Cambridge" must mean something of what we Oxford men thought about Cambridge soon after the middle of the nineteenth century. No doubt it was a tissue of delusions, but I have no difficulty in recalling it. In the first place, we thought that Cambridge men were roughs—that they smoked strong pipes and drank too much beer; that they delighted in the company of bargees, and in the lower forms of sport; and that even their highest attainments in scholarship and science were concealed from view by a studied rudeness. Dean Stanley, himself the fine flower of Oxford culture, wrote, about a brother-clergyman, that he had "some of the savage qualities of the Cantabrigians." We at Oxford prided ourselves on our refinement and good manners, and even Thackeray (who disliked us) was careful to point out that the foolish Mr Fitzroy Timmins was "an Oxford man, and very polite." When that fearfully precocious youth, Edward Gibbon, went up to Magdalen College, Oxford, he found the

Dons of that glorious place "steeped in port and prejudice"; but they did not drink beer. When the Oxford tutor, in Henry Kingsley's delightful tale of *Stretton*, desires to worm a secret out of his unsuspecting pupil, he asks him to supper, and plies him with White Hermitage, saying: "You won't find any beer here, Maynard; that infernal compound of malt, hops, and raw beef, which is good for nothing but to irritate the temper, and which accounts for so much of our national history."

But, just when Kingsley was writing that pungent sentence, a bright light of the University of Cambridge —the incomparable "C. S. C."—was singing a very different strain—

> Say, what is Coffee, but a noxious berry,
>   Born to keep used-up Londoners awake?
> What is Falernian, what are Port and Sherry,
>   But vile concoctions to make dull heads ache?
> He that would shine, and petrify his Tutor,
> Should drink draught Allsopp in its native pewter.

In that contrast you have the difference between Oxford and Cambridge as we then understood it.

As regards external characteristics, I was quoting the other day from Chaucer to show that, five centuries ago, smart clothing, and a tendency to "show off," were regarded as typical of Oxford men. The smart clothing, or at least a scrupulous neatness, lasted into my own time; whereas we believed that Cambridge men habitually ran about their town (Oxford is a City) with bare legs and shrunk flannels, and that the wearer of a tall hat, even on Sundays, would soon find it bashed about his ears.

As regards more important characteristics, our sublime self-complacency bore us triumphantly through. We firmly believed that our ethical standard was infinitely higher than that of Cambridge, and we used to observe, with a truly Pharisaic satisfaction, that there was no district of Oxford which at all corresponded to Barnwell. Now, all this was probably great nonsense; but we, who believed it, were not really much to blame. All we knew about Cambridge was drawn from novels written by Cambridge men, and those authors were certainly at some pains to display the seamy side of Cambridge life and character. Thackeray did his best to be impartially disagreeable as between the two universities; but, when he was narrating the adventures of Pen and George Warrington, and Harry Foker and Lord Glenlivat, we knew very well that his "Oxbridge" was to be found on the banks of the Cam. Indeed, "Stunning Warrington," with his beer and his pipe and his mathematics, his victory over Bill Simes the bargeman, and his partiality for "the Miss Notleys, the haberdashers," might have stood, in Oxford eyes, for a type of Cambridge. *Sketches of Cantabs*—an extraordinarily clever little book of pen-and-ink caricatures—gives the lighter side of what seemed a disagreeable society. The chapters afterwards expurgated from *Alton Locke* were written with the express purpose of showing Cambridge at its worst; and Dr Farrar, in *Julian Home*, drew a peculiarly unpleasant picture of a Cambridge undergraduate's downfall.

Every now and then it happened that the difference, clear enough as a general rule, between an Oxford man and a Cambridge man was obliterated in a particular instance. The Rev. E. M. Young, sometime Head Master of Sherborne, and formerly Fellow of Trinity College, Cambridge, was distinguished by a refinement so painfully oppressive that Mr W. E. Forster was beguiled into exclaiming: "One could have sworn, without being told, that he was an Oxford Don"; and a graduate of Trinity, speaking of a graduate of King's, said: " I call —— a typical King's man, and by that I mean a Cambridge man who wishes to be like an Oxford one"—a deep saying, which none but Cantabrigians can interpret.

So much for "something about Cambridge," as high-sniffing Oxford viewed her in the 'seventies. The second part of my theme is not so easily handled —"The influence of Cambridge on the Liberal thought and action of the nation." It is rather a far cry to Bacon and Milton and Newton; and, though it is true that those three great men were reared at Cambridge, one scarcely dare affirm that Cambridge made them what they were, or can claim their influence as a creation of her own. In a later century, Cambridge has spoken through her poets. The nursing-mother of Byron and Coleridge, and Wordsworth and Tennyson may indeed make her boast of "Poets whose thoughts enrich the blood of the world"; but did their influence go to help "Liberal thought and action"? Byron, yes—"the passionate and dauntless soldier of a forlorn hope, who, ignorant of the future and unconsoled by its promises, nevertheless waged against the conservatism of the old possible world his fiery battle; waged it till he fell—waged it with such splendid and imperishable excellence of sincerity and thought." Byron died young, and perhaps it was just as well for Liberalism that he did; for his later life might possibly have belied the heroic promise of his youth. Coleridge, who began life as Radical, Republican, Pantisocrat—Heavens, what a word!—became, as Matthew Arnold said, "wrecked in a mist of opium," and abandoned poetry and philosophy for the unheroic task of "writing MS. sermons for lazy clergymen." Wordsworth had known what it was to "stand on the top of golden hours," in the glorious dawn of the French Revolution; and he lived to be the "Lost Leader" and the author of the *Ecclesiastical Sonnets*. Tennyson, in "Locksley Hall," fired the hearts of English boys with the promise of a time when mankind should be delivered from the tyranny of the purse and the sword, and when reason and love should rule the world—and he ended with "Hands all round!" and an ode to the Duke of Argyll. Even more painful was the apostasy of Kingsley, who had given us "The Poacher's Widow" and "Alton Locke's Song"; and yet sprawled in homage before Governor

Eyre, and extolled the House of Lords as representing "all heritable products of moral civilization, such as independence, chivalry, etc." That *etcetera* cannot easily be beaten.

There was another Cambridge man, of whose services to Liberal thought I should feel much more confident. Macaulay was a typical son of Cambridge, in his independence, his thoroughness, and his rugged self-confidence. He was, indeed, a Philistine; inaccessible to ideas, concentrated on the things of time and sense, and contemptuous of all who had a wider vision. But he was, in every fibre of his vigorous nature, a lover of civil and intellectual freedom; and modern Liberalism, though he would never have accepted all its ideals, owes a great debt to his zeal for personal liberty. Limits of space would not allow me to enumerate all the names—Connop Thirlwall and Julius Hare and John Sterling and the like—which spread the influence of Cambridge through literature and philosophy. She may even claim a share in Maurice, whose better part perhaps belonged to Oxford. But, when we have reviewed them all, it still is difficult to be certain of their effect on "the Liberal thought and action of the nation." Perhaps the reason of the difficulty is that Cambridge, probably owing to the character of her special studies, has always tended rather to contemplation than to action. It is not for nothing that Cambridge had her school of Platonists while Oxford was fast bound in misery and iron of Aristotle. It was not without reason that, at the crisis of the stormy 'forties, Cambridge took Plato for the subject of her prize poem and Oxford took Cromwell. When the religious world in general, and Oxford in particular, was distracted by the controversy about the long-forgotten *Essays and Reviews*, Kingsley thus recorded his observation:—

> Cambridge lies in magnificent repose, and, shaking lazy ears, stares at her more nervous sister and asks what it is all about. . . . That is the Cambridge danger—cool indifferentism; not to the doctrines, but to the means of fighting them.

That sentence seems to cut much deeper than the surface of a theological controversy. There are "doctrines" of vastly greater importance than those promulgated by the Essayists and Reviewers. There are doctrines of ethics and politics — of life and conduct and civil duty — doctrines of the relation between the unseen and the seen—which will always stir Oxford to her depths, and "the means of fighting," whether for them or against, will never rust for disuse. Cambridge has produced great men: Oxford produces great movements.

X

THE JUBILEE GARDEN-PARTY[1]

A FALLING glass, a leaden sky, a breathless atmosphere—all threatened rain. "This is the break-up of the fine weather," cried the croakers. "Nothing but the Queen's presence can stave off rain," said the more hopeful; and the hopeful people were right. The invitations to the Royal Garden-Party summoned their recipients "from five to seven," but long before the appointed hour all the avenues to Buckingham Palace were besieged by strings of carriages. Not only the great entrance facing the Mall and the privileged side-door opposite Buckingham Palace Hotel were opened, but the private entrances in Grosvenor Place threw back their accustomed doors. Not for full fifteen years had the Palace Garden witnessed such a function, and six thousand invitations—so rumour had it—were issued. Few Londoners even, and certainly no stranger from the provinces, have any notion of the extent of the handsomely wooded park or pleasure-ground which, modestly styling itself a garden, covers a square enclosed by

[1] June 29, 1887.

THE JUBILEE GARDEN-PARTY

St James's Park, Constitution Hill, Grosvenor Place, and Buckingham Palace Road. It is only just over the tops of the towering belt of trees that one can discern the topmost windows of Belgravian houses bounding the distant view. In the forefront stands the stately though rather ponderous façade of the Palace, a classical design in white stone which London smoke has long since subdued to its own tint. The wide lawn is encircled with thick plantations, where Lord Beaconsfield's peacocks, transported from Hughenden, dispute the territorial ascendancy of the Queen's pheasants. A large piece of water bears an abundance of light craft, manned by the Royal watermen in their picturesque uniforms of scarlet. One long marquee contains every variety of light refreshment; a smaller one facing it on the other side of the lawn, and banked up with the choicest flowers, is destined to house the Queen and her family and guests. The Beef-eaters, with their quaint doublets and ruffs, keep guard on the Terrace. The band of the Royal Marines discourses delicious music, and a vast and variegated crowd is dispersed over the lawn. As an effect of colour, it is unfortunate that the men's black coats and hats are not relieved by any vivacity in the ladies' costumes. White is almost universally worn by the younger ladies, and black or purple or deep green by their elders. A lady who has ventured into pink or yellow or crimson, or even displays a red parasol, is a public benefactor to the æsthetic sense.

The sombre effect of these costumes is deepened

by the darkening sky. The air is deathly still, and there are ominous rumours of an impending storm. Suddenly there is a rift in the clouds. The sun bursts out; a light breeze moves the Royal Standard, which, floating from the Palace roof, announces that the Queen has arrived. There is a sensation, a flutter, a sigh of relief. The Royal charm has triumphed over the barometer. It is Queen's weather again, and the Queen comes with it. There is a flash of scarlet in the distance as the Royal carriages drive into the garden. Sir Spencer Ponsonby-Fane, Secretary to the Lord Chamberlain's Office, and virtual dictator of all courtly revels, hurries up to Lord Salisbury, who, badly dressed and looking jaded, is surveying the animated scene through his characteristic eyeglass. He is summoned to greet his Sovereign; and now, "God save the Queen" bares all heads. A long lane is formed across the lawn. The Lord Steward and Lord Chamberlain, with their subordinate officials, walking backwards, prepare the way. Bareheaded we all are as the Prince conducts his mother. Dressed in slight mourning, supporting herself with her folded parasol, and wearing a happy smile, the Queen advances with that inimitable mixture of grace and dignity—that swimming, sweeping gait, which reminds one of some old-world figure-dance, and which compensates for the want of height and the departed elasticity of youth. Deep are the obeisances on either hand. The magnificent Countess of Lonsdale seems to sink into the earth and to reappear. Indian

THE JUBILEE GARDEN-PARTY

Princes, one blaze of scarlet and gold embroidery and diamonds, make their beautiful salaams. Right and left the Queen bows, pausing every few minutes to make more deliberate acknowledgments, and shaking hands with old friends whom she recognizes in the crowd. And so she gradually makes her way to her tent, and behind her files the long row of her children and grandchildren and princely visitors, all decorated with the new Jubilee medal, and brightly but not sumptuously apparelled. The dusky Queen of the Sandwich Islands walks with a singular freedom and dignity, and makes up by benignity of bearing for conversational deficiency — her only English being contained in the brief sentence, learned by rote, "How do you do? Pray sit down." All eyes are fixed on the Crown Princess of Germany, looking very young, and plainly dressed in black and white, as she holds an animated conversation with the Papal Envoy. The Envoy, a slight man of middle age, has the typical countenance of the Italian priest — subtle, intelligent, refined, and inscrutable. His curious costume—a cassock and a tall hat—attracts amused regards, but it is no joking matter, depend on it, which is the subject of conversation between him and the sagacious and politic daughter-in-law of the great Protestant Emperor. The same subject probably engages them which has been present to the minds of all who noted the Envoy's reception at Marlborough House and his invitation to dine and sleep at Windsor —the renewal of diplomatic relations between England

and the Holy See, with a special reference to troubles in Ireland.

Meanwhile the victorious sun streams down upon what Lord Beaconsfield called "a brisk and modish scene." Everyone who is known in politics, in the Church, in the services, in art, in literature, in mere society, is here. The grouping is interesting and picturesque. Mr Chamberlain displays a white orchid. Lord Hartington strolls by with an umbrella. Conversation is rapid and exhilarating. Hunger and thirst, in delicately modified forms, assert their claims. Some people seek coolness on the water, and some rest on the too few garden-seats. Rapidly the gay minutes pass, and suddenly, almost before we are aware, we see the Royal procession reforming; again the long lane shapes itself in the crowd, again the Queen goes smiling and bowing and scattering her gracious greetings. "God save the Queen" announces her departure. The Royal Standard disappears, the vast gathering breaks up, and at 8 p.m., though darkness is falling on Belgravia, the streets have scarcely ceased to echo the hoarse shouts of linkmen, or the thundering chariot-wheels of belated guests departing from the Jubilee Garden-Party.

XI

AN ODOROUS TASK

SOME years ago I had the pleasure of seeing my favourite actress, Mrs John Wood, play the congenial part of Mrs Malaprop. Through all the rollicking fun of the performer, and all the dignified absurdity of the character, I kept watching for the beloved and familiar phrases. One by one they came, each charged with that immortal fun which is the joy of life; but one was missing, and, when the curtain came down, I missed it still. A few days afterwards I had an opportunity of telling Mrs Wood how much I had enjoyed the play; "but why," I asked, "did you cut out the most characteristic of all malapropisms—the one which belongs as peculiarly to her as 'To be or not to be' to Hamlet?" "I cut nothing," replied the great actress. "I spoke the lines exactly as they were written. But I know what you are thinking of —'Comparisons are Odorous.'" "Yes, I am." "Well, let me tell you that it isn't a malapropism at all. It is so like Mrs Malaprop that generations of players have introduced it into the part. But it rightly belongs to Dogberry." Well, a phrase written by

Shakespeare and attributed to Sheridan has a double sanction, and exactly fits my present task. Some twenty years ago I published, in a series of the Queen's Prime Ministers, a short *Life of Mr Gladstone*. This book has lately fallen into the hands of one of my unknown friends, and he seems to have found food for reflection in the words in which I tried to describe the condition of Liberalism at the beginning of 1869, when Gladstone had just become Prime Minister for the first time. Here they are: "Those were golden days for the Liberal Party. They were united, enthusiastic, victorious; full of energy, confidence, and hope. Great works of necessary reform, too long delayed, lay before them, and they were led by a band of men as distinguished as had ever filled the chief places of the State."

It may be well, in passing, to recall the names of Gladstone's first Cabinet. At the head was the towering figure of the Prime Minister, who, though he only grasped the supreme prize of public life when he entered his sixtieth year, was at the very height of his physical and mental powers, and, besides all this, was the most indefatigable worker of his time. With him were associated Lord Hatherley, Lord de Grey (afterwards Lord Ripon), Lord Kimberley, Lord Clarendon, Lord Granville, Lord Hartington, the Duke of Argyll, John Bright, Robert Lowe, Henry Bruce, Edward Cardwell, Hugh Childers, George Goschen, and Chichester Fortescue. Such was Gladstone's first Cabinet, and people, noting the elements of which it was composed, went back for a nickname to the beginning of the century, and labelled it as "All the Talents."

But now comes my friend. "When," he says, "I read those words, I naturally thought of the position of affairs at the present time, and I wondered whether, taking the Ministry of 1869 either as a whole or man for man (but excluding Gladstone himself), they were really equal in ability to the present Ministry."

Thus my new friend Verges, to whom, playing the part of Dogberry, I reply, "Comparisons are odorous, brother Verges; but, as you seem bent on comparing two sets of eminent and excellent men, I will try to aid your task. I will set forth what I remember of the earlier set, and will leave you to draw the comparison."

Verges rightly excludes the central figure of that great Administration, realizing, no doubt, that such gifts as Gladstone's are not easily matched. Let me take the rest of the Cabinet one by one, and note the faculties and qualities of each. We begin, as in duty bound, with the Lord Chancellor—Lord Hatherley,—of whom it may be said without offence that he was stronger as a churchman than as a lawyer, and by his munificence and piety won for himself the title of Lay-Bishop of Westminster long before he was Lord Chancellor of England. That he attained the Woolsack was due to the fact that he was willing, when Sir Roundell Palmer was unwilling, to disestablish the Irish Church. When that act of justice had been accomplished, Lord Hatherley had served his turn, and was cast aside in favour of Lord Selborne, who was said to possess in the highest perfection "the Chancery mind"; and this, to the uninitiated, seems to mean an infinite capacity for splitting straws. Lord de Grey we all remember as Lord Ripon. He was the first man of rank and wealth to throw in his lot with the Christian Socialists, and his countrymen should always hold his name in reverence for the skill and firmness which he displayed in persuading America to accept arbitration in the "Alabama" claims. Lord Kimberley was a man whom rank and wealth certainly pushed forward in public life, but who would have been notable and successful in any class or career. His mind was both rapid and vigorous and his memory tenacious. He was perfectly independent in opinion, forming his own clear judgment on every problem, and resolute in sticking to it. He was perhaps the most fluent speaker in England, and his fluency in French and German equalled his fluency in English. He served the State in a vast variety of offices, and was equally at home in all. As the "General Utility man" of politics, he has never been surpassed. Lord Clarendon (who died in 1870) is now only a name, and barely that; but the present generation will soon learn all about him, for his Memoir is, rather late in the day, to be published. He was a genial and accomplished man of the world, and an eminent instance of the ornamental Whiggery which used to contribute so largely to Liberal Cabinets. An even more conspicuous instance of the same kind was Lord Granville, whose strength lay in tact, geniality, and commonsense. He kept England out of war at a period when all the nations of Europe were straining to fly at each other's throats, and he led the Liberal Party in the House of Lords for more than thirty years, without once losing his temper. These were no ordinary achievements. That Lord Hartington owed a great deal of his political power to the fact that he was bound to be Duke of Devonshire he would have been the last to deny—a great deal, but not all. He had a clear, cool, mathematical head; great powers of "grind," when grinding was a necessity; and a faculty of unadorned yet vigorous speech which created the not quite accurate impression of dogged strength. The Duke of Argyll was a Whig of another type. His cleverness verged on genius. He had thought both widely and deeply; realized, as mechanical politicians never do, the unseen forces of society; and was an orator of the very highest type. Gladstone, from whom he perpetually differed and often broke away, always said that he was one of the three men of his generation who had the greatest faculty of public speech. John Bright had no gift of extempore eloquence, but his prepared orations will be read as long as men care to study written eloquence. Aided by the charm of voice and gesture, his pungent sarcasm, his rich humour, and his irresistible pathos dominated his audience; but he was the splendid organ of a narrow theory, and belonged, as far as his political ideals were concerned, to a type which has passed away. He very unwillingly accepted the yoke of office, and wore it rather uneasily; detested the drudgery of a department, but excelled in dealing with a deputation and sending it away in good temper.

Robert Lowe — what quaint and contrariant memories surround his name! An exquisite scholar, but a sarcastic opponent of classical education; a consummate master of the English language, but incapable of uttering a sentence without a manuscript: most formidable in attack, but in defence, as Gladstone said, "as helpless as a beetle on its back": an advanced Liberal in matters educational and religious, but the most embittered foe of democracy; a jovial, genial, and brilliant member of society, but a savage controversialist and a domineering official. He was the ablest man in Gladstone's Cabinet, and the most disastrous failure. Of Henry Austin Bruce, afterwards Lord Aberdare, we need only say that his attempts at Licensing Reform were so unsuccessful as to accelerate his retirement from the Home Office. Edward Cardwell, esteemed in his younger days one of the most brilliant of the Peelite group, accomplished the reform of the Army (including the abolition of Purchase) and was never heard of again. Hugh Childers was a deft and capable administrator, but a most unfortunate financier. Goschen, on the other hand, was a financier first and foremost; and, if it had not been for his blind fear of democracy, would have been a valuable asset to the Liberal Party.

AN ODOROUS TASK

Chichester Fortescue, afterwards Lord Carlingford, was exactly like a "Portrait of a Gentleman" in the Royal Academy, and left no kind of impression on the public mind or the history of his time.

It must be frankly confessed that Gladstone was singularly unfortunate in some of his colleagues. That so many of them were Whigs, who sate in the Cabinet by a kind of hereditary right, was a circumstance which did not recommend them to the rank and file of the Party; and others, who were not Whigs, contrived to make themselves offensive. They imposed vexatious taxes; they haggled about the amount of water in the sailors' grog, and the price of the window-curtains in a public office; they were assailed by insurrections of half-starved match-girls whose wretched bread their Budget imperilled; they were nightly ridiculed on the stage before delighted audiences, till they ran to the Lord Chamberlain for protection against the scoffers. There were resignations, and rumours of resignations. On the ear of memory comes back the song from *The Happy Land* which night by night brought down the house at the Court Theatre. It enumerated the most unpopular members of the Government, with a characteristic trait of each in turn, and the refrain to each verse was—

>And yet he is a most popular man—
>Nobody wants to turn him out.

Imagine the emotions of Lord Sandhurst and Mr Brookfield, if such a libretto were submitted to their judgment!

XII

FLOWERS

> Just when the red June roses blow,
> She gave me one—a year ago.
> A rose whose crimson breath revealed
> The secret which its heart concealed,
> And whose half-shy, half-tender, grace
> Blush'd back upon the giver's face.

WHO she was, and what I did with it, are questions of no importance, and perhaps it was rather more than a year ago; but the quotation fits the day, and may serve to recall the memory of a true and tender poetess whom nowadays nobody reads. But, even if her verse had not been there to tempt me, I must this week have written about flowers; for the "Royal International Horticultural Exhibition" has filled my mental eye with a vision of glory—a "pomp and prodigality" of colour—which excludes all else. Yet I do not purpose to describe the Exhibition—partly because, in the gracious phrase of the day, it has been "done" by innumerable pens more graphic than my own, and partly because the attempt to describe horticulture always exposes the writer to a double peril. If he tries to be vivid and picturesque, he commonly falls into hopeless confusion, and, in a sense not intended by the poet,

> Gives to the poles the products of the sun,
> And knits the unsocial climates into one.

On the other hand, if he aims at science and accuracy, he "murders to dissect," and makes his paper as dull as a seedsman's catalogue. Flowers in literature should be treated broadly and generally, perhaps even vaguely—just as the eye drinks delight from a field of poppies or a wood carpeted with wild hyacinths; taking no account of *genera* or *species* and ignoring the jargon of "frond" and "stamen" and "pollen." Matthew Arnold wrote to his friend Grant-Duff: "You first led me to try and know the names and history of the plants I met with, instead of being content with simply taking pleasure in the look of them; and you have at least doubled my enjoyment of them by doing so." But, with all deference to my great teacher, I doubt if this is the common experience. Would Wordsworth really have enjoyed the lesser celandine, or Burns the mountain daisy, more keenly because some botanically-minded friend had lectured on their characteristics? Science is too often "at enmity with joy," and the physical delight of beauty is not, I think, enhanced by chemical or structural analysis. Scientific nomenclature is always hideous, and the botanical habit of labelling or libelling innocent flowers and plants with Latinized nicknames is even painfully incongruous. English names have a tenderness and beauty all their

own, simple and homely—yet romantic—rose and
pink and lily of the valley, and lilac (better pronounced laylock); primrose and daffodil and snow-
drop, heartsease and pansy, cowslip and buttercup
and forget-me-not, meadow-sweet and love-in-idleness,
foxglove and bluebell, even cherry-pie, dusty-miller,
and old-man's-beard. Over against such names as
these set fuchsia, dahlia, calceolaria, pelargonium,
ampelopsis Veitchii, odontoglossum, madevallia,
Harryana, Blairii No. 2, and Dorothy Perkins, and
no one who has ears to hear can doubt that our
English forefathers knew better than their descendants
the true language of leaf and flower.

Every year, as the 19th of April comes round,
the hard-pressed paragraphist discusses the question
whether "*his* favourite flower" meant originally Lord
Beaconsfield's or Prince Albert's; and, if he be unusually well-read, he announces that in *Lothair*
primroses are recommended for salads, and in
Coningsby are said to resemble the fried eggs round
our breakfast-bacon. But, putting aside this hard-
worked and vulgarized flower, we know that Lord
Beaconsfield genuinely loved a garden, and—which
is much the same thing—detested gardeners, "from
the days of Le Nôtre to those of the fine gentlemen
who now travel about, and, when disengaged, deign
to give us advice." "The gardener, like all head-
gardeners, was opiniated. Living always at Vauxe,
he had come to believe that the gardens belonged to
him, and that the family was only occasional visitors;

FLOWERS

and he treated them accordingly." At "Brentham" —(alas! poor "Brentham," now perfumed only by sewage and chemical works, and rejected as a gift by County Councils),—at Brentham the same tyranny was attempted, but partially defeated. "How I hate modern gardens!" exclaimed St Aldegonde. "What a horrid thing this is! One might as well have a mosaic pavement there. Give me cottage-roses, sweet-peas, and wall-flowers." And he got what he wanted in Corisande's garden. There, instead of "hard and scentless imitations of works of art," you found huge bushes of honeysuckle, and bowers of sweet-pea and sweet-briar, and jessamine clustering over the walls, and gilly-flowers with their sweet breath. There were banks of violets which the southern breeze always stirred, and mignonette filled every vacant nook." As you entered this delicious pleasance, "it seemed a blaze of roses and carnations, though one recognized in a moment the presence of the lily, the heliotrope, and the stock." Never were the pleasures of scent more feelingly described, and no doubt they are required for the perfection of a garden; but the eye has' even more commanding claims. A pergola of laburnum, raining gold; a wistaria veiling with its clusters the grey stone of a Gothic oriel—these, once seen, are treasures for ever. St Aldegonde's indignant protest against the mosaic-like flower-beds of Brentham is susceptible of a much wider extension. Whoever tries to formalize and regularize flowers, and make them stiff and hard and geometrical, sins at once against Truth and Beauty. The heralds are bad enough, with their parti-coloured roses and their golden lilies; but the worst offenders in this respect are the ladies who decorate churches. Their chief endeavour is to make flowers look like the products of the bonnet-shop. They strip them of the leaves which Nature gives as the grateful foil to vivid colour; they arrange them in all sorts of odd shapes and patterns, sometimes even as symbols and initials; and they bring to their assistance in their unhallowed work an instrument of tin, painted green, something like a glove with too many fingers, which would make even Dog-roses or May, when inserted in its clutch, look artificial.

And, yet again, he who truly loves flowers must be on his guard, in this as in everything else, against the insolent aggressiveness of wealth. We must cling fast to the truth which Ruskin taught us, and must insist, in season and out of season, that a thing which costs nothing may be beautiful, and a thing which costs a fortune hideous. I felt the need for this protestation when I stood among the gaping crowd before the amazing pyramid of orchids at the International Flower Show. Beyond doubt, all were costly; but not all were beautiful. The *Cattleya* is indeed one of the most exquisite of flowers, with its grace, its luxuriance, and its colours like the shoaling waters of an amethystine sea. But I believe it is one of the cheapest and most easily procured of orchids; whereas a sum which would equip an army was expended on expeditions to South America in quest of that skimpy stalk with rare and exiguous tufts of brown and yellow, which so closely resembles *Baccopipia gracilis* in Lear's *Nonsense Botany*.

Away with artificiality and ostentation! Back to Nature and pure beauty—to the vintage-like pendants of purple Clematis, and the bold splendour of Hollyhocks and Sunflowers and Tiger-lilies; nor must I forget my favourite Peony, which, if the Rose is the ruby, may rank among flowers as the carbuncle among precious stones. Is there in the world a scent more ravishing than Syringa, or a prettier shade of pink than Ribes? I end as I began. "I have been in Corisande's garden, and she has given me a rose."

XIII

SOME USES OF WEALTH

An unknown friend writes as follows:—"From time to time you say a good deal about the claims of Labour and the sufferings of the poor. You seem to be half a Socialist. Do you really despise wealth, or dislike the rich?" The question is something of the abruptest, and I prefer to answer in what Matthew Arnold called a "sinuous, easy, unpolemical manner"; so I will begin with an anecdote.

An inquisitive gentleman who haunts Pall Mall found himself during his summer rambles in the neighbourhood of a ducal castle on the day of the week on which it was opened to the public. After he had duly admired the chapel and the armoury, the picture-gallery and the plate-room, he resolved to penetrate a little further, and induced—I should not like to say "bribed"—the housekeeper to let him see the Duke's private dining-room. The Duke was a widower, and the dinner-table was arranged for his short and solitary meal. Returning to Pall Mall, the inquisitive tourist moralized to his fellow-clubmen in a style quite worthy of Seneca or Marcus Aurelius,

SOME USES OF WEALTH

"I wouldn't have missed the sight of that dining-room for anything. It impressed me deeply. There was a man with three castles, 200,000 acres of land, and £1000 a day; and yet he could only eat three courses at dinner, and had no occasion for more than two wine-glasses. I noted them particularly: a sherry-glass and a claret-glass, no more. The housekeeper told me that he could not touch champagne, on account of the hereditary gout. I am a champagne-drinker myself; and it made me feel that, after all, human lots are very equal."

This deep reflection

On Man, on Nature, and on Human Life

helps me towards an answer. Do I really despise the Duke's wealth, or dislike him for possessing it? Not at all. Wealth in itself is never despicable, because it is always powerful; and, before we dislike the possessor, we must know how he uses it. Personally, I dislike a man who hoards. Mr Gladstone has left it on record that he was by nature "thrifty and penurious," and that by the time he was eight he had "accumulated no less than twenty shillings in silver. My brothers judged it right to appropriate this fund." The brothers were quite right. What they did I also should have done. One of Lord Beaconsfield's characters says that the comfortable thing is to have £10,000 a year and be supposed to have only £5000, "for then fellows don't try to borrow of you, and go about calling you a screw if you refuse." Presumably that philosopher spent five thousand and hoarded the other five, and him I should have detested. Hoarding apart, a man who spent all his wealth upon himself would also be detestable; but fortunately this is very difficult. "If," said Mr Pecksniff, "we indulge in harmless fluids, we get the dropsy; if in exciting liquids, we get drunk. What a soothing reflection is that!" And so with all simply personal pleasures—a yacht or an opera-box, a deer-forest or a trout-stream or a string of hunters, a good cook and an "interesting" cellar (I borrow that epithet from a member of the present Cabinet)—none of these things, nor all of them together, can exhaust a rich man's income; as riches are understood in the estimation of the present day. As long as he has sense enough to keep clear of the Turf and the Stock Exchange, the excess of income over expenditure will still be considerable, and we must know how he employs that excess before we can say whether we dislike him or admire him. What, then, should the Rich Man do with his riches?

In the first place, he should be a great church-builder. If he believes in the humanizing effect of transcendent architecture, he should plant, in the dingiest and dullest quarter of each dull and dingy town, such a church as Lord Beaconsfield described in *Sybil*. "Beautiful its solemn towers; its sculptured western front; beautiful its columned aisles and lofty nave; its sparkling shrine and delicate chantry; most beautiful the streaming glories of its vast orient light."

The church, thus grandly conceived and adequately endowed, should be, in the noble words inscribed by the late Lord Addington on St Alban's Holborn, "free for ever to Christ's poor"; and so wealth should be made to serve the social needs of humanity by offering to every child of toil a resting-place, a sanctuary, and a home.

I put church-building first, on the simple ground that eternity is more important than time, and the soul than the body or even the intellect. But the Rich Man should minister to all the complex needs of humanity, and Art would be one of his most effective agencies. A man who forms or inherits a really grand gallery of painting or sculpture, and then (like Lord Glenconner) throws it open for the gratuitous enjoyment of his fellow-creatures, renders an inestimable service to his day and generation.

But art is not all. Life and health are more. The Rich Man, before he begins to collect pictures or statues, should buy some slum-property in an industrial town, make a clean sweep of insanitary areas, and secure open spaces for Public Gardens and playgrounds for the children. If this process involved the destruction of workmen's houses, he should contribute to "Garden-Cities," taking pains to secure that only a "living rent" should be demanded from their tenants. Hospitals again—here is a boundless field for the Rich Man's activities. It would be no contemptible ambition to build, in the heart of some great city, or on the hills which surround it, an imitation of the German Hospital at Alexandria, with its miles of marble corridors and its plenitude of appliances which make illness a luxury; all worked by "sweet societies" of trained Deaconesses, who labour for no other reward than the love and gratitude of their patients. Only let the Rich Man beware lest the disingenuousness of "research" bring evil out of his intended good, and pervert the place of healing into a torture-chamber or a shambles.

I will assume that our Rich Man has some political convictions. I will even imagine—and this is a more daring assumption—that he is a Liberal. If so, some of his wealth must go to the furtherance of the cause in which he believes. When I have been asked why I am a Liberal, my only, but adequate, reply has always been, "Because I can't help it." And in this one respect I could wish, like St Paul of old, that all who hear me were both almost and altogether such as I am. I remember once, in the House of Commons, drawing down upon myself the rebuke of Mr Jesse Collings by stating that my politics were part of my religion. But so, in spite of the Grand Old Man of Birmingham, they are. Because I am a Christian, I believe in Freedom, I believe in the cause of Labour, I believe in Social Reform; and, if our Rich Man felt as I feel, he would spend large sums in serving these high ends. But here a personal factor enters into the calculation. One must know the man whom one is trying to help into Parliament, or else, in times of political unrest, when "sects and schisms" are rife, and false doctrines masquerade under orthodox names, one might find that one had really helped the wrong cause. So, if I were a Rich Man, I should not entrust my subscription to the Party-chest, but should choose my candidates by personal inspection, should satisfy myself that they were sound in the Liberal creed as I understand it and meant to work for the causes in which I believe; and then I should run the man of my choice for all I was worth, and should live again, in his career, the strifes and the victories of my own early manhood.

I have spoken of helping young candidates into Parliament; but the Rich Man's services to youth need not stop there. "The Youth of a Nation are the Trustees of Posterity," and to invest money in the rising generation is "a pleasant exercise of hope and joy." To express that "exercise" in its lowliest form, there is a rewarding sense that one is really giving pleasure when one slips a sovereign into a schoolboy's hand, even though one knows that it will immediately be expended on an ill-assorted meal of strawberries and ices, chocolate and sardines. If one thought that the recipient was likely to eschew these pleasures of the palate and invest the tip in a Tennyson or a water-colour, I suppose one would feel a more spiritual joy. But, in either case, one has established a hold upon the boy's regard, and so may be able to lead him in some direction where he, in turn, can serve another. Let Rich Men who have nephews or acquaintances at Public Schools run down before this term ends, and improve, out of their abundance, on the hint now given.

But, as I near the close of this chapter, I am constrained to make, as the French say, a return upon myself. Am I quite sure that, if I were in the case contemplated, my conduct would be as exemplary as my ideals? With regard to a well-known and emotional family, who excelled in writing letters of condolence at seasons of bereavement, a candid friend observed: "If their lives were only half as good as their letters, they would indeed be a family of saints." Similarly, I feel a kind of misgiving that I have been vastly more benevolent and unselfish on paper than I might be in practice. The contrast between the theories and the actions of humanitarianism has been, times out of mind, the theme of satirists. "A sees B in distress, and thinks that C ought to give him something." It was when the Needy Knife-grinder suggested sixpence for a pot of beer that the Friend of Humanity burst upon him with the immortal imprecation. Let him who lectures the rich on the employment of their riches take heed lest he fall short of the ideal which he has upheld. A multi-millionaire once said to me: "The only really pleasant things in life are eating and accumulating. Eating, alas! requires youth and health; but accumulating becomes pleasanter and pleasanter the longer you live." It would be a dreadful fate if, after bodying forth the admirable uses of imaginary millions, one should find oneself in actual life possessed by the demons of avarice and malevolence, and should end by giving joy only to the Chancellor of the Exchequer. A happier lot be ours!

XIV

"JOHN INGLESANT"

"Some books, which I should never dream of opening at dinner, please me at breakfast and *vice versa*." The sentence occurs in Lord Macaulay's journal, and Mr Gladstone thus commented on it: "There is more subtlety in this distinction than would easily be found in any passage of his writings. But mark how quietly both meals are handed over to the dominion of the master-propensity!" Such indulgence was all very well for the celibate historian, who breakfasted and dined, at the hour which suited him, in "chambers every corner of which was library," but most people are forced to think of catching the train or the tram about 9 A.M., and to share their evening meal with "a howling herd of hungry boys." And yet I think that everyone who has read with the heart as well as the head, and has really assimilated his reading, must feel the suitability of certain books to certain moods—and the converse not less acutely. One would not choose *The Bride of Lammermoor* to enhance the merriment of Christmas, nor ponder *The Ring and the Book* in the delirium of a contested election. But spring never returns without recalling all true Wordsworthians to "The Daffodils," and at Christmas the hymn "On the morning of Christ's Nativity" is as inevitable as *Adeste Fideles*.

Writing now amid the solemnities of Holy Week,[1] my thoughts turn to the notable book which is named at the head of this chapter; for, more than most, it is pervaded by that penetrating sense of Religion, without which all ecclesiastical observance is "a tale of little meaning, though the words are strong."

The genesis of *John Inglesant* was certainly remarkable. Joseph Henry Shorthouse was a Quaker, and a manufacturer (I think of vitriol) at Birmingham. The painful affliction of a paroxysmal stammer unfitted him for society. His business was not exacting; and he had no children to occupy his thoughts at home. So he became a student, at first reading discursively, but tending, as years went on, to concentrate on a line of mystical piety. From his Quakerish antecedents he derived a profound belief in the Inward Light, and a love of that impalpable theology which goes by the name of mysticism. From mysticism he passed to the idea of a visible church, and of the material *media* of spiritual realities; so he was baptized, and became a devoted adherent of the Church of England, yet never surrendered his perfect freedom of judgment. "I distinguish absolutely," he said, "between sacra-

[1] 1912.

mentalism and sacerdotalism; they seem to me mutually destructive. So long as the clergy confine themselves to their sacramental office, I look upon them as THE channel of grace. When they depart from this, and act and talk out of their own heads, I pay no more attention to them than I do to laymen." Plato, and Molinos, and Jacob Boehme had been Shorthouse's favourite authors; and now he began to realize the refined beauty of Anglican devotion, and became an enthusiastic admirer of such men as George Herbert and John Evelyn. By degrees, his shadowy conceptions of religious truth crystallized into a definite theory; and he cast that theory into the form of what he termed a "Philosophical Romance," naming the book *John Inglesant*. It occupied his leisure for several years, and was completed in 1877. At first it was privately printed, handed about among friends, and read with secret bewilderment in the villas of Edgbaston. Eventually he resolved to publish it, and sent it, with ill-success, to a famous firm of publishers, my friend James Payn rejecting it as unreadable. In a moment of happier inspiration, the house of Macmillan accepted it; and, when in 1880 it was given to the public, its success was instantaneous and universal. Some of this success no doubt was due to its style, a little archaic, and not always quite correct, but full of light and colour and stately music—some to the peculiar vein of religious philosophy, which few could understand but all could admire—some to the graphic

"JOHN INGLESANT"

pictures of life and society at one of the epoch-making periods of modern history. But, successful as the book was, it never lacked critics; and it is instructive to recall the comments—not of the "old Liberal hacks" whom all Religion infuriates—but of dispassionate and instructed readers. In 1881 Dr Liddon wrote:—

> I have been reading *John Inglesant*—the writer knows a great deal about the seventeenth century, though I should suppose that some of his knowledge was unbalanced. The book gives me the impression of being written by a man who had taken up the study of the classics (especially Plato) and of theology late in life, and was overpowered by his acquisitions, or at any rate unable to digest them. . . . In the description of the Renaissance (life and art), on which he has expended much pains, I trace the influence of J. A. Symonds and Pater.

These criticisms strike me as perfectly fair, and, read in their context, they make me feel sure that Liddon, whose theology was accurate and logical to the last degree, was repelled by the mysticism—or perhaps he would have called it mistiness—which from first to last marked John Inglesant's religion. Lord Acton approached the book from the historical side. He notes a mistaken date, a misunderstood event, a misinterpreted character. He perpetually asks, with the rather tiresome insistence of the historian, "Did this or that actually happen, at the time stated, under the circumstances described?" And, when he has answered his own questions in the negative, he seems to think that he has seriously disparaged what professes to be a "philosophical romance." And yet, after all said and done, he wrote: "I have read nothing more thoughtful and suggestive since *Middlemarch*," and this was no light praise from a critic who ranked George Eliot with Shakespeare, and first saw revealed in *Middlemarch* "her superiority to some of the greatest writers."

John Inglesant is a book easily accessible to all my readers, and, I suppose, abundantly familiar to most; so I must forbear to trace the fascinating, though rather morbid, story of the hero's religious development, and the strange vicissitudes, political and theological, through which it led him. As my space is limited, I will confine myself to indicating a few passages of peculiar interest and beauty, closing with one which has a special appropriateness to a world making ready for Easter Day.

The story of *John Inglesant* falls naturally into two parts; the scene of the first is laid in England, of the second in Italy. I will take them in inverse order. Shorthouse has a fine passage describing the sunset as it gilds the spires of Rome, and Lord Acton observes, with his habitual pungency, "There are no spires in Rome," but incidentally goes on to say—what was true—"I hear that the author has never been in Italy," adding, with characteristic candour, "That accounts for many topographical mistakes, and leaves a margin to his credit." The Italian part of the book contains, amid much that is beautiful and much that is exciting, one passage charged with a purely ethical message. In describing the midnight ride from Florence to Pistoia, Shorthouse attained the highest perfection of his descriptive style; and made, as he himself avowed, his anxiously considered contribution to a sacred cause which Romance too often blasphemes. I return now from Italy to England, and here, though perhaps the interest is less intense, the atmosphere is clearer and the life more natural. To achieve successful word-painting when one is describing a country which one has never seen, is an achievement of genius; but Shorthouse seems happier —more at his ease—when he is reproducing an English landscape, with its meadows and woods and running waters, its grey churches and its moated halls. In Shropshire and in Worcestershire, in Oxfordshire, Wiltshire, and Huntingdonshire, his observation is equally close and his touch equally felicitous.

Not long ago I avowed in print my detestation of ghosts and spooks and apparitions and all forms of sorcery and necromancy; but one must confess that these things have laid a strong hold on human imagination, and they find a natural place in a philosophical romance. Whether Shorthouse believed in them, I know not; I only know that the scene where the betrayed Strafford appears in a vision of the night to his faithless King is one of the most powerful scenes in this strangely powerful book. But we must not end on a note of censure even when the subject is Charles I. There were holy and loyal souls that loved and honoured him to the end, and in such devout company John Inglesant first caught sight of that beatific vision which, through all the subsequent permutations of his life, served to quicken his conscience and to nerve his wavering will. The scene is laid in the parish church of Little Gidding, and Inglesant is awaiting the mysterious summons which will soon call him to take his part in the desperate encounters of that troublous time:—

Above the altar, which was profusely decked with flowers, the antique glass of the east window, which had been carefully repaired, contained a figure of the Saviour of an early and severe type. The form was gracious and yet commanding, having a brilliant halo round the head, and being clad in a long and apparently seamless coat; the two forefingers of the right hand were held up to bless. Kneeling upon the half-pace, as he received the Holy Things, this gracious figure entered into Inglesant's soul, and stillness and peace unspeakable, and life and light and sweetness filled his mind. He was lost in a sense of rapture, and earth and all that surrounded him faded away. Heaven itself seemed to have opened, and One fairer than the fairest of the angelic hosts to have come down to earth.

XV

A GREEK REQUIEM

A WESTERN eye is always struck by a superficial resemblance between a Greek church and a Jewish synagogue. There is something in the same basilican form and arrangements, the same rounded arches, the same blaze of gilding and mosaic, the same suggestion of the more sacred *arcana* withdrawn from the gaze of the general congregation, the same melancholy unaccompanied music, the same Oriental aspect of the bearded officiants. So much the Church of the Holy Wisdom, in Moscow Road, has in common with its neighbour the Synagogue in St Petersburg Place. So much but no more, for in the Greek churches the Divine Symbol of the cross is everywhere —on the altar, in the priest's hands, on the vestments of the clergy and of their attendants, in the devotional action alike of clergy and people. To-day [1] in the fine basilica in Moscow Road was celebrated, after the ordinary litany, a solemn Requiem for the Greek soldiers who have fallen fighting against Turkey.

A catafalque was placed in front of the sanctuary

[1] June 27, 1897.

gates, and draped in the Greek colours of blue and white, mingled with black badges of mourning. It was guarded by four tall candles similarly draped, and the bulk of the congregation was draped in black. The liturgy proceeded in ordinary course. The priest and deacon wore splendid robes—half cope, half chasuble—of crimson and gold. The "great entrance" of the clergy bearing the sacred elements into the sanctuary was, as always in Oriental rites, the most impressive scene visible to the worshippers, for the most solemn portions of the service are transacted behind the closed and veiled gates of the sanctuary. After the actual Communion had been made, the priests and deacons, attended by a corps of choristers and acolytes in white surplices, with the crossed stoles and black bands on their arms, bearing the ceremonial candles in their hands, grouped themselves around the catafalque. The choir chanted its wailing supplications for the departed, which moaned through the church like the voices of the martyrs beneath the apocalyptic altar, and then the priest recited the prayers, strikingly primitive and non-Roman in spirit and language, with which the Holy Orthodox Church commends its departed children to the Divine Compassion, and implores for them a place in the resurrection to eternal life. Many of the congregation—probably the near kinsfolk of the gallant lads who had fallen in the war—were moved to tears, and to every mind which recalled the processional splendours of this last week must have occurred some compunctious questionings. How long are the army and the fleet of Christian England, which our countrymen have fashioned with their skill and manned with their lives, to support the Great Assassin on his blood-cemented throne? *Usquequo, Domine?* "Lord, how long?"

XVI

A CLUSTER OF ADVERTISEMENTS

"SWEET are the uses of advertisement." Shakespeare's famous line is not half as true as this variant of it. Apart from such gigantic "uses" as we read in *Tono Bungay*, and see every day in our intercourse with commercial millionaires, advertisement has its lesser but still agreeable uses in suggesting reflection and promoting mirth. Many a newspaper enlivens its weekly page of "Facetiæ" with cuttings from the advertising columns of other papers. My friend "Sub Rosa" does it several times a week, and before now I have followed his example. As a rule, the gems of advertisement are not found in clusters: they lurk, singly, in the dark corners of unexpected prints; and the seeker who finds one good specimen after a week's toil counts himself well repaid. But just lately I have been in luck's way. I have "struck oil," as the Americans say; or, to put it more rhetorically, I have discovered a seam or stratum of advertisement, as rich in beauty and profit as the diamond-mines of Golconda. So far it seems to be

A CLUSTER OF ADVERTISEMENTS

known to myself only, and it is not in human nature to disclose my glittering secret. However, I will generously exhibit a few of the gems in my shop-window, and will leave the dazzled passers-by to discover the mine for themselves. To dismiss the language of parable, I may say that all the advertisements which I here present are culled from a single issue of a single newspaper; and the student of sociology may be interested in discovering from the nature of the excerpts the class or layer of society to which that newspaper appeals.

Matthew Arnold once spoke, through the mouth of his friend "Adolescens Leo," of "those toothless old Cerberuses, the Bishops," and the paper from which I am quoting must surely have its circulation in episcopal palaces.

(i.) PAINLESS AND PERFECT DENTISTRY.—Dr ——, Surgeon Dentist, England, and Doctor of Dental Surgery, U.S.A., has been awarded 10 Gold Medals at the Great International Exhibitions for his Dentistry, and has also received the following high testimony—

"MY DEAR DOCTOR,—Allow me to express my sincere thanks for the skill and attention displayed in the construction of my Artificial Teeth, which render my mastication and articulation perfect.

"In recognition of your valuable services rendered to me, you are at liberty to use my name.

(*Signed*) T. BARCHESTER."

(ii.) OLD FALSE TEETH.—We give highest possible price for above. Offers made, and, if not accepted, teeth returned. Dealers in old gold or silver in any form. Bankers' references.

(iii.) OLD ARTIFICIAL TEETH BOUGHT.—Persons wishing to receive full value should apply to the actual manufacturers, instead of to provincial buyers. If forwarded by post, value per return.—Messrs ——. Established 100 years.

(iv.) OLD FALSE TEETH BOUGHT.—Persons wishing to receive full value should apply to us instead of to Provincial buyers. Immediate cash sent, or offer made BY RETURN OF POST.

(v.) OLD FALSE TEETH BOUGHT, any condition. 4d. per tooth given on vulcanite, 1s. on silver, 1s. 6d. on gold, 3s. on platinum. Strictly genuine. Immediate cash sent.

When we consider that these five advertisements are taken from a single issue, we are driven to the conclusion that our "Cerberuses" are even more impotent than when Adolescens Leo jeered at them.

But the loss of teeth is by no means the only misfortune to which this thoughtful journal ministers.

HAIR FALLING OFF.—A Lady who lost nearly all hers, and has now a strong, heavy growth, will send particulars to anyone enclosing stamped addressed envelope to Miss C. M.

While some of us have too little hair, others have too much, or have it in the wrong place. For them, too, Balm in Gilead is delicately advertised.

ELECTROLYSIS antiseptically and effectually performed. Highest medical references; special terms to those engaged in nursing, teaching, clerical work, &c.; strict privacy; consultation free.

From the Bishops, thus rendered articulate and beautiful, we pass, by a natural transition, to the "inferior clergy," and for them also there is joy, in the form of vestiarian history.

STORY OF THE "ENGLESHE SURPELISSE." "It is the most beautiful and dignified Surplice I have ever seen," was the response made by one Clergyman who saw it for the first time. The story of this Surplice is one of small beginnings, and had its origin in a request made by the Chaplain of a Theological College, who, in order to oust the spare, attenuated Vestment which passed for a Surplice, and was very generally worn, asked that Mr —— would make one after the pattern of the Cathedral Surplice of pre-Reformation days. This wish was carried out, and the Surplice taken up by the Candidates who were entering Holy Orders. From time to time their friends saw and purchased for their own wear. Gradually the pattern was improved and perfected—many Clerical Tailors have imitated it, but this "English Surplice" easily holds first place. It is always made in a good material, and the workers have developed such skill, that each Surplice has a distinctive beauty of its own. English Clerics all over the world testify to these facts, while recently it has been winning favour in the United States, where it is passed by the American Customs free of duty, on a certificate that it is for Church use only.

This victory, not indeed complete but still partial, of tailoring over Tariffs, ought certainly to be inscribed among the triumphs of the Church. It is a great and a cheering thought that the "Surpelisse" knits into one the Kingly Commonwealth of England and the Great Republic of the West.

But the cowl does not make the monk, nor the surplice the curate. He needs a further outfit, and he can get a "clerical frock suit" for £3 10s., and "cassocks, gowns, hoods, stoles, hats, and collars" at the lowest price compatible with "fair conditions, and the standard of the Church of England." A post-card, addressed to the proper quarter, will bring him, "free on application," an illustrated catalogue of

> BIBLES, Prayer Books, Hymn Books, Church Services, Daily Service Books, Bible Wallets, Sermon Cases, Motto Cards, Framed Quotations, Pictures, Devotional Books, Christian Literature, Books for Students, Sixpenny Series, and Gem Oratorios.

And he can procure a "beautifully carved crucifix from Ober-Ammergau" (*via* Bristol).

But the curate must not only be properly clad and equipped. He must be taught "How to Speak Effectively," and this he can learn from Mr Hollowell's booklet, price 3s. 6d., "perfect in the clearness and grip of its subject," or in Private Lessons on "Terms for'd."

Even in the matter of his bodily sustenance, the advertisers will help him. If he observes the days of fasting and abstinence, as a good churchman should, he will find himself provided with "vegetarian board (full or partial)," in the "quiet, though convenient, and pleasant situation" of Westbourne Grove; and if it prove too "partial," he can eke it out with "the original Eccles cake," at 1s. 5d. a box. If his constitution requires meat, he can "ensure a good breakfast by buying 'real Wiltshire bacon' direct from the curers"; and he can fill up the chinks with "jams, jellies, and fruits in syrup," or the "new egg-and-milk toffee, brimful of nutriment and overflowing with goodness." He can wash

A CLUSTER OF ADVERTISEMENTS

down his temperate dinner with "pure, unfermented wines," or, should wines of another quality tempt him to inebriety, a "farm colony" will cure him by making him work in its "large garden" for no other reward than an approving conscience. Should he suffer a "nerve break-down," a physician is yearning to receive him into "a large and well-appointed house" near Spithead, which must on no account be confused with a private asylum. If his bodily health should be impaired, he is guarded against the seductive perils of unauthorized practice by "What are we? A question never yet answered by Christian scientists." Should he live to become an "aged invalid," he can be received into a "home, at a nominal weekly charge of 10s. 6d.," and if he wants a little light reading to keep him cheerful, he can buy *Hereafter—Short Studies on Subjects connected with the Life beyond the Grave*. After this, let no man say that the Church of England fails to make adequate provision for her necessitous or exhausted ministers.

In what I have written so far, I may have conveyed the sense that the paper under review is devoted to the interests of a narrow orthodoxy; but this would be quite an erroneous impression. It announces

A PROPOSED MAGAZINE, on modern and progressive lines. To be issued monthly at 3d., which will appeal especially to all Social Workers, and those interested in Religious Work, Art, Music, and Literature.

It advertises a course of

> FRIDAY EVENING LECTURES, in the Green Salon, Eustace Miles Restaurant, 40-42 Chandos Street, Charing Cross. Subject, "The Happiest People in the World; or Society reconstructed on the Principles of the Apostolic Foundation." To be given by the author of *Progressive Creation, Progressive Redemption*, etc.,

And

> A SYSTEMATIC, GRADUATED, AND COMPLETE COURSE OF STUDY in Mental and Spiritual Development, called THE NEW LIFE, is now available for live thinkers all over the world.

It recommends, among "150 of the world's best books," Froude's *Nemesis of Faith*, Renan's *Marcus Aurelius*, and Hume's *Political Discourses*. Lighter recreation it proffers in the shape of jig-saw puzzles and scientific graphology.

It touches that broad human ground where all men are kin, when it offers

> ADVANCES of £100 to £1000 granted at 5 per cent. by an old-established Assurance Society of the highest reputation in connection with Life Assurance.

And it points the way to wealth when it tells us that a collector wants

> COLOURED PRINTS by George Baxter, Silk needlework Samplers and Pictures, Old Cut-glass Lustres and Goblets, Old Coloured Bead-work Bags, Neck-chains, etc., Old Pewter Plates, Candlesticks, and Goblets, Old Staffordshire and China Figures, Well-decorated Old China Tea Services, Old Carved Oak and Mahogany Furniture, Old Silver, small Old Satinwood, Tortoiseshell, and other Tea Caddies. High prices given for fine specimens.

There is a width in this appeal to the lumber-room, which should ensure a rich response.

A CLUSTER OF ADVERTISEMENTS   285

But, if our journal is not sectarian, still less is it the organ of one sex or one class. The reiterated cry of "Blouses! Blouses!! BLOUSES!!!" rings through its columns, and "extreme value is remitted" for cast-off wardrobes. It cheers people of moderate incomes by assuring them that "orchid-growing is not expensive," and at the same time it has its word of hope for the sons and daughters of toil.

BEGRIMED HANDS.—H—'s Detergent has been specially prepared for use whenever soap is ineffectual. Its thorough cleansing power has been described as wonderful by not a few correspondents. Motorists and gardeners will find it very serviceable. It is beneficial to the skin and hair, is antiseptic and refreshing to use. An eminent bacteriologist in giving an order said he liked it very much.

From bishops to bacteriologists is a far cry; but I think I have made good my original proposition that the uses of advertisement are sweet.

XVII

"BOTTLES" ON BOUNDERS

AT the last General Election I went down into my native county to help a young friend in his candidature for Parliament. We had an amusing time, and I lately gave an account of it in a book of fugitive pieces called *Afterthoughts*. My friend, now M.P. for North Loamshire, bears in real life a name both honourable and euphonious; but, unwilling to betray his secrets to the world, I disguised him under a surname on which George Eliot conferred immortality, and a Christian name which seemed to harmonize with it. "Tommy Transome of Transome Hall," when introduced to the world in *Afterthoughts* at once made a good many friends. Several people thought they knew him, and others expressed a wish to hear more about him. In a word he became a favourite with my readers, as, in real life, he had long been a favourite of my own.

Great, then, was my concern when, a few months ago, I received the post-card which I will presently transcribe. It was signed with a name to me unknown, for which we will substitute that of Matthew Arnold's friend, Job Bottles. "Job Bottles, who is on the Stock Exchange; a man with black hair at the sides of his head, a bald crown, dark eyes and a fleshy nose, and a camellia in his buttonhole."[1] Intimately did Arnold know him, and perfectly did he describe him. Yes, Job Bottles shall be my correspondent's name.

Job's epistolary style is of the abruptest. He wastes no time on exordium, but plunges straight into his theme. "It is probably too late to hope that you can be anything but a stout bounder, but why do you draw a character like Tommy Transome in *Afterthoughts,* and say that he is a Harrow boy and an Oxonian? No gentleman from Harrow or Oxford talks like T. T. He is a young G. W. E. Russell bounder: please correct this if the public ('mostly fools') ask for a second edition." This unlooked-for severity caused me to make, as the French say, a return upon myself, and to ask myself point by point, whether I was justly liable to the reproaches thus hurled at me.

1. "It is probably too late to hope" that I can amend. But why? Bottles is, at least in this respect, like the cuckoo in *Thyrsis*—a "too quick despairer." While there is life there is hope. One has heard of conversions in very old age; and, even in the physical world, there is no knowing what wonders might be wrought by a severe course of Turkish baths or an hour's fencing every day before breakfast. I might even acquire a transient celebrity

[1] *Friendship's Garland,* Letter VIII.

by figuring as "Before" and "After" in the illustrated advertisements of Antipon.

2. But why should I desire the transformation? There is no disgrace in belonging to the family of Falstaff, of Charles Fox, and of Sydney Smith. Two of the most eminent statesment of modern times—a Tory Premier and a Liberal Chancellor of the Exchequer—were men whose "lower chest," as the tailors call it, was amply developed. "Laugh and grow fat" is a comfortable proverb; and I firmly believe that the popularity which, in spite of some palpable blots on his character, Henry VIII. has always enjoyed, is due to the fact that he had no "lean and hungry look." The stout and cheerful people have recognized him as a man and a brother, and have made allowances for his shortcomings accordingly.

3. But—"a bounder." Here the dictionaries do not serve me. Yet the word has somehow an offensive sound, and no doubt Bottles used it with an offensive intention. I remember that Lord Methuen, telegraphing home an account of the doings of the Guards at one of the early engagements in the South African War, said that it was a glorious sight to see them bounding from rock to rock; whereupon people called them "Methuen's Own Bounders," and they, when they heard it, were displeased. So it is evident that a bounder, though at present undefined, is something disagreeable; but what of "a young G. W. E. Russell bounder"? This, though it lacks hyphens, is a

truly alarming collocation of words, and bears a startling resemblance to Carlyle's vituperative rhetoric. The sting is not in the first word. The "youngness" will certainly be cured; and, if Tommy were a bounder *simpliciter*, with no qualifying epithets, he might in time learn (from the example of Job Bottles and his friends) to cultivate amenity, good manners, and the art of polite letter-writing. But "a G. W. E. Russell bounder" suggests a more deeply-dyed offensiveness; and even if Tommy lives to be Father of the House of Commons, I fear he will never shake off the effects of this early contagion.

4. It will be observed that Job Bottles finds fault with Tommy's habits of speech; nor do I commend them. The faithful chronicler must report what he hears; but the tendency to slang is always reprehensible. 'Twere much to be desired that the products of our English public schools should talk as the boys in *Basil the Schoolboy* talked about their holiday. "Let us go to Dingley Dell and converse about Byron." "Yes, dear Dibbins, do let's." Or like the monitor in *St Winifred's*, who hoped that a brother-monitor might soon be "what you are most capable of being, not only our greatest support, but also one of the brightest ornaments of our body"; or like the Football-Captain in *The Hill*, who, in the hottest moment of the match, gave his side the Polonius-like advice, "Temper your determination to win with a little commonsense." And fiction yields no finer rhetoric than fact, for, when Gladstone was

leaving Eton, his friend Arthur Hallam said: "I am confident that he is a bud that will bloom with a richer fragrance than almost any whose early promise I have witnessed." Such is the classic eloquence which our Public Schools should, and perhaps at one time did, produce; but I confess that on Tommy Transome's lips it would sound a little unreal. If in Harrow days he had called a schoolfellow "a Bud," I should have thought that he was, in colloquial phrase, pulling someone's leg; though, to be sure, it would have been no worse than a "Nib" or a "Knut." He still talks very much as he used to talk at Harrow and at Oxford; and, if he were suddenly to exchange his expressive vernacular for the style of Dr Johnson and Lindley Murray, I should attribute the change to the unwholesome influence of Parliament. I should fear that my young friend was beginning to take himself seriously; and I might even suspect him of laying himself out for office.

5. "Why," cries Job Bottles, with unreasoning wrath, "why do you draw a character like Tommy Transome, and say that he is a Harrow boy and an Oxonian?" Well, I say that he is, or rather was, a Harrow boy, simply because it is the fact, and in many respects he is a typical product of the school which reared him. "No gentleman from Harrow talks like T. T." Here, for once, Job Bottles must suffer me to contradict him. The Harrow Register reveals the fact that Bottles is not a Harrow man. I presume he followed his elder brother (whom

Arminius von Thunder Ten Tronckh knew so well) to "Lycurgus House Academy, Peckham," which had no doubt a style of speech befitting its traditions. But on the language of Harrow I am, and he is not, competent to speak.

But why, asks Bottles, do I say that Tommy is an Oxonian? The answer is that I do not. Here let me impart to my censor what in slang is called a "wrinkle." Oxford men do not talk of "Oxonians." That word is the exclusive property of the Sporting Reporter, and (in company with the "Cantabrigians") it comes into season at the Oxford and Cambridge boat race, just as "the Battle of the Blues" prevails in June and July, and "Glorious Goodwood" closes the summer. In asking that question Job Bottles has given himself away. Whatever he is, he is not an Oxford man. May I add my respectful conviction that, had he been such, he would have learnt different manners, and would not be so wholly bereft of amenity?

. . . .

I pause on the words as I write them. He? A sudden suspicion crosses my mind. Am I really dealing with one of my own sex, or is my assailant a female Bottles? All Protestants believe that there once was a female Pope, and Freemasons admit that there once was a lady Mason. I turn to the postcard, and scan the signature with careful eye. The writer's indignant eloquence has crowded the signature into a corner, and it is rather a hieroglyphic.

What I took for "Job Bottles" may really be "M. J. Bottles," and, if so, I know where I am, for the great Master of Amenity has introduced me to the circle of Laburnum House, Reigate, where the elder Mr Bottles dispensed an elegant hospitality. "You noticed Mr Job Bottles. You must have seen his gaze resting on Mary Jane. But what with his cigars, his claret, his camellias, and the state of the money-market, Job Bottles is not a marrying man just at this moment. We have heard of the patience of Job; how natural, if his brother marries Mary Jane now, that Job, with his habits tempered, his view of life calmed, and the state of the money-market different, may wish, when she is a widow some five years hence, to marry her himself. And we have arrangements which make this illegal?" The more I think of it the more I am inclined to believe that my correspondent is Mrs Bottles, and that in disputing with Job Bottles I have been barking up the wrong tree. The rather unformed writing, and a visible uncertainty about punctuation, seem to suggest a female hand; but, above all, that word "Oxonian" tells its tale. When I said that "Oxonian" was the exclusive property of the Sporting Reporter, I spoke unadvisedly; I should have added—"and of the lady novelist." "Ouida," I feel sure, must have used it when she wrote of Oxford. It was dear to her who described the breathless contests of the college barges as they raced for Folly Bridge. "'Sit in the bows,' she said, pointing to the stern." It was a lady who drew that scene, and the oarsman thus perversely adjured was "an Oxonian."

. . . .

Hark! I hear a familiar voice, and a footstep—not a very light one—on the stairs. It is Tommy, fresh from Transome, with a huge faggot of spring blossoms in his hand. "I thought these things would brighten you up a bit, as you will stick in this frowsy old town just when the country's about at its jolliest. Hullo? What's all this? Writes all that tosh on a postcard, and talks about 'an Oxonian'! That fairly rings the bell. 'Bounder,' indeed! What price Bottles?"

XVIII

RELATIONSHIPS

THE ensuing chapters were written by request; and as they were received with more than common kindness, I feel a peculiar pleasure in dedicating them to

My Friends in Lancashire.

G. W. E. R.

MOTHERS AND SONS

I know no pleasanter theme for contemplation than this, and it is suggested to me by a letter from Accrington. After referring to the qualities of the *Manchester Guardian*, my correspondent writes:

> I, a working woman, busy week in and week out, feel that I must find time to read its leaders; and some of them, written in times of stress and strain, are filed-up, in the hope that my sons may some day know how their mother treasured these things.

Who the mother is, who tries thus to influence her sons, I cannot tell, for the letter is anonymous; but I hope her lads recognize the fact that in this solicitude of a mother's love they possess one of the two richest boons which life can offer. If the other of those two boons is laid up for them in the storehouse of the unknown future, they are doubly blest; but, be that as it may, let them make the most of the blessing which they have, for it will not last for ever.

> He turn'd him right and round again,
> Said, "Scorn na at my mither;
> Light loves I may get mony a ane,
> But minnie ne'er anither."

It is my deliberate conviction that in one point at any rate—very likely in more—a poor boy's lot is happier than the lot of a boy born into what we call "the Upper Classes," and it is this—that the poor boy has so many more years of that inestimable blessing, a mother's watchful oversight. A mother's love and a mother's prayers may indeed follow their object round the world; but the personal intercourse and daily contact between mother and son have a sacramental virtue in guarding and shaping a boy's course, such as nothing else on earth can supply. Every additional year spent at home, before the age of fourteen is reached, is a boon which cannot be overestimated.

A man whose name would be perfectly well known to all my readers if I were at liberty to mention it has been heard to say : " It is more than thirty years since I lost my mother, but she still is to me an external conscience, pointing me in every exigency of life to the right path, and urging me to take it."

I fancy that the boys at Accrington, whose experience suggested this chapter, have a mother of that type; as they value their future peace, let them make the most of her while they have her. There are foolish people in the world who imagine that from the pulpits of churches called "ritualistic" nothing is heard but formalism and dogma. No one could harbour this delusion who in old days at St Alban's Holborn, had heard Father Mackonochie insist, Good Friday after Good Friday, on the third word from the Cross—"Behold thy son; behold thy mother." I cannot for a moment doubt that those insistent warnings against unkindness, neglectfulness, and undutifulness helped to save many a mother's heart from breaking, and to cheer many a man's retrospect with the remembrance of a sacred duty loyally fulfilled. When Dean Farrar was a schoolmaster, it came to his knowledge that one of his favourite pupils was not as good a son to his mother as he might have been, and the kindly teacher drew thus upon his own experience :—

My mother was, if ever there was, a Saint of God, and I loved her with all my heart; and yet one morning, when a letter brought me the intelligence that the previous night she had gone to bed in perfect health, and yet before morning God had called her to Himself—then my first thought was how much kinder, how much more loving I might have been ; how, in ten thousand ways, by word and deed, which would have cost me nothing, and which would have caused her a thrill of happiness, I might have brightened her earthly life. It was a bitter thought that, much as I loved her, I had not always been so kind to her as I might have been ; and I looked back with joy only to those occasions when I had *not* treated her love for me as matter of course, but had shown, by acts of kindness and gentleness, how infinitely I valued her blessing and her prayers.

There is, I think, no more impressive passage in biography than that which records the spiritual agonies of Monica as she wrestled against adversaries, seen and unseen, for the soul and future of the beloved but passion-driven Augustine. The art of Ary Scheffer has made visible to the eye the yearning of the mother's love, and the struggle with evil in the son's strong soul. It was Monica's hand that dragged Augustine out of the slough, and it was at Monica's feet that he poured out his contrition. Whenever, whether in Catholic or in Protestant theology, men feel the constraining spell of Augustine's teaching, let them give a thought to that long-tried and at length victorious mother who "lifted him out of the mire, and set him among princes."

If the modern Church has ever produced a saint, it was Edward King; and he was pre-eminently a mother's son. To his undergraduate-disciples at Oxford he would say: "Come and talk to my mother. She will do you more good than I can"; and, after her death, he wrote: "How to get on, I don't quite see. I am tempted to fear the loss of her wisdom almost more than the comfort of her brightness; but I know whence it came, and it can come still."

Those wistful words of a man past forty lend a pathetic interest to a letter which I have just received on the subject of Young Men's Melancholy. "Do you not think that the loss of a good mother at an early age often results in this form of Melancholy? I attributed my state of mind in great part to such a loss when I was about thirteen." Yes, indeed! I think it, and I know it. Of course, in what I have written so far, I have had in mind mothers who were not only tender but also wise. Tenderness is indeed the sweetest ingredient in the spell which binds a lad to his mother; but "wisdom is profitable to direct," and not profitable only, but essential. Monica once was over-tender to her son's worst faults; but experience taught her the wisdom of severity. The foolish mother, whose blind idolatry fosters her boy's faults till they grow up into ruinous vices, was drawn for us by Dickens in Mrs Steerforth. George Eliot drew the wise mother—perhaps a little too completely wise—in Mrs Garth. Turning from fiction to actual life, we may see Mrs Garth's substantial but unexciting virtues reproduced in the utterance which Matthew Arnold rather mischievously ridiculed as "Mrs Gooch's Golden Rule." "That beautiful sentence which Sir Daniel Gooch quoted to the Swindon Workmen, and which I treasure as Mrs Gooch's Golden Rule, or the Divine Injunction 'Be ye Perfect' done into British—the sentence which Sir Daniel Gooch's mother repeated to him every morning when he was a boy going to work: 'Ever remember, my dear Dan, that you should look forward to being some day Manager of that Concern.'"

To Matthew Arnold, with his mind set steadily on

the things of the intellect and the spirit, the ideal thus bodied forth seemed inadequate. But I seem to recognize in it, through a medium of commonplace, that sedulous watchfulness of a mother's care, to which so many a many a man is heavily indebted for material success as well as for moral preservation. Anyhow, it is unwise and unsafe to disparage even the most homely manifestations of a mother's love for her son, or a son's love for his mother. Whether wisely or foolishly displayed, whether romantic or pedestrian in its aspect and utterance, that mutual love is a passion which daily inspires heroic deeds, and, when brutally handled, has before now culminated in the ghastliest tragedy. It is not so many years ago that two lads, maddened by the cruelties which their father was always inflicting on their mother, avenged her wrongs by parricide. With that crime, awful in itself and more awful in its consequences, I had, at the time, some personal concern. Many of my readers will remember it; and I only recall it now because it was one of those things which are "written for our admonition." I borrow my last word from Mr James Rhoades—

> O love of Son and Mother!
>   New loves may wax and wane;
> But shall we find another,
>   Nor time nor tears can stain?
> From life's august beginning,
>   Through all her dark extremes—
> Sole love that needs no winning,
>   Nor wastes in passionate dreams.

"More, Please"

My chapter on "Mothers and Sons" has brought an unusually wide and warm response. I delight to think that so fine a theme should have triumphed over defects of handling, and should have touched exactly those for whom the paper was written. The words at the head of this page are quoted from a postcard :—

Manchester, 10-8-12.

I thought you had already reached the top, but to-day's article crowns all. *Deo gratias.* More, please.—Yours to command,

A. B.

The subject is indeed inexhaustible and reaches far and deep. It has been said that there are only two sorts of people in the world—men and women,—and all relations between these two are cleansed and glorified by the idea of motherhood. This the Church of Rome, with her fine sense of humanity, has recognized in the Salutation, three times a day repeated from her belfries—*Ave Maria, gratia plena ; benedicta tu in mulieribus.* It must have occurred to many of us, when gazing at Millet's wonderful picture of *The Angelus*, that English labourers and artisans might well envy his French peasants this reiterated reminder of the glory of motherhood and all that it imports. It was not in a Catholic country—or, rather, not in a Catholic province,—but on the coast of Ulster, that one of the most brilliant and fascinating men of the Victorian age—statesman, orator, author, diplomatist, Proconsul,— the late Lord Dufferin, built a tower which commemorates his mother, the beautiful and famous Helen Sheridan; and Tennyson adorned it with one of his happiest inscriptions:—

> Helen's Tower, here I stand
> Dominant over sea and land.
> Son's love built me, and I hold
> Mother's love engrav'n in gold.
> Would my granite girth were strong
> As either love, to last as long!
> I should wear my crown entire
> To and through the Doomsday fire,
> And be found of Angel eyes
> In earth's recurring Paradise.

That tribute to the mutual love of Mother and Son, as a thing stronger and more durable than stone, has always seemed to me one of Tennyson's finest touches, and, by its ring of intense reality, it suggests that the poet, no less than the statesman, was indeed a Mother's Son. A chivalric writer, depicting some young Crusader-Knights on a Syrian battlefield, just as the hosts of Heathendom were closing in for their destruction, described them as "buoyed up in that moment of surpassing peril by the sublime yet pathetic assurance that He for whom they gave their lives would receive their souls and comfort their Mothers." In all annals of battle, whether romantic or historical, the same thought perpetually recurs, till it finds its homeliest utterance in the words of the dying lad on the field of Belmont—"Tell Mother I'm sorry I ever laughed at her religion. I see now that she was right."

But I said just now that the idea of motherhood covers and sanctifies all human relations. A lad who has really loved and revered his Mother (for love and reverence must go hand in hand) will instinctively regard all women as sisters for his Mother's sake. The one noble element in chivalry, in some respects so mischievous, was that it taught every aspirant to Knighthood that his first duty was to protect the weak, and to shield Womanhood from every touch or even breath of wrong. What Burke so gloriously said of Marie Antoinette—that "ten thousand swords must have leaped from their scabbards to avenge even a look that threatened her with insult"—should be true of every woman who lives in a country where the spirit of chivalry is not dead. She is surrounded by men and boys who have known a Mother's love and profited by it, and in each one of them she can claim a brother. Bishop King, who combined strength and gentleness in a singular harmony, thus advised a lad who sought his counsel:

A very good rule is, never to say anything or do anything to a girl that you would not like another fellow to say to your sister. You know the word "flirt." Don't be one. It is *unkind* to a girl to be played with. Anyone who is a flirt will never be married happily. He will be despised. . . . Treat all those of the opposite sex as sisters; and from this treatment will not only follow repugnance and shame at personal action, but repugnance against others treating womankind not as sisters.

Here is the spirit of chivalry in a modern dress. The late Bishop Wilkinson of St Andrews, who had ministered to Mr Gladstone on his death-bed, made this striking allusion in his Funeral Sermon:

> I like to think of him in his young manhood, on that day when, in the presence of only one intimate friend, he solemnly made up his mind that, whatever else he accomplished in life, whether he succeeded or whether he failed, he would by God's help not rest until he was able to bring back from the dreary wilderness some of those poor women whose lives had been ruined by man's selfishness, man's thoughtless cruelty. I like to see him as the young knight in the ancient legend, girding on his armour for that lifelong effort.

Chivalry again. But, though we are pledged soldiers for a great campaign, we need not always be fighting. Ours must be the attitude of the strong man armed, ready to strike a blow whenever the cause demands it; and our sisters will be all the readier to give us their friendship and their confidence because they know that we should be, if occasion arose, their champions. A woman's perception of the chivalrous nature in man—and its reverse—is the triumph of intuition. Whatever is good in man, woman's influence draws out and makes more gracious. It was a famous saying about a famous woman that "to have loved her was a liberal education"; and the society of good women is the most educative process through which a man can pass. It is not educative only, but disciplinary. A bumptious, or forward, or self-satisfied youth, reminded by a word or even a look that he has gone too far or made too free, has received a lesson by which, if there is any good in him, he will profit to the end of his days. I said when first I touched on this subject, that the great drawback to the system of Boarding-Schools is that it withdraws a boy too soon from his mother's care; and to this might be added, that it secludes him from women's society. It deprives him of those daily lessons in courtesy, chivalry, and self-forgetfulness which the presence of women insensibly impresses; and then, as Gibbon says, outraged nature will have her revenges. When Robert Dolling was trying to evangelize and civilize the slums of Portsmouth, he found that one of the most useful agencies for his twofold purpose was a Parochial Dancing-class. His testimony is worth recalling :—

> It is extraordinary the difference which this has effected in the manners of our people. The dancing is, perhaps, a little more serious than at a ball in Belgravia, for squares are danced with a due attention to the figures. It has given the most happy opportunity of enabling our boys and girls to meet naturally together, and I am more and more convinced by experience that this is one of the greatest wants in a place like ours. Many of our boys and girls have got engaged to be married through this dance, and if any of them gets engaged to a girl outside the parish, the dance gives them an excellent excuse to introduce her to us. It would be very difficult to say, "You must come and see our parson." It is very easy to say, "You must come and see our dancing-class."

Unluckily the sons of the rich have few such opportunities.

A due sense of the beauty and sacredness of womanhood in all its relationships will naturally and rightly affect our judgment on literature and even on history. We feel most at home in the

RELATIONSHIPS

ages when womanhood was honoured; least at home when it was trodden underfoot. Christianity, of course, has done more than any other power to establish woman in her rightful place; but in days long before the Christian dawn we find in heathenism some "shadows cast before" of the higher ideal which was to come.

> Within the pale of that civilization, which has grown up under the combined influence of the Christian religion as paramount, and what may be called the Teutonic manners as secondary, we find the idea of woman and her social position raised to a point higher than in the poems of Homer. But it would be hard to discover any period of history, or country of the world, not being Christian, in which women stood so high as with the Greeks of the heroic age.

And yet, after Christianity, with its revelations of Immaculate Womanhood, had held the earth for sixteen centuries, we find England wallowing in the indescribable beastliness which is set forth in the comic dramatists of the Restoration, and even later in Swift and Fielding and Smollett. It is common to attribute this brutality to the reaction from Puritanism; but Puritanism, in spite of its name, had fallen far below the Christian ideal. One of the amazing fruits of theological partisanship is that we still hear Milton extolled as a great teacher of morality. On this point let Mr Gladstone speak:

> In this matter of Polygamy Milton deliberately rejected the authority, not only of Scripture, and not only of all Christian, but of all European, civilization; and strove to bring among us, from out of Asiatic sensuality and corruption, a practice which, more directly than any other social custom, strikes at the heart

of our religion as a system designed to reform the manners of the world. It seems impossible to deny that this is one of the cases in which the debasement of the opinion largely detracts from the elevation of the man. . . . His conceptions as to the character and office of Christian women, and the laws and institutions affecting them, descend below historic heathenism, and approximate even to brutality.

From this calculated insolence towards Womanhood Shakespeare is wholly free. His heroines are among the most entrancing creations which Genius has ever evoked; but we must have often wished that we could disentangle them from their base surroundings. Scott's girls approach perfection, and Die Vernon is the most attractive heroine in fiction. Tennyson is at his best when he is describing a lad's pure passion and a maiden's response to it; and his lines describing the power of love to elevate and strengthen character ought to be engraven in letters of gold on the walls of every boys' school. Coventry Patmore was peculiarly the poet of womanhood, and *The Angel in the House* contains a stanza, beginning—

<blockquote>He safely walks in darkest ways,</blockquote>

which every lad might profitably learn by heart.

But if I were to set out on a progress through all the poets who have written nobly and beautifully about a subject which others, alas! have polluted and profaned, I should fill my page with quotations. Let one more suffice. After the more vivid colouring of Coleridge and Browning, Wordsworth's love-poetry may seem pale; and yet it has its own peculiar charm, as grateful as a quiet green after a blaze of scarlet, and with it I end:

> He sang of love, with quiet blending,
> Slow to begin, but never ending,
> Of serious faith and inward glee;
> That was the song—the song for me!

TENDER AND TRUE

I head my chapter with the noble motto of the house of Douglas, because it seems to me to convey more exactly than almost any other formula the perfection of the manly character. A correspondent, who has read my recent words about "Mothers and Sons," is moved to ask a question—" Does a mother's influence upon her son tend to develop such virtues as kindness, gentleness, sympathy, thoughtfulness, and unselfishness in the character of the son, *at the expense of other parts of his nature,* such as the sterner qualities connected with manhood? If a boy stays at home during the age of adolescence, and is under the direct influence of a sweet-dispositioned mother, is he not apt to become effeminate?"

That word "sweet," applied to the mother's disposition, gives me pause. "A sweet woman" is not generally an expression of high praise, but rather conveys a notion of foolishness and vacuity. Now, in what I have written about a mother's influence, I have taken for granted that the mother is a wise woman. "Love and reverence," I said, "must go hand in hand," and, though a boy may love an unwise mother, he will hardly revere her. " Tenderness," I said again, " is indeed the sweetest ingredient in the spell which binds a lad to his mother, but 'wisdom is profitable to direct,' and not profitable only, but essential." Wordsworth's "Perfect Woman" was no doubt a perfect mother, and she was formed

> To warn, to comfort, and command ;

and I cannot doubt that to her boys her commands were laws.

Therefore, in answering my friend to-day, I must grant that the experiment of keeping a boy at home during the age of adolescence, with no stronger guidance than that of a "sweet-dispositioned" mother, might very likely make him effeminate, and even selfish and tyrannical. I remember that Miss Florence Montgomery, in one of her delightful stories, describes some spoilt boys who could not carve a chicken, or open a bottle of soda-water, or lace their shooting-boots for themselves; and I suspect that their mother was more sweet than wise.

The "joy that a man is born into the world" is not a fading sentiment. The wise mother, as I have known her, teaches her boy from the first to "endure hardness," to bear little injuries and annoyances without crying or fuming, and to face the small dangers which seem so great, though his heart is in his mouth. My correspondent assumes, and rightly, that the mother's influence will tend to produce 'kindness, gentleness, sympathy, thoughtfulness, and unselfishness" in the boy, but seems to suspect that these virtues will be produced " at the *expense* of the sterner qualities of manhood." Surely this is a groundless fear. Roughness is not strength, and coarseness is not virility. Wordsworth saw " The Happy Warrior "

> Endued as with a sense
> And faculty for storm and turbulence,
> And yet a soul whose master-bias leans
> To homefelt pleasures and to gentle scenes,
> Sweet images! which, wheresoe'er he be,
> Are at his heart ; and such fidelity
> It is his darling passion to approve ;
> *More brave for this, that he hath much to love.*

Among the "sterner qualities connected with manhood" one would, I suppose, reckon self-reliance, strength of purpose, fidelity to pledged faith, and contempt for pain and hardship and popular opinion. All these things a mother can teach, all the more persuasively because of her tenderness. "Tender and true"—the motto holds good in every home where a wise mother bears sway. "Be very kind to your little brothers. Never tease your sisters ; but, when you are with other boys, learn to take your own part. Don't come running home with your finger in your eye every time you get 'cut off' at cricket or shinned at football. When once you have made a promise, keep it, whatever it costs you. Don't be afraid of what other fellows say. Don't be ashamed of goodness. Listen for what conscience says, and, when you hear it, do it." Some such counsels as these are, in substance, uttered every day by wise and tender mothers, and so the sterner as well as the softer elements of character are built up. A man of delicate and beautiful genius told the same tale in better words:—

When I was quite a little boy I passed a pond on my father's farm, then spreading its waters wide; a Rhodora in full bloom, a rare flower in that locality, attracted my attention, and drew me to the spot. I saw a little tortoise sunning himself in the shallow water at the root of the flaming shrub. I lifted the stick I had in my hand to strike the harmless reptile; for, though I had never killed any creature, yet I had seen other boys in sport destroy birds and squirrels and the like, and I felt a disposition to follow their wicked example. But, all at once, something checked my little arm, and a voice within me said, clear and loud, "It is wrong!" I held my uplifted stick in wonder at the new emotion—the consciousness of an involuntary but inward check upon my actions, and then turned homeward. I hastened to my mother and asked what it was that told me "it was wrong." She took me in her arms and said: "Some men call it conscience, but I prefer to call it the voice of God in the soul of man. If you listen and obey it, then it will speak clearer and clearer, and always guide you right; but if you turn a deaf ear or disobey, then it will fade out little by little and leave you in the dark and without a guide. Your life depends upon heeding that little voice."

The cultivation of the conscience in the boy is, I suppose, the noblest of all the mother's functions; and, in comparison with it, all other forms of her affection may seem pathetic and commonplace. Yet life is the sum of trifles, and a good deal of misery may be saved by homely counsels, opportunely delivered. A mother whom I knew well, eminent both for tenderness and for wisdom, spoke thus to her sons, who bore the historic but uncommon name of Wallop,

RELATIONSHIPS

when they first left home for school: "If the other boys chaff you about your name, say, 'There's nothing to laugh at in our name. The verb "to wallop" is derived from it, and, if you like, I'll show you what it means.'"

I now revert to my correspondent's question, because it contains a clause which must materially affect my reply—"If a boy stays at home during the age of adolescence." Here I find a certain ambiguity. If by "staying at home" my friend means an absolute seclusion from other boys—no schoolfellows and no playfellows, but only lessons learnt under the parents' roof—in short, what is generally called "Private Study"—I cannot imagine a training more disastrous for an ordinarily healthy boy. However wise his mother may be, she can scarcely, under such conditions, save her son from namby-pambiness and priggery. The evils of Boarding-Schools I have already stated fully enough; but they are not wholly evil. Even among six hundred irresponsible schoolfellows a mother's influence reaches a boy by letters, by visits, by the intercourse of the holidays, and also by ways less palpable than these. And at a Boarding-School, whatever becomes of the "tender" element in character, the "true"—the hard, firm, and self-reliant element—is pretty sure to be developed. If the choice lies between an absolutely secluded education and education at a Public School, I plump for the School. But I make war on Private Schools, if for nothing else than because they take the child prematurely from his home. If a boy is to go to a Boarding-School at all, fourteen is the best age to start; and then, with a healthy body, a trained conscience, and a mother's influence, unseen but felt, behind and above and around, the boy has a better chance of prospering than if he were the isolated product of the parental library.

But there remains, as in most of the concerns of life, a third and a best course. If the circumstances of the home are such as to enable the boy to attend a first-rate school as a Day-boy or Home-Boarder, he has all the advantages of school in their full perfection, and all its evils reduced to their minimum. He enjoys the Common Life of worship and lessons and games; he feels the stimulus of competition and the inspiration of example; and he goes back each evening to that true sanctuary for body and soul which only a mother's love can provide.

And what is to be the result of all this care and tenderness and wisdom, all these anxious deliberations, all these painfully-weighed decisions? What sort of man is to issue from these processes of formation? I began with a grand motto, and I end with another which is worthy to rank with it. If I violate my own canon of always speaking English, it is because I have not the skill to render Lacordaire's perfect phrase into a worthy equivalent—

> Fort comme le diamant; plus tendre qu'une mère.

Could one conceive a finer combination?

Fathers and Sons

A friend at Birmingham, who was kind enough to like my remarks on "Mothers and Sons," asks for something on "Fathers and Sons." The subject now proposed is by no means so easy as that which suggested it to my correspondent's mind. I imagine that, in the vast majority of cases, the relation between Mother and Son is one of the happiest in the world; but, in the relation between Father and Son, it has been my lot to see not a little unhappiness, not a little unwisdom, not a few disasters. My observation has been both wide and intimate; and it has led me to the deliberate conclusion that, where the relations between a father and his son are strained and painful, the general adage, "Faults on both sides," does not necessarily apply. Where it does, the blame may be fairly apportioned; but there are cases, not a few, of estrangement between father and son where, as far as a third person can judge, the fault is all on one side.

If the fault is on the father's side, it can generally be traced to very ugly roots; indeed, those roots must be ugly and even poisonous which produce the undoing of what might be so beautiful a relation. One of them is simply evil temper. A father's temper, ungoverned and unchecked while the boy is young, produces an habitual terror and a shrinking secretiveness. Mr Arthur Benson says: "To me personally the father I knew in later years, sympathetic, patient, devotedly affectionate, seems a different person from the stately, severe father of my youth, who blew his nose so loudly in the hall, and whom it was almost a relief to see departing in cap and swelling silk gown down the drive." In this case the breach was happily healed by years, but too often it developes into a permanent estrangement.

A still viler root is jealousy. When a father has married young, and, while he is still in the prime of life, sees his son growing into the position, the popularity, and the enjoyments which once were his own, he is sometimes tempted to a most unhallowed bitterness. "He is stepping into my place. He is thrusting me on one side. Every year will make him more of a personage, and me less"—these and such as these are the unuttered sentiments which sometimes turn fathers and sons into rivals, opponents, and even deadly enemies.

A quite different, and much less vile, temptation assails the man who, whether through having married late, or through having had a crop of daughters before a boy was born, is growing old while his son is still quite young. The particular estrangement which arises in this case was drawn with a master-touch in *Vice Versa*.

Mr Bultitude hated to have a boy about the house, and positively writhed under the irrelevant and irrepressible question, the unnecessary noises and boisterous high spirits, which nothing could subdue. He had not the remotest idea what to say to this solemn, red-haired boy, who sat staring at him in the intervals of filling his mouth with preserved ginger.

Divested of its farcical associations, how often have I seen this attitude of Father to Son! the father so far removed from his own boyhood that he is honestly incapable of entering into the boy's thoughts, wishes, or inclinations; and the son simply regarding the father, in the most favourable light, as a paymaster; in the less favourable, as a policeman. And this type of father not only forgets the emotions and experiences of youth, but too often imagines himself to have possessed, in those distant days, all sorts of virtues and accomplishments which his son only too conspicuously lacks. "When I was your age I spent my pocket-money on books, not on pastrycook's trash." "When I was your age I should have been ashamed of myself if I could not translate a page of the *Odyssey* at sight." "Let's see—how old are you? Sixteen! I left school at fourteen, and never cost my Father another penny." These imaginary virtues are intensely irritating to the boy for whose benefit they are evolved; and not seldom, being proved to be frauds, they land the vainglorious parent in contempt and ridicule. Thus I remember a pompous old general, who was noisily sarcastic (before strangers, too) about his son's failure in an army examination: "If such a thing had happened to me, I should have been ashamed to show my face in the county, let alone hunting in scarlet and swaggering at the hunt ball." But, when a contemporary of the general's, pitying the son, pointed out that the Father had entered the army before examinations were invented, it became difficult to maintain filial respect.

Stinginess in a father is another fruitful root of bitterness. When a youth is well aware that his father could, with perfect ease, increase his allowance to a point which would give him the same opportunities and enjoyments as his fellows, he finds it difficult to believe that the paternal parsimony is dictated solely by a desire for his ulterior good; and niggardliness disguising itself as a virtue provokes, at the best, ridicule; at the worst, resentment. When Dick Bultitude, returning to school, asked his father for a tip, Mr Bultitude replied, "If I gave you anything you'd only go and spend it"; as if, says Mr Guthrie, "he considered money an object of art." A goodly company of British fathers spoke in those words of Mr Bultitude; and it is not strange, though it is significant, that a lad who owes money, and is in difficulties about paying it, will always confide his trouble to his mother and try to keep "the Governor" in the dark.

After these very disagreeable causes of estrangement between Father and Son, it is comparatively pleasant to recall another of an opposite type. More than once I have known a lad's character stunted, and his career marred, by his father's undue solicitude for his reputation and success. "Your report from school this Christmas is good; but I shall hope to see it even better next term." "A Second Class in an Honours School is not bad, but I had set my heart on

RELATIONSHIPS

your getting a First." "I didn't like the way you came into Mrs Perkins's drawing-room. You looked as if you didn't know what to do with your arms and legs." "Your speech was certainly good for a first attempt, but you were a great deal too fast." "You've a very fair seat on a horse, but your hands are dreadfully heavy." When constantly assailed by these half-praises and whole-criticisms, a youth is apt to say within himself: "Well, nothing I do will ever satisfy the Governor. I'd better chuck reading"—or society, or politics, or hunting, or whatever it may be—"and go my own way without worrying."

I turn now to the other side of the medal, and survey the case where the fault seems to be wholly with the Son. Here the root of bitterness may be nothing worse than a total lack of reverence. A son may be really kind, in his thoughts and even his actions, but if he is rough or self-assertive or patronizing towards his father, his conduct is hard to bear. It is disagreeable enough to be growing old,

>   to feel each limb
> Grow stiffer, every function less exact,
> Each nerve more loosely strung,

without the additional mortification of being shoved on one side by young self-sufficiency. Sometimes, of course, there is a more diabolical instinct at work than mere rudeness. There may be—one has read of it, and sometimes seen it—an intense ill-will on the part of a son towards a perfectly virtuous and unoffending father. Some frustrated desire, some mortified pride or passion, some implacable jealousy against brother or sister, too indulgently treated, or too liberally provided for, may be the root of this hideous vindictiveness. Or perhaps the source of the evil may be further back in the history of the family, and Heredity may be, at any rate in part, accountable. Jonathan Edwards tells the story of a brutal wretch in New Haven who was abusing his father, when the old man cried, " Don't drag me any further, for I didn't drag *my* father beyond this tree " ; and the same grisly tale is told in other and older literatures.

But, short of parricidal horrors, an ill-conditioned son can do a great deal to make a father's life miserable. Take the case of a lad educated in a rigidly orthodox home, where the traditional views of religion have never been questioned, and are believed to be bound up with temporal and eternal well-being. The son goes to the University, or joins a Circuit, or falls in with free-thinking friends. He acquires just as much of critical jargon as enables him to go home and tell his father that the second epistle of St Peter is manifestly not genuine, or to be sarcastic about St John's " senile iterations and contorted metaphysics." All this may be as a knife running into his father's heart ; and there is no conceivable motive for it except vanity or viciousness. Less bitter, but quite bitter enough, is the experience of a father who, having been, all his life long, devotedly attached to a political party, having worked for it, made sacrifices for it, and perhaps suffered from it, finds that his son has gone over with a rush to the other side, parades his dissent from the faith in which he has been reared, makes common cause with his father's lifelong opponents, and lets it be known that, as soon as he steps into the position which will some day be his, it will be his first endeavour to undo his father's life-work. The cause of the change may indeed be conscientious conviction; but the way of making it known is sheer malevolence.

These instances, taken almost at random, may serve to illustrate my contention that "Faults on both sides" is an adage which, though true enough in most dissensions, does not always hold good of ruptures between Father and Son.

But happily there are cases where tact and judgment in a father may have results which no rebukes or remonstrances or heated arguments or paper-wars would ever have a chance of producing. "I have long since discovered that I cannot drive or lead him, but I find that I can influence him." Those were the words of a very wise father about a very wayward son; and the "influence" brought the boy back to the moorings from which, through sheer wilfulness and love of independence, he had almost slipped away. We have just learned that George Meredith wrote thus to his son: "We have been long estranged, my dear boy, and I awake from it with a shock that wrings me. The elder should be the first to break through such divisions, for he knows best the tenure and the nature of life."

But it would be treason against nature, and a libel on the moral government of the world, if I were to leave the impression that miseries such as these are not daily counterbalanced by instances of mutual love and respect and confidence between a conscientious father and a wholesome-minded son. When King George V. addressed his first Council, on the day of his accession, he said: "I have lost not only a Father's love, but the affectionate and intimate relations of a dear friend and adviser." Thousands of his subjects could, under like circumstances, say the same.

Fathers and Daughters

Before I touch this theme I must revert to the subject of "Fathers and Sons," and I do so only for the sake of saying that what I wrote was not autobiographical. To assume that it was would be as reasonable as to infer that because a neurologist had described several types of nervous disease, therefore he suffered from one or more of them; or that, because a clergyman preached on the Seven Deadly Sins, he had graduated in the School of Satan.

Again, a lady asks: "You have told us some of the causes of estrangement between Fathers and Sons —now may we have the cure?"

I should have thought that the cure was a careful

RELATIONSHIPS

avoidance, on both sides, of the practices which I reprobated. In the distant days, when scholarship and sport were sometimes found in combination, a book much quoted was a treatise on Horsemanship called *Genius Genuine*. It bore on the title-page the name of the famous jockey Sam Chifney (though the style suggests a different authorship), and one of the precepts which I remember best is this—" Ride as if your rein were made of silk and you were afraid of breaking it." Let us apply that saying to the case before us. If a father will use his natural authority over a boy as if it were a silken thread and he were "afraid of breaking it," he will probably find it respected and obeyed. But if he bungles and tugs and tortures, like a heavy-handed rider hanging on to a severe curb, he must not be surprised if the colt rears, or plunges, or even bolts. Which things are an allegory. I must now turn to my prescribed theme.

My readers know, only too well, from my frequent iteration, that my favourite heroine in all fiction is Die Vernon. The glory of Die's character lay in her resolve to sacrifice her dearest hope on earth, and to brave all manner of misunderstandings, that she might save her father's life. And, when at last that object was secured, and Frank Osbaldistone claimed her for his own, his father had sense enough to say, " So dutiful a daughter cannot but prove a good wife." And so she did, if her husband's word may be trusted. " How I sped in my wooing, Will Tresham, I need not tell you. You know, too, how long and happily

I lived with Diana. You know how I lamented her. But you do not—cannot—know how much she deserved her husband's sorrow."

In *Rob Roy* the mutual love of Father and Daughter is seen at its happiest; I turn to another work of genius for a differently-coloured picture of the same devotion, though the transition is like turning from Fra Angelico to Salvator Rosa. *Elsie Venner* is dark with the hues of abnormal tragedy, but the steady glow of a father's love contends with them, and at last subdues them. We must not linger in the enchanted realms of fiction. We must return to history. Everyone who knows anything of the great Sir Robert Peel knows that he was a man of strangely repressed and repressing manners. People who were admitted to his confidence found that under his cold exterior there was a fund of active benevolence; but they were very few, and his children were not numbered among them. One of his daughters told me this curious experience. When she was a girl she was riding with her father, and her horse bolted, carrying her at full gallop all along Park Lane till he pulled up at the gates of the Marble Arch. Sir Robert, too wise to add to his daughter's danger by galloping after her, came up just in time to lift her from her horse, and as he did so he burst into uncontrollable tears. "And so you really do love me?" was her exclamation of astonished delight when she saw the ice-bound nature thaw. This was not the beginning of love, but the revelation of it; and the current never froze again. "Nelly," wrote Matthew Arnold, "is, like Traddles's young lady, the dearest girl in the world"; and I suppose that, in most instances, a Father loves his daughter just for herself, for her prettiness, her brightness, her winning ways—in short, because she is herself and he is her father—and does not reason about it. But surely there often enters another element—the memory of a golden past, "when all the world was young, lad, and all the leaves were green," when the girl's mother was what the girl now is—

> There's music in the gallery,
> There's dancing in the hall;
> And the girl I love is moving
> Like a goddess through the ball.
> You're the queen of all around you,
> You're the glory of the room;
> But I liked you better, Marion,
> Riding through the broom.

That ball, and that ride, were twenty years ago; but now as I watch the dancing I see the same face and form, like a lovely Gainsborough waltzing out of its frame; or, as I cross the common, I catch sight of a figure, and a habit, and a graceful seat on a pretty hack, which somehow seem to stir me with a delicious surprise.

Thrice happy is the man who, with Wordsworth, is permitted to follow the image which he loves through all life's stages—from the days when it is

> A lovely Apparition, sent
> To be a moment's ornament,

through the time when
> He sees it upon nearer view,
> A spirit, yet a woman too!

till with the lapse of years it grows into
> A Being breathing thoughtful breath,
> A Traveller between life and death.

That is the perfect lot. But, if death has drawn its white veil over the picture which I cherished, then surely I must love with double tenderness the visible reminder of a vanished joy. "Child, what has happened? You have become the image of your mother to-night." And although Rufus Lyon knew that Esther was not his daughter, he loved her that night as he had never loved her before.

If we turn to the other side of the relationship, the devotion of daughter to father has been at least as conspicuous a fact in life as in fiction, classical or modern. Goneril and Regan are exceptions to the rule; the world is full of Cordelias. My older readers will recall the peculiar popularity which our own Princess Alice always enjoyed in England, though she left it when she was nineteen, on account of the devotion with which she had tended her father, both in life and in death. A simple and natural virtue, displayed in conspicuous place, seems to knit human hearts together in a singular accord. Daughters are the most enthusiastic hero-worshippers, and the most passionate of partisans. I was infinitely touched by what a lady—the daughter of a very famous man—once told me about a girlish experience of her own.

RELATIONSHIPS

A spiteful neighbour had accused her of an indiscretion. She had no mother, and in her passionate grief she rushed to her father. "As if a child of yours could have done such a thing!" was her indignant cry; and as she told the story, fifty years after the occurrence, she still seemed to feel the reflected blot on her father's scutcheon far more keenly than the direct insult to herself. If I wished to traduce the character of a great statesman, living or departed, I think I should choose any auditory sooner than his daughters. There is no better passage in Macaulay's letters than that which describes the wrath of Lady Clanricarde—Canning's daughter—against the betrayer of her father.

> She and I had a great deal of talk. She showed much cleverness and information, but, I thought, a little more political animosity than is quite becoming in a pretty woman. However, she has been placed in peculiar circumstances. The daughter of a statesman who was a martyr to the rage of faction may be pardoned for speaking sharply of the enemies of her parent; and she did speak sharply. With knitted brow and flashing eyes, and a look of feminine vengeance about her beautiful mouth, she gave me such a character of Peel as he would certainly have had no pleasure in hearing.

This is a good description of an adoring daughter when once fairly started on the war-path. The same enthusiasm makes her the most indefatigable of canvassers at an election; and the same blind hero-worship makes her the worst of biographers. For a woman who has adored her father to write that father's Life is to court disaster; for the reader, turning in dudgeon from an impossible perfection, rushes into the other extreme of unmerited dispraise.

I approach now a department of my subject where I must needs walk very warily, lest I share the fate of him of old, who, rushing into the secret places of femininity, was torn to pieces for his crime. But I think I am not far from the truth when I say that a father-worshipping girl often enters society with a fixed determination that the man she marries shall be such an one as her father is or was or must have been. The father may have been a man of thought or a man of action; strenuous or sensitive; conspicuous in the public eye, or scarcely known beyond his own garden; but, if the girl, brought up at his side, has learnt to look upon him as the most perfect being on God's earth, she naturally desires that her lot in life should be linked with such another. But, happily or unhappily, there is a stronger power in the world than a girl's resolve, and the operations of love cannot be calculated in advance. The girl whose chief delight has been to follow her father across country, rejoicing to see him "cut out the work" for the best men in Loamshire, suddenly finds herself powerless in the grasp of a slum-curate. A girl who has been brought up by an æsthetic sire, amid Morris's wall-papers and soulful-eyed poets with long hair, suddenly links her lot with a soldier or an airman or a hunter of big game. The daughter of a statesman who has held the peace of Europe in his hand finds that true bliss really consists in helping a sympathetic botanist to dissect a weed. In each case, the Father probably objects—indeed, his objections have played a great part in fiction and the drama. If he is a fox-hunter, perhaps he would rather that his son-in-law wore a red coat than a black one. If he loves culture, he would sooner see his girl posed in a studio or a library, than hear of her riding astride on the veldt, or risking her neck in an aeroplane, or transfixing a wild boar in a jungle. The statesman who has pictured his daughter receiving her guests at the Foreign Office, or playing Vice-Queen in some great dependency, looks with ill-concealed contempt on the blameless-lore of stamen and pollen. But, after all is said and done, papa, unless he is exceptionally foolish, remembers that his ascendancy must some day yield to a stronger spell; and realizes that the mildest-mannered suitor may, if baulked, prove to be a second Allan-a-Dale—

> The Father was steel and the Mother was stone;
> They lifted the latch, and they bade him begone;
> But loud, on the morrow, their wail and their cry;
> He had laughed on the lass with his bonny black eye;
> So she fled to the forest to hear a love-tale,
> And the lad it was told by was Allan-a-Dale!

BROTHERS

Mr Horace Vachell's *Brothers* is, to my thinking, a most delightful novel, and, except perhaps *The Hill*, the best thing the author has ever done. But he would scarcely claim a monopoly in so simple a title, and no other would so tersely express the subject to which I am now invited.

A word too lightly uttered has an extraordinary knack of returning after many days and demanding apology or explanation. This truth, or truism, only too familiar to everyone who writes or speaks, has just been illustrated afresh in my own case. A gentleman from the wilds of Shropshire, after saying much that is kind and complimentary, thus questions a recent utterance of mine :—" I am writing to enquire why, in writing the article some weeks ago in which you mentioned the late Mr Gladstone's boyish experience—that when he had saved a small sum his brothers eased him of it,—you rather seemed glad that he was so robbed. I know your intent was to divert your readers' mind from pure miserliness; but I think the young might construe it rather differently, and find authority to rob and pilfer more saving members of their own family and esteem it no wrong."

Now the bare suggestion that I might, all unwittingly, have been destroying the ethics of the Home, caused me to make what the French call "a return upon myself." One cannot always be reading one's own writings, and I had forgotten the peccant passage, but found it after some search in a paper on the uses of wealth. That I may "nothing extenuate" of my wrongdoing, I reproduce the words: "Personally, I dislike a man who hoards. Mr Gladstone has left it on record that he was by nature 'thrifty and penurious,' and that by the time he was eight he had accumulated no less than twenty shillings in silver. My brothers judged it right to appropriate this fund.' The brothers were quite right. What they did I also should have done." So far, my own writing with the embedded quotation. But I feel it due to the memory of the elder Gladstones, and also to the ductility of my younger readers (whom I would not for the world lead into larceny), to complete the record of this forcible transaction. Mr Gladstone says: "I do not recollect either annoyance or resistance or complaint. But I recollect that they employed the principal part of the money in the purchase of four knives, and that they broke the points from the tops of the blades of my knife, lest I should cut my fingers." So there we have the crime—or at any rate the act of deliberate violence—and its extenuation. The infant Gladstone was deprived of his pound, and got in exchange a pocket-knife with broken blades. Certainly it sounds a rather one-sided apportionment, and I am surprised that the little victim felt no "annoyance." That he did not "resist" or "complain" is not so wonderful. If he had resisted, his brothers, all older than himself, would probably have licked him till he gave in ; and, if he had complained to Papa or Mamma, he would have heard about it next time the brothers caught him in a solitary place.

But now I must reconsider my *obiter dictum*—my casual and half-considered saying — "The brothers were quite right." Were they? We must look to motives. If their action was dictated solely by avarice, and the unhallowed longing for new pocket-knives, they were wrong. If their object was to provoke their youngest brother—to make him either fight or whimper—they were extremely wrong. But, if they saw that his infant soul was unduly concentrated on his store of silver; that he sate in sly corners counting it when he ought to have been playing cricket, or was evidently brooding over it when on pony-back or at the tea-table, they were probably right. If—but this is a frightful supposition—if they had reason to suppose that any portion of the fund had been illegitimately acquired, they were certainly right, though I must confess that their moral enthusiasm would have shone out more convincingly if they had not bought those pocket-knives for themselves with their brother's ill-gotten gains. At this point of the enquiry ethics seem to be intertwining themselves with economics. Ought a young boy to have any money? In what way is it lawful for him to acquire it? When he has got it, has anyone else the right to inspect it or invest it? A lady fired with Missionary zeal once addressed her younger friends in this remarkable lyric:

> If you want to be told the best use for a penny,
> I can tell you a use which is better than any—
> Not on toys, nor on cakes, nor on sweetmeats, to spend it,
> But over the sea to the heathen to send it.

Would the elder brother of a boy who possessed the modest coin in question be justified in seizing it for Missionary uses?

I was intimately acquainted with a boy who once won some money at "the Race-Game"—now, I think, gone out of fashion. As the Race-Game, like real Racing, risked money on chances, it was thought wicked in strict families, and the boy was forced, much against his will, to put his winnings into a Missionary Box. Smarting with the sense of injury, he unpasted the bottom of the box, rescued his shillings, and reclosed the aperture. Was he right or wrong? I incline to think right; but, if his brothers had done it for him, they would have been guilty of robbery and sacrilege.

If I even hint that big brothers are capable of bullying or even teasing their juniors, I shall be reproached by tender-hearted people, who will say: "Why! Oh why, do you thus besmirch the most beautiful of relationships?" I had experience of these tender hearts when I was writing about fathers and sons. I write as I do because I know the facts about which I am writing. An elder brother may be the most detestable of bullies, and all the more formidable because he knows exactly the weak points and the tender places. Of course, physical cruelty would be impossible in a decently-ordered home; but there are a hundred ways in which an elder brother can wound and mortify and oppress a younger, while parents do not observe what he is doing, or, observing it, do not understand. Here is a passage from one of Richard Middleton's striking stories which exactly illustrates my meaning. The Elder and the

Younger brother are travelling together, but they find it impossible to converse :—

> The train wandered on, and my eldest brother and I looked at each other constrainedly. . . . I remembered with a glow of anger how he had once rubbed a strawberry in my face because I had taken the liberty of offering it to one of his friends, and I held my peace. I had prayed for his death every night for three weeks after that ; and, though he was still alive, the knowledge of my unconfessed and unrepented wickedness prevented me from being more than conventionally polite. He thought I was a cheeky little toad, and I thought he was a bully ; so we looked at each other and did not speak.

The same unkindness often accompanies brothers to the Private and the Public School ; and away from home it has, of course, fuller scope for its exercise, under the protection of the general principle that anything which hurts or annoys a little boy is good for him. That I may not seem to be exaggerating, let me here record a personal recollection.

I was once talking to an undergraduate friend at Oxford about his family. I knew that he had several sisters, and I asked if he had a brother ; whereupon he said : " No ; I had one once, two years older than myself ; but he died when he was a baby. It was a mercy for me that he did, because we should have been at St Winifred's together, and he would have been just enough older to bully me." There spoke the experience of a Public School. As years go on, bullying of course becomes impracticable; but unkindness may continue, and our social system tends to stimulate it. "The cruelty and wickedness of making eldest sons," against which John Bright always inveighed, lies in this very point, that it tends directly to impair and embitter the brotherly relation. Two boys, within a year of each other in age, born in the same house, reared in the same luxuries and pleasures, educated at the same schools and the same university, find themselves, as soon as the realities of life begin, as differently situated as if they had been born in different worlds. The home, the lands, the income, the sporting rights, the seat in the House of Lords, the political influence, the ecclesiastical patronage, the social consideration, all pass into the hands of the eldest son. The position of the younger sons differs not only in degree but in kind. Broadly speaking, the eldest is everything, and they are nothing. He is a personage, and they are nobodies. His way has been made for him from the hour in which he condescended to be born; they have their ways to make, and, in the vast majority of instances, with equipment very inadequate to the task. Lord Beaconsfield, who knew the working of our social system better than any other novelist, drew out this inequality of lot and its too frequent results in *Sybil*. So skilfully does he enlist our sympathies with the younger as against the elder brother that when Lord Marney is killed by the rioters on Mowbray Moor our liveliest feeling is satisfaction that Charles Egremont succeeds to the estate.

But now, that I may be beforehand with my critics, let me hasten to say that there are plenty of homes in which the brotherly relation is perfectly maintained.

The eldest brother is the watchful and kindly guardian of the "kids"; the example to which they instinctively look; and one of the best influences of their lives. I say advisedly "one of the best," for I do not forget what I have written about mothers and sisters, and about wise and sympathetic fathers; and I must always acknowledge my own immense debt to schoolmasters—not all of them, but some. The conclusion of the whole matter is that Brotherhood may be a most blessed and beautiful relation, if the eldest realizes the responsibilities or strength, and can keep his temper when small and foolish creatures behave after their kind. It may also retain its beauty in maturer life, when the eldest son steps into the father's place, and studies to make the old home a happy centre and rallying-point for a scattered family. But it is the merest flummery to say that this is always the case. We do well to remember who and what he was who first asked the self-excusing question, "Am I my brother's keeper?" And, if we wish to see that primeval tragedy re-enacted on the stage of life—the old spirit amid the new surroundings,—the Irish play of *Birthright* will give us what we want.

HOME

A reader ("a young one," as he tells me), who lives at Pendleton, suggests that my recent chapter on domestic relations may be fitly followed by "Home." Young or old, no reader could have suggested a more attractive theme, and I comply with great goodwill. The only difficulty is where to begin. Perhaps it is better to conceive the Ideal before one comes to discuss the Real; so here goes for "Home! Sweet Home!" That is the song that goes straight to the heart of every English man and woman. "For forty years we never asked Madame Adelina Patti to sing anything else. The unhappy, decadent Latin races have not even a word in their language by which to express it, poor things! Home is the secret of our British virtues. It is the only nursery of our Anglo-Saxon citizenship. Back to it our far-flung children turn, with all their memories aflame. They may lapse into rough ways, but they keep something sound at the core as long as they are faithful to the old home. There is still a tenderness in the voice, and tears are in their eyes, as they speak together of the days that can never die out of their lives, when they were at home in the old familiar places, with father and mother, in the healthy gladness of their childhood."

That is a fine Ideal of the Home; I borrow it from a highly idealistic source; and I confess that I can hardly rise to its full altitude unless I am allowed to imagine that the home is in the country. On this aspect of it, listen to George Eliot :—

> We could never have loved the Earth so well if we had had no childhood in it—if it were not the earth where the same flowers come up again, every spring, that we used to gather with our tiny fingers as we sat lisping to ourselves on the grass—the same hips and haws on the autumn hedgerows. . . . One's delight in an elderberry bush overhanging the confused leafage of a

hedgerow bank, as a more gladdening sight than the finest cistus or fuchsia spreading itself on undulating turf, seems absurd to the Nursery Gardener. And, indeed, there is no reason for preferring the elderberry bush, except that it stirs an early memory—that it is no novelty in my life, speaking to me through my present sensibilities to form and colour; but the long companion of my existence, that wove itself into my joys when joys were vivid.

A man belongs to his belongings, and must speak out of his own experience; but of course I am well aware that great numbers of my fellow-citizens look back to a home in a town with just the same affection as that which a country-bred boy feels towards a home in the country. And yet, when we think of homes in towns, a darker side of the picture forces itself on attention. There is a widespread stratum of society in which a single room suffices for a whole family; and of course there are hundreds of cases where the overcrowding is still more scandalous. "For all who live under these conditions the word 'Home' has ceased to have a meaning. What memory does it hallow? What moral stability does it foster? What spiritual growth does it permit? What experience does it embody to which we can appeal, when we bring news of a Home in Heaven and a Household of God?" What can home mean to a child whose clothes have been pawned for drink, or who has learnt to recoil in affright from the reeling footsteps of the brute whom he calls father?

A prime duty of good citizenship is to make such homes as these impossible, and thereby to avert the horrible evils which they breed. But, happily, bad homes are not the universal rule, even in the land of poverty. "Home! Sweet Home" is still a possibility, and a good home is the nursery of all virtues and all graces. The goodness of a home is not dependent on wealth, or spaciousness, or beauty, or luxury. Everything depends upon the Mother. Her love is a sacramental benediction, and her watchfulness a spell which Satan fears. The Prophet of old time, when he desired to heal the noxious stream, "went forth unto the spring of the waters, and cast the salt in there." A Mother's influence on the home is the salt cast in at the spring of the waters. "There shall not be from thence any more death or barren land." From a good home, thankfully and reverently used, flows the stream of a good, a pure, and a profitable life.

One of the instances in which the beneficent action of a Mother's influence is most clearly seen is the relation of brothers and sisters. When the Mother has been wise as well as tender, there will be no bullying, no roughness, no undue emulation, among the boys; nor yet that incessant bickering about trifles which is not the least vicious, but so intolerably tedious. Among the girls there will be no jealousy, no spite engendered by suppressed vanity, no selfish struggle for the most conspicuous part or the most attractive amusement. The boy will be to his sister Knight-Errant, Champion, and Hero; and she will be to him the Queen of Beauty (till, in the course of nature, a Being with a big B displaces her). But 'tis not ever thus. A lady, who possesses a scientific knowledge of cricket, once said to me at Lord's: "I had by nature a very fine, free style of batting—but it never was cultivated. When my brothers came home from Eton for the holidays they made me field all day; and, when we had a Professional bowler, they never let me have an innings." In this case, I think the maternal wisdom must have been lacking, though the scene of oppression was one of "the stately homes of England." A happier case is that where a brother, honestly proud of his favourite sister, introduces his closest "pal" (to whom he has talked incessantly of her charms), and so begins a process which will some day make the "pal" a member of the family. But, good or bad, happy or miserable, the old home will not last for ever. It belongs to the Educative Stage of life, and passes away in its appointed season. Sooner or later comes the dissolution of the old home; and perhaps the first stage in the process is the death of a child. The brothers and sisters see death for the first time; and this sight sometimes makes an abiding impression on a thoughtless boy. But more often the brothers and sisters forget it soon enough. It is the parents who say (with Matthew Arnold): "*We* shall remember him and speak of him as long as we live, and he will be one more bond between us, even more perhaps in his death than in his sweet little life."

Remembered or forgotten, the first death is the beginning of the end. Perhaps it comes through the death of an elder brother whom we have worshipped —like a schoolfellow of my own, the idol of a large family, killed in an instant by a cricket ball, in the golden afternoon of Midsummer Day. Or perhaps the first to go is the Father, the Breadwinner, on whom all depended; and with him too often goes the home itself. The saddest break of all is the Mother's death—a loss of which no one can measure the consequences. Yet even here one has sometimes seen the compensatory action of a new virtue, when a widowed father has set himself, with resolute tenderness, to be Mother as well as Father to the Children whom perhaps, till now, he has treated only as the playthings of his leisure hours.

Wordsworth describes the life of nature as

> A constant interchange of growth and blight.

It is the same with the life of the home. The dissolution of the old Home is the beginning of the new. (1) To form a home for oneself is to take up the burdens and duties of citizenship, as well as its pleasures. (2) The Home is the basis of the State. The life of the nation is built on the life of the family. It is, I think, an absolutely sound rule, to try all social theories by their bearing on the Home. It will help to save us from perplexities and aberrations, if we apply this test to such questions as these— Communism and Socialism; Divorce and Remarriage; alteration in the Prohihited Degrees; and what is euphemistically called "Neo-Malthusianism." (3)

The anticipation of a home is a strong safeguard in early youth. "The greatest protection to a young man's character is a virtuous attachment"—they were the words of a statesman whose name the whole world venerates. All kinds of evil may be banished by what Chalmers called the expulsive power of a new affection.

> Who is the happy husband? He
> Who, scanning his unwedded life,
> Thanks God, with all his conscience free,
> 'Twas faithful to his future wife.

(4) But marriage, though the usual, is not an indispensable condition of the home. Nothing can be a nobler act in a young man than to make a home for his widowed mother, so as to soften the shock of her altered life; or for orphan sisters, who might otherwise be exposed to privation and even peril. I have known an eldest brother deliberately defer his marriage because he wished to make a home for, and to educate a younger brother, and could not afford to marry until the process was complete.

(5) Home is the test of Character. It is there that manly virtue is shown in gentleness, unselfishness, considerateness for others, willingness to be put out of one's own way, reverence to parents, kindness to those who are younger or weaker or unduly sensitive. A lady once asked the American evangelist, D. L. Moody, "How am I to know whether I am converted or not?" He replied, "Ask your servants." Hypocrisy which may deceive the world is speedily

pierced by the searching scrutiny of home; and the difference between what a man is, and what he would like to be thought, is mostly clearly discerned by those who live under the same roof.

And now I turn again to my friend at Pendleton, who, as he is "young," is presumably still happy in the enjoyment of the old Home; but who, unless he is strangely unlike others of his age, is probably dreaming of the New Home which he will some day fashion to be the sanctuary of his life. Let me assure him that, in both Homes alike, the really important thing is the educating power of domestic affection. "For it is only through our mysterious human relationships; through the love and tenderness and purity of mothers, and sisters, and wives—through the strength and courage and wisdom of fathers, and brothers, and teachers—that we can come to the knowledge of Him, in Whom alone the love, and the tenderness, and the purity, and the strength, and the wisdom of all these, dwell for ever and ever in perfect fulness."

XIX

FRIENDSHIP

THESE chapters about Relationships have brought me an unprecedented amount of correspondence. I hope to deal in turn with each point raised, whether in the way of censure or of approbation; and now I reply to a letter dated "12th of October, 1912." The writer demands an article on "Friendship." "This subject," he says "has an attraction for me, inasmuch as, although I have crowds of acquaintances—some of whom I value very much indeed,—there has never, since I left school, been anybody with whom I would, without hesitation, have shared my innermost feelings, and this I take to be the test of true friendship."

That test, I think, is sound; but the writer follows it with some questions which will be better answered indirectly than directly.

In the first place, let me say that, if my correspondent will procure a copy of *The Hill*, by Mr Horace Annesley Vachell, he will find that its alternative title is *A Romance of Friendship*; and that it is dedicated to the present writer, who "gave the author the principal idea." It is, I must confess, a book in which I feel a peculiar interest, for, if I could write fiction, I should have written it long ago. Even as things are, I was allowed to make some contributions to the narrative; and it embodies in a delightful form my views on the subject proposed to me to-day. But in this column those views must be given in more general terms, and must cover a wider area than that which is dominated by *The Hill*.

For boys and young men—I am not careful to discriminate between these two classes—friendship is a prime necessary of existence. When a man has established himself in life, and the interests of home and wife and family have absorbed him, he may, perhaps, dispense with friendship. But as long as he is young, unmarried, and unsettled, he is as dependent on friendship as on air or food. Even as I write the words I bethink me that there are such things as relaxing air and poisonous food. There are friendships which relax the moral muscle, and, if they are allowed free scope, will fatally affect the life.

> Hast thou so rare a poison? Let me be
> Swifter to slay thee, lest thou poison me.

Too often friendship, or, rather, the world's base substitute for it, means simply an alliance for mutual degradation. But friendship, in its high and only true sense, is the supreme grace and choicest gift of human life. "Among the many words which our common conversation debases from their true significance, the word *friend* is perhaps the most lightly used." There are friendships in which "Satan is transformed into an Angel of Light." The friend may be brilliant, sympathetic, amusing, delightful; a model of all the accomplishments and qualities which young men admire in their fellows; and yet his influence may be polluting and debasing. "Can two walk together, except they be agreed?" That question was asked eight hundred years before the Christian Era: but the lapse of time has not blunted its point.

A man who is in earnest about his moral being will find it impossible to keep company with drunkards or blasphemers; with men who are unscrupulous about their ways of getting money, or are unchivalrous towards women. Perhaps he cannot help being thrown with them in business or society, but he can help making friends with them. While he is courteous to everybody, and carefully avoids all censoriousness and priggishness, he reserves his friendship for men like-minded with himself; and, in intimate association with one or two of these, at once getting good and doing good, he enjoys a priceless privilege. The joys of life are more than doubled when we can share them with a friend, and when dark days come a Brother is born for adversity. As Adam Lindsay Gordon said:

> Life is mostly froth and bubble;
> Two things stand like stone—
> Kindness in another's trouble,
> Courage in your own.

An intimate friendship is at once a safeguard and

FRIENDSHIP

a stimulus. It is a safeguard in recreation and social enjoyment, for a man thinks twice before he plunges into surroundings which he knows that his best friend would condemn. It is a stimulus, because in work or business or even play a man does not willingly lag behind while the friend is forging ahead. In common endeavours for good causes, religious, or social, or political, friendship is a powerful inducement to self-forgetting activity. I saw somewhere a fine saying which, though it fell from a Jesuit, might be treasured by the stoutest Protestant: "Anyone can do a great amount of good in this world if only he does not care who gets the credit of it." A poet who wrote for boys threw exactly the same thought into a football song:—

> When you've had the toil and the struggle,
>   The battle of ankle and shin,
> 'Tis hard in the hour of triumph
>   To pass it another to win;
> But that is the luck of the battle,
>   And thick must be taken with thin.
> They tell us the world is a struggle,
>   And life is a difficult run,
> Where often a brother will finish
>   The victory we have begun.
> What matter? We learnt it at Harrow,
>   And that was the way that we won.

For a "human document" of what friendship at its best may mean, I always cite the instance of Mr Cyril Digby Buxton, who in 1888 was Captain of the Cambridge Cricket Eleven, and also represented his university at racquets and tennis. He died young and suddenly; and after his death his parents found, among a few papers which he had preserved, a letter from a friend, which must tell its own tale without note or comment :—

I could not bear saying good-bye to you, old chap; perhaps for so long; but I hope not. You have been the best friend I ever had, Cyril, and the only one I love as much as my own brother, and even more. I wonder if you noticed any change in me since we came to know each other. It was from knowing you that I came to see what worthless fools some fellows are. You were always so unselfish and straightforward in everything, and you made me feel that I was exactly the contrary, and that you could not care for me at all, unless I improved a bit. So you have done me more good than you can imagine, and I am very much obliged to you for it. Now, Cyril, please forgive this rot, and don't think me a fool or a hypocrite, for I really mean what I say, and I am one of those who cannot keep their feelings to themselves.

Of course, I am assuming throughout this paper that the friendship which I extol is not a mere easygoing comradeship dependent on fair weather and happy circumstances; but has in it the stuff which stands the stress of life and the strain of adverse fate. Two eminent men of Queen Victoria's reign—Lord Houghton and Mr W. E. Forster—had once been chatting in a group of friends, and when Lord Houghton left the room, one of the company said, "That's the man to whom I should turn if I were in trouble"; to which Forster rejoined, "He is the man to whom I should turn if I were in disgrace." A man of whom that could be said by one who had known him long and intimately must have been a friend indeed.

In friendship, as in every other department of life,

it is wise to erect a high ideal. If we would trust more generously, we should receive more abundantly; and the stronger the demand made on a genuine friendship the finer the response. To lay down life itself for friendship, as Sydney Carton in *A Tale of Two Cities* laid it down, is an heroic achievement; and yet day by day it happens in real life almost without recognition—in fires, in shipwrecks, in boating accidents, on battle-fields. Sir Frederick Treves has told us of the wounded soldier in South Africa to whose parched lips he was offering water, and who waved it from him with the gallant words: "Take it to my pal first—he is worse hit than I am." That generous lad died, and the "pal" recovered. Such high offices of friendship are not vouchsafed to all; but, even if we cannot save a life, we may often save a character and a career. The "word fitly spoken" of counsel or warning—even the look of sorrow bent on some manifest wrongdoing—has often averted a fatal fall, and recalled wandering steps into the right path. No man could wish for himself a nobler fate than that, when he is dead, someone should stand by his grave and say: "There lies the best friend I ever had. He saw me yielding to some base temptation. He warned me of my danger, and he saved my soul."

I began by quoting a novel dedicated to friendship; and, if I were to pursue the same theme through literature, ancient and modern, I should soon transcend my limits; and I have already borrowed too freely. Yet one more quotation must be permitted, if only because the genius of the author, Mr Louis McQuilland, is to me a new discovery, and the haunting music of his verse has fairly obsessed me:

> When I sail to the Fortunate Islands
>   Over the violet sea,
> May one friend, my heart's friend,
>   Be there, a-sail with me.
>
> On the breast of the deep, sweet waters,
>   In the arms of the white spray,
> Sailing, sailing, sailing,
>   Till we come to Haven Bay.
>
> In the peace of the Fortunate Islands,
>   By wood, and hill, and shore,
> May one friend, my soul's friend,
>   Abide with me evermore.

XX

A SILVER WEDDING

THE week ending to-day[1] has contained an anniversary which I could not pass without notice. On the 1st of July 1887, I first saw a piece of my writing in the *Manchester Guardian*; and, though that fact is of no general interest, it stirs in me the egotism of a lively gratitude. For five and twenty years my association with this great newspaper has been to me a source of pleasure and of honour; and I should be less than human if, on an occasion so clearly marked, I forbore to express my thankfulness. I thank those who are responsible for the conduct of the paper, and who, from first to last, have treated me with forbearance and generosity. I thank my readers, who have scarcely ever sent me a disagreeable word, and who, in instances beyond my counting, have become my real, though unknown, friends. Specially must I thank the honoured memory of the high-minded publicist and most accomplished writer, through whose good offices I was first introduced to the *Manchester Guardian* — the late William Thomas Arnold.

[1] 6th July 1912.

Mr Arnold and I had been brother-Scholars at Oxford; but, when we had taken our degrees, our paths diverged; and I had not seen him for a good many years, when, in the summer of 1887, we encountered one another at a dinner-party in London. Before the evening ended, he had suggested that I should become an occasional contributor to the paper, and I had gladly accepted the suggestion. It was the year of Queen Victoria's first Jubilee; the great Service of Thanksgiving was celebrated in Westminster Abbey on the 21st of June, and the festivities were concluded, as far as London was concerned, by a Garden-Party at Buckingham Palace on the 29th. Of that party I wrote an account for the *Manchester Guardian*.[1] Such a freedom would nowadays be out of order, but then it was permitted. The account was delayed by an accident in transit, and it was published on the 1st of July.

It had been a summer of unprecedented bustle and excitement; everyone was more or less exhausted, and the annual dispersion from London occurred earlier than usual. Returning in the autumn, I began to contribute to the London Letter; and soon acquired a fictitious name as the author of that letter in its entirety. It always struck me that people must indeed think me possessed of wide and varied information, when they believed that everything which appeared in the London Letter proceeded from my pen; but it was almost impossible to disabuse

[1] See page 242.

their minds of that delusion. When at length I had persuaded the more teachable that I had colleagues in letter-writing, they still affirmed that they could always "spot" my paragraphs. To a lady who insisted that she possessed this species of literary Second-Sight, I suggested a test. She should every day mark the paragraphs which she believed to be mine; for every instance in which she was right, I was to give her a shilling; for every time she was wrong, I was to receive that sum. By the end of a month, she was so heavily out of pocket that she renounced her claim to second-sight, and left me in peace. In those days I was rather at a loose end as regards regular work, and I amused myself by going a good deal into society. During the years 1888, 1889, 1890, and 1891 there were few social festivals of any kind which I did not describe, more or less fully, in the *Manchester Guardian*. But I presented them merely in their picturesque or instructive aspects, and I sedulously eschewed personalities and gossip.

The year 1892 brought a change. The General Election of that year placed Mr Gladstone, for the last time, in power; and he made a proposal which, if I accepted it, would clearly occupy all my time and energies. In urging me to consent, he wrote as follows :—

This will entail a change in your pursuits, but I cannot help thinking that it will be attended with much benefit, for the function you are understood to have had in hand, as regards the press, has its difficulties and disadvantages.

From 1892 to 1895 nothing, I think, from my pen appeared in the *Manchester Guardian*; but in 1896 I resumed, at first rather spasmodically, my former occupations. My friend James Payn was then alive, but confined to his house by crippling illness. I used to visit him pretty regularly, and did what I could to amuse him. One day he said that, if I would put on paper all I had told him, it would make a book, which his firm would publish. At first I was doubtful; and then I determined to make an experiment. The notions, grave or gay, which occurred to me from week to week, should be sent to the *Manchester Guardian*; and, if they proved acceptable there, I would let them try their luck in a book. They ran through the year 1897, and were then published as *Collections and Recollections*. James Payn died on the 25th of March 1898, and the book which I had hoped to place in his hand I could only dedicate to his memory.

All occupations tend to grow into habits, and, if the occupation is pleasant, the habit soon becomes inveterate. I think I was by nature and instinct a penman. I was composing in both prose and verse before I was twelve. When I was thirteen I first appeared in print; and before I went to Harrow I had published a Tract, which had some success in evangelical circles. At Harrow I wrote incessantly. Edward Bowen, who was my tutor, made essay-writing a regular part of the work done in pupil-room. In nearly every Form we had to write an

A SILVER WEDDING

essay once or twice a term, and in the Sixth Form oftener. It was no small advantage to have the boisterousness of one's youthful rhetoric corrected by such men as Edward Young, Henry Nettleship, and the present Master of Trinity. In addition to this enforced composition, I wrote incessantly for *The Harrovian*, and I twice won the School Prize for an English Essay. At Oxford I made my first experiments in adult journalism; and the habit thus early formed has, like the poet's "fell disease,"

<blockquote>Grown with my growth, and strengthened with my strength.</blockquote>

For the last ten years my work for the *Manchester Guardian* has been one of the chief enjoyments of my life.

I have been asked quite lately, and asked in a way which demands an answer, why I have given myself so whole-heartedly to the service of one particular paper. In the first place, the fact is not as the question implies. I am, in the parlance of Consulting Physicians, a specialist but not an exclusivist. I write regularly for the *Manchester Guardian*, and I also write wherever I see a suitable opportunity. But undoubtedly the *Guardian* has the strongest hold on my affection and loyalty, and for very sufficient reasons. To begin with, it is the first paper (since *The Harrovian*) which invited me to enter its service; and disregard of past kindnesses is not one of my faults. Then Nature implanted in me an independent spirit.

Like Mr Gladstone, I regard my mental freedom as my most precious possession; and nowhere, as far as I know, can a contributor find so much scope for his individuality as in the *Manchester Guardian*. Of course my convictions accord in the main with the great principles on which the paper has been built up. Otherwise so close a relation would have been impossible; but now and then the right of private judgment will assert itself. Perhaps I may have been at one time too little of a Home Ruler; at another, too much of a Disestablisher. Here, the cloven foot of Socialism may peep out from under the decorous garments of official Liberalism; there, my love of the Church to which I belong may obtrude itself unduly on the notice of those who worship at other altars. Yet none of these self-assertions have ever caused estrangement between the rulers of this paper and their unruly scribe. But, putting all personal considerations on one side, I am proud to serve the *Manchester Guardian*, because I esteem it the most high-minded, and the least self-seeking, of all English newspapers. To be disinterested seems to me the highest virtue of journalism; and the episode of the South African War, even if it stood alone, would show that there is at any rate one paper in the country which, when a moral cause is at stake, dares to jeopardize popularity and profit.

Turning from the paper to myself, if for a moment I may speak of what I have written, I will say quite plainly that I have tried to preach a gospel; and Peace, Freedom, and Humanity have been its principal contents. In enforcing these I have brought out of my treasure things new and old, and I have purposely dwelt on the brighter, as well as the graver, aspects presented by "this world of opportunity and wonder." Above all, it has been my endeavour to produce

> Not one immoral, one corrupted, thought;
> One line which, dying, I could wish to blot.

Such have been the objects which, with endless faults and failings, but with consistent purpose, I have pursued during these twenty-five years of connexion with the *Manchester Guardian*. My rewards have been many, and far beyond my deserts; but above them all one stands out conspicuous— I mean the privilege of entering, through its columns, into friendly relations with young men; in some cases, of forming personal friendships with them; and, in many, of helping to shape their thoughts, to enlarge their vision, and even to influence their conduct. This has been to me a source of lively joy. I well remember that when, towards the end of 1897, I brought my *Collections and Recollections* to a close, I quoted a stanza from Edward Bowen's "Fairies," and the ring of the lines woke an echo in at least two young hearts. I received a delightful letter from a couple of lads—I should imagine clerks—who lodged together in Manchester, thanking me for the series of papers then concluded and wishing me happiness. This was the first of a long series of similar letters from young correspondents who have been kind enough to like what I write, and courteous enough to say so. Those letters have a place of their own in my escritoire, and I am not ashamed to say that I often recur to them for stimulus and comfort. I write these words not without emotion—

> And, when I may no longer live,
> They'll say, who know the truth,
> " He gave—whate'er he had to give,
> To Freedom and to Youth."